TENTH EDITION

PARENT–CHILD RELATIONS
An Introduction to Parenting

JERRY J. BIGNER
Colorado State University

CLARA GERHARDT
Samford University

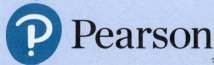

330 Hudson Street, NY NY 10013

Director and Publisher: Kevin M. Davis
Portfolio Manager: Aileen Pogran
Managing Content Producer: Megan Moffo
Content Producer: Yagnesh Jani
Portfolio Management Assistant: Maria Feliberty
Executive Product Marketing Manager: Christopher Barry
Executive Field Marketing Manager: Krista Clark
Procurement Specialist: Deidra Smith
Cover Design: Studio Montage

Cover Art: Shutterstock.com/Dip
Illustrations: Claire Gottschalk
Editorial Production and Composition Services: SPi Global
Editorial Full-Service Project Manager: Herbert Timtim
Production Full-Service Project Manager: Raja Natesan
Printer/Binder: LSC Communications
Cover Printer: Phoenix Color
Text Font: 10/12 New Caledonia

Credits and acknowledgments for materials borrowed from other sources and reproduced, with permission, in this textbook appear on the appropriate page within the text.

Every effort has been made to provide accurate and current Internet information in this book. However, the Internet and information posted on it are constantly changing, so it is inevitable that some of the Internet addresses listed in this textbook will change.

Library of Congress Cataloging-in-Publication Data

Names: Bigner, Jerry J., author. | Gerhardt, Clara, author.
Title: Parent-child relations: an introduction to parenting / Jerry J.
  Bigner, Colorado State University, Professor Emeritus, Clara Gerhardt,
  Samford University.
Description: Tenth edition. | Boston: Pearson, [2019]
Identifiers: LCCN 2017058513| ISBN 9780134802237 | ISBN 0134802233
Subjects: LCSH: Parenting. | Parent and child. | Child development. |
  Families.
Classification: LCC HQ755.8 .B53 2019 | DDC 306.874--dc23 LC record available at https://lccn.loc.gov/2017058513

1   18

ISBN-10:   0-13-480223-3
ISBN-13: 978-0-13-480223-7

Dedication

To our children and their children, who hold the promise
of becoming the future generations of parents.

About the Authors

Dr. Clara Gerhardt

**Professor of Human Development
and Family Science, Samford University**

Clara Gerhardt, MBA, Ph.D., is professor and past chair of the Department of Human Development and Family Science at Samford University. She is a clinical psychologist and a licensed marriage and family therapist, as well as a certified family life educator. Among her many publications, she contributed a number of entries to the *Encyclopedia of Family Studies* (Wiley, 2016). She documented the history of family therapy in two book chapters. She writes a regular guest column for a publication of the National Council on Family Relations and serves as contributing editor for one of their publications.

Dr. Gerhardt has twice served as chair of a State Board of Examiners in Psychology. She teaches university courses on parenting, counseling foundations, and multicultural perspectives. As an internship supervisor she mentors child life and preschool education specialists.

Dr. Gerhardt has professionally presented on six continents, traveled to over 60 countries, and speaks five languages fluently.

Her practical training is constantly updated by being a parent and a grandparent.

The Lifespan of a Parenting Textbook

Tribute to Jerry J. Bigner, PhD. (1944–2011)
by Clara Gerhardt

On my bookshelf are nine editions of the same textbook: *Parent-Child Relations: An Introduction to Parenting*. The first edition was published in the seventies and is a very slim volume. It contains cartoons pertaining to parenting challenges, some a little quaint if viewed almost half a century later. The author of this textbook was Dr. Jerry Bigner, my respected friend and colleague. He conceived the text while in his late twenties and while working as a Human Development and Family Studies Professor, at Colorado State University. He nurtured the book much like a parent nurtures a child. Looking at the nine editions, I see the progression of the book through its own childhood, adolescence, and eventually a sophisticated and fully matured text. After almost 50 years, it is now in its tenth edition and somewhat of a classic.

What makes the nine earlier editions particularly interesting is that that they tell the story of the development of parenting as a special area of interest, but importantly this occurs against the backdrop of the field of Family Science in general. With each new edition, the slow societal changes become more apparent as they affect parents and their families. We become observers not only of the changes of women's roles in society, but also of how men respond to these shifts as their own roles within and outside the family unit are implicated. In one of the later editions, a dedicated chapter on cultural perspectives appeared; parenting should be viewed respecting unique cultural nuances. Increased gender equality and flexible roles within families become more visible.

Dr. Bigner was known for his clear support of human diversity in all its expressions. He was the senior editor of the *Journal of GLBT Family Studies*. It was congruent for him to lend his voice in support of diversity as it occurs and is expressed in parenting and family life. He introduced a chapter on family formation and parenting in same-sex couples, long before this was a topic for discourse in a parenting text.

The text is as familiar to me as the palm of my hand. After all, I have been involved with it since its sixth edition. Like a flashbulb moment I remember where I was when the sad news of Dr. Bigner's death reached me. I was on the Isle of Wight, off the coast of England. In the months before his death, Dr. Bigner and I had frequent discussions about the parenting textbook; its future, how it should adapt and reflect all the changes occurring in society at large and in families in particular. He had made sure he was backing up his work; not on a computer hard drive but by anchoring it in my mind.

Dr. Bigner was a role model to family life educators and over his lifetime his teaching influenced thousands of students. As we present the tenth edition, it seems apt to end with the very last paragraph from the ninth edition: "As we are educating the next generation of parent educators, we hope that they, too, will venture toward securing improved outcomes for children and their parents. After all, public wisdom tells us that there is no better investment than allocating appropriate resources to our children, who, in turn, hold the promise of becoming the next generation of parents." (Gerhardt, In: Bigner & Gerhardt, 2014, p. 348).

> **"Public wisdom tells us that there is no better investment than allocating appropriate resources to our children, who, in turn, hold the promise of becoming the next generation of parents."**
> *Gerhardt, In: Bigner & Gerhardt, 2014*

Preface

NEW TO THIS EDITION

The tenth edition of *Parent–Child Relations* has been dramatically restructured and extensively revised. About 80% of the material was entirely rewritten, and a new test bank was created. The chapters were reconceived. The three sections highlight the context, the developmental process, and the challenges of parent–child relations.

The fifteen chapters provide a suitable format for a typical semester, and the material has been carefully focused to meet the educational requirements of students in parenting.

Two new chapters were added covering family law as it pertains to parenting (Chapter 5) and family composition and dynamics as it influences parenting (Chapter 11). Sections of other chapters were refocused. To make space for these new additions the transition to parenthood, pregnancy, and birth were consolidated into one chapter, and adolescence and teens as parents were merged. Historical and cultural influences were discussed in one chapter as they are intertwined. Theoretical underpinnings were expanded.

Current topics that were incorporated or expanded: coparenting, the effects of globalization on families, only children, military families, fragile families, interrupted parenting, parental rights and privileges, legal concerns, ethics and parenting, intergenerational families, grandparents fulfilling parental roles, diversity within families in terms of roles and function, shifts in gender and parental roles, strengths and resilience within families, and aspirations toward better outcomes.

We trimmed superfluous and repetitive information and added up-to-date research. About 800 current resources were incorporated in an overhauled bibliography, researched by a team of seven qualified research assistants well versed in the field.

The test bank was rewritten to reflect the new structure and emphasis of the 10th edition.

Other new additions were cultural snapshots highlighting diversity, as well as relevant reflections by experts to illustrate pertinent points. We paid special attention to our reviewers, who pointed us in new directions with their valuable and insightful suggestions.

A team of about a dozen subject experts proofed their specific areas of expertise for currency and correctness. Additionally:

- **Frequently Asked Questions** allow students to see parenting concerns through the eyes of a parent or a therapist.
- **Cultural Snapshots** highlight diversity in parenting practices.
- **Learning outcomes** are logically echoed in the focus points within the text and the chapter-end summaries re-address the learning outcomes to come full circle.
- **Website suggestions** contain focus areas so that topics can be researched independently despite websites being dynamic and changing.
- **Video links** clarify pertinent points or introduce readers to relevant researchers in the field.
- **Glossaries** elaborate concepts and phrases highlighted within the text.

SUPPLEMENTS TO THE TEXT

Instructors will be pleased that their favorite topics may be included during lectures to supplement the text. The following online supplements are available to instructors and can be downloaded at www.pearsonhighered.com:

- **Online Instructor's Manual.** This manual provides a variety of resources that support the text, including notes from the author regarding each chapter, suggestions for supplementary lecture topics, and a listing of audiovisual materials that illustrate chapter concepts.
- **Online Test Bank.** The *Test Bank* features evaluation items, such as true–false and multiple choice.
- **Online PowerPoint® Slides.** PowerPoint presentations accompany each chapter of the text. These slides can be customized by adding comments.
- **Computerized Test Bank Software.** Known as TestGen, this computerized test bank software gives instructors electronic access to the Test Bank items, allowing them to create customized exams. TestGen is available in a dual Macintosh and PC/Windows version.
- **Course Management.** The assessment items in the Test Bank are also available in WebCT and Blackboard formats.
- The supplementary materials for this text have undergone major restructuring to lighten the instructor's load.

ACKNOWLEDGMENTS

It takes many musicians to perform a symphony. For any creative endeavor, there is a wide net of people who inspire, support, and simply create the space so that the project can be completed. I had an entire team, not all mentioned by name, guiding and encouraging me. I'd like to express my profound admiration for the next generation of parents, who showed me how they juggle families and careers while parenting respectfully and selflessly.

Some inspired me through their exemplary parenting, shared their expertise and enthusiasm, or poured me endless cups of tea for courage and creativity. In random order, they include: Claire and Edward Gottschalk, Martin and Erika Grotepass, Paul Gerhardt and Jenine Schmidt, Andrew Gerhardt; additionally, the Doctors Christi Gerhardt, Tatum McArthur, David Gerhardt, David Shipley, Christina Ochsenbauer, Irva Hayward, Mary Sue Baldwin, Deborah Burks, Jo King, Jan Robbertze, Jeanie Box, Kristie Chandler, and Celeste Hill. Two inspiring pre-school educators are Marlene Giessen and Melanie Luedders; your dedication touched the lives of many children and their parents. Importantly, my siblings Dr. Frans Grotepass and Dr. Hanna Grotepass. In memory of the late Dr. Willem Grotepass and Dr. Dan Sandifer-Stech; they taught me much about families and life, each in their own way.

Samford University has been the academic home which nurtured and supported me. I am deeply indebted to my colleagues and a truly inspiring team of research assistants. They scoured articles, captured references, found up-to-date graphs and information, and so much more. The fact that 80% of this book was rewritten and about 800 current references were added was made possible by their diligence. Katrina Brown Aliffi (who was a research assistant for the 9th edition), Nicole Smith and Madeline Shipley Llewellyn have Master's degrees and are experts in their own right. These three researchers responded to numerous queries and revisions, while also cheering on the team toward the finish line. My appreciation to Lily Leath, Lindsay Smith, and Caroline Tudor Reed; graduates in Human Development and Family Science who were involved in the early revisions. Some contributors chose to remain anonymous; know that I value your work and I thank you.

As expert readers and contributors I thank the following (alphabetically): Dr. Joe Ackerson, Dr. Sarah Bowers, Matthew Bunt, Marisa Dempsey, as well as the Doctors Ginger Frost, Christi Gerhardt, Bryan Johnson, Walt Johnson, Tatum McArthur, Kelly Ross-Davis, Jenine Schmidt, Dale Wisely, and Patti Wood. Duane Farnell contributed in making Dr. Bigner's dreams for future editions a reality. For generously sharing her photographs and her vision, my gratitude extends to award-winning photographer Carolyn Sherer. To Claire Gottschalk, Industrial Designer, who created the family related logos and virtually all illustrations: My heartfelt appreciation for your support, vision, and artistic contributions.

The thoughtful insights and comments of the reviewers are greatly appreciated: Your insight and expertise guided me toward new directions and improved the overall outcome.

The editors at Pearson were my compass and anchor: Senior Acquisitions Editor Julie Peters and Managing Content Producer Megan Moffo, as well as the entire Pearson team responsible for editing and production, ultimately guided this book to a safe harbor.

Lastly, I convey my love to my inner circle—my husband, Michael, and our children, their spouses, and our grandchildren. They are the ones who turned me into a parent and a grandparent, the most important and rewarding learning school of all.

Brief Contents

Contents

CHAPTER 3
Historical and Cultural Perspectives   63

CHAPTER 4
Theoretical Perspectives on Parent–Child Relations   93

PART I

The Context of Parent–Child Relations

In some ways, we are all parenting experts. We have personally felt the effects of parental and coparental influences. We carry these experiences with us for life. We know about that most sacred of bonds, the one that remains with us forever; as we have been parented or coparented within the diverse context of contemporary family life.

In an ideal scenario, we have been at the receiving end of our parents' and coparents' good intentions. We were the object of their hopes and dreams; we may have witnessed their challenges and sacrifices. In reality, we may have been cared for, but not all of these relationships may have amounted to loving or constructive interactions.

Not all parents can or want to parent.

Not all children take the extended opportunities.

Not all parent–child relationships have successful outcomes.

There are many nuances in the quality of the *caretaker–care taken* configuration. We take it for granted that children are lovingly parented, but the reality is more complicated. Parenting can challenge us like nothing else. It can bring immense joy; disappointment and bitter tears are the flipside of that coin. If these relationships seem like an occasional endurance test, learning from what has worked for others may increase our fitness level to run the (co)parenting race gracefully and with good outcomes.

For as much as parents *parent*, the children do something in return; parents and their progeny do things to each other. It occurs against the backdrop of family histories. Parenting goes forward and backward in time; it crosses generations. We parent in the context of social, educational, and biological influences—factors that limit or enhance our effectiveness. There are many visible and invisible threads that set the loom—the influences we may be aware of, as well as the somewhat imperceptible ones.

(continued)

Parenting and the caring dimensions it represents has the potential for being one of life's greatest joys and ongoing gifts. As students of parent–child relations, we are particularly privileged to be close to the stage, where we can observe, encourage, and cheer on the actors partaking in one of life's true dramas, and where we can become part of the audience eavesdropping on the many dialogues that occur within the sacred space of the family.

"Parents are the architects of the system."

Virginia Satir (1916–1988), American Family Therapist

CHAPTER 1

The Evolving Context of Parenting

Learning Outcomes

After completing this chapter, you should be able to

1. Explain why parenthood is so central in our lives.
2. Identify the context and roles of coparents.
3. Formulate the current views that support formal parenting education.
4. Describe the dimensions of the parenthood role.
5. Illustrate the influences contributing to the parenting style.
6. Specify the social factors affecting parenthood.
7. Review the various family forms and structures.

PARENTHOOD

Children represent our hopes for the future. Children will enter times that parents will not be able to access. The way we treat our offspring is a reflection of our own goals and aspirations. Parent–child relations form the central threads of our lives, as we are touched by their potential and promise. They may be the relationships we have with our own parents in our family-of-origin; alternatively they could be the relationships we have with our children. Either way, there is always a parental connection to be found in our histories, our anticipated futures, and in our present relationships.

The parent–child bond is unique in its biological foundations and in its psychological meanings. For children, this essential relationship ensures survival and helps shape destinies. For adults, it can be one of the most fulfilling human experiences and a challenging opportunity for personal growth and development. Children make us vulnerable and children push us toward greater strengths. In short: one of the most significant and intimate relationships among humans is that between parent and child.

Societies are defined by how they invest in their youngest members. In our society, the parenting role is associated with several different concepts. Originally, the idea of parenthood referred singularly to the prominent aspect of sexual reproduction. Our society, like all others, values the function of reproduction within a family setting because, traditionally, this was the only way to sustain the population: *"Put succinctly, parents create people"* (Bornstein, 2012, p. ix).

Families are formed in various ways and the diversity in family form and function attest to this. Advances in medical technology allow for assisted reproduction, yet the traditional manner of family formation is the most frequently occurring variation. Initial family formation is followed by years of careful supervision of the offspring.

Other ideas are also embedded in our society's concept of **parenthood**—namely, that parents are responsible for nurturing, teaching, and acting as guardians for their children until they reach the age of legal maturity. This extended timespan of providing care for children is unique among most species. Human infants and children have a prolonged period of dependency on adults, partly because of the length of time it takes for maturation of the brain and the complexity of the skills that have to be attained (Dunsworth, 2016).

Parents are considered to be a child's principal teachers. This instructional function and the responsibility given to parents by society to prepare children for adulthood is referred to as *socialization*, or learning how to conform to the conventional ways of behavior in society. Parents serve as educators for their children by teaching them the essential skills needed to survive in society, including social, cultural, and religious values. As the child becomes older, the parents are supported by educational and social institutions that complement and expand on this initial parent–child relationship.

Parents are expected to help children learn the basic rules of social functioning and to impart values to guide the behavior and decisions of their offspring. This is facilitated by the bonding and attachment between parents and children and this unquestioning loyalty will provide the motivation and reason for a kinship-based loyalty that has virtually no parallels.

••

Focus Point. In our society the concept of parenthood implies that parents are responsible for nurturing, teaching, socializing, and acting as guardians for their children until they reach the age of legal maturity.

••

COPARENTING

Coparents can come in various guises and in several contexts. It refers to the people who team up or *collaborate to parent*. Think about the word *cooperate*. It contains the prefix *co*, meaning that it is an activity that we do together or jointly, where we share our resources: in short, where we collaborate. It is much more than an extended form of child care. It is a very legitimate form of parenting and can occur in many settings. It can have legal implications concerning parental rights and responsibilities.

Two factors distinguish coparenting from other serious and ongoing commitments to children. The first is the ability to make decisions for the child, which, hopefully, contribute to the child's well-being. In other words, the coparent can make things happen for the child; there is financial, legal, educational, health-care or other responsibility that places the coparent in an *executive role*, where this parental figure can and should take charge. The coparent may have "ultimate decision-making authority for the child" (McHale & Lindahl, 2011, p. 17).

The second factor has to do with the relationship. Ideally there is an *emotional investment*, a mutual bonding and caring. Not only does the coparent have a serious interest and commitment to the child, but the child has formed or is forming a significant relationship in return. There is "central attachment and socialization" with the coparent (McHale & Lindahl, 2011, p. 17). Ideally coparents are emotionally involved with the children they coparent.

At the heart of coparenting lies the ongoing commitment to a child's well-being in a parental-like manner. Coparents can be biological parents in binuclear families who take on parenting roles from two different households because of divorce or separation. Coparents can be adults who significantly support parents in the parenting role, or may take over the parenting role for an absent or incapacitated parent. In this way, grandparents, supportive family members, friends, and foster parents could act as coparents if they take on permanent and semi-permanent roles with a serious commitment to a child's upbringing. They carry the child's interests at heart and become a significant force in the child's life in a relationship that is ongoing and enduring.

The adults could have a biological link to the child, but they need not have this connection. For instance, parents and stepparents in a post-divorce situation may coparent. Same-sex couples may coparent. Unmarried parents may coparent from two different households. Foster parents could coparent occasionally with a biological parent. The term *co-parenting* has also been used to describe the roles of a married couple in raising the children, although both parents need not be biological parents, as well as of members of intact families fulfilling these roles (Rodriguez & Helms, 2016, p. 437). In short, the role of coparenting has a lot of flexibility, and just as any other significant relationship, the quality of the coparenting can vary to reflect a continuum of attitudes ranging from collaborative and supportive to outright uncollaborative and unsupportive. Nuances of antagonism, cohesion, and balance can all find a varying presence in this unique connection between people who coparent, as well as in the quality of their parenting relationships. In other words, the unhealthy variants of coparenting have undermining agendas, whereas healthy coparental collaborations carry the best interests of the child at heart. Parents post-divorce may find it difficult to separate the concerns that precipitated their divorce from the parental collaboration that has to occur in constructive coparenting. Compatibility between the persons coparenting, as well as educational level and understanding of parenting requirements are all contributory factors in determining the quality of coparenting relationships and outcomes (Rodriguez & Helms, 2016, p. 439)

In summary, "[co]parenting is an enterprise undertaken by two or more adults who together take on the care and upbringing of children for whom they share responsibility" (McHale & Lindahl, 2011, p. 3). The authors elaborate: "This joint enterprise serves children best when each of the coparenting adults is capable of seeing and responding to the child as a separate person with feelings and needs different from their own and when the adults find ways to work together to co-create a structure that adequately protects and nurtures the child" (2011, p. 16).

Coparenting alliances which are healthy and support children in a constructive manner are important because, in contemporary society, family form and function are in flux. The former predictable blueprint of what a typical family looks like is being challenged. Families in transition may necessitate coparenting arrangements, ranging from the conventional to the unconventional. The outcome is important, and can be found in the quality of care the children in these family configurations receive. Coparenting has become a very legitimate caretaking system that was born out of the need to ensure constructive outcomes for parenting challenges while also keeping the best interests of the child in mind (McHale & Lindahl, 2011). It also implies that every child should ideally have the right of access to a parent or parents who will support the child through the tender years toward independence, and beyond.

Another earlier definition is: "Coparenting refers to parents' agreement and communication about how their child should be raised as well as supportiveness of each other's parenting efforts" (McHale, 1995). Importantly the coparental relationship should continue for the sake of the child, even if the parents are no longer on the same page concerning other aspects of their lives (Goldberg, 2015). Research by Goldberg (2015) indicated that the quality of the coparental relationship tended to indicate the willingness and responsibility a nonresident father may display toward financial obligations such as child support. Constructive and mutually supportive coparental arrangements have better outcomes for the children as well as the participating coparents.

Not all coparenting arrangements have happy and constructive outcomes, because frequently the coparenting responsibilities may have been precipitated by disagreement and incompatibility followed by separation or divorce. The factors which broke up the relationship can continue to influence attempts at collaborative parenting. In a study of fathers who participated in interviews for 'Parents and Children Together' (PACT), about two thirds of the fathers stated that their coparenting relationships with their coparenting partners (mothers of their children) were either conflict-ridden or distant and disengaged. Fathers mentioned the presence of arguments, verbal disagreements, and not being on the same page concerning parenting goals and outcomes. Often cooperation was lacking or limited. On the positive side, a third of the fathers felt that as far as the parenting of their children was concerned, they managed to have collaborative and cooperative relationships with the other coparent; usually the child's mother (Holcomb et al., 2015).

Much of coparenting can be seen through the lens of a **parental dyad**, where two parents are involved. If for any reason those two parents no longer reside in the same home, or require ongoing serious support in their parenting roles, coparenting comes into play. With greater awareness of variations of family form and function in different cultural contexts, it is appropriate to expand the notion of coparenting beyond the parental dyad as found in **nuclear families** (McHale et al., 2012). The actors taking lead roles in the parenting can be stepparents, grandparents, same-sex partners, extended family members, and other significant attachment figures.

With so many possibilities, where do we delineate the boundaries of coparental relationships? One useful approach is to look at it in terms of the *executive subsystem*, a term originally coined by Minuchin in 1974 (McHale et al., 2012, p. 76). The persons making the ongoing and truly relevant decisions that affect the child's well-being, and who provide the emotional and physical support and means to carry them through, may well be identified as the coparents. Additionally this can (but need not) overlap with formal and legal designations, such as being a child's guardian, or adoptive parent.

The original meaning references part of the intentions of the "Rights of the Child" manifesto of 1959 (UNICEF. n.d, 1959/1990), whereby a child should be able to have continued access to a parent or both parents, despite the difficulties that these parental figures may have in other dimensions of their mutual relationship.

A parent should be able to remain a parent to their child, whatever challenges the future may hold.

Video Example 1.1 Tips for Successful Co-Parenting

Watch this video on co-parenting. Why is co-parenting necessary for the development of children whose parents are separated/divorced?

(https://www.youtube.com/watch?v=josZkNl34NM)

Focus Point.   Coparents take on permanent and semi-permanent roles with a serious commitment to a child's upbringing. Coparents are characterized by two lead factors: Coparents have executive function and an emotional attachment/commitment to the children they coparent.

PARENTING EDUCATION

"Owning a piano, does not make the pianist." This saying from folklore references a touchy subject: complex skills have to be painstakingly internalized to become our own. The rare Stradivarius violin may document ownership on the insurance papers, but coaxing melodies from it demands a multi-layered blend of talent, musicality, training, practice, and then some. Ownership does not transfer mastery. Likewise for parenting. Becoming a parent does not magically endow us with the gifts that will support a constructive and meaningful lifelong relationship with a child. We may already be in possession of key qualities which promise successful outcomes, but it is not a given. In all likelihood parenting and coparenting in various dimensions will prove to be amongst the most demanding yet also most rewarding tasks we undertake.

When we reflect on our own childhood experiences, several questions come to mind: Why did our parents behave and react the way they did? What would we do differently if we were in their shoes? Are there lessons to be learned that will make us better parents? Are there best practices that we can follow to ensure optimal outcomes?

The need for some formal parenting guidelines has been valued by anxious parents wanting to do the best for their children. A few pediatricians penned best sellers to fill the void. This included the legendary book by Dr. Benjamin Spock, *Baby and Child Care*, published in 1946. The fact that this book was so popular indicated the desire of parents to know more about the topic and to seek information from experts. A much older relic of guidance for parents appeared in a book first published in 1701 and now residing in the archives of the Victoria and Albert Museum in London. It has the promising title: "The School of Manners, or Rules for Childrens Behaviour." It contains advice for children in terms of qualities that can be equally aspired to more than 300 years later (Garretson, 1701/1983, p. 25):

■ "Imitate not the wicked"
■ "Be desirous of Learning"
■ "Be always cleanly" (Written in 1701).

Parenting focuses on nurturing children's growth and development to facilitate socialization and ultimately effective functioning as adults. Parenthood is a developmental role, which changes in response to the needs of the children.

Jozef Polc/123RF.com

Our society goes to great lengths to train people for most vocational roles. A license indicating training and competence is required for a range of activities and vocations. Many teenagers line up with great urgency at the drivers licensing office on the morning of their 16th birthday. They do not want to miss a minute of this rite of passage. In the United States, the privilege to learn to drive a car is part of the ritual of celebrating this milestone birthday, as it also represents the promise of mobility and independence. Other than for special circumstances such as foster parenting, no state or federal statute requires individuals to have training or preparation to become parents, or to practice parenting, even though the stakes are high and the effects are long lasting. Public policy and family law have entered the debate concerning the well-being of children by providing legislation and processes that serve in the best interests of the child, especially in those instances where parents flounder in their duties.

The media provide us with realistic as well as idealistic versions of the challenges of these unique relationships. Sometimes parenthood is portrayed as a happily-ever-after story. But we are not so naïve as to believe that the majority of parents and children have smooth interactions, or that children will invariably turn out well if they have good parents. We know that

greater forces are at work and that parents are not solely responsible for their children's character, personality, and achievements upon attaining maturity.

Learning about parenting in formal coursework, observing parents and children interact in natural settings, and hearing parents share their experiences may contribute to an authentic and balanced understanding of parenthood. Although most parents could profit from learning new ways to be effective in their role, there are so many seemingly conflicting guidelines concerning parenting that it is hard to separate the wheat from the chaff. Researchers continue to make progress toward helping parents find more effective ways of parenting and raising children to become competent adults, while parenting programs are formally assessed regarding efficacy. Experts continue to study parent–child interactions in the hopes of gaining a clearer understanding of how this relationship changes over time and is altered in certain social contexts. They look at the dynamics of parent–child relations and try to distill the essence. Even so, we see the pendulum swing, and our current slightly indulgent parenting practices form a contrast to stricter authoritarian approaches of a century ago.

Contemporary ideas about the nature of parent–child relations are the result of years of social evolution and many historical changes. Our concept of the relationship between a parent and a child contains numerous complex meanings. These in turn influence an adult's decision to become a parent and also shape the subsequent parenting behavior. Disconcerting events occurring in families and in contemporary society underline the urgency of preparing parents and coparents to ensure that they are competent in their roles.

The qualities inherent in parenting relationships can benefit or harm a child's development. The prevalence of destructive behaviors in adulthood is traced to family-of-origin experiences in which poor and ineffective parenting may have played a major role (Murphy, 2014). Family experts are concerned about the effects of emotional, physical, and sexual abuse of children by their parents and close family. Poor preparation for parenthood, inadequate social support, lack of adequate skills for coping with the stresses of parenting, and resource-depleted environments all interact to put families at risk (Thompson, 2015b).

Relationships between parents and children are complex and varied. Parenthood is described as a *developmental role* that changes over time, usually in response to the changing developmental needs of children. In a parenting course, we try to describe the many interacting factors, from individual through to greater societal influences, that contribute to the outcomes of raising children. By recognizing and understanding some of the patterns and learning techniques and approaching parenting as a skill set that can be expanded, parent-child relations can become more rewarding for all participants. Biological parenthood is not a prerequisite; there are many paths toward a caring relationship. We can use these skills in any responsible coparenting relationship involving children and adolescents, and in a variety of professions.

Comprehensive Resources

- **Encyclopedia of Family Studies**
  A comprehensive scholarly resource pertaining to families, presented in four volumes. Topics are arranged alphabetically and authored by leading experts in their respective fields.

  Shehan, C. L. (Ed.). (2016). *The Wiley Blackwell Encyclopedia of Family Studies*. Wiley Blackwell.

  Shehan, C. L. (Ed.). (2016, March). *The Wiley Blackwell Encyclopedia of Family Studies*. http://onlinelibrary. wiley.com/book/10.1002/9781119085621. Online Version.

- **Handbook of Life-Span Development**
  A comprehensive scholarly resource pertaining to lifespan presented in two volumes:
  - Cognition, Biology and Methods
  - Social and Emotional Development

    Lamb, M. E. & Freund, A. M. (Eds.) (2010). *The Handbook of Life-Span Development*. Wiley.

- **Handbook of Parenting**
  A comprehensive scholarly resource pertaining to parenting.
  The five volumes cover the following areas:
  - Children and Parenting
  - Biology and Ecology of Parenting

- Being and Becoming a Parent
- Social Conditions and Applied Parenting
- Practical Issues in Parenting

  Bornstein, Marc H. (Ed). (2012). *Handbook of Parenting*. 2nd ed. NY: Taylor & Francis/Psychology Press.

Under the editorial leadership of Marc Bornstein of the *National Institute of Child Health and Human Development* (www.nichd.nih.gov), dozens of leading researchers in the field of parenting contributed.

- **The Sage Handbook of Child Research**
  Melton, G. B., Ben-Arieh, A., Cashmore, J., Goodman, G. S. & Worley, N. K. (2014). *The Sage Handbook of Child Research*. Sage.

- **Evidence-Based Practice in Infant and Early Childhood Psychology**
  Mowder, B. A., Rubinson, F. & Yasik, A. E. (2009). *Evidence-Based Practice in Infant and Early Childhood Psychology*. Wiley.

The above two comprehensive volumes focus predominantly on childhood.

Parenting Reflection 1–1

At the outset and before having studied parent–child relations, what topics would you include in a course for first-time parents? What qualities would you encourage parents to display? What are some things that you would recommend in terms of parenting?

Focus Point.   As parents raise children, they begin to understand their children's developmental needs and become more effective and responsible in their roles as parents. Parents can improve their skills and parenting outcomes by being exposed to research and outcome-based parenting education. Parenting occurs within the milieu of the family system, as well as social and cultural contexts. Contemporary ideas on parenting roles ideally reflect current best practices.

DIMENSIONS OF THE PARENTING ROLE

The relationship between parents and children is one of the cornerstones of human existence, largely because of its biological basis. It is an essential part of our society, and society requires the addition of new members in order to continue. The unique bond between parents and their children can be examined from an ecological perspective.

Ecology is an interdisciplinary branch of biology that examines the *interrelationships* between organisms and their environment (Kagitcibasi, 2013). Behavioral scientists have placed an ecological perspective on human development and social behavior. Using this approach, the developmental changes in individuals, families, and other social groups take place within the context of interactions with changing environmental systems and bidirectional influence (Bronfenbrenner, 1979; Kerr, Stattin, & Özdemir, 2012). Various environments and contexts influence and shape behavior; parents assume different roles that influence their behaviors as parents. This same ecological perspective is used in the context of describing dimensions of the parenting role.

Family as a System

The family can be perceived as a system. The relationship between parents and children is a subsystem of the larger social system that we call a family. One model for understanding family group functioning is the **family systems theory**. This approach falls within an ecological context (Becvar & Becvar, 2013; Kagitcibasi, 2013). Family systems theory describes family functioning in ways that resemble other systems found in nature, such as the solar system and ecological systems. Everyday functioning takes place in a family, rules evolve to govern the behavior of members, roles are assigned to regulate behavior, and these roles relate to family goals. Family groups strive to maintain stability over time and adapt rules, behaviors, roles, and goals. Family members experience developmental changes, resolve interpersonal conflicts, and confront crises in ways that enhance effective functioning of the system.

Several subsystems co-exist within a larger family system, such as the relationship of the parents versus those of the siblings. A **subsystem** is a microcosm of the larger family system that mirrors the functioning of this group. The same principles and concepts that explain the functioning of the larger family system relate to how subsystems, including the parent–child subsystem, function.

The main priority of the parent–child relationship is to nurture children toward maturity. The parental role is sensitive and responsive to changes within the family system. For example, when one adult is removed from the family through divorce or death, the remaining adult's quality and style of parenting change. The parenthood role is also heavily influenced by factors arising from the larger environment on the family system.

Bidirectional Relationship

The parent–child relationship is **bidirectional**, as described in the by now classic work of Ambert (2001). The flow of influence goes both ways (Kerr et al., 2012). This means that adults and children influence each other.

Children's behavior and development contribute to the quality and scope of parental interactions. As children experience developmental changes, parents change their behavior and adapt by changing the rules, the ways they interact with their children, and their goals for child rearing. For example a baby is parented differently than an adolescent is parented. Interactions between parents and children evolve in tandem with children's developmental changes. Similarly, children respond to changes in parenting behavior in ways that help them achieve the developmental tasks appropriate for their particular life span stage.

Until several decades ago, the relationship between parent and child was described as a **unidirectional** model of socialization (Ambert, 2001; Kuczynski & Mol, 2015). In this model, the adult assumes the role of a teacher who is responsible for encouraging appropriate behavior patterns, values, and attitudes that prepare the child for effective participation in society upon reaching maturity. The child's role is that of being an active learner. According to the model, the flow of information is solely from parent to child. Clearly, the unidirectional model features the adult as having significant power over the child. In contrast, the subordinated child lacks social power. In the past, these were the accepted roles for parents and children, and they received strong support.

Developmental and Lifespan Pursuit

Parenthood is a **developmental** role that can continue over the **lifespan**. Unlike most adult social roles, parenting behavior and interactions must adapt to the developmental changes in children. Changes arising from a parent's own personal development affect the caregiving behavior. The age and developmental status of both the parent and the child affect the nature and context of the relationship at any point in time. Parenting also continues throughout the lifespan although the nature of the relationship will constantly morph to allow for changes in the participants. Initially parents are very protective of their as yet helpless offspring. Physical care may dominate. As the lifespan continues parents age and the offspring become capable adults. At some stage the roles flip when the parents may become frail and dependent, and their own children take on the roles of caretakers.

Social Construct

Parenthood is a social construct, which means that it is influenced by values that are transmitted culturally and in social contexts. The parental role is a social institution based on complex values, beliefs, norms, and behaviors that focus on procreation and the need to care for the young (Noddings, 2013). People who are not parents can also experience the parenting role—for instance,

through coparenting. Coparents are significant persons within a system who collaborate and contribute to the parenting of a child (McHale & Lindahl, 2011; Sterrett et al., 2013).

The role of the parent is universally understood by diverse groups. Every society, culture, and subculture defines appropriate behavior for parents. Some cultural groups may allocate a higher moral stature to parents. On the other hand, some couples make a conscious choice to remain child-free, and these individual choices are respected without affecting their status within a given community.

Parenting Reflection 1–2

Should parents raise their children using identical methods, styles, and approaches? What effects would such uniformity in child rearing have on adult outcomes?

Focus Point.   Current approaches describe the parent–child relationship as bidirectional, meaning that a child is acknowledged as an active participant and contributor to the relationship. Each person influences the behavior of the other. By contrast, parent–child relationships were traditionally and historically described as unidirectional; that is, the adult had complete jurisdiction, power, and control over the relationship. The parenting role can be characterized by four dimensions:

- **Family as a System.** The family systems theory describes parenthood as a subsystem of the larger social system of the family and within an ecological context.
- **Bidirectional Relationship.** Both parents and children actively participate in a bidirectional interaction with mutual influence.
- **Developmental and Lifespan.** Parenting is a *developmental* role and a *lifespan* pursuit: both parent and child undergo developmental changes with time and life span progressions. This continues throughout a lifetime.
- **Social Construct.** Parenthood is a *social construct*. The parental role is a social institution based on complex values, beliefs, norms, and behavior.

INFLUENCES IN THE PARENTING STYLE

Several factors contribute to how people see themselves as parents, and how they behave in this role. A number of themes merge into a workable blueprint that guides the parenting-role behavior. It is as if someone takes the pieces of a puzzle, manages to perceive how they all fit together, and puts them together into a completed object (See Figure 1–2).

Some factors that contribute to an adult's concept of parenting behavior come from past experiences. New ideas are added as the person gains experience in parenting children. The child makes contributions as well, just by who they are and the kind of care they require. Family ecological factors, attitudes about discipline, and an individual's past experiences all influence parenting styles (Pfefferbaum, Jacobs, Houston, & Griffin, 2015).

The factors that combine to influence a parenting style and form a parenting blueprint include the following (See Figure 1–1):

1. *Family-of-origin influences.* The model of parental behavior experienced in the family of origin.
2. *Sociocultural influences.* Social class, background, values, beliefs, education.
3. *Bidirectional influences.* The ways children and parents influence each other.
4. *Developmental time.* Synchrony of parental style and child's developmental stage.
5. *Personality, temperament.* Factors that are unique to parent and child.
6. *Family structure.* Family composition and membership.

Family-of-Origin Influences

One of the major influences in how we parent comes from observing our own parents and close caregivers. We use them as models for how to act (Sigel, McGillicuddy-DeLisi, & Goodnow, 2014). The perceptions we have about how we were raised influence how we approach our own children. Adults who are satisfied with their own upbringing tend to duplicate some of the parenting styles of their own parents.

Unpleasant memories from childhood may be the motivator to drastically change one's parenting style and not emulate one's parents. For example, the child who was somewhat neglected and whose parents never attended any sporting events, may make a distinct effort to be available when their own children require support.

The experiences we have in our childhood provide a blueprint for a number of interactional patterns in adulthood (Galvin, Braithwaite, & Bylund, 2015). There are several sources for this blueprint:

■ The goals our parents had for our growth and development.
■ The model of parenthood we observed from our parents' behavior.
■ The influence of parenting models that were handed down inter-generationally.

The parenting blueprint we assimilate may not be helpful when the time comes to assume the role ourselves. It may be inappropriate or unrealistic because circumstances in our family of origin may not resemble those in our current family.

Not every family system is healthy or well-adjusted. For example, a parent may be affected by addiction disorders, by mental or emotional disturbances, or by living conditions that hamper the ability to parent. Most attempt to hide the emotional pain that results from their inability to function healthily. When this occurs, the adult may adopt parenting behaviors (possibly learned from their own parental models) and assign roles to the children that mirror those in their family of origin, even if these roles are dysfunctional. What affects one person in a family system affects everyone to some degree. Patterns for coping with the stress of an unhealthy family of origin tend to carry over into future generations.

FIGURE 1–1. Interacting factors influencing parental style.

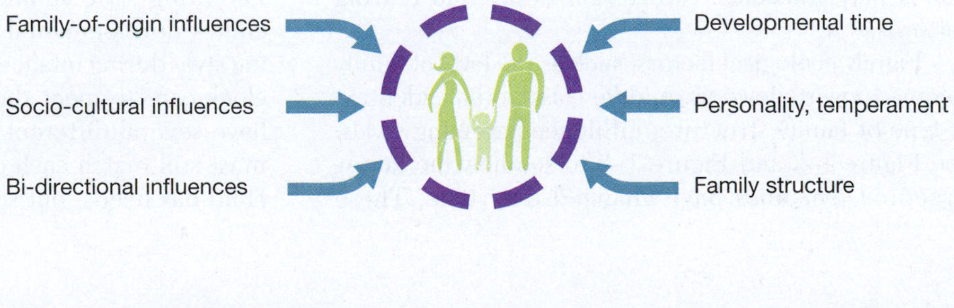

Family-of-origin influences

Socio-cultural influences

Bi-directional influences

Developmental time

Personality, temperament

Family structure

Based on observations of numerous adults acting as parents, several models of parenting behavior have been developed that illustrate how an unhealthy family of origin influences a person's own patterns of parenting (Koerner & Schrodt, 2014). There is never a pure assimilation of one particular model into a person's potential parenting behavior; instead, a composite of behaviors is taken from the various models.

Sociocultural Influences

Numerous studies have reported considerable variations among socioeconomic groups and the ways that children are reared. Values and outcomes may vary greatly, for instance from valuing education highly to discouraging girls from going to school. This can set the trajectory for the future of that child.

Generally there appear to be more similarities than differences in child rearing. This has been somewhat attributed to media presentations of middle-class values, and that more families in developed countries can achieve a middle-class lifestyle through education and rewarding employment. The potential for children's mental growth may be influenced by the differences in language use and teaching styles in the parental home. The middle-class values placed on education and academic achievement may result in patterns of interaction that promote children's problem-solving skills.

Parental behavioral styles are partly guided by the value systems of their social class. Each group maintains essentially the same intention to support children's growth and development, but the styles between groups may differ. Middle-class parents tend to value social achievement, encourage children to acquire knowledge, and expect independence early in their children's lives. Lower socioeconomic groups may have the same intentions, but immediate problems and challenges linked to income potential and the effects of poverty may cloud the good intentions parents have for their children. These differences in values may translate to differences in child-rearing patterns.

Family ecological factors, such as the level of family income (poverty level vs. middle class), ethnic identity, or type of family structure, influence parenting styles. See Figure 1–2 and Figure 1–3 to see how the family structural dynamics have changed over time. These factors also affect a family's ability to provide equipment and services, such as medical or dental care, clothing, and food, which, in turn, influences the quality and nature of the interactions. In this way, parents' goals for their child-rearing efforts may be tempered by a variety of family ecological factors.

Bidirectional Influences

Traditionally, children are seen as learners who require numerous learning opportunities to prepare them for adulthood. They undergo intensive socialization efforts. Typically, the adult assumes the role of teacher and the child the role of learner. This configuration can contain elements of a unidirectional model of socialization, unless the child is encouraged to be an active and participatory learner.

Children are viewed as being in need of adults' protection and they are dependent on parents for a long period. The relationship between parent and child is one in which the social power of the adult is unlikely to be questioned. The greater physical size and strength of adults also contributes to their power over children. In extreme situations where parental intentions are harmful to the child, the child becomes a victim. Some adults destructively use power to control and manipulate, rather than facilitate children's growth and development (Hoffman, 2013).

Family systems theory describes interactions within family relationships that have a reciprocal effect on participants. In some semi-symbiotic relationships, parental health, resources, and aspirations can be influenced by the demands of the child. An instance could be if a parent takes care of a child with special needs, but is not able to access sufficient support from other members of the family and of their immediate social systems. This could contribute to parental burn-out, presenting in less than optimal parenting.

Developmental Time

Parenting style should be congruent and match the child's developmental level. For example, the parenting style during infancy focuses on providing round-the-clock care to meet the infant's needs. When families have several different-aged children, parenting styles must still match each child's developmental level. The child has needs, but so does the parent. For example, parents may have to juggle the demands of their children while also finding ways to maintain job responsibilities. As children gain autonomy, parental styles should allow for this autonomy to blossom in an age appropriate manner. Typically, attitudes guiding parenting behavior can be expected to shift with the changing developmental needs of children.

On a macrosystemic level, the timespan within which we live and the historical and social events of that period can influence the backdrop against which parenting occurs. Bronfenbrenner (1979) refers to these influences as the Chronosystem; events that occur together in time, that occur in synchronicity. For example, if children are part of a refugee generation, the traumatic events of involuntary migration will also influence the parenting they experience.

Personality and Temperament

Parents typically try to actively meet the needs of their children. This ensures the likelihood of the survival of the children and promises the rewards of best outcomes. How the parents meet these needs, and what they perceive as being most important, may relate strongly to the socialization goals as well as cultural practices. There are inherent differences, not only between the children but also between the parents. Parents who have several children often express their amazement that the children may have the same parents yet turn out so differently. Each individual is unique. Even identical twins reveal subtle differences (Claridge, Canter, & Hume, 2013). This can be ascribed to the "nature" part of the nature-nurture formula. Once we add different environmental influences, the disparities may become even more pronounced.

The research by Bell and colleagues points toward the influence of parental temperament on parenting behavior (Garstein, Bell, & Calkins, 201; Lusby, Goodman, Yeung, Bell, & Stowe, 2016). Parental temperament can play a moderating role in parent-child relations. Nurturing behavior of parents toward their infants could be affected in mothers who suffered from perinatal depression (Lusby et al., 2016), although the intensity that the babies were exposed to was also of importance. The effects of maternal depression could be mitigated by coparental influences. If constructive nurturing behavior occurred within the family system,

even during the time a mother was dealing with perinatal and postpartum depression, these other nurturing relationships could minimize the effects on the infant. Supporting the mother toward health and dealing with her depression constructively remain important goals for the family system.

The Neurobiology of Human Attachments. The research on subtle, and possibly epigenetic, influences that may promote the expression of nurturing behavior, reveal complex and interacting factors at work. The role of the hormone oxytocin is increasingly implicated as exerting influence in nurturing and bonding behavior (Feldman, 2017). Parenting integrates the functioning of two neural networks, namely cortical-paralimbic structures which are associated with emotional processing, and cortical circuits which support social understanding. As parents spend time with children and are involved in active childcare, their caregiving experiences become more pronounced. The influences of hormones and how these shape brain behavior and expression are implicated (Abraham, Hendler, Shapira-Lichter, Kanat-Maymon, Zagoory-Sharon, & Feldman, 2014). The research, especially by Feldman and colleagues (Feldman, 2017; Feldman, Monakhov, Pratt, & Ebstein, 2016) points toward the hormonal influences in the brain and ultimately in attachment, nurturing, and parenting behavior. These hormonal influences also are noted in the subtle differences between mothers and fathers as they pertain to parenting (Kim et al., 2014).

Family Structure

Family size and family membership plays a significant role in parenting behavior. Families can be very diverse. They can be three generational families, single parent families, or blended families to mention a few variations on the theme. The effects of being a single child or the youngest child with much older siblings, have been well documented, as this places much attention on the child, with varying outcomes (Claridge & Canter 1973/2013). Family size has shrunk over the past decades, and the overwhelming responsibilities of having a family with a dozen kids is almost unthinkable in developed countries considering our current contexts. Refer to Figure 1–2.

FIGURE 1–2. Average number of own children per family (for families with children under 18), 1955–2016.

Source: U.S. Census Bureau, Current Population Survey, Annual Social and Economic Supplements, 1955, 1960, 1965 and 1970 to 2016.

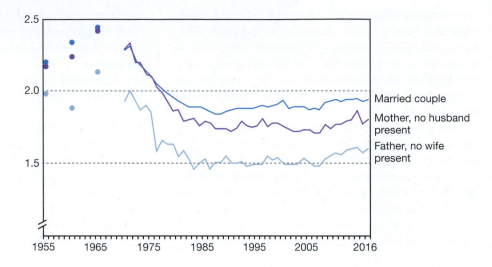

Married couple

Mother, no husband present

Father, no wife present

Video Example 1.2 Functions of the Family

Watch this video on the different types of family structures. How does family structure impact a child? (https://www.youtube.com/watch?v=nOng7C5rRhU)

Parenting Reflection 1–3

Consider how your own disciplinary style could be influenced by various interacting factors. Would you or wouldn't you adopt the disciplinary style that you experienced in your own youth? Justify your choice.

Focus Point. Parenting styles reflect the interaction between individuals and their child-rearing goals.

SOCIAL FACTORS AFFECTING PARENTHOOD

Throughout the 20th century and beyond, child-rearing approaches gradually eased up from restrictive and authoritarian to increasingly permissive. As the more punitive approaches decreased, physical punishment was discouraged. As children were studied in a developmental context, numerous child-rearing experts offered detailed, at times conflicting, child-rearing advice.

Family form and function can vary greatly. Many roads can lead to good parenting outcomes, just as many family forms can harbor and shelter their members in optimal ways. This historic photo, taken in 1905, depicts Jakob Mittelstadt, right, his wife and their eight children at New York's Ellis Island, just after the family arrived in New York.

This original photo can be found at North Dakota State University, Fargo, ND. source: https://library.ndsu.edu/grhc/articles/newspapers/news/ellis_island.html

Source: Sherman, A. F. & Mesenhöeller, P. (2005). Augustus F. Sherman: Ellis Island Portraits 1905–1920. Reading, P.A.: Aperture.

The emphasis became more psychological, inspired by techniques and concepts from developmental, clinical, and counseling psychology. Behavior modification based on positive reinforcement or reward became popular, especially in educational contexts and in managing certain behavior clusters, such as attention deficit disorders.

A number of contemporary social issues impact parent–child relations directly or indirectly. The larger society affects individuals and families to some degree, and the reverse is true as well with a bidirectional influence. Some of these issues are controversial and can be divisive in nature.

■ The roles of both genders are evolving and are sustained by the gender equality movement. Social conditions in many arenas cause major ripple effects. Current parents attest to the shared economic roles of partners, closely linked to shared parenting roles.

■ Societal issues pertaining to public education, violence, addiction disorders, economic challenges, and the like, have far-reaching effects on childhood and family life. Resource-strapped families are raising children in poverty, and employment and educational prospects for young adults can be challenging.

■ A significant turning point in American culture occurred after September 11, 2001 (9/11). Worldwide terrorist acts have become more prevalent. Military families, and especially the children in these families, have been deeply affected by deployment and war-related issues.

■ The increasing presence of the World Wide Web via personal electronic devices and the influence of social media, have caused a ripple effect in changing communication patterns, education, and endless other areas of family life in a paradigm shift unlike anything previously experienced in history. Information overload and less real-life face time with significant others are phenomena linked to the digital age.

■ Privacy issues have become a serious concern, as information from the digital world is mined and publicly accessible. This in turn has led to discussions concerning privacy that adolescents demand from their parents, and privacy between spouses.

■ The continuing debates surrounding family formation choices, general civil rights, legal and illegal immigration, displacement of refugee families, and the like continue.

••

Focus Point.   Social changes including greater gender equality, education, scientific and technological advances, expanding civil rights, and more, filter through to the family in a systemic manner, and contribute to family changes in form, function, and structure.

••

DIVERSITY IN FAMILY FORMS AND STRUCTURES

In our increasingly complex society, the family is an important source of stability, refuge and shelter. We have become more conscious of the diversity in our society; there is endless variety based on factors such as age, race, sexual orientation, special needs, and ethnic group identity, to name a few. With increased respect for diversity and the acquisition of multicultural competence in our personal and professional lives, we know that each group has its own strengths. As Americans we can find many threads that connect us in one common fabric, including our desire to pursue happiness. This noble goal is referenced in the U.S. Constitution. As Nobel Laureate Maya Angelou has so poignantly expressed in her poem "Human Family" (1995), in which she states that as humans, we are more similar than we are dissimilar.

These social changes are reflected in contemporary family life in America. For example, a trend reported by the U.S. Census Bureau (n.d.) is an increase in the number of nonfamily households and a decrease in the number of family households. In 1970, 70% of all American households were family households (at least two persons related by blood, marriage, or adoption), while today, these kinds of households are diminishing. Social relationships, such as divorce, families-of-choice, and families with same-sex parents, have changed the face of the American family. Families have changed in size, structure, form, and function and diversity is the norm.

In family forms and functions we concentrate on the configuration of the family. Even so, we cannot discuss every variant contained in our society and, therefore, within families, because members can belong to many different groups simultaneously. Most of the family forms discussed in this text are typically found in mainstream developed and developing countries. We acknowledge that there may be relatively isolated groups, especially in anthropological contexts, where variations occur. These small groups may represent rarer family forms; for instance polygamy; which involves marriage with multiple wives or husbands simultaneously.

To highlight every type of family where parents and children can claim membership would amount to cataloging differences, whereas we are trying to focus on unifying family trends. In this section, we focus on the predominant family types or structures that include children. Some of these variations may include:

- Two opposite-sex adults who are cohabiting or with an intact marriage and their children.
- Two same-sex adults, married or cohabiting, and their children.
- Single-parent adults and their children.
- Blended families composed of two opposite-sex adults who have remarried and the children of one or both.

- Renested families composed of adult parents and their adult children who have returned to the home.
- Custodial (co-resident) grandparent–grandchild families.
- Families of choice: not necessarily biologically related but cohabiting.

Family complexity may be linked to child well-being. Even so, it is not always intuitive and can present differently across family structures (Brown, Manning, & Stykes, 2015). Simply stated, this could mean that a specific family form need not be consistently linked to positive or negative outcomes. In the end, the quality of the relationships within a specific family form, combined with their social support systems and other resources, seem to be the crucial determinants of outcomes in terms of child well-being. Many roads can lead to good parenting outcomes, just as many family forms can harbor and shelter their members in optimal ways.

Two-Parent Families

Traditionally, families are thought to be composed of two opposite-sex, married adults and their children. For generations, this family form was considered the ideal, normative family form in which to produce and raise children to maturity. In contemporary family life there

FIGURE 1–3. Living arrangements of adults 18 and over showing growing complexity: Almost half of adults today do not live with a spouse (Data up to 2014).

Source: Current Population Survey, Annual Social and Economic Supplement, 1967–2016.

Growing complexity
Almost half of adults today do not live with a spouse

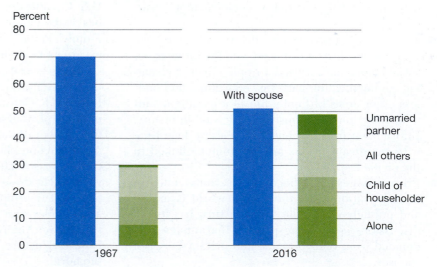

are many variations on the theme. Cohabiting couples with children, and same-sex couples and their children, whether married or cohabiting, form family units facing similar joys and challenges.

With gender equality on the forefront, there has been a welcome move toward *dual parenting*, with the implication that both parents will contribute whatever the parenting situation demands, regardless of traditional gender role stereotypes. In *dual-income* families, the ideal would be that all tasks are shared, from income-producing work and household-related labor, to the nurturing and raising of the offspring (Kotila, Schoppe-Sullivan, & Kamp Dush, 2013). In practice, this is not necessarily true. Dual-income families may have blurred traditional gender role divisions. Dual parenting ideally implies that both parents will contribute equally, responding to what the specific situations may demand, rather than giving a response based on traditional gender roles, even though each parent may bring different strengths to the parent–child relationship.

Androgynous parenting is sometimes used to describe roles that are either gender neutral or that are performed by the opposite-sex parent from the one who stereotypically assumes the role. An example would be strengthening the nurturing aspect of fathers, whereas in the previous century, mothers were the primary nurturers. The blurring of gender roles in the parenting context, specifically, can enhance a greater sense of gender equality in the children. Members of Generations X and Y are more likely to be *dual centric* or *family centric*, meaning that they emphasize work and family *equally*, actively planning to allocate sufficient time to family life. These are the cohorts who were born in the 1970s and 1980s (Dawson, Sharma, Irving, Marcus, & Chirico, 2015; Kray, Galinsky, & Thompson, 2002).

Much of the information on parent–child relations is derived from research based on individuals living in two-parent families. As such, it continues to be the predominant family form in the United States (U.S. Census Bureau, n.d.). In the general population, this family form is declining. This decline is often attributed to changes in attitudes that have made adult *cohabitation*, or living together without benefit of marriage, and divorce less stigmatized and more acceptable throughout American society (Wagner, Schmid, & Weiß, 2015). In addition,

the downward trend in two-parent families is contrasted with the upward trend in single-parent families in the United States.

Despite the decline in this traditional form of family, most children in the United States experience growing up with two parents (Vespa, Lewis, & Kreider, 2013; U.S. Census Bureau, 2016). Many adult couples choose to cohabit rather than marry, while raising the children of either or both partners (Richards, Rothblum, Beauchaine, & Balsam, 2016). From the statistics it is apparent that:

■ The number of adults who cohabit rather than marry is increasing (Lofquist, Lugaila, O'Connell, & Feliz, 2012; U.S. Census Bureau, 2016; Vespa, Lewis, & Kreider, 2013).

■ The nature of the relationship of a cohabiting couple closely resembles that of a married couple. The couple can face risk of separation and distress, similar to marriage partnerships (Manning, 2015).

■ Cohabitation does not necessarily lead to marriage (Rose-Greenland & Smock, 2013).

■ About one in nine cohabiting couples is in a same-sex partnership (Carl, 2012).

See Figure 1–4.

Single-Parent and Binuclear Families

One of the more common types of families in the United States today is composed of one adult parent and one or more children under age 18. Whether headed by a man or a woman, this unit is called a single-parent family. A **binuclear** family refers to children who have *access to two families*, usually as a result of parental divorce.

The number of single-parent families, whether by necessity or by choice, is increasing more rapidly than any other family form. It may be as a result of divorce, although many unmarried women choose to have children and express the wish to remain single by choice. In 2010, there were about 75 million minor children ages 0 to 17 in the United States. About two thirds of the youngsters were living in dual parent households, while a third lived in single parent set-ups. The number of children living with both parents decreased by about 10 percent between 1980 and 2010. Older children were less likely to live with two parents. Of the

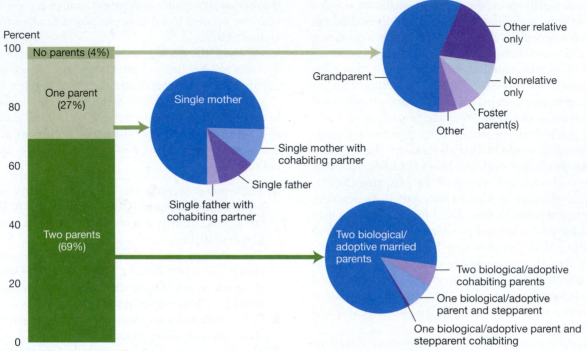

FIGURE 1–4. Percentage of children ages 0-17 living in various family arrangements, 2015.
Source: U.S. Census Bureau, Current Population Survey, Annual Social and Economic Supplement.

children in single-parent households in 2010, 23 percent lived only with their mother, 3 percent lived only with their father, and 4 percent lived with neither parent (Federal Interagency Forum on Child and Family Statistics, 2015).

Single-parent families accounted for about 26 percent of all families with children in 2010. Single-parent families are more prevalent among African Americans as a group (U.S. Census Bureau, n.d.).

A single-parent family is created through (1) divorce, desertion, or separation of the adults; (2) the death of one adult; or (3) having a child while unmarried. The most common means is through divorce. The vast majority of single-parent families are headed by women because U.S. courts typically award full physical custody of younger children to the mother, while also considering the best interests of the child.

Quality of life is a major issue for many single-parent families (Mikonnen et al., 2016). Any type of disruption in family life can produce a crisis, and divorce is one of the most stressful experiences of adulthood. It can also be traumatic for children. Although divorce has become commonplace, it is a crisis event that forces many short- and long-range adjustments.

The experience of being a single parent differs for women and men. Women generally expect to have financial difficulties, and there are significantly more children who live in poverty because they live in a single-parent family headed by a woman (Federal Interagency Forum on Child and Family Statistics, 2015). The implications for children growing up in single-parent families, especially those headed by mothers, can be serious. While most studies report that children generally fare well while living in a single-parent family, those who live in poverty are at greater risk for problems at school, teen parenthood, unemployment, and lower wages when entering the labor force.

Life is not easy for most single-parent families. Yet many persons choose divorce over an unhappy relationship, even though a multitude of difficult adjustments are inevitable. This type of family arrangement can be more efficient and harmonious than a household marked by tensions and strife between the adults, especially if abuse is part of the scenario. Same-sex married couples may face similar stressors of divorce (LeBlanc, Frost, & Wight, 2015).

● ●

Parenting Reflection 1–4

You have been elected mayor of a large city, having run your campaign on social reform. What are some of the things that you can do in your official capacity to improve the quality of life for single-parent families?

● ●

Blended Families

Blended families are formed when at least one of the adult partners remarries or when a couple cohabit and children are involved. Because the vast majority of single-parent families are headed by women, the person usually filling the vacant adult role in the new blended family is a man (Nixon & Hadfield, 2016). He may or may not have been divorced and may have children of his own. Same-sex couples can also choose to live in blended families while being married or while cohabiting.

Remarriage is popular, although these relationships have a higher risk of ending in divorce than first marriages (Carl, 2012; Kennedy & Ruggles, 2014). The median length of first marriages in the United States is about 7 years. Most persons who divorce remarry within 3 years. Second marriages tend to last about the same length as first marriages. It is unusual for an individual to have been married three times or more. Blended families, by definition, involve the children of one or both remarried partners, although many remarried couples have at least one child from this new union (Aughinbaugh, Robles, & Sun, 2013).

Popular perception holds that blended family life is highly problematic for all involved. Researchers have found that this family form may be no better or worse than other family forms, although the challenges are unique. These challenges include dealing with a complicated extended family network, difficulty in establishing stepparenting roles, and the unique developmental tasks associated with forming a new and cohesive family identity (Zeleznikow & Zeleznikow, 2015).

Families With Renested Adult Children

Families with renested adult children are a modern phenomenon. The renested family emerges when children who have been launched into independence return home to their family of origin. Young adult children, or emerging adults, are also referred to as *boomerang kids* (South & Lei, 2015). Some estimates suggest that more than 60 percent of all young adults between age 18 and 30 will, at some time, return to their family of origin to live temporarily. It is estimated that about 56 percent of men and 43 percent of women between age 18 and 24 live with one or both parents (Vespa, Lewis, & Kreider, 2013). During extended economic downturns, these numbers tend to increase.

The phenomenon of *renested* families occurs primarily when young adult children experience some type of transitional life crisis, such as job loss or divorce, and turn to their families for support. Young adults in stable partnerships are less likely to return home, whereas single moms are more likely to return to the parental base (Hayford & Guzzo, 2016). Some renested families are formed when adult children return to their elderly parents' homes to care for them, while others need grandparental support in raising their own children, especially if they are single parents.

Renested families need to adapt and respond to the development of a young adult. Family rules may need to be changed and new boundaries established as parents and emerging adults adapt to new ways of managing family life. The kind of arrangements derived will involve new definitions of family relationships that reduce the social power of the parents. Parents feel more positive about the arrangement when their boomerang kids reciprocate by contributing to the household financially and in kind, and are respectful of family rules. It is beneficial to all parties if the adult children can maintain their autonomy, even while returning to the parental home (Tanner & Arnett, 2016).

The *sandwich generation* refers to adults who are looking after their own parents, as well as their offspring; they are the middle generation with a generation on each side (Bogan, 2015).

Kinship Families

Custodial Grandparents and Grandchildren.
Increasingly American grandparents may be faced with the responsibility of raising their grandchildren,

and possibly providing some financial support for their own children. Typically grandchildren live in grandparent-maintained households, although it can include extended family members who are caring for related children. In 1970, in the United States, there were about 2.2 million of these households. By 2010, this number reached about 7 percent, or 4.9 million children living with a grandparent. A breakdown of these figures indicates that about half of the children in grandparent-maintained households are Caucasian, followed by about a quarter African American and just under 20 percent Hispanic/Latino (U.S. Census Bureau, 2014).

The family that encompasses *three generations* faces special challenges. For the grandchildren, there may be very real reasons why their biological parents cannot raise them. The lives of the grandparents are also transformed in unexpected ways, with considerable financial stressors accompanying their ongoing responsibilities. A significant number of grandparents find themselves overburdened and overwhelmed, especially if the children display behavioral issues or if the grandparents have failing health. The scenario is more positive if the grandparents are healthy, coping, and have the resources to fulfill this variation of the parenting role. For some, it adds meaning to their lives in a joyful and rewarding manner. Even so, postponement of having children may mean that grandparenthood arrives at a later age (Margolis, 2016).

The grandmother maintains the household in the majority of these families, and may be more likely to retire in order to invest time in the grandchildren than a grandfather would (Wiese, Burk, & Jaeckel, 2016). Co-resident grandparent–grandchild families are typically created when parents experience some type of personal problem that prevents them from effectively fulfilling their caregiving role. Examples of such debilitating personal problems include incarceration, addiction and related disorders, child abuse, chronic physical or emotional illness, or even death. Grandparents may step in to assume custody and provide a stable environment rather than the children being placed in foster care. Even so, grandmothers and grandfathers may perceive these challenges differently; depending on how involved they had been with their own jobs and whether they saw retirement in a positive or a negative light (Wiese et al., 2016).

Co-resident families face unique challenges. Grandparents may take on their roles when they are older than when their parents before them claimed the title of grandparent. They may not be as healthy and as able to fulfill a parenting role (Margolis, 2016). Many grandparents, while acting compassionately, find that their plans for a serene retirement must be postponed or abandoned to provide for their grandchildren. Others have to apply for public assistance because of increased expenses challenging an already-limited fixed income. The grandchildren may display problems related to parental divorce, addiction disorders, and inconsistent parenting behavior. Grandparents in co-resident households are more likely to be poor with the associated negative effects. Providing for the educational needs of grandchildren may be difficult if their own education was incomplete. And they may be unsure how to guide the children's educational experiences in a more digitalized world (Choi, Sprang, & Eslinger, 2016).

Focus Point. Diversity, in structure and form, are principle characteristics of contemporary American families. Significant variations in the ways that families are defined and how they are composed reflect changes occurring in the larger society. This in turn affects the parenting role. The influences can be bidirectional.

Families of Choice

The term *family of choice* denotes family formation not exclusively relying on shared genetics, or legal parental status. Family members choose to function as a family and this is the term often favored in same-sex unions. The concept "family" and what that implies is continuously evolving in response to and in interaction with societal and other demands. Additionally, created and assigned kinship roles represent variations in the family bonds. In single parent families, cohabiting and repartnered unions, same sex unions including persons identifying themselves as LGBT, and LGBTQ, as well as transnational families; the expression of a family of creation can be varied, even ambiguous (Cherlin, 2012; Gerhardt, 2016b). Common wisdom tells us that we can choose our friends, but we cannot choose our families. In families of choice these options are expanded.

Cultural Historic Snapshot 1–1

Children in the Civil War

Amidst the devastation of war, children forfeit their childhoods.

As fathers joined the military action during the Civil War in America (1861–1865), women and children waged their own battles sustaining the home front, as they were fighting for survival. Children would help with farming responsibilities, looked after younger siblings, sewed, made soap and candles, or scavenged for food. When their teachers joined the war effort, educations were interrupted, unless children were homeschooled. Here are some authentic reflections by children from this time:

"I was ten years old today. I did not have a cake; times are too hard. I hope that by my next birthday there will be peace in our land."

(Carrie Berry from Atlanta, Georgia)

"We are starving. As soon as enough of us get together we are going to take the bakeries and each of us will take a loaf of bread. That is little enough for the government to give us after it has taken all our men."

(Anonymous child from Richmond)

"In these few months my childhood had slipped away from me. Necessity, human obligations, family pride and patriotism had taken entire possession of my little emaciated body."

(Celine Fremaux from Baton Rouge, Louisiana)

Children on the Civil War homefront encountered trials, hardships, and violence that forced them to grow up quickly amidst a nation at war with itself . . . [Children] comprised a much bigger portion of the US population in 1860 than in the 21st century, with persons under age 19 making up nearly half of the population (compared to less than 25% today). . . . Many soldiers on both sides invoked the future of their children as to why the war should be fought . . . A number of children took up arms with their elders and served as enlisted soldiers or regimental musicians. While we don't know how many children enlisted during the Civil War, we do know that around 48 soldiers who were under the age of 18 won the Congressional Medal of Honor for their bravery and service. (Schwartz, retrieved 2017)

Source: Marcie Schwartz, Children of the Civil War. Civil War Trust. Retrieved from: http://www.civilwar.org/education/history/children-in-the-civil-war/

Military Families

"Soldiers may go to war as individuals but they come from families that are impacted by their deployment" (Myers-Walls, & Myers-Bowman, 2015, p. 2038). Military families face unique challenges, which may be even more pronounced in families with two serving members. Deployed military mothers are a fairly recent phenomenon. During deployment, military families share some of the stressors and challenges with families who function as single-parent units, but they are also subjected to a military environment that, in some ways, is a world of its own. While deployed, parenting from a distance and maintaining family cohesion, is challenging. Simultaneously, the deployed soldier is also forming a surrogate family with similarly deployed colleagues.

Military life (even without deployment) is characterized by some unique qualities that affect marital and family functioning and are closely related to parenting and child rearing. If one person from a family unit is deployed, it affects that entire unit, and the ripple effects are extensive (Oshri., Lucier-Greer, O'Neal, Arnold, Mancini, & Ford, 2015).

In an important review article that provided meta-analyses of studies spanning a decade ending in 2013, Yablonsky and co-authors shed light on themes relevant to military families (Yablonsky, Barbero, & Richardson, 2016). About 2.2 million U.S. service men and women are on active duty, and the number of spouses and children affected number three million. Based on figures released by the U.S. Department of Defense in 2013, about 200,000 persons were actively deployed at that time (Yablonsky et al., 2016). If one includes extended family, millions of Americans have experienced the deployment of a family member.

The cycle and transitions around deployment contain stressors of their own. This cycle contains the stages of pre-deployment, deployment, post deployment and possible re-deployment. Each stage contains particular stressors for the affected children and spouses as well as the deployed individual (DeVoe & Ross, 2012). Military personnel, as well as their families, face significant adjustment when the family member returns from deployment. There may be post-traumatic stress to deal with, the possibility of an injury is a reality, and the entire family has to readjust and rebalance to find a new equilibrium (Willerton, MacDermid Wadsworth, & Riggs, 2011). For some of the families, this adjustment cycle and its subsequent challenges is repeated with redeployment. According to Yablonsky and her co-researchers (Yablonsky et al., 2016), each phase of the cycle can have its own tasks and outcomes:

- **Pre-deployment** phase. Getting ready, facing uncertainty and some emotional distancing.
- **Deployment** phase. Staying engaged by connecting with own family and finding a support or surrogate family in the deployed setting.
- **Transposement** during deployment. This refers to the altering of the family; taking on new roles, challenges of communication.
- **Post-deployment.** Reintegrating with own family. Requires understanding, appreciation, and renewed family bonding (Yablonsky et al., 2016).

Considering that the period of deployment averages about 15 months, the spouses and children in these families are under a significant strain for extended periods of time. They worry about the safety of the family member who is deployed, and they suffer from what has been called *ambiguous loss*, which is the temporary loss of a family member combined with the risks, threats, and vulnerabilities associated with injury and permanent loss of life (Yablonsky et al., 2016). Whether we concentrate on the qualities of temporary single-parent households or the characteristics of long distance parenting, these families face stressors that affect many areas of family functioning, and seem to increase with repeated deployment (Lucier-Greer, Arnold, Mancini, Ford, & Bryant, 2015).

The sustaining and positive factors in these families are the strength and stability of the marriage relationship, combined with their social connectedness to a network of supportive and significant others, such as friends, family, and other military spouses and their families (Saltzman, Lester, Milburn, Woodward, & Stein, 2016). In the work of Karney and Crown (2011), it was found that, paradoxically, deployment increased the stability of many military marriages, but there are many variables that contradict generalizations because marital stability varies according to gender, race, length of deployment, and age at the time of marriage. To quote Karney and Crown: "In short, for the vast majority of the U.S. military, the longer that a service member was deployed while married, the *lower* the subsequent risk of marital dissolution. In these groups, deployment appears to enhance the stability of the marriage. The beneficial outcomes in terms of marital stability seem to increase with length of deployment" (2011, p. 37).

Although the marriage itself may be stable, multiple and prolonged deployments appear to escalate general family related difficulties, and there can be cumulative risks (Lucier-Greer et al., 2015). Ross (2016) found that despite the relative stability of military marriages, the female service members faced almost double the risk of marital breakup as compared with their male counterparts. Soldiers who return with post-combat mental health problems affect the entire family, which can precipitate poor adjustment in the children of these families. Major depression, PTSD, and generalized anxiety can affect as many as one in five soldiers (Ross, 2016).

Clearly, the excellent support networks of the military and the social cohesiveness of military families contribute to *emotional resilience*. The communities' capacity and ability to support military families is crucial in positive outcomes, as well as in providing support for the children in these challenging situations (Oshri. Lucier-Greer, O'Neal, Arnold, Mancini, & Ford, 2015). As civilians, we should understand that there is an immense positive power contained in our expressions of care, support, and appreciation toward military families. Their well-being is also the concern of the greater community, even though the military has built excellent and exemplary support systems and provides expertise in many areas of social concern. The numbers of children involved are large; the cohort represents about two million children, who have to deal with potentially traumatic challenges such

Support networks of the military and the social cohesiveness of military families contribute to their emotional resilience. The military family also faces specific challenges associated with each phase of the deployment cycle—pre-deployment, deployment, transposement and post deployment.

asseparation from a parent and the potential risk to that parent (Wadsworth et al., 2016).

There are several priorities for research about military families and subsequent integration of research findings (Willerton et al., 2011; Yablonsky et al., 2016):

- The deployment cycle; specifically pre-, during, and post deployment, and how one phase affects the next can benefit from further research attention.
- Studying marital and family relationships longitudinally; including deployed mothers, non-partnered mothers, dual military couples, and same-sex couples.
- Studying the effects of deployment on child well-being and parent–child relationships, especially in different service contexts, as the sub-cultures can vary.
- Studying the renegotiation process in military families as they readapt after deployment.
- Examining coping with the psychological and physical wounds of combat, and subsequent transitions.
- Studying the impact of help-seeking behavior in soldiers who are not partnered, as well as help-seeking behavior of related family members.
- Communication styles and modes during these various transitional phases, and especially during deployment.

The support provided to military families can expand and benefit from research findings. Among some of the recommendations are the use of systemic and evidence-based approaches and the power of education to inform and to teach as this will have a trickle-down effect. Information and best practices that are being dispersed more widely snowball in reaching their target audiences. Service members, as well as their spouses, require information and training to safeguard the psychological health of their children and to optimize parent–child relations.

Ethnography: Diverse Family Forms

The family forms described previously are those typically found in developed nations. In remote and fairly isolated contexts, typically described in anthropological studies, other variations on the marriage and family theme exist. Some variations include the following:

Polygamy involves a marriage that may include several adults. Polygamy falls under the umbrella term *polyamory*, which literally means loving several persons or partners. There are specific variations; for example, the family form of a man and several wives is called *polygyny*, literally meaning "many" linked to the Greek root of the word *gyny* meaning woman or female, the same root as found in "gynecology." When a woman is partnered by several husbands simultaneously, it is referred to as *polyandry*. Here the Greek root of the word is "andro," the same root as found in the word describing "androgens" or hormones typically associated with males (Nanda & Warms, 2014, pp. 176–178).

Other variations are endogamous and exogamous marriages; the first require marriages between members of the same group, the latter requires the opposite, namely that the marriage partner does not belong to the same group.

Morganatic Marriage. In certain ingenious cultural and historic contexts, novel ways were found to manage the typical rights and privileges associated with marital unions. Some marriages had to do with transference of power, privilege, titles, property, and rights, especially in noble, powerful, or rich families. A morganatic marriage described two persons who did not have the same social class or rank, for instance a royal marrying a "commoner." In morganatic marriages ways were found to avoid some of the legal rights and responsibilities accompanying marriage. In contemporary societies these practices are typically not legally sanctioned. To prevent certain assets being transferred to the wife at marriage, the marriage was called a "left-hand marriage" where the husband held the wife's hand with his own left hand during the ceremony. As the right hand was thought to be the dominant hand, using his left hand lessened the marriage for all intents of inheritance of privilege or power, such as royal titles. Thus a left-hand wife had minimal or no rights, whereas a right-hand wife (usually the first wife) was entitled to the privileges associated with her husband's rank (Körner, 2016). Nelson Mandela's father, who was a chief of the Thembu tribe in Southern Africa, married his first wife and she could access his rank and his title. In some circles, this marriage to his first wife was thought to be a "right-hand marriage" and the three subsequent marriages were thought to represent "left-hand marriages." (See Cultural Snapshot 1–1.)

Problems and challenges with succession rights were documented in several royal families and have altered the course of history. The current Royal Family in Britain may have been totally different had Edward VIII not abdicated in December 1936 to marry American divorcee Wallis Simpson. Family form and function in terms of access to the throne, were most definitely affected in major ways.

Cultural Snapshot 1–2

Father of a Nation

Family forms vary and are strongly influenced by cultural and religious practices. Family forms and function are transitioning in response to changing norms and cultural practices. What may have been a symbol of status or power a century ago may not convey the same message in more recent contexts. Looking at the family history of Nobel Peace Prize winner, Nelson Rolihlahla Mandela (1918–2013), some of these cultural and historical differences are apparent. Mandela's father was a chief and a person of high status in his Thembu tribal community. Mandela's father had four wives. Mandela was born in Mvezo village as one of four children by the same parental dyad. Mandela's father had a total of 13 children with his four wives. Further offspring from Mandela's father were his three half brothers and six half sisters.

Nelson Mandela's family of procreation was large as well. He was married three times. From his first marriage four children were born, of whom two reached adulthood. Another two children were born from his second marriage. When Mandela married Graca Machel, her two stepchildren and two biological children from her former marriage joined the large extended family linked to Nelson Mandela. Mandela has 17 grandchildren and many great grandchildren.

Nelson Mandela is lovingly called "Madiba" by the South African nation, a word denoting respect and admiration. It is a name from the Thembu clan, who speak Xhosa, and references Mandela's ancestry. Mandela has at times been credited as "*parenting a nation*."

Based on: Mandela, Nelson. (1994). *The Long Walk to Freedom*. London: Little, Brown & Company and on information displayed at the Mandela Museum, near Qunu, South Africa (nelsonmandelamuseum.org.za/).

In most developed countries, variations on marriage with simultaneous commitments to multiple partners are typically not legal or sanctioned by the mainstream societal values or legal systems. There are also strict taboos and incest rules against marrying very close family members who are related by blood, and this is illegal in virtually all cultural and societal contexts.

(Based on: Körner, A. (2016). "Heirs and their wives: Setting the scene for Umbertian Italy. Chapt. 3, pp.38–52. In: Mehrkens, H. & Lorenz F. (Eds). *Sons and Heirs: succession and culture in nineteenth century Europe*. Palgrave Macmillan.)

FAMILY WELL-BEING

The quality of the relationships within diverse families is a key indicator of overall well-being. Making value judgments about one particular family form or configuration over another is not a constructive exercise. Sometimes families choose their composition, but more often than not, life's seemingly haphazard challenges contribute strongly to the configurations. One single mom freed herself with courage and determination from an intensely abusive relationship. She stated: "This was not the life script I had envisioned for myself or my family, but this is what it is. I am determined to give my children the best upbringing I can, no matter the sacrifices."

The relevance lies in how well the members of the family are functioning within their particular family group. Family *wellness* is affected by so many factors, from the economic to the emotional. An entire range of resources are required to ensure that the family unit avoids the pitfalls of becoming a fragile family.

The comments by sociologist Judith Stacey take on a timeless quality. Her perspective on the diversity of family forms seems to endure two decades after it was written:

> The most careful studies and the most careful researchers confirm what most of us know from our own lives: The quality of any family's relationships and resources readily trumps its formal structure or form. Access to economic, educational, and social resources; the quality and consistency of parental nurturance, guidance, and responsibility; and the degree of domestic harmony, conflict, and hostility affect child development and welfare far more substantially than does the particular number, gender, sexual orientation, and marital status of parents or the family structure in which children are reared. (Stacey, 1998a, p. 80)

CHAPTER FOCUS POINTS

Parenthood

■ In our society the concept of parenthood implies that parents are responsible for nurturing, teaching, socializing, and acting as guardians for their children until they reach the age of legal maturity.

Coparents

■ Coparents take on permanent and semi-permanent roles with a serious commitment to a child's upbringing. Coparents are characterized by two lead factors: Coparents have executive function and an emotional attachment/commitment to the children they coparent.

Parenting Education

■ As parents raise children, they begin to understand their children's developmental needs, and become more effective and responsible in their roles as parents. Parents can improve their skills and parenting outcomes by being exposed to research and outcome-based parenting education. Parenting occurs in the milieu of a family system, and within social and cultural contexts. Contemporary ideas on parenting roles ideally reflect current best practices.

Dimensions of the Parenthood Role

■ Current approaches describe the parent–child relationship as bidirectional, meaning that a child is acknowledged as an active participant and contributor to the relationship. Each person influences the behavior of the other. By contrast, parent-child relationships were traditionally and historically described as unidirectional; that is, the adult had complete jurisdiction, power, and control over the relationship. The parenting role can be characterized by four dimensions:
  - *Family as a System*. The family systems theory describes parenthood as a subsystem of the larger social system of the family and within an ecological context.
  - *Bidirectional Relationship*. Both parents and children actively participate in a bidirectional interaction with mutual influence.

■ *Developmental and Lifespan*. Parenting is a developmental role and a lifespan pursuit: both parent and child undergo developmental changes with time and life span progressions. This continues throughout a lifetime.

■ *Social Construct*. Parenthood is a social construct. The parental role is a social institution based on complex values, beliefs, norms, and behavior.

Influences in the Parenting Styles

■ Several overlapping influences contribute to the nature and context of an adult's potential behavior as a parent and influence the configuration of the adopted parenting style. Parenting styles reflect the interaction between individuals and their child-rearing goals.

Social Factors Affecting Parenthood

■ Social changes, including greater gender equality, education, scientific and technological advances, expanding civil rights, and more, filter through to the family in a systemic manner and contribute to family changes in form, function, and structure.

Diversity in Family Forms and Structures

■ Diversity, in structure and form, are principal characteristic of contemporary American families. Significant variations in the ways that families are defined and how they are composed reflect changes occurring in the larger society. This in turn affects the parenting role. The influences can be bidirectional.

USEFUL WEBSITES

Websites are dynamic and change

Administration for Children and Families, U.S. Department of Health and Human Services
www.acf.hhs.gov
Children and youth

American Academy of Child and Adolescent Psychiatry
www.aacap.org
Family resources

American Academy of Pediatrics
www.aap.org
Resources for parents, health advisories, 'Blueprint for Children' report

Centers for Disease Control and Prevention
www.cdc.gov
Healthy living recommendations

Military Child Education Coalition
http://www.militarychild.org/
Research and resources for military families

National Institute of Child Health and Human Development
www.nichd.nih.gov
Research-based information and resources: health of children, adults, families, and communities

National Institutes of Health
www.nih.gov
Health information and research on environmental influences on child health

CHAPTER 2

Parenting Approaches

Learning Outcomes

. . . .

After completing this chapter, you should be able to:

1. Identify the parent–child relationship as being the core of parenting.

2. Summarize a parent's role as the primary teacher.

3. Illustrate the characteristics of appropriate discipline.

4. Distinguish between positive and negative forms of discipline, including the legitimate concerns surrounding corporal punishment.

5. Describe the four main parenting styles and their implications.

6. Illustrate the Parenting Circumplex Model, by means of a diagram.

7. Assess the role that context plays in the implementation of parenting practices.

8. Evaluate the common elements of evidence-based parenting programs.

9. Explain the effectiveness of positive parental discipline.

. . . .

THE PARENTING RELATIONSHIP

At the core of parenting lies the relationship. This is the essential point of departure. Almost everything we expect from a constructive, trusting, and sustaining human interaction is equally applicable to a parent–child relationship. Treat your child with the same respect, dignity, compassion, and love with which you would like to be treated. It is reflected as a core truth in philosophical reflections and in major world religions. Treat your neighbor like yourself. Do unto others what you would like to be done unto you.

The many opinions concerning the best way to raise children can seem like a big fluffy ball of wool, distracting us from the essence. Try unraveling the ball of wool—it ends up with a simple beginning; a parent–child relationship. More than that, ideally it comes from a place where there is true concern for the others' well-being, or the legal wording: "In the best interests of the child." As parents, our first concern should be to do no harm, just as the ethical guidelines caution us in the helping professions: *First of all, do no harm.*

If the central theme concerns relationship building, we need effective communication and listening skills. Similar to good partnerships and marriages, parents and children need to know how to negotiate respectfully, where and how to put boundaries in place, how to participate in the lifelong back and forth of the unique and intimate dialogue between a parent and a child. We have to listen actively. Slowing down to truly focus on our two-year-old, lays the foundation for the exchanges during adolescence. Warmth needs to be displayed; it is part of the nurture component that feeds and sustains the relationship. Relationship-based care practices in infant and toddler care emphasize continuity of caretakers in early developmental contexts, supporting relationship formation and maintenance.

We have borrowed and appropriated information from psychology and the helping professions in general. We have learned from psycho-therapeutic approaches. The study of human motivation has shaped our understanding. Human developmental theory showed us that we are parenting a person who is in flux, changing and evolving over the lifespan. Our interactions need to reflect and respond to these non-static qualities.

The trends in parenting approaches and programs reflect the trends in psychology. For this reason, the theories are relevant, as they show us the underpinnings that lead to a particular approach. They reveal how thinking about children and their caretakers has shifted and changed over the decades. Parenting approaches also reflect what is going on systemically in society at large. A major war, an economic downturn, an influx of refugees; these macro-systemic events trickle down and are echoed, however faintly, in the one-on-one relationships within a family. There are some swings in the pendulum. We leave behind us a history of overly strict, punitive, and authoritarian parenting, while we are moving towards more democratic relationships, based on best practices.

If we consider the evolving parent–child relationship, birth marks a point of extreme dependence and vulnerability for the newborn infant. The power differential is dramatically unequal. The adult is responsible and in control. Factors that should facilitate this caring and nurturing role is the innate instinct to protect our young, and that we want to care for our children as we are heavily vested in their well-being which also represents our own hopes for the future (Children's Defense Fund, n.d.).

As children develop, they will master one task after another, until ultimately they are launched into emerging adulthood and beyond. The bulk of the responsibility has shifted from the parent to the child, as the next generation speeds towards autonomy and independence, while their parents wonder how the kids grew up in what seemed like the blink of an eye. History will repeat itself, one parent–child relationship after the other, linking backwards and forwards in time to become part of the very fabric of society.

Parenting Reflection 2–1

Parenting occurs in the many contexts in which children grow and develop. Reflect on the needs that unify us as parents—what we universally share in our parenting efforts, regardless of ethnicity, culture, or origin.

Focus Point.   The parent–child relationship is the foundation of parenting. This relationship is dynamic and constantly evolving as both parents and children grow and mature. Our knowledge of psychology and human development provides insight into patterns of interaction that lead to positive outcomes.

PARENTS AS TEACHERS

Parents remain responsible for the core of the teaching and learning process; ethics, the value and respect for learning, the attitude towards responsibility and work, and the nuances of what happens between people in relationships. The modeling that occurs day in and day out as children observe their parents may be one of the most powerful yet under-recognized schools of life. These are impactful learning and teaching opportunities and as parents we need to be cognizant of what we gift our children; intentionally as well as inadvertently. In many ways we are our children's first teachers.

Parents have always taught their offspring the skills and knowledge they believe children will need to function effectively as adults. Even so we have outsourced much of the formal education, and parents are supported by educational institutions in a process that lasts a decade or two, but continues both formally and informally for a lifetime.

From ancient times to the present, societies have recognized that parents are their children's first and most important teachers. Long before public school systems were established, parents held the responsibility for training and teaching their children the essential skills and knowledge to become effectively functioning adults. Our cultural traditions are society's way of transmitting customs, values, and beliefs that have served the elders well. It is a form of education. While formal educational functions have been taken on by other agents, society has never relinquished the socialization responsibilities of parents in equipping children with basic skills and knowledge.

Comparing past and present, parenting challenges have shifted. Until very recently, infant mortality took a disconcertingly high toll. The vulnerability we feel when our children are threatened remains a constant and different challenges take their place in the gallery of parental concerns and fears.

The dilemma lies in distinguishing what children truly need in order to flourish, as opposed to what may be perceived as a peripheral luxury. Because it is a moving target that is influenced and determined by context, it is not possible to find the panacea promising good outcomes for all. Parenting and the various systems within which it occurs is subject to many variables. No one size fits all.

It is practically impossible to know what type of occupation children will hold in the future. The vast advances in science and technology make it difficult for us to predict the challenges of the future world. We can make educated guesses, but we do not know. People in developed countries require years of education and training to become competent in an occupation or a profession. Typically, parenting is not held to the same formalities. Preparing the next generation to cope emotionally and to perfect social and interpersonal skills is usually a matter of trial and error. Parents have to be role models of values that will have meaning and usefulness to their children when they are grown, regardless of the changes in society. These may include:

■ Integrity that will guide appropriate civic, ethical, and law-abiding behavior.
■ Self efficacy and the ability to attain goals and objectives, including an education.
■ Interpersonal and coping skills.
■ Respecting the needs of others, as well as one's own.

The childhood experiences of today's parents differ from those that their children will encounter in the future. Additionally, the isolated nuclear family system has few outside supports to assist in its child-rearing efforts. According to the respected historical voices in the field of parenting (Bronfenbrenner, 1985; Kagan, 1976), children generally need several core processes to take place, and remarkably little has changed since these, by now historical, recommendations.

■ To feel valued by parents and a few significant adults, such as a teacher or a relative.
■ To develop their own personal attitudes, values, and opinions in order to become autonomous.
■ To develop and master skills and abilities that are valued by society.
■ To love and to be able to accept love from others, which includes forming secure attachments.

Parental competency requires knowledge of a variety of approaches for guiding children toward adulthood. Parental love and nurture of children is important for their healthy growth and development. Being a competent and effective parent requires additional skills. There are a number of strategies and parenting styles that focus

In addition to providing a loving and nurturing structured environment, parents also foster ethics, communicate value and respect for learning, and teach the skills and knowledge children need as they grow into adults.

Otnaydur/Shutterstock

on fostering the emotional needs and character development of both parents and children. Some strategies are therapeutic, some attempt to resolve conflicts between parents and children and teach interpersonal skills, and some propose a warm, nurturing approach to parent–child interactions.

Rather than offering a recipe for child rearing, these strategies and parenting styles provide parents with skills for raising children to become competent adults.

Focus Point.   As a child's first teacher, a parent is charged to instill values and attitudes that guide children on their journey towards autonomy and adulthood. There are many approaches that parents can follow to become competent teachers and effective socializers. Practicing a variety of these strategies enhances the effectiveness of parenting and improves the quality of parent–child interactions.

Cultural Snapshot 2–1

The Wide Spectrum of the Human Family

In virtually all societies, people group together and form families which are recognized as a specific social form. But not all societies, or all families, look alike or function in similar fashion. A herdsman in East Africa for instance, may regard a very large group of people as kin; large referring to several hundred. Some may be related through the bloodline others by marriage. The Hopi, located primarily in northern Arizona, include married daughters and their offspring as part of the family. Once sons marry they form family entities of their own, and are not regarded as close relatives in the way the majority of North Americans may define that term (Based on: Ferraro & Andreatta, 2014).

"They live at impossible altitudes on the roof of the world, in the extreme north lashed by freezing winds, in baking deserts where they trek from one oasis to another and in the equatorial jungle where the sunlight has difficulty reaching the ground: these are the peoples of the world, the holders of cultural rather than genetic differences, civilizations whose lives follow a rhythm different to that of the industrialized world. They are human groups and societies in continual evolution, with an extraordinary capacity for interchange, which leads to the infinite number of variants that together we refer to as Humanity" (Ferrera, 2005, Back cover).

Among the Gallong people in Arunachal Pradesh, India, the family is patriarchal and patrilineal, which also implies that the oldest son will inherit once the father dies. Occasionally polygamy occurs. These extended families live together, typically in a long house, which is subdivided to accommodate the individual smaller or nuclear family units. Those who live together also share their meals. If a female member of the household is widowed, she goes to live with her younger son. The way a new family unit signals their independence from the rest of the clan, is that they light their own fire and eat separately (Based on Ferrera, 2005).

"The Gallong claim they are descended from the Heaven and the Earth, the two primordial gods from whom the entire universe resulted after a number of divine generations ..." (Ferrera, 2005, p. 147).

Sources: Ferraro, Gary & Andreatta, Susan. (2014). *Cultural Anthropology: An Applied Perspective.* 10th ed. Boston, MA: Cengage Learning.

Ferrera, Mirella (2003). *Peoples of the World.* Vercelli, Italy: Whitestar.

APPROPRIATE DISCIPLINE

Discipline in the context of child rearing should have the positive meaning of instructional *guidance*. For discipline to be effective, parents need to view it in light of the term's original and positive meaning. The term **discipline** contains the root of the Latin verb *discere*, meaning "to learn." It is found in Middle English and is used in the context of instruction. A derivative of the term is *disciple*, which means "pupil" or "student."

The following pertain to appropriate discipline:

■ Effective discipline should be developmentally appropriate.
■ Steer children towards appropriate behavioral choices.
■ Encourage internalization of rules, values, and beliefs.
■ Strengthen self-regulation and self-efficacy.
■ Guide social skills, facilitating work and social interactions.
■ Actions should be positive, reasonable, and temperate.
■ Consistency as well as flexibility, are relevant.
■ Discipline provides structure by developing rules within a family system.

If we can shape and guide children through positive and respectful actions, it is our hope that we can minimize the harsh and humiliating practices that can be disrespectful to a child. Appropriate guidance is preferable to punishment after the fact. Good guidance should be like the navigating devices in our cars. At the first hint of an error the computer modulated voice will pipe in: "Recalculating route." Ideally our interventions should be ongoing and small; they should be based on respectfully guiding and encouraging behavior towards the right direction. If we can convey that we value the developing individual, it paves the royal road towards that person

valuing themselves. The bonus will be that this contributes incrementally towards a good self-concept; one of the cornerstone gifts a parent can facilitate.

These practices are equally applicable to all those professionals working with children and youth: child care professionals, educators, the helping professions in general.

Process and Content

The *process* of parenting refers to the general ebb-and-flow of the parent–child relationship. The qualities that define the relationship are also the qualities that describe the process. It is the vessel that contains the specifics. For instance, the process between two people can be respectful or it can be disrespectful; to use but two dimensions. In reality, relationships are multidimensional and complex.

The *content* refers to specifics. It is how we metaphorically color between the lines, how we fill the vessel. Specifics could refer to the exact bedtime ritual for a child, the specifics of the menu. Basically, it is the detail that makes up the whole. These details are important, in that, added together they set the tone of the relationship which is then expressed in the process. For example, if we are irritable about every detail in our interactions with our children, we can express that in a moment of making a derogatory remark, or not caring about the food we pack in their lunch boxes. But the countless little things that accumulate express how we feel about that relationship. The content contributes to the process.

All's not lost if we get one of those details wrong. As parents and caregivers we are fallible, and at times we suffer from overload, so unintentionally we are definitely going to get a number of the details wrong. But importantly, if the process is good, if our ongoing relationship with the child is positive, then the relationship is in credit, even though the occasional lapse can occur. We can still move forward. Donald Winnicott (1896–1971) was an English pediatrician and a psychoanalyst. He coined the concept of "good-enough parenting" and he said:

> "The good-enough mother ... starts off with an almost complete adaptation to her infant's needs, and as time proceeds she adapts less and less completely, gradually, according to the infant's growing ability to deal with her failure" (Winnicott, 1953).

By *good-enough* we presume he implied that the general process was the intention and practice of good parenting, even as perfection is unattainable; we are, after all, human, and parents can burn-out and despair. We know about the realities of *caregiver despair*. Winnicott also acknowledged the progression of the lifespan, which altered the parenting relationship in a bidirectional manner.

There is a tipping point though. If our relationship consists only of negative input, stacked and multiplied day after day, then the process of the relationship is at risk. Gottman (1994) from a marriage and family therapy context, described qualities such as criticism, contempt, stonewalling, and defensiveness, that ultimately destroy a relationship. He referred to them as the four horsemen, and they tend to usher in destruction. In small doses they may seduce us into thinking they are handy weapons in an interpersonal duel. But they do some immediate harm, and in ongoing large dosages they become sufficiently toxic that they jeopardize and possibly destroy the relationship. Neglectful parenting, in its many forms and expressions, can claim as its victim a vulnerable and defenseless child; something responsible grown-ups should never have on their conscience.

Just as in any other interpersonal relationships, parents and children bring their unique personalities to the table. There is no single perfect way of parenting, just as there is no single perfect way of sustaining a marriage or a relationship. It is about the *process* of the relationship; that has to be mutually respectful and constructive. The *content* of how that happens will vary from one parenting relationship to another. As the proverb states: Many paths lead to Rome. There are also many paths towards a fulfilling and sustaining relationship between a parent and a child.

Positive Self Esteem

Parents have many responsibilities, but one of the central roles is in supporting the development of positive self-esteem and related good self-concept in the developing child. This quality will direct and influence many related facets of the child's functioning.

Parents should be the *guardians* of their children, in that they look after their welfare. The word guardian contains the root "*guard*," which implies that we watch over and ensure the safety of the person concerned. According to the Oxford Dictionary, the word is derived from the Old French "*garden*"; and is also of Germanic origin, as in the noun "*warden.*" As guardians we are not only responsible for the physical and emotional wellbeing of those entrusted to us. We have to actively contribute to supporting the unfolding of a total person, allowing potential to be realized so that children can become the best persons they can be. The image that the child has of himself will form the basis of self-confidence, aspirational goals, and many related endeavors with far reaching effects.

The *process* should serve this outcome. Every time the *content* is negative, we chip away at the self-concept of a developing person. We are slowly and in very small increments doing harm. It may be a one-off occasion for which we can apologize, but as guardians of children we need to be mindful of the ongoing process of shaping an individual. Negative comments are remembered much longer than positive remarks, and the potency of a negative and hurtful remark is thought to have at least four times the power as compared to a positive utterance. Negatives sting more and they are remembered longer.

In the classic French fairy tale by Charles Perrault (1628–1703), with the title "Diamonds and Toads," two sisters fall under the spell of a fairy. The girl who uttered good thoughts had diamonds and pearls cascade from her mouth. The girl with the poisonous tongue released toads and snakes into the world. It is more effective to guide through positive input, as that sets the tone for mutually respectful and supportive interactions. Modeling by setting a good example is a powerful way of shaping behavior.

Nurture and Structure

Combining appropriate nurture and structure are the cornerstones of good parenting.

Nurture relates to all the ways in which we demonstrate love, not only for others but also for ourselves. Nurturing involves touching, noticing, and caring in healthy ways; being appropriately responsive. Nurture and care can be expressed in several variations and often overlaps. Discipline is most effective when provided to children within a nurturing or caring atmosphere. By nurturing their children, parents show them that they are loved unconditionally and are lovable. Nurture involves true concern for the other's well-being and expressing that constructive emotion.

Structure is provided through the internalized boundaries and controls that people acquire through socialization experiences that guide their behavior. Parents provide structure by providing these socialization experiences, instruction, limits, and rules that support self-disciplined actions. When applied appropriately, rules provide children with a sense of protection and foster a sense of trust and security. Parents teach children rules that are rational and that outline the boundaries of acceptable behavior. These boundaries contribute to expanding emotional regulation and internalizing self-discipline.

"Successful parenting is an authoritative balance of love and limits."

(Larzelere & Kuhn, 2016, p. 1551)

Responsive and Responsible Care

Responsive care is expressed when a parent determines what a child's needs are, but this determination can only occur because of the feedback loop between parent and child. The parent acts in a trusting and loving manner that generates a sense of trust. It involves noticing and listening to the child and understanding the cues and requests that the child offers. An example would be when the parent notices the child is getting overtired and initiates the bedtime routine, even though the child protests. The parent asserts the right to implement the intervention that is appropriate while considering the best interests of the child. Another example would be the parent who notices that the child is running a fever, and responds by giving the medically indicated intervention or seeking professional help.

Ideally both parent and child interact in an ongoing bidirectional manner and the parent is sensitive to the needs of the child. The care is derived from love that is unconditional. This means that love is given freely, without expectations, limits, or measure. The parent's message to the child is "I love you because you are who you are."

Unconditional love and acceptance does not mean that negative or harmful behavior is sanctioned and condoned. Instead there is a clear differentiation between the unacceptable behavior, and the unconditional respect for the person. This means that if little Sven scribbles on the white leather couch with an indelible marker, we express our frustration by clearly pointing out that the couch is not the drawing board. Clearly, we do not want a reoccurrence of the event so we need to guide and point out the boundaries. "This behavior is unacceptable because it destroys the couch that we all like to sit on. If you want to draw, use the paper on your drawing board." This is a more constructive approach that also guides towards a solution. Commentaries about the bad character and meanness of the child are inappropriate, as this situation is about the act of drawing in an inappropriate place. It should not be a judgment of character.

Constructive Guidance

The goal of constructive and respectful parental guidance is to foster an understanding of the child. It becomes an extension of the relationship. Knowing the guidelines regarding acceptable and unacceptable behaviors and their consequences in well-functioning families is helpful. In healthy family systems, there are negotiable rules. Children in healthy families learn that the rules are for their protection and freedom. They know that they can talk with their parents about making occasional exceptions to the rules. Rules can be negotiable and non-negotiable. Non-negotiable rules typically involve situations that ensure the safety of the child. Each family system must develop its own rules, policies, and values regarding child rearing and socialization. These evolve from and depend on many factors, such as personalities, family of origin, values, financial and social status, and the number and birth order of the children. Some common guidelines for parents are:

- *Equifinality as it applies to discipline.* The concept of equifinality from family systems theory implies that families attain similar goals in different and varied ways. Different methods for socializing children may still lead to the same outcomes, namely children who will grow up to hold similar values and attitudes. A variety of techniques and practices support socialization. There is no single disciplinary program that will meet all parenting goals.
- *Empathy: Connecting with feelings and motivations.* The goal is for the parent to enter the child's world, to gain an understanding of a child's feelings and motivations. The parent can be attentive to a child's verbal and nonverbal communications and reflect the feelings. This process is based on compassion and empathy. Misbehavior may be a learned response or action that is logical at a particular time. Parents who attempt to understand their children in a loving, noncritical way will feel less overwhelmed. Parents will be more rational and encourage children to think before they act in a developmentally appropriate manner. Empathy supports problem solving, as opposed to angry outbursts.

- **Explaining and reasoning.** Reasoning, combined with non-abusive approaches (e.g., withdrawal of privileges), are effective interventions. These guide children to comply with parental wishes. Developmentally appropriate reasoning is the key. Immediateness of the reasoning is relevant as the child can then associate the explanation with the situation. The intervention should be in proportion to the behavior being guided. Usually, if there is a good relationship between parent and child, an explanation may suffice.

- **Consistency** of the disciplinary approach helps children control their actions and can support emotional regulation. Consistency takes effort, but it provides structure in the form of predictability, and siblings will know and expect fairness in that similar situations will be met with similar disciplinary approaches.

- **Positive reinforcement** and other constructive methods are viewed as desirable in shaping behavior. Appropriate and sincere praise and acknowledgment of the effort invested in a task are powerful. Parents may require an expanded skill set to implement these successfully. Current approaches caution against overuse of hollow and meaningless praise in a uniform manner that does not match the situation or effort concerned. The semi-automatic praise of "Good job" risks becoming meaningless if overused.

- **Facilitate appropriate autonomy.** Children require opportunities to reason and make age appropriate choices. Granting the right to make appropriate personal decisions and to experience the consequences fosters responsibility. The parent's role is to help generate alternatives without supplying all of the answers, options, or solutions all of the time.

The term scaffolding is also used in this context. Decisions must be age- and context appropriate and always keep the safety and well-being of the child in mind. The parent who makes all decisions and accepts all the responsibility fosters dependency rather than autonomy. By making their own decisions and living with the results, children learn to differentiate themselves from others and to establish personal boundaries. Decisions can initially be relatively small such as: "Would you like to wear the brown or the blue shirt."

- **Foster appropriate individuality.** Some family systems value sameness or rigid conformity in all members. Individual differences in values, opinions, ideas, or means of self-expression respect the uniqueness of each family member. Children should be treated fairly and consistently, while also respecting their individuality. Children, especially adolescents, may not think and act exactly like their parents or hold identical values and beliefs. The demand for sameness can destroy a child's spirit and self-perception as an autonomous human being who has the right to be unique and true to her own self.

···

Focus Point. Despite the common view of discipline as a form of punishment, appropriate discipline should include encouragement, positive messages, nurture, and guidance. Discipline is used to help children acquire socially appropriate behavior according to the patterns supported by their family system. Effective discipline should be moderate, developmentally appropriate, and acknowledge the particular child's needs.

···

Cultural Snapshot 2–2

Children are Treasured Gifts

In American Indian and Alaska Native families, children are typically seen as treasured gifts. Parents and other extended family members are charged with discovering the unique characteristics of a child at birth to determine her or his place within the tribe. For several months an infant is carefully observed to learn about his or her nature. The child's name is based on the characteristics that family members observe. Only then is the naming ceremony conducted, sometimes many months after birth.

Parents usually teach their children traditional values based on the practical application of personal belief systems. Sharing personal resources, thoughts, and knowledge is considered appropriate in interpersonal interactions. Things and people are perceived according to intrinsic rather than extrinsic traits and characteristics. Children are taught to be in touch with the rhythms of nature and to be sensitive to the needs of others.

CORPORAL PUNISHMENT

Aggressive acts directed at children violate the trust children have in adults. They take unfair advantage of the vulnerability and power imbalance between the generations. They are also the expression of adults who are bankrupt when it comes to constructive resources and interventions for guiding behavior. Any discipline that is performed in anger implies an irrational parent and a potentially dangerous situation for the child. Similarly, interpersonal violence (IPV) as it occurs in marital or partner relationships, emanates messages of disrespect, loss of self-regulation and control, power imbalances, and victimization.

Corporal punishment is a serious topic as it is damaging and has long range detrimental outcomes. It is a slippery slope when we deal with corporal punishment versus abuse. What parents may regard as well intended "paddling" (hitting with a flat object, like a paddle), may in reality contain all the elements of disrespect, violation of boundaries, and elements of abuse. When it occurs inside the privacy of the home, it may go unreported, but that does not make it an acceptable practice.

In 1979, Sweden became the first country to formally ban all corporal punishment. More countries followed suit and, internationally, the adoption of policies prohibiting corporal punishment is increasing. The *Convention on the Rights of the Child* advocates that all forms of corporal punishment should be ceased. Consequently in virtually all developed countries and a number of developing countries, corporal punishment is now legally prohibited. In the majority of U.S. states this practice is illegal, but the policies are not uniform throughout the United States.

In educational contexts, such as schools, corporal punishment is forbidden, and educators and childcare professionals know from their training that this practice meets with zero tolerance. In North America, children who report their parents for serious corporal punishment, can and have successfully set the cogs of the legal system in motion, with ensuing social worker home visits and probation of the parents.

In practice, even mild forms of physical punishment can easily cross the line to becoming abusive; harming the child. Add to this that parents may differ substantially in what they regard or define as mild versus serious in terms of physical punishment. Parents, especially in very traditional cultural contexts, may state that it is at their own discretion how they discipline their children and that they themselves had been disciplined in this manner.

Parents who model aggressive behavior as a means of conflict resolution are sending a message that they condone this behavior. Considering the danger physically and the negative effects on a child's self-esteem, corporal punishment should never be an option. Depending on the age, size, and strength of the child, physical vulnerability varies tremendously. The emotional scars that this behavior leaves behind are consistently powerful and often influence the victims in their choice of disciplinary approaches once they are raising their own children.

Corporal punishment can be generally described as a form of discipline often defined as the "use of physical force with the intention of causing a child to experience pain, but no injury, for the purposes of correction or control of the child's behavior" (Fréchette, Zoratti, & Romano, 2015).

Other punitive approaches aimed at the body, have varying emotional effects. Thus, forcing a child to ingest noxious substances (e.g., washing their mouths with soap

Parents who have been subjected to physical punishment or abuse as children are more likely to use spanking as a means of resolving conflict.

for telling a lie), pinching, slapping, forcing a child to remain in an uncomfortable position physically, locking them in a confined space, and the like, can be forms of punishment targeting the body. On the extreme end can be heinous acts such as burning, scalding, kicking, pinching and shaking, which clearly can cause permanent damage and represent severe maltreatment and abuse.

Parental interventions which are aggressive can lead to violent behavior in children (Sandberg, Feldhousen, & Busby, 2012). The connection between harsh physical punishment in childhood and violence in adult dating has been documented (L. G. Simons, Burt, & Simons, 2008). Adults, who were spanked by their parents, may revert to similar negative approaches in their own disciplinary actions. Spanking and other forms of physical punishment usually occur as an expression of parental anger, which can represent temporary lessened emotional control, and in turn has the potential of harming the child.

It is most unusual for a child to launch a personal attack with malicious intent. If that occurred, it may be symptomatic of larger problems within the family system or possibly signal behavioral disorders. Parents who are angry and critical when faced with misbehavior, may dictate their own solution to a problem which discounts the child. At times, adults who resort to physical and abusive disciplinary interventions have major problems themselves; some of the perpetrators may be dealing with addiction disorders which in turn influence their behavior. Clearly professional interventions are indicated, and in extreme situations parents may be declared unfit to raise their own children.

On the positive side, in developed countries, greater numbers of parents are moving away from corporal punishment as an option. Younger generations are also increasingly averse to this form of discipline. In the United States, the majority of Americans feel that corporal punishment is not a justifiable practice; not in the home nor in school settings (Downs, 2015). (Refer to Focus On 2-1: Corporal Punishment).

Video Example 2.1 Parenting: Kids and Discipline Across Cultures

Watch this video on disciplining children across cultures. Does the world agree on the best way to discipline a child in order to produce productive members of society?
(https://www.youtube.com/watch?v=9RYO5acAGWw)

Parenting Reflection 2–2

Do we have the right to intervene when parents use physical punishment, especially in public? What would you say to a parent who is a stranger, and who displays this form of parenting interaction?

Focus Point.   Discipline ideally should emphasize the teaching of appropriate behavior through *positive* and preferably *non-punitive* approaches. Discipline can be seen as a form of guiding behavior in which parents explore constructive ways of shaping a child's conduct. Appropriate rules and boundaries provide children with structure and teach them to internalize self-regulatory behavior.

Focus On 2–1:   Corporal Punishment: Aggressive Approaches and Negative Outcomes

Consider these research findings on the effects of corporal punishment on children. The evidence strongly cautions against using spanking or other physical methods as disciplinary measures.

- Adults who spank children are likely to have been spanked by their parents as a primary means of controlling their misbehavior (Taylor et al., 2016).
- There is a very strong association between experiencing harsh, abusive, physical punishment in childhood and being a perpetrator of violence in intimate relationships in adulthood (Sandberg et al., 2012).
- The acceptance of spanking as a means of discipline varies across ethnicities, races, and cultures (Hawkins, Rabenhorst-Bell, & Hetzel-Riggin, 2015; Nadan, Spilsbury & Korbin, 2015).
- Spanking appears to be a prevalent means of child maltreatment, frequently used as a last resort in gaining children's compliance to adult wishes.

- Most spankings occur when adults are angry with children, and fail to effectively control their own emotional outbursts (Rodriguez, 2016).
- Parents who are considered abusive by mental health professionals and by the courts, consider spanking to be an acceptable means of discipline.
- Spanking is frequently used instead of positive reinforcement of desirable behavior (Gershoff, 2013).
- Using information from the fragile families study (FFCW), it was shown that spanking occurred especially in very young children through to adolescence, and that the children would subsequently externalize the behavior as in acting out aggressively themselves. The earlier this pattern was established the more likely it would persist in later life (MacKenzie, Nicklas, Brooks-Gunn & Waldfogel, 2015).
- Children who are spanked exhibit more aggressive behaviors than children who are not spanked (Gershoff, 2013). Spanking is associated with children's negative feelings of self-esteem and personal worth (Gershoff & Grogan-Kaylor, 2016).
- Males are more likely than females to approve of spanking children (Gershoff & Grogan-Kaylor, 2016).
- Spanking may produce a child's conformity to parental wishes in an immediate situation, but its long-term effects may include increased probability of deviance, including delinquency in adolescence and violent crime in adulthood (Gershoff & Grogan-Kaylor, 2016).
- Parents who are members of conservative and fundamentalist religious groups tend to perceive spanking (corporal punishment) as an acceptable form of discipline (Bottoms, Goodman, Tolou-Shams et al., 2015; Holden & Williamson, 2014). Even so, research concerning conservatism in the broader community and correlation to corporal punishment are not conclusive
- Social disorganization and related community factors may be more important than religious or political affiliation in predicting risky parenting behaviors such as maltreatment (Breyer & MacPhee, 2015).
- Individuals who are considered to be bullies have been subjected to physical punishment/abuse as children and have incorrectly learned that the use of physical force is an "acceptable" means of resolving conflicts with others (Zottis, Salum, Isolan, Manfro, & Heldt, 2014); note that this is not mainstream-recommended behavior.
- The use of corporal punishment (including spanking) is controversial. Over 25 countries worldwide prohibit this practice by law (Scheidegger, 2014). Harsh child punishment is also regarded as a topic that deserves to be addressed by human rights (Watkinson & Rock, 2016).

Additional resource: Downs, Jon O. (2015). Positive behavioral interventions and supports vs. corporal punishment: a literature review. *International Journal for Cross-Disciplinary Subjects in Education* (IJCDSE) 6(1): 2126–2132.

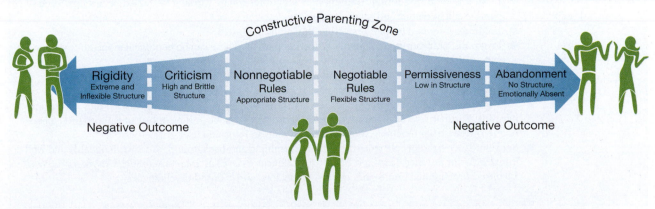

FIGURE 2–1.   Continuum of structure in parenting relationships. The central shaded area represents the zone of constructive parenting behavior.

Focus On 2–2: **The Continuum of Structure in Parenting Relationships**

In the midrange, a constructive parenting zone is created, where balanced parenting occurs. The further we move towards both ends of the continuum, the more dysfunctional the interventions may become. The two central parenting characteristics, namely, **Nonnegotiable Rules** and **Negotiable Rules**, are patterns that support development of appropriate structure and self-regulation and are the most helpful to both children and parents. **Constructive Criticism** and appropriate **Permissiveness** can occur depending on context and the developmental stage of the child.

The pairs of parenting styles at the two opposite ends of the continuum—*Rigidity* on the left and *Abandonment* on the right—do not provide children with healthy structure and are considered to have negative effects. (Figure 2–1).

The visual model was created by Gerhardt, C., in Bigner & Gerhardt (2014, p. 85). Loosely based on concepts discussed by Clarke, J. I., & Dawson, C. (1998). *Growing Up Again: Parenting Ourselves, Parenting Our Children* (2nd ed.). Minneapolis, MN: Hazelden.

Parenting FAQ 2–1

We would like to take a formal parenting course. Any suggestions?

In reviewing parenting programs, an estimated 15,000 different parenting programs are available worldwide and in many languages. Narrowing it down to programs in English still leaves an overwhelming number of choices, adding up to hundreds of options, many of them not reputable. The following decision tree may help:

■ The outcomes of a number of parenting programs have been assessed, and a brief selection is tabulated in Table 2–1 Evidence-based Parenting Programs. These programs meet stringent standards and have been tested in various population groups. There are about 50 programs that meet these requirements, and the list is growing.

■ Determine the age of the child or the needs of the target group. Programs can be quite specific in addressing content areas and age groups. Among the choices are the following:

◆ Programs presented by trained group leaders.
◆ Programs requiring formal training and for professionals working with certain groups, such as youths with addiction and related disorders.
◆ Programs intended for parents within the family context.
◆ Programs requiring group sessions with other parents. These can be beneficial in forming a support group and in understanding what other parents are experiencing.
◆ Programs that can be studied individually, using DVDs and print.
◆ Programs based on different theoretical approaches.

■ Non-evidence-based parenting programs vary tremendously in quality. Some advice may be outright harmful. For that reason, it is important to choose wisely. Look at the context of the program, check online reviews from reputable sources, and become an informed user.

■ Seek guidance from people who, through their training and background, are knowledgeable and well informed—for instance, Certified Family Life Educators (CFLEs), Licensed Social Workers (LSWs), Licensed Professional Counselors (LPCs), educators, and licensed psychologists.

Focus On 2–3:   **Mental Health Resources**

Including Parenting Programs

National Registry of Evidence-based Programs and Practices (NREPP)

www.nrepp.samhsa.gov

The U.S. Department of Health and Human Services maintains an objective and detailed registry of resources related to *mental health promotion* in the broadest sense. Many of these interventions focus on *parenting* and *child-related themes*. Prevention of addiction and related disorders features strongly in the formula for supporting mental health. The NREPP acts as a liaison between persons seeking programs to implement and the program developers. For many organizations and professionals in the helping professions, this is a valued and trusted resource.

This registry is constantly growing, with well over 400 evidence-based interventions, and many more programs in the pipeline for review (SAMHSA, n.d, 2017). A search for programs focusing on *parenting* listed around 50 results, and more programs may be suitable, depending on the age of the child, parental concerns, and the context in which the program is administered.

To be included in the registry, programs need to reflect evidence-based practices, as supported by the quality of the program's research and its readiness for dissemination. Interventions and programs are reviewed by panels of experts and have to meet stringent criteria in several areas, including the availability of materials and support resources for users.

Based on: U.S. Department of Health and Human Services, Substance Abuse and Mental Health Services Administration (SAMHSA, n.d, 2017). *National Registry of Evidence-based Programs and Practices.* (www.samhsa.gov).

TABLE 2–1.   Selection of Evidence-based Parenting Programs

Program	Description
Families and Schools Together (FAST)	A community-building family skills program. Theoretical angle: multimodal incorporating various sociological and psychological theories. Described as a "universal, community-based, public health parenting model to reduce inequalities in health, education and social care" and "recognized by the United Nations as an evidence-based, universal, family skills model for drug prevention" (McDonald, Miller, & Sandler, 2015).
The Incredible Years©	Program has undergone many revisions and is regarded as an exemplary program. Theoretical approach: Cognitive, emotional, and behavioral theories. Focus: Social skills, social modeling, parenting strengths, building positive relationships. Lead author: Carolyn Webster-Stratton.
Nobody's Perfect Program	Community-based parenting program owned by the Public Health Agency of Canada (PHAC). It is described as participant-driven and requires experiential and active learning. Theoretical angle: Multimodal and mutual aid theory providing mutual support. Focus: To maintain and promote health of young children by enhancing skills of parents.

(Continued)

TABLE 2–1. *(Continued)*

Program	Description
Nurturing Parenting Programs for the Prevention of Child Maltreatment	A family-centered program to support prevention of child abuse and neglect. Replacing negative parenting patterns with positive ones. Theoretical angle: positive and negative nurturing; the latter can involve abuse and neglect. Focus: Replacing dysfunctional behavior with functional alternatives. Lead author: Stephen Bavolek.
Parenting Wisely (PW)	Available as a cost effective, computer-based training program for parents and families with interactive instruction. Theoretical approach: Social learning theory. Focus: Aims to reduce child behavior problems and enhance effective parenting skills. Improve parent–child relationships and communication.
Parent Management Training – Oregon Model (PMTO)	Implemented internationally and in a variety of cultural contexts. Theoretical angle: Social interaction learning model (SIL). Focus: Designed to prevent and reduce children's behavior problems. Lead author: Gerald Patterson.
Parents Matter! & Families Matter!	Developed for Sub-Saharan African contexts. Implemented supported by Centers for Disease Control and Prevention (CDC). Theoretical angle: Multimodal; sociological and psychological theories. Focus: Reducing sexual risk-taking behavior in adolescents by enhancing communication skills between parents and their children.
Strengthening Families	Group family sessions providing structured skills training. Variations of the program address different cultural contexts. Theoretical angle: Family systems theory, social learning/efficacy theory, social ecology model, resilience. Focus: Preventive intervention. Lead author: Karol Kumpfer.
Supporting Father Involvement Project	Addresses both parents as well as paternal and co-parenting situations. Theoretical angle: Social contexts, resilience, coping. Focus: Risk and protective factors, social support, coping skills. Promotes positive parent–child relationships.
Triple P – Positive Parenting	Provides a tiered, multilevel system representing support for parents and guiding towards prevention by increasing knowledge and skills. Theoretical angle: Multi-modal. Focus: Skill building and prevention. Program originated in Australia. Spanish and online versions available.

This summary (in alphabetical order) of ten evidence-based programs is based on: Ponzetti, J. J. (Ed.). 2016. *Evidence-based parenting education: A global perspective*. New York, NY: Routledge (Chapters 10–19, pp. 141–307).
This table was previously published in a similar form: Gerhardt, C. (2016). Selection of evidence-based parenting programs. *National Council on Family Relations: CFLE Network*. Winter. 28(1),: 20. Published with permission.

Focus Point. Evidence-based parenting programs and mental health resources range in effectiveness and are available for some parents who need assistance with various aspects of the parenting process.

PARENTING STYLES

Parenting styles refer to those collections of child-rearing behaviors that tend to be global in nature. They refer to an umbrella of parental behaviors.

Parenting styles characterize an overall approach to parenting, while parents can display a variety of behaviors that change and are modified by a number of real-life circumstances depending on context. Parenting styles also reflect a philosophy of parenting that characterizes what parents emphasize in shaping children's developmental behaviors. Parenting styles encapsulate those attitudes and beliefs that form the implicit rules that guide a person's behavior as a parent. These have a significant influence on behavioral choices in interacting with and guiding the child toward adulthood.

Strengths based parenting, also the title of a book (Reckmeyer, 2016), is based on the results of Gallup research into psychological strengths of about one million people (www.gallup.com). The approach focuses on strengths, as the title reveals, and also states that parenting styles vary considerably to accommodate individual differences in children and their parents. Gallup is a major organization concerned with polls and has used the considerable volume of information to focus on strengths.

Parenting is often described on a continuum of four styles, each with differing amounts and interactions of structure and nurture. Behavioral and social scientists recognize a group of basic categories in parenting styles. Initial thoughts about parenting revealed three basic styles: *authoritarian*, *authoritative*, and *permissive*. These approaches are based on the, by now historically relevant, work by Diana Baumrind (1966) and represent some of the earlier attempts to add a theoretical angle to the practice of parenting. The permissive subset can be further differentiated into *permissive-neglectful* and *permissive-indulgent* parenting approaches.

Later another category, namely that of *uninvolved* parenting was added by Maccoby and Martin (1983).

Baumrind (1996) states that *authoritative* parental approaches (the approach she strongly supports), appear to promote healthy, socially responsible outcomes for children that include

■ Acceptance rather than rejection and firm, but not rigid, policies.
■ Emphasis on critical thinking skills, individuality, and self-initiative.
■ Models of the behaviors and attitudes that parents want children to adopt.
■ Parental explanations of the reasons for the rules and the policies.

Critique on Parenting Styles

Some of the critique concerning Baumrind's, by now virtually legendary, approach is that it is a product of its time, the sixties, and therefore a little dated. The social context was a post war baby boomer generation who questioned the authority and control of remaining attitudes from the post Victorian era; the very strict and regimented approaches. These were giving way to person-centered interactions, as the American therapeutic icon, Carl Rogers, made us aware of the virtues of person-centered therapy and unconditional positive regard. The anti-psychiatry movement and anti-authoritarian protests questioned prevailing values and approaches. The spin-offs from anti-Vietnam war sentiments, by a generation whose parents could remember WWII only too clearly, provided fertile ground for 'flower power,' experimentation with hallucinogenic drugs, and a re-examination of psychiatric practices focusing on institutionalization.

The second main point of critique to Baumrind's approach is that it does not sufficiently emphasize the *context* of any given parenting situation. Parents cannot be consistently pegged into one category or another; ideally, they shift through approaches as the situation demands. If a child approaches a potentially injurious or even life-threatening situation, the only correct approach would be very authoritarian. Intervene immediately and strongly to avert disaster. Thus, the context and the developmental stage of the child can and should determine the subtle shifts and changes in parenting. For that reason *responsive* and *responsible* childcare approaches are relevant, as they can react to the context.

It is thought that parents initially adopt one particular style that strongly influences the manner in which they interact with children, but that this position shifts according to particular situations; for example, in public or private settings and in response to children's needs as they change developmentally. Parenting styles are adaptable within family systems as parents attempt to maintain homeostasis within this relationship. For example, when a child is preschool age, appropriate authoritarian-style parenting provides assertive care, and promotes relevant standards for children to expand their emotional regulation. The parenting style shifts toward the authoritative style when children reach school age and supportive care is mixed with assertive care. Later, as children reach adolescence, parenting styles relax and become more permissive as teens take increasing responsibility for their own decisions and actions.

Developmentally appropriate parenting accommodates developmental changes in children. Parenting styles may display variations according to education, ethnicity, culture, and social class. Above all, context remains a serious consideration.

Authoritative Style.

This is the style that is favored and approximates desirable parenting. The overall approach of **authoritative parenting** is focusing on the inherent strengths of the child, as well as on the desirable outcome. It emphasizes the development of autonomy in children, within reasonable and developmentally appropriate limits. When providing structure, authoritative parents may resort to tactics such as reasoning, overt demonstrations of power through modeling and conversations, or psychological reinforcement. The structure is expressed in a verbal give and take, where the reasoning behind the policies is shared with the child. The child's opinion is respected and considered. Children tend to be self-reliant, self-controlled, content, and curious about learning and exploring their environment.

This parenting style is also effective when children become adolescents because it coincides with the appropriate autonomy that young adults seek. It allows for expression of individuality and permits participation in family decision making. This parenting style encourages a child's success in school, development of a healthy sense of personal autonomy, and positive work attitudes.

Authoritarian Style.

If parental rules are critical, judgmental, and unloving positions and promoted by authoritarian attitudes, the resulting discipline and structure will tend to be rigid and inflexible. Such rules and the manner in which parents enforce them can lead to extreme authoritarianism that causes children to acquire a negative self-concept. Children who are raised by parents who use criticism, sarcasm, nagging, discounting, shame, and guilt will think that something about them must be unlovable and wrong to elicit these responses. They are on the fast track towards outcomes that may go hand in hand with rebelliousness and self-destructive behavior.

Authoritarian parenting relies predominantly on controlling children's behavior towards immediate and long-range obedience (Baumrind, 1966). Authoritarian styles are anchored in traditional methods of child rearing. Typically, this parenting style involves controlling children's behavior in every respect. Obedience is obtained in various controlling ways, but physical punishment and other forceful means are often used to gain the child's cooperation. A typical response to a child's questioning of rules (and an authoritarian parent has many, many non-negotiable rules) may be, "Because I said so." Usually, this parenting approach evaluates, judges, and shapes the behavior of a child according to an established and often absolute standard to which the child is expected to conform. The parent's word is law. They are not encouraged to think for themselves or to think critically. Children raised in this way are followers rather than initiators.

Clearly, authoritarian-based programs address the parental need for control, and it can become a *unilateral* interaction, where the parent exerts their will on the child. The research repeatedly emphasizes *bidirectionality* in parent–child relations and responsiveness to infant and child needs in order to lay the foundations for further healthy and well-adjusted development. Authoritarian styles are not especially conducive to promoting emotional health because parents intimidate rather than promote self-worth. Negative criticism, especially if directed at the person in a devaluing manner, brings with it damaging outcomes.

Some current approaches to very authoritarian parenting are not evidence-based. A particularly hazardous approach guides parents toward rigid scheduling of infants, with the advice to let very young babies cry while they are coerced into a schedule. This approach has been associated with *failure to thrive* (FTT) in babies, as well as involuntary early weaning of infants.

Dealing with out-of-control and high-risk teenagers in special educational "boot camp" settings should not be confused with parenting programs for normally developing children. These are therapeutic interventions for select high-risk populations, who frequently already have a history of family court involvement.

Alice Miller (1990) refers to authoritarian parenting in its extreme form as *poisonous pedagogy* because this style appears to promote parenting behavior that is, in effect, emotionally abusive and damaging to a child's self-esteem. Miller believes that the net result of this parenting style robs children of their spirit, promotes the development of self-doubt, and inhibits normal emotional development in later life.

Permissive Style.   This is an indulgent style that displays nurture without the benefit of accompanying structure. The **Permissive parenting** approach avoids excessive control, does not enforce obedience to externally defined standards, and basically allows children to regulate their own activities (Baumrind, 1966). Permissive parents believe that they should respond to their children as individuals and encourage them to be autonomous, often before the children are developmentally ready to do so. In practice it can have the appearance of loving neglect (*permissive-neglectful parenting*). A permissive parent is not interested in being viewed by a child as an authority figure or as an ideal person to be imitated; rather, this parent wishes to be the child's friend, almost like a peer, and displays nurturing behavior. But nurture without much structure can lead to over-indulgence, one of the riskier outcomes of this approach (*permissive- indulgent parenting*).

Permissive parents allow greater latitude in children's behavior. Policies or limits to behavior are determined in consultation with children in an attempt to allow them to voice their own opinions and retain their favor. The anti-establishment movement in the mid-1960s favored this type of child-rearing approach, but the pendulum has swung towards the opposite direction with later generations of "helicopter" parents, who hover over their children.

Uninvolved Style.   Poor outcomes can be expected from *uninvolved* parents, who, in their emotional, and at times physical, absence seem to declare that they do not care about the child. The fourth category that was added to Baumrind's original three, is the uninvolved parent (Maccoby & Martin, 1983). This fourth parenting style is occasionally identified as *neglectful*, as it is low in warmth and low in control.

Uninvolved parents may as well be absent, as they do not provide much input to the child irrespective of whether it is positive or negative input. There simply is minimal input. They skip the teacher–parent meetings, are not seen on the spectator's benches at ballgames, and may have their eyes firmly fixed on the screen of their portable electronic devices. The child can try several strategies to gain their attention. Initially children may escalate their behavior, becoming more and more attention seeking and demanding. If the parents remain in "sleep-mode" like a dormant computer, the children will eventually withdraw and create a world that is separate and even secretive.

The uninvolved parent deprives their child of all the joy that a healthy interaction can bring. There is limited dialogue and reduced investment. In family therapy this mode is also referred to as being *disengaged*. Parents may think they can get away with it, if there are no overt signs of misbehavior. But payback time usually arrives, especially during adolescence, when it will be too late to form the relationship that should have been formed years ago. Teenagers who don't talk to a parent, may have learned the lesson many years earlier, namely that if the child talks, the uninvolved adult does not listen attentively.

The solid, caring relationship that allows for sharing of ideas, hopes, and dreams needs to be built from the earliest point of departure. The bonding and attachment starts forming prenatally as we dream about the person we will meet at birth, and intensifies the minute we hold that baby in our arms.

Think of running a marathon. The participant who casually strolls along the first few miles will never be able to catch up with the other runners who were vested all along. Similarly, the child who was neglected in the early years may not wish to enter a relationship later on. We have seen this repeatedly in the children who were neglected in international orphanages, who failed to attach and thrive once they were welcomed into loving adoptive families.

Parenting cannot be postponed until the child is sufficiently mature to be a grown-up conversation partner and contemporary friend to the parent. That relationship is formed in the tender years, and it needs ongoing and careful nurture and attention. Parents who take the leap to get involved with this person entrusted in their care, may just find that it is the most demanding, challenging, yet rewarding undertaking ever.

Video Example 2.2

Watch this video on parenting styles. What seems to be the most effective parenting style, according to this particular video? Why?

(https://www.youtube.com/watch?v=ZTOICxSvwx0)

FIGURE 2–2.   The degree of structure and nurture displayed in the *three* original parenting styles, described in the historical work by Diana Baumrind (1966). From left to right the figures represent: *Authoritarian:* High in structure, low in nurture; *Authoritative:* Balanced interaction between structure and nurture; optimal parenting style; and *Permissive:* High on nurture, low on structure.

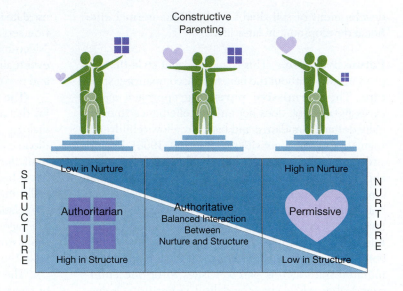

Structure and Nurture Revisited

The three original parenting styles, as well as the fourth added style, can be viewed in the context of structure and nurture; two cornerstone dimensions identified in parenting. We could classify parenting styles using the dimensions of *nurture* (warmth/responsiveness) and *structure* (control/demand) (Maccoby & Martin, 1983). When the basic parenting styles are viewed through these lenses, authoritative styles are seen to be high in warmth and high in control, authoritarian styles are seen to be low in warmth and high in control, and indulgent or permissive styles are seen to be high in warmth and low in control. This may sound like a confusing mouthful, and it may be easier to understand by looking at the figures that illustrate these concepts. Refer to Figures 2–2 and 2–3.

Some rules will be negotiable while others, by necessity, will not. Negotiable rules will lead to healthy feelings of self-esteem in children. On the other hand, rigidity, inflexibility, having mostly non-negotiable rules, and abandonment will damage children's self-esteem. When enforcing rules, it is wise for parents to decide how and when to use their authority, when to be lenient, and when to penalize children for misbehavior. Rules constitute a significant aspect of the patterns that govern the functioning of the family system and the parent–child micro-environment. Without some rules, the family system cannot function effectively. It is essential that rules for children's

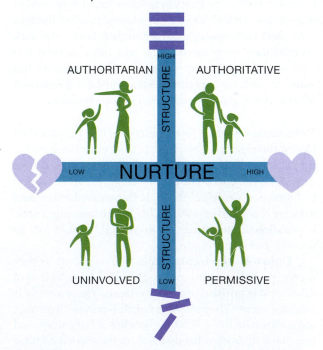

FIGURE 2–3.   Nurture and structure expressed in four traditional parenting styles.

welfare and development be formed rationally rather than emotionally and impulsively. Parents who provide implicit rules that are not expressed clearly, and provide inconsistent experiences leave a message of uncertainty with their children. These behaviors may be likened to very permissive parenting, or even abandonment of children as in uninvolved parenting. Refer to Figures 2–4.

Transitioning to Parenthood: Father Support & Involvement	
Boot Camp for New Dads (1990)	This program is validated by research and best practices and focuses on *father involvement* in pregnancy, birth, and parenting. As such it fills a vital role in strengthening the fatherhood movement and thus the family. It relies on father-to-father support. It is operated by the New Fathers Foundation, Inc. Spanish version available (http://www.bootcamp fornewdads.org/).
The Incredible Years & Incredible Babies	An exemplary, evidence-based program with interlocking subsets. Parents can select the section most applicable to their parenting lifestage. "Incredible Babies: A guide and journal of your baby's first year and organized around developmental stages." By the same author as the "Incredible Years" parenting program: Carolyn Webster-Stratton (http://incredibleyears.com/).
Dad's tuning into kids (2007)	"A program targeting fathers' emotion coaching skills" and
"Bringing Baby Home" workshops	"Fostering emotionally intelligent children, families, and communities": Author: John Gottman & the Gottman Institute
Websites dedicated to fathers:	National Fatherhood Initiative (www.fatherhood.org) National Center for Fathering (www.fathers.com) Also offers workshops and training programs.

Examples of four types of parenting styles

Authoritarian
"Mom, can I go outside and play with Sophia?"
"No."
"Why not?"
"Because I said so; don't ask again."
And "Dad, can you help me with this homework, please?"
"Why isn't your homework done already? Rules are rules, homework before dinner, no if's and no but's."

Permissive
"Mom, can I go outside and play with Sophia?"
"Whatever; you can go outside and play with Sophia, then we'll be late for the movie. Do as you like."
And "Dad, can you help me with this homework, please?"
"Well, you can skip doing it if you don't feel like it."

Authoritative
"Mom, can I go outside and play with Sophia?"
"I don't think that's such a good idea right now because we're running late and we are trying to make it to the movies in time. Remember, we had decided to go to the movies together? There will be another time for you to play with her later, okay?"
And "Dad, can you help me with this homework, please?"
"This seems like tricky homework; let's see if we can find the solution together."

Uninvolved
"Mom, can I go outside and play with Sophia?"
"Go ask your father."
And "Dad, can you help me with this homework, please?"
"It's not my problem."

FIGURE 2–4. Examples of four types of parenting styles.

Focus Point. There are four basic parenting styles: authoritative, authoritarian, permissive, and uninvolved. Each style is characterized by its levels of warmth and control. While many parents often fall into one of the four categories, the style employed by a parent may shift throughout the parenting process as situations change and children mature.

THE PARENTING CIRCUMPLEX MODEL

In the previous discussions and supporting figures, we saw how parenting models gradually evolved. They moved from a model with *three* parenting approaches, to a model with *four* parenting approaches. In the *Parenting Circumplex Model*, an attempt is made to add the relative strength of the expression of a particular parenting approach, with a context in which that parenting approach occurs. This approach focusing on parenting styles is based on, and is an elaboration of, the *Circumplex Model of Marital and Family Systems*, as developed by David H. Olson and his coworkers (Olson, 2000; Olson & Gorall, 2003). The Circumplex Model of Marital and Family Systems is anchored in family systems theory.

The Circumplex Model of Marital and Family Systems is also referred to in a popular context as the Couple and Family Map. This model can illustrate the reactions and adaptations of families to the stressors that they developmentally experience. The original Olson model represents the interaction of dimensions of *cohesion* (emotional bonding) and *flexibility* (stability of a system). This model can illustrate the reactions of families to the stressors that they developmentally experience. Cohesion can be defined as the emotional bonding between members of a couple or a family system. Flexibility is a reflection of how change influences the stability of a system (Olson & Gorall, 2003). Importantly these characteristics are not permanently fixed in position, a couple or family may, and should, have an appropriate range of motion as demanded by the context and by how a system adapts.

Olson & Gorall (2003) describe a skiing analogy to clarify the dimensions of family functioning. In this analogy the focus is on *balanced* versus *unbalanced*. If a beginner on the slopes focuses too much on maintaining balance, it may actually be counterproductive. If we watch experts on their skis, we notice that their bodies adapt. Their torsos may be still while the legs are absorbing the shocks of the moguls. They may re-shift their bodies and adjust to maintain their balance while negotiating uneven terrain and curves. In the same manner a well-functioning couple or family, can adjust their ability to change or remain static (as in the *flexibility* component), and they can vary how emotionally close or distant they are from each other (*cohesion* dimension). Stress and crises will push healthy couples and families towards adaptive behavior, so that they can regain their metaphorical balance and provide the members of the system the required interpersonal support (as displayed by the cohesion dimension). The context will contribute to how they adjust in making the best outcome a reality (Olson, 2000).

Similarly, in parenting, parents can blend various approaches depending on the context, the temperament of their child, and their own personality. Parents do not follow the same parenting approach in all situations and at all phases of the lifespan.

Numerous researchers have added value in establishing the validity and reliability of the circumplex model by applying it to large samples. Over 1,200 studies have been done incorporating this model of family assessment (Olson, 2011). This approach has been explored and adapted by a number of researchers. A similar circumplex approach is applied to different behavioral dimensions in various contexts. For instance, some adaptations are applied in neighboring disciplines such as industrial psychology and psychopathology, as well as in the assessment of personality and of interpersonal styles.

The further a family system's functioning is distanced from the center, the more *extreme* the systemic presentation of the behavioral patterns. The original goal was to try to connect elements from theory, research, and practice. Importantly, a system is not supposed to be fixed in a static point on such a representational map. Families constantly adjust. In times of sorrow and in times of joy, families typically draw closer together, in bonds that may approximate enmeshment. They may also be more chaotic in their structure if they experience great pressure and undue amounts of stress. Depending on the lifespan development of participants, couples as well as families may shift to various positions on the model to represent how they adjust to the challenges of real life.

In parenting for instance, it is presumed that the two dimensions of *structure* and *nurture* are pivotal in

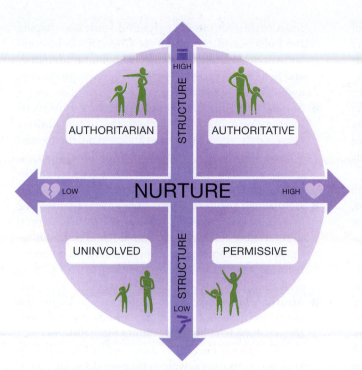

FIGURE 2–5.   In the Parenting Circumplex Model, the two dimensions of structure and nurture are placed on two axes. We can address the variations in parenting styles and the relative strength of the expression of a particular parenting approach. These can occur in parent–child relations in general, but also within one parent–child relationship in particular, as it progresses through developmental stages.

Based on the original Circumplex Model of Marital and Family Systems by David Olson (Olson, 2011; Olson & Gorall, 2003). The *Parenting Circumplex Model* was created by Gerhardt, C., based on information in Gerhardt (2016a, p. 357) and Bigner & Gerhardt (2014).

parenting styles (Bigner and Gerhardt, 2014). If we replace the circumplex model dimension of *flexibility* with *structure*, and the dimension of *cohesion* with *nurture*, we can address the many variations in parenting styles that occur in parent–child relations in general, and also within one parent–child relationship in particular, as it progresses through developmental stages (Gerhardt, 2016, p. 357). This application of the Circumplex Model to parenting approaches is clarified in Figure 2–5.

Acknowledgment: This adapted section on "The Parenting Circumplex Model" was first published in a slightly different form in: Shehan, C. L. (Ed.) (2016). *The Wiley Blackwell Encyclopedia of Family Studies.* Chichester, UK: Wiley Blackwell. In this volume: Gerhardt, C. Circumplex Model of Marital and Family Systems. Volume I: pp. 356–358. Used with permission of the publishers, John Wiley & Sons, Inc.

Focus Point.   The Parenting Circumplex Model is a product of the family systems theory and illustrates the relationship between parenting approaches and the contexts of these approaches. The model relies heavily on the interplay between structure and nurture.

PARENTING PRACTICES IN CONTEXT

No two parents are exactly alike in their parenting. No two contexts are identical. Siblings attest to how different their parents can be to each one of them, even though they are raised in the same household. Clearly each parent–child relationship is complex and brings with it its own unique qualities. Add to that the unique genetic mix, and the nature/nurture theme magically starts playing and finding expression.

Many child-rearing approaches have emerged over the past century, each advocating a particular approach to discipline. Many of these strategies are representative of applied behavioral science and also reflect mainstream psychological approaches. None guarantees consistent results in children's behavior or in parents' interactions with children. Child rearing approaches become relevant when perceived within their *context*. Outcome and research-based information, parental education, and a host of other factors influence prevailing trends in subtle and unsubtle ways. Add sociological, economic, historical, cultural and other complexities into the mix, and it is clear that we are dealing with a shifting target.

Strategies are developed by considering a variety of approaches that will hopefully accomplish something desirable. Parents develop strategies for child rearing as well, endeavoring to promote good outcomes. In the short term, parents may set limits on children's behavior for their safety and well-being and to support socially approved behavior. In the long term, parents may develop rules that teach children the complexities of human interaction, the consequences and importantly the implications of personal values and ethics.

The care parents provide can be both positive as well as negative, and it interacts with the personal attitudes, temperaments, and reserves of the parent. When care is offered positively and consistently, children's development is facilitated in healthy ways. When care is negative and inconsistent, love becomes conditional. This is in contrast to the ideal of unconditional acceptance. Negative care can revolve around indulgence, abuse, and neglect. There is harshness in dealing with children, which results in negative and harmful effects that support unhealthy self-esteem. Parents' treatment of children teaches those youngsters about themselves and allows them to make conclusions about their self-worth.

Clearly then the stakes are very high in the parenting game. We are dealing with the happiness and potential of those entrusted to us, in our roles as parents, as educators, as childcare providers and in related professions.

Focus Point.   While theories and models provide guidelines for positive parenting practices, each parent-child relationship will differ based on the context as well as the dynamics of each relationship.

PARENTING APPROACHES AND THEORETICAL FRAMEWORKS

Systematic reviews of parenting programs identify a number of broad approaches representing various theoretical frameworks (Bunting, 2010). Principles from different approaches tend to spill over somewhat and it is probably not possible to have an entirely purist approach based exclusively on one theoretical model. The following broad classifications pertain:

■ *Cognitive Behavioral Approaches* use principles of behavioral parenting, adding cognitive elements to restructure and reframe parenting, while also shaping the behavior of the children. Cognitive behavioral approaches connect elements of cognition (thinking) and behavior (expressive actions). It is a sophisticated and effective approach.

■ *Social Learning Approaches* are based on social learning principles that include the use of positive role models, negotiation, and finding constructive and positive alternatives to traditionally punitive inputs. It includes modeling, and acknowledging and strengthening appropriate and desired behavior.

■ *Relationship-based Approaches* focus on listening and communication skills. Many basic principles used in counseling are applied to parent–child communications. These approaches are characterized by active listening and respectful parenting in an ongoing dialogue.

■ *Multimodal Approaches* are those combining the elements of various approaches and theoretical models, resulting in eclectic parenting using different elements to reach best outcomes. As it is unrealistic to keep interventions in watertight compartments, there are strands of eclecticism in virtually all approaches.

Different reviews have used different categorizations, and there is overlap between approaches and programs. In general, most parenting programs seem to focus on the *cognitive-behavioral* and *relationship-based* components, although combining approaches as in a *multimodal* approach, allows addressing many aspects of parenting in the most suitable manner. See Table 2–2 for more information.

Cognitive Behavioral Approaches

Cognitive behavioral approaches are action-oriented, in that they seek to find favorable outcomes as reflected by changes in behavior. For this very reason it is a popular therapeutic approach. It does not solely rely on acquiring insight; instead it targets behavior that may be troublesome, while also addressing the accompanying cognitive aspects, i.e., thoughts, beliefs, and attitudes. In adults it is widely used in a variety of conditions including situations addressing emotional regulation, depression, and posttraumatic stress disorders. In parenting contexts, it offers many valuable alternatives to handling potentially difficult situations in a constructive manner.

Cognitive behavioral approaches emphasize an awareness of environmental events and context to fully

TABLE 2–2.   Resources Listing Parenting Programs

Selection of Sources Listing Parenting Programs (In alphabetical order)

Blueprints University of Colorado at Boulder. This registry is constantly updated. *Blueprints in Europe*	■ *Blueprints for Healthy Youth Development:* University of Colorado at Boulder. http://www.colorado.edu/cspv/blueprints/ Social Research Unit at Dartington, U.K. in collaboration with above. Variation of same resource with a focus on programs in Europe.
Evidence-based Parenting Education: *A Global Perspective*: Edited by Ponzetti, James J. (2016) Part of: *Textbooks in Family Studies Series*, published by Routledge.	■ Discusses the fundamentals of parenting programs, and describes ten programs in detail. Contributions frequently written by the authors of the particular evidence-based parenting programs. (Refer to Table 2–1 in this chapter for more information). Ponzetti, J. J. (Ed.). 2016. *Evidence-based parenting education: A global perspective.* New York, NY: Routledge.
National Registry of Evidence-based Programs and Practices (NREPP) U.S. Department of Health and Human Services This registry is constantly updated.	■ The U.S. Department of Health and Human Services maintains an objective and detailed registry of *Parenting* programs, which have met certain standards of evidence-based practice. Program details such as cost, resources, implementation practices and potential target audiences, are also available at this site. www.nrepp.samhsa.gov
Pew Charitable Trusts: Report by Carter & Kahn (1996) (Historical Development)	■ For a detailed summary of major federal initiatives as well as notable parenting and educational programs of the pre-millennial era, refer to an extensive report funded by the Pew Charitable Trusts. Much additional development has occurred since publication, but it remains a comprehensive summary and of historical value. Carter, N., & Kahn, L. (1996). *See How We Grow: A Report on the Status of Parenting Education in the US.* Philadelphia, PA: Pew Charitable Trusts.
What Works: Effective Prevention Programs for Children, Youth and Families: University of Wisconsin-Madison.	■ Detailed listings of evidence-based registries pertaining to specific topics; e.g., violence, suicide, parenting, child welfare, appropriate discipline, corporal punishment. Very comprehensive resource that is constantly updated. http://whatworks.uwex.edu/Pages/2evidenceregistries.html

understand what controls behavior. In the same manner that behavior is learned, it can also be unlearned, changed, or modified, especially if we also pay attention to the cognitive dimension. Individuals adjust their behavior according to its consequences. People tend to behave in ways that result in positive consequences and avoid behaving in ways that result in negative consequences.

One has to consider the complexity of both learning and cognitive elements in this approach. Some of the behavioral components include using behavior modification techniques, which allow parents to teach children acceptable behavior by reinforcing desirable

behavior and weakening undesirable behavior. According to this view, behavior is a learned response with an accompanying cognitive element. Just as children are taught to read, they are taught to behave appropriately in a variety of situations, but as their behavior changes, their thoughts and feelings about the situation change too. Thoughts, feelings and behavior are interrelated and can be mutually influential. A child learns to adopt a given behavior pattern if it accomplishes a desired goal. A parent can intentionally or unintentionally encourage and shape certain behaviors in a child by the manner in which they respond to the child's actions.

Concepts from Behavior Modification.

- Behavior is learned and is a function of its consequences.
- A given behavior is encouraged and taught when it is immediately rewarded or reinforced.
- Reinforcement may be either positive or negative.
- Learning may be generalized from one situation or setting to another.

Reinforcement. Reinforcement maintains that a reward (which serves as the *reinforcement*) must immediately follow a particular behavior to increase the likelihood of that behavior reoccurring in the future. All reinforcers are considered to be stimuli and are either positive or negative.

Positive reinforcement (positive reward) increases the likelihood that a particular behavior will occur again. An example might be praising a child for using good table manners. The positive reinforcement (such as praise) should *immediately follow* the occurrence of the desired behavior. The behavior then becomes associated with its reinforcement. In the real-life example, praising good table manners means that the child is likely to continue displaying good manners because she likes the praise and responds positively to it.

Negative reinforcement occurs when an unpleasant stimulus is removed, increasing the likelihood that the behavior recurs. An unpleasant stimulus associated with a certain type of behavior becomes reinforcing when its withdrawal is a positive or pleasurable experience. For example, *time-out* could be experienced as a negative situation; when it is over, the reward is that this intervention is stopped, which is a positive feeling. *Time-out* is an intervention whereby the child is removed from the social environment and has to sit or stand in a specific spot for a short period of time (depending on the age of the child). This approach is falling into disuse for normal parent-child interactions, as positive reinforcers are preferable.

Extinction. Behavior modification includes the concept of extinction of behaviors that are undesirable or unpleasant. This concept is illustrated by a teacher who ignores the whining of students. The undesirable behavior is not reinforced when the teacher deliberately does not pay attention to it. If the children are not reinforced by receiving attention, they will eventually cease. For many parents this is a difficult process. The number of times a behavior must be ignored is often high, and it may take a long time for the child to eliminate the undesirable behavior from the repertoire.

Reinforcement schedule. The frequency with which reinforcers are used is important. Researchers have found that continuous reinforcement of behaviors is not desirable. Intermittent reinforcement is more effective.

- The desired behavior may be reinforced according to the number of occurrences. For example, a child receives praise only after pronouncing five words correctly.
- The amount of time between behaviors may determine reinforcement. For example, the child may receive reinforcement every other minute while talking, or there may be a variable amount of time between reinforcements, such as once after 1 minute, again after 3 minutes, and again after 10 minutes. Reward schedules that are not entirely predictable are more effective. Another practical example: an antique collector never knows when he will find a treasure at an auction. Because his success is intermittent and not predictable, he may be more motivated to keep on hunting for a bargain.

The use of reinforcement to teach children desirable behavior is a very powerful tool. Because behavior can be bidirectional, children also affect the behavior of adults. Through *reciprocal feedback*, children teach behavior patterns to their parents by applying their own brand of reinforcers. When an adult nags loudly, for example, a child usually tunes out the adult's unpleasant behavior by not listening. Similarly, a child who seeks the attention of parents learns to act in a manner that reinforces parental attention.

Video Example 2.3

Watch this video on reinforcement and punishment for children. What is the difference in using reinforcement versus punishment and how does it shape a child's current and future behavior?

(https://www.youtube.com/watch?v=BVbGS VhKGwA)

Social Learning Approaches

The **social learning theory** is based on the work of Albert Bandura (born 1925). This, and related theories, is especially useful in the context of education and human development, and it explains how socialization occurs and how someone learns appropriate behaviors by *modeling*. Bandura acknowledged many of the concepts from traditional learning theory, but he added a *social* element. Three important concepts in this theory are as follows:

- **Observational learning.** People (and children, in the context of parenting) can learn from social observation.
- **Intrinsic reinforcement.** Internal mental states are part of this learning process.
- **The modeling process.** Several factors can play a role in this process, such as the participants, attention, retention, reproduction, and motivation. Learning something does not necessarily imply that it will result in a change of behavior.

According to this theory, an individual responds to a number of complex stimuli in forming associations between appropriate and inappropriate behavior. Conscious thoughts, rather than an automatic response to a stimulus, assist in shaping behaviors and actions.

This approach focuses on the importance and role of a *model*, or learning through *imitation*. Many behaviors are acquired by observing the behavior of others and then replicating them. Research shows that children learn to express social behaviors such as sharing and cooperation, as well as aggression and violence, by seeing a model demonstrate such behaviors. Models include actual people and characters in media presentations.

Research indicates that when children see a model being rewarded for acting aggressively, they are more likely to demonstrate the same kind of behavior in their own play. Bullying may be one such negative example.

Social learning theory also explains how people acquire social values and attitudes. Social roles are learned and children imitate the behaviors that they observe in adults and in other children who serve as role models.

Parenting Reflection 2–3

When parents model undesirable behavior, for instance, prejudice and discrimination, they are teaching their children these values, attitudes, and behaviors by example. Explain how appropriate parental modeling could contribute to multicultural competence.

Video Example 2.4

Watch this video on Bandura's Bobo Doll Experiment. According to Bandura, are aggressive behaviors learned? Explain.

(https://www.youtube.com/watch?v=dmBqwWlJg8U)

Developing a deep understanding of the family system as the child's model for all social interactions can encourage parents to utilize relationship-based principles such as replacing concrete rewards with encouragement, replacing punishment with logical consequences, and holding regular family meetings.

Andy Dean Photography/Shutterstock

Focus Point.   Behavior modification is a reliable method to elicit desired behaviors. It applies effective, conscientious, and positive reinforcement. Behaviors can be shaped by using reinforcement and paying close attention to the time when the reinforcement is given. Social learning theory emphasizes the influence of modeling and observation in learning a variety of social behaviors and roles.

Relationship-based Approaches

The relationship-based strategies focus primarily on the communication skills developed by the parent and a method for resolving the conflicts that occur between the parent and the child.

A number of positive parenting programs rely heavily on improving the communication and the relationship while teaching parents how to be more effective in their caregiving and disciplinary activities. Many current programs are anchored in a solid relationship-based foundation (Bunting, 2010). A number of parenting programs incorporate basic counseling techniques that can be applied in communication situations across disciplines, for example, with children, in marriages, and at work. An earlier program that seems to have withstood the test of time is Parent Effectiveness Training (Gordon, 1975/2000), which represents a humanistic strategy for promoting a healthy relationship between parents and children. Another older parental educational curriculum is Systematic Training for Effective Parenting (STEP).

As with other humanistic approaches, such as those promoted in the historic yet ground breaking work by Haim Ginott (1922–1973), these strategies teach the parent when to act as a counselor to children regarding their behavior (Ginott, 1965). These approaches are firmly grounded in proven counseling techniques as applied to parenting skills. Although these techniques are effective when performed appropriately, their overuse may lead a child to tune out the parents, and parents need to remain sincere lest they want to sound like scripted actors.

Communicating With Children

In essence, the following proven counseling principles are applied to achieve a more effective manner of communicating and interacting with children:

Active listening.   The parent engages in active listening, a common therapeutic technique used in counseling.

Instead of rescuing the child by offering solutions and suggestions for solving the problem for the child, the parent listens to the child and sifts through the child's statements to determine the feelings being covertly communicated. The parent then sums up the perceived problem. The goal is for the parent to empathize with the child, providing a nurturing response, and objectively reflect back to the child the parent's perception of the problem. The child is allowed to search for his or her own solution.

"I" Messages.   Parents can express their feelings to children about troublesome behavior in *non-damaging* ways. On those occasions when a child's behavior is a problem to a parent, the child may not know that he or she is causing a problem, or the child may be testing a parent's limits. At times, children just can't seem to resist the temptation to misbehave, even though they know that they will get into trouble for doing so. In such situations, the parent "owns" the problem. The child's behavior is problematic because it is troublesome to the parent. A trusted technique used in many applications of good communication is to reframe messages so that they are "I" messages. In other words, the child is not attacked by the parent; instead, the parent describes the effect of the behavior on him- or herself.

Without having learned to do otherwise, most adults, when discussing someone's offensive behavior, begin with *you*: "You're acting stupid." "You are doing that all wrong." or "You are driving me crazy with all that noise." Such "you" messages often occur in cases where the adult is angry about the other person's behavior. A more effective presentation, especially when an adult wants a child to listen to what he or she is saying, takes into consideration the following:

- Begin the message with the word "I."
- Next, add how the parent feels ("I feel disrespected . . . ").
- Then label the problem ("I feel disrespected when you carry off my personal things, like my iPad, without asking me").

"I" messages differ from "you" messages in that they enable a parent to effectively communicate a message to a child without damaging the child's self-esteem. "You" messages can contain content that would hurt the child's self-esteem, such as "You are acting stupid" or "You are doing that all wrong."

"I" messages are used to get a child to listen to what an adult has to say, to communicate facts to the child, and to help the child modify the unacceptable behavior. When parents learn to use this format, children also acquire the skill and begin to express their feelings to parents in non-damaging ways. "I" messages place the responsibility for changing the child's behavior on the child rather than on the parent, and they are less likely to promote resistance and rebellion in children. The communication has to be adjusted to meet the developmental level and characteristics of the child concerned.

Negotiation skills and conflict resolution.   In essence, this process is based on a bidirectional interaction, where both parties bring something to the table and a mutually agreeable resolution is sought. Families mistakenly believe that in resolving conflicts there must be a winner and a loser. This tends to pit children against parents in a power struggle, each attempting to gain their own way. A solution based on a compromise may satisfy all involved. A logical sequence for working through a problem may contribute to a better outcome. This applies to work and partnership situations as well, and it also is an element of good negotiation skills. Keys to good conflict resolution practices include the following:

- Identify the conflict and share the responsibility for conflict resolution.
- Generate possible solutions, which also develop the child's cognitive skills.
- Evaluate the solutions, increasing communication between parties.
- Decide on the best solution, avoiding destructive emotional outbursts.
- Implement the solution without the parent exerting power over the child.
- Evaluate the solution, while encouraging the child's autonomous behavior.

In *bidirectional* parenting, it is helpful to recognize the influence of children's behavior on parents and to teach children to recognize the rights and needs of parents. *Respectful* parenting allows both parents and children to interact on a more equal basis instead of relying on power-assertive methods that damage children's self-esteem.

Interacting With Children

Logical Versus Natural Consequences.   A key element of this strategy is teaching children the logical consequences of their behavior as opposed to using rewards or punishment. The child assumes personal responsibility for her actions reducing the need for authoritarian behavior by the parents. For example, if you touch a hot stove, you get burned. Natural consequences are sometimes either too dangerous to be allowed or too remote in time to be effective for teaching children about the results of their actions. In such cases, the parent must substitute a logical consequence—a consequence that is a rational result of a given action. For example, if a child arrives home after the evening meal has been served, the logical consequence of the child's tardiness (which should have been established and agreed to by all family members in advance) is that the child must prepare a meal or eat cold food. When administered consistently, the child concludes that being punctual avoids unpleasant consequences.

This technique places the responsibility for the choice of behavior, as well as its consequences, on the child, not the parent. A child learns to think, make plans, weigh the consequences of decisions, and accept responsibility for those decisions. A consequence must be experienced fully and consistently by a child before it can be an effective learning tool. In situations that are not life threatening and cannot cause long term damage, parents should allow children to experience the consequences (obviously with the best interests of the child in mind).

Encouragement Instead of Reward or Punishment.   A major tenet of this strategy is that stimulation from within is more effective in producing desirable behavior than outside pressure. Encouragement replaces reward, and a logical consequence replaces punishment. Encouragement and reward are different in timing and effect. Encouragement is given *before* an act takes place; a reward is given *after*. Encouragement is given when an attempt is made, regardless of any difficulty or failure experienced. A reward is given only when the child succeeds. Current parenting approaches emphasize the benefit of acknowledging the effort a child invests through encouragement and acknowledgment. Reward for mediocrity is not encouraged as it can devalue the reward.

Age Appropriate Autonomy.   Parents should respond to their children's needs and individual differences with acceptance and involvement. As part of the authoritative parenting style, we find some tried and tested techniques in which children are provided with positive guidance while also strengthening their age appropriate sense of autonomy. Providing choices, redirecting, and solving problems can be constructive ways of managing situations.

A Selection of Parenting Interventions

Positive guidance to gain co-operation. While interacting, we can gain the child's cooperation by providing age appropriate choices and positive guidance:

> *"Would you like to wear your blue or your grey sneakers today?"*
>
> *"Shall we walk to the house on the grass or on the sidewalk?"*
>
> *"Would you like to eat your soup with a spoon, or using a sippy-cup?"*

Problem solving. Solving problems asks for the child's input and suggestions in resolving a situation:

> *"I need your help in tidying up these toys, how can we do this?"*

Providing age appropriate choices. Combining the problem-solving approach with choices is often effective:

> *"We need to get your hair washed. How are we going to do that?"* and then adding the choice can be helpful: *"Shall we wash your hair using this cup or the hand sprayer?"*
>
> *"We need to get dressed for school today. Would you like the green or the purple sweater?"*

Positive language and acknowledgment.
Instead of the negative version:

> *"Don't throw your shoes at the furniture!"* it is more helpful to focus on the positive:
>
> *"We need to put on shoes if we want to walk outside."*

Use clear short sentences and instructions that are developmentally appropriate.

Remember to thank your child for being helpful:

> *"Thank you, that made it easy for both of us!"*

Redirecting. Redirecting looks like this:

> *"I can see you want to eat this candy, but that isn't a healthy breakfast. We can save it for later. Have you seen this yummy sandwich? Let's try a bite."* Try to make the candy disappear; out of sight out of mind.

Encouragement. Additionally, we can encourage good behavior by providing positive commentary as appropriate. In short, speak to your child as if she is your equal in terms of respect; it is a loving approach that contains a lot of conversation. The child is a participant in that conversation, and there is responsiveness to the child's needs and wishes creating a constructive acknowledgment of the child and his or her personhood.

> *"You did a great job clearing the table, I appreciate that. Now we have more time for bedtime stories."*
>
> *"Thank you for getting into your car seat; that makes the school trip so much easier and safer for all of us."*

Anticipatory Structure. If children can anticipate events, they are more likely to cooperate. It is a good parenting practice to warn children in a supportive way that a transition in activities will soon occur. Children can change their pace as they have time to adjust to new aspects of the routine. This type of structure can support both children and parents to avoid a battle of wills. Here are some examples:

> *"In ten minutes we will stop playing and begin getting ready for bed."*
>
> *"We will read two bedtime stories, then its sleepy time."*
>
> *"In five minutes we will wash our hands and get ready for a snack."*

Counseling principles such as active listening, negotiation skills, and conflict resolution focus on constructive and respectful communication. These techniques are used in a developmentally appropriate manner.

Parenting FAQ 2–2

Constructive Choices Versus Threats

"If you don't stop doing that, I'll throw you out of the window!" The preschooler may not fully grasp all the implications, namely, that the threat is dangerous and irresponsible to enforce, nor may the child understand that the parent will not carry out the threat. The threat may instill fear and mistrust. Threats seem to be a "last resort" approach, but as a parenting technique it is a dead end.

Why do we talk? We talk to establish a relationship, to communicate, and to support self-efficacy in the child. Threats do not do any of this. Instead they communicate anger, and are a misuse of power. If threats are overused, they will be discounted and perceived as hollow and inconsequential. When one parent plays off the other by invoking the powers of the absent parent to strengthen his own authority, it may sound like this: "Just wait till your mother comes home; she will really give it to you!" The absent parent is pulled into an unsolicited battle she did not choose.

Choices provide positive alternatives and elicit cooperation. Instead of: "Get your shoes on right now! Or else . . . " a parent will be more successful to bypass the issue of the shoes and focus on the choice: "Would you like to put on your blue or your red sneakers?"

Make the consequences clearly identifiable. Give the child time to mentally and physically complete a task which in turn fosters time management skills. Remember the courtesy of saying "please" and "thank you." These should be modeled to show respect and appreciation, and be aware that the tone of our voices can communicate so much more than our words. Here is an example of a threat and an appropriate alternative:

Threat: "This is the last time I'm telling you to stop playing, else you'll go hungry tonight!" This situation may end up in a battle of wills, which is not recommended as it is stressful for all involved.

Respectful alternative including anticipatory structure: "We'll be having dinner in about 10 minutes. Please finish up what you are doing." Then in five minutes the request can be repeated: "We are about to stop playing, in five minutes you can start putting away your toys so you'll be ready for dinner. Thanks for doing this!" Do not include too many anticipatory messages. Usually about one or two will be sufficient. Keep the tone friendly and supportive.

Nonnegotiable Situations

Importantly: When children's safety is endangered or there are time pressures, it is the adult's responsibility to behave in the best interests of the child, keeping safety in mind.

In practice that means that the responsible adult makes an appropriate decision and the situation is nonnegotiable. The rules are:

- Safety first
- Consider the best interests of the child

Focus Point. Bidirectional communication between parents and children allow both parties to actively participate. There are times when adults can simply listen to the child's problems, using active listening techniques. When a child's behavior is offensive or problematic, parents need to point this out by using "I" messages. When there is mutual respect during conflict resolution, we learn to compromise in socially accepted ways.

Multimodal Approaches

Multimodal approaches take the best from various other approaches and integrate them in an eclectic manner. For a formal program to be truly multimodal it would incorporate various theoretical principles, best suited to particular areas they wish to address.

Approaches and programs which are multilevel target various parent education strategies and use a collection of ways to address parenting topics and concerns. This means that a heterogeneous parent population can be reached; there is something for everybody (Bunting, 2010). One such exemplary evidence-based program is the Australian Triple P – Positive Parenting Program. It has a three-decade development history and has been used in over 25 countries. This program can target different groups such as families during separation and divorce (Transitioning program), families dealing with disability (Stepping Stones Program) and families displaying socioeconomic and cultural diversity (www .triplep.net). An American program that is regarded as

Parenting FAQ 2–3

Our children play us off against each other. "But dad said . . . " is a common refrain. Where from here?

We are parents and we are individuals. Differences happen. But there should be a united front in terms of outcomes, for the sake of the kids. Parents who do not agree with each other may have to consider looking at their own relationship and figuring out how they can compromise and meet each other midway to reach consensus. Otherwise they undermine each other's parenting efforts. What is the intent of the parenting approach, what is the outcome we wish for our children? If we can agree on that, we can express that in different ways while still traveling to the same place.

exemplary is the program by Carolyn Webster-Stratton, called "The Incredible Years" (www.incredibleyears .com). A summary of ten leading and exemplary programs can be found in Table 2–2: Selection of Evidence-based Parenting Programs.

Family Meetings.   One starting point for developing an effective, loving relationship with a child is for the adult to learn about the impact of the *family system* in shaping the child's emerging patterns of behavior. The family system is seen as the child's model for all social interactions with others. The democratic basis of this strategy is reflected in the use of family meetings to reach agreements, communicating effectively, and helping children participate. If meetings occur on a regular basis, children can have an equal voice in family decisions. Reserving family meetings for crises only give them a negative flavor. Decisions may relate to establishing logical consequences for family rules, determining the use of family resources, and resolving disputes among family members. Family meetings typically involve the nuclear family, usually the people having dinner together. Hence the dinner table is a good place for informal, pleasant family meetings. Families do well if they get together regularly, for instance for meals. Reserving family meetings for disciplinary actions or negative content creates unwanted associations. Family meetings are a way of ensuring that regular communication channels remain open.

Research has shown that families who eat together, and who celebrate together, display greater cohesiveness and mutual support (National Center for Education Statistics, n.d.). PISA, the acronym for Programme of International Student Assessment, examined student scores in science, reading, and mathematics literacy in more than 70 countries and education systems (www.oecd.org/pisa). In the United States, the organization is affiliated with the National Center for Educational Statistics (NCES). The

PISA study showed that educational outcomes are better for students from cohesive and supportive families. Families who, for example, regularly eat a meal together. It is not the meal in itself that emits the magic higher educational scores, instead it is what the meal tells us about that family's organization. Parents who make time to spend with their children, who celebrate together and parents who stay up to date with their children; these families can expect the better civic and educational outcomes. All these factors promote a supportive family environment that builds resilience and promotes a better family climate, including improved social and scholastic outcomes. The idea is that the family as a system works at developing strategies for mutual support.

POSITIVE PARENTAL DISCIPLINE

Research over the past decade or so reflects what we may have suspected intuitively. In a review and meta analysis of 77 published articles that evaluated parent training and outcomes, the bottom line was that the more positive, encouraging, and supportive approaches were preferable and had better outcomes, as compared to the continuum of negative and punitive angles, which historically included corporal punishment (Kaminski, Valle, Filene, & Boyle, 2008).

Parenting skills that ranked high were ones that reflected consistency, constructive communication skills, and the benefits of parents trained in applying principles of parenting programs, as these provided skills that were proven to be effective and appropriate. In this analysis, the use of time-out featured as an important option with the provision that parents were trained in how to use it appropriately (Kaminski et al., 2008).

The **exclusively positive parental discipline** approaches, as described in popular self-help books, tend to see the world of discipline through rose-tinted glasses. As much as positive approaches are generally favored in the arsenal of parenting techniques, the *exclusively* positive approaches have been subjected to critique. Researchers have cautioned that we need to consider *context*. The bigger picture may determine the most appropriate disciplinary response (Larzelere, Gunnoe, Roberts & Ferguson, 2017). What can we recommend to parents and teachers who have to discipline oppositional, defiant children, or preteens and teens who are clearly pushing the limits with antisocial, self-harming, or even unlawful behavior? The parenting programs listed by reputable sources such as NREPP (National Registry of Evidence-based Programs and Practices), categorize parenting programs according to target populations, age groups, professional support, training, and the like. One such program focusing on positive approaches is the "Triple – P: Positive Parenting Program" which is regarded as exemplary.

The quality of parenting and outcomes of parental interventions can to an extent be a reflection of the reigning cultural climate within a particular societal group and also reflect some of the child rearing trends within a society at large. For instance, over the past century parenting has shifted from being predominantly authoritarian and punitive to leaning towards indulgent. Public policy and public health initiatives, can have a responsibility to support parents and families in meeting their parenting roles optimally (Sanders, 2012).

Because early and middle childhood experiences can influence later outcomes, children should ideally be exposed to relatively intact worlds with positive feedback that shapes behavior respectfully. It sets the tone for much of what is to come. Competent parenting that includes appropriate structure and is represented by predominantly authoritative approaches facilitates pro-social behavior in youths (Carlo, White, Streit et al., 2017). In a study of youths and neighborhood influences, those approaches which were supportive and protective were more effective than punitive interventions (Emery, Trung & Wu, 2015). In this study, neighbors intervened to support pro-civic behavior.

But as we know from some international adoptions, where children have been exposed to extreme duress in the first years of their lives, these at times traumatic socialization experiences can lead to diverse behavioral outcomes. Many well-intentioned foster parents have had moments of despair fighting the scars inflicted by previous, possibly abusive, parenting and coparenting scenarios. Those behaviors in turn require varied interventions.

Another point of view acknowledges that we cannot shelter children from all adversity. When slightly older children are exposed to age-appropriate hardship and

frustration in manageable doses, as real life presents it to them, it may be unavoidable. Later on in their lives, they will meet similar lessons in dealing with challenges, emphasizing that context is very important when talking about resilience (Dagdeviren, Donoghue & Promberger, 2016). In the adult world, many situations do not provide a true and consistent reward for behavior. Take, for instance, paying taxes and bills on time, driving safely, or being civil and courteous to colleagues and friends. Our societal contexts offer many examples of situations when noncompliance is punished with fines, citations, social isolation, and the like. Credit cards, for example, have very slim margins of tolerance. As a responsible member of society, we are expected to display civically engaged behavior, thinking of the well-being of our neighbor and fellow citizen.

The child who meets with punitive boundaries in response to antisocial behavior, may learn about the control exerted by appropriate structure, even though this elicits frustrations and sends the message "No, not all behavior is OK or acceptable." It may also be an opportunity to foster resilient behavior, and learn to toughen up in an appropriate manner, taking responsibility for actions. The word of caution is that the situations need to demand age appropriate responses and disciplinary interventions which are pedagogically and psychologically sound, considering the context. Researchers Larzelere et al. state: "Exclusively positive parenting needs to be supported by stronger research, including randomized trials with oppositional defiant children, before being accepted as definitive" (2017, p. 24).

Positive approaches are preferable to negative and punitive approaches. The various *contexts* will determine to what extent exclusively positive guidance is feasible. As child related professionals we have to tread cautiously when working with diverse groups of children and adolescents from different backgrounds. They have probably been exposed to a wide range of socialization experiences (not all of them positive) and subsequently present with an array of behavioral responses. We may have to deal with situations where an exclusively positive approach is not possible at all times, and structure and boundaries can be part of a constructive parenting approach.

One of the frustrating and realistic aspects related to childcare and parenting is this phrase: "It depends." Exclusively positive parenting is an appropriate ideal to strive for, but maybe not for every child in every situation, and we need more research. Hopefully, we can work towards therapeutically positive outcomes and attain a situation of trust and mutual respect which ultimately fosters the best outcomes for each child.

Focus Point. Positive approaches are preferable to negative and punitive approaches. The various *contexts* will determine to what extent exclusively positive guidance is feasible. Children and adolescents from different backgrounds have probably been exposed to a wide range of socialization experiences and subsequently present with an array of behavioral responses. Some situations may not allow for an exclusively positive approach, despite maintaining trust and mutual respect. Structure and boundaries are aspects of appropriate disciplinary interventions.

"Time-out" as an Intervention

Time-out, the once favored approach, is morphing into new forms. Time-out has a good track record of being effective, but could be problematic if parents use it incorrectly (Larzelere & Kuhn, 2016). Potential difficulties arise if it is overused, if it becomes a threat and gains predominantly negative associations. Time-out should ideally occur in a neutral environment and under supervision of an adult. Larzelere & Kuhn (2016, p. 1549) provide some pointers, including: making sure that the child understands the expectations, using a timer for a maximum of five minutes and requiring compliance with the original request. It is best to use this technique only for certain misbehaviors, it should not be an overused catch-all.

The traditional time-out version requires removing the child from the challenging situation, putting them on a little mat, or on a stool so that they can reflect or regain composure. Minutes of time-out are tallied with the age of the child in terms of number of years, with a maximum of five minutes. An eight-year-old can expect five minutes of time-out. Once they calm down they can return to the group activity after an apology. This apology is thought to help the child gain insight that the particular behavior was disruptive or inappropriate. This approach is based on behavioral principles of reinforcement and extinction; where undesirable behavior is not given undue attention or even ignored, whereas appropriate behavior is acknowledged, and thus reinforced (Larzelere & Kuhn, 2016). In the case of time-out, there is some removal of privileges involved, in that the child is removed from a situation in which they want to participate (albeit disruptively).

Some parents send their children to their bedrooms. Sending a child to their room for time-out can be tricky as they then associate their safe and personal space with punishment. This room is also where they sleep, and where some of their personal possessions are kept, and ideally should not be tainted by the negativity of punishment. But in cramped living arrangements, choices for time-out may be limited.

A constructive re-interpretation of time-out suggested by the author (Gerhardt), is described in "Parenting FAQ 2–4," and is referred to as "Take-a-minute" or "Time to Regroup." Importantly, this does not only target the child, it also addresses the adult who has to regain composure; after all, it is an interaction between a parent and a child. It supports emotional self-regulation and, with some added regular deep breathing, can be effective in a very short time.

Ineffective Disciplinary Methods

A review of the literature on parental discipline suggests that some practices have worse outcomes than others (Painter & Corsini, 2015):

■ Discipline or parental behavior that is inconsistent.
■ Irritable, explosive practices, including shouting and threatening.
■ Inflexible, rigid discipline, extremely authoritarian discipline.
■ Low parental supervision and minimal involvement; neglect.

Inconsistency in parental behavior and discipline serves primarily to confuse children about how they are expected to behave. Children receive mixed signals when a parent is inconsistent in enforcing rules and the attendant consequences. When parents fail to agree on certain policies about children's behavior, children are quick to pick up the parental inconsistency.

Some parents appear to have only one type of reaction to children's transgressions, for example, loud emotional outbursts such as yelling, screaming, or exhibiting violent physical acts of aggression. The intensity of the parental reaction and the degree of punitiveness usually escalates in relation to the frequency that the child misbehaves.

When parents employ inflexible, rigid discipline, they rely on one type of punitive strategy regardless of the transgression. No matter what a child does, the parent reacts the same way. What is lacking is a *hierarchy* in an organization of parental reactions that links the seriousness of the offense to the nature of the parental reaction. Typically, when parents rely on this inflexible approach, they do not employ verbal reasoning. Rather, the parent reacts in the same manner providing the child little assistance on how to learn from the mistake.

Parenting FAQ 2–4

Sometimes our children have meltdowns, or we as parents suffer from caregiver despair. How do we handle these difficult situations when we feel as if it's all getting too much?

Take-a-minute: Time to Regroup

The best interventions occur when parents as well as their children are calm; when they are able to communicate respectfully. It's the same in other relationships, including marriage. Do not discipline in anger. Do not spout ugly words you will later regret. Do not accuse or abuse. Never belittle, especially not a child who does not have the weapons to retaliate. Communication is about exchanging ideas, finding good outcomes. It should not be about warfare and the home should never become the battlefield. Interventions should also be developmentally appropriate.

Take-a-minute is an effective way to interrupt negative and disruptive behavior. Importantly, it allows both the child and the parent an opportunity for self-regulation, which, from a neuro-psychological point of view, is relevant and valuable. Add some deep breaths, and the regrouping time can be doubly effective.

It is time away from play or from disruptive behavior. For adults, it can be that moment of counting to ten and regaining composure. It can be that pause provided by breathing deeply and becoming mindful. After all, we should resolve issues when we can talk and listen calmly, not when anger clouds our heads. Here are some helpful guidelines:

- Importantly, this technique targets not only the child but also the parent. A parent who is out of control or seething with anger, can potentially be a dangerous parent, and not in a position to guide a child.
- Calm down time should preferably not be punitive in a negative way. Rather it is a moment to catch our breaths, regroup, regain composure.
- Often a minute or two is sufficient. "Let's stop and calm down" or "Let's take a minute."
- It is preferable not to send the child to his room as a punishment, because he may develop a negative association with his own room. On the other hand, when it is a situation of merely regaining calm and a quiet oasis is needed, the bedroom is a good place for reflection and regrouping.
- Stay in the vicinity to supervise the child and to ensure her safety, but do not interact verbally to allow some time to calm down. The tone should be supportive and positive. Encourage the child to breathe deeply and calmly: "Let's take a few deep breaths."
- When parents and children are calm, it may be a good opportunity to explain why we needed to take a minute to regroup, and why the particular behavior was unacceptable.
- After regrouping, do not continue to remind the child about poor behavior or temper outbursts, or even worse, shame the child about the behavior. Take-a-minute should be a period that ends with a brief explanation and the child's apology, if that is appropriate. The intention is that the child learns from the situation and it is resolved in a constructive and supportive manner.
- Regard take-a-minute as one approach among many and use it only when the situation calls for it.

When parents fail to provide good supervision and are minimally involved, children feel abandoned and emotionally neglected. Left to their own devices, children are at risk for a wide range of behavioral problems, poor school performance, and failure to develop effective interpersonal skills.

Parenting Challenges

How we were parented ourselves, can have an *afterlife* in how the next generation is parented.

Unfortunately, not all families are healthy nor do they parent children with positive outcomes. In reality, some parents can be abusive to children. The blueprints for both positive and negative parenting styles are acquired by observing and modeling the behavior of our parents in the family of origin. Social learning theory supports that many of our social behaviors are acquired through observation while growing up.

Toxic Parenting.   Several parenting models, along with their common traits, are described below.

Demanding parents often conduct child rearing using an authoritarian style. These parents require children to believe that they must live their lives according to the adult's standards and ideas about what is

Historical Cultural Snapshot 2–3

"Children Are Just People . . . Let Them Be"

Read the following statements written in the early seventies by Arthur Janov (b. 1924), in his book *"The Feeling Child"* (1970). Janov was a psychologist who was also trained as a social worker. He authored another book titled *"The Primal Scream."* Janov thought that early childhood could be traumatic, including the event of birth. Clients were encouraged to get in touch with some of this original pain, hence the reference to "primal scream." In scholarly circles his work was thought to be somewhat controversial.

He sympathized with the so-called "Anti-Psychiatry" movement of the sixties and early seventies, although he was not a leading figure in this movement. A movie from this time, *"One Flew Over the Cuckoo's Nest"* (1975), was based on an earlier book with the same title (1962). The film depicted the at-times disturbing hospital conditions for patients labeled as mentally ill. The implication was that an unhealthy society harbored the problems, as opposed to the patients themselves. This period witnessed a movement that was critical of psychiatry and included anti-authoritarian sentiments; hence the name "anti-psychiatry" (Nasrallah, 2011). Leading exponents

included Thomas Szasz, David Cooper, and Ronald Laing. Some of these anti-authoritarian undertones can be detected in Janov's quotes about children:

> "Children are just people. There are no special rules about relating to them that do not apply to any and all relationships. There's not much you have to do to children. You don't have to discipline them, lecture them or punish them. All you have to do is talk to them, listen, hold them, be kind and free, spontaneous and easy, and just let them be" (1970, p. 197).

> "... actions and interactions between parent and child are only important insofar they reflect feeling. The fact that there are hundreds of books written on child-rearing implies that children are a separate species requiring special treatment. They are just people needing exactly what parents need. The question is not 'How should I handle my child?' it should be 'How do you treat people you love?' A parent isn't someone who lays down rules. He is a loving friend" (1970, p. 197).

Almost half a century later one can ask to what extent his points of view are valid or invalid, in terms of current approaches to parenting.

Source: Janov, A. (1973). *The Feeling Child.* Simon Schuster.

---

acceptable and appropriate. Guilt and manipulation are used. Children are treated consistently as if they are totally helpless and must be dependent on their parents, regardless of their abilities or age. Children react to such treatment over a long period of time by developing a high need for parental approval, as well as exhibiting learned helplessness or practicing deception.

Critical parents interact with children by criticizing and being judgmental. This tactic can be used as a means to achieve control over children. Such behavior can motivate both the parents and the children to maintain a high degree of family secrecy. Substantial personal boundaries minimize intimacy, and rigid rules regulate behavior. Both the adults and the children suffer from low levels of personal esteem because of the pervasive air of failure that permeates their relationship. Children have overdeveloped feelings of guilt and sensitivity when errors are made.

Overfunctioning parents send consistent messages to children about their ineptitude that sustain the parents' overprotective behavior. These parents feel overly responsible for a child's actions and manage almost every aspect of a child's life. Some family therapists feel that overfunctioning parental behavior arises out of a deep fear of being abandoned.

Disengaged parents are emotionally uninvolved. These individuals appear to be too busy or self-absorbed to function adequately as parents. They might not have learned to love or be loved as children, and as parents they are unable to express these emotions. Depression in parents can make it very difficult for them to engage in social contexts. Chronic illness, disability, and mental illness can intrude on a good parent–child relationship and represent an obstacle in establishing and maintaining appropriate parenting behavior.

Ineffective parents are incapable of meeting the needs of children and accepting the responsibilities of parenting. Many reasons may underlie this parenting model, such as addiction and related disorders or chronic illness. Children assume roles that are far beyond their abilities—for example, when an older child assumes the full-time care of younger children.

Abusive parents harm children emotionally, physically, and even sexually. These parents were often abused by their own parents and are prone to repeating such actions. The emotional scars left on children take much effort and time to heal when they become adults (Sandberg et al., 2012).

It is possible to alter one's parenting style by consciously becoming aware of one's actions and how these actions impact a child's growth and development. Working with a competent family therapist is one way of making constructive changes.

Normal Behavioral Problems

Context. Frequently, there are conflicts between parents and children over socialization tasks, relationship concerns, and gaining compliance from children. Many situations that are termed normal behavioral problems are actually a problem for the adult and not the child. Similarly, many problems are simply a normal part of development as children strive to accomplish specific tasks but experience difficulty in mastering them. These may relate to the age of a child: What is normal behavior at one stage may be problematic at another and may indicate some type of developmental or emotional disturbance.

Importantly, the context of the behavior will contribute to determining if it is within the boundaries of normalcy, or whether it warrants further examination by a professional team. Parents need to be aware of the difference between normal behavioral problems and problems that are indicative of a more serious disorder that calls for professional attention and intervention.

Parenting Reflection 2–4

Reflect on the parenting style/model exhibited by your own parents. Based on what you observed and what you remember, can you predict what model/style you will adopt when you become a parent?

Focus Point. There are many ineffective disciplinary methods that result in poor parent–child relationship quality and unhealthy development. Toxic parenting methods, such as demanding or disengaging practices, can be damaging and even passed from generation to generation.

CHAPTER FOCUS POINTS

The Parenting Relationship

- The parent–child relationship is the foundation of parenting. This relationship is dynamic and constantly evolving as both parents and children grow and mature. Our knowledge of psychology and human development provides insight into patterns of interaction that lead to positive outcomes.

Parents as Teachers

- As a child's first teacher, a parent is charged to instill values and attitudes that guide children on their journey towards autonomy and adulthood. There are many approaches that parents can follow to become competent teachers and effective socializers. Practicing a variety of these strategies enhances the effectiveness of parenting and improves the quality of parent–child interactions.

Appropriate Discipline

- Despite the common view of discipline as a form of punishment, appropriate discipline should include encouragement, positive messages, nurture, and guidance. Discipline is used to help children acquire socially appropriate behavior according to the patterns supported by their family system. Effective discipline should be moderate, developmentally appropriate, and acknowledge the particular child's needs.

Corporal Punishment

- Discipline ideally should emphasize the teaching of appropriate behavior through *positive* and preferably *nonpunitive* approaches. Discipline can be seen as a form of guiding behavior in which parents explore constructive ways of shaping a child's conduct. Appropriate rules and boundaries provide children with structure and teach them to internalize self-regulatory behavior.
- Evidence-based parenting programs and mental health resources range in effectiveness and are available for some parents who need assistance with various aspects of the parenting process.

Parenting Styles

■ There are four basic parenting styles: authoritative, authoritarian, permissive, and uninvolved. Each style is characterized by its levels of warmth and control. While many parents often fall into one of the four categories, the style employed by a parent may shift throughout the parenting process as situations change and children mature.

The Parenting Circumplex Model

■ The Parenting Circumplex Model is a product of the family systems theory and illustrates the relationship between parenting approaches and the contexts of these approaches. The model relies heavily on the interplay between structure and nurture.

Parenting Practices in Context

■ While theories and models provide guidelines for positive parenting practices, each parent–child relationship will differ based on the context as well as the dynamics of each relationship.

Parenting Approaches Based on Theoretical Frameworks

■ Cognitive behavioral approaches are action-oriented, in that they seek to find favorable outcomes as reflected by changes in behavior. For this very reason it is a popular therapeutic approach. It targets behavior that may be troublesome, while also addressing the accompanying cognitive aspects; i.e., thoughts, beliefs, and attitudes. Cognitive behavioral approaches include elements of behavior modification to elicit and strengthen desired behaviors.

■ Social learning theory emphasizes the influence of modeling and observation in learning a variety of pro-social behaviors and roles. Many programs are multimodal, in that they include elements from various theoretical approaches.

■ Bidirectional communication between parents and children allow both parties to participate constructively using active listening techniques. When a child's behavior is offensive or problematic, parents need to point this out by using "I" messages. When there is mutual respect during conflict resolution, we learn to compromise in socially accepted ways.

Positive Parental Discipline

■ Positive approaches are preferable to negative and punitive approaches. The various *contexts* will determine to what extent exclusively positive guidance is feasible. Children and adolescents from different backgrounds have probably been exposed to a wide range of socialization experiences and subsequently present with an array of behavioral responses. Some situations may not allow for an exclusively positive approach, despite maintaining trust and mutual respect. Structure and boundaries are aspects of appropriate disciplinary interventions.

■ There are many ineffective disciplinary methods that result in poor parent–child relationship quality and unhealthy development. Toxic parenting methods, such as extremely authoritarian, demanding, neglectful, and disengaged practices, can be damaging. Through family of origin influences these toxic methods can be passed on emotionally from generation to generation.

USEFUL WEBSITES

Websites are dynamic and change

American Academy of Pediatrics
www.healthychildren.org
Family life and family dynamics

Australian Institute of Family Studies: Parenting Styles and Strategies
www.aifs.gov.au/cfca/
Parenting styles

Children's Defense Fund
www.childrensdefense.org
Child welfare

Institute for Education Sciences: What Works Clearinghouse
www.ies.ed.gov/ncee/wwc/
Corporal punishment, discipline, social learning theory

National Institute of Child Health and Human Development
www.nichd.nih.gov
Responsive care

National Society for the Prevention of Cruelty to Children in the United Kingdom
www.nspcc.org.uk
Resources for parents, and research initiatives. U.K. based. Very user-friendly.

CHAPTER 3

Historical and Cultural Perspectives

Learning Outcomes

After completing this chapter, you should be able to

1. Discuss how attitudes toward children have shifted over the centuries.
2. Identify the forces that contributed to a more developmentally appropriate approach to childrearing.
3. Illustrate the roles of socialization, cultural identity, traditions, and assimilation in effective parent–child relations.
4. Assess the challenges faced by ethnically diverse families.
5. Summarize the process of globalization and its impact on families.
6. Investigate the possible outcomes, both positive and negative, of family migration.

THE EVOLUTION OF CHILDHOOD

The essential love between parents and their children has probably not changed over time. There is a deep bond between parents and their children and even if times were different, we would find the elements of this caring relationship documented through works of art as well as archival documents.

Parents and their children are better understood against the backdrop of history. These same influences are absorbed into our culture. History tells us about our roots and our

63

heritage; the foundations on which we build. The history of our own families also highlights the prevalent cultural influences of the time. Sociocultural history is a description of a culture at a particular time in history; how people lived, the fabric of their social lives. In that respect, history and culture overlay one another and have mutual influence.

Our culture gives us a complex societal context. **Culture** is relative to each particular group and is characterized by some flexibility because it can change over time. Culture cannot be contained within tight boundaries; instead, it permeates into many areas of life and has fuzzy edges. No one story can tell the entire tale. Culture is influenced by history; hence the discussion of historical and cultural perspectives in this chapter.

There are multiple levels of consequence as individuals can influence a culture and culture, in turn, can have an effect on its group members. The cultural exchange is modified by the context within which cultural events are embedded, and this includes the historical context. Culture influences parent–child relations and defines a range of family systems. History and culture go hand in hand, there is an interrelatedness that helps us find meaning and greater understanding in why parenting is the way it is today in this particular cultural context. When we want to know about how people lived, how they parented, and what their attitudes towards children were, we enter the domain of *sociocultural history*.

The way we parent and the way our great-grandparents approached these child-rearing challenges may seem poles apart. But then, we live in different times, with different concerns and mindsets, while our ancestors faced different challenges. The nature and quality of parent–child interactions are influenced significantly by the historical context as well as the cultural values of a particular society in which we live. As our oldest ancestors pass on, we also lose that link to the history that they represented in our personal histories. We have to rely on what has been documented and preserved. Similarly, our knowledge of history before documentation is scant and is limited to archeological finds, decorations on art objects, cave paintings, and other expressions including possibly some oral traditions. These combine to tell us that once someone was inspired by relevant imagery from a time long ago. Considering these restraints, our best knowledge of the history of children comes from the most recent centuries.

Our society tends to be child centered, but this was not always reflected in customs, laws, or how children were treated by adults. Generally, our current culture values the well-being of children and social institutions like the family, schools, and social service agencies, focus on meeting children's needs. We see childhood as a special time in the lifespan, a time of preparation and education for the later years. Childhood is hopefully a time for happiness and freedom from anxiety. We believe that children have unique needs that are first met in their family system and later by educational institutions, groups, and agencies outside of the family system. Our ideas about the intrinsic nature of childhood developed over many years of social transformation in Western culture (Heywood, 2013).

Childhood, parenthood, and the family were viewed differently in yesteryears. Most social historians agree that changes are noted in the ways that adults define and conduct appropriate parenting behavior. Although parenting has always had a strong nurturing component, the way that adults express this love and care has changed in culturally supported ways. Child-rearing practices have evolved throughout history to reflect the changing ideas of what children need from adults to prepare them for their own future as adults (Bigner & Gerhardt, 2014).

Adult Lifespan and Infant Mortality

Where there are adults, there must have been children, and the history of humankind is also the history of childhood. Our knowledge of children during prehistoric times, including the times of hunter–gatherers, is limited to archeological and paleontological data (Volk, 2011). We know that the lifespan was much shorter, and many people died before reaching their milestone 50th birthday. Childbirth was a high risk undertaking, and claimed numerous maternal lives (Tew, 2013). Child mortality rates were disconcertingly high, and from archeological findings, the estimates are that around half of the children never reached adulthood. Extended families and social groups were necessary for survival. Stating this bluntly:

> In many ways, the history of childhood is perhaps best described as a history of death. Infant and child mortality rates appear to have been shockingly high for all but the most recent part of the history of childhood (Volk, 2011, p. 475).

Johann Sebastian Bach's work has endured over centuries, and to many he justly ranks amongst the greatest composers of all time. Bach (1685–1750) was prolific and endowed the world with an extraordinarily large musical legacy. In his personal life, he and his first wife Barbara had seven children by the time she died at the age of 36. With his second wife, Anna Magdalena, the couple had another 13 children. In short, out of 20 children, 10 reached adulthood (Washington, 1997).

The threat of death forced parents to be both invested and disinvested in their offspring. They invested strongly in these bonds to increase the odds of survival as children represented their lineage, the hope of a next generation. At the same time, the many circumstances accompanying high child mortality demanded a certain resignation and disinvestment. Refer to Reflection 3–1, Family Life and Infant Mortality in Victorian England.

Reflection 3–1
Family Life and Infant Mortality in Victorian England

In Victorian times, the loss of a sibling was a likely occurrence, and it exerted an emotional toll on the entire family. The loss of a parent proved to be disruptive to the family structure and devastating to the children who were sometimes sent to live with extended family, which was not always a loving environment. The surviving parent very likely remarried, even if it was only to keep the household intact.

Walter Littler, the 14th of 18 children, describes his Victorian childhood in his memoir. Within a dozen years, eight of his siblings had passed away from infectious diseases such as measles and scarlet fever; illnesses, which a century later, would be fairly well controlled (Frost, 2009). In the Foakes family, the mother, Grace, had 14 children, of whom only five reached adulthood, while nine died in infancy or childhood.

[The loss of a child is] an almost unimaginable loss to modern eyes. Parents faced such grief with resignation, but when siblings died, children were both frightened and saddened, a state sometimes aggravated by the Victorian custom of keeping the body in the parlor or kitchen until burial. The death of a contemporary was a shock, one that forced children to face the reality of mortality. (Frost, 2009, p. 21)

Source: Frost, Ginger S. (2009). *Victorian childhoods*, Chapter 1, page 21. In the series, Mitchell, Sally (Series Editor). *Victorian life and times*. Westport, Connecticut: Praeger. The following source is referenced by Frost (2009): Littler, Walter. (1997). *A Victorian childhood: Recollections and reflections*. Belbroughton, Worcestershire, England: Marion Seymour.

Recorded Beginnings

With the absence of a long-lasting oral or written history, the details elude us. The review of the evolution of childhood begins with the ancient cultures that influenced contemporary Western societies, and where we have greater access to more detailed historical data.

The Greek philosopher Plato (427–348 BCE) is credited with saying:

Do not train a child to learn by force or harshness; but direct them to it by what amuses their minds, so that you may be better able to discover with accuracy the peculiar bent of the genius of each.

In the light of our current insights from developmental psychology, the above statement would pass as a mature and insightful approach to children. In ancient times, only two stages of the human lifespan were recognized: childhood and adulthood (Heywood, 2013). Adolescence and emerging adulthood were identified much later in history.

Adulthood was considered to be the culmination of childhood experiences. Childhood was the time for preparing to become an adult. Achieving this status was the primary goal of an individual's developmental progress. The boundary between childhood and adulthood was distinct. Childhood commenced at birth and usually ended at surprisingly young ages when they were ushered into the world of adult roles. During what we would currently describe as the pre-teen years, these children assumed adult status, along with the associated responsibilities and behaviors.

Children's preparation for their future roles as adults was a concern. Although schools taught a wide variety of subjects, parents were responsible for teaching their children basic skills and knowledge. Education was considered to benefit the well-being of the community and the state, rather than the welfare of the individual. In these cultures, a formal education was a privilege that was restricted to men while women acquired domestic skills related to home management and child care.

The family was recognized as the core element in many of these early civilizations. The father was the family leader, and the mother was regarded as a child's first teacher. Women and children had very few rights and were considered to be the property of an adult male. Children could be sold into slavery or even abandoned. By the 5th century, rewards were given to families who gave asylum to orphaned or deserted children, marking early beginnings of socially sanctioned interventions that served better outcomes for children.

Disturbingly for present day cultural standards, child sacrifices, infanticide, and slavery were common during these historical eras. On the authority of the father, infants who were deformed could be left to the elements, drowned, or suffocated.

Middle Ages. The Middle Ages (400–1400) were times in which family life centered primarily on an agrarian lifestyle; that is farming or looking after livestock. Families were structured in *extended families*, with several generations living together. Formal education was minimal and mainly restricted to the clergy of the Catholic Church.

We do not have full insight into how children were truly treated, or what they meant to their families. Because it is not extensively documented and illiteracy was the norm, we have neither a complete nor accurate picture of childhood before the 15th century.

Renaissance. Over the next two centuries, 1400–1600, Europe experienced a period of cultural revitalization that was marked by voyages of discovery, scientific exploration, and an explosion of artistic creativity. Adults explored their inner environments or personalities, attempting to discover their true selves. This social and cultural expansion subtly filtered into a desire for greater understanding of children and parenting. New insights in some areas fostered simultaneous revision of ideas in others.

Gradually a new approach towards children began to emerge. This contributed to changes in attitudes about the nature and status of children in society. During the late 1500s, artists gave more attention to children in their artwork. Another indication of greater concern and attention was the creation of special clothing styles just for children. Until this time, children had been dressed in replicas of adult costumes. This change in clothing style signaled that children, at least those of the nobility, were seen as distinct and separate entities (Cohen, 2013).

By the late 1500s, additional distinctions between the world of adults and that of children emerged. Recreational activities, stories, and types of medical care between the two groups began to differ. Advice on how to provide discipline and guidance in child rearing became more widespread (Bigner & Gerhardt, 2014). Over the next 200 years, the rate of social change would accelerate, bringing new adjustments to the ways that people viewed parenthood and childhood.

The Industrial Revolution. The Industrial Revolution, typically thought to have started around 1790, produced dramatic changes in family life and roles. The father's central role consisted of providing the economic support and moral and religious education for children. He also acted as the disciplinarian. Authoritarianism and fatherhood became intertwined. During and following the Industrial Revolution, fathers were increasingly employed in factory related jobs, which separated them from their families for long periods. Mothers in turn assumed responsibility for the character development and socialization of children. The mother became the instructor and central family figure in a child's life, and the nurturing aspect became stronger. In some very religious families, physical punishment for character molding continued.

•••

Focus Point. While history and culture are fairly fluid constructs, their intersection sheds some light on the evolution of childhood and parenthood throughout history. Most of our knowledge of ancient family life comes from archeological findings, literature, and the visual arts, which tend to tell us that, due to high infant mortality rates, parenting centered around survival rather than nurture. Children were given tasks and some adult responsibilities. They had to actively contribute to the household.

•••

Earlier Perceptions of Children

We surmise that in earlier centuries the needs of children were not particularly considered. There was no documented concept that infants needed to learn to trust their caregivers, or attach to them. That made it an easy decision to send a child away from home. It was common practice among west European nobility to send their infants to live with wet nurses who were peasant women who had infants of their own and looked after children to supplement the family income. The wet nurse usually cared for the nobility's infants for about 2 years. Because there were no infant milk formulas, and no standards concerning infant care, these women would also breastfeed the infants. Apparently, the biological parents were not particularly concerned about the quality of care given to their infant during this time (Harlow & Laurence, 2010).

Assimilation into the adult world came early, usually during the period we currently describe as middle childhood. A child's education, as there was no formal schooling, came from observing and imitating adult role models. Children in well-off families might have been individually tutored. Parents probably felt that younger children needed adult supervision and care, but this did often not extend to close emotional ties. Parents did not appear to provide warmth or nurture to children, possibly because many children died in infancy and childhood from diseases that are preventable today. Even so, we are not sure of the facts and the reality may have been different.

During this period, parenting was only one of many functions of the family, and no high priority was attached to it. Families were most concerned with the production of food, clothing, and shelter to ensure daily survival. Intense emotional investment in children was associated with risks, as death claimed so many of these young lives and interrupted relationships before they had a chance to blossom.

The thought that children were regarded as "miniature adults," was largely based on the work of Aries (1962), and a number of recent researchers in the field of the history of childhood maintained that his views should be seen as a thesis, not as fact. A good half century later, his once popular statements are being questioned and current researchers strongly caution against stereotypical historical views of children, especially as being smaller versions of adults (Kindleberger, 2016, p. 155). The thinking tends to steer more towards the individualistic nature that is inherent in parent–child relations; not all parents behave the same way towards their offspring despite the social norms of the time.

The thesis of children as small adults was based on their adult-type clothing and that they were given responsibilities at an early age. The lives of children and adults paralleled closely. Children were exposed to adult behavior and living conditions. For example, many children were apprenticed to learn a particular trade. Children had to help on the farm, look after younger siblings and generally bring their share towards what was generally required to support the survival of the family. It seems counterintuitive that mothers and fathers did not bond with their offspring.

In the Foundling Museum in London, information surrounding foundling children from the Victorian era (mainly 1800s) is documented and preserved. These children were abandoned in churches and on orphanage steps in the hope of a better future. Their mothers simply could not take care of them as the mothers were unpartnered, very poor, lacked family support, and were at the mercy of the exceedingly harsh judgment and discrimination against unwed mothers. Seeing the love tokens these women left with their offspring leads one to believe that this forced child abandonment was heartbreaking and haunted the mothers for years to come. Clearly, many of the parents who lived centuries before us must have had tender feelings and deep attachment towards their offspring.

DEVELOPMENTALLY APPROPRIATE APPROACHES TO CHILDREARING

Historically, a child was seen as an object to be socialized by the parents. This was a *unidirectional* model of socialization. The adult's behavior was the *stimulus* that caused or produced a *response* or outcome in a child. If adults taught their children well, meaning if they socialized them to meet the norms of society, then the children would become good persons. Adults could achieve their parenting goals if they provided appropriate care giving. Following this logic, the formula for effective parenting was based on consistently good parental performance during child rearing. Society made judgments about how child-rearing success was attained.

Approaches to child rearing were also influenced by the earlier writings of John Locke (1697). Locke was known for his *tabula rasa* (blank slate) theory of development. In this view, children were believed to be born with their minds and personalities empty like blank slates and impressionable for influences by adults. The child-rearing experiences emphasized the traits manifested in adult personalities. This is a cause-and-effect view of child rearing. It was more moderate. Parents were role models for their children, influencing future character development. Much later in history, in the early 20th century, John Watson, a Behaviorist psychologist, picked up a similar tone indicating that children could and should be influenced by the adults who could serve as moral examples. These approaches grappled with the nature/nurture question and placed their bets on the nurture part of the formula.

Another voice at this time was that of Jean-Jacques Rousseau (1712–1778) whose theories on childhood sounded good on paper and many of his quotes are still circulating today:

> We are born weak, we need strength; helpless, we need aid; foolish, we need reason. All that we lack at birth, all that we need when we come to man's estate, is the gift of education.

In his personal life he was said to have faced challenges in his fathering role, and rumor has it that one or more of his children became guests of the local orphanage.

If children did not behave appropriately, it was because they did not know any better. Parents were advised not to be overly concerned about breaking a child's will, but they were also warned against indulging a child. The historic booklet: *The School of Manners or Rules for Children's Behaviour* (Garretson, 1701/1983, p. 39–40) provided lists of things children should and should not do. From a list of 26 "Rules for Behavior in Company," here is a small selection:

- "When thou blowest thy Nose, let thy Handkerchief be used, and make not a noise in so doing."
- "Gnaw not thy Nails, pick them not, nor bite them with thy teeth."
- "Spit not in the Room, but in a corner, and rub it out with thy Foot, or rather go out and do it abroad."
- "Read not Letters, Books, nor other Writings in Company, unless there be necessity, and thou ask leave."
- "Let thy Countenance be moderately Chearful, neither laughing nor frowning." (sic)

Even so, the introduction makes it sound as if parents need fortification against the unruliness of their children, lest the latter overrule. Paraphrased in modern English the essence is, that the younger the child when we approach the task of disciplining, the better the outcome is likely to be. We can still "mend and reform them," using the guidelines in this very early version of a self-help book. One can detect some vague elements of the beginnings of developmentally appropriate parenting in these words, quoted as they appeared in the 1701 format:

> … And that is the proper and peculiar part, both of Parents at Home, and Masters at School, towards the good and accomplished educating of youth, as to Manners may be the more early, their desires and endeavours the more successful … occasioned by a long and troublesome observation of Childrens

Book first published in 1701, *The School of Manners, or Rules for Childrens Behaviour* (sic). It contains advice for children in terms of qualities that can be equally aspired to more than 300 years later (Garretson, 1701/1983).

rudeness in behavior, both at home and abroad, and of Parents perpetuating intreaties, tiring the instructors of their Children with importunate demands … those documents which may tend to mend and reform them. (sic) (1701/1983, p. 18).

Environment and Discipline

The cultural and religious conditions that existed at the time that America was colonized contributed to a unique view of children and the provision of care by their parents. Colonial America spans from about 1600–1750. Children were seen as inherently depraved. Adults thought that children were basically bad and in need of correction and guidance. It was thought that parents could overcome this by providing particular child-rearing experiences. Many parents believed that if they administered stern discipline through hard labor, children would become self-denying, pious adults upon maturity. Adults prized children for their usefulness and for being a source of cheap labor. Their value in the colonies increased because of the high rate of infant mortality.

The premise that the nature of children was sinful stemmed primarily from the rigid Puritan religious views of the colonists (Cohen, 2013). These are illustrated in the *Day of Doom*, a catechism written by Michael Wigglesworth (1631–1705), which was learned by almost every child in Puritan New England. Puritan parents were responsible for providing rigorous moral and religious training for children, which included stern discipline. These parents believed it was their responsibility to bring children to religious salvation or conversion. This was accomplished when children were able to recognize and admit their own sinful nature and become Christians. The earlier this occurred, the better, from many parents' point of view. To help children achieve religious conversion, they were taught that they must always obey their parents unquestioningly, especially their father. They were taught to curb their natural inclination to commit sins. Aspects of childhood that are considered acceptable and developmentally appropriate today were, in Colonial times, viewed as manifestations of sin. Play was considered slothful, and children were kept occupied by memorizing scripture and religious songs. This approach to child rearing placed authority and the welfare of children squarely in the hands of parents. Based on this approach, the unidirectional model of parent–child relations became the primary model of child rearing.

During Colonial times, adults approached their parenting role in ways that we would today label as overly involved and borderline abusive. Stemming from what we think may have been selective indifference toward children during the Renaissance, this represented a pendulum swing toward the opposite stance. There was a heavy emphasis on religious matters and the use of harsh disciplinary methods to achieve children's salvation and obedience. Despite the punitive image, parents had great affection for their children and showed concern for their welfare in ways that were thought to be appropriate at that time.

On the positive side: increasingly children's needs were acknowledged. Historians tell us that children had toys; not in abundance but playful activity for the sake of playing was acknowledged. Some of the earlier material specifically written for children were the stories of "Mother Goose," in the late 1700s. Fairytales (for instance those captured by the brothers Grimm) told parables to young and old alike and captured tales from oral history and translated them into the more permanent written form. These were published in the mid 1800s but circulated in oral tradition for many centuries previously.

Bend the Tree While It Is Young

Because religion may include a focus on morals and ethics, historically it had a clear influence on child rearing approaches, and may continue to do so to the present. The child rearing guidelines were inspired by religious movements that supported rigid and extreme beliefs. Essentially, these somewhat radical approaches focused on the burden of sin and, by implication, the inherent wickedness of children. This view advocated stern, harsh use of physical punishment and strict moral instruction for youngsters, such as found in a strong, authoritarian child-rearing style. The saying *"Spare the rod and spoil the child"* and *"Children should be seen, not heard"* are examples of this attitude.

Children were like saplings or young trees, which had to be bent and guided towards the correct outcomes while they were still flexible and their ways could be influenced and modified. Contrast that with the contemporary respectful approach acknowledging that children are developmentally in flux and have to be constructively guided and supported towards appropriate choices. How a parent trained a child determined the outcome in terms of the child's character in adulthood (Downs, 2015).

Susanna Wesley's (1669–1742) life is unique and almost surreal for the 21st century reader. Her child-rearing techniques and her life were documented in her diaries, which ultimately became accessible to scholars. She was born the youngest of 25 children, a family so large that it finds few documented counterparts even at that time in history. She married at the age of 19, and with her husband Samuel Wesley, they had 19 children. Two of these children were the brothers John and Charles Wesley, attributed with founding the Methodist religious movement, a variation on Protestant values.

In her diary she wrote about the duties she had as a mother and that she tried to spend individual time with each child, but that in practice she had to do that on different days for each child. Consider the logistics; if she were to take half an hour individual time with each one of her children, she would be spending more than an eight-hour workday doing just that. About the harsher side of discipline Susanna Wesley wrote that her own children would cry softly in fear of punishment. It would appear that children as young as a year old were harshly corrected. This was thought to promote quiet children and tranquil households (Cunningham, 2005). She described correction as follows:

> . . . when turned a year old (and some time before) they were taught to fear the rod and cry softly, by which means they escaped abundance of correction (Cunningham, 2005, p. 53).

Expanding Child Focused Values

The time period we are focusing on here is about 150 years starting in the early 1800s and reaching forward to post WWII. Clearly, social trends develop gradually and cannot be put into watertight time-related compartments. The prevailing thoughts of the day influenced what people perceived as desirable and correct behavior. The time frame under discussion includes the Victorian era in Britain which coincides with the reign of Queen Victoria (1819–1901), and is accessible because of the wealth of documented information.

Historian Ellen Ross (1993) states that the real life changes that occur within a family, frequently happen at a slower pace than what is observed in political and industrial contexts. Ross references the concept of "family time" attributed to Tamara Hareven (1982), who discussed the relationship between families and work. Thus Ross states that the clock measuring "family time", does not tick at the same pace as time in political and other social contexts (Ross, p.26). She elaborates this by stating that many core aspects pertaining to family life remain relatively static.

Several major views about parenthood and childhood emerged, and continued to exert an influence. Positively, approaches that emphasized the beginnings of lifespan developmental principles were finding their way into mainstream culture. There were also philosophies focusing on behavior learned from the environment, justifying strict discipline. Religious principles provided guidelines concerning moral and ethical guidelines.

Beginnings of Developmental Approach

Obedience was valued, but it could be coaxed from children in more humane ways, such as by being firm, using persuasion, and giving rewards rather than physical punishment, as described in 1863 in the historic guide with the title: *Moral Culture of Infancy, and Kindergarten Guide.* This early guide referenced Mrs. Horace Mann, the wife of an educator, and was published by her sister Elizabeth Peabody (Mann & Peabody, 1863/2015). This book can be considered to be one of the earliest written

Since World War II, changing economic conditions and the rise of the Women's movement have left families with new ideas about gender roles involving working mothers. The current norm is a two-income family with the vast majority of women working outside the home throughout their children's childhood years.

documents concerning developmental approaches to children and it emphasized:

- Meeting children's developmental needs.
- Including in the parental role the shaping of children's personalities.
- Encouraging age-appropriate nurturing and gentler care.

Even so, much moralizing was taking place, making the outcomes for unmarried mothers exceptionally difficult, and the fact that some parents with special needs children were known to go to great lengths to hide their "shame" was described in the book *Family Secrets: Shame and Privacy in Modern Britain* (Cohen, 2013). Historian Ginger Frost sums up key elements concerning parents and their children from this era. Refer to Reflection 3–2.

Reflection 3–2

Parenting in Victorian Times

- Family life in the Victorian period was most influenced by middle-class domesticity, which stressed the parent–child bond. For the aristocracy, nannies still did much of the day-to-day parenting, but for the rest, mothering, particularly, was key to healthy childhood development.

- Religion was a major part of parenting in the Victorian middle class. Most parents believed in God sincerely and were anxious about their children's spiritual health.

- Working-class parents, who often had many children, showed their love through hard work and were less religiously-minded. Poor mothers labored continually to keep up appearances on little money, and child-care was shared in working-class communities with neighbors and kin.

- Fathers' main duty was providing in all classes; however, historians have shown that fathers had many other roles, as the "fun" parent, the repairer of shoes, even the caretaker during illnesses. Most Victorian men took fatherhood very seriously.

- Though children were valued, parents made the major decisions and emphasized discipline, duty, and thrift to their children. Middle-class parents tended to use guilt more than corporal punishment, but in the working class, hitting children was common. Overall, children were not spoiled. Parents were far more likely to fear over-indulging a child than spanking a child.

- The number of children per family lowered throughout the century, but differed by class. The middle class was the first to limit births, while the working class was the last. Thus, more children got individual attention toward the end of the century in middle-class homes.

- Birth order and sex determined much of a child's life for the working classes. The eldest child in a poor family was expected to leave school and go to work as early as possible, and also to help care for younger siblings. Older girls were most prone to be out of school as "mother's helpers." This led to conflict when states began compulsory elementary education.

- Problem parents (alcoholics, criminals, abusers) lost their children to state care, which was often crude in the Victorian period (e.g., workhouses). Thus, children often preferred the indifference of drunken or abusive parents to orphanages or state institutions.

- In the early 20th century, European states began instituting programs such as school lunches, medical inspections, and free milk to pregnant or nursing mothers. These programs were helpful, but also meant more state intrusion into family life.

References: Leonore Davidoff and Catherine Hall, *Family Fortunes: Men and Women of the English Middle Class, 1780-1850* (Chicago: University of Chicago Press, 1987); Ginger Frost, *Victorian Childhoods* (Westport, CT: Praeger, 2009); Lydia Murdoch, *Imagined Orphans: Poor Families, Child Welfare and Contested Citizenship in London* (New Brunswick, NJ: Rutgers University Press, 2006); Claudia Nelson, *Family Ties in Victorian England* (Westport, CT: Praeger, 2007); Julie-Marie Strange, *Fatherhood and the British Working Class, 1865-1914* (Cambridge: Cambridge University Press, 2015).

Published with permission of the author of this reflection: Ginger S. Frost, PhD, Research Professor of History, Samford University, Author of: *Living in Sin* (1995), *Victorian Childhoods* (2009), & *Promises Broken* (2011).

Child Focused Mindset Gathers Momentum.   The more child-focused mindset developed parallel to the early focus of psychology. During the late 19th and early 20th century, movements in both Europe and America were established and early childhood education with nursery schools and kindergartens was advocated. These approaches acknowledged the developmental nature of children and that we should treat children age appropriately in child-friendly settings. These are some of the educators and programs that are still favored to this day. The following persons and their approaches reflect a paradigm shift in how childhood education was viewed and, importantly, how it was practiced.

- **Charlotte Mason** (1842–1923) was a British educator whose ideals were that all children should have access to an education. She is credited with the quote: "Education is an atmosphere, a discipline, a life."
- **Maria Montessori.** In the 20th century, Maria Montessori (1870–1952), an Italian physician and educator, expanded on the developmental approach to early learning. The well-known *Montessori* schools are named in her honor.
- **Waldorf or Steiner Education.** Based on the philosophy of Austrian-born social reformer **Rudolf Steiner** (1861–1925). His philosophical view emphasized the great potential of the human mind. Child's

play was regarded as a valuable expression, which deserved incorporation into educational programs. The first *Waldorf* school opened in 1919 in Stuttgart, Germany.

- **Reggio Emilia.** Developmental approaches found stronger expression in early educational and pre-school contexts. Post WWII, in a town called Reggio Emilia in Italy, educator **Loris Malaguzzi** (1920–1994) was a major initiator of the pre-school education movement.

The focus on children and their needs gathered momentum and was acknowledged in legal and educational systems, and in the social support provided to families and children. Social policy gradually changed not only children's and parental rights, but also all the systems that supported the family (Refer to TABLE 3–1: Families in Victorian England).

TABLE 3–1. Childhood and the Family in Victorian England

	Influences of Victorianism occurring from 1815–1914
Industrial Revolution: Mid-18th to mid-19th century	Childhood differed depending on the class, the generation, and the gender of the child (Frost, 2009). Breakup of the extended family. Increased urbanization as fathers, who were the breadwinners, took on factory jobs; 80 percent of the people lived in cities, often in poverty. Less support from the extended family. Class differences were based on education, financial prospects, and family background. Children were exploited, often laboring in factories.
Early Victorian: 1830s–1840s	Queen Victoria's reign from 1837–1901. Upheaval in the economic, political, and social arenas. Depression in industry and in agriculture. Potato blight in Ireland, resulting in mass immigration to the United States. Victorians idealized the family and the middle class. Reality was different, with poverty and persons in the lower classes struggling. This had a direct effect on family life and children. At worst, children were exploited, died early of infectious diseases, missed out on education, and were sometimes sexually and socially abused. At best, children were idealized for their innocence and seen as central to the family. Childhood was a very short period, and children could start working as early as age 7.
Middle Victorian: 1850–1875	Relative prosperity. Large families and low life expectancy. Children could be orphaned or have to deal with stepparents. Children born out of wedlock were stigmatized and were either absorbed by maternal families or left as foundling children to be raised in orphanages. Class differences set the stage for the different experiences of childhood. Highly religious society.
Late Victorian: 1875–1914	Rise of new technology like the telephone, chemicals, and electricity. This period culminated in World War I. Large families and high infant mortality. Frequent loss of a parent as life expectancy was short. Children were often socialized by their siblings. Family size declined in middle-class families. Children's rights became a topic for discussion. Some social reform. Alternatives other than prisons and workhouses for troubled children. The length of childhood increased as children were schooled longer. Children entered the workforce later.

TABLE 3–1. (*Continued*)

	Influences of Victorianism occurring from 1915–1914
General Themes: Attitudes toward children	Gradual increase in awareness of the importance of parenting. Gradual change in children's roles with the understanding and insight that childhood had its own characteristics and demands. Childhood and youth were not the first stage of adulthood, but a separate entity. Slow but steady social and legal reform occurred, fueled by political changes, and these reforms spread throughout the social classes. Child rearing entered the realm of public policy.
Discipline	Typically, harsh discipline, treating children as if they were innately bad and needed correction. Corporal punishment. From about age 12, children were treated as adults. No extended transition into adulthood. No juvenile legal system; children were punished in the same manner as adults, or placed in harsh reform schools. Social reform initiated in the late 1800s.
Homeless children and orphans	Children born out of wedlock were mostly absorbed by maternal households, although some children were abandoned as a result of dire poverty. Increasing social reform movements to help these children (e.g., orphanages, schools, foundling homes). Many institutions were founded by religious groups (e.g., the Salvation Army).
Abuse and neglect	Dire social conditions, including poverty, violence, and alcoholism, set the stage for child abuse (including some sexual abuse) and neglect. Prudery in middle-class families did not make them immune to the neglect and abuse of children.
Toys and play	The late Victorian period recognized the importance of play, and children had toys and playtime. Games could be seen as being educational as well as recreational. These insights represented the fragile beginnings of child centeredness. Books for children were being printed.
School	Initially, there was no compulsory schooling; children often left school during late childhood or early adolescence to learn a trade. Education was incomplete. Sunday schools were established to teach literacy, as well as religious concepts, to working children. England had a national school system by 1870, and compulsory schooling followed by 1880.
Child labor	Child labor continued throughout this era, up to World War I. In the late Victorian period, much of the child labor was part time, at least until school-leaving age, which was 14. Interrupted education precluded the hopes for a good economic future, with far-reaching effects on families.

Based on Frost, Ginger S. (2009). *Victorian Childhoods*. In the series, Mitchell, Sally (Series Editor). *Victorian Life and Times*. Westport, Connecticut: Praeger.

Focus Point. Compared to today's bidirectional model of parenting, most historical periods were characterized by an authoritarian, unidirectional parenting style in which strict guidelines and harsh punishments were encouraged. Only in the late 1800s did a more nurturing, developmentally-minded approach to parenting begin to formalize.

Video Example 3.1

Watch this video referencing the influences parents have on their children. What kinds of influences do parents exert on their children?

(https://www.youtube.com/watch?v=8b9dE4Szu88)

Library of Congress

As legal and educational systems became more child-focused, organizations such as the Children's Aid Society emerged. These organizations served children and families by providing social support and advocacy for child-focused policy.

PARENTING AND CULTURE

Because parents are the main socialization agents of children in their younger years, they are also the transmitters of cultural values. As the child's world expands, other socialization agents are also at work, for instance, for the adolescent, the peer group is important in conveying values and norms relevant for that age group. Teenagers may attach great value to the cultural norms of their peer group, sometimes to the dismay of their parents. Outward expressions of identity, for instance the way we dress, or the style of our haircuts, can be strongly influenced by subcultures, which in turn follow fashions and trends.

The **parent–child relationship** provides an opportunity for the psychosocial development of both children and adults, especially the adults. Parents are assisted in their growth and development as adults by parenting children, while children are socialized into adulthood by parents. The parent–child relationship mirrors the larger family process, and, in turn, aspects of cultural norms. The cultural values will shape and direct the

behaviors of all members within the family system, and, in turn, the family unit or the extended family can create its own mini subculture, with traditions and values that are unique to that specific family.

Although parents have a strong and vital influence on children's development, other factors, especially cultural influences, play a major part. The *bidirectional* model portrays the give-and-take of information and influence between culture and families. Cultural norms impact behavior in powerful ways.

Child rearing is a unique statement of personal and family philosophy, while also reflecting the cultural values and norms of the family and the larger society within which that family is embedded.

Focus Point.   While cultural values shift dramatically throughout history, the impact that the culture has on parenting and the family unit is a fairly consistent phenomenon.

The Role of Culture

The cultural dimension describes what families value and believe to be important, and guides the behavior of members of a particular cultural group. **Culture** is a virtual shorthand between persons sharing the same cultural context; it allows them to assume content and meaning without further clarification because, as members of the same cultural perspective, they have been *enculturated* in a similar manner. According to Fukuyama (1995, p. 211): " . . . culture is not an unbending primordial force but something shaped continuously by the flow of politics and *history*" (italics added). Culture is not static; it changes and responds to the environment. What has gone before may influence future cultural expressions.

Culture has similarities with a computer operating system; it forms a basic layer on top of which other programs can run. Similarly, in a group of people who share cultural values, there are rituals, values, beliefs, and ways of doing things that are shared unquestioningly. This adds to the harmony within a group because there is a cohesiveness that results from these shared values, customs, and belief systems. Being part of a cultural group, members absorb the values seemingly by osmosis. In reality, culture is learned behavior that is transmitted initially in the parent–child relationship, and later by all those who assume coparenting, supportive, and other social roles in a child's life.

Cultural Snapshot 3–1

Harajuku Fashion and Street Culture

In the district of Harajuku, in Shibuya, Japan, there is a small yet world famous subculture where fashion is extreme, predominantly interpreted by the youth. For the emerging adults concerned, this is an expression of identity and autonomy, and a way of making visible and noticeable statements concerning their individuality. They follow and mix international trends and prefer certain brand labels, with the proviso that it is radical. Fashions have a quick turnover time and even last month's fashion may be out of date today. Clothes are matched and mismatched to create eye-catching, attention grabbing combinations. Some of the individuals' appearances are influenced by comics and fantasy figures. For instance, fairy tale and Disney figures such as Little Red Riding Hood, or Mini Mouse may find new life interpreted through clothing.

Each outfit represents a blended and unique fusion between Japanese and American cultural expressions. Any unconventional expression of individuality is applauded. Clothing choices and combinations are once-off, but certain themes may predominate while they are fashionable. Unconventional hair and makeup are encouraged. On Sundays, the areas around Harajuku station, as well as the close-by Meiji Shrine become a fashion catwalk, where dramatic and bold fashions are displayed. The point of dressing so radically, is to be noticed, photographed, and admired; but most importantly to serve as an expression of autonomy and individuality.

(Based on material retrieved from: www.japanesestreets. com/harajuku-fashion/. Retrieved January 2017).

Feije Riemersma/Alamy Stock Photo

The style of the Harajuku district of Shibuya, Japan, is known for its mix of international trends, eye-catching color combinations, and influences from comics and fantasy figures.

Cultural Historic Snapshot 3–2

Culture Is Like a Map

Definition of Culture by Kluckhohn (1949)

Some of the early and poetic definitions of culture, are by American anthropologist Clyde Kluckhohn (1905–1960) who ended his academic career at Harvard University. His area of expertise was Native American culture, specifically the Navajo. In his classic book, *Mirror for Man* (1949), he explained culture to lay readers. Many of the isolated communities he studied during his lifetime have since been exposed to aspects of westernization and it is becoming increasingly rare to find enclaves with pure traditional cultural values.

   Some of his descriptions concerning culture and "culture building," a term he used to indicate the adaptive way in which culture is shaped, addressed this topic from various angles:

   Comparing culture to a map. Kluckhohn (1949) uses a metaphor from cartography and geography to describe the landscape of culture. In the same way that a map of a given territory is only an abstract representation of that geographical area, culture is an approximate description of the qualities and characteristics found within a given social context. We use maps to direct us, to find our way. In a similar manner, if we understand the landmarks of a culture, we can feel our way through the social customs and the semi-obscure layers of customs, values and beliefs within a given societal group.

   Cultural fragments caught by an imaginary sieve. Kluckhohn (1949) thinks that history precipitates fragments of culture. A metaphorical sieve catches the nuances of cultural meaning as these were crystallized by history. As members identify with any given cultural context, they will be able to recognize the cultural messages, and thus have access to those cultural fragments. Combined these precipitated fragments create cultural meaning.

   Acknowledging the function of culture. Kluckhohn (1949) is of the opinion that cultural content can only remain viable, if it is functional. Remove the usefulness of these cultural strands and they will atrophy or die off. This also explains why culture changes over time in response to the demands of current and changing environments

Source: Kluckhohn, C. (2009). "Queer Customs." In G. P. Ferraro, *Classic Readings in Cultural Anthropology* (2nd ed., pp. 6–12). Australia; United Kingdom: Wadsworth Cengage Learning.

One of the functions of shared cultural knowledge is that it provides information that can support the survival of the group subscribing to that culture. Ways of doing things, rituals for dealing with lifespan transitions, all the implied ways in which we can behave, can be guided by the reigning cultural value systems. Culture shapes the rules or social norms that outline appropriate behavior in a variety of contexts, such as the roles that persons fulfill and the notions of acceptable and unacceptable actions. Importantly, it links them to individuals, agencies, and institutions that transmit these values and beliefs, and may impart a sense of belonging. For example, for some, these values are derived from the larger ethnic group with which they identify (Matsumoto & Juang, 2016); for others, these values come from religious beliefs and philosophies. Usually, all of the contributing agents are so intertwined that there is little point in teasing out which system contributed what in terms of culture. Matsumoto and Juang (2016, p. 8) reference Lonner and Malpass (1994) when they state that: "Culture, in its truest and broadest sense, cannot simply be swallowed in a single gulp."

   This reflects the complexity of this multifaceted topic. Regardless of the origin of the values, parents are charged with transmitting this cultural heritage to their children. It also plays into the scenario that children's brains are equipped with what neuroscientists call *mirror neurons*, which support children in mimicking and copying behavior, especially language, in a virtually involuntary manner (Cozolino, 2014). This ability is also believed to play a supportive role in the acquisition of culture.

   Cognitively, children learn values, attitudes, and beliefs by parental example. Negative prejudices can also be learned, which underlines the necessity of parent–child relations that focus on values and behaviors that will support and enhance *multicultural competence* in the child's later life. According to Ryder and Dere

(2010), cultural competence should be regarded as a general orientation. It is also aspirational and can be fostered and strengthened with "knowledge about and comfort with the implications of cultural difference" (Ryder & Dere, 2010, pp. 11–12). These same authors use the concept *cultural humility* to describe the quality required in a professional clinical relationship.

An informal description of culture compares its effects to a global positioning device, which directs, and gently redirects, the user back to a preset destination. In cultural terms, it would mean that ongoing minor behavioral adjustments are made to meet cultural expectations. Members of a cultural group share and can reference the symbols and behaviors pertaining to that group. It becomes especially apparent in rituals for life transitions, for instance, lifespan rites of passage surrounding birth, marriage, and death.

The formal definitions of culture may seem simple, but encapsulate complexity. Matsumoto and Juang (2016, p. 404) define culture as "[a] unique meaning and information system, shared by a group and transmitted across generations that allows the group to meet basic needs of survival, pursue happiness and well-being, and derive meaning from life." Shiraev and Levy (2016, p. 4) describe it in the following manner: "Culture is a set of attitudes, behaviors, and symbols shared by a large group of people and usually communicated from one generation to the next."

According to Nanda and Warms (2014, pp. 52–54), who describe culture from an anthropological perspective, the following commonalities recur in definitions: It is learned behavior, it uses symbolic "shorthand" or sets of symbols, it is integrated in a logical manner, the material is shared by members who subscribe to a particular culture, and culture adapts and changes over time. "Culture is also a way that human beings adapt to the world" (2014, p. 65).

Even though cultural constructs have a degree of permanence, there is also fluidity, allowing for change. The change can be rapid, as in some small subcultures, or relatively slow, as in intergenerational changes. Culture has blurry or indistinct boundaries in that there is no clear demarcation where the influences of culture begin or end. We live in more interconnected ways through mass media, global communication, travel, immigration, and other effects of globalization, and therefore cultures become less stable because there are so many layers of bidirectional influence.

Applied here, culture serves as the lens through which parenting behavior may be observed regarding the proper ways to raise children to maturity in accordance with cultural values and beliefs (Prioste, Narciso, Gonçalves, & Pereira, 2015). More specifically, each culture is likely to have its own particular ways of defining proper child rearing. From this vantage point, culture becomes a worldview possessed and practiced in unique ways by each culture or subculture.

Large societies, such as that of the United States, often consist of a variety of subcultures that are differentiated from the larger society according to distinct sets of behaviors, values, and beliefs. These subcultures may be based on features held in common, such as ethnicity, nationality of origin, sexual orientation, age, gender, political affiliation, religious belief, or geographic location. It is possible that individuals may ascribe to more than one subculture based on these factors. Blending or fusing cultures may allow for both a *heritage* culture and a mainstream culture (Ryder, Alden, Paulhus, & Dere, 2013).

Enculturation and Acculturation

In the United States, where the population has been largely derived from immigrants of many different groups over the years, multiculturalism encourages and allows various subcultures to retain their basic features while also coexisting with others as one nation. Immigrants can maintain a *heritage culture* while simultaneously assimilating to the *host culture*; leading to bi- and multicultural identities (Ryder et al., 2013). The first or original cultural imprinting is called *enculturation*. The process of acquiring a second culture, layered on top of the first or integrated with the first, is called *acculturation* (Doucerain, Dere, & Ryder, 2013; Shiraev & Levy, 2016).

Individualism and **collectivism** are two cultural conceptions of value systems (Shiraev & Levy, 2016). The various cultures around the world are characterized by the manner in which these two value systems are blended or balanced. Essentially, *individualism* in a culture values the person and what can be accomplished on one's own. Individual identity and self-expression are valued as well. *Collectivism* as a cultural trait emphasizes the interdependence of the individual with the larger community. Collectivism encourages people to fit in and adapt to the characteristics of the larger community. Collectivism is frequently associated with cultural groups in Asia, whereas mainstream North America is generally regarded as individualistic. Note that collectivism and individualism occur on a continuum and that varying degrees of each dimension can occur.

These two cultural conceptions have direct application in parent–child relations in that they influence how parents translate cultural values into interactions with their children. For example, parents in cultures characterized as *individualistic* tend to:

■ Encourage autonomy, independence, and self-reliance in children.
■ Foster children's personal achievements.
■ Support children's competitiveness.
■ Allow children to question and explore.
■ Allow children to participate in decision making.

In contrast, parents in cultures characterized as *collectivist* tend to:

■ Have closer emotional ties to children for longer periods in infancy and childhood.
■ Emphasize the extended family network in teaching children what is valued.
■ Stress obedience to all authority, especially to parents and older family members.
■ Emphasize children learning and respecting social norms governing appropriate behavior.
■ Emphasize the sharing of property and belongings.
■ Shape children's behavior to demonstrate responsibility and obligation to others (Prioste, et. al., 2015).

There is some interplay between collectivism and individualism. Parents who emigrate from typically collectivistic cultures may find it difficult to assimilate into individualistic cultures. The family cultural values may be at odds with the mainstream cultural values of the host country.

In the teaching–learning environments of educational systems, individualistic approaches emphasize dialogue, independent exploration of ideas, creativity, questioning, and active participation in the teaching–learning process (Ralston, et. al., 2013). Traditional collectivistic environments tend to put the teacher or professor into an authoritarian position as the expert, whose opinions may be accepted unquestioningly, while placing the student into a more passive learning role. In an individualistic teaching–learning environment, original thought and action may be prized. For parents (and for teachers) in general, it is a constructive challenge to impart values promoting some cultural cohesiveness while also allowing individualistic, yet pro-social, expression.

Heritage Culture. The aspects of the cultural heritage to be maintained, versus the aspects to be silenced by the assimilation process, may contribute to adaptation to the host culture. The willingness of migrants and immigrants to find the level of assimilation best suited to integrate successfully may contribute to the family's well-being (Dere, Ryder, & Kirmayer, 2010). Typically, the assimilation and integration process occurs and strengthens from one generation to the next. Each subsequent generation becomes more assimilated into the host culture. The language of the country of origin is usually lost by the third or fourth generation post initial immigration. The United States is an example of such blending of many immigrant voices into one choir.

Cultural Translators. First-generation immigrants may bear the brunt of new cultural challenges, while second-generation immigrants (the offspring of the immigrants) may thrive as cultural "translators," understanding both the culture of the country of origin and the culture of the adopted home country (Zolfaghari, Möllering, Clark, & Dietz., 2016). It is also possible for both these qualities (collectivism and individualism) to be present at the same time, depending on the context. Cultural transitions can elicit feelings of both individualism and collectivism, depending on the situation and on which cultural values are dominant at a given time.

A person who is familiar with both (or several) cultures becomes a cultural translator. One such multicultural person described herself as standing with each one of her feet in a different "cultural shoe." She could step forward and backward into different cultural contexts. She also mentioned that as a teenager searching for a personal and a peer group identity, she felt like a cultural outsider belonging neither here nor there. As she matured she found she could join several cultural groups, as she understood and could translate elements of each cultural language.

Ethnocentrism. Behavioral scientists who study cultural influences warn us about the problems of *ethnocentrism* as we study our culture in the United States in comparison with that of others. This occurs when we use the understandings of our culture to compare, evaluate, and judge those of others. Implicit is the conclusion that our culture is superior and preferable to that of others (Matsumoto & Juang, 2016). For example, the use of physical punishment by parents with children has different meanings and different values from culture to culture and even from one subculture to the next. In another example, although American parents typically value children becoming autonomous at an early age, this practice is viewed as unusual in some cultures.

Cultural Universalism and Cultural Relativism

In studying parents and children, as well as families, we should strive to recognize that there are patterns that are likely to be shared across subcultures, as well as patterns that are unique to each, recognizing the functioning of *cultural universalism* versus *cultural relativism* in influencing our perceptions. In cultural relativism, the *cultural context* within which any cultural expression occurs is emphasized, increasing the understanding and tolerance of cultural expressions that may occur beyond the mainstream (Shiraev & Levy, 2016).

Etic and Emic.   Additionally, the concepts *etic* (culturally universal) and *emic* (culturally specific) are of importance. Etic (pronounced to rhyme with "poetic"), draws together those cultural components that we share universally. It is sometimes referred to as an outsiders view of culture, or as viewed by an observer. On the other hand, emic (pronounced to rhyme with "scenic") refers to that which identifies us, or makes us culturally unique, sometimes referred to as a cultural insider's view; someone belonging to, or a participant of the culture. (Shiraev & Levy, 2016).

Three examples illustrating funeral rites, marriage rituals, and parenting better illustrate the interplay between etic and emic qualities.

Funeral Rites.   It is a universal quality (etic) that we grieve our dead. How we go about the *funeral rites* is culture specific (emic). We may find extremes in funeral practices; certain groups in the Himalayas lay out the corpses with utmost dignity to be devoured by vultures. In this particular context, that may be regarded as the best culturally accepted option. Other cultural contexts may be to cremate the dead in public funeral pyres, such as we could observe in Varanasi, India. In the North American contexts, funeral rites are mainly delegated to formal funeral undertakers or directors, following the accepted norms of that particular cultural group, often strongly influenced by prevalent religious practices. But what connects us all universally, is that we mourn our dead, and we treat them with respect. This universal quality would represent the etic perspective.

Marriage Rituals.   The second example concerns *marriages*. It is culturally universal that couples get married (etic perspective). The specifics of how that ceremony takes place are culturally specific (emic perspective). For instance, traditionally, Hindu brides wear red saris, Japanese brides may be dressed in a festive Kimono, and according to western practices the bride wears white. Currently, western couples try to focus on making some elements of their ceremonies unique, so that their special day is infused with memories that they have personally made and that mean a lot to them (emic perspective). As cultures begin to fuse or people adopt bicultural lifestyles, both traditional and contemporary cultural practices may be involved. The Korean bridal couple may initially have a traditional ceremony, dressed in traditional costume, and midway change to western bridal attire. In this way, the couple feels they acknowledge all the cultural elements within their personal histories. For traditional Indian brides, their wedding sari is red, whereas western brides tend to wear white.

Parenting.   The third example pertains to *parenting*. It is culture universal (etic) that parents in healthy family contexts want the best for their offspring. They may be ambitious and protective on behalf of their children, they may serve as role models to learn a variety of roles, values, social conduct, and more. Cultural contexts which are culture specific (emic) may focus on a variety of child-rearing approaches. For instance, Japanese parents tend to value control of emotions and do not display their emotions as flamboyantly as Mediterranean cultures might; French and Italian parents are emotionally more interactive with their children. Authoritarian practices were valued by some groups and corporal punishment was regarded as accepted, whereas, in northern America, corporal punishment is typically frowned upon (Shiraev & Levy, 2016). When it comes to rituals such as baby blessings, and rites of passage ceremonies, these can vary dramatically from culture to culture and are also influenced by religious practices.

Clearly, one has to be cautious of stereotypes in making these statements, and must be aware that for every generalization there are exceptions. In reality, culture-specific and culture-universal qualities are not always at opposite ends of the continuum. Depending on cultural contexts, there can be flexibility and overlap.

Cultural Snapshot 3–3

Gifts, Promises, and Commitment

The western practice of getting engaged with a diamond solitaire ring for the bride is not culturally universal. Grooms typically do not wear equivalent diamond rings, although increasingly men choose rings to express their individuality. The diamond engagement ring specifically, has gained popularity in the past century, fueled by intense advertising. Other cultural contexts have varied ways of indicating marital status. For instance, in the traditional Indian context, the bride may signal her marital status by coloring the parting of her hair with a bright red pigment, such as henna, or wear a toe ring, called *bichiya*. Ornate bangles may also be a wedding gift.

In some countries such as Germany and Russia, the wedding band was traditionally worn on the right hand, although that is changing as cultures influence each other. As people are increasingly exposed to varied cultural practices, they may incorporate symbolism from more than one cultural context, as they themselves may be exposed to fused cultures in their personal lives. This is also proof that cultural practices are in flux, they can change over time to incorporate new and relevant themes, while other themes are maintained to acknowledge their cultural underpinnings.

As far as parenting is concerned, new mothers may be gifted with an item of jewelry at the birth of a child, to mark this momentous and joyous occasion. The child may also receive gifts as friends and family celebrate the new arrival. The practice of gender identification by color seems to have gained ground, and a pink or a blue ribbon on a mailbox in northern American contexts unmistakably signals whether a boy or a girl was welcomed into that household.

Some examples are based on: Shiraev, E., & Levy, D. A. (2016). *Cross-cultural Psychology: Critical Thinking and Contemporary Applications* (6th ed.). New York, NY: Psychology Press, Taylor & Francis Group.

Socialization

The family is a universal social institution. This group has the responsibility of producing children and socializing them to become well-functioning members of the larger society in which their family is embedded. Although families have always been the basic building blocks of a society, they have also changed significantly over the past century in terms of composition, size, and functioning, as well as the characteristics that give them meaning.

Years of social evolution have produced changes in families themselves, as well as in the umbrella societies under which the families are sheltered. Family functions have altered over time as societies have changed. Of all the functions that families originally had in society, the socialization of children to prepare them for their participation in society is perhaps the principal task to which parents in contemporary families continue to subscribe.

While there are various definitions of what **socialization** comprises, we will use this term to mean "the set of interpersonal processes through which cultural meaning is passed on and changed" (Peterson, Steinmetz, & Wilson, 2005, p. 10; Park, Coello, Lau, 2014). In a more practical vein, socialization is what parents do to teach children to conform to social rules, acquire personal values, and develop attitudes and behaviors that are typical or representative of their culture at large. Socialization occurs through the many ways that culture is transmitted to children by parents, the media, institutions, and agencies.

This process begins in earnest when children are toddlers and preschoolers, when parents and other caregivers take an active role in teaching and socializing children. The lessons are not always given in formal, verbal instruction; many are learned by children when they observe the behaviors of their parents and caregivers. Young children are excellent imitators as young brains are programmed to copy. This is a powerful way of socializing children, as well as transmitting culture, even at an early age (Jensen & Arnett, 2012).

Depending on the nature of a particular family system, certain standards may be promoted more than others. Despite the diversity of families today, almost all teach certain kinds of behaviors and values to children. Embedded in the guidance about acceptable behaviors are lessons about undesirable behavior as well. All of this is based on the assumption that there are shared meanings for *acceptable/desirable* versus *unacceptable/undesirable* behaviors that are taught by all parents and other agents in society that influence individuals and families.

Espies/Shutterstock

The cultural dimension in the context of family life is a cornerstone that reflects, among other things, the values, beliefs, and attitudes of persons sharing a culture, and these in turn influence rituals, family life transitions, parenting, and more.

Families can be socialization agents and function on a rigid to flexible or even permissive continuum, as reflected by their parenting styles. This depiction of socialization as a unidirectional model fails to accurately describe what truly happens in families when parents are raising children for adulthood. In reality, the process of socialization is *bidirectional* in nature because children play a role in this process. Parents change and shape the lessons of socialization based on the developmental stage and personal abilities of the child. This is also referred to as *developmental* parenting, meaning that it is appropriate for a particular child, acknowledging their individual and unique abilities while also considering their developmental age.

Focus Point.   Parent–child relations are influenced by and take place within a cultural context. Socialization is the way that parents and other societal entities teach cultural norms to children. Socialization is bidirectional in that children and their parents participate in this process, and society in turn influences the family unit.

Reflection 3–3

Try to predict how marriage, parenthood, and parent–child relations will be conceptualized in the year 2100 or even 2200. How would you rate contemporary families in their abilities to socialize children effectively for their future?

ETHNIC DIVERSITY IN FAMILIES

Cultural diversity has always been a hallmark of American society; it is the product of the immigration of various ethnic groups to the United States since pre-Colonial times. In recent years, ethnic identity has been reemphasized as Americans have become more curious about their family roots. Americans have always considered themselves to be a culturally diverse society. This diversity is reflected in the numerous ethnic and racial groups that have emigrated from other countries to make their new home in the United States (Glick, 2010).

Ethnic identity is a central family ecological factor that influences how most of these family systems are organized and how they function. It continues to play a role in each subsequent generation. Many ethnic minority families have created new lives and discovered new opportunities, but they have also struggled with the prejudice and discrimination that limits educational experiences, job opportunities, and the ability to function fully in communities. Because of these issues, family systems with minority ethnic and racial backgrounds experience problems that are not usually shared by those with a Caucasian, middle-class background.

Researchers examining family structure and functioning have tended to classify families in minorities according to the stereotypes promulgated within the larger society. Families are increasingly affected by mainstream cultural influences within their country of residence because the mass media is so powerful in exposing individuals to a variety of values, cultural norms, and marketing pressures.

In historic approaches to parenting, the challenges faced by parents and children were sometimes described within the context of the cultural and racial groups that represent a cross section of families in the United States. This approach in 21st century America may become a collection of stereotypes, rather than a description of authentic differences and similarities. A study of culture reveals that where different cultural groups live in close proximity they form friendships and work networks, as well as numerous formal and informal relationships. In the United States, we are also connected through a common language. Groups of people meet and cultures *fuse*. Ultimately, best practices are blended in ways that suit individual and family needs, and cultural influences are more prevalent in rituals, some aspects of religious practices, food choices, and cultural norms than in actual child-rearing practices. Because children receive similar schooling, and are acculturated in the same mainstream culture, cultural boundaries fade.

Cultural Respect.   We should, ideally, first focus on the generalities that connect us as humans and avoid the risks of *stereotyping* specific groups. There is also the risk of *ethnocentrism*, whereby we judge people from the perspective of our own cultural heritage. Acquiring *cultural humility* and *cultural respect* is the process of

counteracting the potential pitfalls of an ethnocentric approach. With cultural humility the person attempts to understand the "insider's" perspective, which in turn facilitates multicultural competence. It is similar to the process of "*empathy*" as found in counseling and therapeutic interactions.

The process of describing the American population in terms of five major ethnicities as represented in the United States, has been called *ethno-blocking* and is also informally referred to as "hyphenated Americans" because each group tends to be described by hyphenating or linking these Americans to the original geographic and ethnic roots. The U.S. Census Bureau designations are based on race, rather than ethnicity or cultural background, and comprise the following: Non-Hispanic Caucasian, African American, Asian, American Indian or Alaska Native, and Hispanic or Latino (Carl, 2012, pp. 40–43).

It is appropriate that we are concerned about building bridges between all families that make up American society (Sanagavarapu, 2010). Diversity, and its essential importance in our society, is a critical element that has made American society what it has become today, and it predicts how the future will unfold. Ethnic diversity is a part of the sociocultural system in which we live. It encompasses people's values, how their families operate as a social system, how they teach their children to function effectively, and how resources are used to promote daily functioning.

Multicultural Competence.   Diversity is a hallmark of family systems in American society, each family attempts to accomplish a common goal but in different ways: for example, raising children in the midst of uncertainty about the future, to become effectively functioning members of this society and ensuring that the children acquire *multicultural competence* (Dere et al., 2010). Multicultural competence is also an important and often required asset for the workplace, and requires respectful understanding of the unique cultural views to which another person may subscribe.

••

Focus Point.   America, historically known as the "melting pot," is a country rich in diversity. Helping children develop *multicultural competence* is a large part of the parental role of socialization. The current approach is to see society as a "mosaic" in which numerous individuals from a variety of cultures and ethnicities contribute to the larger whole or "Gestalt."

••

Multiracial and Interethnic Families

The number of multiracial and interethnic married couples has increased significantly; approximately 9 million individuals (or 2.9 percent of the population) described themselves as multiracial (Humes, Jones, & Ramirez, 2011). As early as 1761, colonial laws prohibited marriage between people of different races, but in 1967 the U.S. Supreme Court ruled such laws unconstitutional. International and interethnic adoptions have also created families with blended ethnic backgrounds, an enriching experience for every family member.

Research of multiracial interaction is an expanding area and may focus on strengths and defining identities in several cultural contexts (Dere et al., 2010). Similar to being multilingual, multiethnic persons can serve as cultural go-betweens, as they have access to more than one culture. This can be a considerable and highly valued skill in international relations and diplomacy. The positive outcomes can be found in the efforts of parents to provide effective adult role models in multiethnic and family contexts. Generally, there has also been a focus on increased multicultural competence.

Children in multiracial and interethnic families develop increased multicultural competence because of effective adult role models in multiethnic family contexts.

Diverse Influences

The diversity of families in American culture has meant that we can learn from each other when it comes to parenting. A large wave of immigrants from a variety of cultural backgrounds arrived between 1840 and 1930. The modern-day middle class also emerged from this group following the Great Depression of the 1930s. Many of these values pertaining to a working middle class became a dominant force in influencing the entire culture of the United States to this day.

In that time period, a number of differences could be observed between families and child rearing practices. What realistically may have been at work were family ecological factors, such as significant differences in family income, quality of housing, availability of health care, provision of adequate nutrition, and the availability of time to devote to parenting children.

Middle-class values continue to play a major role in providing a template for what is termed appropriate. Even so, the degree of materialism associated with middle-class success may not always grant peace of mind (Samuel, 2013). The conspicuous consumerism of the middle-class may eventually lead to an erosion of certain moral and ethical values, although economic pressures provide a counter influence. The diversity in families provides several models of parent–child relations that demonstrate both *cultural universalism* (etic) and *cultural relativism* (emic) in child rearing.

Education and Multilingualism

Educational achievement is highly valued amongst most families. Apart from the desire to improve their immediate and extended families' economic futures, education serves as an additional motivator fueling the desire to immigrate to the United States from other countries. Education is perceived as providing additional opportunities to the children of these families (Alba & Holdaway, 2013). Paradoxically, it is not unusual for educational attainment to be assigned a low priority by parents and other family members if it conflicts with a child's allegiance to the family (Roopnarine & Johnson, 2013).

Globally, more than half the world's population speaks at least two languages (Spitzer, 2016). Many families maintain the language from their culture of origin in addition to the language of the host culture. Hispanic children may initially find it socially and educationally challenging to acquire English as a second language, yet the benefits of bilingualism may surface later. Most learn Spanish as the primary language spoken at home and in the community. Hispanic parents generally favor this approach because it appears to support their children's cultural heritage, and bilingual classes may facilitate children's learning of the English language. Research clearly points toward the many advantages of bi- and multilingualism (Diamond, 2010; Sun, bin Sallahuddin, & Kaur, 2016). Some of the advantages appear to include superior social skills, improved problem solving abilities, flexibility in thinking, improved communication skills, and possibly improved memory. It appears that the neuro-linguistic connections that are made in bilingual and multilingual brains can have profound and long term effects. The term *cognitive reserve* is used to denote the positive outcomes of early bi- and multilingualism, and this reserve appears to postpone the onset of Alzheimer's disease (Spitzer, 2016).

Educational achievement is highly valued among Asian American parents. For example, more than half of Asian Americans have completed 4 years of college or more, which is an increase from the previous Census. Of all minority groups, these graduates tended to have the highest average earnings (Humes, Jones, & Ramirez, 2011). First-generation immigrants from Asia may subscribe to collectivism, whereas mainstream North America tends to be more individualistic. In immigrant families, fathers became more prominent in the lives of their children, as influences in the adopted country subtly change parenting patterns. For example, promoting interdependence, obedience, and cooperation (aspects that support collectivism) was not entirely compatible with the challenges faced in more individualistic environments (Prioste et. al., 2015).

Focus Point. Issues confronting newly arrived immigrants may involve cultural marginalization. Economic difficulties, problems in acquiring and using another language, and general acculturation issues present a special challenge for immigrant parents and children. It may be difficult to merge the *heritage* culture with the *host* culture. Bilingual children can act as cultural translators as they have access to two cultures and two languages. Generally, it is a desired outcome and opens job opportunities where these unique skills are desirable.

GLOBALIZATION AND PARENTING

The demographics of families in the early 21st century are changing rapidly and dramatically, often driven by the direct and indirect effects of globalization. As it is a process that is constantly evolving, globalization defies a tight definition. Family forms that were the norm until recently are adapting and changing. Families relocate and are separated through voluntary migratory patterns, involuntary choices related to survival, and the hope of better opportunities. The demands of cultural uprooting and assimilation place parents in different cultural contexts from those of their own offspring and affect parenting. High-pressure economic demands alter parenting practices. There has been a multilevel shift concerning the family as an institution, in some ways intentional and in some ways unintended. It is changing the cultural fabric of societies. Serious efforts are required to balance the far-reaching effects of globalization while also nurturing those initiatives that carve out better futures for the world's families, by supporting diverse family forms and functions.

FIGURE 3–1. Percentage of children ages 5–17 who speak a language other than English at home and who have difficulty speaking English, selected years 1979–2014.

Source: U.S. Census Bureau, Current Population Survey and American Community Survey.

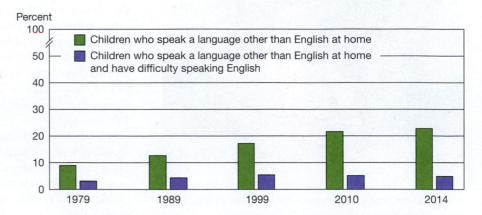

Globalization refers to increasing interconnectedness worldwide. According to Pieterse (2015, p. ix), "as the dynamics of globalization change … so do not just the tides but the shorelines of culture."

The repercussions are numerous and affect many platforms including economic, political, and human endeavors. The outcomes range continuum-like from positive to negative. According to Pieterse, the gains from globalization include rationalization, standardization, and control. The losses include alienation, disenchantment, and displacement (Pieterse, 2015, p. 45). Globalization brings with it opportunities while also making demands.

In terms of family form and function, globalization precipitates similar dual outcomes; the effects can range from beneficial to destructive. Worldwide mobility, as a result of various voluntary and involuntary migratory patterns and the concomitant effects on families, has ripple-like intergenerational effects. Some families have the choice of being mobile, leaving their countries of origin to permanently emigrate, seek educational opportunities, or temporarily live and work in other contexts. Others undergo the transitions involuntarily, for example, having to flee from a war zone or being forced to leave an area as a result of crippling poverty and conditions that do not support family survival. The overall picture of families on the move incorporates both the brightest and the darkest prospects.

The United States was formed by the merging of many different nationalities and ethnic groups into a nation. Large numbers of persons arrived in this country to pursue their dreams of freedom, wealth, and personal happiness. Whether individuals and families arrived legally or were undocumented, their dreams were to eventually assume respected positions in their adopted communities. The amalgam of so many different ways of life, languages, family structure, parenting styles, and perspectives has given strength to the diversity of American culture. Even though many of these persons may not have translocated during their own lifetimes, they are descendants of the original immigrants and represent a blending and meeting of ethnicities and cultures.

Focus Point. Globalization directly and indirectly impacts families of all backgrounds. Depending upon the circumstances, the effects of globalization can range from helpful to harmful.

Challenges to Migrating Families

Parents make great sacrifices in pursuing better outcomes for their families. Asian immigrants to North America have been known to send their infants and toddlers back to relatives in their countries of origin so that, as parents, they can pursue the "dream" (or more realistically the required sacrifice), leading to better economic and educational opportunities and the prospect of social mobility for the next generation. In order to obtain the required education, or meet the stringent labor demands of the new host country, immigrants may ask their own parents in another cultural context to raise their preschool children. Children who exemplify this form of parenting have been called "satellite babies" and "satellite children" (Bohr & Tse, 2009). The

FIGURE 3–2. Percentage of children ages 0–17 living in poverty and type of poverty measure, 2014.

Note: These data refer to the civilian noninstitutionalized population.

Source: U.S. Census Bureau, *Current Population Survey*, Annual Social and Economic Supplement.

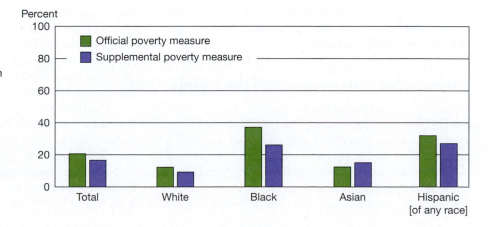

children are reunited with their parents when the time comes for them to be educated, only to face major challenges regarding a potential lack of emotional attachment to a set of parents who may seem like friendly visitors. They also have to begin the arduous process of negotiating their new host culture and language. The reverse situation also occurs. Immigrants have offspring in their new host country. These children are sometimes called "anchor babies," as their birth in the host country might provide legitimate access to legal residence for the child's parents. This term has gained negative attention as the motive for having a child should not be self-serving, mercenary, or for implied gain and benefit; especially if it does not serve the best interests of that particular child.

Under the best circumstances, these children from dual contexts may reap the benefits of having two or more cultures at their fingertips, making them a good fit for jobs on the international stage. The long-term and more pervasive effects relating to attachment and family loyalties are unclear and can vary greatly depending on numerous factors, most importantly the quality of care and the opportunities that the grandparents or extended family can provide.

Another mobile family form is that of the "traveling breadwinner." The breadwinner may skip borders and cultures in the quest to provide for his/her family, but in doing so there is much coparenting from a distance. The parent who is the constant point of reference for the children may be a virtual single parent and the dominant influence on the children. In the case of men, such traveling breadwinner fathers have been nicknamed "astronaut husbands" as they may seem to disappear into outer space until the next family rendezvous (Bohr & Tse, 2009). In other cases, the family lives as expats and frequently the older children have to attend boarding school in the country of origin to create any semblance of continuity in their education.

Globalization, Migration, and the Family

Globalization and migration are related processes that feed off one another. Delving back into our own roots as a species, we know that many families adopted a nomadic lifestyle. Humans followed the lure of food and as hunter-gatherers they uprooted regularly for survival. Once agriculture and livestock provided more predictable options, families could afford to be vested in their

land. Permanence versus mobility seems to ultimately pivot on the instinct for survival.

Numerous factors may contribute to why families undergo the potential upheaval that can result from migration due to the global marketplace. They may be legal immigrants, they may be illegal or legal refugees, they may move temporarily to study or for employment, or they may move to be reunited with family members or loved ones. In addition, individuals may have been adopted internationally, or family breadwinners might work under the umbrella of a company as expats in countries other than their own, for instance for large international concerns, for the military, or in international relations. Underlying these demographic shifts are economic and social pressures and prospects (Ager & Brückner, 2013).

Family scientists are concerned with the effects of these transitions on families, and specifically the children in the families. Every move is accompanied by various degrees of expected and unexpected disorientation, even trauma. Involuntary moves may be of greater concern; large segments of families on the move have little or no choice in being uprooted. Global movement may split up families or separate families from others of their society. Children may have to be raised inter-generationally by grandparents or other family members while the mobile units of the family seek their fortune and try to feather a nest in the new host country. Their circumstances may preclude an informed choice and severely limit options.

Contemporary Migration and Poverty.   From the results of the 2010 U.S. Census we know that about one-fifth of children living in the United States have one foreign-born parent. For each of these children there is a story. Each probably has a language other than English; has a culture of origin; and has faced challenges relating to adaptation, assimilation, and ultimately integration into the mainstream or host culture (Dere et al., 2010). For most of these families, poverty is also part of the packet of challenges. In the United States, 3 percent of children are foreign-born themselves and have one foreign-born parent.

If we take a closer look at living conditions, and how they affect relocating families, poverty undeniably is a distinct force. Immigrant parents and their offspring may find it harder to get a grip on the economic ladder and on employment opportunities because of language barriers, educational limitations, and acculturation problems. The U.S. Federal Interagency Forum on Child and

Family Statistics reported in 2011 that one-third of the foreign-born children living in the United States were living in poverty, and living conditions were characterized by overcrowding. For a child growing up in this milieu, the simplest tasks such as doing homework may represent an obstacle. Add English as a second language and the scholastic challenges escalate further. On the positive side, immigrant parents are well aware of the doors of opportunity opened through education, though they may go to the other extreme of pressurizing their children to achieve and excel. With youth on their side, the younger generation has the distinct advantage of being able to master English more easily than their parents. These children become the literal and cultural translators for their families and represent a bilingual and bicultural segment of their host society.

Focus Point.   While it can offer children a unique, multicultural experience, family migration often presents many challenges for families, including instability, separation of family members, and assimilation to new cultures.

Globalization, Culture, and the Family

The cultural dimension is a cornerstone in the context of family life. It is of utmost importance because it reflects, among other things, the values, beliefs, and attitudes of persons sharing a culture, and these in turn influence rituals, family life transitions, parenting, and more. Religious values and beliefs incorporate dimensions of cultural values and beliefs, and vice versa. Culture's visible and invisible tentacles reach into the furthest corners of family life, to the extent that the dominant cultural values within a family will become a virtual instruction manual as to how things are done in that particular family or group. Cultural values are referred to by the larger cultural context within which the family is embedded, and there is a bidirectional influence.

Definitions concerning culture in the psychological sense typically assert that there is a shared information base that contains values, attitudes, and beliefs and that these dimensions are transmitted intergenerationally and between members. It is a sophisticated process of teaching, learning, and imitation. Change is possible, the tempo of the change being dictated by several interacting factors. This information base enhances chances for survival and can contribute to perceptions regarding quality of life (i.e., the extent to which people have what they consider to be important) and hence it links to the experience of well-being. It provides a platform for stability as the shared content becomes a shorthand and a code for participating members. Subscribing to the same culture imparts a sense of belonging and understanding, because members of a cultural group become insiders and privy to understanding the code of that specific culture. When a family makes a global move, it is immersed in change, much of it cultural change, and this can be bewildering and challenging.

Changing cultural contexts underlie the cultural disorientation felt by transitioning persons. When we change the country or region in which we live, there is a good chance that we also change the cultural context. Regular travelers, expats, and so-called citizens of the world may find it easier to negotiate these changes, as they may have experienced them often enough that they may subscribe to a "third culture"—the product of blending cultures of origin with host cultures. Changing cultures may be as disorienting as music changing mid-dance. When one is still anticipating the rhythm of a familiar tango, the sudden change to a waltz requires a whole new angle of attack. It is one thing if one knows and anticipates that this may happen, but another if one is facing the unknown. For refugees and persons seeking opportunities for economic survival, the luxury of "cultural acclimatization" is out of reach, and it may take an entire generation for a family system to slowly conform to the beat of a different cultural drum.

Historically, large waves of immigration have occurred and have shaped nations. One example is the emigrants who left Ireland during the potato blight of the mid-19th century, pinning their hopes on foreign shores. Religious persecution has been the motive for numerous displacements. The Huguenots left France to seek religious freedom in new countries, and by the 18th century many of them had found refuge elsewhere. After the partition in India, countless families relocated. Countries and nations have been shaped by their immigrants. The United States is one country with very strong immigrant underpinnings. When the relocations are initiated by political unrest, persecution, war, or major threats to survival, they are typically accompanied by much pain and suffering and an entire generation may be scarred by the emotional trauma that these events elicit.

The globalization of families in the 21st century has had far-reaching effects that have not been faced in this exact form in previous centuries. Tighter border control and immigration regulations have resulted in physical boundaries as well as bureaucratic obstacles, which have served as barriers to prevent uncontrolled influx of migrants. When the pressures are great enough, refugees and illegal immigrants will risk their lives in the pursuit of the hope of a better quality of life or just mere survival. In doing so, family units can be fragmented, lives can be lost, and the hope for a better future may remain elusive.

Economic Implications for Families. Globalization has created opportunities in countless contexts. There is a constant exchange of goods and ideas. The interchange may advance the goals of the party initiating the exchange. However, the flipside of the coin reveals a disturbing truth, which has to be addressed through public policy and legal reform. Sherif-Trask (2010) states that at the heart of globalization we may find controversial twins: poverty and inequality. Globalization is emphasizing economic disparity, widening the gap between poorer and richer countries. According to Polakoff (2007), free trade and the international collaborations that have been sanctioned through economic globalization have left large segments of the population in developing countries and in countries delivering labor in manufacturing plants and other production facilities vulnerable to abject poverty and exploitation. These conditions draw in children as well. Although there is a strong movement to abolish child labor and to stringently regulate labor practices, the risk remains and there is tangible evidence that the exploitation of illegal child labor has yet to see its last day. When it comes to underage labor, the entire family is involved because the family may not see any other opportunities for survival but for children to be employed. Additionally, the children producing the work are precluded from educational opportunities and may be exposed to dangerous environments and practices, precipitating human rights violations with lifelong effects for the children concerned.

There is a clear and definite link between globalization, world poverty, and child labor. These practices foreclose on the childhoods of individual children and on their educational opportunities and therefore their future employability (Polakoff, 2007). This in turn affects both their families of procreation and their families of origin, and fixes an intergenerational cycle of poverty. It is crucial that international as well as domestic laws prohibit practices involving child labor and child exploitation. These practices extend beyond the factory floor; children are exploited for warfare and for the sex trade. Based on its ongoing research, UNICEF estimates that the number of victimized children worldwide runs into the millions. This refers to children who are victims of large-scale political and economic scenarios. It excludes individual situations of, for instance, bullying. Children are used and exploited in dangerous situations such as in wars and in mines, and in the sex trade they suffer serious psychological and physical harm.

Migration and Emerging Adults. One of the important developmental tasks of adolescence is the formation of a personal as well as a cultural identity. Adolescents have to take a position towards values; beliefs; notions about relationships, spirituality, and religion; politics; social constructs; and more. These cumulatively contribute to their personal identity. Clearly, adolescents and emerging adults have to find their way through a variety of cultural contexts to integrate these aspects into their personal self-concepts, and a formal process of "cultural integration" occurs in which they choose and integrate the components of various cultural inputs. All adolescents, regardless of immigrant status, must go through this process; it is a "cultural identity path" that adolescents have to carve out for themselves (Jensen & Arnett, 2012). Jensen and Arnett favor the term "emerging adults" as it acknowledges the extended transition from adolescence to adulthood.

In the 21st century, globalizing world, few adolescents or emerging adults grow up in an isolated, monocultural context bypassing the effects of media culture (Jensen & Arnett, 2012). If they live in developed countries the chances are great that—via social media, the Internet, and television and cinema—they will become aware of the complexities of diversity and global influences.

Adolescents may find it remarkably difficult to emigrate and relocate, despite their emotional willingness to explore the world of adults. They have formed peer groups and they attach utmost value to this social system that extends beyond the family. If traumatic circumstances force them to relocate, as in the case of being refugees, additional trauma occurs. Identity formation, which is also anchored in cultural identity, extends well into emerging adulthood (Jensen & Arnett 2012). The risk of being flung across cultures like jetsam is that it may invite antisocial and anti-civic behavior patterns. These potential outcomes occur because the identity with and loyalty to the new culture of the host country have not yet been crystallized, and there is a void where the culture of origin previously was. Adolescents may feel marginalized as they are crossing the bridge between cultures. They have left behind one familiar cultural context but have not yet been fully acculturated into the host culture. The need for a peer group and the urgency to feel included can lead to poor choices, especially if the host culture's cultural codes are unintelligible. It opens the door to falling in with the wrong crowd and to behaving in ways that may have undesirable outcomes. This is a time when parental guidance is crucial, but, if parents are both working long hours to secure the family's survival, parental supervision may be at its lowest. Frequently, adolescents have to be substitute parents as they babysit younger siblings, placing additional strain on the system and leaving little time to dedicate to scholastic pursuits.

Clearly, cultural globalization has implications for parenting practices as well. For families migrating from rural to urban contexts, from developing to developed countries, from agricultural to industrialized environments, and from collective to individualistic societies there are giant adjustments to be made to cross the geographical and cultural divides. Much of the global movement is from developing to developed countries, as families are seeking to improve their living conditions. This may include the wish for better educational opportunities for their children, a higher standard of living, improved medical care, and a peaceful environment away from the ravages of war and economic instability.

Migration and Assimilation.   Frequently, the destination culture is idealized until the family settles in it. After joining the host culture, the challenges of assimilation may appear more challenging than originally anticipated. This process may contribute to the idealization of the culture of origin. In the old country the ways were familiar and the social exchanges understandable. How do parents raise their children in this new environment, and to what cultural values will they subscribe? It

depends on how different the culture of origin is from the new host culture. Ultimately a hybrid style develops. A point of contention between parents and their offspring is frequently the degree to which each culture can play a role in personal lives. Parents and children who have immigrated come from two different cultural places; the children can never be enculturated in exactly the same way as the parents were, as they have to find their feet and assimilate into the new host culture. If enculturation refers to the acquisition of primary cultural references in the culture of origin, acculturation refers to the second layer of culture imparted by the host culture. Successful assimilation requires a blending, merging, and reevaluation of cultural concepts from a variety of sources (Shiraev & Levy, 2016).

As much as the parental dyad may feel proud that their offspring are absorbing the language of the host culture by virtual osmosis, and can act as literal and cultural translators, the parents may add yet another layer of demands on their offspring stemming from the bicultural situation. Parents may place visible and invisible cultural demands on their children—visible and tangible especially in terms of dress code and less tangible in terms of cultural values (Matsumoto and Juang, 2016). The family may continue to follow dietary preferences from their culture of origin, seek out these foods, and expect their children to fall into the same patterns. Food preferences are remarkably consistent even as families are exposed to globalization, and it can become the connecting factor that binds the family, especially during celebrations and days of religious significance. The parents, or the immigrating dyad, may have made the physical move to a new cultural context, but they maintain their separateness as they hold onto some expressions from their culture of origin, and they are cautious concerning the ways of the host culture.

Parents may demand various degrees of conformity, going as far as the choice of a life partner. In some cultures the pressures are high to marry within the same cultural, racial, and/or religious background. This may be taken as far as matching a future spouse from the country of origin. When these marriages occur, there is often a dissonance in terms of level of cultural adaptation. The newly "imported" spouse may experience culture shock, while the spouse who has been partly assimilated into the host culture may not fully understand the challenges their partner is facing. Marrying from the same cultural background has both advantages and disadvantages. The interpersonal demands that contribute to the success of a partnership remain the same, and a merely cultural match cannot ensure a successful pairing. Mutual understanding of the partner's cultural background may be a facilitator in that the couple can understand and access shared cultural codes. Going beyond the shared cultural heritage, the individual challenges of acculturation remain. Being part of a supportive community, and engaging in pro-civic behaviors that are vested in the host country, contribute to a successful transition. Parents also have to realize that their children can never share the cultural content of the country of origin totally, as the children are being raised in a different cultural context, and their acculturation to the host culture demands bicultural values and experiences.

Gender Roles

Another implicit area of influence is growing gender equality. In the postmillennial developed countries, more women are reaching for higher education than at any previous time in history. Professions that were dominated by one gender in the past are welcoming both genders (Hannan, 2013). As families from non-western cultures seek their fortune in western contexts, the families gain higher aspirations for their own daughters (Sanagavarapu, 2010). They want their female offspring to be protected from the inequality and bias experienced in the countries they left behind. Having to survive and earn a living in a competitive arena, education, and the acquisition of skills required in the labor market are keys to better career prospects. But this too has its own unintended backlash and one has to look twice at the costs-to-benefits ratio of the effects of globalization on families (Sanagavarapu, 2010). In seeking tertiary education and better career opportunities, women have less time to devote to seeking a life partner and to building a family. These life choices are interpreted in various ways, depending on which age group's point of view is examined. Sherif-Trask (2010) states that genders differ in how they experience the effects of globalization, especially on the inner sanctum of family life. Factors that contribute to these varied experiences include race and ethnicity, socioeconomic class, and regional differences.

Older generations may be subject to greater cultural and traditional pressures and they may try to resist the notion of changing family roles and family structure. As family life is altered, the care of the elderly faces new challenges as well (Sherif-Trask, 2010). In the leading developed countries, adults are less likely to be in long-term stable partnerships than in the mid-20th century, and family size has shrunk, in some nations to lower than replacement value. Slowly but surely the population size in these countries is shrinking. It may continue to do so unless it makes gains through immigration. At the same time, population growth in developing countries is exploding, typically accompanied by the lack of economic, educational, medical, nutritional, and other resources to sustain that growth and offer hopeful futures to families living within those contexts.

Acknowledgment: This adapted section on globalization and parenting was first published in a slightly different form in: Shehan, C. L. (2016). *The Wiley Blackwell Encyclopedia of Family Studies.* Chichester, UK: Wiley Blackwell. In this volume: Gerhardt, C. *Globalization and families.* Volume II. pp. 979–986. Used with permission of the publishers, John Wiley & Sons, Inc.

Ripple Effects on Parenting

Organizations such as UNESCO are raising awareness concerning the global state of families. Developed nations have a responsibility to initiate family-friendly policies and workplaces, accessible education, and health care while also taking a stance against child and gender-based exploitation and discrimination. Serious efforts are called for to contain the destructive effects of globalization on families while also nurturing those initiatives that carve out better futures for the world's families and their children.

The demographics of families living in the 21st century are changing rapidly and dramatically. Family forms that were the norm a few decades ago are transforming to meet 21st-century demands. Longer educational training, dual-career families, commuting, and high-pressure economic demands are redefining parenting. Couples marry later, if at all, and in leading developed countries fertility has declined. Each one of these alternatives may have different outcomes, which in turn directly affect parenting. There is a multilevel disinvestment in the family as an institution, in some ways intentional and in other ways unintended (Gerhardt,

2016c). This affects the larger systems within which families are embedded and is changing the cultural fabric of society and the futures of families and their children, and importantly how those children are parented.

Focus Point.   Similar to the changing of a song mid-dance, changing cultures can be a disorienting transition. Extreme outcomes of migration can include sex slavery, child labor, poverty, and exploitation. The extent to which parents encourage and allow assimilation of their children into a new culture varies from family to family. Many organizations are working to implement policies to protect migrating children and families against exploitation.

CHAPTER FOCUS POINTS

The Evolution of Childhood

■ While history and culture are fairly fluid constructs, their intersection sheds some light on the evolution of childhood and parenthood throughout history. Most of our knowledge of ancient family life comes from archeological findings and literature, which tell us that, due to high infant mortality rates, parenting centered around survival rather than nurture. Children were frequently depicted as miniature adults and were expected to take on many adult responsibilities.

Developmentally-Appropriate Approaches to Childbearing

■ Compared to today's bidirectional model of parenting, most historical periods were characterized by an authoritarian, unidirectional parenting style in which strict guidelines and harsh punishments were encouraged. Only in the late 1800s did a more nurturing, developmentally-minded approach to parenting begin to formalize.

Parenting and Culture

■ While cultural values shift dramatically throughout history, the impact that the culture has on parenting and the family unit is a fairly consistent phenomenon.

■ Parent–child relations are influenced by and take place within a cultural context. Socialization is the way that parents and other societal entities teach cultural norms to children. Socialization is bidirectional in that children and their parents participate in this process, and society in its turn influences the family unit.

Ethnic Diversity in Families

■ America, historically known as the "melting pot," is a country rich in diversity. Helping children develop *multicultural competence* is a large part of the parental role of socialization. The current approach is to see it as a "mosaic" in which numerous individuals from a variety of cultures and ethnicities contribute to the larger whole or "Gestalt."

■ Issues confronting newly arrived immigrants may involve cultural marginalization. Economic difficulties, problems in acquiring and using another language, and general acculturation concerns present a challenge for immigrant parents and children. It may be difficult to merge the *heritage* culture with the *host* culture. Bilingual children can act as cultural translators as they have access to two cultures and two languages. Generally, it is a desired outcome and opens job opportunities where these unique skills are desirable.

Globalization and Parenting

■ Globalization directly and indirectly impacts families of all backgrounds. Depending on the circumstances, the effects of globalization can range from helpful to harmful.

■ Although it can offer children a unique, multicultural experience, family migration often presents many challenges for families; including instability, separation of family members, and assimilation to new cultures.

■ Similar to the changing of a song mid-dance, changing cultures can be a disorienting transition. Extreme outcomes of migration can include sex slavery, child labor, poverty, and exploitation. The extent to which parents encourage and allow assimilation of their children to a new culture varies from family to family.

USEFUL WEBSITES

Websites are dynamic and change

Child Welfare League of America
www.cwla.org
Publications on excellence in child care and other topics

United Nations Children's Fund (formerly United Nations International Children's Emergency Fund [UNICEF])
www.unicef.org
Initiatives and reports concerning children

United Nations Educational, Scientific and Cultural Organization (UNESCO)
www.unesco.org
Publications and research reports including "Education for the 21st century"

Urban Institute
www.urban.org
Research reports focus on public policy

CHAPTER 4

Theoretical Perspectives on Parent–Child Relations

Learning Outcomes

After completing this chapter, you should be able to

1. Identify the characteristics of a theory and its functions.
2. Summarize the notion of theories as building blocks.
3. Describe the idea that parents are socialization agents.
4. Evaluate the different attachment theories connected to parenting.
5. Examine the concept of reciprocal interaction as it relates to parent–child relations.
6. Distinguish between behavioral, cognitive, and social learning theories.
7. Determine the factors that influence functioning in family groups.
8. Describe each level of Bronfenbrenner's ecological systems model.
9. Recommend ways in which families can adapt to stressors.

THEORIES AND THEIR FUNCTION

In most theories pertaining to parents and their children, we can see the personal connections between the lives of the theorists and the content of their theories, or their ways of explaining the world. A theory is usually the theorist's way of trying to connect the dots and to create meaning and relevance out of information. Theories are not the truth, but they deal with aspects of the "truth" or reality as perceived at the time a theory was conceived. In that way, theories are flexible and can evolve or, alternatively, become obsolete.

Theories are ways of grouping facts together to organize what we think about a given topic. Thus, a theory can be very personal to the theorist presenting it. If, for instance, Sigmund Freud, the "father of psychoanalysis," expressed his view (or theory) on how we function as human beings, he would be influenced by a host of things. His thinking would be different from somebody like Carl Rogers, an American therapist who lived considerably later than Freud. Both legendary therapists would be influenced by what other scientists and theorists were thinking; the prevailing Zeitgeist or intellectual climate of the time, and the context of the time in which they lived. Both would rely on personal subjective experiences and more objective observations. To illustrate this, let us grossly oversimplify aspects of Freud's (1886–1939), Frankl's (1905–1997), and Rogers' (1902–1987) theories and try to briefly shadow them as they reach their conclusions.

Because Freud is of such great historical and theoretical significance, the author (Gerhardt) visited Freud's therapy rooms in both Vienna, Austria, and in London near the current Tavistock Clinic. Being in the actual homes where Freud had lived and worked was the closest I could get, in trying to empathize what it might have been like in his world, at that time.

Freud's life coincided with the end of the Victorian period and beyond, nearly up to WWII. The women's rights movement was making itself heard, but the rights had not been won. Medical science had not yet liberated reproductive decisions. Victorian and general middle class values were conservative and often hypocritical. Families were presented in idealized form but the reality could be less savory (Cohen, 2013). Pick out a few things in Freud's theories which resonate with this context. Freud talked about men as the superior gender, and women in turn have "penis envy," a term first used by Freud. Without a vote, with restricted independent economic powers, with no say over reproductive choices, and with limited opportunities for an education, women in Freud's day may well have been envious of the world men inhabited. Seen in the context of his time, Freud's use of the term seems less out of touch then, as compared to the 21st century reality.

If brutal behavior toward children or within marriages was a hush-hush secret when trying to present the perfect facade to the world, then it follows that we can repress this content and it gets stored in the unconscious from which it can only peek out in distorted form, such as in dreams or through jokes. Remember, this is an extreme oversimplification of the theory. Freud embellished it in much greater detail. He is so revered because he caused a major paradigm shift in thinking. He entered the annals of history because he put in motion a new way of seeing the human psyche. As far as parenting is concerned, we can thank Freud for the insight that traumatic events during childhood can play a role in later life.

Viktor Frankl was a therapist of note whose lectures I attended several times. He was a Holocaust survivor, a psychiatrist, and he authored books, including the famous *The Will to Meaning* (Frankl, 1969/2014). He sacrificed virtually everything of significance in the concentration camps, including his spouse, mother and brother, intellectual property (he lost the manuscript of his book), and freedom. Yet he rose Phoenix-like out of the ashes. Could you imagine what his theory looks like? His theory's central theme concerns the dignity with which we suffer and resurrect. We may not be able to control what we lose, but we can address the attitude with which we deal with that loss. His was a most powerful theory, from someone who paid the highest price. Readers of his books pay tribute to his ability to resurrect himself without turning bitter or being defeated.

Fast forward to Carl Rogers. Rogers spoke in a public presentation at the university where I studied and I had the distinct privilege of attending this historical event. Admittedly, I was in my early training as a clinical psychologist, but the thought of having heard this legendary therapist in person, adds to the fascination.

Rogers is a child of the 20th century and his life spans the greater part of it. He lived against the backdrop of two world wars, followed by the Vietnam War, which affected many American lives. Note that he lived more or less in the same time frame as Frankl, yet the two approaches differ greatly, as each theory is an expression of the individuality and the life experiences of that theorist. The most central part of Rogers' theory reflects his sense of optimism, and a humanistic dimension toward the "self" or psyche of a person. His genuine respect for his fellow human beings has colored therapeutic approaches to this day, and we find elements of this respect in parenting techniques as well. In his theory are concepts like "congruence" or genuineness, and unconditional positive regard. In relationships, including therapeutic and teaching relationships, the attention should be focused on the other; he called it "client-focused." A mature or fully functioning person would self-actualize and seek opportunities for joy within their world. In this manner, his theory is hopeful, positive, and reconciliatory. Apply some of these attitudes toward people to the children we parent, and we have the essence of a respectful and positive parenting approach.

A meta-analysis of several studies trying to establish the most influential psychologists of the 20th century showed that Freud and Rogers ranked among the top ten. When the study narrowed down the most influential therapists, Freud and Rogers occupied first and second positions (Haggbloom et al., 2002). It is unequivocal that both influenced our thoughts about parent–child relations.

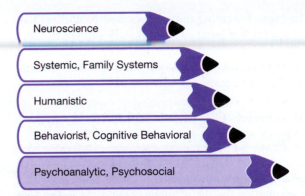

FIGURE 4–1. Psychoanalytic, Psychosocial and related approaches.

Focus Point.   Theories are flexible ideas that reflect on observations or realities, or try to find meaning and order from those observations. They are influenced by the social context, experiences, educational background, and opinions of the theorists behind them.

THEORIES AS BUILDING BLOCKS

Standing on the Shoulders of Giants.   Numerous theories have influenced our current perspectives on parent–child relationships. Each one builds on the insights of previous theories contextualized within a given time period. In this chapter, we discuss the most significant theories in greater detail, and we briefly summarize this progression of theoretical approaches and developments in Figures 4–1 and 4–6. Core ideas are highlighted and summarized in Table 4–4, appearing near the end of this chapter.

We can view five major shifts in thinking about parent–child relations as linked to the bulk of theories supporting specific approaches. Other authors and sources may prefer different approaches, for instance chronological approaches, which are very helpful. Heath (2013, p. 3) provides a clear table of historical progression, based on a timeline. This is one way of organizing the information. The approach we are following in this chapter is to highlight major shifts in thinking, irrespective of the specific time context in which they occur.

Psychoanalytic, Psychosocial, and Related Approaches

Psychology is a relatively young science, and its diffuse beginnings tend to coincide more or less with the end of the 1800s and the beginning of the 1900s. There is no clear beginning to psychology; no official birth date. Early approaches with a psychological angle tried to differentiate from especially philosophy and medicine, but overlap between various sciences, which is a good thing, as it provides context (Hergenhahn & Henley, 2013). We also find that psychologists can come from several backgrounds in terms of foundational academic training.

The predominant early approach studied the individual and specifically the psyche of the individual, hence the name psychology. Using the word intrapsychic refers to the processes that happen within the psyche of an individual. Psychosocial refers to what happens in the psyches of participating persons in a social context. The psychoanalysts (e.g., Freud) and neo-psychoanalysts (e.g., Jung, Adler) would subscribe to a predominantly intra-psychic approach. The psychosocial approaches (e.g., Erikson) would focus more on psychic components as they interact with social and relational aspects. Most of the researchers exploring aspects of attachment (e.g., Bowlby, Ainsworth) emphasize psychosocial dimensions.

Parenting Implications.   In terms of parenting, supporters of the Psychoanalytic, Psychosocial and related theoretical approaches, would pay attention to factors that traumatized the child, repression of traumatic memories, and how the child could be supported in terms of therapy. Parenting approaches and conditions that are harmful, for instance neglect, lack of opportunities for attachment, abandonment, and over-indulgence can contribute to sub-optimal outcomes in terms of child rearing.

Behaviorist, Cognitive Behavioral, and Related Approaches

The Behaviorist, Cognitive Behavioral and related approaches were not focused on what happens inside the psyche, or the art of introspection (as in the first group). They are predominantly interested in what happens outside the psyche. They study the things and conditions that influence behavior and how what we learn influences that behavior. If we bring the nature/nurture formula into the conversation, then this group focuses on the nurture (or environmental) aspects that influence behavior. Early work focused on learning as a behavioral modifier and examples of theorists in this group would be Pavlov, Watson, and Skinner. Reward and

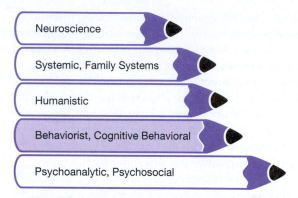

FIGURE 4–2. Behaviorist, Cognitive Behavioral and related approaches.

punishment as motivators for learning and conditioning feature strongly. See Figure 4-2.

As with the previous group, the idea of modifying the initial concept by adding the social dimensions resulted in a slightly looser and more palatable angle. Persons supporting social-learning, learning within

Cognitive, behavioral, and related approaches advocate for providing socially supportive contexts to maximize learning in children. The ways in which parents interact with a child and provide a variety of physical and social experiences are an essential component of a child's development.

a social context, and hence the social components that contribute to that learning, would include, for instance, Bandura, Vygotsky, Piaget, and Bruner. In other words, the learning opportunities are mellowed and contextualized by the social context in which they occur.

Parenting Implications.   Learning principles are especially important in educational contexts. Some of the good as well as the poor habits that children learn may influence parenting outcomes. As parents and as educators we need to be cautious as to what behavior we model and also support good learning outcomes by providing socially supportive contexts in which that learning can occur. As an incentive, reward is preferable to punishment.

Humanistic and Related Approaches

Humanistic and related approaches were established from the mid 1950s and beyond; WWII has ended and there is a sense of optimism, leading to larger families (these are the baby boomers being born). The sense of optimism filters into therapeutic approaches that focus on our humanness and our spirituality. We have hopes for a better future and the luxury of thinking about our personal dreams and aspirations; hence the emphasis on self-actualization and fully functioning personhood. Initiation of this emphasis is credited to Rogers, although Allport and Maslow also feature strongly. The approach changes the techniques and anticipated outcomes of therapy. The goal of therapy is to become the best a person can be, fully functioning and self-actualized. These approaches also contributed to stronger focus on individuality. Popular psychology was quick to join the conversation with self-help books and books for parents. See Figure 4–3.

Parenting Implications.   The science and art of therapy grew dramatically and this spilled over into parent–child relations. What worked in therapy would also work in terms of parents and their children. Focus on attentive and active listening, unconditional positive regard, truly focusing on the child as an active participant in the relationship and fully bidirectional parenting were encouraged. Good parenting would support children in actualizing their potential.

Systemic, Family Systems, and Related Approaches

The previous approaches have focused on the psyche, on social contexts, on learning, and on the self reaching its potential. The next leap is even bigger. The focus shifts again, this time to the forces that act between and within systems and how they provide contexts of varying influence. Importantly, each previous step forms a foundation for the next approach. See Figure 4–4, Many therapists are eclectic by incorporating different angles into their approaches. The two most frequently used therapeutic approaches are cognitive behavioral and systemic approaches (Gurman & Kniskern, 2014). The Family Systems approach acknowledges the family as a system with its own rules and effects as a result

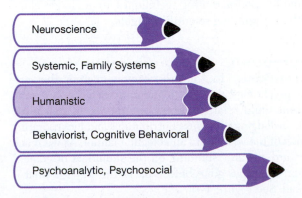

FIGURE 4–3.   Humanistic and related approaches.

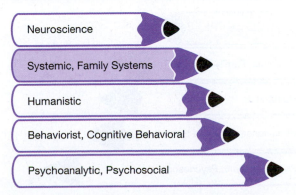

FIGURE 4–4.   Systemic, Family Systems and related approaches.

of the relationships between members of that family. Behavior is not generated within one person only; a relationship can elicit its own behavioral outcomes. That explains why people function well in some relationships and poorly in others; it is contained within the system. Zooming out even further, a theory like Bronfenbrenner's shows that the influences that affect any individual child relationship can extend further to include school systems, culture, public policy, and the like.

Parenting Implications.   A child's behavior is, among other things, a function of the system within which that behavior occurs. Family members become co-actors; hence it is about parent–child relations. The behaviors are bidirectional in that the parent influences the child and vice versa, but the societal and larger influences likewise have a role to play.

Neuroscience and Related Approaches

Neuroscience and related approaches appeared post Millennium, but with underpinnings from the previous decades, providing leaps in how we view children and their interactions with their parents. Our insights are aided and expanded by scientific research, supported by computer science, imaging techniques, and other technological developments See Figure 4–5. These approaches provide constantly shifting and expanding horizons. Some recent topics of interest pertaining to parenting include the effects of attachment or the

lack thereof on brain development. Neuroplasticity, epigenetics, and the potential of different outcomes are explored. The word "imprinting" is used in a new context, namely, as in "genomic imprinting," referring to different gene expressions depending on whether the gene has been inherited from the mother or the father, and depending on different environments contributing to gene expression. These approaches provide greater understanding of genes and stem cell research. The study of the teenage versus the adult brain, has shown distinct differences affecting a number of critical areas of functioning. Neuroscientists have learned that there are critical window periods for attachment, as well as for acquiring skills such as language. Emotional regulation, self-efficacy and self-regulation can strengthen as the child gains developmental and cognitive maturity. Neuroscience has expanded our understanding of cognitive psychology and related fields. In short, greater insight into neuroscientific dimensions of human behavior, provides insight into the functioning of the brain in a variety of contexts.

Modern science has led to artificial reproductive techniques (ART) and put parenthood within reach of a greater group of potential parents. This in turn added to the diversity in family forms. Many more topics will gain relevance as scientific research continues and the future will reveal our ever-expanding insights.

Parenting Implications.   Neuroscience and related approaches enable understanding behavior in terms of physical development, particularly brain development, pre-empting the contributors to challenging situations and possible interventions. Research-based and outcome-focused parenting techniques are included along with incorporating scientific insights.

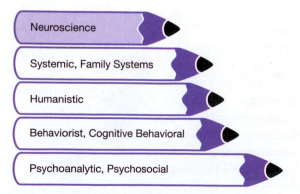

FIGURE 4–5.   Neuroscience and related approaches.

Focus Point.   In a macro-systemic manner, the various psychological theories and approaches concerning parent–child relations build one on top of the other, acknowledging previous contributions and incorporating much of the wisdom in an eclectic manner. As we reach forward, we are "standing on the shoulders of giants," where what has gone before paves the way for what is ahead. See Figure 4–6.

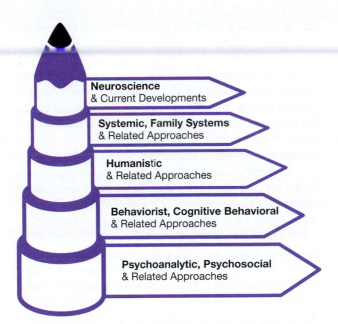

FIGURE 4–6. Theories and approaches build on each other extending the knowledge base.
The major theoretical shifts in psychology affect how we view parent–child relations. In multi-modal and eclectic approaches relevant parts from several theories are combined. Newer approaches do not necessarily exclude or invalidate previous theories. Theories can evolve over time.

PARENTS AS SOCIALIZATION AGENTS

Most of the theories presented in this chapter directly or indirectly address parent–child relations, and the theories and their concepts may enhance our understanding. Historically, a child was seen as an object to be socialized by the parents, often in a very authoritarian manner. This was a unidirectional model of socialization. If an adult behaved well as a parent, the child would become a good person. Adults hoped for good outcomes if they provided appropriate caregiving. Following this logic, the formula for effective parenting was based on consistently good parental performance during child rearing.

Behavioral and social scientists who studied parent–child relations realized that this traditional idea of parenting was too simplistic and it truly needed to

address additional aspects. The bidirectional model is a more accurate depiction of parent–child relations. This model portrays the give-and-take of information and influence between parents and children; each person influences and has an impact on the behavior of the other.

Several theoretical explanations describe the bidirectional parenting process more realistically and provide an understanding of the influences and how they change over time. Child rearing is a unique statement of personal and family philosophy. Adults shape and adjust their parenting behavior, and so do their counterparts; the children. The parent–child relationship mirrors the larger family process. Using this perspective on family systems, it is possible to describe how the developmental changes being experienced by all members affect everyone within the family system.

Historical Underpinnings of Democratic Approach. Historically, the democratic approach to child training is based on the work of Alfred Adler (1870–1937) and is incorporated into Adlerian psychology and the related work by Rudolf Dreikurs. Adler was one of the pioneers who focused on the unique needs of children. He is credited with opening the first parent–child guidance clinic in Vienna, and he made a significant contribution to mental health and the prevention of mental disorders. Adler thought that good parent–child relations were a key factor in achieving mental health and parental education was emphasized. He ultimately emigrated from Austria to the United States in the early 1930s and took up a professorship at the Long Island College of Medicine.

One of the early and historically relevant parenting educators was Rudolf Dreikurs (1897–1972). He was an Austrian-born American psychiatrist, and was inspired by some of Adler's ideas. He wrote a string of books, many of them still available, updated by various co-authors. One of his earliest publications, in 1946, was *The Challenge of Parenthood*. The core of his thinking revolved around the child's need to feel valued and loved, and how parents can facilitate this. Behavior can be understood within its social context and belonging to social groups is a basic need, regardless of age. Democratic approaches such as encouragement, setting appropriate limits, practicing mutual respect for family members, and collective decision making are important (Dreikurs, 1946; Dreikurs, 1948). Some of these concepts have a timeless quality as we recognize them in current parenting approaches.

Democratic child training recognizes the impact of a child's sibling subsystem in influencing behavior. Dreikurs, following Adler's premise, believes that birth order and position among siblings in the family system act to shape the child's life plan. Within a given family, there are differences in the siblings and their life plans as the participants vie for parental attention, sibling alliances, and varying parental expectations.

••

Focus Point. As the behavioral and social sciences moved from a unidirectional to a bidirectional model of parenting, theorists began to focus on children's needs and the impact that parenting, either positive or negative, could have on children later in life.

••

ATTACHMENT THEORY AND PARENTING

John Bowlby and Mary Ainsworth

Attachment Theory is based on the work of John Bowlby (1907–1990) and Mary Ainsworth (1913–1999) and is also referred to as the Bowlby–Ainsworth Perspective (Posada, Longoria, Cocker, & Lu, 2011). Bowlby was a British psychologist, psychiatrist, and psychoanalyst, and Ainsworth was a Canadian developmental psychologist. Both studied at Tavistock Clinic in London where they met as colleagues. Bowlby eventually became the mental health consultant for the World Health Organization. Ainsworth is known for her contributions to play therapy with children, where she used play to explore emotions, including grief. Both Bowlby's and Ainsworth's life work centered on the effects of maternal separation on child development, now expanded to include significant and ongoing caregivers and coparenting situations.

The central tenet is that children brought up with consistent, loving parents or significant, reliable caregivers can develop a foundation of trust and attachment and can grow up to be well-adjusted adults who are capable of forming trusting and loving relationships. If the stability is interrupted for any reason, such as maternal deprivation, problems can manifest as separation anxiety. Particularly during the first 2 years of an infant's life, the care should be constant and preferably provided by the dominant attachment figure. Often this is the mother, although different parenting configurations are becoming more common.

Ainsworth identified initially three styles of attachment, and later added a fourth: secure, ambivalent, avoidant, and disorganized attachment. She observed these styles in the well-known "Strange Situation" in which an infant and his caregiver were left alone in an unfamiliar playroom, with a one-way mirror for observation. The caregiver would leave the room and later return, which offered opportunities to observe separation and reunion behaviors. In her publications she elaborated with longer descriptions. Many contemporary parents leaving their children in a childcare setting, have experienced similar reactions when dropping off their child.

- *Secure attachment.* Regarded as successful attachment. Provides a sound basis for current and later relationships.
- *Anxious-ambivalent attachment.* The child is anxious in the presence of strangers, even if the primary caregiver is in the room. Child displays some insecurity.
- *Anxious-avoidant attachment.* The child tends to ignore the caregiver and not display much emotion. Limited display of emotion regardless of who is present in the room.
- *Disorganized/disoriented attachment.* Disruption of attachment and freezing. This seems to be the "strategy of desperation" as the child feels overwhelmed.

(Based on: Ainsworth, M., Blehar, M. C., Waters, E., & Wall, S. (1978). *Patterns of Attachment: A Psychological Study of the Strange Situation.* Psychology Press and Routledge Classics Editions.)

Bowlby believed that an infant's attachment was instinctive, and that both mothers and infants have a biological need for each other. This is another twist on the concept of *bidirectionality* in the context of parenting relations. Attachment is strengthened by care and responsiveness.

John Bowlby is also remembered for the report that he wrote for the World Health Organization in 1950 entitled "Maternal Care and Mental Health," which emphasized that children's early experiences of care and parental interactions were crucial to overall healthy development and well-being, and that parental deficiencies could have far-reaching implications with detrimental outcomes.

Both Bowlby and Ainsworth certainly contributed major insights into aspects of attachment within the caretaking relationship, specifically parenting. Nowadays, we take much of this information for granted, but it was groundbreaking when first studied.

Melanie Klein

Attachment theory has several earlier, as well as later, underpinnings as a number of researchers and therapists each contributed insight to flesh out the overall theory. The work of the psychoanalyst Melanie Klein (1882–1960) laid some of the foundation. To place this in a historical context, Klein was born in the year that Charles Darwin died. One of her themes was that, to an infant, the mother represented completeness, and Klein talked about the good versus the bad breast, where the "good" refers to the nurturing aspect and the "bad" refers to the emotionally absent mother. She was also working with troubled children and used toys in her therapeutic sessions.

Initial attempts to study the effects of early nurturing experiences for infants began when investigators examined institutionalized infants and children in the 1940s and 1950s. At that time, infants and children who were abandoned or orphaned were placed in large group homes, where they received minimal care and attention from only a few adults. Researchers found that these children exhibited delayed development in many areas, which was attributed to inconsistent "mothering" and lack of nurture (Bowlby, 1952; Goldfarb, 1945; Ribble, 1943; Spitz, 1945). Historically, children raised in institutions were frequently suffering from malnutrition, especially protein deficiency. This could coexist with emotional and psychological difficulties such as developmental retardation, apathy, sleep problems, and depression. The sensory deprivation and the malnutrition would have played a role, as well as the lack of ongoing, predictable nurturing and trusting relationships with caretakers. Symptoms of physical and mental illness in many of these children were attributed to the lack of appropriate interactional experiences.

René Spitz and James Robertson

Other contemporaries who explored aspects of relationships and bonding included René Spitz (1887–1974), who studied grief in children, and who linked inappropriate early care to expressions of grief. James Robertson (1911–1988), a psychoanalyst, and Bowlby collaborated in making a film in 1952 about a two-year-old, named Laura, who is going to the hospital. In the film, Laura is initially very upset about being separated from her parents. As the separation continues, she eventually calms down. The adults think that she has adjusted to the situation, but in reality she is grieving and withdrawing. This film is disturbing, and raises questions concerning the ethics of allowing this situation to progress and to be filmed. With our current research practices and ethical responsibilities of not doing harm, such observations would have to be interrupted in the interests of the child's well-being.

William Goldfarb, Anna Freud and Jean Piaget

Several researchers contributed to the general attachment concept. William Goldfarb (1915–1995) wrote case studies near the end of World War II based on what he witnessed in orphans who suffered from the effects of parental loss and separation, as well as intense trauma. Anna Freud (1895–1982), Sigmund Freud's daughter, studied children in particular, and she formulated some of the work on defense mechanisms. She, too, observed children who had been separated from their significant and trusted caregivers during the war (World War II). Jean Piaget (1896–1980) was influential during this same period. Piaget's emphasis on cognitive development and cognitive processing was acknowledged by Bowlby as he endeavored to clarify aspects of attachment.

Harry Harlow

Harry Harlow (1905–1981) was an American psychologist who studied maternal separation, social isolation, and aspects of caregiving and attachment behavior. Behavioral scientists realized that it would be unethical

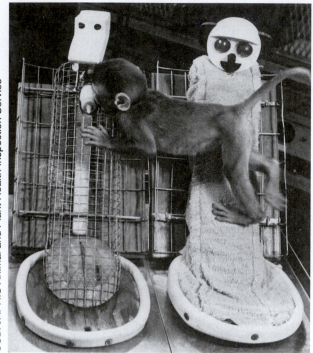

USDA/APHIS Animal and Plant Health Inspection Service

Wire-mesh and terry-cloth surrogate mothers used in Harlow's research on attachment.

Photo courtesy of the University of Wisconsin Primate Laboratory and Harry F. Harlow.

and immoral to deprive a human infant of mothering experiences and chose instead to study the short- and long-term results of the lack of adequate, appropriate mothering in animals. Harlow and his associates (Harlow, 1958; Harlow, Harlow, & Hansen, 1963) examined the effects of depriving infant monkeys of significant mothering experiences. Harlow found that separating infant monkeys from their mothers following birth resulted in severe emotional trauma in the baby monkeys. The infant monkeys' lack of direct physical contact with their mothers was identified as contributing to their disturbed behavior patterns when they grew to maturity.

Harlow initiated various studies. In one study, infant monkeys were separated from their natural mothers and placed exclusively with one of two artificially constructed surrogate mothers. One group was allocated to surrogates built of bare wire mesh; the other to soft terry cloth covered surrogates. Both structures could dispense nourishment.

Monkeys reared with the terry-cloth surrogate were found to be more curious, more interested in exploring the environment, and better adjusted socially than those who were "reared" by the wire-mesh surrogate. Nevertheless, both groups developed in unhealthy ways into their adulthood. Neither group acquired normal monkey social skills; they were overly aggressive, preferred isolation to intimacy with other monkeys, and lacked sexual mating skills. Other behaviors included staring into space, stereotyped rocking movements, and poor social interactions with other monkeys.

In another experiment, the animals could move freely between two surrogate monkey structures. They received nourishment only from the wire-mesh surrogate, yet they preferred the soft-textured surrogate and spent most of their time with the latter. This result stressed what Harlow referred to as **contact comfort**, or an infant's need for soft, comforting, nurturing sensations provided by a caregiver. Harlow also found that monkeys who were raised in total isolation for the first months of their lives, never recovered from this severe form of social isolation. Nurturing environments later in life did not appear to undo the profound effects of this early childhood trauma which had occurred during a critical attachment period.

These animal experiments are regarded as controversial and subsequent initiatives towards implementing guidelines and legislation regarding the ethical treatment of laboratory animals is thought to have been partly triggered by these studies.

Video Example 4.1

Watch this video on the Harlow Monkey Experiments. Describe the Harlow Monkey Experiment. What theory does it explore?

(https://www.youtube.com/watch?v=9wmvZH 5lX_U)

Video Example 4.2

Watch this video on Harlow's studies on the dependency in monkeys. Why do you think the monkeys chose the cloth monkey over the monkey providing nutrition?

(https://www.youtube.com/watch?v=OrNBEhzjg8I)

Konrad Lorenz

Konrad Lorenz (1903–1989), a joint winner of the Nobel Prize in 1973, studied medicine and had a passion for zoology. He studied instincts in animals and is known for his work on attachment. In the context of ethology (the scientific study of animal behavior), he explored bird and mammal behavior and noted that they bonded during a critical attachment period shortly after birth. Of significance in the context of attachment is that Lorenz found that the recently hatched goslings that the researchers were feeding followed the person who wore a specific pair of rubber wading boots. Lorenz thought that the birds became permanently imprinted at an early age with significant caregivers to whom they were most frequently exposed, even if the caregivers were human. When different caretakers wore similar-looking boots, the goslings would follow the person wearing the boots.

As a result of these findings, researchers were alerted to the critical post-birth period when imprinting occurs and early bonding patterns are laid down. This knowledge is currently applied to human birthing practices, where newborn babies are placed on the mother's stomach for skin-to-skin contact as soon after birth as possible. Fathers are encouraged to be active participants during the birth and after in order to encourage bonding. Parents and their infants should have the opportunity to bond during the sensitive days and weeks following the birth.

Another situation in which we can see the effects of attachment or the lack thereof, is in international adoptions. Understanding the role of the earliest childhood experiences in orphanages prior to international adoptions has elicited further investigation, as well as recommendations for best practices. Children who are adopted fairly late during their first or second year frequently present with attachment disorders and difficulties in forming trusting relationships. These children may have spent their early months in overcrowded and understaffed orphanages. Attachment and trust issues are more recognizably expressed once they have acculturated to the new environment. Currently, pediatricians and other professionals who deal with adopted children are alert to these possible outcomes of early deprivation, and research is continuing.

According to Posada et al. (2011), the Bowlby–Ainsworth view integrates perspectives from various fields, including evolution, psychoanalysis, ethology, and cognitive psychology. It points out the range of implications that early attachment can have in later life, such as the formation of intimate relationships, the sense of self, and emotional security.

In *deployed military families*, we are faced with long-distance coparenting situations that are unique in terms of stressors and outcomes (Posada et al., 2011). An understanding of the implications of attachment plays a distinct role in legal decisions concerning child custody, adoption, and foster parenting.

Focus Point.   Attachment Theory focuses on the connection between an infant's early bonding experiences with a parent or caregiver and their ability to form trusting and loving relationships later in life. Multiple theorists have linked a lack of consistent nurturing in early childhood to various mental illnesses and attachment disorders in adulthood.

PSYCHOSOCIAL DEVELOPMENT THEORY AND PARENTING

There has been a foundation of developmental research that preceded the systemically oriented theories. Major influences were exerted by leading figures such as Sigmund Freud, Alfred Adler, Jean Piaget, and Erik Erikson. They focused on various aspects, including cognitive and social development. The key characteristics of the theories of the major contributors, as well as the implications for parent–child relations, are summarized in a table are summarized in Table 4–1.

Most modern theories focus on the development of a child during the years between birth and the end of adolescence. Many explanations consider the interaction between heredity and environmental influences in individual development. Until a few decades ago, the years of childhood and adolescence received the greatest attention. Few developmental theorists attempted to explain or interpret what took place in the various stages of adulthood (i.e., early, middle, and late adulthood). The psychosocial theory of Erik Erikson (1950/1993, 1964, 1982; Erikson, Erikson, & Kivnick, 1986) was a notable exception. Erikson's theory features developmental change as a process that continues throughout the life span between birth and death, not just during the growth years of infancy, childhood, and adolescence.

Erikson's theory is, in part, an extension of Freud's psychoanalytical approach to explaining human personality development (Allen, 2015). For the most part, classical psychoanalytical theory is not embraced by contemporary theoretical thought in explaining human development. Some of the symbolic situations Freud refers to, such as the Oedipal complex, are not easily tested by research. The Oedipal complex refers to unconscious feelings of sexual attraction toward one's own mother and is named after the fifth-century Greek mythological character Oedipus who marries his mother after unwittingly killing his father.

This brief example does not do justice to the complexity of Freud's work, which may be better understood within the context of his time as well as the rest of his theory. Freud is important in that he contributed to a paradigm shift in thinking, and the direct and indirect influences of psychoanalysis permeated not only the social sciences, but also the arts and literature. His teachings are believed to represent the beginnings of academic thought about how humans experience personality development.

Erikson's approach was regarded as more realistic, although it did not generate a vast body of supportive research. In another notable exception to Freudian thought, Erikson believed that development occurred throughout a person's life span. Each stage of the life span has its own developmental theme, which Erikson terms a **psychosocial crisis**, or a challenge to attain a healthy rather than unhealthy attitude or generalized feeling. Developmental change is enhanced or retarded by a person's experiences in confronting and handling each psychosocial crisis that occurs within each stage of the life span. The person must confront a central problem—a specific psychosocial crisis—at each life stage and is given the opportunity to develop strengths and skills leading toward a particular attitude that is healthy or unhealthy. Provided with a social and psychological environment that is conducive to developmental change, an individual faces each problem during that stage with the potential for healthy, normal accomplishment. If the person experiences overwhelming difficulty in accomplishing what is expected during one stage of the life span, the result will be difficulty in dealing with the psychosocial crises during future stages.

Developmental change does not occur within a vacuum, free from other influences. The process is structured so that a person faces the challenges and trials of life with the support of others. Developmental change occurs first within the context of a supportive family atmosphere, then within an increasingly wider social radius of friends, and later within the school environment, and so on, as life progresses. **Significant others**—those who are singularly important to a person—assist or inhibit the developmental progress at each life stage. An individual proceeds to the next stage after meeting the particular requirements of biological, social, and psychological **readiness**. This readiness to progress further along the developmental path is significantly influenced by others in the social environment. In the case of a developing child, the parents are close at hand.

The psychosocial crises during each stage of the lifespan present the individual with the challenge of acquiring what Erikson calls **psychosocial senses**. These are attitudes or general feelings that result from how adequately a person can meet and master the crisis at a particular stage of psychosocial development.

Erikson describes eight stages of psychosocial change over the life span and labels each in terms of healthy or unhealthy psychosocial development. It is important to note that a person's mastery of a psychosocial attitude or sense is not an all-or-nothing matter; instead, it is continually being weighed on a balance. It is possible to gain some measure of unhealthy, as well as healthy, feelings related to the psychosocial attitude associated with a particular life stage. In the balance of experiences, attitudes and feelings that promote healthy psychological development derive from attaining healthy experiences that outweigh those that are unhealthy. In early childhood, for example, children are thought to experience a psychosocial stage during which they have opportunities to acquire the ability to function independently, or what Erikson calls a sense of autonomy. Positive experiences that lead children to conclude that they can function autonomously result in a healthy sense of autonomy. Negative experiences, if occurring with sufficient consistency and intensity, lead the child to feelings of shame and doubt concerning the ability to function autonomously. The result is an unhealthy sense of shame and doubt. In Erikson's theory, at each of the eight stages, progress in development occurs when the healthy attitude in that stage is acquired, whereas future difficulty in psychosocial development will occur when the unhealthy attitude dominates.

Erikson uses a timetable to illustrate his eight stages of psychosocial development. Although the ages listed are flexible guidelines for the times at which people experience the stages, the first five occur during the growth years of infancy, childhood, and adolescence, and the remaining three occur during adulthood. See Table 4–1 for an overview of Erikson's developmental stages.

Application to Parent–Child Relations

Erikson does not specifically indicate in his theory how it might be applied to parent–child relations, but we may infer from his writings how this may be accomplished. His theory provides a basic framework for understanding the psychosocial changes experienced by an individual. A family system is composed of several individuals of differing ages and developmental levels, each involved in resolving the challenges of their own particular psychosocial stage. The parents are at the stage of psychosocial development of generativity versus self-absorption. If a couple has several children, they are all likely to be at different developmental stages. For example, the oldest child may be involved in accomplishing the tasks leading toward a sense of industry versus inferiority, the middle child may be addressing the tasks involving initiative versus guilt,

and the youngest may be learning to accomplish the tasks of basic trust versus mistrust.

This intertwining or congruence of developmental stages being experienced by parents and children is referred to as *reciprocal interaction* in family systems theory. In the everyday interactions taking place between parents and children, each participant in this subsystem promotes the acquisition of the healthy psychosocial sense being experienced by the other. The provision of appropriate parental care assists children in achieving the particular psychosocial attitude that they are mastering at a particular developmental point. The children, in turn, provide the parents with the opportunity to provide care. Thus, children assist their parents in mastering their sense of generativity.

In this manner, parenting behavior adapts and is modified as children grow older. By passing through the various stages of psychosocial development, children's needs change, and parenting styles are adapted to meet these new needs. Using the concepts of reciprocal interaction and adaptation, homeostasis is achieved in parent–child relations when parenting behavior is congruent with meeting the needs of children at their different stages of growth and development. For

TABLE 4–1.   Erikson's Developmental Stages

Psychosocial Crisis	Ages Persons Involved	Persons Involved and Theme
I. Trust vs. Mistrust	Birth to 18 months	Maternal Person. Theme: To receive and to give, learning to trust, first relationships
II. Autonomy vs. Shame/Doubt	18 months to 3 years	Paternal Person. Theme: To hold on and to let go, early initiatives in self-care
III. Initiative vs. Guilt	3 to 6 years	Family. Theme: To make, to imitate, exploration, expanding developmental world
IV. Industry vs. Inferiority	6 to 12 years	School, neighborhood. Theme: To make things, to make together, social connectedness
V. Identity vs. Role Confusion	12 to 18 years	Peer groups. Theme: To be oneself, to be with others, individuation, autonomy, and peer relationships
VI. Intimacy vs. Isolation	18 to 24 years	Partners in friendship, relationships, competition. Theme: To find oneself in another, relationships, and intimacy
VII. Generativity vs. Self-absorption	24 to 54 years	Partner. Theme: To take care of, including empathy and concern for others
VIII. Integrity vs. Despair	54 years to death	Humanity. Theme: To reflect on being and not being, existential reflections

Source: Based on E. H. Erikson. (1959). Identity and the life cycle: Selected papers. *Psychological Issues 1*(1).

example, a child who is striving for autonomy during the latter part of infancy prompts entirely different patterns of caregiving from parents than were called for when the child was focused on developing a sense of trust. The course of parent–child relations proceeds according to these interactional sequences: The child assists or inhibits the parents in their development of a sense of generativity as the parents assist or inhibit the child in meeting the challenges of each developmental stage. Like the larger family system of which it is a part, the parent–child subsystem must adapt to changes in the individual participants to maintain stability and effective functioning.

Parenting Reflection 4–1

What are some ways at each of Erikson's developmental stages that inappropriate and ineffective caregiving by parents could impede a child's psychosocial development and encourage the acquisition of an unhealthy attitude?

Focus Point. Erik Erikson's framework for explaining the process of psychosocial development over the lifespan provides another means for interpreting the relationship between parents and children. He describes eight psychosocial stages. The framework focuses on developmental changes in individuals that occur in association with the passage of time. These changes occur within the context of the social environments that individuals experience throughout their lifespan. Parent–child relations change in response to the concept of reciprocal interaction.

THEORIES RELATED TO BEHAVIOR, COGNITION, AND SOCIAL LEARNING

Learning Theory

Learning theory encompasses several different explanations of how individual behavior is modified or changed as a result of experiences and interactions with external factors. The explanations discussed here as they relate to parent–child relations include: (a) operant conditioning

or behavior modification (Skinner, 1938), and (b) social learning theory (Bandura, 1977).

Operant conditioning, or **behavior modification**, is a powerful tool that parents can use to shape children's behavior. Briefly, behavior modification emphasizes the role of rewards or reinforcers that are associated with particular acts. If a parent wishes to teach a child a new skill or help acquire a new type of behavior, then a reward given immediately following the child's action or behavior would reinforce that behavior. Positive rewards have been repeatedly shown to be very powerful in changing a child's behavior or in teaching new skills. Positive rewards may also be social in nature, such as a hug, smile, or praise—for example, "I'm very proud of you for doing that!"

Little Albert. A classic case study in psychology is *Little Albert*, who, in the 1920s, was exposed to classical conditioning by psychologist John B. Watson. This same case also showed the effects of the generalization of conditioned responses. Baby Albert was about nine months old, and in a sequence of conditioned responses and associations, he acquired a fear response toward a furry, white rat. He generalized this response toward a bearded Santa Claus mask. Possibly the most important long-term outcome of this experiment is the stringent ethical guidelines and rules concerning experimentation with children. In today's climate, this dubious experiment with an infant would not have been permissible, and nowadays there are several safeguards in place to ensure that ethical and responsible research standards are met, especially with minors.

Social Learning Theory explains how learning may occur when there is no visible reinforcer or reward. This theory is especially useful in explaining how socialization occurs or how someone learns appropriate behaviors based on family beliefs and values. According to this theory, an individual responds to a number of complex stimuli in forming associations between appropriate and inappropriate behavior. Conscious thought, rather than automatic response to a stimulus, assists in shaping behavior and actions.

This approach focuses on the importance of the role of a *model* or the effect of observation learning, also known as imitation. Many kinds of behaviors are believed to be acquired by watching the behavior of another person and then replicating the observed behavior in one's own actions.

Research shows how children learn to express such social behaviors as sharing and cooperation, as well as aggression and violence, by watching such behaviors demonstrated by a model. Models include both real people and characters seen in media presentations. Research reveals that when children see a model being rewarded for acting aggressively, for instance, they are more likely to demonstrate that same kind of behavior in their own play.

Social learning theory also explains how people acquire social values and attitudes. Social roles are learned in this manner. Children imitate behaviors that they observe in adults and in other children they perceive as models. For example, social learning partly accounts for how gender-role behaviors or scripts are acquired in childhood.

When we look at the cultural and social contexts within which certain theories were developed, we can see that theories reflect some of the greater societal and intellectual reference points of a specific time. See Cultural Snapshot 4–1.

Cognitive Theory

Several theoretical approaches explain how people acquire their thought processes and problem-solving abilities, as well as organize and use information. The theories by Jean Piaget are relevant in the context of parent–child relations. His writings on this topic were based initially on observations of his own children (Piaget, 1967; Piaget & Inhelder, 1969). One of the co-authors of this book (Gerhardt) met one of Jean Piaget's personal assistants in Switzerland. The assistant, by then progressing in age, recounted how many of the experiments were conceived and then executed to determine cognitive processes in children. She also elaborated on what it was like to be part of Piaget's research team. Even at that time, it was a great honor to work in his laboratory, and his assistants were well aware of his eminence. Her description of Piaget was that he was somewhat eccentric and was confident in taking the "path less traveled" in his research. This encouraged his coworkers to think outside the box as well. On a personal note, she remembers that Piaget used to cycle to work, past several farms, and that Piaget did not appreciate it if dogs chased him while he was on his bicycle. He was particularly upset when on one of his cycling trips he was bitten by a farmer's dog. In short, Piaget's human qualities resonate positively with readers who only know him through his work.

Cultural Snapshot 4–1

Three Theorists, Three Cultural Contexts, Three Points of View

Freud, Rogers, and Skinner represent three major points of view within psychology, namely: psychoanalytic, humanist, and behaviorist. Each person was influenced by the culture, the time, and trending research during their lifespan. Freud lived at a time of gender inequality, where women's roles were predominantly confined to the home, and university education was a rarity. Rogers had studied religion and history as an undergraduate and was intensely interested in the psychotherapeutic process. Skinner was a controversial figure who, in essence, was of the opinion that free will was an illusion, and that consequences shaped behavior. Unlike Rogers, he was not interested in the workings of the psyche. All three made major contributions to the understanding of behavior and psychology. Each point of view is relevant, similar to the classic tale of the three men who described an elephant from different angles, thus highlighting very varied characteristics. By reading a brief quotation by each theorist, note how they reflect some of this greater context within which their personal views are embedded.

- The great question that has never been answered, and which I have not yet been able to answer, despite my thirty years of research into the feminine soul, is "What does a woman want?"

  Sigmund Freud

- Experience is, for me, the highest authority. The touchstone of validity is my own experience. No other person's ideas, and none of my own ideas, are as authoritative as my experience.

  Carl Rogers

- I did not direct my life. I didn't design it. I never made decisions. Things always came up and made them for me. That's what life is.

  B. F. Skinner

Several concepts are central to Piaget's thoughts about the development of intellect. *Cognition* and *cognitive development* are terms that refer to the way in which humans come to know and understand the world or the environments in which they live. A variety of related processes—perception, problem solving, judgment, and reasoning, for example—are involved in how people organize their mental life. Cognitive development also refers to the changes that take place as people acquire a general understanding of their environments. See Table 4–2.

Cognition is based on the acquisition of *schemes*. This refers to a consistent, reliable pattern or plan of interaction with the environment. Schemes are usually goal-oriented strategies that help a person to achieve some type of intended result from his or her behavior. For example, a rudimentary scheme is built or acquired that serves to guide a child's behavior in

TABLE 4–2. Piaget's Stages of Cognitive Development

Sensorimotor (Birth to 3 years)

■ Establishment of sensorimotor schemes
■ Assimilation and accommodation, modification of schemes
■ Elementary understanding of cause-and-effect relationships
■ Emergence of object permanence
■ Emergence of elementary logic

Preoperational-Intuitive (3–6 years)

■ Emergence of language helps to establish cognitive schemes
■ Preoccupation with classification tasks
■ Thinking becomes intuitive in nature
■ Development of large database of knowledge and information
■ Cognitive flaws include egocentrism
■ Perception is based upon appearances

Concrete Operations (6–11 years)

■ Understanding relationships between events and things
■ Operating objects, symbols, and concepts to acquire this understanding
■ Internalizing the outer environment by using mental imagery and symbolism
■ Other cognitive attributes:
  ■ Centering
  ■ Mastery of conservation problems
  ■ Reversibility
  ■ Black-and-white thinking

Formal Operations (Adolescence and older)

■ Increasing use of scientific reasoning
■ Decrease in egocentricity
■ Increasing ability to empathize
■ Emergence of personal meanings
■ Emergence of higher order moral reasoning

Based on Piaget, J., & Inhelder, B. (1969). *The Psychology of the Child.* New York: Basic Books.

picking up an object that draws his or her curiosity or attention to explore by touch, sight, and even taste. This scheme acts as a script of sorts that becomes a permanent part of the child's mental abilities in learning how to manipulate objects and learn about their nature. Once the scheme is acquired when learning about one object, it can be generalized to be used in learning about all objects that a child is interested in manipulating.

Piaget believed that there are two basic types of schemes that are formed throughout infancy, childhood, and adolescence:

1. *Sensorimotor schemes,* Formed in infancy and childhood, are based in motor acts and serve to help the child understand how the world operates in very rudimentary terms.
2. *Cognitive schemes.* More like ideas or patterns based on symbolism and abstract reasoning, formed from early childhood into adolescence and older years, that also permit problem solving and attainment of certain goals, for example, mathematical processes such as addition and subtraction.

Schemes evolve, once formed, from basic to more advanced and complex natures. Essentially, we are able to modify existing schemes by two processes:

1. *Assimilation.* Occurs when new information is incorporated into an existing scheme.
2. *Accommodation.* Occurs when an existing scheme is altered to bring about congruence with reality. For example, an infant acquires the basic scheme for sucking on an object. After this is mastered, the baby will attempt to suck on anything that comes near his or her mouth, such as fingers, toes, and so forth. He or she may learn from interactions with parents that sucking is most appropriate with a nipple or pacifier.

Piaget proposed that individuals experience a series of four stages in infancy, childhood, and adolescence in acquiring an understanding of the world. Development proceeds from a general to a more specific understanding as children acquire greater experience with their environments. The ages at which people proceed through these stages are somewhat variable, but Piaget believed that the sequence of the stages is invariable.

The cognitive theory is a comprehensive guide to understanding mental processes and how these are acquired and change as a person grows and develops from birth through childhood and adolescence. Central to Piaget's explanation is the role of personal experience with one's environment, both physical and social, in influencing how we think and reason. The ways in which parents interact with a child and provide a variety of physical and social experiences are an essential component of a child's development. For example, parents provide physical experiences for infants through toys and food, and in the places in the community where they take children. These shape children's understanding of their physical environment and how they can operate in this setting. Parents also provide a social environment to their infants by talking and playing with them, and teaching them rudimentary social skills in late infancy. These parental actions continue throughout childhood and adolescence. For example, when parents read to their children and encourage them to look at picture books, the children learn that information can be acquired from printed materials. What parents provide as experiences for children influences the quality of their cognitive development.

Sociocultural Theory. Lev Vygotsky (1962, 1987) is a Russian psychologist who proposed a perspective of psychological development known as the **sociocultural theory**. This approach emphasizes the social aspects of cognitive development; that is, intellectual growth is stimulated by interactions with others, especially parents. Vygotsky stated that

■ Development during infancy and early childhood is specific to a particular historical time in which a person lives. Differences in development depend on when and where someone grows up.
■ Development takes place when a child observes an activity in group interactions and then internalizes this activity.
■ Symbols such as language assist in internalizing activities.
■ Culture is learned through interactions with others from the same culture.

Vygotsky proposes that children accomplish many developmental tasks within the context of what he terms the **zone of proximal development (ZPD)**. Many tasks that are too difficult for children to master alone can be accomplished successfully with the guidance and assistance of adults who are more skilled than children. The lower limit of the ZPD is what a child can accomplish in learning a task independently—without adult assistance. The upper limit of this zone is what can be accomplished when assisted by an adult. The ZPD represents an idea of a child's learning potential. It emphasizes the interpersonal context in which learning tasks occur by implying that learning is a shared experience.

Young children are assisted by parents and other caregivers who motivate their interest in successfully accomplishing a task that appears difficult to achieve. By providing children with verbal instruction and by helping them do things themselves with guidance, parents and others assist children. The children, in turn, organize the information in their existing mental structures and transform it to accomplish increasingly difficult tasks.

Application to Parent–Child Relations

Some researchers use the term **scaffolding** to refer to any parental behavior that supports a child's efforts at more advanced skill acquisition until the child becomes competent at that behavior. We refer to such assistance as *assertive* and *supportive care*, which includes nurture and refers to the ways that parents provide appropriate and healthy support to their children. When parents instruct their preschool-age child in this manner, it may happen in the following sequence:

1. Recruiting the child's interest in performing a task or activity.
2. Simplifying the task to a number of steps that lead to a correct solution.
3. Maintaining the child's interest in the task.
4. Pointing out errors as they occur and providing guidance toward correction.
5. Controlling the child's frustration by discounting the distress caused by making mistakes.
6. Demonstrating or modeling correct solutions (Astington, 1993; Rogoff, 1990).

When seen in this manner, children learn best when parents model problem-solving skills or mentor the child in ways of reaching solutions to the problems. Vygotsky's views approximate that of social learning theory but are nested within the cultural context in which development occurs.

Monkey Business Images/Shutterstock

Parents scaffold by supporting their child's efforts at more advanced skill acquisition until the child becomes competent at the behavior; children learn best when parents model problem-solving skills or mentor the child in ways of reaching solutions to the problems.

Vygotsky incorporates the concept of interdependence as a central part of development (Rogoff, 1990). This runs against the parenting philosophy frequently displayed in the United States. In our society, child-rearing practices tend to promote individualism as a valued trait. For example, infants are placed in separate sleeping quarters from parents and are expected to learn to comfort themselves while going to sleep. Children also conduct their own play activities with a minimal amount of adult guidance. School performance is based on competition with others, and individualism is highlighted by the heavy emphasis on personal performance in sports and athletic activities, for example. Other cultures promote collectivism rather than independence in child rearing. In Vygotsky's view, optimal development occurs within the collectivist context of relationships among individuals.

Cognitive Learning Theory. Jerome Bruner's (1966) work on children's cognitive development reflects a rich understanding of the role of one's culture in influencing the acquisition and evolution of thinking processes. Like Piaget, Bruner believes that ideas are based on the ability to categorize according to similarities, as well as differences. Bruner proposes three modes of representation that are acquired in learning to understand one's environment: (1) enactive or action based, (2) iconic or image based, and (3) symbolic or language based. In applying these concepts, Bruner believes that new material is acquired by experiencing these three types of representation sequentially. One of Bruner's central tenets in educational theory is that anything can be learned at a very early age if it is properly organized. This notion is in sharp contrast to Piaget's approach.

Parenthood as a Developmental Role: Developmental Interaction

We have presented and discussed a number of different, but related, ideas about the nature of the parenting role, the variety of factors that are thought to influence parental behaviors, and how these relate to child outcomes. It is important to reemphasize that individuals experience changes in how they conduct themselves in their role as a parent. These changes are developmental in nature and occur in association with the passage of time. Like other patterns observed in family systems, the parenting role must evolve in relation to the needs of the children and the parent(s). Most people enter this role with ideas about what it is like to be a parent, and what might be expected from children. Parents need to change and evolve their parenting skills and abilities, often in response to the developmental changes that children experience. Several writers, including Ellen Galinsky (1987), have developed the topic in greater detail.

Parenthood is traditionally considered to be a developmental task of adulthood. Although this is not necessarily an essential component of adult development, many people experience a sense of generativity by becoming a parent. Galinsky describes six stages in the evolution of one's parenthood role that were observed in individuals as they grow and change in response to the developmental changes being experienced by their children. We refer to this process as **developmental interaction** (sometimes called developmental parenting), which is the motivating factor that produces such mutual developmental changes in parents and children.

Drawing from the theoretical work of Levinson (1978) and Erikson (1950) on adult development, Galinsky outlines the following six stages of parenthood:

1. **Image-Making Stage.** During this period, a potential parent uses imagery to rehearse what it must be like to be a parent. This is a time for individuals to develop their vision of what kind of parent they wish to be. It is a time for preparation for parenthood that is particularly stimulated by the initiation of a pregnancy. Pregnancy brings many changes, especially for a woman. Her body changes, her image of her body changes, and she experiences the unique feeling of a new life developing within her body. This image-making stage is a time for individuals to examine their relationship with their own parents, a relationship that often serves as a guide for how they themselves may act as a parent. It is a time for evaluating how changes might occur in the relationship between partners. Ultimately, this stage is also a time for preparing for the child's birth and confronting fears, especially those of the unknown if this is the first pregnancy.

2. **The Nurturing Stage.** The major focus of this stage of emerging parenthood is establishing an attachment to the new infant. For new parents, this involves reconciling the reality of what the child is actually like with how they may have imagined him or her to be. This stage necessitates redefining a couple's relationship and their relationships with their parents, in-laws, friends, and coworkers. Paradoxically, by getting to know the baby, each parent has the opportunity to get to know him- or herself even better than before. The experience of nurturing a baby reflects back to the parent the kind of person that she or he is.

3. **The Authority Stage.** This period is characterized by the realization that parenthood involves a strong element of adult authority. This is partially stimulated by the changes taking place in children that allow them to master an increasingly wider range of skills that challenge parental interactions. The changing nature of children at this time calls for greater reliance on the parent as a person of authority who decides much of what is right or wrong, appropriate or inappropriate, regarding children's behavior. Essentially, this is the time when adults must accept the responsibility for guiding the life, behavior, and development of the child. The

authority stage involves the emergence of rules as a means for governance and the clear establishment of personal boundaries between parents and children.

4. **The Interpretative Stage.**   At this time, adults assume the responsibility of acting as interpreters of the world for their children. This means that they begin to impart their interpretation of their own particular worldview or family values to their children. Parents answer children's innumerable questions, help them to acquire skills for making personal decisions about their behavior, and pass on family values. This stage ends with the child's entrance into adolescence.

5. **The Interdependent Stage.**   This period includes parenting adolescent children and demands that adults reexamine the issue of parental authority and how this is to be played out. The new child who emerges during adolescence is one who increasingly demands to be independent from parental control and authority. The reality of development for both adults and children is that although parents must recognize this desire for independence, it is not reasonable to permit adolescent children to have complete control over their decisions and behavior. The challenge of this stage of parenthood is for parents and adolescents to adapt and redefine their relationship to allow negotiation and discussion of rules, appropriate behavior, limits, and so forth.

6. **The Departing Stage.**   At this time, parents reexamine all of their experiences in raising children. Parents begin to let go of their children and relinquish authority over them. They recognize that their parenting career is coming to a close and that the tasks of parenthood are almost completed. To be truly mastered, the relationship between adult children and parents must be redefined to encompass the new adult status of the children. This means that the relationship takes on an adult-to-adult quality in which the authority of the parent is no longer paramount.

Parenting Reflection 4–2

How has information from the behavioral sciences contributed to the understanding of parent–child relations?

Focus Point.   Theoretical approaches may be useful in understanding the social context of parent–child relations. Learning theory components (e.g., behavior modification and social learning) explain how parents teach children by using rewards to reinforce desirable behaviors and by serving as models of behavior. Cognitive behavioral theory stresses the importance of the experiences that parents provide for children as a means of shaping their mental life. These can be both physical and social in nature. Vygotsky's views expand on social learning to explain how parents teach skills to their children. Important concepts in this model are scaffolding and zone of proximal development.

THE FAMILY AS A SYSTEM

Families can be regarded as the building blocks of society. Families have the power to influence society, just as they themselves are being influenced. There is interrelatedness, a give-and-take, among all of these components. If the society at large faces a recession, the families within that society will struggle. Going one layer deeper in this nested configuration, we know that individual family members are affected by what is happening within their family, and the members, in turn, have the ability to influence the climate of their family group. We are all interrelated in this complexity and the influences act in both directions; they are **bidirectional**. Anyone who has built a house of cards, stacking the cards as high as possible, knows that one false move can cause the entire structure to come tumbling down. That is because the pieces of that structure are dependent on one another; they can no longer be seen in isolation.

Present-day family life provides options that were not possible in the past. Clearly families are not static. Family sociologists speculate that these variations reflect the family's adaptation to societal change. Families have morphed in size, structure, composition, and function in response to changes in the society within which they are embedded. In the past, a significant portion of family life was devoted to the nitty-gritty of socioeconomic survival; hands-on food production plus cultural and social demands filled the hours of each day.

Today's families are still on the treadmill of survival, but there is fairly extreme job specialization requiring education and skill building. Children require a longer childhood to fit in all this training and education; hence we have a period of "emerging adulthood," representing a time for staggered shouldering of adult responsibilities. Family functioning also focuses on the luxuries of psychological expression and fulfillment. The emotional and social needs of family members matter; generally, we seek the happiness (or something close to it) that we have been led to believe is our birthright. To reach this complex and often abstract level of self-actualization, our children require quality relationships with parents, who in turn support and model the ways toward becoming fully functioning members of society. Importantly, that implies challenges beyond earning a living; it should also involve how we navigate the psychic landscape of our lives and how we deal with all the people in our personal worlds. In today's smaller families, interactions within the family group are intense and frequent. The survival and continuation of families may depend on how well each member's personal needs are met by the family group.

Many families are unable to adapt to the complex demands placed on them. Family life today is occasionally described as asynchronous; meaning that family leaders (the adults) depend on personal past experiences to guide their current behavior and to prepare their children to function as adults. There is no guarantee that the future will be anything like the past, especially if societal changes continue to occur as rapidly as they have over the past 50 years.

The ways we define parenthood vary depending on how family ecological factors are experienced by each family system. Almost every family system adheres to the central role expectations of parenthood, including an emphasis on nurturing, teaching, and caring for children. Because of cultural and environmental variations, it is impossible to define families according to only one form, structure, or approach. At different times, theorists have added various approaches that explain child rearing and family functioning. Combined, all of these factors illuminate the relevance of family functioning against the backdrop of history.

Family Systems Theory

Family scientists have been inspired by general systemic approaches in the physical sciences and these represent the historical underpinnings for the systemic family approaches that followed (Von Bertalanffy, 1974). The systemic perspective explains the complex workings of naturally occurring systems such as biological ecological systems and the solar system. When applied to families, systemic approaches describe them as operating in similar ways to other systems observed in nature. The family is described as a *social* system (Becvar & Becvar, 2012).

Systems theory can explain the complex interactions of a family and the factors that regulate family behavior. The intent of a family system is to maintain the stability of the family group over time. The theory also explains how a family responds to change, both developmental changes within family members and external changes that challenge the family's ability to function effectively as a group.

Several subsystems exist. For example, the relationships between parents and children, between the adult spouses, and among siblings are recognized as subsystems. The *family systems theory* is important in the context of the study of families, and specifically parent–child relations, because it also represents the dominant theoretical choice in family therapy. Almost all marriage and family therapists are trained in family systems theory together with cognitive behavioral therapy; the systemic approach counts amongst the most frequently used therapeutic approaches (Gurman & Kniskern, 2014). We will summarize some basic concepts of this approach.

Wholeness.   A family is more than a group of individuals who function independently. A family operates on the principle of *wholeness*. The family group must be considered in its entirety. In other words, using a principle from *Gestalt* psychology, a family is greater than the sum of its parts, in this case its individual members.

Interdependence.   Interdependence is related to the principle of wholeness. What affects one, affects all to a greater or lesser degree. A mobile is a good way to illustrate this concept. All parts of a mobile are connected, so when one part is moved abruptly, other parts are affected and respond accordingly, although to a lesser degree (Satir, Gilmore, & Golden Triad Films, 2004). The parts of the mobile represent different family members, and the strings connecting each piece of the mobile represent the different relationships found in a family system. The mobile illustrates the interdependence of family members. See Figure 4–7.

When one person in a family system experiences some type of change, such as becoming seriously ill, leaving the family, or receiving a job promotion,

FIGURE 4–7.   A mobile can illustrate family interdependence.

to some degree everyone in the system is affected. Whether the change is good or bad, beneficial or detrimental, all members of a family system react and attempt to compensate for the imbalance caused by a change that directly affects just one member. The objective is to return to a state of balance, called *homeostasis*, which existed prior to the change that caused the imbalance.

Patterns.   Within a family system, patterns evolve that serve to regulate the behavior of members and allow members to anticipate each other's behavior. These patterns are unique to each family system, although some patterns follow general guidelines that are common to all family systems. The patterns that are usually found in most family systems include rules, roles, and communication styles.

Rules.   A family system typically develops rules to govern members' behavior. Rules provide common ground for understanding which behaviors are acceptable and appropriate within each family system. In turn, the consistent application of rules helps to maintain the stability of a family system over time in general and especially in times of uncertainty or crisis. The rules in each family system evolve, usually through the negotiations of the adults. In many instances, the rules that become established in a family system have their roots in the adults' families of origin.

Rules can be explicit or implicit. **Explicit rules** are known, stated, and outlined clearly so that all people in the family know and understand them. Explicit rules are often stated verbally, especially when transgressions occur: "You know, the rule is that you must be home by 10 o'clock."

Implicit rules are unspoken and are often inferred from nonverbal behavior. Implicit rules are not usually discussed openly, yet everyone is expected to know and obey them. For example, some family systems do not allow the expression of anger. In such families, everyone is expected to be pleasant and to not engage in open conflict. When conflict is imminent, family members could leave the group, be in denial about the underlying emotions, or defuse the potential conflict. It is difficult to discuss such rules and to change them because they are not readily acknowledged despite their strong influence. Generally, *healthy* family systems operate with an abundance of explicit rules and few implicit rules, while those that are unhealthy have a greater number of implicit rules (Duncan & Fiske, 2015).

Rules can also be **negotiable**, or *non-negotiable*. In the first instance, parents practice flexibility in the enforcement and children may contest these rules. For example, a negotiable family rule might relate to coming to dinner when called. A **non-negotiable rule** on the other hand, might require children to always inform parents of their whereabouts when away from home. Families vary in what is negotiable or non-negotiable and there is no single standard. Each family generates rules frequently based on rules in the families of origin of the parents. Rules may change in response to the developmental stage of the child. For instance, they could be non-negotiable to protect younger children, or negotiable to reflect children's increasing autonomy.

Roles.   Roles are used in family systems to outline acceptable behavior and to regulate the system's functioning. Rules may evolve to describe and outline roles. For example, to be a good mother, a woman should attend all school-related functions of her children, maintain a clean and orderly home, be employed outside the home, and the like. Rules that describe the child's role might be that the child should be a willing learner and be able to perform some family tasks. The rules provide the script to be enacted by the person filling a particular role in a family system.

Unhealthy families often develop implicit roles that are governed by implicit rules. Because such families do not always cope with stresses effectively, one family member may assume a role to act out the stress on behalf of a particularly dysfunctional member (Becvar & Becvar, 2012). For example, a child may act as the family scapegoat by becoming depressed or acting out to detract from the parents' unhealthy relationship. In this instance, the child's role draws attention away from the parents. In a different family system, a child's implicit role may be the "best little boy." In this system, the role carries the expectation of perfectionism and conformity.

Communication Styles.   Three basic styles are found in most families: verbal, nonverbal, and contextual (Becvar & Becvar, 2012). *Verbal* communications relate to the words used to convey information among persons in the family system. *Nonverbal* communications can accompany a verbal message and include tone of voice, facial expression, body posture, and hand gestures. The purpose of the nonverbal message is to inform the receiver about what to do with the verbal message. It hints at the intent of the message and often contains an implicit command or request. *Contextual* communication refers to where and under which circumstances the verbal and nonverbal communications occur.

Reciprocal Interaction and Feedback

Systems theory does not support a cause-and-effect process of interaction among members of families or family systems. Rather, causality is seen as a *reciprocal interaction* between people and systems (Becvar & Becvar, 2012). Essentially, systems theory stresses that people in a family system influence each other's actions. Behavioral interactions become intertwined as one person reacts to another, setting up a chain of interactional sequences. One person's action serves as a stimulus that elicits a reaction or response from another; this reaction, in turn, acts as a stimulus that elicits a different reaction or response; and the cycle continues. Behavior serves as both *stimulus* and *feedback*. See Figure 4–8.

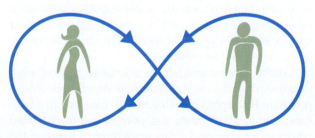

FIGURE 4–8.   Reciprocal interaction.

Boundaries

Boundaries establish limits that distinguish a family system from all others. It can also differentiate the members of a particular family system (Minuchin, 1974; Galvin, Braithwaite, & Bylund, 2015). These abstract, psychological dividers outline who participates in a particular subsystem and their role in that subsystem. Boundaries also keep subsystems distinct. A family member can participate in several family subsystems. Boundaries prevent overlap between subsystems. For example, when conflicts occur within one subsystem, boundaries help contain the conflict from spreading. For instance, when the adults in the committed relationship disagree, the boundaries help to ensure that the relationship with their children is not affected.

Boundaries regulate the degree of closeness or intimacy permissible (Sharaievska & Stodolska, 2015). Although boundaries can be changed and may vary, families typically have either flexible or rigid boundaries. These result in open or closed family systems. For example, a healthy family system maintains closed boundaries for the expression of the adult couple's intimate relationship. It is private and does not include the children or other family members. An *open* family has flexible boundaries that permit the easy exchanges with other individuals. Essentially, healthy families operate as an open system (Robinson, 1980). Personal boundaries among family members in a closed system, can become fused, or *enmeshed* (Minuchin, 1974). For example, children are not encouraged to differentiate themselves as individuals. Similarly, families who are emotionally distant, function on parallel tracks that do not meet, and are *disengaged*. See Figure 4–9 for illustrations of these two types of family boundaries. In healthy family systems, boundaries are valued because they help personal individuation and appropriate autonomy (Barbera, Bernhard, Nacht, & McCann, 2015).

Equifinality

All subsystems have goals that support the reason for their existence. Likewise, all family systems develop goals that influence functioning and behavior. The concept of *equifinality* means that families share common goals but they reach these goals in different ways. For example, constructive parent–child relations may mean

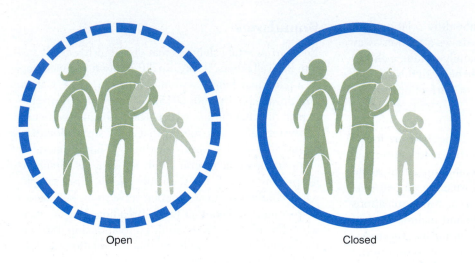

FIGURE 4–9. Open and closed boundaries in family systems.

Open

Closed

different things in different families. Each family will find their own path toward reaching the goal. The saying: "Different strokes, for different folks" comes to mind.

Homeostasis

The ultimate goal of family system functioning is to maintain stability, or *homeostasis*. This is also known as *dynamic equilibrium*. The word **dynamic** refers to constructive changes that will contribute to better outcomes, and hence contribute to stability. Healthy family systems try to maintain homeostasis by balancing appropriate change as well as appropriate stability. During times of stress, appropriate change or appropriate sameness may be desirable, depending on the context of the situation.

Application to Parent–Child Relations

Family systems theory depicts the parent–child relationship as one of several *subsystems* within a family. Other subsystems include the marriage or committed relationship between adults, the relationship among siblings, the relationship within the extended family (e.g., grandparent–grandchild), and relationships with the larger circle beyond the nuclear family (e.g., school, church, neighbors).

Parent–child relationships are also subject to rules, and follow communication patterns described earlier. *Interrelatedness* means that what affects an adult will also affect children, and vice versa. If a child develops a chronic illness, this condition alters the relationship with the parent and other family members. If the adults divorce, we can expect children to experience related effects.

Boundaries outline acceptable and unacceptable behaviors within this relationship. Our culture specifically prohibits sexual activity between parents and children as it is considered totally inappropriate and unhealthy for all parties. We tend, as a culture, to separate the world of children from that of adults. There is a *family hierarchy* separating the parental dyad from the children.

Adaptation and *reciprocal interaction* may be observed. For example, parents may have more nonnegotiable rules in place for younger children. These are relaxed when the children mature. Parents usually change the rules when they are no longer effective. Parents continuously monitor various issues intended to maintain family homeostasis and will make adaptations when necessary.

Equifinality is observed in the number of equally acceptable strategies for raising children. Not everyone will agree on a particular approach, but there is an understanding that no single or absolute approach will fit all situations. Family theorists are often *eclectic* in their approach, as they apply various theories in different settings, depending on context.

When parents seek advice, assistance, and information they may wish to stabilize their situation or solve a problem. By displaying willingness to have an open family system in problem solving, parents can work toward constructive change. In this way *stability* is promoted while chaos and disruption are avoided.

Parenting Reflection 4–3

Family therapists predominantly use variations of the systemic approaches. Explain why a systems approach lends itself to working with families. How could the principles of a systems approach be applied in other social situations (for example, work environments, committee participation, sports, church groups).

Focus Point.   Family systems theory explains the complex interactions of a family group. It addresses the factors that influence how the group makes decisions, sets and achieves goals, and establishes patterns that govern behavior. It explains how group stability is maintained. Concepts central to this theory include wholeness, interdependence, patterns (i.e., rules, roles, and communication styles), reciprocal interaction and feedback, boundaries, equifinality, adaptation, and homeostasis. The relationship between parents and children is one of several subsystems that make up a family system.

ECOLOGICAL SYSTEMS THEORY AND PARENTING

The **Ecological Systems Theory** (also called bio-ecological systems theory) proposed by Urie Bronfenbrenner (1917–2005) (Bronfenbrenner, 1979, Bronfenbrenner, 1986, Bronfenbrenner, 1993) leads our attention to the role of different environments and how these affect individual and family functioning, including parent–child relations. It also represents a *sociocultural* view of development. Bronfenbrenner, a cofounder of the federal Head Start program, felt strongly that various systems in a child's life could be influential in promoting the best outcome. He focuses on the role of five distinct but related environmental settings to explain how individuals and their family systems are influenced in their development, how relationships function, and how interactions take place. A person is at the center of a set of environments that can also be described as multiple *nested* layers. From this standpoint, an individual is not a passive recipient of interactions with other people and other environments, but is actively involved in direct interactions. In fact, the interactions are *bidirectional*.

Initially, the child only interacts with those closest to him or her, but these circles widen and become more complex with increasing maturity. See Figure 4–10, which depicts the ecological system of development.

The first environmental setting with which a child interacts is that which comprises the environments provided by the family, peers, a school, or a neighborhood. This is known as the **microsystem**. The next environment is known as the **mesosystem**, which encompasses the microsystem. This system involves relations between the first and all other systems that affect the person. For example, the family has relationships and interactions with the school that the child attends. The child's relationships at school, then, are influenced by what takes place in the family setting, and vice versa. For instance, if one or both parents have some type of addiction or related disorder, this will affect a child's interactions and relationships within the family setting and influence interactions and relationships within the child's school setting. Academic performance and social relationships and interactions with peers and teachers are influenced by what happens in the child's family life, and vice versa.

An **exosystem** also influences the individual. This setting may be visualized as encompassing the mesosystem. The individual does not have an active role in this context, but is influenced by it nevertheless. An exosystem may be government agencies, community programs, the employment settings of parents, and so on. For example, the work responsibilities or assignments of one parent may change, requiring different and extraordinary work hours. When the parent begins to work longer hours, or at night rather than during the day, the parenting experiences of the child are affected accordingly. Another example would be how the quality of the child's life is affected by funding cutbacks to community recreation programs sponsored by local governmental agencies.

A **macrosystem** is an even larger context that affects an individual. This environment involves the larger culture in which the individual lives and encompasses the exosystem and what it contains. In this context, the person is affected by the broad, generalized beliefs, behavior patterns, and value systems deemed appropriate by most members of a particular society. These influence how a person interacts with all other environmental settings. Culture would fit into this system as well.

The last environment is the **chronosystem**, which encompasses the entire network of other systems. This

FIGURE 4–10. In Bronfenbrenner's theory, a system can be viewed in terms of interrelated, nested layers.

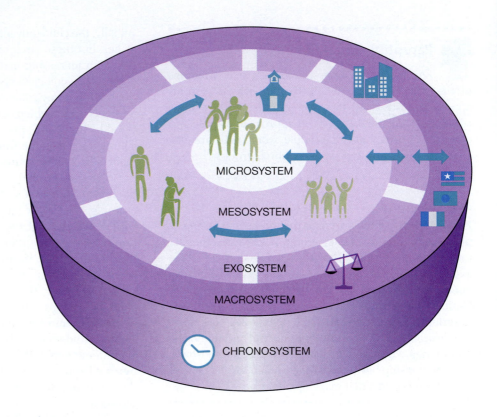

context involves the organization of events and changes over the lifespan of an individual at a particular *historical time*. For example, we know that adults are influenced in their current behaviors and interactions by events and interactions that took place during earlier stages in their lives. It is generally understood that if a person was abused as a child, the effects can last a lifetime. With therapeutic assistance, these effects can be minimized but perhaps not completely ameliorated and can continue to influence the person in various ways for years. Likewise, changes in cultural attitudes are reflected within the chronosystem and affect individuals at different historical times. Attitudes about gender roles in society are different today than 100 years ago. Androgyny, for example, is more acceptable today than a century ago. The chronosystem may also refer to the influences that an entire cohort experiences—for instance, a generation affected by the Great Depression or, in our current context, a generation that grows up with the World Wide Web and highly accessible communication technology.

It is possible to view society as an immense collection of families. As such, what goes on in families is also reflected in society, and vice versa. A family system cannot function independently from the physical, social, economic, and psychological environments of which it is a part. The ecological systems perspective outlined by Bronfenbrenner emphasizes the *dual influence* between families and societies locally and throughout the world. Essentially, what happens in one environmental aspect influences what occurs in others, as well as in families that make up a society. Likewise, what occurs in families affects the various environments in which they live. The family ecology view leads to an examination of the ways that various sociocultural environments influence family form and functioning. Bronfenbrenner did adapt his theory over the years, and slight variations have occurred as the theory evolved (Tudge, Mokrova, Hatfield, & Karnik, 2009).

This model has at times been misinterpreted in the literature, and various interpretations have led to some conceptual confusion (Tudge, Mokrova, Hatfield, & Karnik, 2009). Bronfenbrenner referred to the combination of "process-person-context" to highlight the interrelatedness and complexity of influence between various components at different levels of a system (Bronfenbrenner & Evans, 2000). See Table 4–3.

TABLE 4–3.   Bronfenbrenner's Ecological Systems Theory

The Roles of the Layers in Parent–Child Relationships

Layer	The layers have a **bidirectional** influence on one another.

Microsystem	**Micro** comes from the Greek *mikrós*, meaning "small" (think of a microscope with which very small objects can be viewed). The *microsystem* refers to the smallest or innermost system. It encompasses the very personal influences of family, neighborhood, and school. In parent–child relations, this layer would represent the relationship that is closest to the child, namely the parental relationship, as well as close family ties and the immediate environment.
Mesosystem	**Meso** comes from the Greek *meso*, meaning "in the middle." In this model, it is the middle layer sandwiched between the inner (microsystem) and the outer (exosystem) layers, and its function is to connect the structures in the child's world. For example, the teachers and the parents could be connected to each other through the *mesosystem*, yet both have an influence on the child. The mesosystem conducts (or facilitates communication) between the microsystem and the exosystem.
Exosystem	**Exo** comes from the Greek *exo*, meaning "outer." One could view it as the *buffer zone* between the inner circles known to the child and society at large (macrosystem), which may be anonymous to the child. The *exosystem* has an influence on the child because people and organizations from this layer interact with the parents and have an influence on the parent–child relationship. Examples from this layer are community programs, agencies, and services that may support the family.
Macrosystem	**Macro** comes from the Greek *makrós*, meaning "large." The *macrosystem* represents the largest of the nested layers. Aspects within this layer influence the child in an indirect manner. The aspects are present, and in the parent–child relationship one can feel the influence, but they may not always be apparent, as they could be somewhat abstract. Examples include cultural beliefs and values. The influence from this system can ripple right through to the parent–child relationship.
Chronosystem	**Chrono** comes from the Greek *chrónos*, meaning "time" (think of a chronometer, a very accurate timepiece). The *chronosystem* is an extra dimension. Imagine the model to be three dimensional. The chronosystem affects all of the other layers. It encompasses *time-related influences*. Examples are persons who all experienced the Great Depression or a major war, or Millennials who are all familiar with technological innovations such as the internet, or similar time related experiences that influence the generation experiencing them.

This is a summary of the five distinct, but related, multiple nested layers and their roles in the parent–child relationship. Based on the work of Urie Bronfenbrenner (1979).

....

Focus Point.   Bronfenbrenner's ecological systems theory explains how individuals and families are affected by a variety of interacting environments in a bidirectional manner. An individual's family, by being part of the total environment, is also influenced by these other systems. The systems are nested within each other.

....

Video Example 4.3

Watch this video on Urie Bronfenbrenner and Ecological Systems Theory. The Ecological Systems Theory outlines the various environmental influences on families and their children. Can you name and describe some of these influential systems?

(https://www.youtube.com/watch?v=moa-MY9EpZY&t=9s)

SYSTEMIC FAMILY DEVELOPMENT THEORY

The emphasis in this approach is on the word: *development*. As an undergraduate topic for study, most family science students take several courses in Human Lifespan Development. When we study the *individual* human lifespan, we notice that a person goes through various stages, and that these stages greatly determine the relevance of what occurs when. Similarly, we can think of the family unit as progressing on a *family* developmental lifespan. For instance, a young nuclear family will face different challenges than an older more established family.

Just as individuals follow predictable stages in their personal development, families also experience stages that follow a predictable course (Bohn & Berntsen, 2013). The progression of stages that a family follows from its establishment to its demise has been labeled the *family life cycle*, although it is not cyclic in the true sense of the word (Nauck, 2016).

A realistic model that describes how families change in association with the passage of time is the *systemic family development theory* model (Laszloffy, 2002). The systemic model proposes that families are both similar and diverse in their intergenerational composition.

A family system provides an expressive function for members. Family members are dynamic, developmentally changing individuals, who are contained within the unit of their family. Hence that family unit or system must also change its response over time (DeHaan, Hawley, & Deal, 2013).

Many years ago, pioneer sociologist Ernest Burgess (1926, p. 3) described the family as a "unity of interacting personalities." Unity in this context alludes to the concepts of *wholeness* and *interdependence* as currently used in family systems theory. The reference to interacting personalities denotes Burgess's observation that interaction among family members serves a vital purpose in the functioning of a family system by promoting the psychological welfare of each family member.

Stressors in Families

Families share a common process of developmental change over time, marked by individual details and stressors (Laszloffy, 2002). These stressors force family systems to adapt. Stressors can be positive (eustress) as with happy events, such as a marriage. They can be negative (distress) when they imply loss or destruction. The transition typically produces changes in family roles and relationships. Sometimes a family has difficulty making a successful adaptation. The experience of a single stressor can usually be dealt with using helpful resources. For example, the birth of a child is stressful and the routine in the home is altered. People make changes in their roles and routines to adapt to the needs of the new baby. Stressors only become problematic when several occur simultaneously or in rapid succession. Refer to Focus On 4–1.

Intergenerational Families in Developmental Time

Theoretical approaches that are systemically focused emphasize a strong sociological component. These approaches are valuable in understanding the extended contexts in which families function. They also form the basis of much of the therapeutic work relating to the family. We can further enhance our understanding by looking at the lifespan challenges of the diverse family members who make up a particular system.

In looking at families in a systemic manner, we can stack the lifespan expectations of each participating family member. We may find for instance, that while the baby is learning to walk, the grandmother is dealing with balance loss. There is a subtle irony in the fact that some of the challenges in early and in later life display similar qualities; as we struggle to gain a skill in early life, we may struggle as we lose that skill during later life.

The family systems approach clarifies that families are systems. But these systems are also intergenerational, because obviously family members come from different age groups. It is possible that four generations could be interacting at any given time. Each generation is on its own timeline. For that reason, each generation is also at a different point in their lifespan, facing the challenges of that particular stage and age group.

Intergenerational family systems renew themselves. As the oldest generation passes on, the next generation becomes the oldest. In some ways, it is like the progression that occurs when a senior class graduates. As the oldest cohort leaves, a new group of freshmen will be entering, who will slowly mature until they too, become graduating seniors. In families, new generations are added while older generations fall away.

Focus On 4–1:   **Stressors in the Family**

Examples of Stressors Common to Families (listed alphabetically)

- Birth of a child, adoption, infertility
- Boomerang kid moving back to the parental home
- Career, work, dual careers, income
- Chronic illness, disability, death of a family member
- Dating, marriage, separation, divorce, remarriage
- Deployment in military families
- Developmental stages of children
- Mental illness, addiction, and related disorders
- Mid-career changes, lifelong education
- New family roles (e.g., in-laws, blended families, a stepparent, grandparents)
- Relocation, moving, downsizing
- Retirement, redundancy, financial problems
- Sandwich generation, looking after elderly parents
- Simultaneous stressors occurring in all generations

A metaphor for visualizing this intergenerational family system is to view it as a layered structure. The oldest, or foundational layers, disintegrate while simultaneously new layers are added on top. This layered structure has been likened to a layered cake (Laszloffy, 2002). We view the structure as a whole, just as we must view an intergenerational family in its totality in order to understand it. The individual building blocks of the structure are like the individual family members. Individuals form a family when brought together through marriage, birth, adoption, or by choice. By losing layers of the structure (generations dying) and adding new ones (new generations being born), adjustments occur. See Figure 4–11 for a visual representation of the intergenerational family system dynamic.

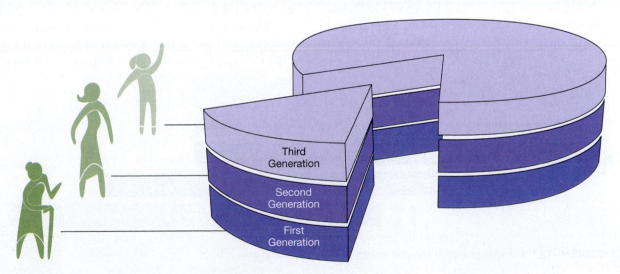

Third Generation

Second Generation

First Generation

FIGURE 4–11.   Intergenerational family system.

To perceive what may be occurring developmentally in an intergenerational family system, we would observe the entire family group for a short time. A cross section of family life offers a *snapshot* in time (Laszloffy, 2002). By examining the family's place in developmental time, we can see the adjustments each generation is making. Family members can realign their roles which ideally would lead to improved family cohesion. This approach can also place the individual within the context of other family relationships, and could be extended to include a cultural context (Hardy & Laszloffy, 2002).

Lifespan Tracks

Typically, generations are about 20–30 years apart. By the time the fourth (or youngest) generation is born, the first (or oldest) generation is dealing with late adulthood and end-of-life themes. If we imagine each generation's life span as a track, we can stagger these tracks or life paths and see where they overlap and intersect. This would provide us with a developmental slice of the intergenerational family in terms of developmental time. Each generation is at a different point in the life span, but chronologically, we are looking at this intergenerational family system at one particular moment in the family's history. See Figure 4–12 for an illustration of Intergenerational Lifespan Tracks in developmental time.

These intergenerational moments can be clearly observed at family gatherings and family transitions. If the extended family gathers for a joyous or a sad occasion, they offer each other support. It is also the time when all generations are present, allowing the observer a chance to delve into the family history and gather the anecdotes that become so precious once a generation has passed on.

Family Genograms

Genograms allow the conceptualization of family development (Dykeman in: Capuzzi & Stauffer, 2016). They place the person within the generations of their family, or within an intergenerational family system. A genogram is a form of family notation, similar to a family tree. It has the added ability to indicate family relationships such as emotional qualities between the members. Genograms can document a number of events that take place within family systems. By using various symbols and annotations, relational aspects can be documented. Genograms can be works in progress, where they become more intricate as the family evolves. It is based on the work of McGoldrick & Gerson (1985) and has been expanded by several contributors. It is frequently used in family therapy, and students who study families should be familiar with this form of family notation (Ballard, Fazio-Griffith, & Marino, 2016).

For this intergenerational genogram, we meet an imaginary multigenerational family—the Smith and Johnson families: paternal grandparents William and Ava Smith, and maternal grandparents Jacob and Olivia Johnson. Their children Liam Smith and Sophia Johnson marry and have two children: Noah and Emma Smith. The first and last names of this family are amongst the most frequently occurring names in the United States according to the U.S. Census of 2010.

The first genogram depicts a family with young children, and the genogram is straightforward (See Figure 4–13). In the second genogram about twenty

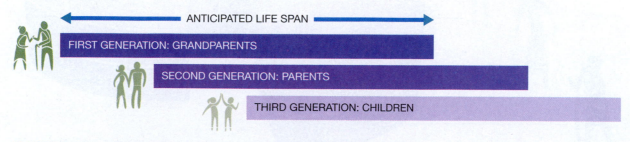

FIGURE 4–12. Intergenerational lifespan tracks in developmental time.

FIGURE 4–13. Genogram of a family with young children, depicting three generations.

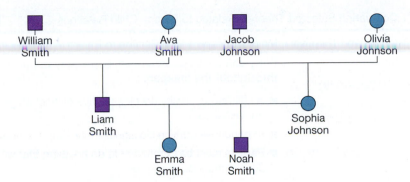

years later, the family has experienced the death of a parent, divorce and the formation of a new relationship to form a blended family. This progression in lifespan tasks is depicted in the greater complexity of the second genogram (See Figure 4–14).

This simple family genogram depicts three generations. Men are depicted with squares and women with circles. Genograms can document a number of events that take place within family systems.

The families twenty years later.   In this genogram, a line between Dan Matthews, to the right of Sophia Smith (née Johnson), represents a second marriage for Sophia and a blended family system for the children. This genogram is increasingly complex, as it shows the death of the maternal grandmother, the divorce of the parents, and the formation of a blended family system.

Parenting Reflection 4–4

How can families locate resources to help them cope with stressors even before they occur? Does advance knowledge help prepare people to react appropriately? Try to illustrate this with a practical example from your own experience.

Focus Point.   Systemic family development theory allows us to understand the complexity and diversity of families. By examining a family at a particular point in its developmental time, it is possible to see that families share common stressors that challenge each generation. This model has significant practical applications. Variations are to depict the families on a lifespan track, and these bear a resemblance to the generations depicted on genograms.

FIGURE 4–14. Genogram of the same family 20 years later, depicting death of a grandparent, divorce of the parents, and remarriage of one parent.

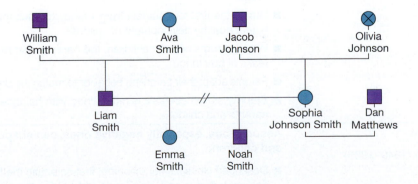

TABLE 4–4. Comparing Selected Theories Related to Parent–Child Relations

Selection of Theories and Theorists	Major Concepts/Ideas Related to Parent–Child Relations
Psychoanalytic Sigmund Freud (1886–1939)	**Early childhood experiences, especially the traumatic ones, can play a role throughout the lifespan.** ■ A child's personality develops in five distinct stages from infancy through adolescence. ■ Experiences early in life significantly shape later development. ■ Parents must be careful not to do anything that will fixate (stagnate) a child's development at any stage. ■ Parental strictness/restrictiveness inhibits children's healthy personality development. ■ Adult/child neuroses are caused by psychological trauma. ■ Parents must do and say the right thing at the right time to influence healthy development.
Psychoanalytic: Neo-Freudian Alfred Adler (1870–1937)	**Overindulgence, as well as neglect, of children (disengaged parenting) can cause problems in adulthood, especially in relationships.** ■ Our current focus on three parenting styles is partly attributed to Adler's work. He opened the first child guidance clinic in Vienna in 1921 and was a pioneer in developing parent education programs. ■ Social interest plays an important part in behavior. Behavior is motivated to maintain one's social interest. ■ Everyone strives for perfection/superiority in their behavior and interactions. ■ A child's personality is highly influenced by her or his birth order; parents treat children differently according to their birth order. ■ Boys are held in higher esteem than girls (masculine protest). ■ Behavior focuses on meeting goals, finding purpose, and channeling ideals. We are drawn toward the future rather than motivated by our past.
Psychosocial Erik Erikson (1902–1994)	**Healthy development at each stage lays the foundation for the subsequent stage. A good childhood is the foundation for appropriate adult development. Eight stages are described.** ■ Personality development occurs in *eight* distinct stages over the lifespan. An individual must master a crisis or challenge in order to move to the next stage. ■ During the first four stages, from infancy to adulthood, parents can assist or hinder healthy development of children. ■ When parents care for children, the parents also master major developmental tasks of adulthood. ■ Parents adapt their parenting behavior to match the developmental stage of the child. ■ Stability or homeostasis is maintained with balanced interactions between parents and children.
Behaviorist Ivan Pavlov (1849–1936)	**Associations, especially negative ones, can shape behavior in both animals and children.** ■ Described classical conditioning; first scientific method of learning demonstrated in animals. Conditioned a dog to salivate at the sound of a bell. ■ Behavior can be established and shaped by structured learning experiences; learning occurs strictly by association.

TABLE 4–4. (*Continued*)

Selection of Theories and Theorists	Major Concepts/Ideas Related to Parent–Child Relations
Behaviorist John B. Watson (1878–1959)	**Strong focus on the nurture component of the nature/nurture debate.** ■ Attempted to extend Pavlov's findings to human infants and children; "Little Albert" experiment (later ruled unethical). ■ Careful structuring of parental behavior produces certain predictable outcomes in child behavior. ■ Children's behavior can be carefully altered through conditioning experiences.
Operant Conditioning B. F. Skinner (1904–1990)	**The principles of conditioning can be found in certain disciplinary approaches in the form of reward and punishment.** ■ Parent's use of rewards and punishments enhance learning in children. ■ Positive reinforcement (reward) is a powerful tool in encouraging appropriate behavior in children. ■ Parents use operant conditioning when a child makes an association between an act and a consequence for that act. ■ Rewards can be used excessively; parents should use a mixed reinforcement schedule to extend the life and effectiveness of positive reinforcers. ■ Children can habituate to parental overuse of rewards. ■ To be effective, a positive reinforcer should immediately follow the desired act of a child.
Social Learning Albert Bandura (b. 1925)	**There is an emphasis on self-efficacy and self- esteem, which, if nurtured in children, will contribute toward success in adulthood.** ■ For learning to be successful, children must be motivated to learn. ■ Children learn by watching others' behavior (observational learning). ■ Internal mental processes, such as pride, enjoyment, and happiness facilitate learning. ■ Children can learn new information without any other behavioral changes. ■ In order to learn, children must pay attention; something that is new or interesting gains their full attention. ■ Children must retain information in order to perform a specific act. ■ Encouragement also promotes a child's learning experience. ■ A child's belief that she will succeed in learning, solving a problem, or mastering a situation, influences the behavior directed toward the task.
Cognition & Social Context	**Vygotsky, Piaget, and Bruner all emphasized that learning happens within a social context. This has far-reaching educational implications.**
Cognition Lev Vygotsky (1896–1934)	**Children learn while being scaffolded (supported) by significant adults in a zone of proximal development.** ■ Social interaction is the basis of a child's quest to find meaning and understanding of the world. ■ In children, social learning precedes and promotes development. Culture shapes cognitive development and understanding of the world. ■ Children are curious and are actively involved in their own learning process. ■ A skillful tutor acts as a More Knowledgeable Other (MKO) who models appropriate behaviors and provides instructions for understanding the world. Parents, peers, significant others, and objects can be sources for learning.

(Continued)

TABLE 4–4.   (*Continued*)

Selection of Theories and Theorists	Major Concepts/Ideas Related to Parent–Child Relations
	■ In the Zone of Proximal Development (ZPD) a child can accomplish tasks independently or with some help and instruction. A more knowledgeable other can support the learning process and promote skill development and higher mental functioning. It is similar to learning to ride a bike while being supported by training wheels. ■ Language is a child's tool for powering mental development.
Cognition Jean Piaget (1896–1980)	**Piaget emphasizes cognitive development (mental and thinking abilities), which parallels the physical development of the child.** ■ Innate mechanisms and processes allow children to learn how to organize their understanding of the world and how it functions, leading to the ability to use logic and form hypotheses. ■ Mental development is organized into five distinct, but related, stages—from infancy to late adolescence. ■ Experiences with the world form the basis of understanding; children spend much of their time developing a database of meanings by which to understand the world. ■ Language is the tool that accelerates mental development and enhances the ability to use thought and images to form mental representations of the world. ■ Symbolic thought emerges in childhood as children learn how the world operates; this limited understanding is later transformed into a more fluid way of understanding how the world operates in late childhood and adolescence. ■ Scientific thinking emerges in late childhood and adolescence based on the child's experiences in understanding how the world operates. ■ Parental guidance and help are important in providing a wide variety of experiences that help children learn how to organize their thoughts and promote advanced learning and understanding.
Cognition & Social Context Jerome Bruner (1915–2016)	**Bruner is credited with the concept of scaffolding (also used by Vygotsky). Interactions need to be framed within a social context. The role of culture is recognized.** ■ Children must learn how to represent their environment(s) in various ways in order to learn how to think and to think creatively. ■ Interactions with others, especially parents, as well as with cultural technologies, are important for promoting mental development. ■ Children (and adults) learn to represent their environment in three distinct, but related, ways. ■ Children of any age are capable of learning anything as long as it is properly organized. ■ Parents can help promote a child's mental development by providing stimulating language experiences.
Developmental Interaction Ellen Galinsky (b. 1942)	**Parents evolve parenting skills in response to their children's' developmental stages.** ■ Six developmental stages of parenthood.

KEY CONCEPTS

Several different, but related, theories can be applied to understand and study parent–child relations. Each provides insight into a particular aspect of this relationship. Some describe how the relationship changes over time; others describe how the relationship functions.

Theoretical Approaches

- *Attachment theory* is attributed to the work of Bowlby, who emphasized the importance of the early mother and infant relationship in terms of trust, nurturance, and responsiveness. He believed that this mutual focus on each other is instinctual. Several other important researchers, such as Klein, Ainsworth, Lorenz, and Harlow, added to our understanding of attachment and bonding. The theory is important in our understanding of early child-care situations. It has implications for international adoptions where some children spent their infancy in orphanages. It is also of importance in the legal setting, with implications for custody, adoption, and foster parenting.
- *Ecological systems theory* proposed by Bronfenbrenner, offers a way to understand family functioning against the backdrop of increasingly larger social systems. Bronfenbrenner suggests that five distinct environmental settings influence persons in their developmental progress. These are the micro-, meso-, exo-, macro-, and chronosystems. The relationships function in interaction with various environments and the people in those environments. The environments are nested within each other. This theory is also referred to as an ecological theory of development.
- *Systems theory* has been applied to the study of families. Family systems theory is useful in explaining the processes by which a family group makes decisions, sets and achieves particular goals, and establishes methods for governing the behavior of its members. This theory is helpful in describing how these processes work to maintain the stability of a family group over time and how the family reacts to changes that affect individual members and the group. According to this theory, several subsystems can be found within the larger family system—for instance, parental systems and systems comprising the children. These are usually based on relationships between two or more members, such as the adult spouses, parents and children, or brothers and sisters. Each subsystem has its own patterns that mirror those of the larger family system.
- *Family systems theory* uses several concepts to explain family functioning: wholeness, interdependence, patterns (i.e., rules, roles, and communication styles), reciprocal interaction and feedback, boundaries, entropy, equifinality, adaptation, and homeostasis. This approach is especially popular in the context of marriage and family therapy.
- *Systemic family development theory* is an extension of family systems theory that is useful in understanding how a family group changes in response to stressors that occur as part of the normal developmental processes of individuals. This realistic model of family life recognizes that families are complex and are composed of several interrelated generations. By taking a snapshot or slice of developmental time being experienced by a family, it is possible to examine the stressors that affect each generation in a family and study how a family responds to and copes with these stressors. By making adaptations in patterns, families are able to make the necessary changes to reestablish the stability in their functioning.

Erikson

- Erikson proposes a theory of eight stages that describe the psychosocial development of individuals over the life span. The stages start with trust versus mistrust in infancy, with resolution of the psychosocial crisis at each stage, and culminate with integrity versus despair in middle to late adulthood. This theory stresses
- The continuity of developmental changes over a person's entire life span.
- The resolution of a central crisis or challenge in each stage.
- The mastery or acquisition of a healthy or unhealthy psychosocial attitude at the completion of each stage.
- The assistance and support from significant others who assist or impede an individual's developmental progress.
- Erikson's theory may be applied to parent–child relations by examining the congruence between the psychosocial stages of parents and children. The concepts of reciprocal interaction and adaptation explain the changes in parenting behavior in response to the changing developmental needs of children. In turn, children help parents achieve their particular psychosocial attitude as they are the recipients of the caregiving behavior.

(Continued)

Other Theories

■ Other theories can be applied to parent–child relations. Learning theory stresses how behavior is modified through rewards and by observing the behavior of others. Cognitive theory, as described by Piaget, focuses on the cognitive development of the child and the role of physical and social experiences provided by parents in shaping how children come to understand their world. Vygotsky's observations emphasize how parents structure learning experiences in teaching children to master skills.

Developmental Role

■ Parenthood is a developmental role experienced in six distinct stages as proposed by Galinsky. These stages start with the image-making stage and proceed through the nurturing, authority, interpretive, and interdependent stages, culminating in the departing stage. The changes in the parental role are stimulated by the developmental changes in the child as the child grows older.

Christingasner/123RF.com

Approaches to parenting evolve and grow, using theories as points of departure.

CHAPTER FOCUS POINTS

Theories and Their Function

■ Theories are flexible ideas that reflect on observations or realities or try to find meaning and order from those observations. They are influenced by the social context, experiences, educational background, and opinions of the theorists behind them.

Standing on the Shoulders of Giants

■ In a macro-systemic manner, the various psychological theories and approaches concerning parent–child relations build one on top of the other, acknowledging previous contributions and incorporating much of the wisdom in an eclectic manner. As we reach forward, we are "standing on the shoulders of giants," where what has gone before paves the way for what is ahead.

Parents as Socialization Agents

■ As the behavioral and social sciences moved from a unidirectional to a bidirectional model of parenting, theorists began to focus on children's needs and the impact that parenting, either positive or negative, could have on children later in life.

Attachment Theory and Parenting

■ Attachment Theory focuses on the connection between an infant's early bonding experiences with a parent or caregiver and his or her ability to form trusting and loving relationships later in life. Multiple theorists have linked a lack of consistent nurturing in early childhood to various conditions and attachment disorders in adulthood. The theory is important in our understanding of early child-care situations, and can give insight into international adoptions, custody cases, and foster parenting.

Psychosocial Development Theory and Parenting

- Erik Erikson's framework for explaining the process of psychosocial development over the lifespan provides another means for interpreting the relationship between parents and children. He describes eight psychosocial stages. The framework focuses on developmental changes in individuals that occur in association with the passage of time. These changes occur within the context of the social environments that individuals experience throughout their lifespan. Parent–child relations change in response to the concept of reciprocal interaction.

Theories Related to Behavioral, Cognitive Behavioral, and Social Learning

- Theoretical approaches may be useful in understanding the social context of parent–child relations. Learning theory components (e.g., behavior modification and social learning) explain how parents teach children by using rewards to reinforce desirable behaviors and by serving as models of behavior. Cognitive behavioral theory stresses the importance of the experiences that parents provide for children as a means of shaping their mental life. These can be both physical and social in nature. Vygotsky's views expand on social learning to explain how parents teach skills to their children. Important concepts in this model are scaffolding and zone of proximal development.

The Family as a System

- Family systems theory explains the complex interactions of a family group. It addresses the factors that influence how the group makes decisions, sets and achieves goals, and establishes patterns that govern behavior. It explains how group stability is maintained. Concepts central to this theory include wholeness, interdependence, patterns (i.e., rules, roles, and communication styles), reciprocal interaction and feedback, boundaries, equifinality, adaptation, and homeostasis. The relationship between parents and children is one of several subsystems that make up a family system.

Ecological Systems Theory and Parenting

- Bronfenbrenner's ecological systems theory explains how individuals and families are affected by a variety of interacting environments in a bidirectional manner. An individual's family, by being part of the total environment, is also influenced by these other systems. The systems are nested within each other.

Systemic Family Development Theory

- Systemic family development theory allows us to understand the complexity and diversity of families. By examining a family at a particular point in its developmental time, it is possible to see that families share common stressors that challenge each generation. This model has significant practical applications. Variations are to depict the families on a lifespan track, and these bear a resemblance to the generations depicted on genograms.

USEFUL WEBSITES

Websites are dynamic and change

Attachment Parenting International
www.attachmentparenting.org
Parenting support, role of attachment in parenting

Bronfenbrenner Center for Translational Research, Cornell University
www.bctr.cornell.edu
Ecological systems theory

Erikson Institute, Graduate School in Child Development
www.erikson.edu
Child development

Jean Piaget Society, Society for the Study of Knowledge and Development
www.piaget.org
Cognitive theory

CHAPTER 5

Parenting: Rights and Responsibilities

Learning Outcomes

After completing this chapter, you should be able to:

1. Discuss the legal system's role in creating and enforcing parental guidelines.

2. Explain how the Constitution protects parental rights.

3. Identify the legal rights and responsibilities that parenthood entails.

4. Assess the responsible decisions parents need to make on behalf of their child.

5. Discuss the role of the government in child maltreatment.

6. Discuss the positive and negative outcomes of the current foster care system.

7. Differentiate between various types of parental custody.

8. Name some benefits that Parenting Plans offer families going through divorce.

9. Illustrate how the well-being of children is promoted at the state, federal, and global levels.

THE PRIVILEGE OF PARENTHOOD

Parents have rights, responsibilities, and privileges. What happens in the inner sanctum of the home may largely be their private concern. Presuming they have dependent children, parents can make many major decisions concerning those children, and in all likelihood there will be minimal interference by the law and those who enforce it. They will be guided in their decision making by policy and laws pertaining to the family, combined with their personal values and ethics; but generally, they can fly solo within the parameters of what is regarded as acceptable behavior, bearing good outcomes in mind.

There is a major and important proviso; their actions and decisions need to be in the best interests of the child, while also considering the well-being of the child's extended context, namely, the family and society at large. It follows that children have rights as well, and these reciprocal rights exert an influence on the parents and the way that they fulfill their roles in this capacity (Baumrind & Thompson, 2002).

Boundaries of Parental Autonomy

Parents can raise children with a great amount of autonomy. Even so, there is an invisible hand that regulates our behaviors as we are meeting societal demands and acceptable practices. We are socializing our children so that they can become fully functioning members of a particular society, and can benefit from the privileges and responsibilities that membership confers (Baumrind & Thompson, 2002). One of the functions of culture is that it is an intergenerational passing on of values, customs, beliefs, and generally useful information that is relevant for survival within that particular societal system or cultural group (Shiraev & Levy, 2016). In this context, culture exerts an influence on parenting practices as well.

The legal system (including public policy) similarly exerts a "guiding hand" or an "invisible hand" of subtle and not-so-subtle influence. What society requires from its members can be encouraged and, importantly, can also be discouraged by legal and ethical guidelines. Ethical and legal guidelines overlap, but whereas some of the ethical principles are only aspired to, the legal ones are enforceable. In law enforcement the punitive implications can range from mild warnings, reprimands, fines, and monetary obligations to the more serious, namely, loss of parental rights or imprisonment—which, in essence, represent loss of freedom and privileges. At the furthest extreme of punishment could be loss of life itself, the consequence of having willfully taken a life.

The phrase the "invisible hand" is attributed to the Scottish economist Adam Smith, who, in 1776, reflected about the economic influences in a society. He described the delicate balance between supply and demand. If the marketplace wants something, people will produce that item. The quantities and the price will be influenced by how much is available and who wants it. Think of the juggling of oil prices, or the price of land that is highly desirable and scarce, for instance on a beachfront. This principle is one amongst many forces that guide the economy.

Public policy and the law exert similar, seemingly undetected influences. As long as we function within the parameters of acceptable ethical and legally condoned behavior, we may never truly feel the guiding hand of the law. We may think that parents can raise their children in any way they like and have a lot of freedom in their parenting choices. But push at the edges of those parameters, or break them, and we may experience a ripple effect of far reaching consequences, typically with the intent of pushing us back towards where we fulfill our duties in legally condoned ways. Even so, the welfare of both children and their parents is of importance to the state. As Baumrind and Thompson state (2002, Vol V, p. 18):

> The State has considerable interest in the well-being of children. After all, children are citizens, as are their parents. But children are citizens with different qualities . . . they require special protections [and restrictions] that are not offered other citizens . . . that are suited to children's unique characteristics and needs.

Parents Causing Concern

After parents have provided cause for concern and the authorities have become involved, the law with regard to parenting can restrict parents in what they are doing. Alternatively, the law can require them to do things that are not required of the population in general— for instance, participate in drug screens, give up their parental time to the other parent, complete a parenting course, or even lose custody of the child concerned.

For every case of suspected or real abuse, an investigation should be initiated. Looking at the numbers of maltreatment cases reported, we notice that some do and some do not reveal a justifiable cause warranting further investigation and intervention. In 2013, in the United States, over 2 million cases were investigated out of concern, but not all these cases had cause.

Cultural Historical Snapshot 5–1

Cultural Paradigm Shifts

The Century of the Child

The 20th century promised to become the *century of the child*. Swedish reformer Ellen Key stated in 1909, that she anticipated that radical changes would occur in how we thought about children and that these shifts in turn would herald changes in our treatment of children:

> From the late 19th century onward, research on children has moved steadily from the margins to the center . . . during the [twentieth] century children's welfare and children's rights have become increasingly politically important (Montgomery, 2009, p. 1).

Mothering as Child Nurture

At more or less the same time in England, just preceding WWI, the *Infant Welfare Movement* was trying to positively transform child rearing conditions and approaches by offering mothers programs and help (as well as occasional threats). The goal was to reimagine motherhood and its role, not only in a woman's life, but also in the context of her family and in society at large. Reformers were intent on changing social policy, and one group specifically targeted the welfare of infants. At that time in British society, as may still be the case in many poor families to this day, the lower socioeconomic classes had to focus intently on day-to-day survival; making ends meet, feeding mouths while also providing clothing and shelter. The awareness that, as parents, they should also be concerned with the social and emotional development of their children hardly featured at the top of their priorities, as there were so many other pressing needs.

> Although much maternal passion and interest went into keeping the children fed and well, and mothers' relationships with their children could be intimate and satisfying, women's principal identity during this period remained that of managers of their households, rather than nurturers of their children. The "maternalist" Infant Welfare Reformers . . . thought that *mothering as child nurture* (italics added) should require new kinds of work, some of it defined by doctors, and should occupy a more central position in an adult woman's identity (Ross, 1993, p. 195).

Sources: Montgomery, H. (2009). *An Introduction to Childhood: Anthropological Perspectives on Children's Lives.* Oxford, U.K.: Wiley Blackwell.

Ross, Ellen. (1993). *Love and Toil. Motherhood in Outcast London*, 1870–1918. NY/Oxford: Oxford University Press.

This translates to about 29 potential concerns per 1,000 children, or almost 15% of children. Actual cases of proven maltreatment lowered the numbers to about 10% of all children (Herrenkohl, Leeb, & Higgins, 2016). These authors state that the incidence is probably higher if children were asked directly, as opposed to relying on reported incidences. The 10% average is in close accordance with the estimates by the Centers for Disease Control (CDC, 2014a) who reported maltreatment occurrences of about 9.2 per 1,000 children in the year 2012 in the United States.

Sometimes a report is made concerning the abuse of a child and the state, for various reasons, might not respond adequately. It may be difficult to fact check and prove a suspicion of abuse. On the other hand, a one-off incident may require the same rigor while investigating the full extent of the maltreatment claim. For example, a professional dad who threatened his son with a blunt butter knife became the subject of home visits by the social workers and an interlude in family court; all for having lost his temper. The fact that he did not have a history of violence, and was not serious with his intentions, mattered little in the short term, because the son had called the police. At that moment, the father's threat became the concern of the state and the wheels to protect the well-being of the minor son had been set in motion. In protecting minors, it is better to err on the side of caution, than to miss a genuine case of maltreatment.

The legal systems can regulate both desirable and undesirable behavior, but as long as we are acting within the parameters of the law, the guiding principles will shift into the background while we are getting on with the important task of living our lives and raising our children, or as the U.S. Declaration of Independence aptly describes it, as concentrating on: "Life, Liberty and the pursuit of Happiness" (Declaration of Independence, 1776).

Our parental independence is a little like finding a parking spot on a busy university campus. As long as we park in the appropriately assigned spaces, we will never know about the traffic warden. But park in that fire lane and the next thing, we find a ticket on our windshield representing a warning or a punishment.

Because parenting is usually done in partnership with another parent or coparent, the legal system is also utilized to referee the competing rights of noncooperating parents, for instance separated partners or divorced parents who find it difficult to collaborate in their parenting tasks. This can be likened to vigorously competing for the same parking spot. We call upon the judicial system to set parameters for parents who are not able to function as a unit.

Ethics of Parenting

> The ethics of parenting begins . . . with the assumption of responsibility for offspring by parents. Although parents do not alone have the responsibility for the welfare of children—the state . . . also has important obligations to children—parental responsibilities are first and foremost. (Baumrind & Thompson, 2002, Vol. V, p. 28)

A very general description of ethics in the context of the helping professions, is that it is a set of guiding principles to ensure best outcomes for the participants of and those affected by those relationships (Wilcoxon, Remley, & Gladding, 2013). In this context, helping professionals, are multi-disciplinary team members who work with families and children in a variety of contexts. The parties who may be directly or indirectly affected by ethical principles and guidelines are the participants of the helping relationship, in other words, the client and the help provider. A third party is involved, namely, the public or the society within which the behavior occurs. The latter group is affected by the responsible versus the irresponsible practice of a profession within their community and they provide the greater context or platform on which the ethical principles and guidelines are played out.

Many professions have ethical codes, and these codes may vary as different facets are emphasized, and the occupation requires a range of skills in varying contexts. As an example, the profession of locksmithing may have an ethical code of not misusing their privileged position of having access to homes, workplaces, and security

systems; and their code of ethics may also emphasize best interests and doing no harm. Simply stated, if a locksmith were to misuse her skills and privileges to gain unlawful entry into a home, that professional would be acting unethically and in the process also breaking the law. In many areas, ethics and the law overlap. (Linde & Erford, 2018). Professional organizations that regulate a particular profession may be assigned the role of enforcing the ethical conduct within their given profession. Family related professions can adhere to various codes of ethics, depending on the registering body providing licensure to their particular profession. Thus, there are codes of ethics for social workers, licensed counselors, psychologists, family life educators, and the like.

If parents are instrumental and major role players in the very complex relationships with their children, parents too may benefit from guiding principles. At this point, no formal ethical code for parents exists, but we do have the suggested "Rights of the Child" (UNICEF, n.d.) as a point of departure and various nations have created amendments to best meet their unique cultural and social needs.

Best Interests and Doing No Harm

Ethical principles contain the double faceted guide of:

- *Best interests* (beneficence)
- *Doing no harm* (nonmaleficence)

Best Interests and Doing No Harm.   The principle of best interests implies **beneficence**. It means thinking of the child's best outcomes, what is ultimately good for the child. This tends to be a *proactive* gesture, in that good outcomes are actively sought after. Additionally, parents should do no harm; in ethical contexts referred to as **nonmaleficence** (Erford, 2014, p. 67). Parents may try to justify their own behaviors or not realize that severe neglect or maltreatment represents harm to the child, and it is harm that is instigated by the party that the child should be able to trust, namely, the parent. Parents should go beyond being *reactive* in that they do no harm, they should also be *proactive* in their parenting relationships, so that they do good. In practice, these principles go hand in hand, although there are subtle differences and overlap.

Hippocratic Oath.   We can look back to the ancient Greek philosophers for inspiration on this topic. The best-known example of such a commitment to act ethically is the *Hippocratic Oath* (Emery, 2013). It contains the following commitments among many others quoted from the translation of the original Oath as well as from a later translation by Lasagna (1964). Note that the reference to doing no harm is contained within the first quotation, and forms part of the Hippocratic Oath:

> Into whatever houses I enter, I will enter to help the sick, and *I will abstain from all intentional wrongdoing and harm* . . . (italics added)

> I will remember that I remain a member of society, with special obligations to all my fellow human beings, those sound of mind and body as well as the infirm.

Oath of Maimonides. Some regard the *Oath of Maimonides* as a more recent supplement to the Hippocratic Oath. The words in this Oath are attributed to Moses Maimonides (1135–1204), a rabbi, scholar, and physician, and the Oath ends with:

> Thou hast appointed me to watch over the life and death of Thy creatures; here am I ready for my vocation and now I turn to my calling. (Seeskin, 2006)

We as parents, coparents, and persons concerned with the welfare of children, are the ones who have been appointed to watch over them and implement our calling to our best abilities. Most parents with good intentions tend to follow their inner compass of moral behavior and will often sacrifice everything in favor of the child entrusted to them. The problems arise with the minority who, for a range of reasons, both obvious and obscure, turn the sacred parent–child relationship into an unequal battleground, and exploit, abandon, and hurt those entrusted to them. Indeed, harm can be done.

• •

Recommended Resource on Ethics of Parenting

Baumrind, D. & Thompson, R. A. (2012). The Ethics of Parenting, Volume V: Pp. 3–34. In: Bornstein, M. H. (Ed.) *Handbook of Parenting*. New York, NY: Taylor & Francis, Psychology Press.

• •

Laws Reflect Culture

Laws reflect the culture of a society and are anchored in our ethical aspirations. Laws pertaining to the family serve to support and protect the family unit and its members. The parent–child relationship exists within this cultural context. Culture determines, among many other things, the roles and values that are passed down through generations. Laws in turn inscribe culture. They are the written forms of the policies, values, and norms of that particular society or nation. In the United States, the law is found in the federal and state constitutions, statutes, administrative rules, and executive orders, as well as in the judicial branch of the government that interprets laws. In this way, it can permeate society at all levels. The many tentacles of the law can reach out and touch and affect us in very obvious as well as virtually imperceptible ways.

> The ethics of parenting embraces both broadly generalizable . . . and culturally specific considerations. It could not be otherwise, respecting as we must the constructions of children's needs and parenting responsibilities that characterize cultures and cultural groups (Baumrind & Thompson, 2002, Vol V, p. 17).

Across the globe and across the parenting life cycle, the laws of a society strongly influence and determine many parental functions. Procreation, and its counter form, not procreating, is a personal decision and right. What may be taken for granted in some contexts may not be applicable in others. For instance, the decision to become a parent has been regulated in China by its one-child policy, replaced recently by a two-child policy (Attané, 2016). Although illegal, in some countries honor killings of young girls are implicitly sanctioned by the existence of legal loopholes for the perpetrator (Sev'er, 2012). On a positive note, providing generous support for parents through paternity and maternity benefits in terms of leave, pay, and child care, are examples of public policy that strongly support family life (Allen et al., 2014).

Cultural Change. As a society experiences cultural changes, the law often responds. For example, since the beginning of this millennium, attitudes towards same sex marriage have shifted. In a 2001 poll, only 35% of Americans supported same-sex marriage. Contrast this with the 55% support in 2016 (Fingerhut, 2016). Laws are revised and expanded to remain up-to-date and reflect current concerns. The area of parental rights and duties for same sex couples is one such area undergoing major revisions.

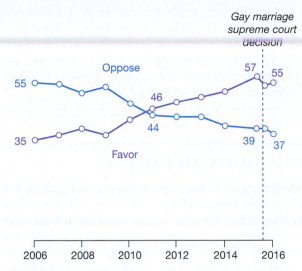

FIGURE 5–1. Support for same-sex marriage after 2015 Supreme Court ruling, percentage respondents opposed and those in favor.

Based on Survey conducted March 17-26, 2016 by Pew Research Center.

Laws can follow as well as initiate cultural change. The cause and effect is bidirectional. A change in the law can anchor a change in culture. For example, the Civil Rights Act of 1964 created a climate for change, but was also a response to a need for change (Inglehart, 2015). The act not only changed the law but also slowly impacted attitudes regarding equality for all races. In the 1970s, divorce laws eliminated the "fault" requirement as a necessary ground for dissolution of a marriage and made it easier to obtain a divorce (Leeson & Pierson, 2015). As more divorces occurred, there was less societal stigma attached to being a divorced parent or a child of divorce.

Focus Point. There is a subtle interplay between public policy, legal guidelines, and the wishes and actions of individual parents. Parents can express individual parenting styles, goals, and dreams for their children, hopefully with the proviso that they are in the best interest of the child and they follow the general ethical and legal guidelines of the society within which they are embedded. However, the law steps in when these guidelines are not upheld.

Parenting Reflection 5–1

When it comes to parenting, to what extent are parents free to implement their own choices while also considering the ethics, laws, and public policies of society at large?

What happens when parents disagree about a major aspect of parenting?

LAWS AND RIGHTS

Reproduction and the related outcome of parenting, is an individual right. This right to parent is preserved unless a parent is unfit or unable to provide for the care of his or her children. Linked to having children, as well as the alternate choice of *not* having children, are the rights pertaining to privacy and the right to procreation.

The 14th Amendment of the United States Constitution states "no state [shall] deprive any person of life, *liberty*, or property, without due process of law." (14th Amendment to the U.S. Constitution, n.d.). In a case in 1923, the United States Supreme Court upheld that liberty "denotes not merely freedom from bodily restraint but also the right of the individual to . . ." "*. . . establish a home and bring up children . . . according to the dictates of his own conscience . . .*" (emphasis added)

The laws of a society strongly influence and determine many parental functions throughout the parenting life cycle. An understanding of the court process and of laws pertaining to the family, can help practitioners and families navigate the complex legal system.

(Meyer v. State of Nebraska, 1923). Parents have a superior right to decide how to raise their children even if they are not following best parenting practices.

Grandparents

In a more contemporary case, grandparents asserted visitation rights, which were denied by the mother of the children (Baumrind & Thompson, 2002). This is the setting that led up to the court ruling in favor of the mother. Tommie Granville and Brad Troxel had a romantic relationship. They never married, but they had two daughters, Isabelle and Natalie. After the couple separated, Brad lived with his parents and regularly brought his daughters to his parents' home for weekend visitation. Brad committed suicide in 1993. After their son's death the grandparents continued to see Isabelle and Natalie on a regular basis. The children's mother exerted her rights and wished to limit visitation. Ultimately in the appeal, the United States Supreme Court found that the grandparent visitation statute violated the Federal Constitution. The Court cited the fundamental *liberty* interest, as a constitutional right (Troxel v. Granville, 2001).

This implied that parents *can* make decisions for their own children. The United States Supreme Court stated "it cannot now be doubted that the Due Process Clause of the Fourteenth Amendment protects *the fundamental right of parents to make decisions concerning the care, custody, and control of their children.*" (emphasis added) (Troxel v. Granville, 2001) The case described is a binding federal case law today, in that it must guide both federal and state courts in deciding similar issues.

Focus Point. The right to reproduce and parent children according to one's moral compass is outlined in the 14th Amendment of the Constitution. This section also upholds the parental right to make decisions for their children who are not yet of legal age.

THE RIGHT TO PARENT

When it comes to laws concerning parenting, there is a relationship between federal and state laws. An understanding of how the court system works and which courts hear what types of concerns is important knowledge for family life educators, social workers, and other family related professionals, as they provide support for a family enmeshed in a complex and sometimes confusing legal system (Johns, 2014).

Unless the issue at hand involves a federal question such as violation of the United States Constitution, legal issues pertaining to family life and parenting are a matter of individual state law. It is more likely that a family life professional or social worker will be called to testify or provide educational and background information in a state court. States have laws that regulate adoption, divorce, child custody, age of majority, emancipation from parental control, and rights of inheritance between children and their parents. There is a variation in these laws among states. As long as the state law does not run afoul of the United States Constitution or other federal law, they may vary from state to state.

Parenting FAQ 5–1

Does a divorce have to be by mutual consent? How is child support determined? What happens if my partner doesn't comply with the terms of our divorce agreement?

Most states have no-fault divorce laws, and all it takes is for one person to declare legally that the marriage is irretrievably broken and the divorce proceedings may begin. You will need to consult a lawyer for legal advice. Many states have a formula by which child support is determined. Usually, a couple's gross annual income forms the basis to determine how much each adult will contribute to child support. In some states, this formula may include how health insurance, childcare, and/or educational expenses are shared by each adult. The divorce agreement will include stipulations about child support and visitation. You can return to court for legal redress of your complaints regarding any violations of the divorce agreement, and/or you can call upon the county sheriff's office for assistance in having the terms of your agreement enforced. Mediation may be helpful.

Rights and Responsibilities

The **right** to parent is a bundle of rights, including much more than the right to decide with whom a child may visit. Health care, education, religious affiliation, and extracurricular activities are areas in which parents make decisions for their minor children. When parents are unmarried or divorced, certain legal parameters are in place to ensure a child has access to both parents and that both parents are able to participate in raising their child. The child has a right to emotional, physical, and financial support from both parents. Parents have a right to a relationship with their child. The parent–child bundle of rights is bidirectional.

With rights come **responsibilities** of parenting, and the law holds parents accountable for meeting the basic needs of their children. Legally mandated parental duties come primarily from state laws, although federal legislation has provisions to which states must adhere in areas such as child abuse, foster care, child support, education, and interstate custodial issues.

The role of a family life professional, social worker, or family related service provider includes that of educator and advocate. It is vital for these professionals to become familiar with the legal environment in which they and their clients operate. Knowledge of the legal context means resources can be tapped and rights accessed that may benefit the family (Johns, 2014).

Many times a parent will not have enough information to ask the right questions. A trained advocate fills the gap and enhances healthy parenting. The list of questions that a family life educator, social worker, or helping professional may be called upon to answer are endless. Where does a single mother who cannot afford a lawyer go to get child support from the father of her child? How can an unmarried father establish visitation with his child if the child's mother denies him access? What practices should be avoided or put in place in an adoption so that both the biological and adoptive parents are protected and the adoption creates a secure permanent environment for the child? What happens to children when they do not have a parent willing or able to care for them? Are children with disabilities entitled to any special protections and rights?

Preventing Delinquency.   As long as a child is a minor, the adults in a child's life have a responsibility to guide the child towards healthy development, general

FIGURE 5–2.   With rights come responsibilities of parenting, and the law holds parents accountable. Laws pertaining to the family serve to support and protect the family unit. Laws reflect the culture of a society and are anchored in our ethical aspirations.

welfare, and best outcomes. There are state variations concerning the age when the minor transitions to adult status in the eyes of the law. As long as the child is of *minor* status, parents, guardians, and other specified adults such as teachers, have a responsibility towards that minor. An adult who fails to prevent unlawful behavior or actively leads a minor astray is implicated. For instance, if an adult exerts a negative influence over a minor, such as by condoning or facilitating substance abuse, or supporting and encouraging unlawful behavior, or engaging in sexual activities with the minor, that adult failed in their expected legal and ethical role towards the minor. In legal terms this can be seen as causing, inducing, abetting, encouraging, or contributing towards waywardness or delinquency of a child and is punishable by law (Wilcoxon, Remley, & Gladding, 2013, p. 274).

Responsible Parenting

The task of parenting continues throughout the parental lifespan, even though the nature of that relationship alters to reflect developmental changes in both parents and offspring. The rights, duties, and responsibilities change accordingly. Those who practice family law, or work in areas related to family support in legal contexts, know that every stage of the lifecycle can be affected. The influences start prenatally, proceed through raising children, and they continue till after death. Part of this cycle will focus on marital, cohabiting, and other partnerships.

In the lifecycle, we make promises, maybe supported by formal contracts. Ideally, if all were well in the world, and we all behaved like exemplary citizens, then we would not need so many legal guidelines. But typically the trouble starts when we seek to enforce the "exit clause"—when we no longer want to be with this particular partner, if we can no longer support our child, if parenthood had not been on our agenda in the first place.

Who is responsible for the children if we have children? What happens to the children if we divorce? Who supports them and until when? And once we die, can our children inherit and benefit from our assets? Clearly these questions have become a part of the recent history of humankind, and the legal system has taken on the task of finding responsible ways through this maze of human decision making and behavior. Even so, there can be state-specific variations.

Age of Majority.   A look at the *age of majority* illustrates this variation. A child becomes an adult for many legal purposes when they reach the age of majority. Parents are no longer legally responsible for the child's care and financial support. A person reaching the age of majority is able to enter into a contract without parental consent. The ability to contract is important if a young person wants to buy a car or rent an apartment without parental involvement. The age of majority in the United States is typically 18 for most purposes, but in some states it can extend until the age of 21 (National Conference of State Legislatures: Termination of Support—Age of Majority, 2015).

Pregnancy and Prenatal Responsibilities.   The choice to have children as well as the alternative, namely to remain childless, is not regulated; it is regarded as a private and personal choice (Duncan, 2016b). A person needs to give consent for their own permanent surgical sterilization and if married, the spouse needs to be part of that decision-making process. Whether a couple wants children or not, should be one of the key conversations they have *before* legitimizing their relationship. However, asking about intent to have children and similar family related questions are not appropriate in, for example, formal job interviews, and cannot be used in a discriminatory manner.

Prenatally, parents, and especially the pregnant mother, are responsible for a lifestyle that should support healthy outcomes for that pregnancy. Public policy has guided towards best practices. Mothers who inadvertently were exposed to teratogens that affected the unborn, e.g., medications and other harmful substances, have been part of class action suits against pharmaceutical and other companies who contributed to the detrimental outcome, even if this was inadvertent. The Thalidomide tragedy around 1957, when the drug was first marketed, is such an example (Källén, 2016). Children were born with limb deficiencies and severe disabilities. Another situation with extremely negative outcomes that affected many couples, surrounded an intrauterine contraceptive device that led to severe infections and in some cases sterility. These lawsuits not only fulfill a compensatory role; they also serve to heighten responsibility so that these types of outcomes are avoided in the future. Many states have enacted criminal laws prohibiting pregnant women from *intentionally* using substances that negatively impact an unborn child (Gaspari, 2016).

Reflection 5–1

A Father's Letter to an Unborn Child

In the 1970s a contraceptive alternative in the form of an intrauterine device (IUD) was introduced and used by millions of women. For some women, these devices caused infections, leading to infertility and sometimes death. The company producing the devices faced around 350,000 lawsuits and declared bankruptcy (Grunwald & Adler, 1999, pp. 607–608). Here, a few sentences from a father's letter to the child he would never have:

> Dear Son or Daughter, I write this letter to you because I don't know what else to do. You never existed. You were never born. You never even had a chance to be born because of a mistake your mother and I made a long time ago.

The father then continues to explain that his wife had a hysterectomy as a result of an infection caused by the IUD. He laments that the child they had wished for will never join their family. In his letter he ends with:

> "I feel the same way as I started . . . empty. Your father who never was nor will be . . ."

Based on: Grunwald, L., & Adler, S. J. (Eds.). (1999/2008). *Letters of the Century: America 1900–1999.* New York, NY: The Dial Press.

Focus Point.   Parents can make personal and private choices concerning the right to procreate, as well as the right *not* to have children. As such, either of these choices is legally protected and privacy is respected. A person who chooses to become a parent is legally responsible for that child from pregnancy until the age of majority.

Parenting Reflection 5–2

Do you think there may be any situations in which the right to have a child or to *not* have a child could be legally regulated? Be warned that these topics can lead to heated and divided discussions as they touch on intensely personal values and convictions. Persons do not all share the same point of view.

LEGAL PATERNITY AND MATERNITY

Assisted reproduction has brought a new set of legal issues. Some states have responded with laws regulating the practice, while other state laws are silent. Battles between would-be parents ensue, to determine *legal paternity* and *maternity*. There are those disputes that arise because multiple couples or individuals want to raise the child and enjoy the benefits of mutual love and affection characterizing a healthy parent–child relationship. They desire that the child benefits from their social security, military, or other financial rewards to which only a legal child is entitled.

Typically, sperm and ovum donors, who wish to remain anonymous and supply their services in commercial contexts, as well as gestational carriers, relinquish their rights to claim parenthood. The first baby produced from genetic material from three parents, was born in 2016. The maternal mitochondrial material was supplied by a donor as the mother carried a gene that put her offspring at risk for severe and debilitating disease leading to miscarriage or death in infancy (Hamzelou, 2016).

Because human beings are who they are, and because circumstances and minds can change, these situations have been contested. Legal advice before considering these complex relationships is strongly advised. Contracts are typically mandatory when using commercial sperm and ovum banks. Not all would-be-parents follow official guidelines when it comes to achieving parenthood. Some create their own informal arrangements, and once the context of that situation changes, a lot of second guessing can occur. Assisted reproduction such as the use of a surrogate may cloud the issue of parentage creating a disparity between biological and legal parents. Ultimately, the best interests of the child should be considered, including emotional attachments the child has formed. Unfortunately, in many of these cases legal parental rights may trump best interest.

For as many happy outcomes, there are also heartbreak stories. One well publicized case concerned an international gestational carrier, who gave birth to twins, one healthy female and one male with a chromosomal abnormality. Once the twins were born, the biological donor parents took the healthy, female twin back to Australia but rejected the male twin with Down's Syndrome, leaving him to be raised by the surrogate mother (Schover, 2014).

Establishing Paternity and Maternity

The contemporary family comes in many variations, with fatherhood, and even motherhood, not always easily discernible. A child has a right to a relationship with both parents and to be supported by them during minority. Parents have the responsibility to register the baby's birth. In the United States, about four out of every ten children are born to unwed mothers (National Center for Health Statistics, 2016). Determination of not only paternity but also maternity may depend on the legal process. Same sex married couples face a fluid legal environment in establishing both partners as parents.

Federal laws provide parameters for determination of paternity. The National Conference of State Legislatures has summarized a number of requirements supporting best practices that include allowing paternity to be established at any time before a child turns 18. A court can order genetic testing even if paternity is denied, both parents need to be informed of the implications if paternity is established, genetic tests are accepted as evidence, procedures are in place at hospitals and birth record agencies to acknowledge paternity, fathers are permitted to establish paternity, and several other related guidelines exist ("Child Support 101.2: Establishing Paternity," 2014).

When a child is born to a legally married couple, the husband is presumed to be the father and the wife is presumed to be the mother. A birth certificate reflects the names of the parents and is recorded with the appropriate state agency. When nonbiological parents legally adopt a child the original birth certificate is changed and an amended one is issued.

If a child is born to an unmarried mother and the father is present and willing to sign an affidavit of paternity in the hospital, he becomes a *presumed father*. His name is placed on the birth certificate. A presumed father's status does not equate with that of a legal father, but gives the presumed father parental rights including the right to be notified regarding legal matters concerning the child and the responsibility for support of the child. The father or mother may bring an action in court to judicially establish paternity. The court usually addresses custody and support in a paternity hearing. An order by a court requiring support from a parent implies legal status of a parent. This can become a burdensome undertaking for someone who did not intend nor wanted to be a parent.

. . . .

Parenting Reflection 5–3

Reflect on the greater diversity of family form and function in the 21st century by considering the advances in assisted reproductive techniques, as well as sophisticated contraceptive choices. These have allowed individuals to make diverse reproductive decisions that suit their personal circumstances. Have these choices been accompanied by new legal challenges?

. . . .

Paternal Rights.   If it is alleged that a man is the father of a child, although no legal determination of paternity has been made he is a *putative father* under the uniform Paternity Act that some states have adopted (Child Welfare Information Gateway, 2014b).

As a **putative father**, a person may still have a limited degree of due process rights as far as notification of legal proceedings affecting the child. By registering as a putative father within the appropriate time frame, the father is entitled to notice of adoption proceedings concerning the child. This process does not guarantee that an adoption will not be granted. Instead it gives a person who believes he is the father of a child the right to be heard on the issue of paternity. Putative father registries give potential fathers rights when a mother cuts off all ties with the father and refuses to reveal her whereabouts during pregnancy and birth. Previously, there was little recourse for a father if a mother named the father as "unknown" and gave consent for an adoption without a fair determination of paternity. The advancement and accuracy of DNA genetic testing has changed the field of paternity determination dramatically. Testing results can determine or rule out paternity or maternity with 99.9% accuracy (Ryan et al., 2013).

Dependency

In most contexts, parents have a responsibility to provide for the care and support of their children. The law neither defines the "ideal" parent nor requires a parent to meet that standard. If parents do not meet the basic needs of their children, if they neglect, abuse, or allow their child to be abused, the government will step in to protect the child. Many factors contribute to identifying the basic standard a parent must meet including cultural norms, availability of financial and educational resources, special needs of parents or children, and extended family support.

Under the doctrine of *parens patriae*, translated as "the parent of the nation," the government has the right and duty to protect those who cannot protect themselves. A *dependent* child is a child who is in need of protection because her parents will not or cannot provide for the basic care of their child.

Medical Treatment

The ethical principle that is a guiding force in the context of medical decision making is: *"First of all, do no harm."* If an intervention can intentionally worsen the situation, it clearly should not be the first choice.

Constitutionally protected rights are not absolute. Does the *right to parent*, and does the First Amendment right to *freedom of religion*, include the right to withhold lifesaving medical treatment from a critically ill or even dying child? Generally the answer is no, although some children do not receive the optimal medical care due to a parent's religious practices. Each situation may be different but generally if it is a life-or-death decision, the courts can overrule the decisions of the parents, considering the best interests of the child.

A situation that implicates quality of life and prospects for recovery may be more complex. For instance, a child in a long-term coma—where tests found no brain activity and no independent breathing ability—could be taken off life support, despite parental wishes to the contrary, once the courts have made that decision. In other words, that decision cannot be made solely by the parents or the hospital staff (Burkle & Pope, 2015).

Living Will

For adults, having a living will may simplify matters as it intends to express the wishes of the person concerned, but when minor children are concerned these are complex decisions and individual situations differ. These situations can also be contentious when parents disagree. The same can also be true when the state will not allow the parents to take their child off life support. Several big cases have helped determine the "Right- to-Die." In short, these situations are very complex (Campbell, 2017).

More common and less dramatic are choices related to vaccination of children. Indirect pressure is exerted because educational institutions require proof of certain vaccinations, or alternative medical documentation if a child has not been vaccinated. These vaccinations are available at minimal or no cost at public clinics.

Video Example 5.1 In Brief: The Science of Neglect

Watch this video on child maltreatment and neglect. How can maltreatment and neglect cause lasting harm to the development of young children?

(https://www.youtube.com/watch?v=bF3j5UVCSCA)

Education

Responsibility to Educate.   In developed countries, one of the ongoing duties of parenthood is to ensure that children are educated. Typically, parents and their children can access free public schooling, which is usually compulsory until the age of 16. To support these educational efforts, transport to and from schools can be free as well, and some schools provide lunch programs at no cost to children who do not have secure access to food. In America, children with special needs have access to the specialized care and support in an appropriate school environment that acknowledges their unique needs.

Home Schooling.   Parents who decide for whatever personal reason that they do not want to use public schooling and basically do not want their children exposed to this form of education, have the option of placing their children in private schools and footing the bill for that, or they could home-school. But homeschooling in the United States does not confer a carte-blanche to the parent. Homeschooling parents have to follow a curriculum, belong to a homeschooling organization, and generally ensure that their children receive the benefits of an extended and structured

Just over a century ago, children were still laboring in factories in the United States. Compulsory schooling has helped improve conditions for U.S. children. The original caption of this historical photo was: "Hattie Hunter, spinner in Lancaster Cotton Mills, S.C. 52 inches high, worked in mill for 3 years. Gets 50 cents a day. Dec. 1, 1908. Location: Lancaster, South Carolina."

education. The U.S. Department of State publishes details concerning homeschooling requirements as well as resources and some recognized homeschooling programs. Kunzman & Gaither (2013) published an extensive review on the research and scholarship surrounding homeschooling.

Religious and Other Education.   When it comes to religious education, it is generally regarded as the personal responsibility and privilege of the parents, especially as church and the state are separated in the United States. In many contexts, sex education is also the parents' responsibility and privilege, although most schools offer formal and developmentally appropriate sex education programs to children. Parental consent may be required to attend the information sessions. Outlines of sex and relationship education guidance for the United Kingdom emphasize the broader context of sexuality in terms of relationship education.

Discipline and Control.   Generally, it is the privilege of the parents to discipline and guide their children. Note that corporal punishment is generally not sanctioned in the United States and can elicit legal response. But laws in this area are in flux, and some states do not have laws that prohibit corporal punishment—paddling may still occur in some school situations. Clearly, punishment that leans towards abusiveness, or is abusive, is treated with the same seriousness as maltreatment of the child, as the differences can become indistinguishable.

• •

Focus Point.   Parents have both the right and responsibility to guide their children in all aspects of life, a task often influenced by cultural norms, availability of resources, special needs of parents or children, and extended family support. Aside from providing care and support to meet the child's basic needs, parents are also responsible for making decisions about their child's medical treatment, education, and discipline.

• •

CHILD MALTREATMENT

The 1874 child abuse case of Mary Ellen McCormack sparked a movement that continues today to prevent child maltreatment. At that time in the United States,

there were no laws specifically protecting *children* from parental abuse and so the case of Mary Ellen was brought to court by the American Society for the Prevention of Cruelty to *Animals* (American Humane Society, 2016; Coller, Stewart-Brown, & Blair, 2015). See Historical and Cultural Snapshot 5-2. Victorian England grappled with similar challenges and passed the "Children's Charter," formally known as the "Prevention of Cruelty and Protection of Children Act of 1889." It allowed the state to take permanent care of children who had to be removed from cruel, abusive, and harsh home environments. Legislation surrounding child labor was also introduced (Ross, 1993, p. 24).

Video Example 5.2 The NYSPCC- History

Watch this video on the "United Nations Conventions on the Rights of the Child." How does this treaty aspire to improve outcomes for children
  (https://www.youtube.com/watch?v=VgoRJH6n61g)

For a child to become dependent and thus enter the child welfare system, numerous family stressors may contribute (Kisiel et al., 2013). Addiction disorders interfere with the ability to parent and can have long lasting negative effects on children. Relapse from addiction is common and creates family instability (Child Welfare Information Gateway, 2014a). Incarceration, death, or mental illnesses are also factors that may lead to dependency. Today's extended family is often geographically scattered, and there may be no safety net for some parents experiencing extreme difficulties. Unfortunately, negative coping mechanisms sometimes lead to child neglect or mental and physical abuse.

Today *mandatory* reporting laws require some individuals, such as health-care workers, teachers, and social workers, to report suspected child abuse (Lynne, Gifford, Evans, & Rosch, 2015). If a person is not a mandated reporter, they can still report an abuse situation to the appropriate state agency. A non-mandated reporter is called a *permissive reporter* and may be following best practice. Each state has a designated agency to deal with these complaints (Child Welfare Information Gateway, 2016).

According to federal requirements in the Adoption Assistance and Child Welfare Act of 1980 and the

Cultural Historical Snapshot 5–2

"Inhumane Treatment of a Little Waif," 1874

Testimony in court by 10-year-old Mary Ellen McCormick on April 9, 1874. *The decision in this case is considered to be the first adjudicated case of child abuse in the American court system.*

"I don't know how old I am. I have no recollection of a time when I did not live with the Connollys. I call Mrs. Connolly mamma. I have never had but one pair of shoes, but I can't recollect when that was. I have had but no shoes or stockings on this winter. I have never been allowed to go out of the room where the Connollys were, except in the nighttime and then only in the yard. I have never had on a particle of flannel. My bed at night has been only a piece of carpet stretched on the floor underneath a window, and I sleep in my little under-garments, with a quilt over me. I am never allowed to play with any children, or have any company whatever. Mamma (Mrs. Connolly) has been in the habit of whipping and beating me almost every day. She used to whip me with a twisted whip—a raw-hide. The whip always left a black and blue mark on my body. I have now the black and blue marks on my head, which were made by Mamma with the whip, and also a cut on the left side of my forehead, which was made by a pair of scissors. (Scissors produced in court.) She struck me with the scissors and cut me. I have no recollection of ever having been kissed by anyone—have never been kissed by Mamma. I have never been taken on my mamma's lap and caressed or petted. I never dared to speak to anybody, because if I did I would get whipped. I have never had, to my recollection any more clothing than I have at present—a calico dress and shirt. Whenever Mamma went out I was locked up in the bedroom. I do not know for what I was whipped—Mamma never said anything to me when she whipped me. I do not want to go back to live with Mamma because she beats me so. I have no recollection of ever being in the street in my life."

Postscript: The rulings from these court proceedings recommended removal of Mary Ellen from the home where she had been abused and termination of parental rights. She was initially placed in a home for "delinquent" teenagers, as it was referred to at that time, which was not ideal. Later she was welcomed by a supportive family. She married at age 24, had several children, and was a responsible and caring mother. She died in 1956 at the ripe old age of 92. By all accounts, she appeared to parent her own children lovingly and constructively, overcoming her own experiences of abuse and maltreatment.

Quotation of the child's testimony is in the public domain. Source part of the court records of 1874. Subsequently recounted in an article by physician and medical historian Howard Markel. Quote in this historical snapshot published in the Milbank Quarterly: Op Ed by Howard Markel: December 2016.

Retrieved from: https://www.milbank.org/quarterly/articles/neglected/

Markel, H. (2009). Case shined first light on abuse of children. *New York Times*, December 14. March 21, 2017. Another version of this article appears in print on December 15, 2009, on page D5 of the National edition with the headline: The Child Who Put a Face on Abuse.

Retrieved from: http://www.nytimes.com/2009/12/15/health/15abus.html?_r=0.

Adoption and Safe Families Act of 1997, states must use *reasonable efforts* to prevent removal of children from their own homes, or reunify the family if children must be separated from their parents. Services such as therapy, supervised visitation, child care, transportation, and drug screens are offered to parents who try to keep or to regain custody once their children enter the child welfare system. There are exceptions to the *reasonable efforts* requirement for particularly flagrant conduct on the part of parents. For example, if a parent abandons a child or has been convicted of murder of another child in the family, the state is not obliged to rehabilitate the offending parent.

Best Interest of the Child

State juvenile or family courts have jurisdiction over dependency or child protection cases. Either by state mandate or *best practice*, the court appoints an attorney advocating for the best interest of the child. The attorney or advocate is known as a *guardian ad litem*.

The best interest standard is the *overriding guideline* in juvenile court proceedings where parental rights must be balanced with the safety and well-being of children. A guardian ad litem differs from an attorney appointed by the court to defend a child who has been charged with a juvenile offense. The juvenile attorney is appointed to ensure that the child's rights are protected, including making the state prove beyond a reasonable doubt that the charge against the juvenile is correct. The best interest standard used by the guardian ad litem may or may not coincide with what a child wants. Nevertheless, the guardian ad litem should professionally know the children she represents and explain legal directives in a developmentally appropriate manner while also following best practices.

Focus Point. Due to progress in child protection laws, mandated reporters and court-appointed advocates are among the roles that have been established to detect and prevent child abuse. If abuse of a child is suspected, it is the job of the legal system to protect that child, often to the point of revoking parental rights.

CHILDREN IN FOSTER CARE

In 2014 in the United States, there were over 400,000 children in foster care. Of these, more than half were in non-relative homes or group homes (Children's Bureau, 2015). Figure 5–3

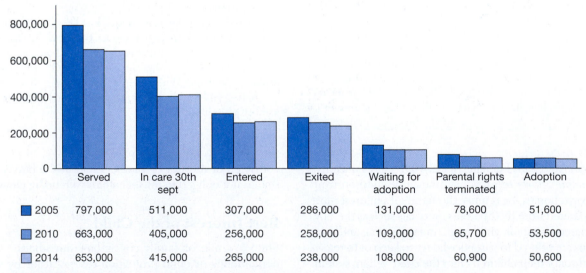

	Served	In care 30th sept	Entered	Exited	Waiting for adoption	Parental rights terminated	Adoption
2005	797,000	511,000	307,000	286,000	131,000	78,600	51,600
2010	663,000	405,000	256,000	258,000	109,000	65,700	53,500
2014	653,000	415,000	265,000	238,000	108,000	60,900	50,600

FIGURE 5–3. Trends in Foster Care and Adoption: FY 2005-FY 2014.
Yearly cut off date for data is 30th September.
Source: AFCARS data, U.S. Children's Bureau, Administration for Children, Youth and Families.

New York Foundling Asylum - Sister Irene and her flock. This historical photo from 1888 depicts children in care and was originally titled: "The New York Foundling Asylum: Sister Irene and her flock"; the word 'asylum' meaning a place of shelter. Through social reform and public policy guidelines, significant progress has been made in working towards improved outcomes for children.

Although the goal of the child welfare system is to achieve *permanency* in a child's living situation, this goal is often not reached. Family reunification is not possible for all children. Finding adoptive homes for older children, special needs children, and sibling groups, is more difficult than placing healthy newborns. Adverse childhood experiences such as abuse, neglect, and family dysfunction have a negative impact on well-being (Lereya, Copeland, Costello, & Wolke, 2015). Children living in foster care are more likely to have experienced at least one or even multiple adverse childhood experiences than children living with two biological parents. More than half the children in foster care had experienced violence by their caregiver in one study. Almost two-thirds had lived with someone with addiction-related problems (Bramlett, & Radel, 2014).

Multiple placements cause instability, yet they are common in the foster care system, often out of necessity. A child may experience several placements before finding a "forever home." A change in placement may disrupt a child's education and can create stress as the child repeatedly has to adjust to a new environment. Being uprooted does not foster bonding, attachment, or emotional investment. This is also reflected in poor school performance. School aged foster children rank amongst the bottom 30% and only half will graduate. Even fewer will succeed at college level (The Stuart Foundation, 2013).

After foster children come of age or become emancipated by a court, few resources assist them with the transition to adulthood. The federal government has recognized the importance of providing transitional services. The "Fostering Connections to Success," and "Increasing Adoptions Act of 2008," extend the age for foster care services from 18 to 21 years. Risks of unemployment, homelessness, incarceration, and other negative outcomes are higher in children growing up in foster care (Barn & Tan, 2015; Courtney et al.; 2011).

Children can languish in the foster care system while reasonable efforts are made to rehabilitate their parents. Federally mandated timetables limit the time that children can be in state custody. Federal policy and law seeks permanency for children. Courts are required to review the case of a child in foster care every six months and a permanency hearing must be held once a year. If parents cannot be rehabilitated, a placement with a relative is sought. Nowadays, grandparents may be raising their grandchildren if parents dismiss their responsibilities for the care of their children (Kirby & Sanders, 2013). If there is no suitable relative, the state will seek to *terminate* parental rights so that a constructive adoption outcome can be sought. Refer to Figure 5–4.

The picture for foster children is not all bleak. Some foster children exhibit admirable resilience. Factors that build resilience, such as emotional support, and an ongoing and permanent relationship with a suitable mentor can be life changing. Dr. Norman Eggleston was a respected and accomplished social worker and academic. He spent much of his childhood in foster care with multiple placements. He ascribed his success to the ongoing interest and mentorship of his social worker. He was honored with a scholarship named after him and he was inducted into the Alabama Hall of Fame for Social Work (2002).

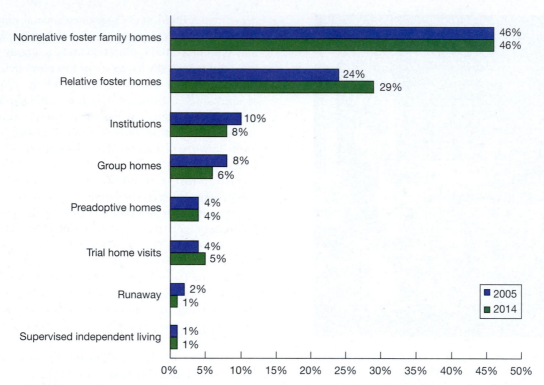

FIGURE 5–4. Placement Settings for Children in Foster Care on September 30 in 2005 and 2014.
Source: Children's Bureau, Foster Care Statistics 2014.

Focus Point. Children living in foster care are more likely to have experienced abuse, neglect, and general family dysfunction. Commonly, multiple placements disrupt the child's day-to-day routine, adding stress and preventing adequate bonding. Once a foster child reaches the age of majority, resources are scarce to assist them as they transition into adulthood.

Guest Reflection 5–2

The Two Sides of Parenting:

Life in the Foster Care System Is Consistently Inconsistent

When I was eleven years old, my mother fetched my sister and me from school early. We got into my grandmother's car, innocently and trustingly thinking we were going on a field trip, after all we left school early. We arrived at a very big building where we were met by a man we did not know. Instead of the early school break that promised to be a nice adventure; these were the first few hours towards a place I hope no child has to go.

Like a bombshell, my mother shattered our world with a few sentences. She explained that she was incapable of taking care of us, and she promised she would turn her life around and come back for us in a few weeks. That was then, and we believed her.

My mother had left us in what seemed like an overwhelmingly huge building with people we did not know. We were taken for a physical examination to rule out maltreatment. Being so young we did not fully understand that our mother struggled with drug abuse and depression. Now I know that she did not make this decision lightly, and at the time she must have hoped it was for the best. Nevertheless, we felt abandoned.

A few hours later, two women picked us up with "We're going to take care of you both for a while." The first week was very hard, and it took me many years to fully accept my mother's decision. My time in the foster care system consisted of five different schools and numerous foster parents. Some parented better than others, although most of them meant well. There were times when the foster parents fulfilled the roles of parental figures, other times they were emotionally absent. The ones who tried, recognized my needs and met them, enrolling me in tutoring when I was struggling academically, and taking me to weekly psychotherapy when I felt overwhelmed.

Being a child in the foster care system meant my biological parents surrendered their legal rights as parents, and relinquished them to the court system. For ten years, I had monthly meetings with a social worker. Sadly, it was hard to keep the same social worker which added to my struggle with rejection and abandonment. At one point, my sister and I were separated, which really felt as if I had lost the last close relationship.

And then, slowly, things started turning around. In eighth grade, I was placed with a new social worker. She was honest, compassionate, and I recognized her sincere desire for my success. We are still friends, and have coffee whenever I'm in town. In my freshman year of high school, I was finally placed in a nurturing and supportive home. It was with these parents that I was cultivated towards being a healthy person. They taught me how to communicate, how to trust, how to be myself without the fear of rejection. I was treated in a way that gave me self-confidence and my self-esteem grew. I slowly learned how to love and trust and how to receive love from others.

With the support of my family, the court system behind me, and my personal determination, I have grown into that person nobody imagined I would become. I have graduated from a four-year private university, paying my own way. I have aspirations to work in the international domain and to support the process of creating family policy. I believe I will achieve those dreams. Despite the past, and at times my lack of having been parented, I not only survived—I thrived.

The reasons why I have been successful are because of the relentless support of my parents; they believe in me and encourage me to do the best I can. When I made mistakes they did not stop loving me or give up on me. They reiterated their love and helped me fix my mistakes. My parents taught me what was right and wrong, but allowed me to make my own mistakes and were there to help me when I needed them. I was taught that I wasn't the mistake of my biological parents, that I was a person in my own right and that I had the capability to better myself. I took the circumstances that I was given and I did not let them define me, but looked for opportunities that would allow me to grow and give me purpose.

Importantly, somewhere in this reflection, I started referring to my foster parents as my parents. They did the work of parenting, they enveloped me with love, and ultimately they made me whole. That's what good parenting can do.

(Based on true experiences, published with permission of the author, who chose to remain anonymous.)

DIVORCE

The dissolution of the parental partnership elicits new challenges, as it directly impacts the child. The process of divorce can be stressful for all family members. Although allegations of fault are no longer necessary to obtain a divorce, fault may play a part in how a court divides assets and child custody determination. Thus, in a litigated divorce the parties, generally through attorneys, will expend emotional and financial capital over a sometimes lengthy period of time.

Alternative Dispute Resolution (ADR)

Alternative Dispute Resolution is a form of resolution that has proved to be a more productive way of settling disputes in terms of money, time, and stress (Taylor, Harper, Jurecko, Melowsky, & Towler, 2015). In this type of resolution, the parties to a lawsuit resolve their differences outside of court with the help of a trained facilitator. After an agreement is reached, the parties present the agreement to the Court to be considered, ratified, and made into an order that is the final decree of divorce. There are two main types of ADR used in divorce cases—*mediation* and *collaborative divorce*. Both are beneficial to children. Arbitration and neutral evaluation are also valuable tools in settling potential disputes.

Mediation

Mediation is the process in which couples negotiate and work together to create a parenting plan, divide the family assets, and settle other post-divorce issues with the facilitation of a trained neutral third person, the mediator.

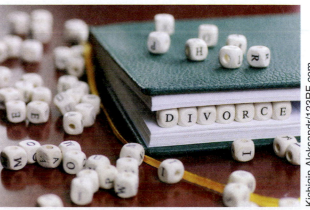

During the divorce process, methods of alternative dispute resolution (ADR) and support with parenting plans that keep the child's best interests in mind are critical in alleviating and managing the stress on the family.

Collaborative Divorce

Collaborative divorce is a newer method for resolving conflicts in family law. When a divorcing couple is committed to resolving their conflicts outside the adversarial environment, they can agree to engage in a collaborative divorce. Each party hires a specially trained collaborative lawyer to assist and advise them in creating their divorce settlement. The parties sign a contract that specifies their commitment to a non-litigated divorce and agree not to use the litigation process. If an agreement is not reached and parties choose to litigate, they must hire another lawyer who was not part of the collaborative agreement. Other professionals participate in the collaborative process. Mental health coaches and a financial expert are common members of the collaborative team. A child expert may provide information on the best interests of the children.

••

Focus Point. There are many avenues that divorcing parents can take in order to reduce conflict and stress during the divorce process. Alternative Dispute Resolution and Collaborative Divorce are two methods that allow for a more positive experience for everyone involved.

••

PARENTING PLANS

Perhaps the most important legal aspect of a divorce for children is a *parenting plan* decreed by the Court divorcing the parties. In the United States, parenting plans vary from state-to-state but most parenting plan include provisions for *child support* (Drozd, Olesen, & Saini, 2016). It also includes where the child will spend her time and with whom. Parenting time during school days, weekends, summer vacation, and holidays is addressed specifically.

Custody

In deciding where a child will live after a divorce and who will take care of the child's needs, two aspects of *custody* are considered, namely legal and physical. **Legal custody** refers to decision making about the major aspects of a child's life such as medical, educational, religious, and extracurricular activities. It is not uncommon for divorced parents to share *joint legal custody*. Often one parent is designated the "tie breaker" if parents cannot come to an agreement on a particular issue.

Physical Custody and Visitation. Physical custody refers to where a child will live. If one parent is designated the *primary physical custodian* the child will live with that parent. The non-physical custodian will be allowed to exercise **visitation rights**, meaning legally mandated access and right to spend specific times with their child. If parents live in close proximity it is possible for parents to share physical custody, equally dividing the time spent with their children. If a plan becomes unworkable because circumstances change, parents may go back to court to seek a modification of their parenting plan. This is a separate legal action and can be the source of more litigation. Alternative dispute resolution is available and may be advisable for modifications.

Most parents who do not live together are eventually able to parent together in a non-marital partnership. The term *coparenting* includes this type of parenting and is in the best interest of children.

In very high conflict situations another approach may be the safest and best way for a child to have access to both parents. With **parallel parenting** parents have limited contact with each other. Communication is usually by email or through a third-party intermediary.

••

Focus Point. Parenting plans can be very beneficial to families who are going through divorce. They establish written guidelines for each parent to follow, outlining issues that may arise, such as requiring child support and a well-defined schedule of each parent's visitation rights.

••

THE GLOBAL WELL-BEING OF CHILDREN

The **Convention on the Rights of the Child**, drafted by the United Nations Children's Fund in 1949 (UNICEF, n.d.) and formally adopted in 1990, reflects a concern with the global well-being of children and is an intentional approach to create and maintain a comprehensive national agenda for children. The rights address the best interests of the child, the protection of rights, nondiscrimination, parental guidance, and survival and development to name just a few. There are 54 articles focusing on rights, as well as the implementation of measures. Although these suggested rights are not legally binding in the United States, many countries have adopted them as a guideline and aspire to implement them through public policies. The Declaration also serves as a global platform for discussions concerning the rights of children and has definitely heightened awareness concerning this important area of concern.

Declaration of the Rights of the Child

On December 10, 1959, the General Assembly of the United Nations adopted the Universal Declaration of the Rights of the Child. The United Nations recommended that the declaration be publicized, especially in educational institutions, with the intent that ultimately it will be adopted universally. Here are some of the stated children's rights:

Children should be raised by their family or by those who will best care for them.

Children should have access to enough food and clean water.

Children should be raised under at least adequate circumstances.

Children have the right to health care and education.

Children with disabilities should have access to special care.

Children have the right to play.

Children have a right to safety and should not be hurt or neglected.

Children should not be abused as child labor or trained to fight.

Children have the right to express their own opinions.

Children should be allowed to speak their native language and practice their own religion and culture.

Children should be taught about peace and tolerance.

Source: Based on United Nations, Declaration of the Rights of the Child (Plain Language Version). In the Public Domain. Retrieved from http://www.un.org/cyberschoolbus/human-rights/resources/plainchild.asp

Video Example 5.3 United Nations Conventions on the Rights of the Child

Watch this video on the "United Nations Conventions on the Rights of the Child." How does this treaty aspire to improve outcomes for children?

(https://www.youtube.com/watch?v=TFMqTDIYI2U)

Focus Point.   The right to parent is an umbrella right that covers education, health care, and a variety of other responsibilities. Because laws on parenting differ from state to state, family life professionals offer their services to help families navigate the often complex legal world.

FINAL THOUGHTS

The rights and responsibilities of parents and their children are complex and challenging. Children may need extra protection from society, especially if disputes arise, and if parents, for whatever reason, cannot shoulder their responsibilities. Entire professions and disciplines devote their expertise to the many challenges of family life and parenting. This chapter is by no means exhaustive, instead it serves to highlight a few family-related concerns, focused on supporting those members of society who may be most vulnerable or at risk; namely the children.

> **The ultimate test of a moral society is the kind of world that it leaves to its children.**
>
> *Dietrich Bonhoeffer (1906–1945)*
> *German theologian*

CHAPTER FOCUS POINTS

The Privilege of Parenting

■ There is a subtle interplay between public policy, legal guidelines, and the wishes and actions of individual parents. Parents can express individual parenting styles, goals, and dreams for their children, hopefully with the proviso that they are in the best interest of the child and they follow the general ethical and legal guidelines of the society within which they are embedded. However, the law steps in when these guidelines are not upheld.

Laws and Rights

■ The right to reproduce and parent children according to one's moral compass are outlined in the 14th Amendment of the Constitution. This section also upholds the parental right to make decisions for their children who are not yet of legal age.

The Right to Parent

■ Parents can make personal and private choices concerning the right to procreate, as well as the right *not* to have children. As such, either of these choices is legally protected and privacy is respected. A person who chooses to become a parent, is legally responsible for that child from pregnancy until the age of majority.

Legal Paternity and Maternity

■ Parents have both the right and responsibility to guide their children in all aspects of life, a task often influenced by cultural norms, availability of resources, special needs of parents or children, and extended family support. Aside from providing care and support to meet the child's basic needs, parents are also responsible for making decisions about their child's medical treatment, education, and discipline.

Child Maltreatment

■ Due to progress in child protection laws, mandated reporters and court-appointed advocates are among the roles that have been established to detect and prevent child abuse. If abuse of a child is suspected, it is the job of the legal system to protect that child, often to the point of revoking parental rights.

Children in Foster Care

■ Children living in foster care are more likely to have experienced abuse, neglect, and general family dysfunction. Commonly, multiple placements disrupt the child's day-to-day routine, adding stress and preventing adequate bonding. After a foster child reaches the age of majority, resources are scarce to assist them as they transition into adulthood.

Divorce

■ There are many avenues that divorcing parents can take in order to reduce conflict and stress during the divorce process. Alternative Dispute Resolution and Collaborative Divorce are two methods that allow for a more positive experience for everyone involved.

Parenting Plans

■ Parenting plans can be very beneficial to families who are going through divorce. They establish written guidelines for each parent to follow, outlining issues that may arise, such as requiring child support and a well-defined schedule of each parent's visitation rights.

The Global Well-Being of Children

■ The right to parent is an umbrella right that covers education, health care, and a variety of other responsibilities. Because laws on parenting differ from state to state, family life professionals offer their services to help families navigate the often complex legal world.

ACKNOWLEDGMENT:

Sarah Bowers, LCSW, JD, co-authored the initial draft and served as legal consultant for this chapter on family law as it pertains to parent–child relations. Her expertise and contributions in this collaboration are gratefully acknowledged and much appreciated. Used with permission.

USEFUL WEBSITES

Websites are dynamic and change

Administration for Children and Families
http://www.acf.hhs.gov
The Child Abuse Prevention and Treatment Act—A History from Gateway (2014)

American Academy of Pediatrics
https://www.acpeds.org
Parenting and divorce, related topics

Behind Closed Doors
http://www.unicef.org
Impact of domestic violence on children (UNICEF Study)

Family Impact Institute: Purdue University
http://www.purdue.edu/hhs/hdfs/fii/
Using Research to Build Better Public Policy for Families

Futures without Violence
https://www.futureswithoutviolence.org
Domestic violence and related themes throughout the lifespan

National Conference of State Legislatures
www.ncsl.org/
Human services, family law related concerns

Up to Parents
http://www.uptoparents.org
For separated and divorced parents: building better futures for children

PART II

The Developmental Process of Parenting

Parent–child partnerships are never static. They are a work in progress, they are multidimensional, they grow and evolve; just like other significant and meaningful relationships. For parents, there is an element of wonder, as they witness their children progress through the lifespan. The person, who was parented as an infant, a toddler, a child, an adolescent, an emerging adult and beyond, is a miracle of transformation. But that represents only one side of the relationship.

The parents are changing too. They are maturing, becoming better acquainted with their parenting roles and hopefully wizened by life's lessons. Somewhere within this constantly evolving partnership, the core relationship between a parent and a child is forged. If it starts out on a solid foundation, each next phase can be built on that secure footing. Days will turn into months and years.

If we are privileged enough to be part of the unique bond between a parent and a child, we will in all likelihood experience one of life's truly rewarding relationships, one that touches us to the core and continues over a lifetime.

**"Other things may change us,
but we start and end with family."**

Anthony Brandt

CHAPTER 6

The Transition to Parenthood

Learning Outcomes

After completing this chapter, you should be able to

1. Label the various forces that influence a decision to parent.

2. Differentiate between families of origin and families of creation.

3. Recognize factors that contribute to healthy pregnancy outcomes.

4. Recall the various stages of the prenatal period.

5. Explain the role of the childbirth educator.

6. Assess the effects of postpartum depression on the parent–child and parent–parent relationships.

7. Describe several alternative avenues to parenthood, including reproductive technology.

8. Evaluate the challenges associated with intra- and intercountry adoptions.

9. Assess the effects of the foster care system on attachment and healthy development.

A TRANSFORMATIVE RELATIONSHIP

During our lives some transitions will change us; they will touch us in a manner unlike anything we have known before. We will experience the joy of new life, but we will also be subjected to the heart wrenching pain of losing a loved one. These events will alter us in ways that we cannot anticipate. We are protected by not knowing how deeply we will grieve the loss of a loved one, until we are facing that despair. Similarly, we may think that we know what it will be like to parent; yet when we undertake the task with our own families of creation, it seems different because we cannot compare it to anything we have encountered before. Just as we can try to learn to swim by watching seasoned swimmers or even imitating the movements on dry land; we will be dealing with a fresh set of experiences once we immerse ourselves in the liquidity of water and are surrounded by its gravity-altering qualities.

Many of us seem to know this truth instinctively. We display an urgency to adopt that most challenging of roles, and are deeply motivated to embrace the revered role of a parent. Of course we have to acknowledge that we have an instinctive voice luring us towards procreation. The biological way to defy death is to create, leaving behind a younger version so that the cycle of life can continue as it has done for eons before us. But there is more. How can we explain the selflessness with which parents welcome children into their homes, who were birthed in other families or on other continents, and the focused manner in which couples deal with the countless hurdles of assisted reproduction?

Parenthood counts among our most valued educational opportunities. Although, as folklore warns us: "Life gives the exam first, and the lesson afterwards." It has the potential to radically change us, to enrich our worlds, and to shake our self-centeredness out of our systems. There are few, if any, equivalent experiences. After all, how many other relationships are lifelong, demand that we always give our best, encourage us to focus on the well-being of the other, and become part of our core identity? Admittedly, it is not the only path towards a life well lived. Increasingly, individuals consciously decide to remain child-free; this particular role does not speak to them. Even so, they may choose to be deeply involved with children in extended family; in their professional, mentoring, and volunteering capacities; and in other instances in which they can have a significant and long-lasting impact on young lives.

The transition to parenting is complex and multifaceted as described by Heinicke who spells out the multifactorial intricacies (Heinicke 2002). These include pre-birth determinants and the stability of the marriage as well as parent characteristics. For those who have chosen to parent and to coparent in a variety of situations and opportunities; the parent–child relationship can be a transformative experience that finds virtually no equivalent in other domains of the human journey (Demick, Bursik, & DiBiase, 2014; Heinicke, 2002; Rilling & Young, 2014).

Parenthood and Committed Relationships

The committed relationship of a couple acts as the foundation for their family-of-creation. Forming such a relationship of trust and intimacy requires time, effort, and emotional investment. The first years of a marriage or partnership are usually devoted to these outcomes.

Our culture supports romantic notions about parenthood and child rearing that may deceive adults about what these roles require. Folklore or common beliefs imply that parenthood improves a couple's marital relationship and that a truly successful marriage is one in which happiness predominates all of the time. Many childhood fairy tales end with the words " . . . and they lived happily ever after." We grow up with the unrealistic expectation that somehow marriage is the panacea for all of life's challenges.

Reality introduces the couple to their parenting roles. Like other everyday routines, becoming a parent requires restructuring and reorganizing of a couple's committed relationship. A new baby, especially a first-born, elicits both positive and challenging reactions. Often we have heard guest speakers in our parenting classes say that once they cradled that newborn in their arms, they felt an overwhelming sense of responsibility, even fear, as the task of keeping their seven-pounder alive seemed daunting. The arrival of the firstborn brings with it mixed emotions of intense joy and gratitude, while insecurity and stress wait in the shadows (Doss & Rhoades, 2017).

On the positive side, couples who have a strong and secure relationship before the birth of a child, and importantly are *mutually supportive,* can anticipate better outcomes. If one of the partners is *undermining* concerning parenting roles, it will negatively influence the parenting prospects in terms of adaptation, not just for the parent at the receiving end of the negativity, but for both as together they form a parental dyad (Le, McDaniel, Leavitt, & Feinburg, 2016). Women especially are susceptible to signals of support from their partners, and they interpret these as reflections of romantic interest as well, although men are less inclined to make that connection (Le et al., 2016).

For millennial women, the fact that their partners are actively involved in the parenting, is the new norm towards shared responsibility within the marriage, which importantly includes childcare and related parenting activities (Fillo, Simpson, Rholes, & Kohn, 2015; Yavorsky, Kamp Dush, & Schoppe-Sullivan, 2015). Despite changing norms, mothers still seem to be shouldering more of the childcare responsibilities, even if they are employed outside the home. The particular responsibilities of parental involvement depend to some extent on the gender of the parent, the specific parenting domain, and in a more complex sense, psychological adjustment. Jia, Kotila, Schoppe-Sullivan, & Kamp Dush (2016) describe patterns of "*mother step in*" and "*father step out*" as father involvement can decrease while mothers take up the slack. Le and co-researchers (2016) emphasize that partners in parenting influence one another in a reciprocal manner over time as they are a twosome or dyad. It is almost intuitive that support begets competence; whereas subtle and overt boycotting will spread its own poison.

Researchers who study the effects of parenthood on marital satisfaction have consistently reported that rather than improving a couple's relationship, the presence of children is initially associated with decreasing marital satisfaction (Belsky & Rovine, 1990; Bouchard, 2016; Johnson, 2016). The quality of marital satisfaction begins to decline following the birth of the first child. It continues to do so as the child grows, culminating in its lowest point when the child reaches middle childhood, and then just when we second guess ourselves regarding the decision to become a parent, the quality improves as the children go through adolescence and head on towards early adulthood, while the parents regain a little of their independence. When we compare parents to non-parents the levels of content merge as the children become older (Doss & Rhoades, 2017). Accessing support- and educational parenting groups can be crucial in

smoothing over the difficulties associated to this phase and facilitate better communication. Attitudes such as decreased contempt and increased expression of positive emotions were outcomes of targeted interventions (Shapiro, Gottman & Fink, 2015).

Putting this into a bigger perspective, these feelings could also be seen in the light of lifespan and role changes, and importantly, the intrinsic qualities partners bring into the relationship. The timing of parenthood in terms of the lifespan is also noteworthy (Bouchard, 2016). Early marriage may be benefitting from the spillover of the honeymoon effect. It seems a little unrealistic to expect the marriage not to alter, as new lifespan demands surface. There are challenges in comparing non-parents to parents, even though this has been done repeatedly in research, because the parenting role in itself brings about some transformational changes. In short, the problems that exist in the pre-birth relationship, may be magnified and predict greater challenges post birth. Similarly, the couple with greater emotional resources, good support systems, and a firm committed relationship can expect to access these same resources in managing life with an infant. Even so, there can be additional stressors in the form of infants with difficult temperaments, and parents who are poorly attached to their newborns (Doss & Rhoades, 2017).

Historically, it was taken for granted that married couples would have children if they were biologically able to do so. With medical advances, circumstances have changed. Family formation can be planned, even timed, and assisted reproductive technology can help certain couples move toward their dreams of parenthood. People have greater freedom of choice, but this, too, has been accompanied by some unique challenges.

Ideally, couples emotionally plan to have children long before conception and birth. Partners should discuss how many children they want and prepare for the entry of children into their family system. They should be in agreement, so that the future child will be welcomed into a stable and committed relationship. Couples who seem to face greater challenges are ones dealing with unplanned pregnancies, especially before the relationship of the parents was sufficiently secure (Bouchard, 2016).

Complex issues are considered in making the parenthood decision. Nowadays, economic considerations play a central role (Lindert, 1978/2015). In developed countries, children are no longer considered to be the economic asset they were in the past. Instead, they are a financial obligation, even though it is a liability or "burden" that parents are happy to shoulder. Average marriage age is older, and for couples seeking an education, childbearing is delayed, often until couples are well into their thirties. Reasons for the delay vary; the couple may want to establish a sound financial base first. Others delay having children until lifestyle goals have been achieved. In addition, a variety of social pressures, as well as emotional factors, contribute to the decision to become a parent (Klobas & Ajzen, 2015). Potential parents must examine the role that children play in fulfilling the different needs, values, and functions within a particular family system. Parent–child relations are a lifelong commitment and partnership, and they will demand that we as parents intend to give even more than we may ultimately receive.

Union Instability and Union Disruptions

Disconcertingly, those couples exposed to *union instability* and *union disruptions*, can expect significantly greater challenges, and importantly, these disruptions tend to implicate the offspring. Amato & Patterson (2016) state that instead of looking only at divorce as a disrupter, unstable partnerships carry their own hazards, which can act out intergenerationally. By accessing data from the National Longitudinal Study of Adolescent to Adult Health, these researchers showed that parent and offspring disruptions were positively linked. Youth who had been subjected to parental union instability were more likely to be unstable in their own partnering patterns. *Parent discord* was also a significant factor, in that strife between parents trickled down to the next generation in terms of their own partnering outcomes (Amato & Patterson, 2016).

Parenting Reflection 6–1

Some couples remain child free by choice. Others definitely want a family. Consider both points of view and what may justify these opposite choices. If the two partners in one relationship differ in their choices concerning having children, what implication does that have for their shared future?

Focus Point. The birth of a child invokes a range of emotions, from joy to feeling overwhelmed. Modern trends, including increased gender equality, have led fathers to take a more active role in parenting. Ideally, the choice to parent includes consideration of many factors such as parental leave, economic stability, and emotional preparedness. Parental union instability and disruptions have an undesirable effect on the offspring.

Video Example 6.1

Watch this video of Dr. John Gottman explaining the research about relationship shifts after having a child. What are some of the research findings concerning changes in relationships after having a baby?

(https://www.youtube.com/watch?v=KNa1Vxrn ZBE&t=2s)

Economic Factors. Folklore may soothe us promising that every child is born with a bread under his arm; meaning that every child will be cared for even though as parents we do not know how. Sadly, this optimism is misplaced. Worldwide, millions of children may never reach optimal outcomes because they are growing up in underserved and deprived circumstances (Lamanna, Riedmann, & Stewart, 2014).

The transition to parenthood (TTP) challenges the parents concerned emotionally, physically, and economically. Persons considering parenthood carefully consider the financial implications of having children, possibly because they still have a choice whether or not to become a parent. Economic factors relate to a couple's desired lifestyle and educational aspirations and can contribute to delayed parenthood. Although the costs of childbearing and child rearing vary widely, it has been estimated that for a middle-class working family in the United States, about one fourth of the total lifetime income is devoted to meeting the costs of raising a child from birth through age 18 (Lino, 2014).

To raise a child is an expensive undertaking. A middle income family with a child born in 2013 can expect to spend a quarter of a million dollars on child-related expenses until the child reaches age 18. Adjust that for anticipated inflation and the estimates can increase by up to 20%, which are staggering sums (Lino, 2014).

Thus, family expenditures to provide housing, to meet the general and educational needs of children, for transportation, and for food consume the majority of a family's income (see Figure 6–1).

Opportunity cost is another hidden price tag attached to child rearing, and represents the potential loss of family income while one parent is not gainfully employed. Sometimes this is counterbalanced by saving on expensive childcare alternatives. In about 20% of American families, the female partners have higher earning ability than the income potential of their male partners (Wang, Parker, & Taylor, 2013). Increasingly fathers have taken on child-rearing responsibilities while mothers have become the lead breadwinners. Some parents choose not to reenter the workforce until the youngest child enters kindergarten. The ability to raise children with full-time parental supervision is regarded by some as a valuable privilege, even if it is accompanied by financial and career sacrifices.

Structural Factors.   The marital and employment status of the parents are an important consideration when planning to have a family. Single mothers, even if they are single by choice, tend to have significantly

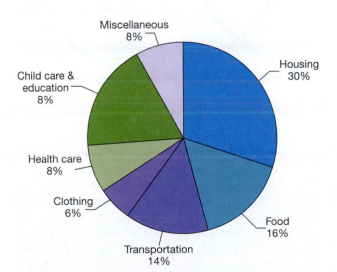

FIGURE 6–1.   Expenditure shares on a child from birth through age 17 as a percentage of total child-rearing expenditures, 2013.

Note: U.S. average for the younger child in middle-income, husband-wife families with two children. Child care and education expenses only for families with expense.

Source: Lino, Mark. (2014). Expenditures on Children by Families, 2013. U.S. Department of Agriculture, Center for Nutrition Policy and Promotion. Miscellaneous Publication No. 1528-2013.

lower household incomes than married women who can pool resources with a spouse (Ermisch, 2003/2016). A younger single mother might interrupt her education for parenthood, and this might close the door to obtaining higher wages from jobs that require a longer educational path. Additionally, a single mother carries the burden of an entire household, whereas in a partnership or marriage, this responsibility would be shared.

Child care is a top priority when both parents return to the workforce. Finding reliable, high quality child care, calls for careful consideration. Many families in the United States rely on relatives or in-home (family) care of children. Others rely on agencies, nonprofit organizations, co-ops, mother's day out programs affiliated with churches for child care. Child care has become a reality for dual income families, which in turn represents the majority of families with young children (Rathbun & Zhang, 2016). High quality care requires continuity of the significant caregivers, a structured curriculum, and accreditation or licensing of the facility to mention but a few of several factors.

Our cultural attitudes tend to be child-friendly and pro-birth; married adults are socially coerced to become parents. Grandparents especially may send unsubtle messages expressing their desire for grandchildren. Simultaneously, there is a veiled message to couples to have smaller families, implying the concerns of overpopulation and related economic resources. A group's *fertility rate*—the number of biological children that a woman has—can reflect varying cultural norms. For instance, Hispanics are currently a fast-growing group in the United States, partly because they favor larger families (Brown, 2014).

• •

Parenting Reflection 6–2

What are some advantages and disadvantages of having children in this day and age? How can society's expectations of parents become more realistic?

• •

Psychosocial Factors.   Complex and interacting psychosocial factors contribute to the decision to become parents. The reasons for having children have shifted from the need for a strong familial workforce in the past to reasons of a psychological and social nature. The many factors that affect the decision are shown in Figure 6–2.

FIGURE 6–2. Complex interrelated factors influence decisions concerning parenthood.

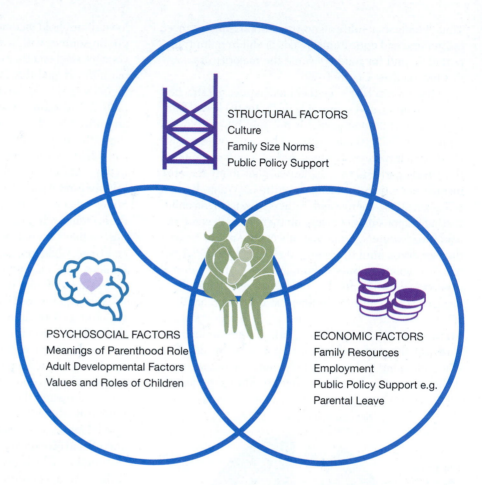

STRUCTURAL FACTORS
Culture
Family Size Norms
Public Policy Support

PSYCHOSOCIAL FACTORS
Meanings of Parenthood Role
Adult Developmental Factors
Values and Roles of Children

ECONOMIC FACTORS
Family Resources
Employment
Public Policy Support e.g.
Parental Leave

Reasons for becoming a parent. Many personal reasons enter into a person's decision about whether to become a parent, and most people genuinely appear to want children. These reasons are anchored in the family of origin values, social class, ethnic group, cultural traditions, and more (Overall, 2012). When children are born, adults' underlying reasons for becoming parents may be played out in their child-rearing efforts. Although these reasons are highly personal and unique to each individual, there is a strong *psychosocial* theme that reflects pleasure in child rearing, feelings of love and affection, and attitudes of generativity.

Some aspiring parents view procreation as one of the primary reasons for their existence, and may be supported by their religious beliefs. Children represent a continuation of the family name and hence the genetic line. In some cultures and family systems, there may be special significance attached to male heirs. This gender-biased thinking in select communities, has led to a surplus of male offspring causing an imbalance in the next generation, which in turn creates a shortage of marriageable partners; an unanticipated domino effect.

Having children can be an *altruistic* and unselfish desire to express affection and concern for children. Parenthood provides an outlet for the fulfillment of our psychological desire to be needed. Parents hope that by producing offspring, they prove their maturity as sexually mature adults. It is also related to the need to conform to peers. Parents may hope that their children will be a source of emotional security and love, but there is no guarantee that children will reciprocate the parental investment.

Parenting is occasionally seen as a second chance at life. Some parents may try to relive their own childhood through their children, while others hope that their children will do better in life than they did themselves. Becoming a parent may be an effort to secure an intimate relationship. The belief that a child can rescue a troubled marriage is usually erroneous, as the reality of increased strain on the partners can escalate difficulties. On the other hand, older first-time parents and parents with good support systems report positive outcomes from having children (Myrskylä & Margolis, 2014).

Role Strain

By adding a child to a family, that system becomes more complex (see Figure 6–3). The parents feel pulled in all directions by juggling multiple demands which lead to *role strain*, and in turn can contribute to some marital dissatisfaction. **Role strain** occurs when adults attempt to succeed at several competing social roles. In practice, this means that both parents try to cope with a variety of roles, including that of breadwinner, home manager, parent, marriage partner, plus a few more. In trying to perform all these roles as best they can, the task becomes overwhelming. Think of the circus artist who is spinning several plates on top of sticks. Each one needs constant attention and within a minute of inattentiveness it can all come crashing down. For a new parent, the last straw may be the lack of personal time for self-renewal; combined with the lack of sleep we have the perfect formula for melt down.

Couples do well to develop a strong and committed relationship *before* having children, because their relationship will suffer some neglect while they are actively raising their new child (Doss & Rhoades, 2017). Most couples anticipate that their lives will change. Others are surprised that with children they have to reexamine their roles within the family. The generation of millennial men who are becoming parents, are hands-on, involved, and dedicated fathers. They take pride in knowing how to soothe and care for their children, and the traditional gender lines are fading fast for this younger generation.

Support groups and parenting classes offer information and education about parenthood (Fine, 1989/2014). These groups assist in several ways by giving people the chance to meet peers facing similar circumstances. It allows for sharing, mutual support, and social networking. Expectations about parenthood and child rearing can be explored in a safe environment, while up-to-date accurate information and resources are provided. These groups have been shown to enhance marital quality as well, as it helps parents access their resources and improve communication (Shapiro, Gottman & Fink, 2015).

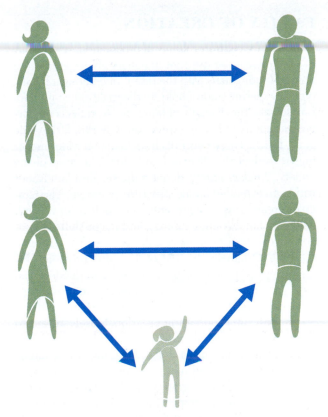

FIGURE 6–3.   The addition of a child into the family unit adds to the complexity of the system.

Focus Point.   Parenting often carries considerable financial obligations, adding stress especially to families living in poverty, or families not benefiting from generous parental leave options. Pressure from friends, family, and society may influence a couple's decision to have children. Many parents experience role strain, an outcome of altering the makeup of their family system.

Video Example 6.2

Watch this video of Carolyn Pirak talking about the Transition to Parenthood. What is the biggest thing soon-to-be parents fail to think about when preparing to bring home a baby?

(https://www.youtube.com/watch?v=KNa1Vxrn ZBE&t=2s)

FAMILY OF CREATION

'**Family of Creation**', 'family of procreation,' and 'family of making' can be used interchangeably to denote the union of individuals with the intent of creating a family, typically sharing a household. In the reality of contemporary society, the diversity of family forms reflects numerous variations in family expression (Cherlin, 2012; Jojic et al., 2012). These concepts have taken on wider meanings to reflect the diverse family forms in an evolving society. '*Nuclear family*' denotes the smallest family unit within an extended family structure or system. The family of creation usually presents in a nuclear form. With changing family demographics, and major shifts in gender, race, ethnicity and roles, the concept has a flexible meaning. Originally the root of the word 'procreate' literally implied producing offspring by reproduction. The term '*family of creation*' is often preferred as it side steps some of the original literal meanings (Gerhardt, 2016b).

Family of Procreation/creation loosely refers to the creation of a family unit by two or more persons. Children may, but need not be present in this family form. The family need not all reside in the same place as may be the case in migrating families. The goals of the family of creation are to provide physical and emotional shelter to the members of that family. Ideally. a family of creation nurtures its members and provides a place of trust, intimacy, and authenticity. There are benefits and responsibilities derived from pooling economic and other resources.

The concept of 'family of procreation' is juxtaposed to '*family of origin.*' Additionally, from the point of view of adult offspring, they can see themselves and their sibling system as the family of procreation, created by their own parents. The family of origin implies the families from which individuals originate and which represent and contribute unique family values, ancestry, and dynamics (Galvin, Braithwaite, & Bylund, 2015). In its most commonly used context, the family of procreation will bring into the newly created family some of the values, customs, heritage, and ancestry of two families of origin; traditionally representing maternal and paternal sides.

Families are components of the larger system of society. In this manner, the influence is dynamic and bidirectional as both individual families and the larger context of the society in which these family forms are expressed, will influence and be influenced by one another (Bales & Parsons, 2014). Role expectations within and outside households have changed, and in parallel manner the implicit rules of the family of procreation also morphed into new configurations. The number of women choosing to remain child free by choice has increased over the past three decades. The trends surrounding family formation continue to alter and same-sex couples, cohabiting couples, single adults, as well as interethnic and interracial liaisons are some examples of persons fulfilling family roles and establishing households.

Nuclear Family

When the family of creation is seen in the light of being a *nuclear family*, multigenerational factors of stress as well as resilience occur in the larger system within which the nuclear family is embedded, and these will affect this family form (Gerhardt, 2016b). Although the family of creation may strive to function as an autonomous household, there are influences from families of origin which can reach back several generations and can find expression within the family of procreation.

Nuclear families are subject to several differentiations within the unit itself. Examples can be a parental dyad consisting of the couple who takes on the major responsibilities heading the household. Levels of functioning within a family of procreation can be hierarchical, adding to the complexity of the family unit. Triads or triangles and other alliances can occur. Their current expression is frequently influenced by the families of origin. These variations are described in the classical and established approaches to family systems theory (Bowen, 2015; Titelman, 1998). In practice, a family does not function as an island, instead it is related to its own ancestral roots and a multitude of family-related forces can express themselves in new contexts. There is an intergenerational transmission of values which affects the functioning of the family of creation. Murray Bowen emphasized various emotional family processes in his theory (Bowen, 2013). He highlighted the role of differentiation, in which individuals as well as families can strive to find what is unique or autonomous to them; especially the components that support constructive functioning. These varied influences from families of origin can influence couple functioning and stability in the family of creation and then also find expression in the ways offspring are parented.

Importantly, the intergenerational continuity of a family system can ideally contribute towards the shelter that an individual or a newly forming couple may seek and experience while embarking on the creation of a new family (Gerhardt, 2016b).

Acknowledgment: This adapted section on Family of Creation was first published in a slightly different form in: Shehan, C. L. (2016). *The Wiley Blackwell Encyclopedia of Family Studies.* Chichester, UK: Wiley Blackwell. In this volume: Gerhardt, C. Families of Procreation. Volume II. Pp. 755–757. Used with permission of the publishers, John Wiley & Sons, Inc.

....

Focus Point. Our families of origin consist of our own parents and our own siblings. Contrast this to our families of creation. This is the family we create with a partner and can include our own children. When the family of creation is seen as a nuclear family, the influences from previous generations will filter down to this family form. These can be positive or negative influences. The continuity of a family system contributes to the shelter that an individual or a newly forming couple may seek and experience while embarking on the process of forming a new family of creation/procreation.

....

PLANNING FOR A FAMILY

Responsibly managed parenthood is a major challenge for which parents need all of the information, support, and medical care they can get in order to contribute to an optimal outcome. Ideally, a visit to a gynecologist or health care provider at least 3 months *prior to conception* promotes planning for a successful pregnancy and addresses current medical issues (American Pregnancy Association, 2017). Prospective parents may also be urged to attend a "Well Baby" clinic prior to conception so that they can receive guidance concerning best practices and preparation for a pregnancy. Prospective parents should access some of the excellent material regarding parenthood that is available in print and on websites. Parenting and birthing classes will also provide information and recommendations (The American Congress of Obstetricians and Gynecologists, 2017).

Genetic Counseling

Some of the greatest advances in planning for a pregnancy have occurred in the area of genetic counseling and the availability of sophisticated genetic screening tests. This remains a rapidly developing area of research and the knowledge base is constantly expanding. For persons who know of genetic conditions in their own family tree, it can be most helpful to have their risks and outcomes professionally assessed *before* contemplating a pregnancy, as it facilitates planning for best outcomes. Potential parents can be given information, based on a combination of genetic testing, detailed family history, and statistical analyses.

Genetic carrier screening, which is a DNA test, can provide more detailed information. Depending on medical advice, couples with known risks may opt for in vitro fertilization where *preimplantation screening* can reduce the possibility of passing on certain debilitating medical conditions. Miscarriage screening can determine if a pregnancy was lost because of genetic abnormalities. More than half of miscarriages in first trimester are attributed to chromosomal abnormalities. The outcome may assist couples in making decisions regarding planning of a pregnancy (The American Congress of Obstetricians and Gynecologists, 2017).

Intensive research to learn more about hereditary influences as related to birth defects has led to the development of remarkable new diagnostic tools. Prospective parents, as well as parents who have had a previous child with a birth defect or a hereditary disease, benefit from the information provided by genetic counselors and genetic screening.

Preparation for Conception

"We are pregnant" or *"We are trying for a pregnancy"* means just that: it involves *both* parents. The prospective mother as well as the prospective father should adopt healthful lifestyles. Fathers should optimize their health in order to produce healthier sperm, as certain substances and environmental factors can have a detrimental influence. For example, abnormal sperm development can be attributed to a man's exposure to lead, recreational drugs such as marijuana and cocaine, cigarettes, alcohol, radiation, and environmental chemicals such as pesticides (Sharma, Biedenharn, Fedor, & Agarwal, 2013).

The Preconception Medical.   Medical screening allows for treatment of STIs or other conditions that require medical attention, before conception. Routinely, blood groups of parents are checked to avoid Rhesus incompatibility, a condition that can severely affect the first pregnancy, but importantly, future pregnancy outcomes.

Under medical supervision, prospective mothers should be weaned off medications that may be harmful to a developing child. Prospective mothers also try to take a "pill break" from contraceptive pills, well in advance to trying to start a family. Prospective parents need to stop smoking (fathers included). Nicotine use during pregnancy leads to lower birth weight and a pregnant woman should not have to inhale smoke passively because her partner is smoking. After the birth passive smoke inhalation is harmful to the infant. Children who were exposed to the smoking of their parents, tend to have a higher incidence of asthma and other respiratory illnesses (Burke et al., 2012).

Prospective parents who have addictions and related disorders should undergo rehabilitation *before* considering pregnancy, because a child could suffer severely from parental abuse engendered by poor lifestyle choices. Destructive behaviors, such as using illicit drugs, misusing prescription drugs, and imbibing alcohol, are detrimental to a healthy pregnancy. For example, infants born to women who are addicted to crack cocaine (cocaine in a smokable form) are also addicted and must receive special medical care following birth. These infants are colloquially referred to as "crack babies" and suffer as a result of prenatal cocaine exposure. Similarly, alcohol use can lead to fetal alcohol syndrome (FAS), which is a debilitating condition in infants and is associated with maternal alcohol abuse. Any recreational drug use amounts to parental irresponsibility that can lead to many problems in later parent–child relations. Such problems are frequently linked to other challenging issues in *high-risk* families.

A prospective mother's health can be adversely affected by her emotional state. High levels of anxiety and depression before a pregnancy may signal other stressors that require expert medical and, possibly, psychiatric attention, and should be regarded as part of the planning to transition into parenthood.

Maternal Health

A number of factors are important for good pregnancy outcomes. The field of maternal–fetal medicine, also known as *perinatology* has emerged in recent years to address the management of pregnancy, including high-risk pregnancies, and to detect and treat conditions while the fetus is still in the uterus. Ample pregnancy-related material is available on reputable websites, and is provided during prenatal clinic visits. Adequate prenatal supervision may be an important factor in reducing the incidence of low birth weight and prematurity in infants (Till, Everetts, & Haas, 2015). A woman's educational and socioeconomic level affects whether she seeks prenatal care (Heaman et al., 2015).

The nutrition and health of a pregnant woman influence the quality of development of the growing child. These factors have a strong impact on the wellbeing of both the fetus and the mother (Bhutta et al., 2013; Center on the Developing Child at Harvard University, 2016). Weight gain is monitored. Some nutrients may play a critical role in influencing the quality

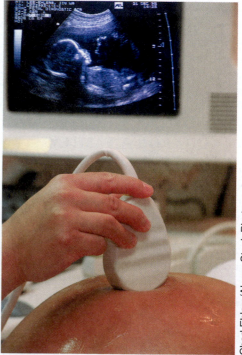

Chad Ehlers/Alamy Stock Photo

Access to prenatal care and screening, advances in maternal-fetal medicine, and ensuring that healthy nutritional practices are followed are all aspects that help pregnant couples adapt to the physical, emotional, and social changes associated with pregnancy.

and nature of a baby's development before birth. For example, an adequate amount of folic acid (a type of vitamin B) appears to counteract the risk of spinal cord defects (e.g., spina bifida) in a developing baby (Czeizel, 1995).

A note of caution is warranted as certain medical conditions may require additional medical attention; expectant mothers need to follow the guidelines provided by their physicians very carefully. Some examples of these medical conditions are poorly controlled diabetes, high blood pressure, pregnancy-induced hypertension or preeclampsia, hypo- and hyperthyroidism, heart disease, and placenta previa, which may cause excessive bleeding. Typically, mothers of multiples are monitored and regarded as high-risk pregnancies.

A number of drugs and other chemical agents are known to have *teratogenic* effects; that is, they cause the abnormal development of an embryo. The most common ones include some of the psychotropic medications and drugs used to treat cancer, acne, and psoriasis, to name but a few (Tantibanchachai, 2014). A woman should never self-medicate while pregnant, or if she suspects that she may be pregnant. Even over-the-counter medications and herbal products can be harmful. It is important to review every substance that one considers taking with the medical team that is providing the prenatal care. Other substances to be avoided during pregnancy include alcohol, nicotine, and caffeine.

Several infectious diseases, including STDs, can be transmitted from mother to child. Some diseases are known to damage the baby's central nervous system during the fetal stage of development, for example, cytomegalovirus (a herpes virus) and toxoplasmosis. The latter is linked to a parasite that can be found in cat litter boxes, among other places. The Zika virus, transmitted by mosquitoes, has been associated with microcephaly in the unborn, with devastating outcomes (Centers for Disease Control, 2014b).

Parenting Reflection 6–3

What are the pros and cons if couples who anticipate starting a family undergo genetic and health screening for potential problems that may influence a future pregnancy?

Focus Point. Responsible parenting begins before conception and a preconception medical may be recommended. With the help of genetic counseling, parents can be informed concerning the risks of possible genetic concerns and determine the best way to proceed. Both women and men should prepare for conception by adopting healthy lifestyles and avoiding stressors. All medications, including over-the-counter products, need to be approved by the medical team. Prenatal care is important to ensure optimal pregnancy outcomes.

Timing of Parenthood

Both parents contribute genetic material to their offspring, so mothers as well as fathers have been implicated in the etiology of neurodevelopmental and other disorders. Older women experience higher rates of miscarriage and are more likely to give birth to children who have some type of genetic disorder. For example, the incidence of Down syndrome, a genetic disorder that presents with a number of medical conditions and associated developmental delays, increases significantly among women who bear children after 40 years of age, although the father's age has also been implicated (Fisch et al., 2003). Noninvasive prenatal tests (NIPT) can report gender, and certain chromosomal abnormalities, from about the 9th week of pregnancy onwards, using a blood sample of the mother.

The age of the father appears to be significant. Mutations in paternal genetic material increase exponentially with paternal aging. Some of the findings presented in this section are based on the work of Kári Stefánsson and his colleagues in Iceland, who compared the whole-genome sequences of 78 trios of a mother, father, and child (Callaway, 2012; Sun et al., 2012). Many of these mutations are harmless, but there is strong evidence that some mutations contribute to neurodevelopmental disorders (Callaway, 2012; Hoischen, Krumm, & Eichler, 2014; Iossifov et al., 2014). Couples in stable relationships with good earning potential as a result of completed education, face better outcomes than couples who do not have the resources for this responsible life challenge, or who have to interrupt their education to accommodate the needs of a child.

Unintended Pregnancy.   Despite many available contraceptive choices, unplanned and unintended pregnancies are a reality. These parents transition into parenthood possibly impulsively or more often than not, because they do not see pregnancy as something happening to them. The accompanying emotions may range from joy to despair. An estimated 50% of pregnancies in the United States are unplanned and, clearly, this also affects the way in which parenthood as a role is perceived (Centers for Disease Control, 2015b). Some of these pregnancies will be welcome, but others are unanticipated and act as stressors that precipitate a number of problems. Many of these are attributed to adolescent parents, but committed and married couples can also be surprised by an unplanned or unintentional pregnancy (Guttmacher Institute, 2016b; "National & State Data," 2016).

Couples, especially ones whose relationships are not stable or are in the early stages of relationship formation, may push the idea of a pregnancy from their minds as something that only happens to other people and definitely not to themselves (feeling invincible). This is one of the predominant reasons for teenage pregnancies. Not planning on using contraception can escalate into an unplanned pregnancy because "Life happens" (Centers for Disease Control, 2015b). Outcomes vary depending on support systems and accessible resources.

Even under the best circumstances, a planned pregnancy demands responsibility and commitment. Bringing a child into the world has lifelong repercussions, even if these are joyful ones. Put bluntly, once a woman and a man have merged their genes and a child is born, there will be a connection ever after. The child they conceived together will be a reminder of this connection, irrespective whether as a couple they remain committed to each other or not.

• •

Focus Point.   Current research has shown that the lifestyle choices, ages, and genetics of both the mother and the father can affect the future outcome of the child they plan to conceive together. Ideally, pregnancies should be planned and include a preconception medical consult to ensure optimal outcomes. Despite a feeling of invincibility, an estimated 50% of all pregnancies in the United States are unplanned.

• •

PREGNANCY AND BIRTH

The birth of a first child transforms individuals into parents; it is a significant event for the family system it joins. People evolve into their parenthood roles as they assume increasing responsibility in raising and caring for children. For as many couples who carefully plan and time the conception of their children, there are almost equal numbers who enter the parenthood phase without premeditation, and pregnancy may be unintentional. This nine-month period provides the first parenting opportunity to offer nurturing care to the unborn child. Pregnancy and childbirth are important aspects of parenting. The pregnancy and the first three years of life are regarded as most important foundational phases and have the potential to set the tone for much of what is to follow (Amato, 2014; Center on the Developing Child at Harvard University, 2016).

Prenatal Development

The time before birth or the *prenatal* period, is significant and unique because of the effects on the later stages.

1. *Critical period of human development.*   The embryo is vulnerable to many factors that can enhance or hinder its development. Environmental and genetic influences can set the stage for adult wellness, or the lack thereof. These factors can result in congenital birth defects, miscarriage, prematurity, low birth weight, and tendencies toward certain behavioral traits. The biological father's health is relevant in determining the quality of sperm, which, in turn, contributes to the outcome of the pregnancy. It is also the genetic material contributed by the father that will determine the sex of the infant (Moore, Persaud, & Torchia, 2011).

2. *Shortest stage of the lifespan.*   The average length of pregnancy is 280 days (about 40 weeks), although this period can vary. During this relatively short time, a one-celled organism at conception grows to more than 200 billion cells.

3. *Most rapid growth and development during lifespan.*   The first trimester (90 days) of pregnancy is the *embryonic stage*, or the formative phase; the fertilized egg differentiates into specialized cells that make up the systems of the body. By the end of this embryonic stage, the body has a distinctly recognizable human form and contains all the organs

Cultural Snapshot 6–1

Pregnancy and Folklore

Historically, much of what occurs during pregnancy was hidden from direct observation, so the beginnings of life were largely misunderstood and were explained through superstition and speculation. Folklore about pregnancy encouraged the belief that almost everything a pregnant woman experienced would ultimately affect the developing child. Physical defects in a baby were believed to be caused by maternal experiences. For example, birthmarks were thought to result from the mother spilling wine or eating too many strawberries during pregnancy, or being hit by a falling cherry.

A facial cleft deformity, previously referred to by the now defunct term *harelip*, was thought to result from the mother having seen a hare or rabbit. Similarly, it was believed that if a pregnant woman read a lot of classical literature, the child would have strong literary tendencies. These examples illustrate the belief that random events could permanently influence the unborn child, which put misplaced guilt on the mother if something went wrong during pregnancy. Such "hear-say" myths have been discarded as scientists have gained information about how life begins, how the genetic code is transmitted, and how genes are expressed.

A manual of women's health, dating from the 11th century, delivered advice for the birthing process. It could be speeded along with herbal baths and ointments, such as violet and rose oil. Encouraging mom-to-be to sneeze might encourage progress, and a little pepper could be helpful in this regard. Eating butter with labor encouraging words carved into it, and a snakeskin tied around her hips might just have the desired effect (Chadwick, 2011).

---

essential for functioning after birth. The second and third trimesters are the *fetal period* of the pregnancy. During this time, the fetus experiences refinement and the most rapid increase in weight and length. Full term birth weight averages 7½ pounds (Moore, Persaud, & Torchia, 2011).

Adjusting to Pregnancy

A pregnancy affects the couple in several ways, although the experience is unique to each parent and each couple. An expectant mother undergoes a variety of physical, emotional, and social changes. These include adjusting to a changing body image as the pregnancy progresses, challenges to physical and psychological well-being, feelings about what it is like to be pregnant (especially for the first time), dealing with fears of the unknown, and shifting moods that may be related to fluctuations in hormone levels (Mayo Clinic, 2017a).

For the most part, women and their partners react favorably and with great anticipation to the news that a pregnancy has been confirmed. This appears to be especially the case when the pregnancy is desired and the first one. Like parenthood, pregnancy has different connotations and meanings for different individuals. For some, pregnancy validates one's sexuality and reproductive ability. For others, the initiation of a pregnancy revives childhood memories.

Less positive reactions are attributed to other sources: frustration with the economic issues that plague families, especially among young starter families; lack of social support from families of origin and other networks; feelings of uncertainty about whether one wishes to continue a relationship with a partner or that the pregnancy is generally poorly timed for current circumstances.

Aspiring parents will reflect on what it will be like to have a child and what kind of parents they will be and what kind of person the child will become. Expectations of parenthood include how each partner will contribute to this effort, which has important bearings on what happens after a child is born (Biehle & Mickelson, 2012). One of the benefits of the 9 months of pregnancy is that it allows mental preparation. Expectant parents have time to think of themselves as a family rather than as a couple.

Prenatal Screening and Diagnostic Tests.   Prenatal screening and diagnostic tests are listed chronologically in Table 6.1 as they can occur during pregnancy. Not all tests are indicated for each pregnancy, and this list is not exhaustive. Even though the table has been laid out in trimesters, tests can overlap trimesters, and some tests can be repeated.

Courtesy of Dr. Tatum A. McArthur

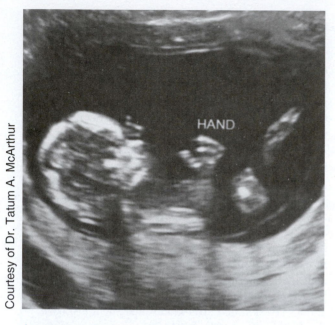

A sonogram of a fetus can assist in determining important information such as fetal age and sex, and in ruling out possible abnormalities.

Courtesy of Dr. Tatum A. McArthur

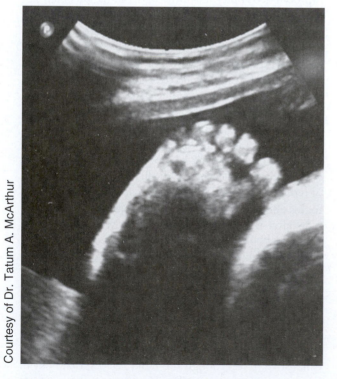

This is an ultrasound image of a normal intrauterine pregnancy (IUP) at 25 weeks. During the anatomy scan which is performed during the second trimester, the extremities are evaluated.

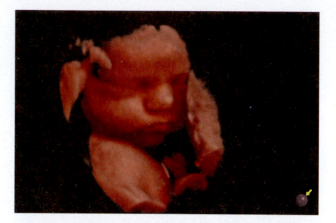

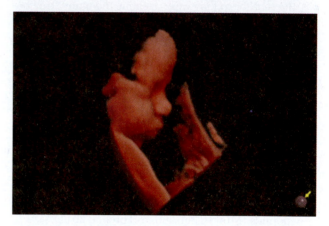

3-D ultrasounds images are used to enhance diagnosis. As shown in the images above, 3-D ultrasounds have the ability to provide clear images.

Focus Point. Short- and long-term outcomes are related to intrauterine conditions before birth, making the period before birth one of the key developmental stages of the life span. Certain risk factors are related to the father. Various factors contribute to *developmental plasticity*. This means that a given genotype can be expressed in different ways in response to environmental factors.

Fetal Origins of Adult Disease

Barker Hypothesis.   Research indicates that the prenatal period of a person's life appears to be one of the crucial periods in determining the later spectrum of health and disease (Cosmi, Fanelli, Visentin,

TABLE 6–1.   Prenatal Screening and Diagnostic Tests

FIRST TRIMESTER SCREENING	Tests are usually performed near the end of the first trimester or around weeks 9–14. Usually first trimester screenings are not invasive and are not known to cause miscarriage or other complications.
NIPT	Noninvasive prenatal test. Analyzes placental DNA through a blood sample of the mother. Can be done as early as 9 weeks. Used for gender reporting except where it is illegal.
Blood tests	Can assess for increased risk of chromosomal abnormalities. Some early tests can provide false positives which are distressing to parents. Rapidly evolving area of diagnostics.
Ultrasound tests	Ultrasound waves make the fetus "visible." Usually it is the first time the parents "meet" their unborn child. There are several types of prenatal ultrasound tests.
Standard ultrasound	This two-dimensional imaging technique provides information concerning the size, location, and development of the fetus and placenta.
Advanced ultrasound	Targeted ultrasound using more sophisticated equipment. Indicated in high-risk pregnancies.
Transvaginal ultrasound	Provides a clearer image of the fetus than transabdominal ultrasound. Can also screen the cervix and pelvic area of women who are not pregnant.
Fetal echocardiography	Provides more information on the fetal heart; anatomy and functioning.
SECOND TRIMESTER SCREENING	These tests are usually performed during months 4-6 of a pregnancy.
Ultrasound tests	Standard care throughout pregnancy.
Blood tests	The quad screen measures the levels of four substances in maternal blood. Results are compared with the first trimester screening results. Rapidly evolving area of diagnostics.
Amniocentesis	These three tests can detect certain genetic abnormalities and other conditions.
Chorionic villus sampling	
Percutaneous umbilical blood sampling (PUBS)	Only done if specifically indicated and carries risks of miscarriage and fetal death.
THIRD-TRIMESTER SCREENING	These tests are usually performed during the last 3 months of the pregnancy.
Ultrasound tests	Throughout pregnancy, in all trimesters, part of standard prenatal care.
Fetal nonstress test	A noninvasive test: monitors baby over 20–30 minutes, recording movement, heart rate, and heart rate in response to movement.
Maturity amniocentesis	To determine maturity of the lungs and anticipated function.
Doppler ultrasound	Measures blood- and blood flow-related conditions within baby and between placenta and baby.
3-D ultrasound	This technology is similar to CT and MRI scans, and is used to enhance diagnosis. It provides a fairly clear image. The 3-D image is still, in 4-D it can be a short sequence of the baby moving.
4-D ultrasound	

Based on information published by the Mayo Clinic (2011, pp. 305–319) and the American Pregnancy Association (2012), www.americanpregnancy.org

Trevisanuto, & Zanardo, 2011). One theory associated with this premise is sometimes referred to as the *Barker hypothesis*, attributed to David J. P. Barker, a British physician and epidemiologist who first published the theory in 1992 (Cooper, Phillips, Osmond, Fall, & Eriksson, 2014; Daniels, 2016).

Barker and his co-researchers refer to factors that contribute to *developmental plasticity*. This means that a given genotype can be expressed in different ways in response to environmental factors (Bavis & MacFarlane, 2016; Gollin, 1981/2012; LaFreniere & MacDonald, 2013). In other words, a given developmental situation, such as intrauterine development, can develop in many directions, ranging from optimal to threatening to the development of the fetus. Various factors will interact to contribute to the outcome, and in this manner the fetus has developmental plasticity, or the potential to be molded by the situation.

Barker and his colleagues studied the relationships between prenatal (in utero) conditions influenced by intrauterine growth and maternal nutrition and some of the following conditions and diseases: coronary heart disease, high blood pressure, stroke, type 2 diabetes and obesity, osteoporosis, aging, and breast and ovarian cancer.

Mothers in both developed and developing countries can unwittingly influence later health outcomes for their unborn children by being poorly nourished and/or chronically malnourished (Barker, Eriksson, Forsén, & Osmond, 2002; Bhutta et al., 2013). Many chronic disorders that present themselves in adult life can be linked to prenatal conditions (Barker, 2004; Hanson & Gluckman, 2014). Mothers who live in poverty and are malnourished and underweight can present with intrauterine conditions that result in low birth weight and prematurity, both of which can have long-ranging health effects. One of these effects is the development of a "thrifty metabolism," meaning that the fetus protects itself against malnutrition by using calories in a conserving manner.

When the infant is later exposed to overnutrition, as is common in our society, that child is at greater risk for obesity and all the complications of obesity, including type 2 diabetes and coronary heart disease. Further research has shown that mothers with a high body mass index at the beginning of their pregnancies, as well as those gaining an excessive amount of weight during pregnancy (for example, overweight and obese mothers), could also unwittingly be setting up their offspring for later obesity and possible type 2 diabetes, because insulin sensitivity and insulin production rates may, to an extent, be established in the womb (O'Reilly & Reynolds, 2013).

Developmental Plasticity.   This hypothesis about developmental plasticity emphasizes the crucial importance of good prenatal nutrition, general prenatal care that promotes intrauterine growth, and factors associated with preventing premature births (Hanson & Gluckman, 2015; Parlee & MacDougald, 2014). This very sensitive period of an infant's life, namely the *prenatal* (before the time of birth) and the *perinatal* (around the time of birth) periods, can determine many facets of her future well-being, as well as disease development. This is one of the many reasons why, ideally, mothers should receive early prenatal care and babies should be monitored and delivered in hospital environments with specialized care, where *optimal outcomes* are more likely.

PREPARATION FOR BIRTH

Birth preparation classes are helpful to most couples, especially when expecting a first child. Prospective fathers will learn how to support the mother during childbirth. These classes will also focus on breathing exercises that assist the mother during labor and delivery. A couple will be advised to think about a "birthing plan" that encompasses where the mother will deliver the baby and pain management during labor and the delivery.

Prospective parents are encouraged to take an infant and child cardiopulmonary resuscitation (CPR) class during this time, and many hospitals with birthing centers will offer these as part of the preparations. Parents should also choose a pediatrician so that all support systems are in place. Parents can visit the hospital or birthing center to familiarize themselves with the environment and the procedures. Good preparation, both mental and physical, will help parents to avoid panic and incorrect decisions when time is of the essence. It also creates an emotionally supportive environment when parents know in advance what to expect.

Childbirth Education

A childbirth educator or a labor support companion (also referred to as a *doula*) emotionally cares for the mother and her partner while she is in labor and sometimes for a period before and following the delivery (Mayo Clinic, 2017b). For centuries, they have been present in numerous cultures. Although they are certified, doulas are not medically trained, nor are they midwives. For that reason, they *do not* deliver babies and they do not have a clinical role.

Doulas act in an emotionally supportive role as a labor coach and companion for the parents. Doulas are frequently also responsible for childbirth classes during

Cultural Snapshot 6–2

Baby on Board: Attitudes to Pregnancy

Whether we live in a fairly remote environment such as rural Namibia or in the heart of a pulsing city such as Boston or Beijing, the physiological process of pregnancy is a rite of passage that unites us in a culturally *etic* manner. What is culturally unique (*emic* concerns), is how our cultural attitudes towards pregnancy can differ, and how the rituals surrounding pregnancy and birth can carry unique cultural stamps. Shiraev & Levy (Shiraev & Levy, 2016) state:

> Attitudes towards pregnancy . . . differ. In traditional collectivist countries, such as Malaysia, Singapore, Indonesia, Philippines and Thailand, pregnancy is more family centered with active participation and guidance from the family. In individualist societies, childbirth tends to be a rather private affair (p. 234).

They seem to mean that it is private in terms of medical support and the actual birthing experience, in contrast to the acknowledgment of being pregnant, which is often announced publicly with joyful anticipation.

Jhumpa Lahiri, a Pulitzer Prize winning author, contrasts American hospital births to a traditional Indian perspective in *The Namesake*:

> Ashima thinks it's strange that her child will be born in a place most people enter either to suffer or to die . . . In India, she thinks to herself, women go home to their parents to give birth, away from husbands and in-laws and household cares, retreating briefly to childhood when the baby arrives (Lahiri, 2003, p. 4).

In London, pregnant women can wear a pin with the words: "Baby on Board" while traveling on the Underground. That signals to other passengers that the expectant mom should be offered a seat in a crowded subway. It also reflects a very public way of acknowledging pregnancy. In the post WWII years, most developed countries have gradually adopted a less guarded approach concerning pregnancy. Couples are increasingly open about their fertility struggles and acknowledge if a baby was born as a result of fertility support. The openness towards what used to be a more guarded family secret as in "being in the family way," is also noticeable in more informal and body hugging clothing, as mom's proudly display their "baby bump" as a cause of celebration.

Research with international exchange students studying in North America, indicates that these students think of Americans as being very open about what is regarded as a rather private matter in some cultures.

> People make official announcements, inform relatives and friends, and throw parties to spread the word about their condition . . . in many countries, such as Russia, pregnancy is commonly kept secret until the changes in a woman's body become obvious (Shiraev & Levy, 2016, p. 235).

Typically, husbands in Russia would not be present at births (Shiraev & Levy, 2017). Importantly these authors warn us not to make stereotypical judgments, as cultures are in flux and norms change, including attitudes and customs surrounding pregnancy and birth.

Sources: Lahiri, Jhumpa (2003). *The Namesake*. NY: Houghton Mifflin. Shiraev, E., & Levy, D. A. (2016). Cross-cultural Psychology: Critical Thinking and Contemporary Applications (6th ed.). New York, NY: Psychology Press, Taylor & Francis Group.

pregnancy, so that rapport is established and there is continuity in the persons the parents trust when the time of labor arrives. After all, labor and delivery is a very private and important event in their lives. These individuals provide useful social, emotional, and some physical support for new parents and have a positive impact on the mother's experiences during the days following the birth. They also coach the father on how to be supportive. They provide continuity when some of the medical attendants may change. Women who have the support of a doula or childbirth educator are reported to cope more effectively with the responsibilities of being a new mother. Information is available from DONA International (www.dona.org).

•••••••••••••••••••••••••••••••••••••••

Guest Reflection 6–1

Sharing One of Life's Most Intimate Events

The day of the childbirth is a powerful and formative day in a couples' relationship. For me, it was a day that was eagerly anticipated, but arrived too soon as I went into labor at 27 weeks. Even so, my labor was long and difficult. During those hours, my husband, the kindest most servant-hearted man I know, sat at my bedside feeling out of place and clearly beyond his comfort zone. He gave me ice chips and spoke encouraging words, while also feeling helpless. After 36 hours, our first son was born. He was healthy and perfect in every way and the joy of his arrival was the most important thing on our minds.

After taking time to process my delivery and reflect on the experience, I felt there had been something missing. That kind, selfless husband of mine had felt very helpless and unable to effectively comfort me during labor. I began to question how husbands can support their wives and contribute to creating a positive labor experience. I knew my husband would have done any of the things I was reading about, but we were not educated and had not been exposed to those suggestions.

In the coming months, I began to volunteer in the hospital's antepartum department and realized my story was not unique. There were many fathers who felt poorly equipped and helpless during their wives' delivery. My quest to help families in the birthing room started at that time and led me towards becoming a certified childbirth educator and a certified doula. I felt strongly that the birth experience should be a positive and engaging experience for *both* parents of the child-to-be-born.

I believe that many of us were created to be helpers and fixers and what better time to connect to those competencies than during labor? After gaining experience and successfully completing the certification process, I was seeing my theory come to life in the families I coached. In childbirth classes, I would begin each series explaining why these competencies were relevant, not just for the mother-to-be, but also and especially for her partner. As a couple, they were going to learn ways to support one another, thus creating a better birth experience.

As a doula, I would talk to the spouse about how he could comfort his partner during labor. I would gauge his comfort levels and step in and out of the situation as needed. My desire as their labor support was to see their bond strengthened and for them to work through labor together; because at the end of the day, I will be leaving, whereas the couple will continue their parenthood journey together. They need to find the ways in which they can parent and nurture not only their baby, but also their relationship.

My joy was seeing dads thrive while embracing their position in labor. When birth partners feel empowered to actually make a difference, it transforms the labor and delivery for everyone. The parents invest in one another, they share an exceptionally intimate event, and importantly they bond with their child.

When couples work together to achieve a positive birth experience, they gain the required confidence to enter parenthood with their hearts firmly anchored, enabling them to nurture and shelter the fragile life now entrusted into their safekeeping.

Marisa S. Dempsey, B.A. Human Development & Family Science, Certified Doula and Certified Childbirth Educator. Used with permission.

•••••••••••••••••••••••••••••••••••••••

•••••••••••••••••••••••••••••••••••••••

Focus Point. The prospect of becoming parents brings about changes for both partners. Women who anticipate motherhood positively adjust better to pregnancy, labor, and delivery. Expectant fathers play an important role and may need assistance in successfully transitioning into their new role in the family. Hospital births with medical support optimize good outcomes and are recommended for all births. It minimizes risks should unforeseen complications occur.

•••••••••••••••••••••••••••••••••••••••

THE BIRTHING EXPERIENCE

The birth of a baby is a momentous event for a family. Current birthing practices support the family and encourage the involvement of the father. Medical teams are aware of the emotional and social aspects surrounding birth, and these needs are respected and incorporated into contemporary birthing practices. The interior architecture of modern hospitals caters to the family's comfort and well-being, and labor rooms and the rooms where the parents subsequently stay are designed to promote family cohesiveness in order to facilitate bonding with the new infant. If the newborn is healthy, she will stay in the room with the parents. A lactation specialist will guide the mother to facilitate nursing. There may be a sleeper couch in the room so that the father can stay at the hospital to support the mother in this new and challenging adventure while both parents get to know their newborn.

Emotional Aspects

Childbirth is recognized as being both a psychological and a physical event that has implications beyond the immediate. Reactions to childbirth range from ecstasy and intense spirituality to negative. *Skin-to-skin contact* between each parent and the newborn, as well as the expression of physical affection and eye contact, are believed to facilitate emotional bonding (Feldman,

Cultural Snapshot 6–3

The Birth of a Child Is a Joyous Occasion

If circumstances are optimal, the birth of a child is a joyous occasion in all cultures. People from different ethnicities celebrate this occasion differently. In the United States, the gender of the child is often "color coded" with pink or blue, although in an increasingly gender equal environment, this practice is not followed in all circles. We can all share in the joy of this new life, even if we do not know the family personally.

In Mexico, a pregnant woman may attach two safety pins in the form of a cross to her underwear to protect the unborn child. This is believed to be especially important during a lunar eclipse due to the Aztec belief that a bite had been taken out of the moon and it was feared that a bite could be taken out of the baby's mouth. Folklore advises women not to cut their hair during pregnancy, and some think it may have to do with diminishing strength. In some Latin American cultures, food prohibitions are taken very seriously. Mothers are discouraged from eating strawberries in order to prevent the baby from being born with a red blemish (e.g., a hemangioma). In Mexico and Central America, la cuarentena refers to the 40 days after the child's birth when a mother is expected to rest and adjust to motherhood while another member of the family takes care of household tasks and any other children. There are also home remedies for postpartum depression.

Rosenthal, & Eidelman, 2014). Family-centered childbirth methods enhance the process. A birth experience that promotes bonding between the parents and the infant contributes toward preventing later parenting difficulties. Even when prolonged separation is necessary, as with a premature birth that requires neonatal intensive care, health-care professionals will guide the parents to be actively involved in the infant's care, facilitating bonding.

For parents who are having their second or third child, there continues to be some stress associated with childbirth. This may be related to the memories of past experiences. These stimulate a more realistic appraisal of the impact that a newborn has on family life, routines, and resources. Most fathers are deeply touched by the miracle of birth. Some women experience an emotional letdown following birth as an expected outcome of the delivery process, and this can be hormone-related.

Postpartum Depression.   An estimated 15 percent of women suffer from significant depression, perinatal mood and anxiety disorders, and related conditions. These can occur regardless of age, income, race, or ethnicity (Postpartum Support International, n.d.). These reactions occur much more frequently than the general public realizes.

Postpartum depression is a serious condition that requires medical intervention; the mother needs intense and ongoing support until she is healthier. Sometimes a mother is unable to report how she feels, or tries to keep up appearances. For that reason, family members and friends need to be alert; if they suspect depression, they need to call in medical help immediately. Ignoring this condition can have very serious repercussions for both the mother and the infant because the mother is sometimes unable to recognize her infant's needs, leading to *failure to thrive* in the child and this in turn can have long term detrimental effects (Pratt et al., 2015). Suicide and infant homicide have also been reported, underlining the seriousness of this condition.

Postpartum depression is a type of clinical depression that includes feelings of not wanting to provide care for the infant, severe mood swings, continual fatigue, lack of joy in life, and/or withdrawal from relationships (O'Hara & McCabe, 2013). It is treatable, often with antidepressants in combination with psychotherapy and pulling in family support systems to help with childcare. Of particular concern is the interference that can occur in the attachment process between the mother and the child. Postpartum depression seems to have a clear organic basis, but there can be contributing psychological factors as well. It is helpful to acknowledge that parental strain and despair are among the feelings that parents experience, and that sleep deprivation and lack of social support are likely contributors to the strain. Fathers can also experience postpartum depression, although their depression may be reactive in nature. Fathers can also feel overwhelmed, which may result in a depressive episode (Biebel & Alikhan, 2016).

The symptoms of these depression-related illnesses can vary, and it is advisable to get medical advice. Several factors can interact to precipitate the condition. Researchers have shown that mothers who were exposed to stress and even violence during pregnancy may be more prone to depression after the birth, and their infants show higher than normal levels of stress hormones in their blood. Prenatal exposure to maternal stress can have lifelong effects on the offspring (Brunton, 2013; Glover, 2014).

Some of the factors that increase the risk of postpartum depression include the birth of multiples, fertility treatment, preterm births and subsequent time in neonatal intensive care unit, complications during pregnancy, medical conditions, poor social support systems, and abusive relationships, including intimate partner violence (IPV) (Gaillard, Le Strat, Mandelbrot, Keïta, & Dubertret, 2014; Hawes, McGowan, O'Donnell, Tucker, & Vohr, 2016).

Postpartum Psychosis.   Mothers who experience **postpartum psychosis**, a serious psychiatric condition, may lose contact with reality. They may have delusions, such as believing that their child is evil and will do them harm. Hallucinations can also occur. Some mothers with this condition have harmed or even killed their children during psychotic episodes.

Pregnancy and Infant Loss

Miscarriage.   Known also by the term spontaneous abortion, a **miscarriage** is a pregnancy that spontaneously ends within the first 20 weeks of gestation, although most end within the first trimester (American Pregnancy Association, 2017). The rate of pregnancy loss is estimated at about 10–15% of all recognized pregnancies. The reasons are varied and can be linked to maternal health, hormone levels, issues with implantation, and chromosomal abnormalities within the developing embryo, to name a few. Genetic testing of miscarriages indicate that almost half of these are attributable to genetic abnormalities (Suzumori & Sugiura-Ogasawara, 2010).

The risk of miscarriage increases with the mother's age. Physical trauma (such as being involved in an auto accident) can also be a factor. Depending on the reasons for the loss of the fetus, and the individual circumstances surrounding family formation, the distress associated with a miscarriage can range from mild to severe. For some parents who went through lengthy treatment for infertility, the loss of a pregnancy, perhaps one of many, can be devastating. They will experience repeated cycles of grieving as their hopes for biological parenthood seem to have been shattered. Several factors can aggravate the couple's distress (Huffman, Schwartz, & Swanson, 2015):

- A history of infertility and ART interventions
- Whether it was a planned pregnancy, and whether there have been previous live births
- Whether the loss is recent and whether there is a medical explanation.

Infant Loss.   Carrying a baby virtually to term and then facing a stillborn delivery is extremely traumatic. There are several situations for which parents require ongoing emotional support in addition to medical intervention: infertility, preterm birth, miscarriage, stillbirth, early infant death, and SIDS. Women who have experienced any of these losses can be devastated, and it can present as guilt, anxiety, depression, and grief (CDC, 2016). It is important to acknowledge the presence and the importance of the lost infant in the lives of the parents. Parents are encouraged to name the child and to go through culturally appropriate mourning and burial rites. Parents also need to see the baby, even if it was stillborn, because this can facilitate a farewell and ensue closure.

Professionals who deal with grief and loss are available in most hospitals and can guide the family toward the appropriate support systems. Professional counselors can help the family overcome emotional difficulties. For grieving families, volunteer associations offer support groups for miscarriage and infant loss. The national *Share* organization is one such network that guides participants toward help and support (www.nationalshare.org).

In some instances, a doula or birthing companion may assist the parents emotionally, especially if the parents know from tests that the baby will be stillborn. After the birth, parents are allowed unpressured time with their baby. Some parents have a naming ceremony in the presence of a pastor or other religious figure, and invite closest family like grandparents to pay their respects and say their farewell. Hand- and footprints are made as a keepsake, and some parents keep a tiny lock of hair. Depending on personal preferences some parents dress the baby and take photos. Above all, the child is acknowledged as a family member. This allows parents to grieve for a person they knew, however briefly and under very painful circumstances. Hospital staff are trained to treat parents with the utmost respect and frequently a symbol is placed on the parents' room-door to alert staff concerning the situation (Ellis et al., 2016; O'Connell, Meaney, & O'Donoghue, 2016).

Rainbow Babies.   A **rainbow baby** is the term used to describe a healthy baby born after previous infant loss or miscarriage. For parents, this is an important and emotionally healing event. In all likelihood parents carry the burden of emotional trauma subsequent to previous unsuccessful pregnancy outcomes. Live birth success is a joyful outcome for parents who have struggled with fertility-related challenges, or who have grieved a stillborn child.

Focus Point.   Many hospitals and birthing centers encourage parent–child bonding by providing various resources and accommodations. Postpartum depression is more common than most realize, and can include mood swings, fatigue, and a lack of joy. Attachment and bonding are implicated and this in turn can contribute to the baby failing to thrive. This condition is serious and requires medical and family support. Parents who experience a miscarriage or infant loss are encouraged to access support from professionals who can assist them with the grieving process. A rainbow baby is the term for a live birth after previous infant loss.

ALTERNATIVE AVENUES TO PARENTHOOD

Medical technology has advanced to levels that were unimaginable a few decades ago, and children have been born despite challenging reproductive circumstances (see Figure 6–4). Worldwide it has been estimated that about 5 million children have been born as a result of assisted reproductive technology (ART) (Okhovati, Zare, Zare, Bazrafshan, & Bazrafshan, 2015). Persons desiring biological parenthood are willing to endure significant hardships and economic challenges. Others fulfill their parenthood role by welcoming children into their hearts and homes through adoption and foster-care.

Guest Reflection 6–2

Empty Arms, Grieving Hearts: Supporting Families through Loss

Working in a hospital with families who have lost a child through miscarriage, stillbirth, and newborn death has been one of the hardest, yet most sacred experiences of my life. The grief that overcomes these parents as they hold their child is raw and brutal; I cannot forget it—it is etched in my mind. My role is to support these families as they make arrangements for their children, create keepsakes to remember their son in tangible ways, take pictures of their beautiful daughter, and wait alongside them until they are ready for the final reluctant farewell.

As I have heard others comfort the grieving mothers and fathers, I have been encouraged by some of their compassionate gestures. A simple: "I am so sorry," "I am here for you anytime," "I will be bringing you dinner this week," "I can't imagine the pain you are experiencing," or remaining silent and grieving with them, is the most treasured gesture to offer these families. The gift of a friend's presence and care is sufficient. The loss can be appropriately acknowledged by remembering them on special days like their child's due date, death date, or Mother's Day, and allowing them the freedom to "not be themselves" for the amount of time it takes to process their loss. One can never gauge parents' grief when they have lost a child. It shouldn't ever be assumed that grief of an early miscarriage will be any different than that of a parent who lost a term child. Each parent walks their own unique path through grief. We respect and honor that.

Clichés and easy answers are disheartening and seldom helpful. Grieving parents do not need theological justifications, or intellectual band-aids. They will express and address their Faith in their own time. This is not the moment to be told they could "just" have another child; nor that "this happened for a reason." In many cases, the medical team may not know why the unthinkable happened. Telling parents there was a "reason" gives them the desire to seek a solution to questions that have no answers.

Children are not replaceable. At the point of their loss, families need to focus and mourn this child; this child they waited for, dreamt of, and had anchored in their hearts. The power of presence, pursuit, and passionate love, is what these families desire. They do not need many words, just space to grieve and the knowledge that you are with them every step of the way, now and in the days to come.

Marisa S. Dempsey, B.A. Human Development & Family Science, Certified Doula and Certified Childbirth Educator. Used with permission.

FIGURE 6–4. Outcomes of Pregnancies That Resulted from ART Cycles Using Fresh Nondonor Eggs or Embryos, 2013.

Notes: Maternal deaths prior to birth are not displayed due to small number (n = 5).

Total does not equal 100% due to rounding.

Source: CDC.

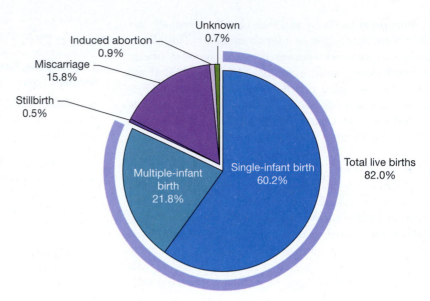

A number of techniques are available and some of the better-known approaches include:

- Fertility drugs
- Intrauterine insemination (IUI): sperm donor could be used
- In Vitro Fertilization/Embryo Transfer (IVF-ET).
- IVF combined with intracytoplasmic sperm injection (ICSI)
- Gamete intrafallopian transfer (GIFT)
- Zygote intrafallopian transfer (ZIFT)
- Donor ovum and/or donor sperm and donor embryos provide genetic material
- Traditional gestational surrogacy (genetic connection with the carrier): A woman may carry a baby to term as a gestational carrier, and her own ovum is fertilized by a donor. The couple raising the child know that the father is also the biological father.
- Gestational surrogacy (no genetic connection with the carrier): the host carries a fertilized ovum to term. The chromosomal material of the embryo is that of the biological donors and the gestational surrogate does not have a genetic link to the embryo.
- Three-parent offspring where the maternal mitochondria come from the third party (Fogleman, Santana, Bishop, Miller, & Capco, 2016).

Based on: National Institute of Child Health and Human Development: U.S. Dept. of Health and Human Services (www.nichd.nih.gov)

Mayo Clinic: Patient Care and Health Information: Infertility (www.mayoclinic.org)

Challenges

A number of ethical, legal, and psychosocial issues are involved in artificial reproductive techniques (ART), some related to the cultural values associated with parenting. As assisted reproductive techniques are becoming a mainstream option, the legal and ethical issues have been largely addressed. Undoubtedly, new challenging concerns will arise, but the current approach is to attempt to clear the legal requirements *before* proceeding with the interventions.

The experience is emotionally, physically, and financially demanding. The process is psychologically invasive and areas of private life become the object of medical concern. Clinic staff and professionals are empathic, and patients receive emotional support and counseling before, during, and after the procedures. Grieving occurs if the technique fails, and the couple has to revisit the trauma of loss.

An increasingly open approach allows children insight into their unique histories at the appropriate developmental time. Research on the long-term implications for the children concerned continues (Hart & Norman, 2013; Talaulikar & Arulkumaran, 2013). The legal and ethical study of assisted reproduction has become a rapidly evolving area of specialization.

For those who experience the gift of parenthood through ART, the transition can seem very fragile and almost surreal. Having probably had repeated disappointments as a result of pregnancy loss, nothing can be taken for granted, and they can be fearful to get their hopes up. Once parenthood is a reality, many treat it as a precious gift and invest constructively in their children.

Guest Reflection 6–3

Transitioning from "Couple" to "Family"

For most of my adult life, I was convinced I had no maternal instinct. I viewed the offspring of friends and acquaintances who'd reproduced in college or grad school much the same as I'd view an exotic yet ferocious animal . . . interesting from a distance, but nothing I'd want living in my house. Then, in my late twenties, my biological clock went off, and it was determined to make up for lost time. Thankfully, after eleven years as a "couple" — seven of those married — my husband was on the same page.

The next three years held one miscarriage, countless rounds of infertility treatments, an equal amount of tearful disappointments, and an adoption application. Had my husband and I not had so many years to hone our partnership, I can easily see where such an emotional roller coaster could have left us both motion sick and ready to end this marriage ride. But we held firm, and "one last try" resulted in that long-sought plus-sign on the pregnancy test stick. Even though I suffered constant nausea and wound up hospitalized for high blood pressure, we reveled in every moment of my pregnancy, devouring book after book on parenting and child development. We'd waited so long for this chance, my husband and I swore we'd do everything in our power to get it right.

Once we finally had our baby boy in hand, our attachment was immediate and fierce. Every move our son made was fretted over or applauded. Long married— and having already weathered years of emotional and physical challenges during our infertile years— my husband and I saw rearing our baby as an extension of our already strong partnership which made for a relatively smooth transition from "couple" to "family."

Jodi Burrus reflected on her personal journey towards parenthood. Used with permission.

Parenting Reflection 6–4

Is it likely that in the future an even greater number of pregnancies could be managed by artificial reproductive techniques? Name some circumstances that could benefit from such developments?

Focus Point.   While alternative methods of conception and fertility support allow numerous families to experience the joys of parenthood, multiple ethical and legal questions are raised by some of the techniques. The coming years will shed more light on the positive and negative outcomes of such practices.

PARENTING AND ADOPTION

When a couple decides to grow a family-of-creation, they usually envision having a baby. They start thinking about children, and what this new life would mean to them; where the youngster would fit into their lives and how much they would love her. In a way, they create an emotional space for that child to enter their worlds. The infant of their dreams may or may not have a name, but slowly he becomes a virtual presence. As they tentatively start thinking about children and their friends may be having offspring, the call towards parenthood becomes louder and more insistent.

But biological parenthood is not guaranteed. Sometimes because it does *not* happen, or cannot happen, parents explore other avenues to welcome children. Fertility challenges are not the only reasons for thinking about a wider circle of bringing a child home. Numerous parents have raised biological children, but they feel it their emotional, moral, altruistic, or religious calling to offer a good life and a home to at least one child (http://adopt.org).

The reasons for choosing to become adoptive parents may vary greatly. Some couples with genetic predispositions towards certain illnesses, do not want to pass these on to a next generation. Other adults feel that their lives are rich and plentiful and welcoming another child to benefit from a stable family life seems a way of sharing the abundance. As for the particular child who joins their family, his world may change from hopeless to hopeful. Same-sex couples may decide to grow a family through adoption, rather than go through costly assisted reproductive options (Duncan, 2016a).

Second-Parent Adoption and Kinship Adoption

There are other variations on the theme, linked to legal reasons. If a stepparent legally adopts the biological children of their spouse, it may be the final way of unifying the family, before the eyes of the law, and is called second-parent adoption. Grandparents may adopt grandchildren to ensure their well-being in the future. Not only can children be adopted, adults can be adopted too, to seal the permanence of relationships and treat someone like a legal child, with the same rights and privileges. This may be a consideration in inheritance matters. Kinship adoption is a common variety, and usually serves to keep families united, and, importantly, there is the consideration of "the best interests of the child."

Historical Underpinnings

The history surrounding adoption tells us a little about societal attitudes towards children, and some of the historic facts certainly do *not* evoke our proudest moments. Adoption was shrouded in secrecy in Victorian England, although kinship adoptions were fairly frequent (Cohen, 2013). Child abandonment, foundling homes and orphanages, and the not so savory truth of using orphans as cheap or free labor, are facts we should revisit to remind us how far we have come and need to go in changing these social injustices (Duncan, 2016a). Between 1854 and 1929 the "Orphan Trains" in the United States transported about 200,000 abandoned, homeless, and orphaned children to supposedly better futures. What happened in reality was unregulated and depended greatly on the ethics, goodwill, and morals of the family or persons extending their hospitality to a particular child. There are documented stories with good, but also ones with sad, outcomes (http://www.pbs.org/wgbh/amex/orphan/).

Biological matching was the emphasis in the period between 1930 and 1950. Secrecy surrounded adoption, adoption records were sealed, and birth parents and their children had no hope of ever being reconciled. The thinking of the day was that if the adopted child resembled her adoptive parents as closely as possible in terms of biological characteristics, the matching process promised better outcomes (Duncan, 2016a). Fast forward to intercountry adoptions which contributed to removing the stigma and secrecy of ancestry. Transracial adoptions became common and helped create greater understanding of diversity and supported the development of multicultural competency.

When adoption laws were originally written in the United States, a significant emphasis was placed on

In an initiative starting in 1855, about 3,000 children per year were sent across the United States to be welcomed in homes all over the country. Some of the wording in this relatively recent poster of 1910 reads: "These children are of various ages and both sexes, having been thrown friendless upon the world. They come under the auspices of the Children's Aid Society of New York . . . the citizens of this community are asked to assist the agent in finding good homes for them."

Source: "Extra! Extra! The Orphan Trains and Newsboys of New York" by Renée Wendinger is an unabridged nonfiction resource book and pictorial history about the orphan trains. ISBN 978-0-615-29755-2

the importance of blood ties among family members. This was relevant in terms of family property rights and inheritance. In more recent times, U.S. laws have been revised to make adoption more accessible. It is possible for parents with diverse backgrounds to welcome children from a variety of settings and circumstances. There is also a movement to encourage fostering with the hope that it turns into adoption: "Foster to adopt" (Foster Care to Adopt, 2017). This also implies finding "forever homes" with "forever families."

Some families celebrate the day they welcomed a child into their home. This can be a yearly celebration, in addition to the child's birthday. These celebrations can secure the bonds of the family and lead to greater family cohesiveness. On the other hand, the day itself is also a reminder that somewhere, a child's birthparents had to make difficult decisions and sacrifices. Families can decide individually how they choose to mark these events, while also respecting the complexity of the situation that preceded welcoming a child into a home, whether through fostering or adoption. The important message should be that the child feels truly welcome, allowing her to find stability, security, and love in what hopefully promises to become her forever family.

Several factors are associated with the decision to grow a family through adoption and parents need to know in advance that difficulties and obstacles can arise (Child Welfare Information Gateway, 2013; Smalley & Schooler, 2015):

- The reasons for welcoming a child through adoption are varied and diverse, and can include fertility challenges, unique situational factors, age, and importantly altruistic reasons.
- Foster to adopt is an initiative to adopt children from the U.S. foster care system.
- Domestic adoption has been supplemented by international adoptions (also referred to as inter-country adoptions).
- Most single mothers retain custody of their children. They are supported by extended family. Alternatively they tend to choose kinship and open adoptions where parties maintain contact.
- Children who are adopted into stable homes may benefit from the welcoming family environment.
- Some placements may be challenging, such as children with special needs, children who have cycled through numerous foster families, and children who spent their early months or years in depraved circumstances.
- Although there is a preference for welcoming newborns into adoptive homes, this is seldom feasible for international adoptions. On the other hand, domestic adoptions through agencies tend to predominantly be newborn adoptions (Kreider & Lofquist, 2014).
- As far as international or intercountry adoptions are concerned, the highest number of children came from China, followed by Ethiopia and South Korea. Especially if they were born in China, a greater number of girls were available, making up two thirds of adoptees (U.S. Department of State, Bureau of Consular Affairs, n.d.).

- The adoption process can be lengthy, expensive, and frustrating. Not every application for adoption is approved by a particular agency, and not all result in a completed adoption. Potential adoptive parents can expect several hurdles as they attempt to achieve parenthood, such as background screenings, home visits, waiting for an agency to make the adoption a reality, and finally legalizing the adoption. From first application to actual adoption can stretch from months to over two years and varies.
- Parents can choose the situations best suited to their needs as there are several types of adoptions. These include agency adoptions versus private independent or lawyer assisted adoptions. Private independent adoptions handled by a lawyer tend to involve direct contracting with the birthmother and can be more expensive.
- Closed, Open, or Semi-Open Adoption refers to the amount of contact between the birthparents and the family initiating an adoption. Almost all recent adoptions are open or semi-open. Children and their parents have access to information records including identity of the birthparents, and contact may be possible. With open adoption contact is possible. A semi-open adoption permits access to information for all parties, but without contact.

Transracial Adoption (also referred to as Inter-racial Adoption) can be described as the placement of a child from one racial or ethnic group, with parents of another racial or ethnic group.

- Transracial adoptions are occurring frequently, and are also a reality in international adoptions.
- Transracial adoptions encourage individuals to embrace diversity and allow communities to grow toward greater multicultural competence.
- Children may require support in strengthening their unique ethnic, racial, and country-of-origin identity. This can be achieved by encouraging diversity in family friendships and civic engagement.
- Research has repeatedly demonstrated the constructive outcomes of transracial adoptions (Younes & Klein, 2014).
- The Multi-Ethnic Placement Act of 1994 and the Adoption and Safe Families Act of 1997 prohibit the delay or denial of placement of children on the basis of disparities between the race, color, or national origin of foster and adoptive parents and that of the child (Lercara, 2016).

Guest Reflection 6–4

Transitioning to Parenthood: Welcoming Our Daughter

Our adoption of a girl from China has been an "into the woods"-like journey. The path has not been straight and we certainly didn't know it well when we began, but like the song with the same title, "we couldn't tell, didn't know, what was waiting down the dell."

On a rainy December morning, eight months after completing our dossier, we received the call that our referral had arrived. With trembling hands, we opened the packet. The paperwork stated that the female child assigned to our application had been born. Included in the packet was the expected small passport-like photo as well as a second larger color photo of our assigned girl sitting on the floor on a pink blanket. She is staring straight at the camera with a content quiet look on her face. In the small photo she holds the same steady stare against a classic China red background. I don't know how many words these pictures were worth, but I do know they received thousands of return stares. We made copies and put the photos around our house. Like visual mantras we turned to them through the day. Our back and forth stares laid down the first threads of connection and love. To this point, the adoption process had felt like applying for a ramped up passport application. With the photos the process became relationally real for the first time. I would be kissing those puffy cheeks. That stare, one day, would gaze upon me.

Fast forward to China a few months later. Unlike the labor and delivery in childbirth, in adoption both individuals in a couple can take active roles in the tender experience of bringing a child into the family. We wondered so many things about our daughter. Would we recognize her? Would we feel love for her from the first moment? Could we comfort her? Would it take time to bond? The social worker accompanied us down the hall and we entered a room. We easily recognized the girl whose photo we had been staring at for weeks. She was dressed in thick padded yellow clothes. The social worker introduced her to us. The sounds of the other girls and the Chinese conversation of the adults filled the room.

To our surprise we learned that our new daughter had been raised by a foster family shortly after being brought to the orphanage at less than a week old. We were given a stiff laminated photo and a letter sent from the foster mother. The photo was of our new daughter, the foster mother, and the foster grandmother. The verbal translation of the letter included information about food types and feeding times. The letter ended with a request for us to send future photos to the address provided. Clearly a bond had been made. We left the busy room—taking our first steps as an expanded family of three.

In the short 15 yards down the hall to our hotel room we had carried our daughter away from an Asian, Chinese, world we knew little about to a new, Western, American world—an uprooting with incalculable differences and consequences. The first wave of those differences was certainly sensory—seeing unfamiliar people and surroundings, hearing different language sounds and cadence, smelling different bodies and foods and tasting different liquids in bottles. Back in our room we removed the thick, snowsuit like padded jumper. Out of the clothes she was much smaller and lighter than she had first appeared. Our daughter cried and whimpered for a good hour before falling asleep. My wife and I did our best to comfort and soothe her. Once our daughter was asleep I had the common culture shock thought of "how can two places so different share the same planet."

I also noticed my attention had tuned to the in and out sounds of our new daughter's breathing from the portable crib. Like the automatic wifi search made by modern electronic devices, without willful intention, my heart had done a signal search and locked onto the life sounds for which I was now responsible.

Making physical and emotional space and adding the new child to set routines, is an overarching task for new parents. On our first morning as a family of three our former "in and out" breakfast routine felt transformed to a desert caravan departure loaded with weeks of provisions. The next morning as we began to play she looked us directly in the eye and smiled for the first time. The letter we had received from the foster mother began, "Dear parents, we really appreciate that you are adopting an orphan. She is a healthy and bright girl. I took care of her for 9 months and she has a very regular life." We understood our daughters crying to be in part about being abruptly and radically separated from her foster family and her "regular life." Experiences of loss and grief lie at the core of adoptions. Our daughter's smile thrilled us. It gave us some needed assurance that our adoption would also bring some joy.

The return to the USA from China with our new daughter marked the end of the first phase of our adoption journey. We were exhausted and proud. We had chosen and traveled a significant distance down an unknown path. We had pushed through to a new place in life. We had fresh stories and experiences to assimilate and an expanded family identity to solidify. We didn't know the turns that lay ahead.

Author: Dan M. Sandifer-Stech, PhD. (1959–2016), Parent, Ordained Minister, Therapist, Educator. Published with permission.

Parenting Reflection 6–5

You are the parent of a child and this was an international and transracial adoption. You've been asked to address a group of potential adoptive parents who are likely to pursue similar options to create a family. What advice would you give? How could you support your child in maintaining aspects of her cultural heritage?

International Adoption

International adoptions (also referred to as inter-country adoptions) are noted for their high risk and difficulty, especially because transnational welfare practices are not universal (Chen, 2016). The health histories received may be inaccurate or falsified, increasing the risk of adopting a child with unanticipated special and medical needs. Prospective parents must pay significant fees, such as all agency and in-country expenses, medical checkups, documents, and visa and travel expenses. These costs can run into thousands of dollars. In addition, the difficulties in gathering a health history for the child and government restrictions may make for a daunting obstacle course (Child Welfare Information Gateway, 2012).

Ultimately, the success of an inter-country adoption may depend on several factors and for every heartbreak story there may be an opposite tale of joy and fulfillment. There have been unsuccessful inter-country adoptions, in which the adopting parents wanted to return the child after finding that the challenges were insurmountable. Some cases of aggressive children who were exceptionally hostile towards their adoptive families have been documented. Contributing factors are early and severe neglect, parental deprivation, and *disorders of attachment* (including *reactive attachment disorder* and *disinhibited social engagement disorder*.)

Children who were welcomed from transracial and inter-country contexts, may require strengthening of their unique identity. This can be achieved by encouraging diversity in family friendships, civic engagement, and multicultural competence. If some family friends and peers have similar racial and ethnic backgrounds, it provides a variety of role models for the child, which in turn facilitates positive self-concept and identity formation.

Reactive Attachment Disorder is characterized by "withdrawn behavior and restricted positive affect."

Disinhibited Social Engagement Disorder is characterized by "disinhibited social behavior and repeated violations of conventional interpersonal boundaries" (Black & Zeanah, 2015).

Some of the antecedents to these situations include the following:

■ The adoptive parents may get insufficient or inaccurate information about the child, and the medical histories are incomplete. With limited background information on the biological parents, it is difficult to ascertain whether the child was at risk prenatally, for instance through alcohol or drug exposure.

■ According to ethical adoption practices, children should be clearly identified as having special needs or medical concerns so that adoptive parents know how to offer the relevant support and are informed of the unique challenges.

■ If a monetary exchange is involved, which it usually is, it becomes difficult to draw the line between necessary expenses and a possible profit motive on the part of international agencies in the countries of birth of the adoptees. It is unethical to ever attach a dollar amount to the life of a child.

■ Problems with lengthy stays in overcrowded orphanages, extreme neglect, sensory deprivation, and the absence of constant caregivers have been linked to changes in brain development presenting as reactive attachment disorders, developmental delays, and disinhibited social engagement disorder (Belsky & de Haas, 2011; Black & Zeanah, 2015).

■ Interventions and psychological techniques aimed at addressing the outcomes of early parental deprivation and concomitant disorders of attachment are being researched (Belsky & de Haan, 2011).

. . . .

Focus Point. Adoption, chosen for a variety of reasons, can be a costly, time-consuming, beautiful avenue by which to grow a family. Contrary to historical adoptions, modern adoptions are often characterized by open celebration. Inter-country adoptions present greater challenges due to the varying ethical and legal guidelines of each country, and the age at which some of the children can be welcomed by adopting parents.

. . . .

FOSTER PARENTING

Some parents have to temporarily or even permanently sacrifice their right to parent. Underlying these outcomes may be a history of maltreatment and/or neglect. Families who experience poverty, mental illness, or addiction disorders translate to a distressing number of children who have to experience out-of-home placements. When a community or state agency has determined that children are not safe in their parents' home or that it is not in their best interest to be exposed to an unhealthy parent–child environment, children can be legally removed.

The most common placement is into *foster care* or family foster care. In this setting, children are cared for by screened, trained, and licensed adults who provide substitute parental care. Some of these homes are intended for children with special needs. Foster care could also be provided by a child's relatives and is called *kinship care*. In each of these settings, the foster parents are compensated for the services they provide, although expenses typically exceed the amount that is provided by the supervising agency. The economic gains should never be the sole incentive. Children who settle into a permanent placement refer to this as finding their "forever family."

Foster Care in the United States

The federal government collects information related to foster care and publishes this information annually (Children's Bureau, 2015).

■ The number of children in foster care in the United States in 2014 was over 415,000, indicating a mildly declining rate over the previous decade. Numbers of children being fostered and waiting to be adopted also declined slightly. In 2014, over 100,000 children in the United States were waiting to be adopted from foster care.

■ Annually about 50,000 adoptions are finalized, and about the same figure applies to parents whose rights had been terminated in 2014.

Parental abuse and neglect are the most common reasons for placement into foster care. As many as 80 percent of all families involved with child protective services are affected by poverty, mental illness, addictions, and related disorders (National Conference of State Legislatures, 2016).

Foster parents may be single or married and come from all social backgrounds (Children's Bureau,

2017). Every state has its own criteria for foster parenting. Some criteria for foster parents include that they undergo foster care and parenting training, that they have no criminal record or history of child maltreatment, and that they have an income (which reduces the risk of fostering for the wrong reasons).

Adults who become foster parents are often motivated by their own childhood experiences in foster care or by an altruistic desire to meet the needs of children who come from difficult family circumstances. Foster care has a darker side as well, as not all placements have happy endings. Many of the children struggle with emotional, attachment, and behavioral problems and may have been cycled through various homes. They may have started life in circumstances that cannot support good outcomes. These shadows from the past will reappear and some parents do not have the training, patience, or other superhuman qualities it may require to see the task to completion. Some misguided foster parents may see this as a source of income, but that in itself should be a warning light that they are not truly cut out for this type of sacrifice. Foster parents deal with a variety of challenging issues that are not typically experienced by other adults who care for children.

Another very realistic problem is that foster children can be claimed back by biological parents, sometimes at very inopportune moments. Children may bond with new foster families, only to have that attachment severed, and have to return to an unstable, unpredictable family life, where they are bound by their genetic ties.

The hopeful stories are those in which foster children are integrated into families and eventually are adopted by those families. There is a strong movement to urge suitable foster parents to *"foster to adopt"* so that the cycle of uncertainty can be interrupted and the child can establish roots in a stable and loving environment.

The National Foster Care Association emphasizes that fostering is something we do for a child (National Foster Parent Association, 2016). They state that it is not about financial outcomes, nor should it be entirely about our own needs. Instead, it ideally is: "A chance to make the world a better place—one child at a time."

"A population that does not take care of the elderly and of children and the young, has no future; because it abuses both its memory and its promise."

Pope Francis (b. 1936)

Parenting Reflection 6.6

You are developing a training program for potential foster parents. The course consists of ten classes. What major topics would you include? What outside speakers would you invite to speak on which topics?

Focus Point.   When children are removed from their parents' care, they are placed into foster care or family foster care. This frequently occurs due to parental abuse or neglect, and it is intended to be a temporary solution. Data collected by the federal government indicates that for most children the length of stay in the foster care system is far from temporary. In addition, certain demographic variables are associated with children in foster care.

A foster parent is usually not related to the child being cared for, although some children are welcomed by relatives. Foster parents resemble other adults in most communities and must meet criteria established by state social agencies in order to be able to take on this role. In addition, they must complete approved training to be foster parents. These foster parents face challenges that are unique to their situation by offering a home to neglected children, whose birth parents may not be in a position to provide adequate care.

CHAPTER FOCUS POINTS

A Transformative Relationship

■ The birth of a child invokes a rainbow of emotions, ranging from joy to fear. Modern trends in parenting and greater gender equality, have led fathers to take a more active role in parenting. Ideally, the choice to parent includes consideration of many factors including economic stability and emotional preparedness. Parental union instability and disruptions have an undesirable effect on the offspring.

■ Parenting often carries considerable financial obligations, adding stress especially on families living in poverty. Pressure from friends, family, and society may influence a couple's decision to have children.

Many parents experience role strain, an outcome of altering the makeup of their family system.

Family of Creation

■ Our families of origin consist of our own parents and our own siblings. Contrast this to our families of creation. This is the family we create with a partner and can include our own children. When the family of creation is seen as a nuclear family, the influences from previous generations will filter down to this family form. These can be positive or negative influences. The continuity of a family system contributes to the shelter that an individual or a newly forming couple may seek and experience while embarking on the process of forming an own family of creation/procreation.

Planning for a Family

■ Responsible parenting begins before conception. With the help of genetic counseling, parents can be informed concerning the risks of possible genetic abnormalities and determine the best way to proceed. Both women and men should prepare for conception by adopting healthy lifestyles and avoiding stressors. All medications, including over the counter products, need to be approved by the medical team and prenatal care is important to ensure optimal pregnancy outcomes.

■ The lifestyle choices, ages and genetics of both the mother and the father can affect the future outcome of the child they plan to conceive together. Ideally pregnancies should be planned and include a preconception medical consult to ensure optimal outcomes. Despite a feeling of invincibility, an estimated 50% of all pregnancies in the U.S. are unplanned.

Pregnancy and Birth

■ Short- and long-term outcomes are directly related to intrauterine conditions before birth, making the period before birth one of the key developmental stages of the life span. This critical period forms the foundation on which the later stages will be built. Various factors contribute to developmental plasticity. This means that a given genotype can be expressed in different ways in response to environmental factors. Certain risk factors are related to the father.

Preparation for Birth

■ The prospect of becoming parents brings about changes for both partners. Women who anticipate motherhood positively, adjust better to pregnancy, labor, and delivery. Expectant fathers play an important role and may need assistance in successfully transitioning into their new role in the family. Hospital births with medical support optimize good outcomes and are recommended for all births. It minimizes risks should unforeseen complications occur.

The Birthing Experience

■ Many hospitals and birthing centers encourage parent–child bonding by providing various resources and accommodations. Postpartum depression is more common than most realize, and can include mood swings, fatigue, and a lack of joy. Attachment and bonding are implicated and this in turn can contribute to the baby failing to thrive. This condition is serious and requires medical and family support. Parents who experience a miscarriage or infant loss are encouraged to access support from professionals who can assist them with the grieving process. A rainbow baby is the term for a live birth after previous infant loss.

Alternative Avenues to Parenthood

■ While alternative methods and complex fertility treatments allow numerous families to experience the joys of parenthood, multiple ethical and legal questions are raised by some of the approaches to reproductive technology. The coming years will shed more light on the positive and negative outcomes of such practices.

Parenting and Adoption

■ Adoption, chosen for a multitude of reasons, can be a costly, time-consuming, beautiful avenue by which to grow a family. Contrary to historical adoptions, modern adoptions are often characterized by open celebration. International or intercountry adoptions present greater challenges due to the varying ethical and legal guidelines of each country, and sometimes the age at which a child can join an adoptive family.

Foster Parenting

- When children are removed from their parents' care, they are placed into foster care or family foster care. This frequently occurs due to parental abuse or neglect, and it is intended to be a temporary solution. Data collected by the federal government indicates that for most children the length of stay in the foster care system is far from temporary.

- A foster parent is usually not related to the child being cared for, although some children are welcomed by relatives. Foster parents resemble other adults in most communities and must meet criteria established by state social agencies in order to be able to take on this role. In addition, they must complete approved training to be foster parents. These foster parents face challenges that are unique to their situation by offering a home to neglected or at risk children, whose birth parents may not be in a position to provide adequate care.

USEFUL WEBSITES

Websites are dynamic and change

Academic Pediatric Association
http://ambpeds.org
Baby's health

American Congress of Obstetricians and Gynecologists
www.acog.org
Women's health, pregnancy, and childbirth

American Pregnancy Association
www.americanpregnancy.org
Conception, pregnancy and childbirth, labor and delivery

National Foster Parent Association
www.nfpaonline.org
Education on fostering, resources for foster parents

National Institute of Child Health and Human Development
www.nichd.nih.gov
Mom and baby's health

Postpartum Support International
www.postpartum.net
Postpartum depression, women's mental health

U.S. Department of Health and Human Services, Administration for Children and Families
www.acf.hhs.gov/
Adoption, foster care

CHAPTER 7

Parenting Infants and Toddlers

Learning Outcomes

After completing this chapter, you should be able to

1. Describe infancy and a parent's responsibilities related to this stage.

2. Summarize the importance of the infancy stage.

3. Illustrate the importance of attachment in healthy infant development.

4. Distinguish between the safety concerns of infants and toddlers.

5. Assess the ways in which parents grow and develop.

PARENTAL RESPONSIBILITIES

Birth and the subsequent period of infancy, are amongst the most sacred times in parenting. A baby has joined the family, and for first-time parents this is a major excursion into the land of parenthood. During the pregnancy, the baby was on an "auto pilot" of sorts, incubated in the safest place it could be. The mother could sleep, hope, and dream; the as yet unborn would be nourished and taken care of in a temperature controlled and perfect environment.

Birth changes all that. The baby has become an independent, yet also highly dependent, separate entity. Parents are typically overwhelmed with wonder, gratitude, joy, plus the nagging little refrain regarding whether they will be able to meet this new person's

Andy Dean Photography/Shutterstock

The birth of a baby also marks the birth of a parent; it indicates a time when parents and caretakers must become responsive to and in tune with the unique and very personal language of infants.

needs. It is an awe inspiring task, yet also among the most responsible and time-consuming challenges parents can ever face. After the first few weeks, moms and dads have been known to sigh with relief at having kept the baby *alive*; so daunting did this challenge appear to them.

One of the first and most crucial parenting tasks is to learn the infant's unique and very personal language. As parents, we have to tune in to become acutely aware of what the baby is communicating to us, we need to be at a heightened state of responsiveness; babies need caretakers who are *responsive*. As tiny as this person is, his or her needs are incrementally bigger; often the smaller the baby (as in premature births), the greater the caretaking challenges. But we have not been taught this magical language,

as each child arrives with a new version of communication that we have to decode. A fellow parent stated: "Each child arrives with a unique genetic code that we have to decipher and then try to program" (Steward, 2016).

Infancy is the period of the life span that extends between the birth and the first year following the birth. Recent research findings about the nature of infant development depict an infant as showing highly competent behaviors and being actively involved in learning to master interactions with the environment (Stahl & Feigenson, 2015). Most people are aware that infants require much attention, supervision, and care to grow and develop. Theorists and researchers also acknowledge infancy as a landmark stage in the human lifespan (Bornstein, 2014).

Parenting Reflection 7–1

What are some sources of contemporary ideas about what infants are like? Are these depictions realistic in preparing parents for the reality of first meeting their newborn?

Focus Point.   Parenting an infant, particularly a first child, can be exhilarating and exhausting, terrific and terrifying. Within the first few weeks, parents must learn the new infant's communication patterns to provide proper care. The period of infancy requires parents to be extremely attentive and responsible as the baby transitions from womb to world.

Cultural Snapshot 7–1

Words of advice to Balinese parents:

At birth, your child will be divine, closer to the world of the gods than to the human world. Having just arrived from heaven, your infant should be treated as a celestial being. Provide the attention that a god deserves, and address your child with the high language suitable to a person of higher rank. You should hold your newborn high, for gods and members of higher rank should always be elevated relative to their inferiors. For the first 210 days (or 105 days, depending on region and status), never put your baby down on the ground

or floor, which is too profane for a god. Until then, your baby should be carried at all times (Diener in DeLoache & Gottlieb, 2000, p. 105).

Sources: Diener, M. (2000). Gift from the gods: A Balinese guide to early child rearing. In J. G. DeLoache and A. Gottlieb (Eds.), *A World of Babies, Imagined Childcare Guides for Seven Societies* (pp. 97–116). Cambridge, England: Cambridge University Press.

Harkness, S. & Super, C. M. (2002). Culture and parenting. In: Bornstein, M. H. *Handbook of Parenting*, Volume 2, p. 253. New York, NY: Psychology Press; Taylor and Francis.

LANDMARKS OF INFANCY

The baby travels a journey from complete dependence and helplessness toward the independence and autonomy that are ultimately attained in adulthood. It is a carefully orchestrated interaction of numerous subtle factors that combine towards dynamic outcomes.

Infancy displays unique developmental tasks and landmarks that lay the foundation for future developmental progress. The developmental events that occur in infancy are the outcomes of maturational changes. As the baby grows and develops, changes in size and body proportions become apparent. These in turn influence the development of particular physical, social, and emotional skills. Healthy adjustment in infancy focuses on appropriate developmental tasks which serve as landmarks. Early testing of infants focuses on these observable dimensions (Illingworth, 2013).

Knowledge of developmental events at each stage is important to parents and caregivers. These events are cues to those caring for the infant and will guide and influence the caretaking behavior. This is also the core of the dynamic *bidirectionality* of parenting; as the baby changes, the response of the caretaker should change. In ever circular fashion they continue to influence each other in so many subtle ways. This backwards and forwards responsive interaction is known as *"Serve and return"* (Harvard, The developing child, 2017).

. . . .

Focus Point.   Development in infancy lays the foundation for each consecutive stage of life. Parents have the responsibility of providing appropriate care in order to maximize healthy development.

. . . .

Video Example 7.1

Watch this video on developmental milestones in infants and children. Identify some of the major stages of growth and development in infants and toddlers.
      (https://www.youtube.com/watch?v=SBFnO2FCdeE)

PARENTING INFANTS

Infants demand an extreme degree of dedication from parents and caregivers. This dependence on adults is necessary for survival and for enhancing a child's developmental progress; in turn, adults need to be *responsive*. Learning to become a "baby whisperer" or someone who knows how to soothe babies, means that we need to attune to the individual communication of that child. We need to be intensely focused so that we can read the tiniest signals. The beauty of learning to communicate with a baby is that we will also become sensitive to what they are trying to convey to us, and in response we have to react. Every minute communication, whether it is to indicate comfort or discomfort, may elicit a response. We may intervene to relieve the discomfort; for example, the baby who cries because she needs to be fed, diapered, or cradled in our arms, is telling us something. We have to figure out their needs.

For new parents this can be difficult, because we do not yet know the range of communication, and we have to learn about the cues the baby will give us. Babies signal through their body language and facial expressions, through their body tone and other subtleties, whether they are in a good space or not. Newborns sleep about 16–17 hours of the day (Stanford Children's Health, 2017). Every parent or caretaker of a newborn can attest that that does not translate into only 6-8 hours of caretaking per day. We check babies regularly, we initially keep them in the same room as us, so that there is constant visual monitoring. After all, they are so new to this world and we as parents are so new to them; we both have to learn from one another.

When we talk about "serve and return" we are referring to this process of reacting to the child. The baby may send us signals; it is "serving." Think of a tennis game; we serve a ball, and then we expect our coplayer to return that ball, else there is no interaction, and in essence it is "game over." When the baby is "serving" us with a cue, we need to react appropriately (Center on the Developing Child at Harvard University, 2017). We have to respond in the manner required. This is a two-way street of communication. We as caretakers and parents also serve items to the baby. We touch, we coo, we talk to him, we rock her.

What we are doing on an observable level in terms of interaction, is also happening within the brain of the child. The brain forms an intricate network of neural connections. These neural connections talk to each other through the tiniest of electrical impulses. When a neuron is appropriately stimulated it knows to respond. It will encourage the neural network to grow and form new connections. It is like adding more memory to our computers by adding an extra memory card. We are growing the extra memory and cognitive potential, by growing the neural network. If we do not use certain areas of the brain, those neural networks will be pruned and reduced. It truly is a matter of "use it or lose it." The neural networks are grown by being stimulated. When the "serve and return" sequence plays out within the brain, it means that there is appropriate stimulation which allows for response, which in turn leads to growth (Holland et al., 2014; Kugelman & Colin, 2013; Lebel & Beaulieu, 2011; Moore, Bocchini, & Raphael, 2016; Mundasad, 2013).

Appropriate Engagement

Earlier in this description of "serve and respond" we commented that if no one returns the serve, then the game is over. Similarly, if a child is not appropriately stimulated and engaged, the neural pathways do not grow. It is a misconception that the newborn baby is too young to know. Newborn babies benefit from skin time and appropriate touch, where they can feel the parent and it promotes bonding and attachment. Newborns respond positively to being breastfed, they have an instinctive latching ability, they are preprogrammed to latch-on and suck; it means survival.

In humans, the nature and degree of dependency in infancy and childhood differs from that observed among the young of other species. It takes much more developmental time for the sophisticated and intricate neural connections that characterize mature functioning. For example, the brain at birth weighs only 25 percent of its total adult weight, but by age 3, the brain has attained about 90 percent of its adult weight. Socialization and education continue throughout life. For most of infancy, parents provide intense, hands-on, and continuous caregiving. As children grow older and become more autonomous, the focused physical caregiving diminishes while psychological caregiving takes on new dimensions to become developmentally appropriate.

For the newborn, it is all about creating the environment in which the baby can thrive and grow. With the extensive amount of literature on hand, we have excellent guidelines for new parents.

Sleep–Wake Cycle

A popular belief about infants is that they sleep a great deal of the time, although individual sleeping patterns are subject to wide variations (Stanford Children's

Health, 2017). Informative material, based on best practices, is available to guide parents concerning their child's sleep (American Academy of Pediatrics, 2017b). Sleep during the first few months after birth is interrupted only long enough for the baby to feed. This round-the-clock pattern of alternating periods of sleep with feeding extends to longer intervals of wakefulness after the third month. During the remainder of the time until the infant approaches age 2, sleep decreases to 10 to 14 hours daily.

Resources for Caregivers

Two reputable sources for information about infant care:

- *American Academy of Pediatrics:* "Caring for your baby and young child." (www.aap.org) and (www.healthy-childcare.org).
- *Mayo Clinic:* "Mayo clinic guide to your baby's first year - From doctors who are parents too." (www.mayoclinic.com).

Both sources offer guidelines for health-related aspects pertaining to children, including bringing a newborn home.

Mothers who have missed a lot of sleep because of night time feeding sessions, are cautioned not to fall asleep in armchairs, rockers, recliners, or couches while nursing a baby. If the baby were to fall it could cause serious injuries. Feeding in bed is less dangerous in terms of falling, but again mothers need to place the baby back in her bassinette after the feed, and not fall asleep with an infant in bed (American Academy of Pediatrics, 2017a). Bedsharing with infants, especially babies under the age of six months, could lead to asphyxiation and sleep related death (Moon, 2016).

Sleep Related Infant Deaths

These deaths are associated with suffocation, asphyxia, strangulation, and SIDS (sudden infant death syndrome). Children younger than six months should sleep in a bassinette in the parents' room so that they are monitored at all times. Pillows, soft toys and crib liners or bumpers, may look attractive in a store display, but they are not safe and should be removed from the crib. Infants should sleep in sleep sacks on a relatively hard mattress with no loose bedding. Mothers who nurse infants need to be careful that the infant does not fall if the mother falls asleep while nursing. Babies should sleep on their backs "back to sleep," in a prone position. Daytime, supervised "tummy time" will allow infants to strengthen their backs and necks, but monitoring this carefully is crucial. Co-sleeping is inadvisable. Parents and siblings should never bedshare with a young infant or baby.

Communication and Infant Crying

An infant's first attempts at communication with the world come in the form of crying. Parents soon learn that they must decipher the meaning behind a particular cry in order to meet an infant's needs. For example, a fussy, tearful baby who cries relentlessly may be experiencing colic, a problem resulting from an immature digestive system. A baby may be expressing discomfort as a result of teething, sickness, a wet diaper, feeling lonely, being hungry, or needing comfort and human attention. Determining the cause of a baby's crying is learned by spending time with the baby. Infants communicate their desire to be held, nurtured, and comforted through their cries or their body language. Infants respond to being walked, rocked, and to calm music like lullabies.

Importantly, parents need to know about these despairing situations that can be triggered by infant crying, so that maltreatment of children and especially "Shaken Baby Syndrome" can be avoided. Excellent material is available explaining the phases and duration of infant crying. This is especially valuable to parents who may feel that the crying is endless, and who slide into cycles of despair related to infant caregiving. Studies on infant crying have found that babies cry for a variety of reasons, not all of them related to pain or hunger. Some seem to have inbuilt clocks, as the crying invariably starts early evening. Other babies may be colicky and they can outgrow this phase, although pediatric support may be necessary (Barr, Rajabali, Aragon, Colbourne, & Brant, 2015; Sung et al., 2014)

"The Period of Purple Crying" (http://purplecrying.info) provides greater detail on phases and variations in infant crying patterns. A number of professionals such as pediatricians and psychologists have been involved with the development of this major initiative (Barr et al., 2015). Note that crying has a beginning and an end. "PURPLE" is an acronym for words describing the crying of babies, and the characteristics of the crying behavior are described as follows:

- **P**eak of crying
- **U**nexpected crying
- **R**esists soothing
- **P**ain-like face
- **L**ong lasting
- **E**vening

Various aspects can be observed when it comes to infant crying. There can be a peak of crying and crying that may resist soothing and occurs unexpectedly. The crying may seem to continue a long time and occur at certain times of the day such as late afternoons and early evenings, which may also be the peak crying times. Sometimes the baby appears to be in pain and may resist soothing. For a parent, this may be very distressing and knowing that there is a support network makes all the difference. Parents who feel isolated may succumb to feelings of despair more readily (National Center on Shaken Baby Syndrome, 2017).

Important warning:

Those caring for children, and other support persons, need to know that extended crying spells wear down the caregivers and can lead to irrational behavior in caretaking which should be avoided at all cost. Caretakers who are struggling, need support. Extended infant crying is a valid and real reason to ask for and to extend support. A number of initiatives exist to network young parents. Frequently, the prenatal classes form the basis for later parent support groups for new parents. These vary from community to community.

It is also advisable to use the pediatric and general medical team available to rule out serious conditions requiring medical attention. In other words, even though some babies cry more and longer than others, call in an experienced person, or visit the baby clinic to check if the crying behavior falls within normal parameters, or whether the baby is communicating something more serious.

The ultimate goal is infant safety, and that includes the peace of mind of the caretakers and appropriate knowledge concerning childcare. Refer to Figure 7–1, Figure 7–2.

Feeding and Breastfeeding

To promote the health of both infants and their mothers, the Centers for Disease Control and Prevention (Centers for Disease Control and Prevention, 2017a) recommend breastfeeding. There has been a steady rise in exclusively breast-fed infants, especially at 3–6

SAFE SLEEPING

- *Back-to-Sleep*. Infants should sleep on their backs in a supine position.
- A firm crib mattress, covered by a tight-fitting sheet, should be used in a safety-approved crib.
- There should be no bedding; loose and soft bedding and soft toys in the crib can contribute to suffocation.
- Swaddling infants older than 2 months for sleep is not recommended because it increases the risk of sudden infant death syndrome (SIDS).
- One-piece clothing for sleeping is recommended, depending on the temperature.
- Infant should not overheat; be aware of the room temperature.
- Infants should not nap or sleep in a car safety seat or a bouncy seat, instead of a crib. If an infant falls asleep in a car safety seat while traveling, remove the child immediately upon arrival and place the infant in a supine position in a crib. Monitor the child while traveling.
- Avoid baby necklaces, bibs, or anything around the baby's neck that could cause strangulation.
- There should be only one child per crib—no crib sharing.
- Infants should not sleep in adult beds, nor should they bedshare with an adult.
- Pacifiers may be used, but consult the safety protocols.
- Infants should be observed by sight and sound at all times.

Based on the recommendations of the National Resource Center for Health and Safety in Child Care and Early Education (2017), www.nrckids.org.

FIGURE 7–1. Safe Sleeping for Infants.

CAREGIVER DESPAIR

- Parents and/or caregivers who are sleep deprived or exhausted may act in irrational and desperate ways. They may become frustrated and angry, losing their ability to adapt and to be resilient.
- Recognize that caregiver despair is a real feeling that needs immediate intervention to prevent harm to the child.
- Establish a support system *before* despair sets in. Recognize and *anticipate* when caretaker's emotional resources are approaching depletion.
- Plan for some time off, utilizing support from family and friends or a caregiving facility to give the parent or caretaker a chance to recuperate. Make time for self-renewal and know that it is a valid need that has to be addressed.
- While the infant is young, try to sleep when the infant sleeps, even if this is during the day.
- If a caretaker feels that he or she is losing a grip on his or her emotions, it is necessary to call for help immediately. If that is not possible, the infant should be put in a safe place, such as a crib. The caretaker should then initiate an action which will interrupt the emotions of despair, such as counting to 50, breathing deeply, splashing one's face with cold water, phoning a friend and telling them of the despair, or calling a neighbor to come over. Hopefully, this short break is enough to regain control over one's emotions.
- Social isolation can contribute to the feelings of despair and depression that young parents may face. On becoming a parent, it is important to establish a peer network of fellow parents in an appropriate civic group and to solicit the support of family members, neighbors, and friends who will occasionally help with the caretaking tasks and who will respond in times of need.
- Recognize the despair, acknowledge that it is a valid emotion, and interrupt the overwhelming feeling so that no child is at risk at any time.
- As a parent and a caretaker, learn to anticipate and regulate your own emotions appropriately.
- More information on infant crying can be obtained at Period of Purple Crying® (www.purplecrying.info). This program is part of the National Center on Shaken Baby Syndrome (www.dontshake.org), whose mission is to reduce infant abuse, including shaken baby syndrome (see FIGURE 7–7). This evidence-based *infant abuse prevention program*, which educates parents and warns them about the dangers of shaking an infant, also explains the role of crying in infants.

FIGURE 7–2. Preventing Parental/Caregiver Despair.

months. This implies that mothers are nursing longer and both the mothers and the infants receive the health benefits. The statistics for the United States are encouraging and indicate that about 75 percent of children have been breast-fed at some time, meaning that some nursing occurred, supplemented with formula. Refer to Figure 7–3. At least a third of all mothers have managed to exclusively breastfeed until the baby was 3 months old; in several states, this figure was as high as 50 percent, meeting one of the goals of Healthy People 2020 (Office on Women's Health in the Department of Health and Human Services, 2014). There are distinct cultural

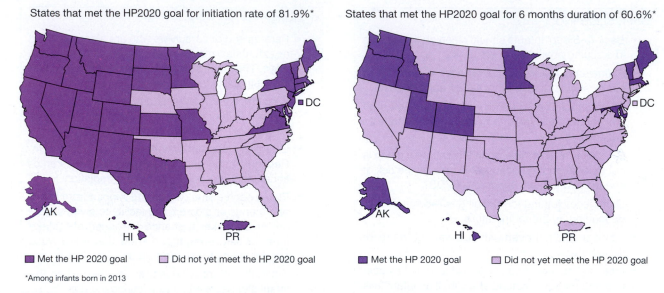

States that met the HP2020 goal for initiation rate of 81.9%*

States that met the HP2020 goal for 6 months duration of 60.6%*

■ Met the HP 2020 goal   ☐ Did not yet meet the HP 2020 goal

■ Met the HP 2020 goal   ☐ Did not yet meet the HP 2020 goal

*Among infants born in 2013

FIGURE 7–3.   States that Met the HP2020 Breastfeeding Goals. HP denotes Healthy People - www.healthypeople.gov. *Source:* CDC, Breastfeeding Report Card, Progressing Toward National Breastfeeding Goals, United States, 2016.

variations, with 80 percent of Hispanic/Latina mothers initiating breast-feeding.

One of the initial decisions in providing infant care is to commit to breastfeeding for at least 4–6 months so that the mother's antibodies (proteins that fight infection) can be transmitted to the infant through her breast milk. This, in itself, is a priceless gift that helps the infant to develop increased immunity against disease. Almost all fathers are supportive and encourage breastfeeding for their newborns because they have been educated regarding the many benefits to both the mother and the infant. Hospital lactation specialists, specifically "Certified International Board of Lactation" consultants, can guide the mother in establishing good lactation patterns and coping with nursing. The lactation specialist will also counsel mothers concerning pumping breast milk for feeding when she is not available to nurse and supplementation with formula, if needed. Ideally, the mother will produce as much milk as the infant requires. It is optimal to exclusively breastfeed for 6 months (American Academy of Pediatrics, 2012b and 2017b), followed by the addition of complementary age-appropriate foods.

The benefits of nursing extend well beyond the actual infant feeding process. Infants who have been breast-fed are less likely to become obese and develop diabetes in later life (Office on Women's Health in the Department of Health and Human Services, 2014). Mothers who have nursed lower their risk for breast cancer, diabetes, and heart disease (Kelly, Chopra, & Dolly, 2015; Ross-Cowdery, Lewis, Papic, Corbelli, & Schwarz, 2016). Additionally, the mothers who nurse lose the weight gained during pregnancy faster. The time spent nursing is an excellent bonding opportunity for the infant and the mother. Some family-friendly workplaces and childcare centers will provide a lactation room for nursing mothers to pump milk or to nurse if the baby is with them. Childcare regulations have been adjusted nationally to support nursing mothers, and it is regarded as a *best practice*. Research supports breastfeeding because the health-related benefits far outweigh any perceived inconvenience (American Academy of Pediatrics, 2017b).

On the other hand, under certain medical conditions, a mother *should not* nurse because infectious agents can be transmitted via the breast milk (e.g., hepatitis, untreated tuberculosis, and HIV). In addition, certain medications and other substances can be excreted in the milk of lactating mothers. Also, lactating mothers should abstain from nicotine and alcohol and greatly limit their caffeine intake. With regard to medications, mothers should take the same precautions during lactation as they did during pregnancy. Medical guidance is indicated (National Medical Association, 2017). For the same reasons, and to ensure safety, unscreened human milk should not be fed to another mother's child; preferably, an infant should receive the milk from its own biological mother.

Under some special circumstances, such as extreme prematurity and when babies are fragile, breast milk can be purchased if it is not available from the mother. This breast milk and the donor mother will have been screened and the milk pasteurized. Some hospitals maintain milk banks that adhere to strict guidelines of the Human Milk Banking Association of North America. Nursing mothers who are able to do so can donate their surplus human milk to milk bank depots.

The **sucking reflex** is one of the earliest reflexes to appear during prenatal development and is exceptionally well developed at birth in full-term newborns. This necessary reflex, which is easily elicited by almost any stimulation to the lips, cheeks, or mouth area, ensures that an infant can obtain nourishment before teeth emerge for chewing. The infant also has a rooting reflex, seeking out the mother's breast in order to nurse.

Most normal infants require feeding every 2 to 4 hours during the first few months after birth. After adding solid foods to a baby's diet, usually after about the sixth month (American Academy of Pediatrics, 2012b), the number of feedings is reduced and continues to decline as the infant grows older. Mothers can continue to supplement feedings with breast milk.

Parenting Reflection 7–2

Explain some of the far-reaching positive outcomes of breastfeeding for both mother and infant. How can fathers be supportive in meeting the needs of a new baby?

Focus Point. A parent should actively engage the infant to encourage healthy communication and bonding. As crying is such an integral part of an infant's communication patterns, it is the parent's responsibility to decipher what each cry means. Studies have been conducted to show the benefits of breastfeeding. Many of these benefits manifest themselves later in the child's life.

Health and Medical Care

If a mother had an uneventful pregnancy, then it is likely that the baby will also enter the world in a healthy state. Certain physical conditions that appear to be of concern could be relatively normal for infants (KidsHealth, n.d.), although regular pediatric checkups are recommended:

- Spitting up or vomiting; the infant should be adequately burped after each feeding to prevent bloating and cramps. There are various techniques for doing this.
- Sneezing and hiccupping, especially during the first few months following birth.
- The appearance of the stool varies by age and diet of the infant. The stools of breastfed babies typically are mustard-yellow, runny, and seedy or curdled in texture. Rashes are common, especially in the diaper area.
- Other skin conditions may be observed, such as cradle cap (seborrhea), heat rash, and if breastfed, occasional skin rashes and slight breast budding or swelling, caused by hormones in the lactating mother's breast milk.
- Obstructed tear ducts sometimes occur, and in the majority of cases there is spontaneous remission within the first year.

It is important to follow up with well-baby medical care that will allow health-care professionals to examine the baby regularly and to judge whether any conditions require medical intervention and treatment. Many physical disorders can be detected early. Immunizations during infancy provide protection from communicable diseases such as measles, diphtheria, mumps, and polio. A schedule of planned vaccinations is recommended. While most families have medical insurance to cover this care, families living in poverty will be able to get all vaccinations and care at no cost at public clinics (Benefits.gov, 2017).

Parenting and Brain Development

Parents play an important role in promoting an infant's brain development. This influence begins with the environment provided by the mother during pregnancy and continues following the birth of the child with the provision of adequate nutrition, health care, stimulation, nurture, and interaction.

An infant's brain experiences rapid growth during the first 2 years following birth. At birth, the brain is functionally operational, but lacks the ability to perform critical thinking skills and to use language. The neonatal reflexes that are present at birth, such as sucking and grasping, are formed at the subcortical level. This part of the brain contains those mechanisms that regulate heart rate,

---

Focus On 7–1   **Early Warning Signs and Infant Care**

It is important to know that an infant does not have the same resilience as an adult. It is better to be over-cautious and to get medical advice as soon as problems manifest, because the consequences can be irreversible if there is no speedy intervention. For instance, diarrhea can cause dehydration very quickly and can be life threatening. Be informed so that, as a parent, you recognize early warning signs that warrant professional intervention. Regard the medical pediatric team as your support system in raising infants optimally.

---

respiration, sleeping patterns, and so forth. These reflexes are important in that they serve as the first avenues for allowing the infant to interact with its environment. These reflexes lay the foundation for all mental functioning during this stage and in the stages that follow.

At birth, there are immense numbers of neurons in the brain that are unconnected. The infant's brain is basically in an unsculpted state at birth regarding these neural connections that allow for the development of many physical, motor, and cognitive skills (The Urban Child Institute, 2016). Meeting an infant's nutritional needs and providing appropriate sensory stimulation is critical for these brain changes to take place.

Parents play a particularly important role in providing stimulating experiences and interactions that promote brain development (see Figure 7–4). The quality of parental caretaking, especially in how nurture is expressed to an infant, plays a critical role (Richter, 2004; Siegel, 2015). When a parent holds an infant in a nurturing manner (with a loving touch) while he is being fed, looks into her eyes (visual stimulation), and talks soothingly (auditory stimulation), then several sensory modalities are being stimulated simultaneously. Later, as the baby grows older, the brain appears to be constantly fine-tuning the neural connections, as well as continuing to develop new ones. This is dependent, in part, upon parents and family members continuing to provide nurture and interactions that help infants learn to be curious and to want to explore, touch, taste, and thoroughly experience their world through their senses. Social and physical stimulation are important and necessary components of providing appropriate infant care (Walsh & Walsh, 2014).

Mirror Neurons.   Later, cultural aspects are transmitted via language, observation of family and community members, and by socialization experiences provided by the parents and significant caregivers. The young brains are equipped with *mirror neurons*, which support this imitative behavior (Ferrari & Coudé, 2011; Gerson & Woodward, 2014). Sensorimotor associative learning is thought to be supported by these neurons in an abundant environment characterized by the "wealth of the stimulus." In other words, the environment needs to provide appropriate stimulation which triggers sensorimotor associative learning to occur (Cook, Bird, Catmur, Press & Heyes 2014).

"Parenting Begets Parenting"

In a research article with the title "Parenting Begets Parenting," authors Lomanowska, Boivin, Hertzman, & Fleming (2017) state that the quality of parental interactions with their offspring will influence the behavior of those children and ultimately shape the later parenting and nurturing behaviors of those infants. It starts very early, as the developing brain of the baby is shaped by environmental influences and these importantly include social interactions with primary caregivers. They state: "Parenting is considered the cornerstone of early socioemotional development and adverse parenting style is associated with adjustment problems and a higher risk of developing mood and behavioral disorders" (2017, p. 120). Importantly too, genes and early experience interact in epigenetic fashion and subtly shape the parenting behavior displayed (Lomanowska et al., 2017). Mothers seem to be especially susceptible to the influences of how they themselves have been parented and early life adversity can be detrimental in unanticipated ways by reaching far into the future. Both fathers as well as mothers can be influenced by genetic, hormonal, and neurotransmitter interactions that support bonding and

PARENTING AND CHILDREN'S BRAIN DEVELOPMENT

- For optimal development, infants and children need ongoing, consistent, responsive, loving, and constructive parenting and care (Miller & Commons, 2010).

- A current theme in child development and in parenting concerns the effects of extreme childhood adversity and brain development, as well as subsequent developmental implications (Lanius, Vermetten, & Pain, 2010).

- Cutting-edge research questions the relationship between parenting and later emotional, cognitive, and social outcomes (Bernard, Lind, & Dozier, 2014; Choe, Olson, & Sameroff, 2013).

- Most of the studies examining the link between parenting and brain structure have focused on high-risk groups, such as children in settings with severe institutional deprivation and neglect as well as maltreated children (Bernard, Lind, & Dozier, 2014; Obadina, 2013; Riem, Alink, Out, Ijzendoorn, & Bakermans-Kranenburg, 2015).

- Certain areas of the brain appear to be adversely affected by deprivation and trauma during sensitive periods in infancy and childhood (Marshall, 2011; Moutsiana et al., 2015).

- It is presumed that, because not all sections of the brain develop simultaneously or at the same rate, the outcomes of early experiences, including the effects of parenting behavior, can differ, depending on when these influences occur (Nagel, 2012; Newman, Harris, & Allen, 2011; Vanderwert, Marshall, Nelson, Zeanah, & Fox, 2010).

- Research seems to support the hypothesis that children, and thereby their developing brains, differ in their responses to varying parenting behaviors (Belskey & de Haan, 2011; Bernard et al., 2014; Whittle et al., 2014).

- Research outcomes also suggest that there is a link between emotional and social trauma in early childhood and the development and function of brain structures (Belskey & de Haan, 2011; Lanius, Vermetten, & Pain, 2010; Newman et al., 2011).

- Delayed maturation and reduced functional connectivity of the frontal cortex, as well as the involvement of other areas of the brain, may contribute to scholastic and emotional difficulties in children with a history of deprivation, abuse, and neglect. The neurodevelopmental effects appear to continue post institutionalization (Bernard et al., 2014; Nagel, 2012; Pollak, et al., 2010; Riem, et al., 2015).

- It is important to establish whether subsequent optimal parenting, as well as therapeutic interventions, can ameliorate the effects of earlier trauma and deprivation (Briere & Scott, 2014).

- Further research is necessary, especially examining the outcome of parenting under relatively normal circumstances with subjects who have not endured extreme adversity (Belskey & de Haan, 2011; Ellis, Boyce, Belsky, Bakermans-Kranenburg, & Ijzendoorn, 2011; Ungar, 2015).

Based on Belskey, Jay, & de Haan, Michelle (2011). Annual research review: parenting and children's brain development: the end of the beginning. *Journal of Child Psychology and Psychiatry* 52:4 (2011), pp. 409–428. Oxford, UK: Blackwell Publishing.

Nagel, M. C. (2012). *In the Beginning: The Brain, Early Development and Learning.* Sydney, Australia: Australian Council for Educational Research.

FIGURE 7–4.   Parenting and Children's Brain Development.

attachment behavior, which in turn influences the quality of parenting (Feldman, Monakhov, Pratt, & Ebstein, 2016; Lomanowska et al., 2017).

Thus, maltreated toddlers are subject to the *cascading* effects of placement instability in fostering contexts, as they are at greater risk for insecure attachments. Multiple primary caregiver changes can be challenging for the very young during formative stages when secure attachment formation should be one of the primary concerns (Pasalich, Fleming, Oxford, Zheng, & Spieker, 2016).

Goodness-of-Fit

Babies display individual temperaments. Some babies are more easygoing than others and parents of several children confirm that each youngster is different. Sensitive infants may be more difficult to please and require their own brand of parental care. Others may thrive with increased levels of stimulation. For example, some infants like to be held and cuddled, others seem to find closeness uncomfortable. If a parent wants to hold and stroke the baby and the baby resists, the adult caretaker may question his own ability to parent.

The stage is set in infancy for the dance that occurs between the parent and the child. Parents of larger families soon learn to accept each child as an individual with a one-of-a-kind style and personality. Each child demands an individual approach that takes into account their unique temperament and needs. When it comes to parenting, one size does not fit all.

Both parents and children will benefit from a variety of life experiences as perceived and interpreted through the unique temperaments of their children. Children, in turn, get to know their parents, and preschoolers may already know how to pull a parent's heartstrings in remarkably sophisticated ways. It is expected of the parent to adjust to the temperament of the infant. This is implied with the remark that one of the most impactful relationships in our lives is the one where we have no say over the personality and characteristics of the person with whom we share this lifelong relationship. In this instance, the temperament of an infant and that of her parents influences how parenting may unfold, while also acknowledging that this interaction occurs against the backdrop of context. This context can include socioeconomic class, resources, educational level, culture, ethnicity, and a range of other variables.

It follows that parenting skills contribute powerfully to parenting children with different temperaments. Any parent or child care educator can attest to this, namely that children differ in their temperaments and personalities, and that as parents and educators we have to find the most constructive and competent ways of parenting and interacting with that child. Each parent–child dyad differs, and our parenting styles have to adapt to the unique nature of a specific child, given the context within which that relationship occurs.

Although some of the basics of temperament may be inborn, understanding the unique temperament of each child enables the parent to develop an understanding of the ways that children express themselves and guide the child towards optimal development, within a given context. Nature and nurture go hand in hand. Parents need to take responsibility for their actions, and that includes their parenting skills.

As parents, our relationships with our children are "for better or for worse; till death us do part," a similar sentiment as expressed in some wedding vows.

Historic Research. Historically we can reference the work of both Belsky and Heinicke who, in 1984,

proposed two models concerning personality and parenting (Belsky & Barends, 2002) and which are discussed in the Handbook of Parenting (Bornstein, 2012). We detect the influences of systemic thinking and these models have been referenced in subsequent research on parent–child relationships and were influential in modern research on parenting (Belsky & Barends, 2002, p. 422).

Belsky's Process Model. Belsky (1984) wanted to throw more light on what was, at that time, perceived as a neglected area of research, namely socialization of children and contributing influences. He was also interested in factors that facilitated child maltreatment, abuse, and neglect.

"The Determinants of Parenting: A Process Model" is the title of the historic work by Belsky and refers to the reciprocal influences between parents, their children, and a given context. Belsky identified three sets of influences or "domains of determinants" as he called them. These were "the personal and psychological resources of the parents, the characteristics of the child, and contextual sources of stress and support" (Belsky, 1984, p. 83). The context included sources that contributed to support, as well as stress; positive and negative influences. Of these three domains, Belsky thought that the parental personality was the most influential. Parents who fulfill their parenting obligations well, require a balanced and competent personality, good impulse control, and they feel satisfied and secure within their own lives. These facets reflect a mature personality as referenced by Carl Rogers (1961).

Belsky formulated a hierarchy of influences:

- The effectiveness of a parent is influenced by several factors.
- These contextual factors include stress and support.
- These, in turn, affect the parent's psychological well-being.
- This, in turn, shapes the parenting behavior.
- The personal psychological resources of the parent are important buffers to ward off stress.
- These parental qualities are more effective in mitigating stress than the characteristics of the child (Belsky, 1984).

What this can mean in present day parenting is that the adult member of the relationship holds the greater responsibility concerning the outcome of that parenting relationship. In the pre-adolescent parenting years, the outcome depends mainly on the parent not the child, as the young child is developmentally not equipped to solely determine that relationship outcome. Parents can act as a shield, in that they can envelop their children with their parental love to give them greater resilience. The opposite is also true, as in maltreatment cases; parents acting out with children as their victims, putting those children at great risk physically, emotionally, and socially.

As a practical example and back to Belsky's research interest of child maltreatment: parents who maltreat and abuse their children should not place the blame squarely on the children to excuse themselves. Think of previous historical times when children were unjustly subjected to extreme punishment because children were thought to be "evil" and in need of correction from their innate "sinful" natures. At that time, the children were blamed for the acts of atrocity committed by the grownups, under the guise of "discipline." According to Belsky, three domains interact, and among these the competence and inner resources of the parent may play the greatest role.

Heinicke's Framework.   Heinicke (1984), a contemporary of Belsky, also proposed a model that focused on the influence of parenting behavior on infants. He focused on the interaction between parental characteristics, family support, and how these factors could determine quality of parenting. The quality of the marriage before the child was born also featured strongly, as this represented the relationship into which the child would be welcomed. He specified the three factors in greater detail: ". . . parent adaptation competence, capacity for positive sustained relationships, and self development" (Belsky & Barends, 2002, p. 422). These factors are intertwined and can relate to how the parents themselves had been parented, and the quality of their own childhood experiences. Of importance was whether the couple had had time to form a cohesive relationship before the birth of their child, as this would provide the positive impetus required for nurturing behavior, especially during stressful times. As far as parental self-development was concerned, Heinicke related this to self-esteem and self-confidence, as well as the ability to function *autonomously*; a concept we also find in Murray Bowen's work on the family.

Video Example 7.2

Watch this video on infant brain development. How can parents and childcare providers contribute to healthy foundations in the developing brain of an infant?
(https://www.youtube.com/watch?v=_0EYXx9iI64)

Attachment

Attachment is an attraction to someone that is based on psychological bonding. It is also described as a strong affectional tie between an infant and his or her primary caregivers (Ainsworth, 1973; Cooke, Stuart-Parrigon, Movahed-Abtahi, Koehn, & Kerns, 2016). This tie affects both the parents and the infant. It is one of the few developmental phenomena that appear to be found universally in all humans and in all cultural settings. It is essential for an infant's survival and well-being. When an infant fails to attach properly to caregivers, the consequences are damaging to his or her emotional, physical, social, and psychological well-being.

Attachment is constructed through the interactions of an infant with the primary caregivers. An infant who is experiencing normal developmental progress behaves in

Kati Finell/123RF.com

Attachment, attraction to someone that is based on psychological bonding, is a universal developmental phenomena found across cultural settings in all humans.

ways that signal a desire to be near caregivers, and the behaviors usually serve to attract the caregivers' attention. Infant behaviors that stimulate attachment to caregivers include crying, smiling, clutching, and touching. Such infant behaviors elicit *responses* from the caregivers that facilitate the attachment process, for example, smiling at, gently handling, stroking, feeding, and talking to the infant.

Attachment between the infant and the primary caregivers is believed to occur in four phases and progresses developmentally. Thus, very early attachment may have elements of being undiscriminating, but as the infant attaches and bonds to the primary caretakers this response develops into being discriminating (Bowlby, 1982). It is this progression that caused subsequent researchers to recommend earlier rather than later age of adoption of children. Children welcomed through adoption thrive if this occurs as early as possible, allowing the infant to bond with the family it is joining. Children who spent longer times in orphanages and child homes without the ability to attach to a constant set of loving caregivers, are at risk of developing attachment disorders. Infants who had been neglected and ignored in early childhood, as was the case in some international orphanages, displayed self-mutilating and rocking behavior in an attempt to self soothe. They also failed to thrive (Cole & Lanham, 2011). In some cases, problems with social relationships persisted, despite the supportive properties of stable and loving home environments (Groza & Muntean, 2016).

Age Ranges and Specific Stages of Attachment.

Bowlby describes this progressive development of the stages within a normally developing child, and links each stage to a specific age range. He describes these stages in the following manner:

1. **Undiscriminating social responsiveness** is observed at about 2 to 3 months of age. This stage is characterized by an infant's orientation toward all humans as seen in the baby's visual tracking, visual exploration, listening and becoming quiet when being addressed by someone, and becoming relaxed when held. Opportunities to examine the faces of caregivers appear to facilitate this phase of attachment.
2. **Discriminating social responsiveness** is observed at about 4 to 5 months of age. This phase is characterized by an infant's recognition of familiar persons, by smiling in response, and by restless behavior when the person leaves its field of vision. Also indicative of this stage is anxiety when encountering unfamiliar people.

3. **Active proximity seeking**—that is, seeking physical proximity and contact with familiar people—occurs at about 7 months of age. At this stage, an infant clings to, crawls toward, and actively seeks to touch and have contact with a familiar person.
4. **Goal-corrected partnership** occurs at about age 3 and completes the attachment process. The child has now learned to predict the behavior of the caregivers and to adjust his or her own behavior to maintain some degree of physical closeness to them.

Attachment is important in establishing an infant's sense of basic trust in people and the environment, and in helping the infant feel secure in exploring the environment (Ainsworth, 1977; Davis, Morris, & Drake, 2016). Children who successfully attach to caregivers learn to express curiosity in their world, which helps promote mental and social growth throughout their lifespan. Children who have successfully attached during infancy appear to have a greater capacity to deal with novel situations, cope with failure, exert greater perseverance in problem solving, participate in loving relationships with others, and maintain healthy self-esteem.

Attachment is Bidirectional.

Attachment is not a one-sided affair that only affects the infant. While this is critical for a baby's survival and well-being, parents also must experience a positive, secure attachment to an infant in order to fully provide for its care. The elementary basis of this interactional pattern that helps both infants and parents to bond was explored first through studies of what occurs in infant development when the infant is deprived of adequate parental stimulation and interaction (Raudino, Fergusson, & Horwood, 2013).

Strange Situation Test.

The process of attachment helps to explain why the relationship established between an infant and her caregivers is very important. The classical method for studying attachment was described by Ainsworth (1983) in the by now classical "Strange Situation" test. This test cannot be used across cultures and its validity has been questioned (Ainsworth, Blehar, Waters, & Wall, 2015). A brief description of Ainsworth's test follows as her work is frequently quoted in any discussion of attachment.

A mother and her infant enter a laboratory playroom equipped with interesting, appealing toys, as well as an adult stranger. Shortly after entering, the mother leaves the room and the baby is alone with the toys and the stranger. Observers record the baby's reactions. Later, the mother

Attachment, or attraction based on psychological bonding, between infant and primary caregiver is essential for the survival and well-being of the infant as well as the caregiver.

Yanlev/123RF.com

returns and the infant's reactions are noted. This is repeated eight times. Note that these three patterns (later expanded to four patterns) of attachment are those observed in the laboratory setting and are not the same stages that Bowlby describes *within* one normally developing child (a longitudinal study), described earlier in this section.

Responses in Strange Situation Test.   These three initial optional responses are the behaviors of several children as observed under laboratory conditions and represents a cross sectional study. A fourth response was later added. The reunion with the mother allows the observers to determine the different types of attachment by the infant and these can vary depending on the developmental stage of the particular child:

- **Securely attached** infants are not overly animated when the mother returns and use her as a base for exploring the room and as a source of comfort upon reuniting.
- **Insecure/avoidant** infants ignore or avoid the mother upon her return, do not appear to be distressed when the mother leaves them, and react to the stranger in a similar manner as to the mother.
- **Insecure/resistant** infants are reluctant to explore the playroom, cling to the mother, and attempt to hide from the stranger. These infants initially seek contact with the mother upon her return, but then show signs of rejecting her. These children have been

found to display more maladaptive behaviors and appear to be angrier children (Ainsworth, 1993).

- **Disorganized/atypical attachment** (*added later*). In addition to behaving in accordance with the three main attachment patterns described above, some children respond in an atypical manner that has been described as *disorganized* attachment. Disorganized attachment may lack coherence, display contradictory patterns, and result in disorientation of the child. This kind of attachment may represent the child's response to being frightened of the caretaker or may be the child's reaction to an abusive situation.

In Short: Successful, secure attachment between the infant and the parents affects all participants and influences the infant's later behavior. There is some connection between attachment and a child's cognitive development. Attachment continues to play an important role in a child's social relationships not only during childhood and adolescence, but also in adulthood in social and intimate relationships (Waldinger & Schulz, 2016). Care needs to be both *responsive* as well as *responsible*. See Figure 7-5.

Parenting Reflection 7–3

Explain the long-term effects of the development of basic trust versus mistrust during infancy.

RESPONSIVE AND RESPONSIBLE PARENTING

- Give loving and consistent care that meets and anticipates the infant's needs.
- Provide a safe environment.
- Respond to cues regarding hunger and the need to sleep.
- Provide appropriate stimulation.
- Talk and sing to the baby.
- Hold the infant lovingly.
- Be a responsible, loving, and trustworthy caretaker.
- Seek information on child-care best practices.
- Adjust the parenting style to meet the child's developmental needs.

FIGURE 7–5. Responsive and Responsible Parenting of Infants.

Focus Point. Attachment is a process in which both parents and infants participate. Secure attachment of an infant ensures its survival and impacts its development in other areas. For parents, attachment to their infant facilitates their nurturant caregiving behaviors, which, in turn, support the attachment process of the infant.

Safety Precautions for Infants

Unintended injury is one of the leading causes of childhood mortality. It is important that parents and caregivers be familiar with precautionary safety measures and that they implement them consistently (see Table 7–1). Parents should consult their healthcare provider. Safety precautions for infants, including suggested guidelines to decrease the risk of SIDS, are

TABLE 7–1. Safety Precautions for Infants

Knowledge is key	Take an infant and child CPR course, be prepared, be safe. Read about infant care; consult reputable books written by experts such as pediatricians.
Observe, supervise, and prevent a tragedy	Be close by; supervise and monitor. Never leave a child unattended. Be vigilant during diaper changes, when the child is on a high surface, and while bathing. Never leave an infant in bathwater. Leaving a child unattended in a car is against the law. Multitasking distracts the caretaker.
Remember "Back-to-Sleep" when putting a baby down in a crib	A baby needs to lie on its back. An increased risk of SIDS has been associated with putting babies on their stomachs (prone sleeping); they are not strong enough to roll over or lift their heads if they cannot breathe.
Infant sleep sack and firm mattress	Use an approved sleep sack which looks like baby clothing, but without legs. Use very firm mattress that is endorsed by the Consumer Product Safety Commission (CPSC). The risk of suffocation and asphyxiation increases dramatically with soft bedding, blankets, pillows, soft toys, and crib liners. Do not swaddle infants older than 6 to 8 weeks of age as they can wriggle loose and risk suffocation.
No adult beds, no bed sharing	Never put a baby in an adult bed, or let baby share a bed with sleeping adults. Adults could inadvertently roll onto the infant, or the infant could suffocate. Have a separate baby bassinet close to the adult bed for constant supervision.
Crib safety	Safety standards for cribs changed in 2011. Only buy cribs that meet 2011 CPSC standards. There are to be no more drop-side cribs; in an older crib, such rails should be immobilized. Do not allow babies to share a crib.
Parental bedroom sharing	Very young babies should sleep in their parents' bedroom in their own bassinette or crib and be monitored. Do not let a baby cry unsupervised. A baby is communicating something with its cries.
When feeding, "breast is best"!	The incidence of SIDS is lower in breastfed babies. Burp well during and after each feeding. Never prop up bottles. An infant should not have a bottle in the crib because of the risk of choking. Check the bottle temperature carefully; it should be body temperature, which is lukewarm, not hot.
Pacifiers	Babies can use pacifiers if they are soothed by them. Never fasten a pacifier to a cord around a baby's neck: strangulation hazard.

(Continued)

TABLE 7–1. (*Continued*)

Choking and suffocation hazards	Small objects present choking hazards. Plastic bags can cause suffocation. Button batteries are poisonous and have caused severe harm to toddlers.
Car seats	• Always transport a baby in a car safety seat. It is the law. • Car seats need to be age and weight appropriate, and CPSC endorsed. • Anchor the car seat according to the manufacturer's recommendations. Use the LATCH system in cars (Lower anchors and tethers for children). • History or the safety status of the seat needs to be known. Do not use secondhand car seats with unknown history. • Learn how to buckle in the child correctly. • Follow the recommended guidelines for placing the car seat—use rear- or forward-facing position depending on the age and weight of the child. • Newer model cars automatically disable the airbag if a child car seat is anchored correctly. • A list of inspectors and installers is available on www.seatcheck.org
Supervise your child	Numerous situations and objects can be safety hazards. Be informed and make informed judgments. Supervise your child at all times.

Based on recommendations by pediatricians from the American Academy of Pediatrics (2017c, 2017d), https://www.healthychildren.org/English/Pages/default.aspx

available. Generally, the following guidelines apply to infants under age 2.

Focus Point. There are many steps a parent can take to promote infant safety. By educating themselves on issues such as bedsharing and infant CPR, parents can be prepared for situations that pose a threat to the infant's well-being.

Non-Parental Childcare

In about 48 percent of all married couples in the United States, both adults are employed outside the home (U.S. Bureau of Labor Statistics, 2016). Most single parents are employed as well. The important element of nurturing behavior from caregivers is sensory stimulation that communicates love and nurture to an infant. Touching, handling, and stroking express affectionate attention and care. From the earliest beginnings, individuals learn to experience love and to express it to others. In infancy, this is thought to occur in relation to the development of an attachment between parents and infants. Early experiences in relation to the type of care given to an infant appear to play an influential role in determining later behavior and development.

The topic of childcare justly receives a great deal of attention as it deals with our hopes for the future; our children. Consider the following statistics related to the use of nonparental child care by families of infants and young children in the United States (Federal Interagency Forum on Child and Family Statistics, 2010; U.S. Bureau of Labor Statistics, 2015; U.S. Bureau of Labor Statistics, 2017; U.S. Census Bureau, n.d.):

■ The changing structure of American families has resulted in dramatic increases in the number of single-parent families in which the mother is the primary economic provider and in the numbers of dual-earner families in which both adults are gainfully employed.
■ About 56 percent of all married women over 18 years of age were employed outside the home.
■ About 75 percent of all children in the United States living with two parents had at least one parent who was gainfully employed year-round.
■ About 60 percent of all children in the United States under the age of 5 had been in some type of childcare arrangement since they were born.
■ Even if a mother is not employed outside the home, many families use child care and nonparental child care as enrichment experiences for children and to provide time for the parents' personal enrichment.

Given this information, questions arise about who is raising America's children and the quality of the care being given. Traditionally, children were cared for within the home, typically by their mothers and close family. Many families are finding in-home childcare arrangements difficult and prefer nonparental licensed and accredited child care settings. In some young families, the fathers are the primary caregivers, staying home with young children to reduce the very high costs of child care and because they like the experience of raising their children, combined with a situation that the mother may have the preferable work environment. There can be numerous reasons determining individual choices.

- The quality of the care provided and the continuity of caregivers are among the most important considerations when trying to determine the desirability of nonparental child care.
- Nonparental care of infants can offer an enriching experience that enhances and stimulates developmental progress.
- Quality care for infants has the greatest impact on infants from disadvantaged families.
- Most of the studies have found beneficial effects of nonparental infant care, but it always has to be seen in the context of the quality and the continuity of the care provided.

One of the main sources of nonparental care of infants today is a nonrelative in a private home, or what is known as *family child care* (Federal Interagency Forum on Child and Family Statistics, 2010). *Kinship Care* refers to care provided by a family member. The employment status of mothers contributes significantly toward choosing a childcare provider who is a relative. Forty-nine percent of employed mothers tend to have a relative rather than a nonrelative provide care for their babies (Federal Interagency Forum on Children and Family Statistics, 2016).

The stability or consistent use of a nonparental care provider for infants is a major concern for both parents and researchers. Changes in the nonparental care provider occur less frequently for infants than for older children. In all, only about one fourth of the families change nonparental care providers within a year. Changes are more likely to occur when the provider is not a relative.

Focus Point. Due to the large number of women who are employed outside the home, an increasing number of families use nonparental care for their infants. The *stability of the care* and the *quality of the experiences* are crucial factors in ensuring good outcomes.

PARENTING TODDLERS

Although much parental attention and behavior is directed in ways that communicate nurture to infants and toddlers, when most children reach 18 months of age, a shift occurs toward providing elementary measures of structure. Essentially, from a family systems theory point of view, toddlers discover their ability to set personal boundaries between themselves and others as they discover that they are distinct individuals and not an extension of their parents. A toddler's attempts at self-differentiation are healthy, but may also produce conflicts and power struggles. Striving toward autonomy occurs when a toddler learns to be self-assertive in a variety of ways. Using the word "NO!" to show non-coope-ration with parental demands and requests, trying to dress without supervision, testing parental limits in play, and toileting are examples of how personal autonomy is expanded and mastered by toddlers.

Self-Efficacy and Self-Regulation

The long and gradual process that characterizes the utter dependence at birth and unfolds towards the relative independence during early adulthood, is like watching a carefully orchestrated symphony. As parents we are thrilled with each new subtle sign of the infant mastering her environment. First smiles, rolling, tentative attempts at sitting up, even though supported. First hesitant steps are usually a cause for celebration and some parents note each event in a baby diary.

Emotional *self-efficacy* accompanies physical maturation. Certain developmental markers will only occur once a level of physical strength and development has occurred to make these possible. **Self-efficacy** refers to the ability of the child to manage certain tasks independently and age appropriately. **Self-regulation** refers to the ability to start managing emotions, again age appropriately. These qualities expand with maturity and in accordance with the developmental level of the child.

The parental attention and behavior directed in ways that communicates nurture to infants and toddlers will begin to shift when most children reach 18 months of age as toddlers discover their ability to set personal boundaries between themselves and others.

Pixelheadphoto digitalskillet/Shutterstock

Toileting usually begins between 18 and 30 months of age and is typically completed by 36 months. Focusing on *toilet learning* acknowledges the neurological maturational process that occurs within the child and that allows the child to gain control over elimination (Wittmer, Petersen, & Puckett, 2013). *Toilet training*, in contrast, implies that the activity is adult directed. In reality, these two facets interact, as the parent responds to the cues provided by the child and provides the supportive environment to facilitate toilet learning, hence the term *toileting* is currently preferred.

An early step in the process of toileting is the awareness that elimination is occurring, and this progresses to anticipation of elimination and, later, the ability to void in appropriate contexts and places. Learning bladder and bowel control is usually easily accomplished if the child is developmentally ready. Guidelines can be found in most reputable child-care sources. The use of positive rewards and reinforcement is often the most successful route for encouraging toilet learning. Shaming a child for accidents or mistakes in toileting is likely to elicit a power struggle between the parent and the child and is not recommended. Being exposed in child-care programs to children who have mastered these skills can provide the appropriate behavioral and conformance cues.

Introducing Solid Foods.   Infants and toddlers are introduced to age-appropriate solid foods when they indicate a readiness to begin taking solid foods. Such indications include the ability to hold the head steady and to transfer food from the front of the tongue to the back and to swallow. Infant specialists recommend that solid foods are preferably introduced at about 6 months. If introduced too early, the solid foods can interfere with the intake of human milk (American Academy of Pediatrics, 2012b).

Older toddlers are encouraged to feed themselves, and small food portions that the child can pick up independently, and that do not present a choking hazard, are introduced. Parents learn to be sensitive to cues from the child; when the child has had enough and wants no more food. Responding to these healthy cues can be a step in counteracting the risks of obesity. Contributory factors to obesity include parents over feeding children with inappropriate food, both in terms of quality and quantity. Seek pediatric guidance; well-baby clinics address feeding in detail.

A major concern in the infant's diet is providing adequate amounts of protein, iron, and vitamin D to meet the infant's requirements for growth. Lack of adequate sources of these nutrients can lead to malnutrition and eventually to permanent damage, especially to the brain and central nervous system (Akkermans, van der Horst-Graat, Eussen, van Goudoever, & Brus, 2016; Jin, Lee, & Kim, 2013). It is necessary to follow the advice of a pediatrician.

Opportunities for Play and Appropriate Toys. Infants need appropriate play equipment and materials to stimulate cognitive development and social skills. Simple toys are often all that is necessary. This is especially reassuring for parents who lack financial resources to provide what they see in stores and being used by other families. Infants can develop adequate cognitive skills by playing with toys and equipment that encourages visual and tactile exploration. These also promote the development of curiosity in the world, which will have long-range positive effects.

Safety is an important factor in choosing toys. While most manufacturers meet safety standards, parents need to keep these points in mind when selecting toys for infants and older children: no sharp edges, no small parts that can be swallowed or inhaled, no cords or strings, and no loud noises (U.S Consumer Product Safety Commission, n.d.). Parents can choose age-appropriate toys and play equipment by considering both the chronological age of their child and the developmental readiness of the child to interact in certain play situations.

Cognitive Development

Cognitive development is initially predominantly judged by physical development and reaching developmental milestones. Parents and caregivers play an important role in facilitating cognitive development through their interactions with infants and the experiences that they

Vikulin/Shutterstock

Responsibilities of parenting toddlers include providing appropriate play opportunities to stimulate cognitive development and social skills, supporting language acquisition, and creating a safe environment for toddlers to develop a sense of self efficacy and healthy autonomy.

provide. They provide the *serve and return* loop, which engages the toddler in a mutually satisfying interaction.

Parents guide an infant to learn cues for appropriate behavior, to understand that it is appropriate to experience the world via their senses, and to be curious about exploring their environment. Parents "*serve*" experiences to the toddlers, who then "*return*" that serve in a bidirectional manner. Essentially, when playing with their baby, parents begin to socialize the child into their family values system, their cultural system, and the importance of social interactions.

For instance, as development takes place and interactions continue, an infant will look for an object that's been covered up with a cloth by searching for it. The time-honored game of peek-a-boo is a classic exercise in helping infants to learn object permanence. In other words, with experience, an understanding develops that an object or person continues to exist even though it cannot be seen. In Vygotsky's terms it was described as the *zone of proximal development*. Parents can support and guide infants in activities and interactions that they could not achieve on their own. Research also points to the ability of parents to stimulate their baby's brain development through what are termed *enrichment activities*. These interactions include a variety of play equipment, sensory experiences, the use of language, and social interactions (Renzulli & Reis, 2014). Rewarding or praising the baby when it is responsive to such activities is also important. In addition, when infants are securely attached to parents, their cognitive and brain development are enhanced as well.

Language Acquisition.   The role of *language* emerges during this period as the basis for learning and development during the later stages of cognitive development. Language acquisition is a crucial foundation in development and communication, and parents perform a significant role in helping infants to communicate. The historical work of Chomsky (1975) presumed that there is a basic brain pattern and anatomy to support language development at birth, and this is shaped and influenced by parents when they talk to and interact with their baby, regardless of the particular language spoken in the home. Babies initially babble in universal sounds, but as they are exposed to role models, they imitate the sound ranges found within their mother tongue. The presence of mirror neurons in the brain is thought to contribute to language acquisition (Ferrari & Coudé, 2011).

It is important to talk to babies and infants in order to provide them with communication cues so that they learn the turn-taking behavior in the communication process and can model the language. Under normal conditions, *receptive* language is acquired a little ahead of *expressive* language; in other words, a child will understand more than the child can verbalize. Receptive refers to the comprehension of a language, whereas expressive refers to producing speech and communicating meaning or intent (The American Speech-Language-Hearing Association, n.d.). Later, with complete mastery of a language, these go hand-in-hand. When we learn another language as adults, we experience this same sequence; initially, we understand much more than we can speak until we become more fluent. By 18 months, children can usually use two-word combinations, and by age 3, the basics of a language system are in place—truly a developmental miracle! Linguistic ability forms one of the cornerstones of intelligence testing, and in typically developing children, verbal skills can be a good indicator of mental ability.

Although it is very tempting to use "baby talk" when speaking to a child, which is an emotional expression, it may be helpful to also use simple, correct language, thereby modeling desirable language. Making up sounds and words in an emotionally expressive way, or calling the child by special names, is virtually universal. In all cultures, parents seem to find unique verbal ways of expressing their love for their child. But, ultimately, language connects us, and we have to agree on what words mean and how they are used to facilitate true communication (Refer to Figure 7–6).

We know that bilingualism enhances brain development because the child will engage additional potential (Krizman, Skoe, & Kraus, 2016; Marian & Shook, 2012). Children can become bilingual if exposed to the second language consistently and preferably before adolescence. There truly is a linguistic window of opportunity that should be used during childhood if the child is going to have the privilege of bilingualism, or even multilingualism. Languages should be separated by person or place. For instance, the parents could speak Spanish only, or if English is spoken at school, then Spanish could be spoken at home. Mixing languages within one sentence or providing a poor example of the language is not helpful.

Safety Concerns for Toddlers

When infants and toddlers become mobile, they experience a change in their perspective of their world. A toddler moves with increasing speed and can freely explore

---

FOSTERING LANGUAGE DEVELOPMENT

Language acquisition is a perfect example of the "serve and return" principle.

- Expose infants to language by speaking to and with them.
- Give infants and young children models of verbal expression.
- Allow infants and toddlers to respond to language.

Respond to them when they babble, coo, or communicate in any form.

- Encourage speaking by listening and initiating verbal interaction.
- Encourage interactive activities and stories.
- Read stories; expose children to books.
- Expose children to another language in a consistent manner, if possible.

Based on American Academy of Pediatrics (2012a). *Healthy Child Care America: Fostering Language Development of 3- to 5-Year-Olds*, Standard 2.1.3.6.

FIGURE 7–6.   Fostering Early Language Development.

Focus Point.   As an infant transitions into a toddler, practices such as toileting and the intake of solid foods contribute to the development of autonomy. Parents can support and encourage the development of language by being responsive and communicative in their interactions with infants.

the physical world. Children at this age have a natural curiosity about their surroundings. Maria Montessori (2013), of early childhood learning fame, commented that children are natural learners and explorers and they exercise their curiosity by discovering and experimenting with the things that surround them. Toddlers need opportunities to explore their environment in a safe manner. Infants learn that balls make intriguing movements when they are kicked, bounced, or thrown; pots and lids can clatter; and water is very attractive and makes interesting sounds and movements.

This ability to become involved with the environment creates its own challenges. Most parents can tolerate just so much noise and mess from children. A child's safety also becomes a preoccupation as parents learn that a toddler's movements can lead to dangerous situations, and they react to these behaviors by childproofing the home to ensure that the child can explore and

NONACCIDENTAL TRAUMA

- In the United States, **nonaccidental trauma** is the most common cause of mortality and morbidity associated with child abuse or maltreatment. The term refers to trauma or injury that is willfully inflicted. The phrase *nonaccidental injury* is also in use.
- Such abuse is often inflicted on infants during the first years of their lives.
- Ill-informed, frustrated, tired, and angry parents or caregivers sometimes act out irresponsibly and abusively when an infant continues to cry.
- The outcomes are nearly always tragic. A Canadian study showed that fewer than 7 percent of all survivors of shaken baby syndrome were reported as being "normal." Aside from death and coma, all other victims had lasting neurological deficits, visual impairment, and other permanent disabilities.
- It is important to train parents and caregivers to react responsibly to an infant's crying. If a caregiver feels despair, the baby should be put in a safe place, such as a crib, and the caregiver should step away, breathe deeply, and calm down. The caregiver should get help, such as calling a neighbor or friend, and do something constructive to prevent the cycle of despair and anger. Never ever act out at the expense of an infant; instead, learn to regulate emotions. Respond appropriately.
- Prior to leaving the hospital, every parent should be educated with regard to the following:
  - Adult emotional regulation
  - Methods for soothing an infant
  - Attitudes toward discipline
  - Basic knowledge of appropriate infant care.
- Perpetrators of abuse can be parents, grandparents, caregivers, boyfriends of the mother, or casual babysitters. A recent study showed that male perpetrators can inflict even greater harm. A combination of caregiver despair and a lack of child-care education can lead to a very dangerous situation. Substance abuse aggravates these circumstances.
- Abuse of children, as well as spouses or elders, is a criminal offense that is punishable by law.
- Educational material is available from the National Center on Shaken Baby Syndrome, whose mission it is to reduce infant abuse (see www.dontshake.org).

Based on information from the National Center on Shaken Baby Syndrome (2005), www.dontshake.org and the American Association of Neurological Surgeons (2005/2017) http://www.aans.org/.

FIGURE 7–7. Nonaccidental Trauma.

ABUSIVE HEAD TRAUMA

- Abusive head trauma is a leading cause of death in children under 5, in the U.S.
- Abusive head trauma accounts for one third of child maltreatment deaths.
- The most common trigger for child maltreatment is when the child cries inconsolably.
- The inconsolable crying can elicit caregiver despair.
- Babies in the first year of life are at greatest risk of injury.
- Be informed, have a support network, anticipate, and recognize your stress.
- Ask for help *before* anyone comes to harm.
- Shaking, hitting, or hurting a baby is *never* a right response to a baby crying.
- Abusive child maltreatment should never occur.

Based on: Know the facts about abusive head trauma: Injury prevention and control: Division of violence prevention Center of Disease Control (www.cdc.gov/violenceprevention/childmaltreatment)

FIGURE 7–8. Abusive Head Trauma.

experience objects safely. Cleaning solutions are placed out of the child's reach, breakables are moved from tables, gates are placed across stairways, electrical outlets are capped, and so forth. Parents may provide a selection of toys that stimulate the toddler's curiosity and exploratory behavior, but household objects such as pots are often just as fascinating to a child at this age (see Table 7–2).

The lifestyle of the family responds and is modified by a child's behavior and stage of development. This responsiveness demonstrates the ability of a family system to adapt to the changing developmental abilities of its members. In these ways, parents also provide structure for children's developmental progress. In certain instances, inexperienced and ill-equipped caretakers, cross the boundary and do harm to a child. Both nonaccidental trauma and abusive head trauma are the outcomes of child maltreatment, and are taken very seriously. Suspected and actual child abuse can set the wheels in motion towards termination of parental rights. See Figures 7-7 and 7-8.

TABLE 7–2. Safety Precautions for Toddlers

Useful website	Safe Kids USA (www.usa.safekids.org) provides important information regarding the prevention of injuries.
Supervision and childproofing	Older infants and toddlers are mobile; they can reach and move objects. Supervise and childproof the environment.
Outside the home	Never leave children unattended. Supervise, anticipate, and intervene to prevent injury. Use recommended restraints in vehicles when traveling.
Toddlers can pull things over	Children can pull over televisions. Furniture should be firmly anchored. Be careful with drawers that slide out completely. Furniture that is unstable can fall on toddlers. Doors can slam on little fingers.
Toddlers can get into dangerous places	A mobile child can get to places and objects that present a danger. Use baby gates and lock windows. Every year toddlers fall from unlatched windows; this should never occur. Remove low-level ornaments. Large chests, including freezers, should be locked or have the latches removed so that a child cannot be trapped inside.
Drowning hazards	Be cautious around water. Open toilets and standing water in a bathtub are drowning hazards. Never leave a child unattended in a bathtub or wading pool. Any activity involving water has to be constantly supervised. Washing machines and dryers are potentially dangerous places.
Burning and scalding	Protect children from hot surfaces or objects, including heating devices. When cooking, use the back burners and turn pot handles inward. Do not pour hot liquids while holding a child; do not multitask while scalding objects are being handled. Lower the thermostat of the hot water heater. Bathwater should be lukewarm and checked before a child is immersed. Do not fill a bath with hot water first and then add cold. Mix to right temperature immediately.
Sunburn	Take precautions with exposure to direct sunlight in order to avoid sunburn. Use an appropriate sunscreen on your child.
Choking hazards	Children explore with their mouths, so many objects will go into their mouths. Ban tiny objects that are choking hazards. Nuts, popcorn, and food on which children could choke should only be introduced to older children who understand the importance of chewing foods thoroughly. Button batteries are poisonous and have led to numerous hospital visits.
For poison emergencies in the United States, call 911 or Poison Help at 1–800–222–1222	Lock up poisonous substances, cleaning materials, and medications, as well as button batteries. If your child takes a daily multivitamin that looks like candy, it should be locked up as well. Childproof lower cabinets in kitchens. Avoid poisonous plants in the home and the garden. Keep the number of Poison Help near your phone.

Parenting FAQ 7–1

Bedtime should be a positive experience for our youngster; any suggestions?

Bedtime can be a special catch up time between parents and children. As parents we need to take the time to make it something to look forward to. We add to the quality by being emotionally available. A routine of first supper, then bath time, and ending with bedtime should become predictable. Bedtime should hold the reward of quality time with the parent when we read stories together. Be consistent, by doing the same routine every evening. The child should form pleasant associations with this time of day. Children know if we are trying to rush them or if we are not truly attentive to them. Reframe the experience as a time to be cherished and shared. Remember that in order for this to work in a positive way, you need to be consistent.

Cultural Snapshot 7–2

Bengali Annaprasan or Rice Ceremony

In the book *The Namesake* (2003, p. 38–39), Pulitzer Prize winning author Jhumpa Lahiri describes an Indian immigrant family celebrating their child's Annaprasan in their newly adopted country—America.

" … when Gogol is six months old, Ashima and Ashoke know enough people to entertain … The occasion: Gogol's *Annaprasan*, his rice ceremony. There is no baptism for Bengali babies, no ritualistic naming in the eyes of God. Instead, the first formal ceremony of their lives centers around the consumption of solid food. They ask Dilip Nandi … to hold the child and feed him rice, the Bengali staff of life, for the very first time. Gogol is dressed as an infant Bengali groom, in a pale yellow pajama-punjabi from his grandmother in Calcutta. The fragrance of cumin seeds, sent in the package along with the pajamas, lingers in the weave … "

"[Gogol] wears a thin fourteen-karat gold chain around his neck. His tiny forehead has been decorated … with sandalwood paste to form six miniature moons floating above his brows. His eyes have been darkened with a touch of kohl … " " … The food is arranged in ten separate bowls … the final bowl contains *payesh*, a warm rice pudding Ashima will prepare for him to eat on each of his birthdays as a child, as an adult even … "

Lahiri continues to describe that the child eats some of the rice: "He takes his *payesh* three times." His mother's eyes fill with tears. They then continue with a ceremony intended to predict his future path in life. A plate containing three objects is placed in front of the child; soil from the garden, a pen and a dollar bill. If Gogol chooses any or even all, it may predict his possible future of being a landowner, a scholar or a businessman. The onlookers encourage the child, but the bewildered infant, unaware that this is a symbolic acting out of his destiny, begins to cry (p.40).

Source: Lahiri, Jhumpa (2003). *The Namesake.* New York, NY: Houghton Mifflin.

Childhood accidents and unintentional injuries are leading causes of death in children (National Association of Children's Hospitals, 2015). Parents and caregivers need to be alert and take all of the necessary precautionary measures to ensure optimal safety.

Focus Point. As a toddler becomes more mobile, the opportunities for harm increase. Properly childproofing a home and becoming educated on the dangers of common household items could very well be the difference between life and death.

EVOLVING PERSONAL CONCEPTS OF PARENTHOOD

During this stage of a family's development, parents learn an important lesson about interacting with children: our behavior as a parent must change in tandem with the changing behavior and needs of children. Children have an important influence on how we parent, and in return we influence the outcomes with the quality of our parenting.

Becoming a parent for the first time is a critical adjustment for the adults in a family. The first child has a major role in shaping the emergence of parenting skills for new mothers and fathers. The parenthood role adds a different, and perhaps more meaningful experience to acquiring meaning in life. With children, adults develop ideas about what it means to be a parent, the needs of children, what goals they have in child rearing, and what kind of parenting style they find appropriate. Above all, parenting is an unfailing path of personal growth. No parent goes untouched by the challenges of parenthood. Having to care for a dependent and fragile newborn can feel like being thrown in at the deep end of the pool; it is a huge responsibility and there is much at stake.

We may not think much about parenting or how to behave in this role until the need arises. When children

Parenting FAQ 7–2

Do you have any suggestions on handling a toddler's temper tantrums? The outbursts that occur in public are especially troublesome.

Reacting to temper tantrums is an exercise in parental control. It is helpful to understand that these tantrums are not a personal attack on you, but the outcome of uncontrollable emotions. Adults can have temper tantrums too, better known as outbursts. Children can learn to control these with a fair degree of success if taught by patient parents, and control improves as children learn to *self-regulate*.

With toddlers, you can begin the learning process by remembering to stay calm yourself. Try to analyze why the tantrum is occurring: Is it because the child is tired and needs to nap? If this is the case, just holding the child firmly and rocking gently will often help to calm things down. If the outburst occurs in public, going to a quiet place may contribute toward calming the child. Perhaps if you can reframe the temper tantrum as being similar to an electrical power outage, it can help you to stay calm. We don't plan an outage; it just happens, and often we just need to be patient and stay calm until the power returns. Recent research has also shown that a temper tantrum follows its own predictable cycle. When the child is intensely frustrated, interference by the parent only seems to aggravate matters. Wait until the child calms down a little and is more open to parental reassurance (Green, Whitney, & Potegal, 2011). A discussion about emotions and constructive ways of dealing with future situations can be introduced after the child has recovered and is calm (Giesbrecht, Miller, & Müller, 2010; Webster-Stratton & Reid, 2011).

are born, adults discover opportunities to examine their existing beliefs, attitudes, and behavior as parents. This seems to be the time when we consider and develop the challenging self-regulating patterns for parenting behavior and parent–child interactions. These self-regulating patterns form the basis of how we act as parents, and the rules and roles we assume in regulating and evaluating our children's behavior.

Parents have to find their own parenting rhythm while also learning to collaborate with their partner in this venture. Initially, parents focus predominantly on safety and care for the infant. Later, as the infant gows and changes, parents increasingly provide psychological and social stimulation as well. Later still, especially following the second birthday, parents support the child's socialization and ways of gradually gaining autonomy.

Gender-Equal Parenting Roles

Many men and women who become parents see parenting differently according to how it played out in their families of origin. Increasingly, adults with young children in Westernized countries are moving toward a gender-equal approach toward parenthood. Parenting roles are shared rather than being distinct or based on gender. Fathers are taking on greater responsibility in nurturing their children and are frequently encouraged

to take paternity leave when a baby is born. Although both partners say they want to share parenting responsibilities equally, women continue to perform more of these tasks than men, and this can lead to *role strain*. Many men fully expect that they will be actively involved in providing care and support for their infants (Harrington, Van Deusen, & Humberd, 2011; Jolly et al., 2014; Rehel, 2014).

Focus Point.　Parenting, specifically in the early years of a child's life, provide each parent with countless opportunities for their own personal growth and development. Changes in gender roles have led to greater father involvement in childrearing. Parents are expected to get to know their child's temperament and adjust their parenting accordingly, a process that contributes to enhanced parental competence.

The Highs and Lows of Parenting

Bringing a newborn baby home can be amongst the most joyful and also most intimidating experiences in adult life. The joys of witnessing the unfolding of new life are immense, and the majority of parents actively seek out parenthood. Even so, the period of caring for a newborn,

Guest Reflection 7–1

The Vulnerability of Parenthood

"The parents' age must be remembered for both joy and anxiety."

Confucius (B.C.E. 551–479) Chinese Philosopher

Becoming a parent late in life, around the fourth decade of my life, brings with it an existential challenge that younger parents might not face, at least when it comes to the vulnerabilities of aging. Namely, as I think about my children eventually leaving for college, I realize I'll be simultaneously approaching retirement and that brings certain fears. This isn't to say I wish I'd had children earlier, but older parents do think of older adult fears—sickness and dying—and hope they'll live long enough to see their children into adulthood. At school functions I've been confused for a grandparent and that's amusing, but there is no stronger impulse in me as a parent than the need to see my children into adulthood.

I often wonder if I'm the only parent who thinks about how long he has to stay alive on behalf of his children. In the early years after my first son's birth, this caused enormous anxiety. As much as I had new parent fears for his health and safety, I worried about my own health, about living for his sake. This is the frightening subject of Cormac McCarthy's "The Road," a story about a father and his young son navigating a devastated world and the father's need to stay alive for his child. That's a melodramatic comparison, but the father's claim that "he knew only that his child was his warrant" is itself an acceptance of the potential for devastation. That is the risk any parent takes in becoming a parent; having children means having to accept your own vulnerability, which is rooted in the basic vulnerability of children. What I'm suggesting is that thoughtful parenting means learning to accept feelings of vulnerability, anxieties for which there is no magical cure.

The old Latin saying, "disce pate" (learn to suffer) doesn't quite capture the spirit, but parents have to learn to live with fear. This requires taking care of oneself and remembering that parenting is more than just a lifelong duty to stay alive. Being a worker bee or a guard dog father are easy roles to slip into, but they are joyless. I've been both of those, so I have to remember from time to time to take a breath, enjoy being a father, and remember that I'm not a superhero, the lone guardian of their future. Accepting my own vulnerability as a parent means learning to trust others to be there if I'm not and, more importantly, learning to trust that my children are resilient and capable in their own ways.

Bryan Johnson, PhD, Professor of English. Director, Samford University Fellows and Micah Fellows. Used with permission.

then an infant, and later a toddler can count among the most exhausting and challenging times of the parenthood cycle. This time is very demanding for the caretakers because infants need constant monitoring and intense caring dedication.

The margins for error are virtually nonexistent, as the smallest lapse in attention can cause dire outcomes. Young babies do not sleep for hours on end while the parent can continue life as if nothing has changed. From birth forwards, every step, every move the parent makes, has to be while also considering the best interests of the infant in their care.

In short, some parents find this period magical as the infant is angelical and vulnerable. Other parents struggle with fatigue and sleeplessness, while trying to juggle multiple roles. There is a good reason why societies are moving towards the ideal of parental leave for both parents; this is a time of family formation in the truest sense of the word; and it can be all consuming.

Toddlerhood brings with it a new set of joys and challenges. Every time there is a "first" for baby, the parents rejoice; first smiles, first steps, hesitant mobility, and the like. Slowly the child is displaying the tiny incremental steps and moves on the long road towards autonomy. As parents, we should celebrate these moments and support the child in finding his or her own strengths and skills; a task that will only increase in complexity as we get closer to emerging adulthood.

Parenting Reflection 7–4

What are some pros and cons of using nonparental child care in dually employed families?

Focus Point.   Although the introduction of a child into a family can be difficult and exhausting, joy and laughter often accompany and out weigh the challenges that many new parents face. Each generation of a family has unique roles and stressors that dictate how they interact with the other members of the family unit. The interplay between the generations further contributes to the development of each member.

CHAPTER FOCUS POINTS

Parental Responsibilities

■ Parenting an infant, particularly a first child, can be exhilarating and exhausting, terrific and terrifying. Within the first few weeks, parents must learn the new infant's language in order to provide the proper care. The period of infancy requires parents to be extremely attentive and responsible as the baby transitions from womb to world.

Landmarks of Infancy

■ Development in infancy lays the foundation for each consecutive stage of life. Parents have the responsibility of providing appropriate care in order to maximize healthy development.

Parenting Infants

■ A parent should be actively engaging with the infant to encourage healthy communication and bonding. As crying is one of the infant's first communication mechanism, it is the job of a parent to decipher what each cry means. Studies have been conducted to show the benefits of breastfeeding, many of these advantages only manifest later in the infant's life.

■ Attachment is a process in which both parents and infants participate. Secure attachment of an infant ensures its survival and impacts its development in other areas. For parents, attachment to their infant facilitates their nurturing and caregiving behaviors, which in turn support the attachment process of the infant.

■ There are many steps a parent can take to promote infant safety. By educating themselves on issues such as bed-sharing and infant CPR, parents can be prepared for situations that pose a potential threat to the infant's well-being.

■ Because large number of women are employed outside the home, an increasing number of families use nonparental child care for their infants. The *stability of the care* and the *quality of the experiences* are crucial factors in ensuring good outcomes.

Parenting Toddlers

■ As an infant transitions into a toddler, practices such as toileting and the intake of solid foods contribute to the development of autonomy. Parents can encourage the development of language by modeling communication and being responsive.

■ As a toddler becomes more mobile, the opportunities for harm increase. Properly childproofing a home and becoming educated on the dangers of common household items is an important parental responsibility.

Evolving Personal Concepts of Parenthood

■ Parenting, specifically in the early years of a child's life, provides each parent with countless opportunities for their own personal growth and development. Changes in gender roles have led to greater father involvement in childrearing. Parents familiarize themselves with their child's temperament and adjust their parenting accordingly, a process that in turn contributes to expanded parental competency.

■ Although the introduction of a child into a family can be difficult and exhausting, joy and gratitude often accompany and outweigh the challenges many new parents face.

■ Each generation of a family has unique roles and stressors that dictate how they interact with the other members of the family unit. The interplay between the generations further contributes to the development of each member.

USEFUL WEBSITES

Websites are dynamic and change

American Academy of Pediatrics
http://brightfutures.aap.org
Infant well-being

American Academy of Pediatrics, Healthy Child Care America
www.healthychildcare.org
Focus: Immunization, prevention, and infant health

American SIDS Institute and National SUID/ SIDS Resource Center
www.sids.org
www.sidscenter.org
Sudden Infant Death Syndrome and other sleep-related infant deaths

First Candle: Helping Babies Survive and Thrive
www.firstcandle.org
New to parenting, Parenting infants, Infant mortality

Mayo Clinic, Infant and Toddler Health
www.mayoclinic.com/
Infant and Toddler Healthy

National Center on Shaken Baby Syndrome
www.dontshake.org
Shaken Baby Syndrome

National Resource Center for Health and Safety in Child Care and Early Education
http://nrckids.org/
Health and Safety for Infants and Toddlers

Safe Kids, USA
www.safekids.org
Preventing Injuries: At Home, at Play, and on the Way

CHAPTER 8

Parenting Preschoolers

Learning Outcomes
∙ ∙ ∙ ∙ ∙ ∙ ∙ ∙ ∙ ∙ ∙ ∙ ∙

After completing this chapter, you should be able to

1. Identify the timeframe and key developmental elements of the preschool phase.
2. Summarize how exposure to rich language contributes to a child's brain development.
3. Demonstrate how the interplay of nature and nurture impacts a young child's development.
4. Describe how the cognitive development of preschoolers includes the concept of egocentrism.
5. Assess the elements of respectful parenting.
6. Describe constructive approaches in dealing with challenging preschool behavior.
7. Evaluate childcare facilities based on a variety of factors, including quality, curriculum, and climate.

∙ ∙ ∙ ∙ ∙ ∙ ∙ ∙ ∙ ∙ ∙ ∙ ∙

PRESCHOOLERS: DEVELOPMENTAL ACHIEVEMENTS

During early childhood every day seems to bring a new skill, as well as a new opportunity. Parents are constantly adjusting to a developing child whose behavior and personality traits are rapidly emerging. Between ages 3 and 5 children are known as *preschoolers*, and this is a rewarding and ever-changing phase of childhood. The interactions within a family system reflect the increasing involvement of young children as participating family members. It is during this phase that young children begin to form concepts around "home," "family," and "children" (Mason & Tipper, 2014). The effects and implications of the type of caregiving the child is receiving is also making itself noticeable, and is expressed in styles of attachment, self-regulation, cognitive organization, and more (Siegel, 2012; Zeanah & Gleason, 2015; Britto et al., 2016). In short, every day in a young life counts, as every day represents an opportunity to shape and support neurological, emotional, social, and physical development.

Preschoolers are adventurous, curious, and thirsty to learn. The rate of developmental change is slower than during infancy and prenatal development, but it is still magical as each day seems to usher in a surprising new skill as children's personalities begin to emerge more clearly. Language is developing exponentially and by age three simple yet effective language is in place which helps the child master an ever-expanding world. Motor coordination and physical skills bring new challenges, as the child can explore, but also get in trouble unless supervised.

Regrettably the worldwide reality is depressing and disheartening. In large scale meta-analyses on the prevalence of sexual, physical, and emotional abuse in children as well as neglect of children, the conclusion was that: " … child maltreatment is a widespread, global phenomenon affecting the lives of millions of children over the world … " which clearly is in sharp contrast to the aspirations expressed in the United Nation's Convention on the Rights of the Child (Stoltenborgh, Bakermans-Kranenburg, van Ijzendoorn, & Alink, 2013).

Even so, globally we continue to aspire and work towards improved outcomes. The quality and the quantity of care we as parents and as caregivers can provide, influences the outcomes of our children. The *United Nations' Sustainable Developmental Goals* provide opportunities for implementing best practices and interventions on a large scale, with the goal of promoting early childhood development. Developmental interventions need to occur across five areas: Health, nutrition, education, child protection, and social protection. They need to be targeted widely and be implemented preferably on existing platforms to make them feasible and to ensure scale: " … the evidence now strongly suggests that parents, caregivers, and families need to be supported in providing nurturing care and protection in order for young children to achieve their developmental potential" (Britto, Lye, Proulx et al., 2016). Parenting counts among life's greatest challenges, exponentially increasing in difficulty when support is scant and resources meager. As

professionals involved with childcare and parenting, we do well to be reminded of the value of every little bit we invest towards improved parent–child outcomes. Somewhere one child's life may be different because of the mentorship they or their parents were exposed to.

****

Focus Point. Though not as rapidly as in infancy, developmental changes involving communication skills and personality expression become more apparent in the preschool years. While millions of children are subject to abuse globally, organizations including the United Nations continue to make progress in facilitating safe environments in which children can thrive.

****

LEARNING AND BRAIN DEVELOPMENT

Throughout this highly impressionable phase the young mind is developing, absorbing, modeling, and memorizing. In short, the brain is shaping and being shaped into who we are (Siegel, 2012). Importantly, language becomes the vehicle for socializing.

A preschooler learns and accomplishes monumental tasks during the years before formal elementary schooling. The power of language opens new worlds of interaction and communication. For the parent, language allows an evolving understanding of the child's universe. For the child, it becomes a tool for socialization and personal expression. Language and communication are the bridges that allow parents and their offspring to explore a shared world. Language is also a complex, abstract, and rich set of symbols; a cognitive mode of meaning. Language and meaning are inseparable; the symbols we use are so powerful because they are a shorthand for very complex thoughts and concepts.

The National Association for the Education of Young Children emphasizes the importance of exposing young children to rich and varied vocabularies. By age three children from enriched or deprived environments already show marked differences in verbally skills. Being aware of these challenges encourages us to seek equitable outcomes, so that all children can be exposed to early learning situations that provide a language rich context for language. In a review by researchers from Stanford University, it was found that the number of words and the level of sophistication of the words varied tremendously depending on the early care contexts of the children and that the gap between children from the two socioeconomic groups widened as time continued (Fernald, Marchman, & Weisleder 2013; Weisleder &

Andy Dean Photography/Shutterstock

A preschooler learns and accomplishes monumental tasks during the years before entering formal schooling. Parents can promote this learning through providing literacy-rich environments and situations in which children are frequently introduced to new vocabulary.

Fernald, 2014; Arnon, Casillas, Kurumada, & Estigarribia, 2014). The differences were first noticeable at 18 months, when most children begin to use two-word combinations and became pronounced by the age of three.

Suskind (2015) a former cochlear implant surgeon and author of the book *30 Million Words: Building a Child's Brain*, emphasizes how language and neurological development go hand in hand. We can take advantage of the *neuroplasticity* of the brain by providing stimuli enriched situations, and what better way of doing that than through language? As we follow the principles of "serve and return" we can encourage the brain to develop and grow and access the many resources locked within it. This is how we can support brain development; word by word. In her words: "It comes down to how well the brain had been nourished with words" (Suskind, 2015, Chapter 2). Exposure to language also influences processing speed. Parents vary greatly in how much they talk to their children; from as few as 670 words per day to 12,000 words per day. Children exposed to more language had richer vocabularies and faster language processing. She emphasizes being engaged and attentive, talking more and using a wider range of words, and taking turns when talking, initiating and responding to talk-situations. In a nutshell, and also the subtitle of her book: "Tune in, Talk more, Take turns" (Suskind, 2015). The work of Hart and Risley (1995) is now of historical value as their early studies on enriching language across socioeconomic class in the 1960s has shaped our current thinking about language stimulation.

Introduce novel words and reinforce them, especially in contexts where associations can be formed. For instance, in a zoo, use the names of the animals, in a bakery use the names of the different kinds of bread. For example, when a three-year-old girl looking up at the clear blue wintery sky exclaimed: "Look at that contrail, grandma!" the grandmother first had to look up the word "contrail" and then applaud the engineer father of the three-year-old for exposing the girl to this word. (Contrail is a visible trail left by high flying jets; basically the burning of fuel leads to ice crystal formation. It looks like a cloud-like streak).

The child's basic skills of motion, communication, and interaction are expanding. It is a time for learning the core skills required for socialization. Young children learn through modeling and observation and increasingly they comprehend their parents' expectations and instructions. As they acquire physical and social skills, they become less self-oriented. For instance, parallel play will shift towards interactive play. These changes enable a developing child to capitalize on a wide range of experiences as she increasingly masters her environment.

As with all other life stages, several unique developmental tasks and landmarks are associated with the early childhood stage. Expanding language skills, as well as increased social, emotional, cognitive, and physical abilities, contribute to increasing autonomy. Self-efficacy and self-regulation are continuing to emerge and finding avenues of expression.

Video Examples 8.1 and 8.2

Watch these videos on language development and enrichment in children. What part do parents play in supporting their child's language growth?

(https://www.youtube.com/watch?v=I7HN5LJOc-w&feature=youtu.be)

(https://www.youtube.com/watch?v=IpHwJyjm7rM)

Focus Point. During this stage of early childhood, an environment filled with rich language contributes to a more verbal preschooler, and ultimately a more successful adult. By actively talking and listening to a preschooler, parents enlarge the child's vocabulary and encourage positive communication skills that could last a lifetime.

BOOKS AND READING

- Have children's books in the home and make time to read with a child. Children who shared reading activities with their parents, have richer vocabularies at a younger age. This in turn benefits brain and linguistic development.
- Let children freely tell what they see on the pages, no need to always follow the text.
- Regularly accompany a child to the children's section of the library.
- Be a good role model: Convey your love of books.
- Books are an important part of development: They expand cognitive skills, language development, memorization, pre-reading skills, and much more.
- Stories can convey messages about prosocial behavior and lessons to be learned.
- Stories about a wide range of topics awaken interests in the child and foster the imagination.
- Books can cover many topics, such as stories where an animal is the lead character; books that help children deal with difficult situations; stories exploring feelings, facts, and fantasy worlds; introductions to culturally diverse worlds; rhymes and songs; and many more.
- Major library systems may list genres of books for children and prove to be valuable resources for parents.
- Help children discover at a young age how much joy can be found between the pages of a book!

FIGURE 8–1. Instilling the Magic of Books and Reading.

Guest Reflection 8–1

On Fatherhood

Being a father is a sacred responsibility, worthy of veneration and my highest level of attention. Maybe it's an art, but that too demands attention and devotion. Raised by what I like to call an in-home-child-support-paying father, one who paid the bills but little attention elsewhere, I'm sensitive to the need to spend time, daily, thinking about how I raise my two boys. That's what I mean by attention, serious time spent thinking about what it means to be a parent, not merely reacting to my children as chaotic little creatures. They're mostly predictable, if you actually think about it. In Book II of his Meditations, Marcus Aurelius instructs us to "say to yourself first thing in the morning: today I shall meet people who are meddling, ungrateful, treacherous, malicious, unsocial." He wishes to remind us that the world is intelligible, if we think about it and prepare ourselves for the day. This is a useful way to thinking about raising children, thinking that is. When they behave in ways I don't expect, I can say to myself, "see you could have predicted that, if only you'd been mindful." For daily living, that means turning off the television or the radio, not shutting the car door in the middle of his sentence because I'm in a hurry, listening to his dreams every morning, asking questions, asking more questions.

As a poet I think a lot about what it means to be a maker, to be mindful of how my words form a made thing. My children are more important than my poems. Being a poet helps remind me seriously to look my children in the eyes and listen to what they say. Sure, I respond with my share of thoughtless "uh huhs," "wows," and "awesomes," for what parent doesn't find the chatter tiresome. But I still try to be mindful of my responses, then listen more carefully. I came to fatherhood late in life. My friends warned me that it would steal my "inner life," that I would lose my sense of "Self." Romantic hogwash. My children, my wife, they are my inner life, as much as my poetry, the books I read, the students I teach, the friends and family I love. And that's what I mean to suggest, that if you see your children as something outside yourself, an appendage rather than an essential part of that elusive inner life, then parenting becomes more challenging than it has to be.

Bryan Johnson, PhD

Director, Samford University Fellows and Micah Fellows, Professor of English.

Used with permission.

Self-Regulation: The Golden Thread

Self-regulation is a central theme of child development. Much more than acknowledged in previous decades, current researchers are finding that

Encourage children to discover the joy that can be found between the pages of a book.

self-regulation runs like a golden thread through child development. It is the manner in which emotion is directed, and it facilitates principles that allow for complexity, connectivism, and information processing to occur in an integrated or regulated manner, which supports constructive functioning (Siegel & Brandon, 2014, p. 267).

The foundations of appropriately regulated behavior find an expression in and influence later behavior as well. It allows us to direct behavior, so that we can rank order importance. Self-regulation will facilitate self-denial and postponement of need gratification, so that important goals can be achieved and emotions can be integrated towards this goal. When early attachment is insecure or harmed in any of numerous ways, those early concerns can find expression in disrupted patterns of self-regulation (Siegel & Brandon, 2014, p. 271).

As preschoolers progress developmentally, their ability to self-regulate improves. Self-regulation represents aspects such as expanding self-control; the ability to postpone or delay gratification; and waiting for an appropriate time or place, depending on the circumstances. These basic skills gain in complexity during each developmental stage towards adulthood, when they support longer range planning and aspects of socially acceptable behavior. They represent a cluster of skills which are gradually acquired in sync with cognitive development; as the child develops the capacity to reason and understand why postponing the behavior may be beneficial.

It is a hard earned and complex set of skills that we apply with varying degrees of success. Even as adults we have difficulty with postponement and integration of impulses and desires; our dismal track record of breaking new year's resolutions and the recidivism of weight loss programs are illustrations of our human frailty.

Delaying Gratification.   Adults often ask preschoolers to delay getting what they want. This is a difficult task for a young child. Children are expected to defer having a smaller need satisfied immediately in exchange for receiving a greater benefit later. The classic marshmallow experiment supported these findings (Murray, Theakston, & Wells, 2016). Children were told that if they could wait before eating a marshmallow until the experimenter came back into the room, they would receive a second one. Some children could wait, whereas others found the temptation irresistible (Schmidt, Holroyd, Debener, & Hewig, 2016). This is an important illustration of how the development towards self-control occurs.

Video Example 8.3

Watch this video of the marshmallow experiment. What does this experiment tell us about delaying gratification for young children?

(https://www.youtube.com/watch?v=0b3SWsjWzdA)

Temper Tantrums.   Researchers have studied **temper tantrums** and found that children reveal a somewhat predictable rhythm that can be identified by the sound of the child's crying, as well as some other behavioral clues (Potegal & Knutson, 2013). There are two aspects to a tantrum, but they are not necessarily sequential. They can occur together. On the one hand, there is intense frustration, which can be linked to kicking, yelling, screaming, throwing objects, or pulling things over. The second cluster of emotions has more to do with seeking comfort and can be recognized by whimpering and sadness.

The researchers Potegal and Knutson concluded that the parental intervention should match where the child is emotionally during the tantrum. Trying to get beyond the angriest point is best done by *not* interrupting. Trying to console children while they are angry and frustrated seems to prolong the tantrum and escalate the behavior. Often the tantrum will suddenly "deflate" and be over. Parents learn to recognize the rhythm of a tantrum and to console their child when the child is consolable.

Some children react with a tantrum when they are overstimulated or overtired. It may be tough for a parent, especially if the tantrum occurs in a public place. If that happens, it may be best to leave the public venue with the child as quickly as possible, and to deal with the outburst in privacy. As children learn to self-regulate, they are better able to deal with minor frustrations. At the same time, parents become more competent at parenting appropriately, defusing inflammable situations, and anticipating their child's needs.

Video Example 8.4

Watch this video of a 3½-year-old's dinnertime temper tantrum. What patterns do you see in this temper tantrum example?

(https://www.youtube.com/watch?v=h4cBU0ZGsHM&feature=related)

Focus Point.   The process of learning self-regulation is often difficult for both children and parents. As children struggle to develop self-control, parents must apply healthy strategies to support the unfolding of the child's unique personality.

PARENTING YOUNG CHILDREN

Parenting changes in response to the developmental progress in children. As children grow from infancy towards early childhood, parents have to consider the expanding, yet age appropriate independence of their children and respond accordingly. Preschoolers are supported by parents who are *responsive* to changes in their children. Children, in turn, shape and modify the parenting behavior of adults. Older preschoolers are particularly sensitive to being treated age appropriately. From ages 3 to 5, the child increasingly expresses initiative, and parents know that they can no longer take their child's

behavior for granted. The game of "serve and return" is taking on a new dimension.

As children become verbally more skilled, we as caretakers can react by shifting from physical methods of child rearing to being more verbal. We begin to use increased reasoning and verbal direction in interacting with preschoolers.

Cognitive, Emotional and Social Aspects:

Providing Structure and Nurture.

During early childhood, it is appropriate to introduce *structure* into day-to-day routines. Structure comes in several forms, such as the rules promoted by the family, the roles taught to children, and the ways that family members communicate with one another. In family systems theory, these are referred to as *family patterns*. Young children model the behavior of those around them and appropriate role models are desirable. Expressions of *nurture* occur when parents try to meet the physical and psychosocial needs of their children. Structure and nurture go hand in hand because structural boundaries should be set using a nurturing tone or attitude.

Table 8–1 lists the behaviors that provide structure and nurture.

Rules are a way in which parents can teach structure to their children while also promoting self-regulation that guides behavior (Yuhas, 2015). Families have negotiable and nonnegotiable rules. Nonnegotiable rules cannot be debated or changed, while negotiable rules are subject to discussion and alteration. In healthy families, a mixture of such rules guides the behavior of family members.

Nonnegotiable rules generally relate to safeguarding the children's well-being. These should not be abusive or rigid. The purpose of rules is to teach responsible behavior, good citizenship, and effective interpersonal skills. Nonnegotiable rules define limits and appropriate behaviors with which children are expected to comply for their own well-being. For example, the rule "Play in the backyard, not in the street" informs a preschooler that a parent cares about the child's well-being and is willing to define the places where the child can play safely. Other nonnegotiable rules might include "Do not touch the heater, it can burn you" or "Eat some breakfast, we all have breakfast in the mornings before going to preschool."

Focus On 8–1   Landmarks of Early Childhood

Physical

- Slower rate of growth in weight and height
- Small appetite; may be a picky eater
- Uses a preferred hand
- All primary teeth erupt
- Major gross motor skills are mastered (e.g., running, climbing)
- Fine motor skills emerge (e.g., creation of art, cutting with scissors)
- High energy level

Psychosocial

- Expanding awareness of self, others, and things
- Gaining independence, some self-control and self-efficacy
- High curiosity level
- Beginning socialization experiences (e.g., appropriate social and gender-role behaviors)
- Learns by doing and from trial-and-error
- Play is more social and creative, as well as interactive

Cognitive

- Building a database of information about the world
- Learns to classify and group things
- Expanding vocabulary and language use
- Improving memory and recall
- Childlike thinking, such as egocentrism, animism, self-centeredness, and concrete thinking

---

Negotiable rules can be questioned by children and discussed with parents. Young children quickly learn which rules are negotiable and which are not. For example, an implicit rule in some families is that children are to eat the food served to them at mealtimes, but children may learn that they can question what they are expected to eat. Perhaps children dislike certain foods. They may bargain with their parents regarding what they will eat and what they will not eat until some agreement is reached. In essence, negotiable rules help teach children how to think and use discussion as a means of conflict resolution (see Figure 8–2).

Toxic Parenting

This time of a child's life is also crucial in setting the foundation for good self-esteem. *Toxic parenting*, which can crush the child emotionally, includes belittling, mocking, teasing, inconsistency, sarcasm, ridicule, and discounting the child. The parent–child relationship is not a competition that the parent should insist on winning. It is the parent's responsibility to do everything possible to create an environment that is conducive to the development of healthy emotions and positive self-esteem. The effects of this parental gift of good parenting will accompany the child for a lifetime.

All forms of childcare that negatively affect attachment, including toxic parenting, are situations in which the negligence or destructive interactional patterns of adult caregivers leave the care-taken with the debt. The caretakers do not fulfill their responsibilities, and the vulnerable children who are the care-taken; are the ones paying the excessively high price for this negligence.

TABLE 8–1. Structure and Nurture Are Two Cornerstones of Good Parenting

Behaviors that provide structure and nurture:

- Affirming developmental achievements appropriately
- Providing a safe and loving environment
- Encouraging appropriate and safe exploration of the environment
- Modeling respectful communication and gender-equal behavior
- Encouraging the expression of feelings
- Providing developmentally appropriate information
- Providing appropriate feedback with regard to behaviors
- Explaining the consequences of behaviors
- Communicating clearly—no guilt trips!
- Being consistent and respectful
- Listening attentively
- Having space in one's life for a child

Parenting Reflection 8–1

What are the implications if a family system has too few or too many rules that govern the behavior of family members? What effects would each of these situations have on young children? What would be the implications for the children's future development?

Enforcing rules and the consequences of rules can be problematic for parents, especially for first-time parents or parents who are not particularly structured themselves. It can be challenging to use positive reinforcement to elicit structure. Structure is most effective when administered calmly and lovingly, and should be pre-emptive rather than after the fact. Appropriate structure supports the development of *self-regulation* which is an important life skill.

Young children are supported in the unfolding and strengthening of self-regulation by parents and environments that provide constructive caregiving environments. Appropriate structure provides predictability and trust. Nurture that guides and acknowledges the needs of young children also supports good self-concept formation.

Cultural Snapshot 8–1

Parenting Values and Expectations

Depending on the particular cultural context, parental behavior and styles of discipline can differ considerably. The use of corporal punishment for instance and even developmental expectations may vary significantly. In traditional Cambodian families, child-rearing practices can include punishment such as spanking. The cultural values surrounding the family and reflected in their community may emphasize discipline, and enforcing compliant behavior. Once families from these cultural backgrounds immigrate to a society where this type of behavior is not condoned, their own child rearing practices adapt to match those of the host culture more closely. For Cambodian immigrants to the United States, for instance, physical punishment of children decreased.

Cultures that are collectivist tend to enforce authoritarian and controlling parenting styles, which can be conveyed by demanding compliance to rules, respecting elders, being mindful of what benefits and honors the family and how behavior affects family reputation. Parental expectations can be modified by cultural overlay; for instance, Japanese mothers valued in their young children the ability to be emotionally controlled and to be courteous. They actively encouraged these behaviors even in very young children. In societal contexts that are more individualistic, as mainstream United States tends to be, the parenting styles focus on the self-esteem of the children, encouraging them to be independent and making age appropriate autonomous decisions. Immigrants of Chinese origin valued education highly and were willing to sacrifice for the future of their children. When asked which qualities were deemed undesirable in children, Japanese mothers mentioned social insensitivity and uncooperativeness. American mothers on the other hand discouraged disruptive and aggressive behavior in children.

The way we parent is influenced by how we observed our parents and others within our cultural context perform their parenting roles. Parenting can never be seen in a vacuum; it is embedded within the culture within which it occurs.

Based on: Shiraev, E. B., & Levy, D. A. (2017). *Cross-cultural Psychology: Critical Thinking and Contemporary Applications.* 6th ed. New York, NY: Routledge. Chapter 8: Human Development and Socialization.

FIGURE 8–2. A Balance between Negotiable and Nonnegotiable Rules Maintains Appropriate Family functioning.

Focus Point. As children develop, an appropriate balance of nurture and structure contributes to optimal parent–child interaction. A lack of either structure or nurture could facilitate behavioral, emotional, or social difficulties.

Parenting Reflection 8–2

As a parent of a preschooler, how could you use rules to manage behavior and encourage a sense of initiative that also supports appropriate self-regulation?

Beginning Socialization

Socialization refers to the process of acquiring personal values, attitudes, and behaviors that reflect the demands of the cultural environment. During early childhood the socialization process begins in earnest. Parents and caregivers take an active role in teaching a young child. Some lessons are formally taught, but the majority are modeled and imitated. Young children learn the patterns and adopt the rules, expectations, and boundaries that the family system establishes. A child gradually learns to distinguish appropriate from inappropriate behavior. Depending on the nature of a particular family system, certain standards may be promoted more than others. Despite the diversity of today's families, almost all teach similar behaviors and values to children.

Part of appropriate socialization is learning social skills. Prosocial behaviors promote helpfulness, empathy, and concern for others, as well as controlling impulsiveness, gaining self-control, and limiting aggression. These altruistic behaviors show an awareness of other people's feelings and appropriate ways of reacting to those feelings. Gradually the social skill of *empathy* is developed, which is the ability to accurately comprehend the thoughts, feelings, and actions of others. Preschoolers have been documented as having the ability to demonstrate empathy towards peers (Brownell & The Early Social Development Research Lab, 2016).

In early childhood, empathic responsiveness can be seen when children share belongings or attempt to comfort or help others. These behaviors are not performed as spontaneously or as frequently as parents and others would like to think. When children have opportunities to observe such behaviors, they tend to model them (Flournoy et al., 2016).

Aggression. **Aggression** can be described as a hostile action that can elicit fear (Breggin, 2015). Aggressive actions directed at people or things can be verbal and/or physical. Our culture values nonviolent social assertiveness. An example is a steady, determined, and controlled effort to reach a solution to a problem. In effect, this cultural concept of assertiveness is a logical extension of initiative. Concern arises when aggression is expressed as hostile or violent behavior that harms others or excludes children from social interactions with others.

Aggressive expressions seem to peak in early childhood and then decline. Mild aggression in preschoolers is part of their normal growth and development. It may serve healthy functions such as helping them discover personal boundaries and to communicate or enforce these boundaries (Schonert-Reichl, Smith, Zaidman-Zait, & Hertzman, 2012). There may be a genetic tendency toward aggressive behavior, although the family environment can promote such behavior as well (Clifford,

Lemery-Chalfant, & Goldsmith, 2015). Children who are treated in harsh, aggressive ways by parents learn to act aggressively toward others. Children also adopt the model of aggressive behavior observed on television and in movies. Children are given a confusing message when they are spanked by adults for hitting others, and this is a clear situation in which reasoning is preferable as aggressive acts like spanking can model undesirable behavior. Modeling and reinforcement are powerful in helping children learn to act in nonaggressive ways. When adults positively reinforce prosocial behaviors, children learn that there are more beneficial ways to express themselves (Gabor, Fritz, Roath, Rothe, & Gourley, 2016).

Encouraging Positive Gender-Role Development.   An important aspect of an individual's self-concept is *gender identity*, the knowledge that humans are either male or female. An individual's biological sex immediately predicts a variety of reactions from others at birth. Children first learn gender or sex roles according to parents' interpretations of masculinity or femininity. In early childhood, parents and other caregivers use reinforcement to shape gender identity. These become modified and refined in middle childhood and adolescence. The result of such socialization experiences is that individuals make personal interpretations of masculinity and femininity at later ages. Gender-role development has both cognitive and behavioral aspects (De Bolle et al., 2015). **Gender roles** appear to vary from one culture to another in some respects. For example, the practice, in some cultures, that women and girls are allowed to eat only after the males in the family have eaten is obviously a cultural factor. On the other hand, the fact that males tend to exhibit more aggressive behaviors than females regardless of the culture would point to a biological factor (Lindsey, 2015).

Young children appear to acquire rigid stereotypes of what it means to be male or female (Telzer et al., 2015). It is to be expected that young children understand what they see as something that is factual. For example, preschoolers typically use visible physical cues, such as clothing and hairstyle, to recognize someone as either male or female. It is not unusual for young children to believe that long hair always indicates that a person is female, even when other features indicate that the person is a male.

A child's gender development begins at birth when parents are told, "It's a boy!" or "It's a girl!" This immediate classification is made more permanent and public by naming the child, usually with a name that conforms to the child's gender. From this point forward,

children are channeled into one gender role or another by being dressed and given hairstyles that identify them as male or female and cause others to treat them accordingly (Liben, 2016). Parents who have both sons and daughters state that the children simply are very different in their gender expression in many subtle and overt ways (Leaper, 2015).

A preschool-age child's knowledge of gender-appropriate role behaviors comes from several sources (Halpern & Perry-Jenkins, 2016). These behaviors are reinforced and modeled to children by adults and others in the family system. Reinforcement from other same-sex children also promotes gender-appropriate behaviors. A part of normal development can be that children explore aspects of different gender roles. Some gender-equal behaviors can be encouraged by involvement in activities and with toys that are traditionally associated with one gender only. For example, boys can be encouraged to take on roles such as playing house, and girls can be encouraged to play with building blocks. Even so boys and girls may play differently with toys that are stereotypically associated with a particular gender. For instance, when given a stroller and a doll, the boy may race with it, and try to take off the wheels to find out what makes it move. Importantly, for every generalization there is an exception, and the current attitude is to be accepting towards a wide range of expressions, and to go easy on stereotyping toys and behaviors as being typically associated with one or the other gender.

In addition, observing adult behavior in nontraditional roles can affect children's ideas about gender roles. Researchers have found that men who were raised in a family where the mother worked outside the home tend to be more gender equal in their attitudes (Burke & Major, 2014). Girls who were exposed to mothers who worked outside the home were more likely to seek out any career option, regardless of the prevailing gender stereotypes. These subtle changes contribute to raising future generations that will strive for greater gender equality (Jackson, 2015).

Children form a more balanced impression when they see both parents in a range of activities, regardless of whether these activities are traditionally gender stereotyped. Higher levels of social competence are found among adults who are comfortable adopting gender-neutral (androgynous) social and vocational roles.

Toy stores and play departments are increasingly focusing on skill categories as they group and market activities for children. This is a constructive approach that minimizes gender stereotyping. Toys should ideally represent desirable social values such as inclusivity: for example, dolls and action figures should represent the various ethnic groups the child would meet in a naturally diverse environment. It also allows for children to seek out role model figures of their own racial group to support identity formation.

Gender Roles and Sexuality

Gender roles and sexuality are constantly evolving aspects of early human development that take on a major role by adolescence. Rather than relating just to physiological functioning and behavior, *sexuality* refers to the broad aspects of sexual interests, attitudes, and activities that are an expression of a person's total being. Sexuality plays a significant psychological role throughout an individual's lifespan, not just following puberty.

Young children commonly ask many questions as a means of gaining information about their world, and questions relating to sexual issues and bodily functions are an extension of this interest. A typical question that can be expected from most 4-year-olds is "Where do babies come from?" and typically they do not want or require the entire birds and bees approach. It is also common for sexual themes to emerge in dramatic play activities, such as when young children play house or the proverbial scenario of playing doctor.

Parents are the primary source of sexual socialization and information for young children (Negy, Velezmoro, Reig-Ferrer, Smith-Castro, & Livia, 2016). Most parents are aware of their responsibilities in this regard. Gender roles can be modeled through what is observed in parental relationships. For example, parents heard their two young sons at play and the younger one remarked to the older brother: "When I grow up, I am going to be a doctor like mommy and you can be a university man like daddy … " Fast forward 25 years and that is exactly what happened. One wonders about the ambitions and life dreams of young children.

Although the accuracy of the information that parents provide in addressing young children's sexuality is important, perhaps of greater importance is the emotional tone with which parents communicate. The child can sense if this is a "secret" topic, or one that is best avoided. Importantly, the answers that parents provide need to match the cognitive developmental level of the preschooler. One way around this is to ask the child what he thinks, and then fill in some information at the appropriate developmental level.

An abundance of excellent and age appropriate material is available. Parents could rehearse the answers they might provide to their preschoolers. Parents should understand that the messages they convey about sexuality, both verbal and nonverbal, will affect children's attitudes and values when they reach maturity. Parents are encouraged to take an active role in shaping children's values and attitudes about sexuality in a developmentally appropriate way. Parents can guide their children toward appropriate choices as they mature by establishing a trusting relationship that allows open communication.

Grief in Children

Many parents find teaching children about the realities of death and dying to be especially difficult, and often it is accompanied by grief that may affect the entire family. As unpleasant as this topic may be, parents should attempt to teach young children about mortality (Anthony, 2013; Stevenson & Cox, 2017).

Very young children cannot understand the finality of death. Even as adults we struggle with the finality of it when we lose a loved one. For example, when preschoolers play cops and robbers, they are able to resume normal functioning after playing dead. When they watch cartoon characters experience serious injury, they see them spontaneously recover. Many young children reach the conclusion that death happens only to those who are old, sick, or fatally injured. This belief leads to questions when a parent or sibling becomes ill about whether the person will die. When teaching young children about death and dying, one has to consider the cognitive abilities and developmental stage of the child and adjust the information accordingly.

Children's grief looks different at various developmental levels. They are not only dealing with intense emotions that they may have never felt before, but they are also learning what death is and what it means to be dead. That is why it is important to choose the words used to describe death very carefully when talking with children and allow them to ask questions and to be honest with them.

Video Example 8.5

Watch this video on communicating gender to children. How should parents/caregivers communicate gender and related roles to preschool children?

(https://www.youtube.com/watch?v=6O9BKRJDqNA)

Focus Point.   Socialization of children encompasses a variety of areas, including appropriate expressions of feelings and gender roles. Parents and other key figures are charged with the responsibility of teaching their preschoolers developmentally-appropriate information on complex topics such as sexuality and death.

Attachment Revisited

There are many benefits in acquiring secure attachments in infancy and early childhood, including higher levels of social competence and self-esteem, the ability to function independently, empathy, leadership skills, and problem-solving abilities in novel situations (Britto et al., 2016). Children coming from disadvantaged family systems and inadequate caregiving environments are at a higher risk for developing insecure attachments and the likelihood of problems in these areas. Those parents who developed secure attachments during their own infancy tend to be more responsive to their own children's signs of distress and to respond appropriately (Ainsworth, Blehar, Waters, & Wall, 2015).

In the fifth revision of the *Diagnostic and Statistical Manual of Mental Disorders* (*DSM-5*), a classification system developed under the leadership of the American Psychiatric Association, there is an entry described as a *developmental trauma disorder*. It can result when children are exposed to prolonged multiple, complex traumas. The *DSM* has had several revisions, and the fifth major revision (2013) reflects current approaches in the field of psychiatry. Attachment disorders present as one main disorder if the DSM-5 approach is used, or as two distinct disorders if the ICD-10 approach is used. Mental health and related child and family professionals tend to follow the DSM-5. ICD refers to the "International Classification of Diseases."

Insufficient Care.   The current terminology (DSM-5) used to describe the situations that can produce attachment disorders, are attributed to *"insufficient care."* These represent *inadequate caregiving environments*. In earlier approaches, the conditions that could facilitate the development of disrupted attachments were labeled as "pathogenic care" (in DSM-IV) and "parental abuse, neglect or serious mishandling" (in ICD-10).

DSM-5 requires that children who are diagnosed in this manner are at least 9 months of age or older in terms of cognitive age, so that children who are developmentally not capable of displaying focused attachment are not erroneously identified (Zeanah & Gleason, 2014).

Reactive Attachment Disorder (RAD).   Children who have been traumatized in early childhood through severe neglect or abuse or who spent the early months or even years of their lives in circumstances of severe neglect may present with *reactive attachment disorder*. This condition has been observed in some children who were adopted internationally and who may have spent the first months of life in orphanages, without opportunities for appropriate attachment (Zeanah & Gleason, 2014). Many of these children may ultimately exhibit either *inhibited* or *disinhibited* attachments (Luyten, Mayes, Fonagy, Target, & Blatt, 2015).

Disinhibited Social Engagement Disorder (DSED).   This group of behaviors tends to focus more on aberrant social behaviors (Zeanah & Gleason, 2014). The children may display disinhibited behavior with unfamiliar adults. In familiar settings with familiar caretakers their attachment behaviors can seem more appropriate. Children with a known biological syndrome do not qualify for this diagnosis, and there is some controversy among experts concerning lead characteristics.

These conditions have been most extensively studied in young children but longitudinal studies are required to determine long-term outcomes.

Key Points.   RAD and DSED are disorders that present in some children who have been subject to adverse care conditions such as social neglect, institutional care, or frequent changes in foster care. Importantly, these children have not had opportunities to form selective attachments. There may be an additional factor at play within the child, as not all children subjected to the same conditions display the same outcomes.

We need to increase our knowledge on long term outcomes. RAD seems responsive to enhanced caregiving, but DSED is less responsive. High quality care is a leading factor in the journey towards recovery, but additional factors may also play a role (Based on the review article by Zeanah & Gleason, 2014).

Cultural Snapshot 8–2

They Walk Back into Their World

The way an infant or a child is carried, tells us something about the context of the parent–child relationship. In westernized societies, we transport babies in child carriers, strollers, but also in slings and papooses, usually strapped to our chest, and when they are older on our backs. But for toddlers, a stroller seems to be the preferred mode of transport. The American Indian and Alaska natives used a cradleboard and swaddled the babies tightly. In colder climates the contact was very close, to keep the baby warm. In many cultural groups, a sling enables carrying a baby the preferred mode; on the hip or back (Harkness & Super, 2002, p. 271). Contrast these ways of transporting infants with this charming description of a Peruvian woman, and her children by Stanley Stewart, a renowned travel writer, who met them while hiking (2016). He describes a woman and her child, Alicia and Laura, who are on their way back from a remote market in the Andes and have to walk at least six hours to get home.

> Like most Andean women, Alicia is a tumult of material—layers of wide *pollera* skirts, bands of *puyto* embroidery, a rust colored woollen jacket, cummerbunds, woven bags, wonderful woven shawls or mantas known as *k'eperina*. Laura is a miniature version of her mother; the same patterns, the same layers of intricate design and color, the same tasselled hat. Side by side on the mountain path, they look like two stages of a set of Russian dolls. Inclining their heads together, they speak to one another in Quechua, the soft sibilant sounds of the language of the Inca (2016, p. 95).

Stewart continues with a description of the functionality of their colorful clothing:

> One of the joys of Andean clothes are the storage opportunities. A lamb peers out between the buttons of Laura's woollen jacket. Various items emerge from the inner folds of Alicia's clothing: two apples, a knife to peel them, a bag of sweets, a live trussed chicken. Finally a baby's head appears, four month old Armeta, cocooned somewhere in her mother's *k'eperina*. She wants to see who their strange new friends are … (Stewart, 2016, pp. 95 and 99).

The mother and her children are described as they walk away and disappear in the distance, or "walk back into their world," not only literally but also culturally.

From: Stewart, S. (2016, September). The secret trail to Machu Picchu. Retrieved January 29, 2017, from http://www.cntraveller.com/recommended/amazing-journeys/machu-picchu-peru-tours-andes

Focus Point. Several attachment disorders, including RAD and DSES have been linked to adverse caregiving environments reflecting insufficient care and social neglect. While not all children raised in adverse conditions display these symptoms, many children who were not able to form secure attachments experience the negative outcomes in adulthood, and may benefit from supportive parenting and possibly therapeutic interventions.

COGNITIVE DEVELOPMENT

The preschool years are very rewarding for parents as their children are now little people with individual personalities, who communicate in remarkably sophisticated ways. It is also the time when many parents request some parenting tips and techniques. Accessing one of many evidence-based parenting programs could be helpful.

Children shift to more sophisticated thought processes typically around age three. We can almost hear children think aloud as they solve problems in their play and daily activities. Their memory is expanding and their recall is improving, in tandem with information-processing skills. They also start applying elementary logic (Dawson, 2016). Childhood memories can often be recalled from when a person was about four years old. Photos of events such as birthday parties support recall (Lee, Wendelken, Bunge, & Ghetti, 2016).

Preschool children do not understand or interpret the world the way adults or even as older siblings do. Piaget described preschool thinking as *intuitive*, meaning that children jump to conclusions, make decisions, and interpret the world based on insufficient facts. They increasingly try to classify things in their world searching for similarities. That is why sorting tasks, such as shape and color matching is relevant to them. This stage reflects the beginnings of a more ordered, logical processing of information (Courage, Bakhtiar, Fitzpatrick, Kenny, & Brandeau, 2015). In practice, this also means that preschool and kindergarten environments are stimulating and fun, as it allows children to explore child-centered activities in safe surroundings.

Preschoolers make judgments and reach conclusions in accordance to their cognitive developmental level. They use very few cues because they cannot absorb and apply greater complexity. Mental changes are facilitated by constantly evolving language skills and perceptual abilities, as well as greater sophistication in brain functioning. The child has prelogical skills which lay the foundation for more complex mental challenges that emerge in subsequent stages of the lifespan.

Once young children adopt a particular point of view, they have difficulty understanding another competing viewpoint. This is also referred to as egocentricity in thinking, as the thinking radiates out from their own perspective of the world. For instance, young children use their own vantage point to understand and make sense of the world. For example, a young child on a walk at night might explain that the moon follows her everywhere; after all, that is what it appears to be doing.

This egocentrism is both a joy and a source of frustration for parents. The opportunity to hear their child's charming perspective on the world is refreshing. Parental frustration may be linked to misunderstanding a child's reasoning which is illogical by adult standards. Some parents become upset when they hear their preschooler tell a "tall tale" and punish the child for lying. For example, if a parent confronts a preschooler about a misbehavior, the child might create a story about how he was told to do so by a monster who has now escaped into the wild. For the parent who tries to enter their child's world, these diffuse boundaries between reality and fantasy can be charming (Stewart, 2016). Creativity can be expanded by continuing with the story just to see where it leads. For children who think concretely it can be unrealistic to expect them to understand the abstract difference between a fantasy and a lie. For this same reason children can believe in tooth fairies, Santa, and Fairyland. We should not rob them of their access to these magical fantasy domains; instead we do well if we see it as a normal phase of development. Maybe we as adults can learn a thing or two from our children.

Preschoolers use sensory information extensively and with greater complexity. Appearance is often the only way they judge or evaluate their surroundings. Young children define reality almost exclusively by what they see, hear, and experience through their senses. They have very limited ability to generalize beyond the information at hand. Judgments, decisions, and conclusions are based on what they see and experience in their world and it is and should be age appropriately childlike.

The parents of preschoolers do well if they can adjust their own expectations of the child to this unique way of thinking that is typical for this developmental stage. Hence, parental interventions for this age group will be different to what works for their older siblings. Parents need to make many decisions on behalf of their child to protect the child from harm. Keeping a watchful eye is imperative because children at this age are not completely aware of the consequences of their actions. Constant vigilance and monitoring are indicated, and it is this constant "being on call" that parents find tiring. There simply is no down-time, except when the preschooler sleeps (Feldman, 2015).

Young children concentrate on only one aspect of an object they see or an activity they do. They have difficulty in perceiving other aspects or elements simultaneously. When young children are attracted to the color of something, they usually do not consider size or shape at the same time. They can separate all of the yellow buttons from a large pile of assorted buttons, but the task of separating all of the yellow, wooden, round buttons is too difficult for them. The ability to make fine discriminations such as this occurs at later stages (Goswami, 2014).

Young children typically cannot understand that some actions or processes can be reversed (Barbel & Piaget, 2013). To a young child, things work one way. For example, when asked if he has a sister, a preschool-aged boy replied: "Yes, her name is Charlotte." When asked if his sister has a brother, the boy replied: "No." We cannot expect these youngsters to have memories for complex information, so keeping it simple when communicating will lead to better outcomes.

Comprehension of size, volume, and shape is influenced by what they see rather than understanding how these can be changed without disturbing the content or context of an object (Goswami, 2014). For example, young children will believe that a nickel is worth more than a dime because it is larger in size, or that the tall thin glass contains more water than the shorter wider one. The mastery of classification skills expands and becomes quite proficient by age six. Teaching a child about different animals is one example. At around 3 years of age, depending on individual cognitive development, children think that all animals are alike. Every animal is called a "dog," for example and the same label is applied to all four-legged creatures. Associating the animals to the sound they make can be one way of drawing attention to differences.

Young children tend to believe that all things, including inanimate objects, are alive. This is a charming aspect of preschool-age thinking in which the child ascribes lifelike qualities to inanimate objects (Severson & Lemm, 2016). Stories like the little tin soldier in the toy shop, or all the toys that are animated when the store is closed are favorite themes. The child-centered ballet "The Nutcracker" depicts a fierce battle between the toy soldiers and the mice.

When young children are involved in solitary play and talk to their toys they are using "private speech," conversations intended for the toy as if the toy were alive. In some ways this is an extension of egocentrism and an element of fantasy play. Preschoolers often jump to conclusions. They base their decisions on a limited amount of information or on how closely one event follows another. They simply do not have the ability to use deductive reasoning to reach conclusions.

A teacher in a university preschool program described a memorable episode involving *egocentrism*. The 4-year-olds were playing ball on a slight hill. One ball thrower stood at the top of the incline and another at the bottom. The little boy at the bottom of the hill stopped the game and asked why the ball *always rolled back down the hill after stopping*. Because this was a group of intellectually gifted children, gravity and the shape of the ball came under discussion. While these ideas were moderately interesting, the small questioner looked the teacher squarely in the eye and said: "I don't think you are right! *The ball always rolls down the hill because it knows I'm at the bottom.*"

Parents play an important role in supervising preschoolers' experiences. Shopping at the supermarket, taking a walk, or reading storybooks are examples of how a child's mind can be stimulated. Preschoolers will see their parents as a source of information. This is particularly appealing to a 4-year-old who poses an endless stream of questions. Parents act as interpreters and help give meaning to a child's understanding of the world. In this manner, parents begin to share their family values, beliefs, and worldview with their offspring.

••

Focus Point. Around age 3, children's thought processes become more complex. The egocentric nature of their thoughts can be both charming and frustrating. Parents should allow their child freedom of expression while also encouraging a broader view of the world around them.

••

Play as a Learning Opportunity

Toys and play equipment encourage children to develop skills and abilities. Play is how young children begin to understand their world socially, physically, and mentally.

Preschool-age children explore various types of play as their social and mental skills expand. Three-year-olds may prefer solitary activities without competition. Children at this age find it challenging to share with others and do well playing alone or in parallel play. Four-year-olds are becoming more creative and imaginative and are learning to share and interact with other children. Different kinds of toys and play equipment appeal to children as they master gross motor skills and begin to explore fine motor abilities. Five-year-olds can play fairly well with a small group of children and participate in more complex types of play, such as creating structures with building blocks, engaging in pretend play, doing artwork, and undertaking simple science projects. Many young children are somewhat familiar with computers because they have played games on their parents' phones or tablets.

Keep safety in mind when choosing toys and play equipment. Some communities have toy lending libraries, which are especially helpful to budget-minded families or those who wish to expose their children to a wide variety of toys. Children like fresh experiences. Similarly, libraries can provide a constant supply of new and stimulating books.

Parents can support preschoolers' acquisition of appropriate physical, psychosocial, and mental skills through respectful communication, as well as engaged and responsive parenting.

Tyler Olson/Shutterstock

Historic Research.   Mildred Parten Newhall (1902–1970), an American sociologist and researcher of play in the late 1920s and early 1930s, described various dimensions and stages of play in her thesis of 1929. These came to be known as the *"Parten's Stages of Play."* She described the learning and work dimensions of play as well as the progression through certain stages as observed from children at play. She identified six types of play: unoccupied play, solitary or independent play, onlooker play or onlooker behavior, parallel play, associative play, and cooperative play. Each type of play elicited a slight variation of social engagement and reflected the developmental stage of the child. Thus, younger children were more likely to play independently and the social, collaborative, or interactive components of play were added later, in synch with the social, emotional, and cognitive development of the child. Sometimes children enjoyed being observers in play, and probably learned from their observations (Howard, 2014).

Children's play could also be influenced by factors such as how well they knew each other, whether they were comfortable interacting, and whether they had played together before. In a preschool setting for instance, children in one class are likely to form preferences concerning playmates and types of play activities. Despite the historic context of her work, Parten's stages of play have maintained relevance (Wong & Logan, 2016).

> **"A child who does not play is not a child."**
> *Pablo Neruda (1904–1973), Chilean Poet, Nobel Laureate for Literature*

Parenting Exceptionally Bright Preschoolers

A significant number of potentially gifted children are born each year. Because most schools do not begin to assess for traits, aptitudes, and behaviors of giftedness until about the age of eight, parents are left to recognize and nurture their child's early demonstration of special talents and abilities (Smutney, Walker, & Honeck, 2015). Exceptionally bright children of any age need support and challenge to become confident about their abilities to think and learn. This is especially true for preschool age children who demonstrate early precocious behaviors.

Bright preschool children are enigmatic: they initiate their own learning; they spout facts like a walking wikipedia; they marvel their parents with adult-like conversations; they understand nuances of language; they exhibit curiosity and deep emotional responses to the world around them. In fact, their curiosity is a key hallmark of their high intelligence and creativity. In comparing the exceptionally bright preschool child to what is developmentally expected, the term asynchronous or "out of sync" is particularly appropriate. The more advanced the child's cognitive abilities are the more "out of sync" she will be in relation to other children her age. Her unique traits and behaviors exhibited at an early age can amaze but also challenge her parents.

Although strong parent involvement and/or preschool experiences and instruction are key to a child's acquisition of academic skills, extremely bright children gain skills such as reading, math, writing, and problem-solving at a faster rate than their typically-developing peers. When a parent is in the midst of life with a preschooler who is demonstrating advanced abilities, recognizing the milestones of early precocious development can be difficult. Table 8–2 lists some behaviors that may indicate advanced development in birth through age five children (Preckel, Baudson, Krolak-Schwerdt, & Glock, 2015; Smutney, Walker, & Honeck, 2015; Vernon, Adamson, & Vernon, 2013).

TABLE 8–2.   Behaviors of Exceptionally Bright Preschool Children

Birth to 12 Months	■ Makes eye contact soon after birth
	■ Almost always wants someone in the room interacting with him or her
	■ Very alert; others notice and comment
	■ Vocabulary of 6–20 words
	■ Shows purpose with toys, seldom destructive or arbitrary
	■ Pays attention when read to or watching TV
	■ Follows directions, doesn't miss a thing, knows what's next in routine
One Year to 18 Months	■ Has a "fit" when not permitted to do something himself or herself
	■ Long attention span
	■ Obvious interest in letters, numbers, books, and talking
	■ Combines multiple words to communicate; uses personal pronouns
	■ Good eye hand coordination, shape sorters, puzzles
	■ Uses puzzles and toys that are beyond stated or expected age level
	■ Tries hard to please; feelings easily hurt
18 Months to Two Years	■ Speaks in sentences; clear understanding of others' talk
	■ Pre-academic skills: Knows many letters, colors, shapes, and numbers
	■ Tenacity; needs to do things own way and not done until they are done
	■ Not easily distracted from what they want to do
	■ Can sing songs, knows all the words and melody
	■ Interested in complex activities and devices, e.g., iPad, smartphone.
	■ Bossy; may lose interest in children who cannot do what they want to do
	■ Needs to know "why" before complying
Two to Three Years	■ Excellent attention for favorite TV programs, videos, or computer games
	■ Shows tremendous interest in printing letters and numbers
	■ Will catch your mistakes and not forget promises or changes of plans.
	■ Advanced use of language to communicate; complex sentences

(Continued)

TABLE 8–2. *(Continued)*

	■ Trouble playing with children same age, prefers adults or older children
	■ Has tantrums especially when thwarted in doing something his or her own way
	■ Can play with games, puzzles, and toys that are above age-level
	■ Early reading skills; reads signs, recognizes printed names and words
Three to Four Years	■ Highly inquisitive and talkative
	■ Increasing interest in books and reading and finding answers from print
	■ Can use technology with surprising competence
	■ Loves to debate, reason, and argue
	■ May become fearful of what they do not understand
	■ Shows interest in how and why; asks questions, and listens to answers
	■ Bossy, especially with siblings or age-peers
	■ Creative; curious, and manipulative
	■ Perfectionistic behaviors begin; may demonstrate obsessive behaviors
Four to Five Years	■ Reading skills spontaneously develop; may read chapter books before age five
	■ Understands numerical concepts; can reason mathematically
	■ Enjoys playing board and card games with older children and adults
	■ Huge vocabulary, amazing memory for facts, events, and information
	■ Advanced facility in using technology: tablets, smartphones, computers
	■ Ability to reason abstractly; understands at a conceptual level
	■ Engages with others in meaningful conversations about topics of interest

Focus Point. Preschoolers need developmentally appropriate toys and play equipment to encourage acquisition of appropriate physical, psychosocial, and mental skills.

RESPECTFUL PARENTING

During the preschool years, children require a fair amount of supportive care. Parenting can be tailored to meet the needs of young children and impart family values. In essence, parenting young children is geared toward what works best with a particular child at her unique level of development.

Historic Research. One of the time-tested approaches for helping parents work with children focuses on teaching preschoolers to learn to listen and, in turn, teaching parents how to gain a child's full attention when communicating. On the basis of the historical work of Haim Ginott (1922–1973), an eminent parent educator, methods were developed in progressive nursery schools during the 1940s and 1950s. Ginott's well-known parenting book *Between Parent and Child* (1965) became a trusted resource for an entire generation of parents. Among the book's key insights were guidelines which are as relevant and contemporary as if they had been written very recently:

Communicate Respectfully and Redirect Behavior

Character assassinations are destructive and toxic. Nobody likes to be criticized and children do not appreciate this form of chiding either. It follows then that attacking a child's personality or character with ugly and hurtful remarks is a no-no (Elkind, 2014). Instead focus on the offensive *behavior* and redirect it into constructive outlets. Separate the misbehavior from the child who does it. For example, Ginott suggests we say something like, "We do not paint on walls. If you want to paint here is some paper for painting." Throwing around accusations can be damaging to a young child's self-esteem and fuel guilt, which in turn freezes higher thought processes and prevents critical thinking. Focusing on the action that can be corrected or modified frees up the child to make better choices while also providing a constructive alternative. Get down to eye level with a child by squatting down, sitting down with the child, or holding the child on your lap (Burgoon, Guerrero, & Floyd, 2016).

Comments such as "Stop doing that!" identify unacceptable acts but fail to guide a child toward acceptable behaviors. Alternatives should be given: "If you need to hit something Benjamin, use the sofa cushion, not your sister" or "Use your words to tell your sister how angry you are; don't use your fists to communicate."

Praise Sparingly but Authentically

Slathering children with hollow praise is not effective. The empty refrain of "Good job" can become as meaningless as an auto recorded voice message. This particular aspect has received renewed attention in the literature, where the emphasis is on the process and the effort of accomplishing a task, rather than focusing exclusively on outcome (Gunderson et al., 2013). Children can be exposed to appropriate disappointments, as it's realistic that we cannot win or be the best at everything. The effort we invest is what it is about, and that aspect is encouraged and praised. Use encouragement along with reinforcement, for example, "I can see how hard you've tried; I'm proud of you for giving it your best shot."

Encourage Age Appropriate Responsibility and Choice

A child can learn appropriate self-efficacy when offered choices from among acceptable alternatives. Instead of asking yes–no questions or fill-in-the-blank questions such as "What do you want to wear this morning?" Ginott suggests that parents ask, "Do you want to wear your blue pants or the green ones?" This allows preschoolers a choice or a sense of control. Lack of control is a major source of frustration and can lead to acting out. Limited and age appropriate choices gently guide a child toward greater autonomy and strengthens self-efficacy (Chapman & Campbell, 2016).

Haim Ginott's suggestions continue to be fully in line with the positive principles of child guidance, even

Providing preschool-age children with opportunities to experience the world around them through interaction with nature can facilitate the exploration of various types of play as well as to expanded social and mental skills.

half a century after they were first written. His recommendations are a consistent recognition of a humanistic approach to parent–child relations that recognize a child's contributions to interactions with the parents. These approaches promote effective communication.

Other methods of positive guidance that are found to be useful with preschool children include the following:

- "Use your words" is a phrase that encourages verbal expression.
- Try to understand the child, that in turn may provide the reason for the actions.
- A preschooler behaves in a developmentally appropriate way, i.e., they will act their age.
- Mistakes are human; use them constructively to leverage learning, i.e., if you have lemons, make lemonade.
- Clearly identify what is appropriate and what is not.
- Use logic and calm reasoning to talk through a situation.
- Talk out a problem rather than solving the problem for the child.
- Explain that there are alternative ways of acting and help the child identify them.
- Do not use shame or guilt to motivate a child, that amounts to unfair parenting.

• •

Focus Point. Parent–child approaches which have stood the test of time include respectful parenting and developmentally-appropriate choices for children. Appropriate adversity, combined with loving support by family and friends, can strengthen resilience in children. Praise should be authentic and focus on the effort invested.

• •

CHALLENGING BEHAVIORS

Some behavioral problems can be temporary, but to parents and childcare providers they can be worrisome, even alarming. It is appropriate to seek professional advice to differentiate between what requires an intervention, and what can be a passing developmentally appropriate concern. Several problems are *stage specific*, in that they are unique to the stage of the lifespan, for instance toileting or bedtime routines can provide temporary challenges. Seeking information from reputable sources, such as the websites suggested at the end of chapters, can provide guidance on topics that parents and child caretakers may wish to address.

Bedtime and Sleeping

The most common bedtime challenges among young children include crying, resisting going to bed, repeatedly getting out of bed, and getting into bed with the parents (Mindell, Li, Sadeh, Kwon, & Goh, 2015). Getting too little sleep makes the child irritable the next day. Several issues may account for resistance to sleeping. Some infants normally whimper when they go to sleep. Parents who interpret this as cries of distress and rush to pick up the infant train him or her to expect such attention at bedtime. Eventually, a young child may prefer to go to sleep while being held and rocked by a parent or other caregiver. Creating a constructive bedtime routine should be something both the parent and the child look forward to.

Appropriate sleep routines are promoted if a young child is allowed time to wind down prior to bedtime. Parents can promote sleep routines beginning in early childhood. The period shortly before bedtime should be calming. Rough-and-tumble play should be saved for the mornings when children are alert. Parents can help preschoolers develop good sleep habits that promote relaxation and preparation for sleep. Restful activities such as baths, reading stories, or quiet play serve as signals to preschoolers that bedtime is approaching. One of the more successful approaches is to use *planned ignorance* (Weissbluth, 2015), whereby parents give their full attention to a preschooler during the period prior to bedtime but do not reenter the child's bedroom after the child is in bed. This policy of "once in bed, you stay in bed" is established with the child's full knowledge and expected compliance. Usually, preschoolers will go to sleep within about 20 minutes after being put to bed.

Sleep routines vary with the developmental age of the child. The amount of sleep needed varies. Preschoolers should progress toward sleep that is not dependent on a parent's constant presence. A worst case scenario is parents who share a bed with a child in order to promote sleep. Bed sharing is an undesirable practice for preschoolers. Parents eventually become sleep deprived and fall into parental despair, promoting poor parent–child interactions. It also is detrimental to the marital relationship.

Ideally, good sleep routines should be established with *positive* routines so that children are not left to cry alone. Letting a child cry when attempting to establish good sleep patterns should not be necessary; the same can be achieved with a non-crying approach. Being overly authoritarian, putting a very young child and even babies on an inflexible routine, and not responding to crying have been criticized as being undesirable practices that can lead to *failure to thrive* in children. Failure to thrive means that children do not develop optimally compared with other children of similar ages.

The developmental readiness of a child is critical. Note that there are temperamental differences in children. Some children fall asleep easily, others need more parent time and it will take longer to establish good sleep routines. Regardless, a child should never be abandoned in a crib or bed. Parents or caretakers should check on the child regularly to ensure that the child is well, and they should be within earshot.

Although a bad dream or nightmare may last only a few minutes, a young child may be able to recall it in intricate detail. Night terrors can last longer, and a child usually cannot recall the frightening details. Children experiencing extreme stress, such as parental divorce or displacement, may report bad dreams (Deliens, Gilson, & Peigneux, 2014). Talking about the fears is appropriate. It may also be helpful to hold the preschooler and rock him for a short time. Reassure the child that such a frightening experience is not real but is created by the imagination. Eliminate activities such as watching television shows that stimulate harmful fantasizing. In any case, television viewing should be supervised and very restricted for this age group.

Toileting

Preschoolers can occasionally experience problems with the functions of bodily elimination. Typically, these have to do with regression during times of stress. Loss of control such as bed-wetting (enuresis) and involuntary passage of feces (encopresis), are not considered problematic until a child reaches school age.

Regression in toileting (toilet learning) might occur as a result of any of changes in the family composition, such as the birth of a baby. It can be an expression of sibling rivalry, extreme fatigue, excitement, anxiety, or illness. Some children get so absorbed by play that they forget to answer nature's call.

Commonsense measures help young children overcome these periods of regression. Reminding a child to use the bathroom may be all that is required. Some parents say: "Use the opportunity to go to the toilet" before they leave the home, and before bedtime. This is conveyed in a friendly, non-threatening manner. Protecting a child from situations that are overstimulating or frightening may be another way of supporting appropriate habits. Shaming or humiliating a child is inappropriate. Such negative interactions do not have a place among constructive parenting techniques. In some cases, a medical consultation is indicated (Kaerts, Vermandel, Van Hal, & Wyndaele, 2014).

Meal Times

The foundations for lifelong nutritional habits are laid during childhood, and parents who guide their children toward healthy and nutritious choices give them a gift for life. Early exposure to healthy foods allows the child to form good associations with those choices and they will usually maintain or return to a similar diet later in life. Food choices and taste preferences are reinforced culturally, and children need to be exposed to the same food several times before it becomes familiar and desirable. A child who receives fast food as a treat is likely to return to that eating pattern when under stress.

Young children eat meals with their families and are taught table manners and the use of table utensils. Preschoolers eat similar foods as other family members but in smaller portions. Children require balanced nutrition which includes adequate amounts of protein to support brain development. Preschoolers develop food preferences based on the foods to which they are exposed. For this reason, the early years are pivotal in establishing the foundation of healthy eating habits, which will set the child on the right nutritional path for life. Eating problems can develop as early as infancy and progress in early childhood. Childhood obesity is taking on alarming proportions. Parents contribute to obesity by serving portion sizes that exceed the child's nutritional requirements, not cooking nutritious meals, routinely eating on the run, using food as a reward, and minimizing physical activity (Matheson et al., 2015). If parents model appropriate behavior, which strives toward healthy lifestyle choices, children almost always follow their good example, especially if they are supported in making healthful choices. Good parenting includes giving children the foundations for a healthy lifestyle, and the family system is a strong reinforcer of such behavior. Ideally, candy should be neither a reward nor a bribe, and we do well if we minimize sugar and eliminate all carbonated drinks as these are very high in sugar.

Parents sometimes miss the early signs of childhood obesity, partly because of their own contributory behavior. Additionally, social norms foster an atmosphere of politeness, avoiding topics that may offend. If health-care providers try to steer the family in the right direction, it is the responsibility of the adults to create the supportive environment for the children because the power to change the situation for the better lies within the domain of parental responsibility.

Focus Point. Parents should counteract childhood obesity by being good role models, cooking nutritious meals, and encouraging physical activity. In this way, they establish a foundation of good eating habits, which will set the child on the right nutritional path for life.

Health and Safety

Young children have immature immune systems, and they may not have developed the antibodies to combat a variety of illnesses. The wide availability of immunizations against a large number of formerly debilitating and fatal diseases has helped to extend life expectancy. It is important for preschoolers to have adequate health care, which includes immunizations.

Parents need to teach their children safety rules for inside and outside the home. Some children are more impulsive than others and can experience many injuries and close calls. These children require an extra-strict parental eye and perhaps more intensive safety instruction. Play equipment, both indoors and outdoors, should be safe and age appropriate. Children should never be left unsupervised, and leaving them alone in a parked vehicle for any amount of time is illegal. Although drowning deaths have declined over the past decade, any water activity requires extremely high vigilance, and pool areas need to be secured. Teaching preschoolers to swim can add to their safety (Anderst & Moffatt, 2014).

Most deaths among young children are caused by injury in or near the home rather than illness (Federal Interagency Forum on Child and Family Statistics, 2016). Accidental injury is the leading cause of death during childhood and adolescence in the United States (CDC, 2014b). During early childhood, this can occur in relation to car accidents, being a pedestrian, a passenger, or being on a tricycle. The use of appropriately designed children's car seats is a legal requirement for all children. Other safety measures include the use of helmets while biking and certain sports such as skiing.

Many accidental deaths involve a child's ingestion of poisonous or toxic substances, such as fertilizer, gasoline, cleaning products, button batteries, and medication. While children in the United States are safer on playgrounds, at childcare centers, and in cars than in past decades, there are still too many preventable injuries and deaths. Even though we have become more safety conscious, suffocation and poisoning have increased (Krugman & Lane, 2014). Parents are urged to store medications and other dangerous substances out of the reach of children. It is wise to have the telephone number of a poison control center at hand and to insist on childproof caps for all medications.

Suffocation and asphyxiation can be prevented with good childcare and sleep practices, following the recommendations of the American Academy of Pediatrics. For preschoolers, loose cords on window blinds, necklaces, and strings can present a strangulation hazard. Also keep plastic bags away from young children. Unlatched windows are a hazard and every year children of this age group in particular fall out of windows. Because this age group is mobile and can climb, furniture can topple onto them, causing major trauma.

Focus Point. Accidental injury is the leading cause of death of preschoolers, with the majority of deaths occurring within or near the home.

Parenting Reflection 8–3

How would you advise the parent of a young child that a behavior problem might be serious enough to warrant professional consultation, even though it is not indicative of atypical developmental progress?

CHILDCARE FOR PRESCHOOLERS

Families and Work

Families and Work Institute (FWI) is a non-profit organization focusing on the work of founder Ellen Galinsky, whose approach emphasizes broad lifecycle stages. This institute has worked on the family–work relationship, as well as youth and child developmental concerns (www.familiesandwork.org/about/). The angle of their work includes the lifecycle stages, combined with an ecological approach to examine factors that can lead to constructive action and change. In the arena of family–work, they have examined the impact of parental leave legislation and factors contributing to effective workplaces. The latter work environments are characterized by opportunities for learning, autonomy, a good work–life fit, supervisor support for work success, and satisfaction with earnings, benefits, and opportunities for advancement. Importantly, too, there needs to be a culture of trust (Galinsky, 2016, p. 205).

Galinsky (2010) in her book for the popular press, described seven skills for pre-schoolers. These include focus and self-control, perspective taking, communicating, making connections, critical thinking, taking on challenges, and self-directed, engaged learning.

Supporting Children

Community services that provide alternative forms of nonparental caregiving are more numerous and accessible to families with preschool-age children than to families with infants. In the United States, about 60 percent of all children younger than 5 years of age who were not in kindergarten were in some type of nonparental childcare program; that is, they were not cared for by a stay-at-home biological parent. The type of supplemental care varies according to the age of the child and the type of care desired by the parents (Federal Interagency Forum on Child and Family Statistics, 2012). While infants more typically receive home-based care by either a relative or a nonrelative, preschoolers who are not yet enrolled in a kindergarten program are more likely to be cared for by a relative or placed in a group program.

Slightly more than half of all preschool-age children are cared for by childcare centers and by nonrelatives in their homes (see Figure 8–3). It has become the norm that one or both parents are gainfully employed and high-quality childcare provides enriching experiences that are good for development and skill building. Childcare settings should have developmentally appropriate and planned activities. Staff should respect each child's individual needs and provide opportunities for children to play with peers.

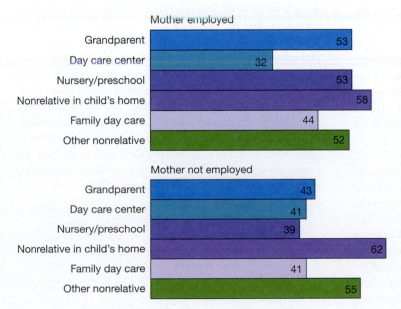

FIGURE 8–3.

Percentage of Preschoolers in Multiple Childcare Arrangements for Selected Arrangement Types, by Employment Status of Mother: Spring 2011.

Note: Employment includes wage and salary jobs, other employment arrangements, and self-employment. Not employed includes those looking for work, in school, or out of the labor force.

Source: U.S. Census Bureau, Survey of Income and Program Participation (SIPP).

Parents choose preschools depending on the location, the affordability, placement possibilities, convenience, reputation, as well as the philosophical approach of the childcare center (although, in reality, this may be a luxury as some of the centers are not available in smaller towns or suburbs).

Historic Underpinnings

There are several approaches to preschool (and school) care, which have strong *historic* roots yet also have a contemporary presence. They are presented loosely in chronological order:

Charlotte Mason. Charlotte Mason (1842–1923) was a British educator and the founder of the "Parents' National Education Union." Her vision was: "A liberal education for all." Another one of her quotes was: "Education is an atmosphere, a discipline, a life." Most of her own education was accomplished at home, by her parents, and as an adult she worked as a teacher. She tends to be associated with the homeschooling movement, although that may have meant something different in the context of her time about a century ago, as compared to the current homeschooling movements. Importantly, too, she was not critical of the educational and public school systems. She felt that if the public schooling system was not accessible to a child, as in child factory workers, or if it did not meet all the requirements that parents had in mind, the parents could take on the responsibility of supplementing or compensating for the educational process by being actively involved in their child's education. Her approach needs to be seen against the backdrop and context of the pedagogy of her time, when great numbers of children were still laboring in factories, and it was particularly difficult for girls to obtain a solid education (de Bellaigue, 2015). Education was also seen as an agent for social change.

Montessori. The **Montessori approach** is based on the work of Italian educator Maria Montessori (1870–1952) and emphasizes the independence and autonomy of the child within a developmentally appropriate context. She graduated as a doctor in medicine in 1896, in Rome, at a time when women were not entering this profession.

One approach used by the *Montessori* method for educating children is to break down complex tasks into simple, easy-to-follow steps. For example, when requesting children to pick up their toys and put them away, parents may find that the task must be broken down. Preschoolers can follow only one concise, simple command at a time rather than a complicated series of actions.

Montessori's classic book (1947) is titled *To Educate the Human Potential*. From it come these two quotes:

This is the secret which the small child himself revealed to us by doing work far beyond our dreams and expectations in all fields, including the intellect and the abstract, provided his hand was allowed to work side-by-side with intelligence.

and

Allow the whole to function together and there is discipline, but otherwise not! Tribes, groups, nations are the results of such spontaneous discipline and association. There is only one problem, and it is human development in its totality; once this is achieved in any unit—child or nation—everything else follows spontaneously and harmoniously.

American Montessori Society: (www.amshq.org/Montessori-Education)

Waldorf. The **Waldorf approach** to preschool and elementary school education is based on the teachings of Rudolf Steiner (1861–1925), the founder of anthroposophy. This was a popular alternative approach in the early 1900s. The first Waldorf school opened in 1919 in Germany, and to this day there are numerous international schools dedicated to his teachings. In Waldorf schools it is presumed that the child has multiple intelligences which need to be addressed and stimulated. Hence, there is a place for music, drama, and crafting, besides the more conventional school subjects such as science and technology. The person is seen as a whole consisting of body, soul, and spirit. Spirituality plays a distinct role and may be the drawing card for parents who choose this type of schooling.

In the educational approach, children were encouraged to develop critical thinking skills and to develop an empathic understanding. From his book on education, comes this quote by Rudolf Steiner (1971):

Where is the book in which the teacher can read about what teaching is? The children themselves are the book. We should not learn to teach out of any book other than the one lying open before us and consisting of the children themselves.

Association of Waldorf Schools of North America (www.Waldorfeducation.org)

Reggio Emilia.   **Reggio Emilia** is the name of an Italian village where the first preschools following a specific educational philosophy were started. The education includes preschool as well as primary education and developed after WWI when people felt in need of uplifting and inspirational outcomes, with a desire to start something different. It is based on the methods and philosophy of Italian educator Loris Malaguzzi (1920–1994). Malaguzzi died in the town of Reggio Emilia, Italy.

One of the characteristics of a Reggio Emilia education is that children should be actively engaged and have control over their learning. This is facilitated if they can touch, move, listen, and observe. Relationships with other children are encouraged to facilitate social outcomes, and clearly children need opportunities to express themselves. Following the devastation of WWI, it was felt that community support and parental involvement could contribute to creating an improved social fabric that recreated hope and more optimistic outcomes.

North American Reggio Emilia Alliance (NAREA): (http://reggioalliance.org)

Video Example 8.6

Watch this video regarding types of preschools. What are the different philosophies of various approaches to preschool education?

(https://www.youtube.com/watch?v=6O9BKRJDqNA)

Parenting Reflection 8–4

Do you think early childhood educational experiences should be required before a child enters first grade? What outcomes can we expect with high quality childcare?

Childcare Centers

Appropriate high quality childcare plays an important role in providing developmental experiences that promote healthy brain development. It can provide the basis for future learning. Several supervisory bodies have published recommended guidelines for early childhood learning environments. Some recommendations and guidelines include the following:

- Stringent health and safety requirements for the facilities, supplies, equipment, and environment
- Licensure and state regulations
- Safe play areas, playgrounds, and transportation
- Nutrition and food services
- Adequate staffing and qualified personnel
- Developmentally appropriate setting
- Curriculum and program activities
- Quality and continuity of care
- Relationship with the caretaker and continuity of care
- Emotional climate
- Opportunities for comfortable play with other children
- Respect for children's individual needs.

Based on National Resource Center for Health and Safety in Child Care and Early Education, 2014.

The context in which young children receive care may be associated with different child outcomes. It is important to take both the *quality* of childcare and the *characteristics* of a family into consideration when examining long-term influences on children's development. For example, young children show increased competence in peer relationship skills when they acquire secure attachments to parents, as well as to nonparental caregivers. This occurs when they have a secure attachment to their childcare provider and their parents. Peer relationship skills can be further strengthened by constructive modeling by nonparental caregivers, even if the parent–child relationship is suboptimal.

When comparing in-home to out-of-home childcare, we need to compare apples to apples. High-quality care that meets all health, safety, and developmental requirements can be optimal in any setting. A problem arises if we try to compare poor in-home parenting with good out-of-home childcare, or we compare excellent in-home parenting with poor out-of-home childcare. In such cases, we are not comparing the same dimensions of care, rather we are comparing apples to oranges. For the present, it may be safe to say that there appears to be little difference in the effects of parental and nonparental care on young children. There is one caveat: The quality of nonparental care must be high (National Institute of Child Health and Human Development, n.d, 2012). The most desirable choices are the ones that serve the *best interests of the child*. The features of each type of supplemental childcare program may vary.

When nonparental care is sensitive and responsive to children's needs, young children are observed to be compliant, cooperative, and achievement oriented. The *relationship* that nonparental adults promote with children has a greater impact than the methods used in working with children. This parallel implies consequences based on the quality of nonparental care. The negative emotional attitudes of nonparental caregivers and failure to respond to children's needs can result in problem behavior. Generally speaking, the intellectual gains offered by preschool programs are greatest for low-income children rather than middle-class children because of the differences in the home environments (Heckman, 2013).

Childcare centers typically offer care of children for a varying number of hours per day, depending on parental needs and work schedules. The kinds of programs most commonly used by families with preschoolers involve groups of children. They operate as a business venture. Some programs are nonprofit and are sponsored by companies, community agencies, churches, or educational institutions. A successful model is the co-op model for preschool, where at least a dozen pairs of parents pool their resources to run a children's preschool and they hire a teacher. Parents volunteer regularly and teach alongside the professional. Parent education and parental skill development is offered as part of this model.

Licensure and Accreditation of Childcare Centers.
During the past few decades, more staff members have been trained in early childhood education. Many universities with programs in child development and child education have childcare centers that fall under the auspices of the university and serve as training institutions while also serving the community. Typically, childcare centers are state licensed. They can also be subject to voluntary national accreditation.

A *licensed* center meets local and state requirements. The guidelines and rules differ from state to state. Guidelines include, for instance, standards and regulations set by a state department of human resources or a state department of health, as well as fire, safety, and other regulations. Licensure of childcare centers is mandatory, and the centers are monitored regularly to ensure compliance.

An *accredited* center meets stringent national standards and is monitored by an overseeing accrediting body. National accreditation is voluntary. An important resource in the United States is the National Association for the Education of Young Children (NAEYC), which is the national accreditation body that sets and monitors professional standards of early childhood education and facilitates voluntary accreditation of childcare centers (www.naeyc.org/accreditation).

Parents should conscientiously check a center's licensure and accreditation status before sending their child there. Some guidelines can be found on state websites, as well as on the U.S government's website focusing on childcare (www.acf.hhs.gov/occ).

Some unlicensed and unmonitored childcare settings in the United States have a questionable reputation and may provide nothing more than custodial care. At times, these settings have become notorious for practices that harm children.

Parenting Reflection 8–5
Explain the implications for the family when an employer provides childcare as an employee benefit.

Preschool Programs

Preschool programs are educational rather than custodial. Most communities have several types of programs available. Preschool programs are typically 2- to 3-hour sessions in the morning or afternoon, and the times can be synchronized to match parental work hours. The number of days that children attend can vary. The more common types of programs are briefly discussed.

Specialized Curriculum Programs.
Some preschool programs offer a particular curriculum, such as one based on the Montessori Method, or an open-classroom model. The theoretical philosophy of a particular program is emphasized over other factors. The curriculum and materials used in a Montessori program foster cognitive skills. Young children are taught to proceed sequentially to reach goals or solutions to problems.

Programs for Exceptional Children.
Some families have a child with atypical needs. These children can benefit from preschool programs that are designed to meet

Bikeriderlondon/Shutterstock

When exploring options for child-care centers and preschool programs, families should seek out high-quality settings that meet all health, safety, and developmental requirements and serve the best interests of the child.

their needs. Such programs typically involve children with special physical or mental challenges. Incorporating children with special needs into mainstream preschool programs allows all children to gain greater empathy through these interactions. The Council for Exceptional Children is a good resource for matters pertaining to special education (www.cec.sped.org).

Programs for the Gifted and Talented.   Typically the programs for gifted and talented children start at elementary school level. Precocious abilities in art, music, language/reading, writing, problem solving, and math may appear at young ages. From the especially creative child to the child who has already mastered learning outcomes to the "twice exceptional" child, exceptionally bright children have a wide range of talents and behaviors that need to be nurtured (Gadzikowski, 2013). Parents of precociously gifted and talented preschoolers often seek guidance on how best to address their child's unique and amazing behaviors. With the current focus on developing and offering preschool programs in public schools, educators are recognizing that preschoolers who come to school demonstrating advanced knowledge and skills need differentiated learning experiences. States like Louisiana and Arizona have developed identification

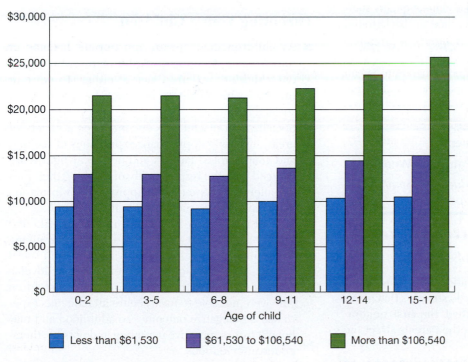

FIGURE 8–4.
Family expenditures of a child, by income level and age of child. Figures have been rounded off to nearest thousand.[1] 2013.

Source: Lino, Mark. (2014). Expenditures on Children by Families, 2013. U.S. Department of Agriculture, Center for Nutrition Policy and Promotion. Miscellaneous Publication No. 1528-2013.

[1] U.S. average for the younger child in husband–wife families with two children.

strategies and programs to meet the needs of the young gifted and talented child (Davis, Rimm, & Siegle, 2010).

Compensatory Programs. Compensatory preschool programs are specially designed to provide a variety of experiences for children from disadvantaged families. Head Start is an example of such a program. Activities promote language acquisition and social and cognitive skills to enhance the child's self-concept and initiative. Nutritional and health needs are also addressed. A unique aspect of such programs is parental and family involvement, which serves to strengthen family functioning.

Excellent long-range benefits result from participation in these programs (Carneiro & Ginja, 2014). Children who have attended Head Start programs score higher on achievement tests and have higher grades in elementary school. These children are also less likely to be placed in special education classes or to repeat a grade (García, Heckman, Leaf, & Prados, 2016).

- -

Focus Point. Many parents access nonparental childcare. Agencies can provide screened au pairs and childcare professionals to provide care in the parental home. The quality of these services should be the most pressing concern, as this is one dimension that affects developmental progress. The care should also meet quality standards. Caretakers should have reference and background checks and impeccable records. A variety of programs supplement parental care for preschoolers. If well chosen, quality childcare and preschool programming can be a very positive and enriching experience for children.

- -

Acknowledgment

Sections on Gifted Education: Patricia F. Wood, PhD

Professor, Director Gifted Education, Samford University. Used with permission.

Parenting Reflection 8–6

If changes in one generation affect the other generations to some degree, how do stressors that occur among the third generation affect the first generation? How does the role strain of the parents affect the children?

CHAPTER FOCUS POINTS

Preschoolers: Developmental Achievements

■ Though not as rapidly as in infancy, developmental changes involving communication skills and personality expression become more apparent in the preschool years. While millions of children are subject to abuse globally, organizations including the United Nations continue to make progress in facilitating safe environments for children to thrive.

Learning and Brain Development

■ During this stage of early childhood, an environment filled with rich language contributes to a more verbal preschooler, and ultimately a more successful adult. By actively talking and listening to a preschooler, parents enlarge the child's vocabulary and encourage positive communication skills that could last a lifetime.

■ The process of learning self-regulation is often difficult for both children and parents. As children struggle to develop self-control, parents must apply healthy strategies to support the unfolding of the child's unique personality.

Parenting Young Children

■ As children develop, an appropriate balance of nurture and structure contributes to optimal parent–child interaction. A lack of either structure or nurture could facilitate behavioral, emotional, or social difficulties.

■ Socialization of children encompasses a variety of areas, including appropriate expressions of feelings and gender roles. Parents and other key figures are charged with the responsibility of teaching their preschoolers developmentally-appropriate information on complex topics such as sexuality and death.

■ Several attachment disorders, including RAD and DSED have been linked to adverse caregiving environments reflecting insufficient care and social neglect. Although not all children raised in adverse conditions display these symptoms, many children who were not able to form secure attachments experience the negative outcomes in adulthood and may benefit from supportive parenting and possibly therapeutic interventions.

Focus On 8–2   **Play Experiences for Preschoolers**

Instead of offering toys haphazardly, consider the specific aspects and skills that a specific play activity or situation may support. A child who could benefit from a sensory experience may require different toys or contexts than a child who is enacting a fantasy story with a playmate. During a day at preschool for instance, children may require a variety of play opportunities depending on their own developmental level, the curriculum, the learning outcomes intended, the strengths to be explored, the child's mood and disposition at a particular time, and the context of the activity. Adult supervision is always recommended.

Promoting gross motor skills

- Wagons, tricycles, scooters, outdoor climbing and play apparatus, ball games
- Playhouses, sandboxes, water-play equipment (supervision mandatory)

Play equipment promoting dexterity and more

- Blocks, simple puzzles, stringing beads, shape-sorting and nesting toys, matching games
- Picture and storybooks, simple computer games and board games

Equipment that encourages creativity

- Arts and crafts supplies (e.g., crayons, chalk, paint, modeling clay, children's safety scissors, paper)
- Rhythm and musical instruments

Dramatic play equipment

- Dress-up clothes and accessories, role-play equipment and mini stage
- Action figures, hand puppets, racially and culturally diverse dolls

Sensory Activities

- Activities involving tangible materials with interesting textures such as clay, playdough, foam, bubbles, shaving cream, water, and sand
- Crawling through a canvas tunnel or exploring body boundaries in a stretchy and breathable fabric "body-sock" can be a fun activity under adult supervision

---

Cognitive Development

- Around age 3, children's thought processes become more complex. The egocentric nature of their thoughts can be both charming and frustrating for parents as they allow their child freedom of expression while also encouraging a broader view of their world.
- Preschoolers need developmentally appropriate toys and play equipment to encourage acquisition of appropriate physical, psychosocial, and mental skills.

Respectful Parenting

- Parent–child approaches which have stood the test of time, include respectful and developmentally-appropriate choices for children. Appropriate adversity

combined with loving support by family and friends, can strengthen resilience in children. Praise should be authentic and focus on the effort invested.

Challenging Behaviors

- Parents should counteract childhood obesity by being good role models, cooking nutritious meals, and encouraging physical activity. In this way, they establish a foundation of good eating habits, which will set the child on the right nutritional path for life.

Childcare for Preschoolers

- Many parents access nonparental childcare. Agencies can provide screened au pairs and childcare professionals to provide care in the parental home. The quality of these services should be the most pressing concern, as this is one dimension that affects developmental progress. The care should also meet quality standards. Caretakers should have reference and background checks and impeccable records. A variety of programs supplement parental care for preschoolers. If well chosen, quality childcare and preschool programming can be a very positive and enriching experience for children.

USEFUL WEBSITES

Websites are dynamic and change

Center on the Developing Child, Harvard University
http://developingchild.harvard.edu
Focus: Preschool and child development

Childcare Resources
www.childcare.org
Focus: Childcare resources

Council for Exceptional Children
www.cec.sped.org
Focus: Education and advocacy for children

Head Start
An Office of the Administration for Children and Families Early Childhood Learning and Knowledge Center
http://eclkc.ohs.acf.hhs.gov/hslc
Focus: School readiness for young children

National Association for the Education of Young Children
www.naeyc.org
Focus: Educating preschoolers

National Association of Children's Hospitals and Related Institutions
Includes its public policy affiliate
www.childrenshospitals.net
Focus: Pediatric advocacy and education

National Child Traumatic Stress Network
http://www.nctsn.org/
Focus: Traumatic stress in children

National Institute of Child Health and Human Development
www.nichd.nih.gov
Focus: Child health and development

National Resource Center for Health and Safety in Child Care and Early Education
http://nrckids.org
Focus: Health and safety in childcare

U.S. Department of Health and Human Services
www.healthfinder.gov
Focus: Health and wellness

U.S. Department of Health and Human Services, Administration for Children and Families
www.acf.hhs.gov
Focus: Children health and nutrition, Parenting,

CHAPTER 9

Parenting in Middle Childhood

Learning Outcomes

After completing this chapter, you should be able to

1. Define middle childhood and its main developmental goals.
2. Outline the landmarks and parental expectations of school-age children.
3. Describe the developmental characteristics of school-age children.
4. Propose actions to support a safe school environment while preventing bullying and harassment.
5. Describe cognitive development in middle childhood.
6. Examine the areas of parental involvement in education.
7. Identify problematic behaviors in school-age children.
8. Outline the educational rewards and challenges of exceptional children.
9. Assess the impact of parental employment status on school-age children.

MEETING UNIQUE INDIVIDUALS

Middle childhood is a rewarding time for parents and children alike, as children are increasingly becoming persons in their own right displaying opinions and unique personalities. As the children are gaining independence, and are discovering their environment, we as adults can share their wonder and their ability to access a fantasy world and still believe in some of the magic of childhood. They seem to be bridging the world from childhood innocence while also tentatively reaching towards growing up. It is a privilege to participate in their domain through their senses as we parent, care for, teach, or mentor this age group. Acquiring the complexities of literacy, numeracy, and other skills adds to the newfound powers of middle childhood. Formally, middle childhood begins when a child enters school; at about 6 years of age and extends to about age 12, or when they become a "teen."

Parents and other grown-ups in the child's world might hold different expectations for school-age children than they did for preschoolers. They take a responsible approach to supervising and providing care for this age group, as the focus on physical safety and survival as seen in the infancy period is diminishing. We can focus on the total social, cognitive, and emotional development and well-being of these developing youngsters. The school years will also be a report card on how well we did during the preschool years; the period before school-age was a critical developmental window laying the foundation for school-age development.

By describing this age group as "school-age" children, we also indicate the prominence of school and education in their world. The educational system in turn faces the challenge of finding ways of reaching and teaching children, that lead to good outcomes and ultimately mastery of age appropriate academic skills. Children spend longer times away from their families and simultaneously the peer group gains relevance. Many supplementary developmental tasks surface during this period. These tasks complement the child's emerging sense of self, the development of a healthy self-esteem and self-concept, which in turn extend to many related aspects of the child's life.

Parenting style and caretaking behaviors are modified in response to the child's development. The methods and techniques of parenting or guiding children that were successful during a child's earlier years have to evolve as the child is gaining mastery over new dimensions. Essentially, parents increase the psychological dimension while toning down the physical-care aspect. The changes in caregiving emerge subtly as a child progresses developmentally. Parenting is a developmental task and it continues to change as children as well as their parents progress on life's path.

Focus Point.   Between the ages of 6 and 12, children in middle childhood further develop their cognitive and social skills with the assistance of parents, peers, and the education system.

PARENTING SCHOOL-AGE CHILDREN

The Decade of Learning

If school is going to become the central focus of the next decade or so of the child's life, it is important that there is "buy in." This valuable period should direct the child towards learning, and schools and parents should be the primary platforms for development of the self that are so closely tied to whether a person thinks they can or will succeed. The awareness of one's own skills and abilities, the self-confidence, combined with environmental and pedagogical support, learning discipline such as long term goals, good study habits, and organization form the psychological foundation that may contribute to whether a child drops out or continues to grad school. Either choice will precipitate a host of consequences that will determine and influence almost all other facets of the learner's life (Adler, 2015).

Schools ideally are social laboratories, incubators of thought, places where curious minds can find the ways and means of finding and researching answers. Teachers and parents should send the message that schools are a safe and privileged space for exploration (Noddings, 2015). If the pre-adolescent is optimally able to learn a language, a musical instrument, or any other specialized skill during this phase of his life, schools should be the places where this can occur.

What happens in schools is so much more than facts and books. Schools are places of civic engagement, they are the venues where children can learn and practice being responsive citizens, and become culturally and economically aware. If parents are involved in the school system, it provides a place to network, a place to form community and more (Martinez & Wizer-Vecchi, 2016). All this relates directly back to the child they are parenting, and orchestrates towards better outcomes, academically, interpersonally, and otherwise.

Because school plays such a significant role during this stage of parenting, school choice is an important way that parents can ensure that the child's educational environment reflects the values parents want to instill in their offspring.

Jovannig/123RF.com

For both parents and their children school choice is important and reflects the values parents want to instill in their offspring. This is the time to invest in a child's education, not just economically but especially emotionally and psychologically, as parental support is one of the most valuable resources to make educational dreams a reality.

Developmental Parenting

As a child reaches elementary school age, parenting changes in quality and style in response to the child's changing developmental needs. The developmental tasks and milestones of school-age children build on those they experienced as preschoolers. During infancy, the focus was heavily on safety and caretaking needs, whereas for early childhood and school-age children, it includes emphasis on social and psychological demands. Physical skills acquired during this period play a significant role in shaping a child's self-concept.

Parenting children in middle childhood, as during the earlier stages, focuses on encouraging them to accomplish essential developmental tasks and milestones. Parents adjust their responses and interactions as part of a developmental parenting process. Parenting styles that worked well with preschoolers lose their effectiveness with school-age children. New accomplishments and abilities emerge during middle childhood. Parents learn that they also need to become psychological support systems for their school-age children.

During early childhood, parents gradually encourage their children towards increased and age appropriate self-control and self-regulation. The experiences from previous stages culminate in greater sharing of social power between the parents and the child. Parents increasingly use psychological insight to help children achieve greater levels of self-control. Reassuring children, encouraging them to recover from social challenges, and giving positive reinforcement for efforts to learn new skills are all helpful. The ratio of assertive versus supportive care shifts during this time because parents expect children to take more responsibility for their actions and decisions.

Parents of school-age children expect them to:

- Refine their social skills, exhibiting an increased ability to cooperate with adults and other children.
- Increase the sophistication of their information-processing skills as reflected in their schoolwork.
- Assume assignments without adult supervision, and complete them according to the standards set by adults.

Focus Point. As a child reaches school age, parenting changes in quality and style in response to the child's changing developmental needs. Parents adopt a variety of interactional styles based on various parenting approaches. During infancy, the focus emphasized safety and physical needs, whereas during early childhood and the school-age years, it expands to increasingly include social and psychological demands.

LANDMARKS OF MIDDLE CHILDHOOD

During middle childhood, developmental events and changes increasingly lead towards maturity and responsibility:

- Acquiring a positive attitude toward assignments and routine jobs; developing of a positive work ethic.
- Mastering the tools of mental and social skills to handle the complexities of formal education: e.g., academic skills including reading, writing, and calculation. Learning group skills through grown-ups, friends, siblings, and peers.
- Acquiring age appropriate responsibility for personal actions and behaviors.

The development of a healthy attitude toward work and duty in performing one's responsibilities means that school-age children are further extending their *self-regulating abilities*. The ability to complete tasks is also supported in the school and home environment. The process of performing tasks to acceptable standards as outlined by authority figures will set the tone for later work and professional skills. The overall feeling that should emerge is pride in accomplishing a variety of skills and being dependable in completing assigned tasks.

Adversity in Context

Children acquire a *work ethic* as they are rewarded and reinforced for a job well done. Importantly, the effort invested is as important as the outcome. Not all children can be top of the class or winners in every endeavor. Encouraging their application to the task, their investment of motivation and energy, are qualities that will serve them well in later life while also providing a reality check in terms of how different people have different talents and skills. Giving everybody on the team a trophy for participation may be an appropriate acknowledgment of

investment and motivation. But even at this young age children have to learn some harsh realities such as only one of the two competing teams will win, and not everybody can be the best at everything all the time. Learning to be graceful and a good team player, even when the winning trophy eludes us, is an important life skill (Greene, 2016).

As parents and teachers, it is a careful balancing act to reward the effort that a child has invested and acknowledging that effort. That is congruent and honest feedback. Pretending that the job is perfect when it is not, with the hollow "well done!" and "good job!" may not do the trick, especially if the child knows that they did not meet the standards to come out on top of the competition (A. L. Brown, 2015; Ricci & Lee, 2016). Parents can be more competitive than the children themselves, and as parents we have to step back and ask ourselves: "Is it realistic what I am expecting?" "In whose interest am I demanding this?" "Is it in the best interest of the child, or are these my own ambitions resurfacing?"

Strength through Appropriate Adversity. The *process* of investing effort, of trying even at the risk of failure, can be relevant and formative as a learning experience. It is about the educational journey as well, not only about the destination. Children learn from this process and as adults we should be supportive and encouraging when the journey is difficult, even at that young age. Perseverance, dignity, keeping an eye on long term goals, behaving in socially acceptable ways; all these qualities add up in positive ways. Ultimately, as parents we cannot fight all the battles for our children. In becoming gradually stronger for the task of dealing with adult life challenges, the child has to be exposed to age appropriate challenges with the proviso that we invest time in guiding them towards coping skills. These coping skills will be the qualities children can come back to as the journey continues or gets more challenging (Anderson, Turner, Heath, & Payne, 2016).

The popular work by Duckworth (2016): *Grit: The Power of Passion and Perseverance*, shows how appropriate stressors such as perseverance and the ability to display strength can lead to positive outcomes. With the tendency to overprotect our children, we as parents may inadvertently have tried to keep them far from all threats, even the expected challenges in day-to-day life. This can be a double-edged sword. Some appropriate disappointments can be character building, especially if the child knows there is emotional support and love of them as a person and they have adults and mentors to turn to for encouragement and advice.

Exploration of the environment should allow for age appropriate challenges and uncertainties, how else is the child going to learn about the bigger challenges that may come their way at unanticipated times? Children who have faced adversity in the form of loss, incapacitation, or the divorce of parents; have overcome these challenges and more as long as there were support persons and mentors in their network (Thompson, 2015c).

In practice it may mean allowing the child to gain freedom to practice making decisions within safe limits. Parents learn that children desire and require increasing degrees of age appropriate freedom. The psychosocial focus is facilitated when the greater desire for independence is supported and opportunities for learning and competency are provided. With these independent actions comes the risk of some disappointments, but if constructively contextualized, these too can play an important role (Ritchhart, 2015).

Self-Efficacy, Self-Regulation, and Co-Regulation

In middle childhood, the youngsters are acquiring skills at a rapid rate, and sometimes they can perform some tasks at adult levels while emotionally still anchored in the world of childhood. For instance, children with special talents such as musical, sport, or dancing abilities may function at very sophisticated levels. These new-found levels of **self-efficacy** seem to know no boundaries and it is an excellent time for parents to invest in coaching and education, as the children absorb new skills enthusiastically.

Self-regulation continues to develop and expand, but is also mediated by the **co-regulation** as exerted by their parents. Appropriate parenting can guide children towards regulation of emotions in socially appropriate ways, because the parent can anticipate difficulties and mediate outcomes. These are useful testing grounds for middle age children.

Lessons From Parents and Peers

It is encouraging that children in middle childhood still greatly value parental opinion; the parent who has a good relationship with the child can be a healthy counterbalance to unhealthy or faddish peer behaviors. For that reason, it is crucial to build and maintain the relationship, and to decide and communicate what is really important in terms of values. Does it really matter if the entire peer group listens to one or another type of

music? Note to self: did we grown-ups not do similar things when we were at that age?

On the other hand, certain topics need to be addressed by parents to prevent harmful peer influence. Talk about sexuality and also, importantly, the dangers of drug and alcohol abuse should be broached in an ongoing yet age appropriate manner. Conversations about these topics should recur at regular intervals, but be adjusted to the developmental level of the child. Regard these talks as a form of immunization, so that the child can internalize constructive parental values in an ongoing and age appropriate manner (Döring et al., 2015).

Entry into the school environment signals changes and adjustments for the child, the parents, and the family system. An additional social group, namely the peers, take on a much greater role. As a child progresses towards adolescence, the peer group assumes an increasingly significant role in facilitating a child's socialization and serves as a reference point for values and social norms. Parents may wonder why the opinion of peers is so important, or why peer opinions and values may spread like wildfire through a group (Wentzel & Ramani, 2016). Part of this has to do with seeking acceptance, wanting to conform to the opinion leaders, and differentiating from parents by finding one's own style, be it for taste in music or the personal expression in terms of clothing.

Importantly, as a parent and an adult working with this age group, be respectful towards them, and learn to differentiate between what is a healthy expression of developing autonomy in the child, versus what can be unhealthy and potentially destructive influences. In short, be involved and knowledgeable about your child's world. They are still at an age where they like this involvement of parents. Once the 16-year-old can take care of his own transport needs it is going to get a whole lot harder; so the foundations need to be put in place during this period.

As the author (Gerhardt) reminds her students in the Parenting class:

Question: "When is the best time to parent a teenager?"

Answer: "Before they become teenagers!"

Lesson-to-be-learned: Middle childhood is very important because of the opportunity for constructive influence; this is the period *before* adolescence, this is the window of opportunity during which values, ethics, norms, work ethic, and the like should be imparted, shared, supported, and encouraged.

Responding to a child's changing developmental demands in middle childhood means adapting parenting demands to this developmental level (see Focus On 9–1).

Throughout these years, the cultural expectations of parents and other authority figures lead to new developmental challenges for school-age children. These social and mental expectations are also supported by school and social contexts and add yet another layer of socialization.

Focus Point. During this developmental stage, parents are charged with the responsibility to teach their children skills such as regulation of emotions and coping mechanisms. The influence of peers becomes increasingly important as children seek acceptance and create deeper bonds with other school-age children. Through continuous open communication, parents can help children develop healthy mindsets and values on topics such as sexuality, religion and spiritual values, friendship, and peer pressure.

Focus On 9–1

The Developmental Characteristics of School-Age Children

General

- Increasing independence
- Tends to be sensitive to criticism
- Enjoys privacy at times
- Becomes increasingly critical of adults
- Becomes more peer oriented

Physical/Motor

- Likes group activities and games
- Gender differences are observable in physical skills
- Well-established hand–eye coordination
- High energy level
- Appearance of permanent teeth
- Changing body configuration

Social/Mental

- Prefers activities with same-sex peers
- Enjoys light competition
- Curious about the world at large
- Develops a series of close friendships
- Improves with regard to group participation
- May construct self-concept based on social comparisons
- Develops reading and calculation skills
- Changes from intuitive to concrete thought processes

Interests

- Enjoys collecting or building on collections
- Enjoys silly jokes and humor
- Enjoys video and computer games and activities
- Likes adventure stories, movies, and biographies
- Likes creative activities and making things
- Acquires skills that display individual talents and abilities
- Enjoys sports, including organized and team sports

Meeting the Needs of School-Age Children

Physical Maturation.   During this time, a number of the school-age children also enter **puberty**, which signals the journey toward sexual maturation. Typically, puberty's onset can be from the age of 10 onwards, but for some children it is earlier. Girls tend to be slightly ahead of boys concerning the onset of puberty. The developmental events and changes that occur during this period lead to increased maturity and responsibilities. Middle childhood is characterized by more advanced levels of developmental abilities, accompanied by greater expectations by parents and others.

Because children are getting stronger, some overzealous parents may try to push their children towards excessive sport involvement, as in pushing them to be competitive beyond their years. Sports injuries and concussions are serious matters. However strongly we feel about sports, we need to also keep the best interests, the safety and health, and the actual physical maturity of our children in mind.

Promoting Competent Eating.   Prenatal maternal nutrition, as well as childhood eating patterns, contribute to adult health outcomes (Ojha, Fainberg, Sebert, Budge, & Symonds, 2015; Brown, 2016). Ultimately, the goal is to establish *competent eating patterns* (Stewart & Thompson, 2015). This paradigm for eating highlights aspects that characterize a competent eater, namely, being positive, comfortable, and flexible regarding food intake. A child needs to know that reliable sources for food are available and that there will be enjoyable and nourishing food at their disposal. Food intake should ideally be internally regulated in response to true hunger. The family's eating patterns should support structured and planned meals (Dwyer, Oh, Patrick, & Hennessy, 2015), and this highlights the importance of the shared family meal. Ultimately, the goal is to maintain a normal, enjoyable eating experience that nourishes the body, yet does not lead to overeating or undereating. Attitudes toward eating should exhibit self-trust that the correct foods will be chosen. In short, a normalization of eating behavior is the desired outcome. Children are responsive to good role models and will incorporate the modeled healthy eating habits.

Of major concern is the increasingly high incidence of obesity and poor nutrition among school-age children.

Food insecurity is also more prevalent in the United States than one would intuitively think, and it is surprising that despite alarming obesity rates, a segment of the population does not know where their next meal will come from (Sun et al., 2016; Chilton, Knowles, Rabinowich, & Arnold, 2015). Obesity and related disorders pave the way toward health problems such as diabetes and hypertension. Several factors complicate this situation:

- Parental role models and the nature and quality of family nutrition
- Lack of knowledge regarding nutrition and a healthy lifestyle within the family home
- Obese parents who condone obesity in their children
- Exposure to fast foods, high-calorie drinks, and inadequately nutritious meals
- Ready availability of high carbohydrate and high glycemic index foods
- Lack of adequate physical activity, while increasing computer and television time
- Skipping family meals because the family is not supporting healthy lifestyle choices
- Chaotic home environments where children resort to "grazing" because there are no scheduled family meals
- Pressures from food advertising in the media and during children's television programs
- Exposure to vending machines and poor-quality cafeteria food in some schools

Childhood Obesity.   Unhealthy eating patterns and weight related concerns may become more apparent during this stage. Sadly, it is so prevalent that even parents do not notice, or choose not to notice, that their child is becoming overweight. As more children become overweight, children will have peers who look similar to them in terms of weight distribution. There has been a steady increase in the number of school-age children and adolescents who are overweight (Federal Interagency Forum on Child and Family Statistics, 2015). About 19 percent of school-age children and adolescents are considered overweight. The incidence is rising; since 1980 the prevalence has almost tripled (Sun et al., 2016; Chilton, Knowles, Rabinowich, & Arnold, 2015). Ethnic heritage and related cultural practices surrounding food can play a role and can contribute to the risk of being overweight. Lower socioeconomic class and poverty, are factors that may limit knowledge concerning wellness and nutrition, and can facilitate unhealthy lifestyle choices in the parental home.

Helping school-age children develop healthy eating habits and food preferences can be challenging for parents and other adults, especially if the older generation is facing weight and lifestyle struggles themselves. The parents are the most powerful influence during early childhood, and how family nutrition plays out in the parental home can set the stage for a lifetime of nutritional choices. One of the greatest gifts that parents can give their children is to instill appropriate nutritional and lifestyle choices from the start. If parents are struggling with food-related challenges, they can be perpetuating the poor habits learned from their own childhoods and inadvertently passing them on to the next generation (Judd, Newton, Newton, & Ewing, 2016). By educating the next generation and by raising awareness, perhaps the cycle can be broken. As a nation, Americans boast some success in decreasing cigarette smoking in adults. Similarly, with collaboration on many platforms, including positive influences in the schools, the incidence of overweight and obesity in children could be reduced, especially since there is so much room for improvement.

School breakfast and lunch programs can also promote good nutrition and eating habits among children at this age by offering healthful food choices through a la carte items and limiting the availability of junk foods in vending machines (Bouchard, Gallagher, Soubhi, Bujold, & St-Cyr, 2015). Recess time offers many opportunities for physical activity, which contributes to good health. Physical education is required in most states at the elementary school level and there has been a movement to try and increase activity in school contexts (Dwyer et al., 2015).

Health and Safety Concerns

Vaccinations.   In addition to promoting good health via healthy nutrition, physical activity, and lifestyle choices, parents have other health and safety concerns for school-age children. Children entering this stage should have received the basic series of vaccinations to prevent many infectious diseases. In the United States, immunizations are usually mandatory for child-care, preschool, and kindergarten enrollment. Some illnesses are common during this period. Because many children are in close contact with each other, it is likely that infectious diseases such as common colds and other conditions will spread easily (Centers for Disease Control and Prevention, 2013b).

Dental and Orthodontic Care.   Because permanent teeth appear at the beginning of this period, dental care is important. Many children are first introduced to a dentist in early childhood, and this becomes even more important in middle childhood. Dental professionals can assist parents in helping children learn the fundamentals of dental hygiene and how to prevent cavities. It is said that about half a century ago the bulk of a lifetime dental budget was spent in the second half of an adult's life. Nowadays, the bulk of the dental budget should be invested before age 20. Orthodontic care has become a virtual rite of passage for American teenagers (Sterling & Best-Boss, 2013).

Vision and Healthy Eyes.   Parents need to make sure that their children are not overexposed to computers and television because this keeps them inactive and indoors. Children should play outside and exercise in environments that require distance vision and outside light. *Outside light* can be tenfold that of indoor lighting conditions. Systematic reviews and meta-analyses of many research studies seem to support that reduced time in natural light and reduced time looking at distant objects, as well as genetic factors, can be contributing factors to myopia (Aries, Aarts, & Van Hoof, 2015). The prevalence of myopia has increased steadily in young adults. Good lifestyle practices, not spending too much time using near vision, and exposure to outdoor and daylight activities in which children exercise and use their distance vision all add up to healthier vision outcomes (Ramamurthy, Lin Chua, & Saw, 2015).

Accidents and Injuries.   Every hour, a child dies in the United States as a result of an injury (Centers for Disease Control and Prevention, 2012). Accidental injury involving vehicles and bicycles are the leading cause of death among children this age (Centers for Disease Control and Prevention, 2015a). Parents need to be assertive in preventing these kinds of accidents from occurring, if possible. Proper supervision during play, using seat belts, wearing helmets while biking and participating in snow sports, limiting where play may take place, and teaching personal safety on the street and in the home are just a few ways that child safety can be promoted. Flat-screen televisions and furniture such as chests of drawers may fall on children if they are not securely anchored.

Particularly alarming is the incidence of gun deaths and related accidental fatalities among children which have been increasing in the United States. Protocol for the safe handling of weapons needs to be strictly followed, as curious young minds may explore objects in the home, without fully realizing the dangers involved. They may have seen guns used freely on video or television, and not realize the extremely dangerous implications in real life. Almost all childhood gunshot fatalities represent some degree of negligence and irresponsibility on the part of the owners of those weapons. Safe storage of weapons is imperative. According to the Centers for Disease Control and Prevention (www.CDC.gov), the greatest number of accidental firearm deaths among youngsters can be traced to inappropriate access to firearms. This can result in self-inflicted deaths, as well as another child inadvertently inflicting the harm (Center for Injury Research and Prevention, 2017).

Head Injuries and Concussions.   Parents and coaches of children who take part in team sports need to be aware of the potential dangers of concussions and repetitive head trauma. New guidelines have been established to better identify and manage concussions, as well as to reduce the number of head impacts during contact sports such as football and soccer. Repeated undetected and untreated concussions can increase the chances of altered cognitive functioning and even permanent brain damage. This is a serious matter as the effects may be lifelong and may not be reversible. About 40 percent of sports-related concussions involved children between the ages of 8 and 13, when the brain is particularly vulnerable to injury. Although concussion is a fairly common injury, it is likely to be underreported, especially among the youngest groups (Weerdenburg, Schneeweiss, Koo, & Boutis., 2016). Every state in the United States has laws concerning the proper identification and management of concussion in youth sports and at their minimum involves obtaining medical clearance before "return to play." There is a growing movement to require schools to develop "return to learn" or "return to think" protocols providing necessary academic supports to students recovering from concussions and other brain trauma. While youth sports provide many benefits to children, understanding how to identify, manage, and reduce the likelihood of concussions is in the best interests of the child and society as a whole (Calisto & Gaines, 2015).

Major research studies and meta-analyses reported the combined findings of over a million children and adolescents diagnosed with traumatic head injury, many of which were single head injuries of milder proportions, also referred to as concussions (Redelmeier & Raza, 2016). The studies emphasize the importance of prevention, (especially in contact sports and on playgrounds), following recommended guidelines for rest and recovery, and avoiding subsequent injury. These conditions with potentially serious outcomes, and it is imperative that they are addressed in a timely manner. Greater awareness in parents, participants in sports activities, coaches, teachers, and medical and related professionals is important to increase prevention and appropriate intervention strategies.

Focus Point.   Although infancy and its central focus on survival are in the past, parents should continue to put great effort into the health and well-being of their school-age children. Both food insecurity and obesity are problems plaguing this age group, either as a result of poverty or poor parental lifestyle choices. Overall health care, including vision, dental, prevention of head injuries and concussions, and yearly check-ups, continue to play an important role in a child's healthy development.

Structure and Nurture Revisited

During middle childhood, children acquire more refined abilities and display greater skill at internalizing their own structure. They are beginning to think more abstractly and these abilities continue to expand. An appreciation for rules helps school-age children internalize value systems, codes of conduct, and social skills while also becoming more self-directed.

Ideally, structure should be combined with nurture. The nurturing of school-age children requires a sensitivity to developmental needs and emerging abilities (Britto et al., 2017). Adapting parenting styles is a major challenge for parents; they must be aware of the developmental and reciprocal nature of parenting. Psychological controls, such as reasoning, are more effective with 9-year-olds than with 3-year-olds. These approaches work best if accompanied by a conversation providing an opportunity for the child to give feedback; the communication component determines if it is a constructive intervention that also makes sense to the child and is therefore meaningful. Responding to a child's changing developmental demands in middle childhood means adapting parenting demands to this developmental level (see Figure 9–1).

(see Figure 9–1).

Parenting Reflection 9–1

Describe some family rules that promote structure for school-age children. Explain both the positive and the negative consequences of such rules.

ADJUSTING PARENTING STYLES

The parenting style should be adjusted to meet the developmental needs of the child. Some behaviors that provide structure and nurture include:

- Affirming developmental achievements appropriately.
- Providing a safe and loving environment.
- Encouraging appropriate and safe exploration of the child's environment.
- Modeling respectful, gender-equal behavior.
- Modeling good communication in the marital relationship.
- Communicating age appropriately and respectfully with the child.
- Encouraging the expression of feelings and responding respectfully.
- Providing developmentally appropriate information.
- Providing appropriate and respectful feedback regarding behaviors.
- Explaining the consequences of behaviors and setting appropriate boundaries.
- Being consistent and trustworthy.
- Providing a home environment that supports social and academic learning.
- Teaching the child appropriate decision making.
- Encouraging the child toward appropriate autonomous behavior.
- Supporting the child's interests and relationships with his or her peer group and friends.
- Teaching the child pro-civic behaviors and values.
- Facilitating engagement in prosocial groups in civic and/or religious contexts.

FIGURE 9–1. Parenting of School-age Children.

Parenting Reflection 9–2

Parents can promote a sense of industry in school-age children by encouraging them to take part in arts and crafts projects. Describe how a parent could use both structured and unstructured projects to promote industry and creativity.

Peer Groups. Our culture is a composite of different subcultures, including various racial, ethnic, and age groups. Individuals have experiences with a number of subcultures throughout their life spans. During the middle years of childhood, children experience one of the first and most important subcultures—the *peer group*.

Peer groups may be formed spontaneously, as with neighborhood children who play together, or formally, as when children are grouped by age in elementary school. In the early part of middle childhood, peer group functioning is less structured and group adherence is loose in comparison with the latter part of this period. Children learn a number of social lessons from the group politics that take place within these groupings (Bingham & Conner, 2015). Like other social systems, peer groups have their own rules, communication styles, and boundaries; they also exhibit other functions:

- Developing companionship, especially for play activities.
- Creating a testing ground for behaviors, acceptable and otherwise.
- Transmitting information, accurate or inaccurate.
- Teaching rules and logical consequences.
- Promoting gender-role development.
- Influencing children's self-concept.

There are many sources that influence the development of a child's self-concept. These include past experiences, hypotheses they generate about themselves, and input from family members and teachers. The feedback provided by a peer group is seen by many school-age children as having a greater degree of truth as compared to other sources. As school-age children grow older, they shift away from using absolutes to determine levels of accomplishment and rely more on *social comparison* based on how they fare in relation to other children their

Cultural Snapshot 9–1

Socrates' Opinion of Children

Every generation's children and teenagers seem to be at the receiving end of criticism from the older generation, who (probably erroneously) believe that their own generation was better behaved and somehow superior. These refrains are not new. Reading Socrates' words from almost 25 centuries ago, we recognize similar themes and complaints. This is what the great philosopher had to say about the youth of his day:

> The children now love luxury; they have bad manners, contempt for authority; they show disrespect for elders and love chatter in place of exercise. Children are now tyrants, not the servants of their households. They no longer rise when elders enter the room. They contradict their parents, chatter before company, gobble up dainties at the table, cross their legs, and tyrannize their teachers.
>
> Socrates (469–399 B.C.E.)

Some things do not seem to change, despite the following explanation of the many factors that influence cultural expression:

> One can begin to understand the significance of culture in determining the "meanings" of social and emotional behavior and development at all levels of social complexity. Clearly, child development is influenced by multiple factors. Within any culture children are shaped by the physical and social settings within which they live, culturally regulated customs and child-rearing practices, and culturally based belief systems … The bottom line is that the psychological "meaning" attributed to any given social behavior is, in large part, a function of the ecological niche within which it is produced (Rubin, 1998, p.612).

Source: Rubin, K. H. (1998). Social and emotional development from a cultural perspective. *Developmental Psychology*, 34, 611–615.

age (Hanus & Fox, 2015). Often, the children that serve as comparisons are considered to be less competent or successful, thereby protecting the self-image. This is a self-serving bias.

A healthy sense of self is promoted when children learn to appropriately explore their personality traits, their collective strengths, and their weaknesses. By not knowing any different, it is natural for school-age children to agree with the criticism and negative input they hear from others their own age. Some children can be very cruel in their comments and actions. Parents and teachers are important as interpreters of reality for children (Merrell & Gimpel, 1998/2014). A parent or teacher who can provide accurate interpretations of others' behavior and unkind words can counterbalance the negative impressions that children receive from peers. This healthy sense of self acknowledges both strengths and weaknesses. School-age children learn that everyone can be vulnerable and that other people have feelings and emotions too. The negatives and weaknesses attributed by peers do not cancel out the positive aspects and the strength of character; but it may take an understanding adult to point that out.

CREATING A SAFE AND RESPECTFUL SCHOOL ENVIRONMENT

Children need to become computer literate to prepare for their future. The use of computers and the Web augment children's learning in both the school and home environments. School-age children should be able to use computers for writing reports, researching topics, and playing educational games. Some children may want to learn to write software and develop website related skills.

Part of the educational responsibility of today's parents, is to guide their children towards cyber safety. If children are allowed to use a computer and access the internet, they also need to be made aware, in an age appropriate manner, of the rules of safe conduct in this arena. Just as learning to drive a car requires exposure to all the traffic rules to safeguard the driver, accessing this medium has responsibilities attached to it. Talking to children about the threats *pre-emptively* helps to minimize or even prevent more serious situations later. Importantly, children need to have a relationship of trust with the parents so that they can confide in them and seek help and support as soon as unexpected events occur (Kochanska, Kim, & Boldt, 2015). Making sure that this relationship of trust is firmly in place is the first step towards cyber safety.

By the same token, children also need to know about the risks of cyberbullying, in which children spread rumors and make derogatory remarks on social media. If peers can be encouraged to support children who are being victimized rather than supporting the bully, then the actions of the bully will be deflated for lack of attention or reinforcement. Peer group empathy training has been shown to have a positive effect on reducing bullying and victimization (Ellis, Volk, Gonzalez, & Embry, 2015).

Most adults are aware that children need supervision when using the internet. Parents need to learn about software filters that protect children from sites containing pornography and chat rooms that can attract people who want to exploit children. Forbidding access to computers and the internet because of the inherent risks is not in the best interests of children because computer literacy is an important educational skill. Instead, it is more constructive that parents guide and monitor their children towards cyber safety.

Parents should develop rules and regulations that outline how much time a child is allowed to use the computer. Additionally, children should be taught never to give out personal information to anyone or to post such information on a website. They should know how to deal with accidental viewing of unacceptable material and how to observe the rules of netiquette (appropriate etiquette while using social media and the internet). Parents should supervise the use of email and instant messaging. If children do not observe the rules, parents may need to install programs that limit internet use (Shin, 2015).

Parents and teachers are aware that some children will not fit easily or readily into peer groups and can sometimes be rejected by other children. When this occurs, adults often seek an explanation about why other children view the rejected child in negative terms. For example, children who are unpopular may be viewed as hostile and overly aggressive, immature, impulsive, different in appearance, or insensitive to others (Tobia, Riva, & Caprin, 2016). Adults should be concerned when children experience rejection because such experiences may contribute significantly to a negative self-image, conflict with other children, and impaired social development in later stages of the life span. Adults can arrange occasions for supervised play with other children so that these children can learn social skills that lead to more positive peer experiences (Harris, 2015).

As schools offer more and more digital learning opportunities, parents must be responsible for guiding their children towards cyber safety and appropriate online behavior.

Cyberbullying

The relentless harassment, intimidation, humiliation, and tormenting of an individual over the internet via social media or by use of other digital technologies—**cyberbullying**—is on the rise. Texting and instant messaging may be used to send hateful messages or threats to a child. The practice of writing anonymous and hateful attacks on a child's character, appearance, or behavior has now moved to modern, digital platforms. Cyberbullying also occurs when a child uses computer software to alter a photo of another child in a demeaning manner.

Parents are usually among the last ones to learn that this type of misbehavior is being directed at their child, and they may not know how to handle the matter. Parents should be able to monitor the use of social media for cyber- bullying. The parent–child relationship should be sufficiently trusting so that a child feels comfortable discussing harassment and threats with his or her parents. Parents should also feel comfortable approaching professionals such as school officials and law enforcement in order to safeguard their children. Teaching a child and modeling that persons who disperse inappropriate content on the web can be blocked, is an important first step in containing and minimizing their destructive attempts. Children may fear the retaliation a parent may initiate as a defensive strategy, and it has to be carefully considered what the best route of action may be for a particular situation. School counselors may be helpful in dealing with the situation in a professional manner.

Parents also have a duty to make it clear to their own children that being a perpetrator who bullies is antisocial and destructive. By discussing these matters with children, parents can encourage empathic and prosocial behaviors. Parents themselves should be positive role models. Both girls and boys have been identified as being perpetrators and victims of cyberbullying; sadly, sometimes the parents of cyberbullies have been implicated as well. Parents are typically most concerned that their own child does not become the victim of bullying behavior. When parents come to the realization that their own child may be the perpetrator and the one who initiates the bullying acts, this situation is sufficiently serious that it may require professional consultation (Stavrinides, Nikiforou, & Georgiou, 2015).

When children are tormented and suffer in isolation, their despair has sometimes culminated in suicide,
sometimes referred to as *bullycide*. This is preventable, and schools are becoming increasingly proactive in curbing bullying and establishing zero-tolerance policies. Effective approaches include calling on peers to support their classmates who are being tormented and teaching children to be empathic. The Web contains many helpful resources for children who are experiencing this type of harassment and for their parents (www.stopbullying.gov).

Bullying and Harassment

Instances of school violence in the United States have prompted parents, teachers, school systems, and communities to examine the issues that have contributed to these tragedies. Several themes have emerged repeatedly:

■ The tendency of some children to become schoolyard bullies and cyberbullies
■ The role of opinion leaders in shaping behavior, both positive and negative behavior
■ The role of the school and peers in preventing mistreatment
■ The long-term consequences of continued mistreatment or bullying

Almost all children experience some form of **bullying** or teasing by another child during the elementary and middle school years. While there are some personal characteristics of victims that may invite bullying, for example, being passive, a loner, or crying easily, children without such characteristics can also be mistreated by a bully (Volk, Farrell, Franklin, Mularczyk, & Provenzano, 2016).

Children who bully others tend to be abused by parents, watch more television featuring violence, and generally misbehave both at home and at school. They feel little remorse for their abusive actions and frequently lie to get around punishment. Many children who are labeled as a bully tend to be characterized as having a callous, unemotional nature that prevents them from comprehending the impact of their actions on their victims (Geel, Toprak, Goemans, Zwaanswijk, & Vedder, 2016).

Bullying and harassment are very real problems of everyday life for many school-age children, and they have long-term consequences. These problem behaviors will not go away on their own. Schools can be bully-proofed, whereby children who are victimized can be taught how to defend themselves, learn how to defuse situations that could lead to victimization, leave situations where bullying can occur, and increase their tolerance of taunts (Midgett, Doumas, Sears, Lundquist, & Hausheer, 2015). Peers can be taught to rise up against bullying and to help defend other children against a bully. The role of peers can be a powerful counterfoil. In addition, schools can implement zero-tolerance policies that, in effect, outlaw bullying (www.stopbullying.gov).

Towards a Harassment-free Environment. Because bullying in schools has escalated over the past decade, schools are increasingly being held accountable to help curb the abuse of children by other children. Between 1999 and 2010, more than 120 bills were adopted by state legislatures to introduce or amend legislation that addresses bullying, harassment, or similar behavior in schools. Almost all states have laws in place that require schools to have clear policies pertaining to bullying (www.nasbe.org/healthy_schools/hs). The safe and supportive schools initiative provides guidance and has released a two-part training toolkit for use by teachers and educators. This training focuses on some of the following elements:

- Developing a supportive classroom environment that includes good teacher-to-student and good student-to-student relationships.
- Establishing a culture of respect for differences. Such a culture increases inter-student competence in interacting with individuals from diverse backgrounds.
- Setting up a network of positive support throughout the school community. Such a network contributes to a bully-proof environment.

Material on training is available from Safe and Supportive Schools (www.safesupportiveschools.ed.gov).

Google's Family Safety Center is just one site that offers guidelines that assist parents in regulating children's use of computers and the Web (see www.google.com/familysafety).

Video Example 9.1

Watch this video on cyberbullying. How can parents get involved to prevent bullying, specifically cyberbullying?

(https://www.youtube.com/watch?v=9s4Vuyf2gz4)

Parenting Reflection 9–3

What are some steps you can take as a parent or a teacher to bully-proof a child who is being picked on constantly by another child? What would you do to help the child who is the bully?

Focus Point. Parents must adjust their parenting styles to the changes occurring in their child's development during this period. As a child begins to rely more heavily on the opinions of their peer group, it is important for parents and teachers to counter the negative effects of bullying and harassment through awareness and possible intervention.

COGNITIVE SKILLS

Middle childhood is fascinating from a cognitive point of view. As far as brain development is concerned, these young brains seem to have an infinite capacity for soaking up information and developing new skills. Before mid adolescence, a young child can learn another language seemingly by osmosis; absorbing it if she is immersed in a context where the language example is adequately available (McIvor & Parker, 2016). During late adolescence and adulthood this window of language opportunity is markedly smaller. Similarly, the younger child can learn a language with a native speaker accent, the older adolescent and adult are likely to carry the accent of their mother tongue into the next language they acquire (Suarez-Orozco, Suarez-Orozco, & Qin-Hillard, 2014). In short, if parents want to encourage their child to learn a second or even a third language, middle childhood is the golden decade to do so.

Similarly, attention to the development of special talents should occur during the middle childhood period. Most dancers of repute have early training, and skilled musicians and visual artists also attest to the value of early exposure to the arts. The skills are learned in a more playful manner, almost holistically. Older learners may face greater hurdles to master certain skills. World-class competitive athletes typically have been exposed to their sport since their tender years.

School-age children increasingly use mental skills as part of their daily lives, many of them involving school activities. For example, children make use of a large database of information that they have acquired earlier in the preschool years and are constantly expanding. By understanding that school-age children still are not able to think logically all of the time and that they are learning the basics of various cognitive processes, parents can customize the ways that they provide structure and nurture at an appropriate developmental level. By understanding that school-age children see the world differently from adults, parents will expect developmentally appropriate outcomes (Weimer, Parault Dowds, Fabricius, Schwanenflugel, & Suh, 2017).

By the time children reach their school-age years, they can understand relationships between events and things. In using and comprehending these relationships, children interact with objects, symbols, and concepts. Their abstract thinking abilities are increasing and they are increasingly able to internalize the environment by using symbolic thought. They learn to add and subtract, classify and order, apply elementary rules of logic to reach conclusions, and apply rules in their choices. They begin to understand the functioning of systems by learning that certain inputs elicit certain outcomes. They are now able to use imagery to perform mental actions (Burnett Heyes, Lau, & Holmes, 2013). Some of the ways of thinking of this age group are the following:

- **Classification** improves as children can attend to several attributes or details of a task simultaneously. This may explain why children at this age are attracted to collecting objects such as dolls, model airplanes, buttons, baseball cards, and the like.
- **Reversibility** allows a child to understand operations such as addition and subtraction. School-age children learn that subtraction is the reverse operation of addition. Science lessons also incorporate this concept as when sunlight is split into its color components using a prism, and by removing the prism, the sunlight is as before.
- **Conservation** problems become better understood during this period. Piaget tested this concept with children by pouring a cup of water into differently shaped containers. Preschool-age children would think that a tall, thin container holds more water than a wide, flat one. School-age children understood that the volume did not change and that it had been *conserved*. Additional experience with the use of mental imagery helps children to work with these concepts.

- **Seriation** is an extension of classification problems where school-age children become able to scale objects according to the concepts of greater than (>) and less than (<). For example, Doll A is taller than (>) Doll B.
- **Understanding time** is important in our culture and has a bearing on daily behavior. School-age children become capable of telling time by reading a clock, and they know the days of the week, the months, and the year. They become more knowledgeable regarding what constitutes the past and the future. An increased ability to understand cause-and-effect relationships helps children to predict what day will occur 3 days from now, for example.

....

Focus Point.   The amount of information that a school-age child can absorb is seemingly limitless as they obtain greater critical thinking skills. By utilizing various thought processes, children begin to understand more concrete as well as abstract concepts.

....

THE WORLD OF SCHOOL

Entry into the school system is a significant event that influences a number of social and cognitive changes in middle childhood. In this setting, a school-age child is introduced to a larger group of peers. The child is also exposed to other adults in authority, such as teachers, school staff, and group leaders (Blatchford, Pellegrini, & Baines, 2015). The school system has gained in significance as our culture has become more technologically-oriented. Parents expect that children will succeed in their learning experiences if they are assigned to trained and skilled teachers. The best arrangement for successful schooling is that parents and teachers work as a team to help children succeed.

Evolving Parenting and Educational Practices

Historically, parenting was an authoritarian affair, and likewise schooling and educational contexts tended to be driven by authoritarian teaching approaches. Children often disliked school with the stereotypical image of compliance, conformity, homework, punishment, rigor, and the like. The stories our grandparents tell us about school attest to this. But a quiet paradigm shift has been taking place inside homes and schools.

Guest Reflection 9–1

Hip-Hop and Hope

Dance provides an opportunity to be challenged followed by the sweet reward of success. I would like to think that these are some of the core lessons we as educators can provide, as success tends to pave the path with motivation which in turn facilitates lifelong learning. As a dance teacher of elementary and middle schoolers, I see the unique transformations in students as a true teaching/learning privilege.

In the lower elementary grades including kindergarten, my end-of-year students seem like totally different people to the children I first met several months earlier. Their surprising sense of creativity, thoughtfulness, and curiosity runs like a golden thread persisting throughout. On a chilly winter day, one of my first graders highlighted these traits as she shared: "Ms. Brown, I have an idea for how we could enter the dance studio today. We could travel along a snowy, cold pathway to the greeting circle, and then we could end by creating a frozen shape that represents all of the different ways that people celebrate holidays; like a Menorah, a Christmas tree, a Mkeka, or a Dreidel!" What a brilliant way to promote unity and acceptance while acknowledging the complexities of culture.

In upper elementary grades, seeing third through fifth graders fall in love with arts education and pursue their new-found passions is an educator's treat. I looped with the same students for my first three years of teaching, and these students will remain imprinted on my mind as the most amazing, stubborn, lively, outspoken, tenacious pupils. They showed me virtually immediately that they were not interested in me or anything I intended to teach, until I committed to them, not only as dancers and students, but as people.

Looping up with these inspiring kids allowed me to pilot and build the dance program at our public charter middle school in Harlem. In building this program together, we developed two major goals for our program:

- To create a school environment where students and teachers reflect deeply about the nature of dance and how dance transcends a particular style or genre and is focused on movement and choreographic inspiration. We contextualized this with the historical roots of dance and the expression of stories and ideas behind a particular movement.
- To give students understanding, appreciation, and strong technical foundations of various genres to strengthen the tools and skills they acquire and then apply beyond their middle school years.

These goals included the importance of peer-to-peer communication, music-to-movement connection, the "why?" behind the movement, and the idea of dance as a story.

One of my most memorable moments occurred as I was walking home one afternoon in May. I saw three of my seventh grade students who had not previously danced and who considered themselves basketball players first and hip-hop dancers second. Walking half a block ahead of me, they were not only practicing the hip-hop piece from class, but also the contemporary dance we were learning. They were doing this in their own time, for the most important reason of all; namely because they were intrinsically motivated. What an important skill to embrace at this young age.

Collaborating with a great variety of students, I can see that dance has become an inclusive and much loved art form. More importantly, I know that irrespective of what these middle schoolers are facing outside class or even outside school, dance represents a constructive and healthy outlet. Dance provides an opportunity to communicate, listen, perform, and observe; qualities we will rely on for the rest of our lives.

Katrina Brown Aliffi (M.S.), Middle School Educator, Dance Instructor. Used with permission.

Parents are aware of *"Responsive"* and *"Responsible"* parenting. In this approach there is the "serve and return" of an ongoing interaction, in which the child receives attention, is responded to, and feels the positive feedback that comes from communication. All this enhances learning and early brain development. Similarly, the early learning and school environments have adopted similar practices. The natural curiosity and willingness to learn is used by responding to the curiosity of children. Children are valued, respected, and encouraged to participate.

Using similar principles as those advocated in parenting education, counseling, early learning, and brain development, schools aim to create *responsive* classrooms as well. It represents social-emotional learning which focuses on educational practices and encourages teachers to modify how they interact with the children they teach. The approach is based on principles from developmental psychology. The change has to be instigated by the teachers, as they are the more powerful figures in the teaching-learning relationship. Similarly, in parenting techniques, the parents are required to initiate the behavior that will bring about the change. It is up to parents and teachers to create an environment that is learner friendly and rewards curiosity and exploration, setting up the intrinsic motivation that will fuel lifelong learning. We have seen echoes of similar philosophies in the teachings of Charlotte Mason, as well as the Waldorf, Montessori, and Emilio Reggio school systems. We have met like-minded vision in the "Problem-Based Learning" (PBL) Approaches (Gerhardt, C, & Gerhardt,C,M, 2009). All contain an element of *active* learning, so that the pupil takes co-responsibility for, and becomes vested in, her own learning.

Some schools support peer group formation through *looping*, a practice that allows children to remain with the same cohort for several years, and the teacher may remain with the same group for more than a year. This provides the stability of ongoing attachments and contributes toward a positive outcome for students, teachers, and families (Ruprecht, Elicker, & Choi, 2016).

Parental involvement.   Parents can assist a child's educational achievement by being involved with the school. Involvement can take several forms; six major areas are identified (National Middle School Association, 2009):

- *Parenting.* Parents acquire developmentally appropriate parenting skills.
- *Communicating.* Parents are informed about, and are interested in, the school community.
- *Volunteering.* Parents participate in volunteer activities to strengthen their relationships with the teachers and other parents.
- *Learning at home.* Parents facilitate the completion of homework through goal setting and providing some parental support.
- *Decision making.* Parents provide input and take some responsibility with regard to school policies.
- *Collaborating with the community.* Parents can become involved with those communities having an interest in this age group, e.g., religious, social, and leadership groups.

Conducive Home Environment.   Giving children their own space for quiet study and schoolwork acknowledges their needs and sends the message that homework and learning is an important and valued endeavor. This is part of creating a *conducive* home environment (Kaplan & Haider, 2015). It is important to provide structure for children, including an appropriate bedtime so that children are rested for school, limiting television or computer games, and having regular mealtimes. Many American children have a television in the bedroom. Television is distracting to children in the space where they also do homework, and it can disrupt bedtime. Children may also be exposed to endless influences via unsuitable programs of which the parents are not aware (Neumann, 2015).

Parents need to find a *balance* between being appropriately involved and genuinely interested versus the two opposite extremes of disinterested neglect, or the alternative of overinvolved helicopter parenting. More supervision is not always better, as it can counteract the child's initiative and ability to explore independently and the development of autonomy.

Soft Skills.   Talking with children about school and afterschool activities, what kind of play takes place with friends, and what projects they are working on also provides support. Structured family mealtimes can provide excellent learning and social opportunities for children. These conversations around the dining table are one way that children learn the many **soft skills** of social interaction that can be an expression of **emotional intelligence** (Devaney, 2015). Such interaction includes behaviors and attitudes that facilitate social engagement, including good manners, punctuality, a work ethic, and respect and appropriate concern for others.

Parents play an important role in encouraging their children's involvement in groups that foster civic engagement, as well as participating in the family's cultural and religious expressions. Children benefit from appropriate role models and mentors who will expand their opportunities for learning social skills that will serve them well in adulthood.

The type of parenting style employed with children this age also contributes to school success (Pinquart, 2016). Children who exhibit academic achievement are more likely to have parents who use an authoritative approach. These children tend to be independently motivated to learn and perform well in school. Children who underachieve and have difficulties at school are likely to have parents who use either an authoritarian or a permissive approach to child rearing. Children in authoritarian homes are likely to depend on extrinsic motivation provided by the parents to perform well academically, while parents in permissive homes do not appear to care how children fare in school (Watkins & Howard, 2015).

Extracurricular Activities

The increased involvement of children with peers, school activities, and activities outside of the family system means more frequent periods of absence from the home. Parents may find it difficult to keep a predictable

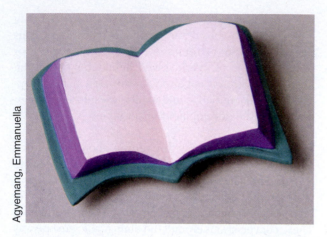

Agyemang, Emmanuella

The peer group facilitates socialization and serves as a reference point for values and social norms. Middle schooler Emmanuella created "Rewritten Rumors," an artwork that comments on the effects of peer-to-peer interaction and the negative impact of gossip.

schedule in the home. Keeping children's schedules from becoming chaotic and allowing periods of unstructured personal time can be challenging. Some parents feel that "more is better" in terms of extracurricular activities. In reality there is a tipping point. Children cannot be randomly overloaded with extracurricular tasks; the choices need to match the interests and skills of the child, considering the ultimate educational outcomes that parents and children themselves wish to achieve.

Letting go of school-age children means that parents accept the reality that they increasingly value peers and best friends as significant others in their lives. This involves allowing them to sleep overnight at a friend's home and, during the later years of middle childhood, go on a camping trip with a youth group. Many children experience their first extended absence from their family during summer camp and visits with relatives.

Parenting Reflection 9–4

Beyond the basics, what are some topics that elementary schools should and should not teach children?

Guest Reflection 9–2

Art, Identity, and Mentorship

An artist can be found within each and every student, and the art classroom honors this belief. When preparing the lesson, while giving feedback, and in showcasing final pieces, it is relevant to acknowledge and honor the person who created that work. Middle school is a time when students are eagerly searching for self-identity and usually experience some self-doubt. Students should be able to find and explore some of their independence and confidence by connecting to their artistic identity.

The first step is for my students to recognize what it feels like to be inspired or "sparked" by something, and to use and nurture that to create artwork that relates to their lives. An art educator's role is as a facilitator of self-expression and to launch a lesson that excites the pupils. Our topics have tackled personal and meaningful themes from speaking out about politics and gender issues, to concerns such as bullying, school staff changes, and family life. Each lesson endeavors to find a personal connection and then explore the most authentic way of expressing one's artistic identity.

The creative process contains many steps including research, journaling, and sketching. Students are required to distill and decipher what they can use. The important connection points are "mini sparks" which guide artistic choices concerning visual symbols, colors, placement, and size. Many students have an initial visual plan that may be modified by research and lead to deeper understanding about themselves and their ideas. These conversations are important moments as they feed the artistic drive to continue working and to recognize the potential of the next point of inspiration.

As students focus on their idea, they are encouraged to use materials that best support their personal vision and identity. Typically, each lesson focuses on a central medium. An open studio with stations for painting, collage, drawing, and sculpture installation facilitates this. The feedback students receive respects their vision. Students are autonomous in their artistic decisions. Modeling is an integral part of the teaching process, yet if a student explores a new approach, that creativity is applauded.

After students complete a piece, it is important to honor their art. Students should feel part of a gallery where their work is displayed. Typically, the art room and parts of the school are transformed into a curated exhibition. Podcasts, docents, and work descriptions are included. This gives students a sense of accomplishment, pride, and confidence—the same magical qualities that professional artists try to capture as they dedicate themselves to their calling.

Lauren Nemchick (B.A.), Middle School Educator in Visual Arts. Used with permission.

Focus Point. Social development in middle childhood relates to adjustment in school and other learning environments, establishing peer relations, and refining the self-concept. During this age (pre-adolescence) the normally developing brain has virtual superpowers to acquire new skills. Educational contexts should be used to promote the building and expansion of these skills. Parents and teachers collaborate in promoting children's academic performance and success.

Sex and Relationship Education

Increasingly *Sex and Relationship Education* (SRE) is seen as one topic, emphasizing the *context* of sexuality (Simovska & Kane, 2015). Parents and schools play an important role in helping children develop healthy attitudes concerning sexual and relationship matters, which should ultimately support safe sexual choices that promote health and well-being. Many school systems in the United States provide developmentally appropriate sex education, beginning in preschool and continuing throughout the subsequent years. These learning units can be presented with input provided by parents who serve on school district advisory committees. Some systems outsource the information sessions to companies who specialize in disseminating age appropriate sex education. In practice, parent initiated conversations, supplemented by school based information sessions, seems to provide good outcomes (Alldred, Fox, & Kulpa, 2016). Many parents appreciate the professional introduction of the topic of sexuality to their children within the educational context of the school. Most teachers in turn, prefer that parents take a more active role in teaching children about sexuality and relationships. In developing countries, there has been an active move towards improved SRE, as one avenue to promote healthier outcomes (Boonstra, 2015).

The important guideline for teaching these topics in school contexts, is that they are conveyed in a 'sex-positive' manner, as opposed to as a topic that is associated with guilt, secrecy, and other negative emotions. To do so effectively, SRE should be taught by expert professionals who can convey that sexuality and relationships are important topics with unique challenges (Pound, Langford, & Campbell, 2016).

School-age children occasionally ask questions about their bodies and sexual matters, and these questions deserve honest answers from parents. Parents should act as interpreters of family values. Parents also have an important responsibility in preparing older school-age children for the physical and psychological changes that they will experience in puberty. Beginning at about age 9, parents can initiate discussions about this approaching developmental event. Opportunities for discussion are important because preteens are more likely to listen to parents' views on sexuality than are children who have already entered adolescence. For example, it is important that girls be prepared for menstruation and that boys understand nocturnal emissions. Many excellent resources are available to assist parents in becoming more knowledgeable about preparing their children for puberty. Socio-biological factors have accelerated puberty in some children, and the changes occurring during this age need to be anticipated and addressed (Collier-Harris & Goldman, 2016).

In some communities, hospitals and other health-related centers provide age appropriate lectures by experts. In a large-scale study of sexual health in Britain, it was found that when information was gained mainly in school contexts, it was more likely to be neutral and health oriented information. Some of the more negative information could be conveyed by peers and by parents who were not professional or expert in providing this specialized type of information (Macdowall et al., 2015). Even so, it is very important for parents to model relationship qualities of interpersonal respect, and to contextualize sex and relationship education with the ethical and religious values they consider to be important for their family and their children.

Importantly, the presenters need to maintain clear boundaries with students. For this reason, it is often preferable that this form of education is outsourced to a team of experts. Some of the goals of SRE is to safeguard and improve the sexual health and decision making of young people, by providing age appropriate information, and guiding them towards constructive choices with healthy outcomes (Pound, Langford, & Campbell, 2016).

TYPICAL BEHAVIORAL PROBLEMS

Part of effective and responsible parenting is imparting prosocial values while encouraging social responsibility and civic engagement in children. These lessons can start on a small scale and they need to be age appropriate to match the cognitive development of the child.

Parents can teach social responsibility by encouraging children to contribute part of their allowance to charity, or by involving children in charitable events such as collecting toys for disadvantaged children. In this way, children are taught the joy of sharing. By discussing social and environmental stewardship and through modeling appropriate behaviors, parents teach children that trash cannot be dropped in public places, composting is environmentally friendly, and we have a responsibility to recycle, to mention a few examples. Parents may choose to use religious instruction to support their values (Döring, Uzefovsky, & Knafo-Noam, 2015). These activities all contribute toward encouraging prosocial behavior throughout childhood. These values will be internalized by the child and will guide their behavior.

Despite parents' best intentions, children may still present with some behavioral problems. The types of behavioral problems observed in school-age children reflect the difficulties they experience in adjusting to the challenges of developmental tasks; therefore, these problems are considered to be age specific. Some, but not all, involve conflicts between parents and children regarding expectations concerning appropriate behavioral standards. Others may be negative, attention-getting behaviors. Some problems, such as learning disabilities, are diverse in their origins and can involve inherent developmental difficulties. Several types of commonly observed behavioral problems are discussed briefly. They include noncompliance, antisocial behaviors, and learning disabilities.

Noncompliance

One of the most common parental complaints is that children fail to comply with parental requests and they disobey the rules established by the family system. This can be called **noncompliance**. This issue, which begins to appear when children are preschool age, can escalate during middle childhood into a full-blown power struggle between adults and children (Sevón, 2015).

Children at this age tend to test the limits of adults' patience, particularly if they are asked to do something they do not want to do. Standard replies to parental requests include, "In a minute, Mom," or "Just let me finish what I'm doing, Dad." Parents are elevating their expectations for children; instead of asking a child simply to get involved in an activity or chore, they insist

that tasks be completed satisfactorily. Some adults may believe that a child should need only one prompt to perform a task before the consequences are enforced. But initially, most parents are patient, understanding that children must adjust as they learn what is expected of them. The patterns of communication we have with our children should be respectful and follow up on the basic principles we put in place during early childhood.

There comes a time when parents know that their school-age child should be complying with the rules without exhibiting great resistance. Some of the most frequently prescribed methods for prompting children's compliance involve the use of behavior modification techniques (Birchler, 2015). One technique teaches parents how to phrase their requests in a way that communicates exactly what is expected of children in keeping with family rules and policies. Essentially, parents are taught how to give clear, concise directions so that school-age children can understand parental expectations. Parents give a child an opportunity to comply, and then provide positive consequences or rewards for appropriate, cooperative behavior.

Antisocial Behaviors

Behaviors that promote ill will, interfere with effective communication and interaction, constitute negative ways of getting attention, and serve as a means of expressing anger and hostility or coping with frustration and anxiety are known as **antisocial behaviors** (Allgaier, Zettler, Wagner, Püttmann, & Trautwein, 2015). Although some of these behaviors begin appearing in the latter part of early childhood, a number are typically observed during middle childhood. They reflect problems in adjusting to the demands of developmental tasks and can challenge effective, healthy functioning. Several behaviors are observed more commonly that cause particular concern among adult caregivers, including lying and stealing.

Dishonesty. Lying refers to the deliberate falsification of information with the specific intent of deceiving the listener. Although young children are often unable to separate fantasy from reality, the ability to understand what is true and what is not follows a child's level of moral and cognitive development. Typically, most children come to understand the importance of truthfulness in their interactions by about age 6 or 7.

- Parents can assist children with problem lying in several ways. It is helpful for parents to model desirable behavior. For example, parental honesty helps children learn how to be trusting and how to generate others' trust in their own integrity.
- When parents observe a child knowingly giving false information, they should tell the child that lying is unacceptable behavior and will jeopardize their effective interactions with others. School-age children can be helped to understand how the consequences of such behavior are related to personal integrity. In such instances, reading "The Boy Who Cried Wolf," one of Aesop's fables, may be effective in instilling the importance of truthfulness.
- Quizzing children about their misbehavior often promotes defensive lying. Parents can avoid this by informing a child that they are aware of the misbehavior. Discussions can proceed from this point in a straightforward manner to resolve the problem behavior.
- Finally, parents should try to determine the causes that underlie a child's lying (Cheung, Siu, & Chen, 2015).

Stealing.   Stealing occurs more frequently among school-age children than most people imagine. Although many parents feel that stealing is an innocuous behavior in early childhood, it becomes a matter of concern among parents of school-age children and adolescents.

Children steal for a variety of reasons:

- They may lack training with regard to personal property rights.
- They may be trying to bribe friends, perhaps to avoid being teased, or to gain their approval.
- Stealing may be a means of coping with feelings of inferiority or of being in some way different from others.
- Children may steal simply because they cannot resist the temptation of obtaining something that they want very much.
- They may steal as revenge against parents or as a means of gaining their attention.

The problem of stealing is handled first by informing children that this behavior is unacceptable. Parents and other adults should deal fairly and honestly with instances of stealing. Again, parental modeling of desired values and actions is important. Attention to the details of property rights is important as well; parents should explain the difference between a child's property and that of others. It may be helpful to give children an allowance if they are not already receiving one. An allowance can help children learn the work ethics of the family system, including how one may obtain a desired object by saving money. Removing temptation, or at least reducing it, by putting money away may also be helpful.

Children With Disabilities

Special Education is a highly specialized field, and children with disabilities require professional assessment and interventions. Typically, schools can guide parents toward accessing these services.

Specific learning disabilities that result in poor achievement in school are frequently observed in association with other types of behavioral problems in middle childhood. Children with behavioral problems also tend to demonstrate other types of maladaptive patterns (Hamid, 2015).

Several conditions are classified as specific learning disabilities, including difficulties with reading, written expression, or mathematics. The *DSM-5* uses the term *specific learning disorders* (American Psychiatric Association, 2013). Researchers generally understand that learning disabilities involve a complex variety of different, but related, conditions and factors that hamper the ability of a child to learn and progress in school. *Autism spectrum disorders* are increasingly diagnosed and require early intervention.

The following factors may play a role in learning and academic achievement:

- *Ability deficits* may account for many of the problems that school-age children experience with school performance.
- *Emotional disorders* such as anxiety, depression, and unhealthy self-esteem may be contributory factors.
- *Biological factors* can account for learning problems that stem from prenatal or postnatal exposure to harmful substances, such as maternal intake of alcohol or cocaine, oxygen deprivation, accidents that affect the central nervous system, infections, and inadequate protein in the diet.
- Children may require techniques and skills that support learning.

In the multi-award winning book *Far from the Tree: Parents, Children and the Search for Identity* by Andrew Solomon (2012), the author describes how parents and families accommodate children and deal with various disabilities and differences; be they physical, mental, or social. He makes the point that there can be power in diversity, including the diversity that is found in our children who may be unlike ourselves (hence the title of the book). Ultimately, as parents, we have a responsibility to accept our children as they are and as individuals in their own right. As parents, we need to support them in attaining the best lives possible in terms of selfhood and quality of life.

Neurodevelopmental Disorders. *Attention deficit disorder* (ADD) is commonly diagnosed in children. When accompanied by hyperactivity, it is called *attention deficit/hyperactivity disorder* (ADHD). These disorders are classified under **neurodevelopmental disorders** in the *DSM-5* (American Psychiatric Association, 2013). They are believed to have strong neurobiological and genetic bases (Numis & Sankar, 2016).

Families, especially the parents of children with ADD/ADHD, experience extreme frustrations while dealing with this condition, and it affects everyone involved. Children with ADHD can be in constant motion from the time they wake up in the morning until the time they finally go to sleep at night. Although the ramifications of this disorder are discouraging for children and parents, the condition is responsive to a variety of treatments (Fabiano et al., 2016), including medication and behavior modification techniques. Family therapy may be helpful in assisting a family system in dealing with the crises associated with a child whose behavior has a disruptive effect on family functioning.

- -

Focus Point.   Many behavioral problems in school-age children are linked to difficulties in achieving developmental tasks; other such problems relate more specifically to difficulties with interactions with parents and peers. Behavioral problems that are related to learning disorders are often displayed in the classroom. A variety of methods may be helpful in dealing with these challenges.

- -

PARENTING EXCEPTIONAL CHILDREN

Our society recognizes that some children have unique needs. These needs can result from a child's strengths, as well as disabilities, and can require an individualized approach by parents, family, and educational support systems. In this regard, individuals who are **exceptional** are in some manner different from their age-peers.

A small percentage of children in this age span may be identified as exceptional in terms of high potential exhibiting special gifts and **talents**. In larger towns magnet schools may attract some of these pupils. Other school districts have programs for exceptional children.

Children and youth with high potential, often referred to as gifted and talented, academically advanced learners, precocious, asynchronous, or intellectually gifted, demonstrate characteristics that can be both positive and "not so attractive." Broadly, characteristics of children with gifts and talents are defined using the following constructs provided by the federal government in the Marland Report (1971):

- General intellectual ability
- Specific academic aptitude
- Creative thinking and production
- Leadership
- Visual and performing arts
- Psycho-motor (not included in subsequent definitions)

Hernendez Lisely

Children and youth with high potential, often referred to as gifted and talented, academically advanced learners, precocious, asynchronous, or intellectually gifted, may be identified as exceptional and be invited to apply for magnet schools or other specialized programs.

Identification procedures for children and youth typically involve administration of tests for intelligence/aptitude, academic knowledge and skills, such as reading and math, creativity, behavior ratings for indicators of traits of giftedness, and assessment of products, work samples, and/or performances (Davis, Rimm, & Siegle, 2010).

On the whole, children and youth identified with gifts and talents are a diverse group; they do not exhibit *all* of the common characteristics *all* of the time. Being gifted or talented in one area does not mean the child will be gifted in all. For example, a child who is an early precocious reader with highly developed verbal skills may or may not demonstrate advanced skills in math. This conundrum or seeming paradox may cause educators and even parents to criticize or show disappointment in an identified gifted child when he or she does not perform highly in all areas, which can lead to emotional issues within the child, such as perfectionism, underachievement, anxiety, and even depression (Gross, 2015).

Children and youth with high potential vary greatly from their age-peers, including behaviorally, socially, emotionally, creatively, intellectually, academically, and in areas of interest. Characteristics of giftedness can be viewed from two perspectives: the "bright" side and the "challenging" side, suggesting that giftedness in children, and even in adults, can be both a blessing and a challenge. See Figure 9–2.

Parenting Children and Youth With High Potential, Gifts and Talents

While parenting the child with gifts and talents is in many ways similar to parenting any child, there are special obstacles and challenges that will require unique strategies. The journey will be filled with extreme highs and lows, joys and frustrations. Issues faced in the home might include disagreements over school work, striving for independence at an early age, sibling rivalry, or problems with peers (Vernon, Adamson, & Vernon, 1977/2015).

Parents can help their gifted child as well as the other children in the family by creating a loving, supportive environment. Parents of children who demonstrate high potential and intellectual strengths could support them in several ways that also reflect good parenting goals in general:

■ Be supportive of your child and her interests
■ Have high expectations accompanied by support
■ Acknowledge and encourage hard work and perseverance in children
■ Consistency in structure, expectations, and consequences
■ Acknowledge that the brilliant mind can be housed in a developing body

TABLE 9–1.   The Two Faces of Giftedness

The Two Faces of Giftedness	
The "Bright" Side	The "Challenging" Side
Learns basic skills better, more quickly, and with less practice than age-peers	Asynchronous or "out-of-sync" development may lead to frustration, especially when pace of classroom learning is too slow or too many repetitions
Works independently at an early age and can concentrate for long periods	Obsessed or fixated when engaged in project of interest; unable to cope when interrupted or switch gears when asked to begin a new task
Develops language and vocabulary early	Argumentative; alienates classmates with advanced verbal skills; asks lots of questions, some inappropriate; dominates discussions; not always a good listener
Learns to read and/or acquire math skills early, often without instruction	Boredom with grade-level reading and math curriculum
Exhibits unusual depth and intensity; heightened self-awareness	Unusually vulnerable; immature; socially isolated

Patricia F. Wood, PhD: Contributing Author for Section on Gifted Education. Professor, Director Gifted Education, Samford University

- Recognize that cognitive, social, and emotional skills can be developing at different rates
- Support your child on the journey towards adulthood, by being an available parent

---

GIFTS AND TALENTS

General Intellectual Ability
- Learns rapidly
- Observant
- Excellent memory for facts and details
- Sees relationships among seemingly unrelated ideas
- Can concentrate for extended periods
- Thinks abstractly

Specific Academic Aptitude
- Enjoys learning
- Develops skills in reading and/or math at an early age
- Exhibits strong problem-solving skills
- Demonstrates persistence and motivation in areas of interest
- Large vocabulary
- Acquires information with ease

Creative Thinking and Production
- Inquisitive, curious
- Sense of humor
- Independent thinker
- Enjoys creative endeavors
- Asks questions, especially "why" and "how"
- Can make connections between seemingly unrelated ideas

Leadership
- Self-confident,
- Responsible, Organized, Charismatic
- High expectations of self
- Good decision-making skills

Visual and Performing Arts
- Creatively expressive
- Highly observant of the world
- Outstanding visual-spatial skills
- Exceptional bodily-kinesthetic awareness and skills
- Driven to produce unique products/performances
- Intensely energetic

Based on: Davis, G. A., Rimm, S. B., & Siegle, D. (2011). *Education of the Gifted and Talented*, (6th ed.), Boston, MA: Pearson.

FIGURE 9–2. Characteristics of Children and Youth with Gifts and Talents.

Children With Exceptionalities

Exceptionalities can involve, for instance, visual, auditory, speech, and motor abilities, or providing self-care, together known as activities of daily living. These special needs can create unusual demands on family systems and parents. In some situations, children have unique developmental challenges that label them as *exceptional*. In addition to educational program in schools, community-based programs for assisting children with exceptionalities and their families have been developed as a result of legislation at the state and federal levels.

The definition of **exceptional children** was formerly restricted to those with emotional, developmental, or intellectual disabilities that placed them at a disadvantage in their ability to function within the larger society. More recently, the meaning of exceptionality has been broadened to include individuals with learning disorders and other disabilities (Individuals with Disabilities Education Act of 2004).

Children with Exceptionalities

The exceptionalities include:

1. Autism Spectrum Disorders
2. Blindness
3. Deafness
4. Emotional Disturbance
5. Hearing Impairment
6. Intellectual Disability
7. Multiple Disabilities
8. Orthopedic Impairment
9. Other Health Impairments
10. Specific Learning Disability
11. Speech or Language Impairment
12. Traumatic Brain Injury
13. Visual Impairment

Children with special needs served under IDEA represent about 13% of the student population of the United States (Snyder & Dillow, 2015). Another category of exceptional children and youth are those who demonstrate high potential and are identified as gifted and talented. Nationally, 6.7% of children and youth are identified as gifted and talented.

In general, males with special needs outnumber females (Robinson, Lichtenstein, Anckarsäter, Happé, & Ronald, 2013). The process for including a child in any of the categories of disabilities involves extensive, comprehensive evaluation by a variety of medical, psychological, and educational professionals. Some children have special needs because of chronic, potentially life-threatening conditions, such as diabetes or cancer. These children may miss school while undergoing treatment and may need some accommodations in the school environment.

Family Reactions

Virtually every parent and every extended family anticipates the birth of a child with joy. When, for any number of reasons, the reality is different, the family will go through mourning and grief. The discovery that a child has special needs represents a loss for most parents, in particular, the loss of future normal developmental progress for the affected child.

Parents experience a variety of reactions which may vary according to the nature of the exceptionality, the degree of impairment, the socioeconomic status of the family system, the availability of professional assistance, the financial resources available, and the presence of other children in the family (Barak-Levy & Atzaba-Poria, 2015). In many respects, the diagnosis serves as a crisis event for a family system. The family as a system must adjust to this newly recognized status of the affected child and begin to search for the numerous ways to meet the child's particular needs and those of the other family members. This process can take months, even years, as the family strives to accept and reconcile their unique situation. Parents must learn ways to strengthen their committed relationship and find ways to find constructive and supportive outcomes for other children in the family.

Those family systems that use the stresses of this situation to their advantage are likely to become stronger by developing healthy coping strategies that may also be applied in future family crises. On the other hand, families who acquire unhealthy coping strategies experience even higher levels of stress and disorganization (Fields, 2015). Many parents experience an adjustment process through which they gain an acceptance of the situation, although others experience ambivalence and even rejection of the child. Ultimately, some marriages will dissolve as the result of the chronic strain of these circumstances.

Parental attitudes about an exceptional child influence the nature and quality of caregiving. Mothers tend to become the family member who assumes the greatest amount of caretaking and nurturing of a child with special needs. Family stress diminishes and becomes more controlled when fathers and extended family and friends lend active support.

The siblings of a child with special needs are also affected (Luijkx, Putten, & Vlaskamp, 2016). Having a sibling with special needs brings some benefits to other children, such as learning empathy, gaining tolerance and compassion, and developing a greater

Having a child with special needs can affect family systems in a number of ways. Siblings have the opportunity to learn empathy, gain tolerance and compassion, and develop a greater appreciation of personal health.

Jaren Jai Wicklund/Shutterstock

appreciation of personal health. On the other hand, siblings often report negative effects such as feelings of jealousy because of a lack of parental attention, resenting the affected sibling's presence in the family, or shamefulness and guilt about the affected sibling. Parents should be mindful of the possibilities of these negative reactions. In addition, girls often complain that brothers aren't expected to assume surrogate parent or caregiver roles to a similar extent. By equalizing the responsibilities between male and female siblings, the psychological risks to girls, especially, are minimized.

The cultural backgrounds of families also influence their reactions to an exceptional child (Khanlou, Haque, Sheehan, & Jones, 2015). For example, in a Caucasian family, a child's disabilities are described and understood in medical and scientific terms; other cultures may attribute the situation to bad luck, an evil influence on the family, or punishment for ancestral sins.

Chronic stress is one of the most frequently observed family reactions (Miodrag, Burke, Tanner-Smith, & Hodapp, 2015). Family members can learn healthy coping strategies, such as attending support groups, keeping a journal, participating in individual and family therapy, tapping into spiritual resources, sharing caretaking responsibilities, and finding time for self-renewal. Networking with other families who are experiencing similar circumstances is also helpful. Unhealthy coping may result in the child with exceptional needs being scapegoated, or emotionally mistreated.

Support for Families With Exceptional Children

Families that have a child with special needs tend to be smaller in size than the average family and have lower incomes than the general population (Stabile & Allin, 2012). Because of their unique circumstances, these families typically make use of more community services and resources in gaining assistance for their child. Several sources provide such support.

Federal Legislation. Federal legislation has helped to address the needs of exceptional children and their families. The Individuals with Disabilities Education Act of 1999 (IDEA: Public Law 94-142, first enacted in 1975) is based on two assumptions:

■ Children with special needs have the right to a free and appropriate education in the public school system.
■ Parents play an important role in the education of their children with special needs.

Essentially, this law gives parents the right to monitor and judge the appropriateness of the educational experiences that their children with special needs receive. The law provides for appointing a guardian for children who are without parents and for funding special education programs.

The law requires that each child with special needs who is enrolled in a public school system be provided with an individualized educational program (IEP) developed by an education specialist working in conjunction with the child's parent(s). The IEP must include a statement regarding the present level of educational performance at the time of the initial implementation, a list of goals and objectives, and the specific educational services and support to be provided. It must also include plans for the child's participation in the classroom, the length of institutionalization (if applicable), and the manner in which the goals and objectives will be evaluated (Liu, 2015).

Amendments to the Individuals with Disabilities Education Act of 1999 (previously Public Law 94-142 and Public Law 99-457) have influenced the assistance provided to families with exceptional children. It requires states to establish comprehensive multidisciplinary approaches to provide early intervention to infants and toddlers with special needs. It extends the ages of the children being served from birth through age 25, emphasizing a focus on services to be provided during the prekindergarten years. This law requires that individualized family service plans (IFSPs) be provided to children with special needs. An IFSP is written for each child between birth and age 3 by a multidisciplinary group of professionals and the parents. It includes the following:

■ An assessment of the child's present level of functioning and developmental status.
■ A statement regarding the family's strengths and needs in facilitating the child's developmental progress.
■ A list of goals and objectives for the child's progress.
■ The means by which the child is expected to achieve these goals and objectives, or the experiences that will promote their accomplishment.

- The means by which the child will be transitioned from early intervention experiences into a preschool program
- The time frame during which these services will be provided
- The name of the child's case manager

Several additional laws strengthened the involvement of families in the process of educating children with special needs. Together, these laws comprise the Individuals with Disabilities Improvement Education Act of 2004. In complying with this legislation, the states have established an Interagency Coordinating Council that oversees the delivery of early intervention services to families and children with special needs. The Elementary and Secondary Education Act of 2001 (also known as the No Child Left Behind Act) contains provisions that address the needs of exceptional children by supplementing other legislation. This legislation allows school districts to provide programming that may increase parental involvement, reallocate financial resources to provide research-based curricula, and heighten the accountability of instructors. The act also permits children with certain disabilities to qualify for special education classrooms and programs that provide financial assistance. The eligibility criteria for special education address 13 categories. The terminology used reflects the categories described in the eligibility criteria published by state educational departments.

Community Services.   The kinds of services needed to assist exceptional children and their families often depend on the age and specific problems of the child. Some problems become evident long before a child enters the public school system. In some instances, these problems are noticed at birth or when expected developmental progress fails to occur within the months or years after birth. Problems can also be discovered through regular screening. When infants and young children are seen on a regular basis by a physician or health-care professional, the doctor or nurse may discover and evaluate the child's current or future developmental concerns. Early detection is crucial because treatment can alleviate some potential difficulties if it is implemented early. Available community services for parents of infants and young children with special needs include childcare centers, hospital programs, public school programs, Head Start programs, and programs offered through colleges and universities.

Respite care is a community service for families and individuals with disabilities. This supervisory service provides temporary relief for the caregivers of developmentally disabled individuals who live at home and also acts as an important element in preventing institutionalization. The service assists families in coping with emergency situations that require the absence of the primary caregivers and also provides relief from the daily stresses involved in caring for a disabled family member. It supports the caretaker in taking some time for self-renewal.

Educational Programs.   School-age exceptional children are included to the maximum extent possible in existing public school programs, a practice known as **inclusion**, formerly *mainstreaming*. These programs are supplemented by special education classes. Because not all children profit from this educational arrangement, some may be placed exclusively in special education classes. School districts offer a variety of programs and services for exceptional children, which vary in response to the needs of the children. These services may include the following:

- *Regular classrooms.* Children receive special attention and an individualized program.
- *Resource rooms.* Children are enrolled in regular classrooms, but they go to a specially equipped room to receive part of their daily instruction.
- *Consulting teachers.* Special education teachers supplement the instruction provided by regular teachers.
- *Day schools.* Special education programs are conducted in a separate room or building for children whose needs cannot be met in a regular classroom program.
- *Residential schools.* These schools provide education and other treatment experiences that cannot be provided through any other means. Such schools are usually reserved for those children with visual or hearing impairment, children with intellectual disabilities, and children with multiple severe disabilities.
- *Hospital or homebound programs.* These programs serve the needs of children who are confined to bed or who experience a lengthy convalescent period and children who are ill.

Other Services.   In addition to involving parents in the educational experiences of exceptional children, some support is offered to the adults and siblings in the family system. These families often need professional counseling, and several helpful strategies have been developed (Hott, Thomas, Abbassi, Hendricks, & Aslina, 2015):

- ■ **Informational counseling** occurs when children are first diagnosed and parents are informed of the test results, prognosis, and treatment approaches.
- ■ **Psychotherapeutic methods**, most prominently behavior modification and reflective counseling, are taught to parents and siblings. Pediatric psychotherapy is offered to the affected child in dealing with emotional and behavioral problems.
- ■ **Group therapy and support groups** place a number of parents or siblings into a support network in which individuals share their feelings, reactions, and experiences to help each other cope with the stresses in their own family system.

....

Focus Point. Parents of children with special needs deal with issues in child rearing that are not usually confronted by other parents. Child rearing in these circumstances can be difficult, but can also have unique rewards. Families experience challenges that influence the quality and the nature of parent–child relations. Federal legislative efforts continue to provide much needed support.

....

PARENTAL EMPLOYMENT AND CHILDCARE SUPPORT

In almost all families, one of the parents is gainfully employed and acts as the lead breadwinner. The stay-at-home parent can be either the father or the mother, depending on the job opportunities, the earning potential, and the psychological temperament concerning the parenting role. There has also been a significant increase in fathers who choose to spend the early years raising their children, and cherish this privilege. The important outcome of these more recent family and work configurations is that stereotypical gender roles have undergone drastic revisions. A new generation of fathers are proud to be able to care for their young children as competently as the mothers, and they want

to be actively involved as parents. In reality, both fathers and mothers contribute unique parenting skills to the family unit, and it is a great privilege for children to have two actively involved parents focused on their well-being.

Lead-Parents

A **lead-parent** or *primary parent* is the parent who is most readily available to meet the day-to-day needs and demands of the child. It is the parent who can respond to the call from school, who can support the child's extracurricular activities, and may spend more hours of the day with the child (Moravcsik, 2015). Fathers who choose to be the lead-parent in terms of parenting may have more flexible work schedules that allow for this involvement. Being the lead parent does not necessarily mean a stay-at-home parent. Another variation on the term that is sometimes used is the *breadwinner* parent, although clearly all these roles can overlap and have flexible boundaries. Lead parents can also shift and change depending on work schedules. For instance, parents who travel regularly as part of their employment, e.g. pilots, flight attendants, travel organizers, site managers, or parents in the military who are deployed, may take on the lead role during the periods that they are at home.

Fathers who are lead parents are slowly gaining momentum in making their parenting needs heard. For instance, they are asking for baby changing stations in men's bathrooms, they participate in parent support groups, and they are challenging the stereotype that tends to put women into caretaking roles. They also seem to flourish in networking with other men who act as lead-parents and generally exhibit competence in their parenting roles.

Work-Family Balance

Increasingly parents seek a **work-family balance** that allows for family time and makes it a priority. Both parents may want or need to be gainfully employed (Molina, 2015), yet parenting and family responsibilities are important. Many parents, especially mothers, would like to re-enter the workforce when their children reach school age because it is easier to coordinate work and school schedules.

The re-entry or return of a parent to the workforce can contain rewarding as well as challenging aspects. On the positive side is the self-actualization of work, using one's skills and education, financial rewards, as well as the social and professional stimulation of a network of colleagues and fellow workers.

The challenging aspects of gainful employment pertain to the juggling of several roles and demands, and finding high quality yet affordable childcare. The change in a parent's employment status affects patterns within family functioning. When one aspect of a system is altered, other aspects have to be adjusted to restore or maintain homeostasis. Family systems strive to maintain equilibrium. The change in one parent's role produces a ripple effect in the behavior and functioning of the other family members. Adjusting to these changes can be challenging. Job-related stress can have a negative impact on parent–child relationships (Figley & McCubbin, 2016). On the other hand, the economic and self-actualization factors that accompany employment contain several positive elements that can affect the family system in rewarding ways.

Many sociological changes have supported these changes in the economics of marriage. Gender roles have become more equal. Women are fulfilling their aspirations for higher education, society is increasingly creating family-friendly workplaces, and a greater choice of child-care arrangements has become available (Pew Research Center, 2015c).

The majority of parents in contemporary American society see their role as provider as part of their obligation within the family system. Currently, most women balance work outside the home with more traditional domestic responsibilities (Parker & Wang, 2013). In 1970, about 90 percent of married couples in the United States had conventional earning arrangements where the husband was the sole provider (Raley, Mattingly, & Bianchi, 2006; Vitali & Arpino, 2016), while only 9 percent of the wives contributed equally to the couple's earnings. By 2015, about 38 percent of wives were earning more than their husbands, implying that the gender wage gap in the United States is narrowing (Campbell, 2015; Schwartz & Gonalons-Pons, 2016).

Many families need the additional economic benefits provided by dual incomes, but many stay-at-home parents have found that full-time domestic roles contain their own challenges. Depression is high among stay-at-home mothers with preschool children (Bean, Softas-Nall, Eberle, & Paul, 2016). Many have college degrees and wish to utilize their educational training.

Parenting FAQ 9–1

My 10-year-old son wants certain items because "Everybody has one." Peers are important, but how do I find the middle ground?

Children at this age are becoming increasingly aware of their peers and what the peer group is doing. They are also beginning to feel the push of peer pressure. At the same time, children are little psychologists who know which buttons to best push with their parents, and whether dad or mom is likely to give in first. After all, have they not spent their entire lifetime studying you, the parent? Ask yourself if the child is possibly modeling examples set in your home? How do you as a family deal with new acquisitions? Do the children get age appropriate pocket money that they can spend in ways of their choosing? Use these situations as opportunities to teach children about managing money and resources in general, but also have reward systems in place for high days and holidays. You can compromise by sharing the expense with him while also learning skills that will be useful in adulthood, such as planning, saving for an object, long term goals, and the like. Put yourself into the child's shoes, ask yourself if this wish is reasonable and appropriate? Does it promote learning and development? There is a place and a time for most things in life, including gifts, rewards, and fun times.

Toward Gender Equality

The effects of women's employment outside the home differs considerably depending on whether the gender roles of the parental couple are egalitarian or non-egalitarian.

■ Family functioning requires adjustments in the roles of all family members. These adaptations relate to household chores, leisure time, recreation, and interpersonal interactions (Carlson, Miller, Sassler, & Hanson, 2016).

■ Marital satisfaction is higher within *egalitarian,* relationships (Sells & Ganong, 2016).

The degree of egalitarianism within the relationship will determine the extent of role sharing. The nature of the couple's occupations and earning potential are also important considerations. If one spouse has the night shift or travels extensively, the roles within the home are obviously adjusted to meet these challenges. In military families, one parent may act as a distant coparent while deployed. These families have to find role arrangements that suit the needs of their specific family challenges.

Adults in a dual-earner family system are challenged to balance work demands with family responsibilities. This can produce stress that is felt throughout the entire family system. Both men and women are able to achieve this balance successfully (Allen & Eby, 2016). Employed mothers may experience **role overload** or **role strain** as they juggle the demands of work and the home, if they continue to bear the principal household maintenance responsibilities in addition to holding a job outside the home (Freese, Smith, & Grzywacz, 2016).

Some factors that contribute to role strain in *non-egalitarian* relationships include the following:

■ The division of family work is inequitable because male partners spend less time on housework or child care.

■ Traditional gender-role attitudes may determine what work is done by whom, even in dual-income couples.

■ Most women would like their partners to be more involved in household responsibilities and child care.

■ Role overload has negative implications for women's health and well-being if they are constantly multitasking and juggling roles.

■ Some men identify more with their work role than they do with a balanced work and family identity.

■ A women's social power within a family system increases significantly after employment. As a woman's level of education increases, there is a greater likelihood of shared household responsibilities with a partner.

Video Example 9.2

Watch this video on changing gender roles at home. Why are gender roles shifting? Do you consider certain jobs to be gender specific?

(https://www.youtube.com/watch?v=ifz4HykIDq8)

Effects on the Children

Many concerns are expressed about how dual parental employment affects children. Many interacting factors play contributory roles, such as the family structure, the ages of the children, the quality and continuity of alternative-care options, and socioeconomic constraints, to name a few (see Figure 9–3). Currently, there are more mothers who are working outside the home than there are those who are staying at home.

As with any other complex issue, researchers report a number of mixed findings on how this situation affects school-age children. Generally, they find no significant adverse effects on children but it depends on the quality and continuity of child care (Felfe, Nollenberger, & Rodríguez-Planas, 2015). Children are thought to receive less supervision, less interaction time, and less discipline than do children in situations where one parent stays at home. Some children have increased television time and an associated higher body mass index (Ziol-Guest, 2014).

School-age boys and girls can benefit from their mother's employment, but girls may be especially influenced in positive ways. For example, the female children of employed mothers tend to have higher levels of emotional maturity and achievement, perhaps because of the roles that their mothers model. Both boys and girls tend to have fewer gender stereotypes and biases when their mothers are employed (Milkie, Nomaguchi, & Denny, 2015). Maternal employment can be a

DUAL PARENTAL EMPLOYMENT

Many factors interact to determine the outcomes of especially maternal employment on children and adolescents, and there is no simple answer to this complex challenge. We do need to distinguish between dual-income couples where both parents work outside the home, and couples where the father fulfills the homemaker role and the mother is the lead breadwinner.

- The father's support and involvement influences the system positively.
- Egalitarian relationships provide better parenting outcomes and work/family balance.
- Maternal employment effects vary by the children's developmental stage.
- Maternal employment effects vary by the mother's age, income, and educational status.
- Maternal employment effects vary depending on the family structure.
- The effects vary depending on the overall family support and economic resources.
- Maternal marital, occupational, and socioeconomic status affect child rearing.
- Maternal employment affects shared family time.
- Racial and ethnic differences affect outcomes.
- Maternal income can add to the economic well-being of the family.
- Other family processes, such as support from the grandparents, play a role.
- Maternal employment can burden older children who then must take care of younger siblings.
- The effects vary depending on the quality and continuity of child care.

Based on the classic research by Crosnoe, R., & Cavanagh, S. E. (2010, June). Families with children and adolescents: A review, critique, and future agenda. *Journal of Marriage and Family, 72,* 594–611.

FIGURE 9–3.   Dual Parental Employment.

positive factor in role aspirations for girls, and boys tend to be more gender equal if they have grown up with mothers working outside the home (McGinn, Ruiz Castro, & Lingo, 2015).

Both boys and girls of employed mothers seem to be more self-sufficient than other children, and they tend to be given more responsibilities by their parents. (Jung & Heppner, 2015). It is reasonable to assume that those

parents who have heavy work schedules or have more than one job are less likely to devote attention to their children and parenting roles and responsibilities.

The *quality* of the parenting time can be influenced by the *quantity* of the time available, unless continuous, quality alternative care is in place.

Focus Point: Dual employment brings rewards as well as challenges. Adults are affected by changes in their family roles and the use of their time. Mothers in non-egalitarian relationships may experience role strain and overload. Parents who are *mutually supportive* experience role enhancement in both their work and their family roles. Working outside the home has economic benefits, widens social networks, and provides intellectual stimulation. Children benefit in various ways from their parents' employment status, both economically and socially. Maternal employment can contribute to more gender-equal role perceptions by their children.

Acknowledgments
Patricia F. Wood, PhD: Contributing Author for Section on Gifted Education. Professor, Director Gifted Education, Samford University
Joseph Ackerson, PhD: Consultant for Section on Head Injuries and Concussions, Pediatric Neuropsychologist. Used with permission.

CHAPTER FOCUS POINTS

Meeting Unique Individuals

■ Between the ages of 6 and 12, children in middle childhood further develop their cognitive and social skills with the assistance of parents, peers, and the education system.

Parenting School-age Children

■ As a child reaches school age, parenting changes in quality and style in response to the child's changing developmental needs. Parents adopt a variety of

Cultural Snapshot 9–2

A Multifaceted Cultural Diamond

Many different threads interweave and are influential in how children acquire their cultural heritage. Children are born into the contexts of their families, and these kinship relationships carry numerous messages and opportunities for learning. The primary caregivers will enact customs from their own cultural repertoire. The child in turn will imitate and mirror many of these subtle nuances. Language will be modeled on the examples provided by significant persons in the child's world. Childrearing philosophies and approaches, as enacted by these caretakers, will include the echoes of the culture within which they are embedded. The larger context of a group, religion or society, provides a further backdrop of influence, and these layers combine to influence child rearing practices.

In short, cultural influences are multi layered. They adapt and change to meet environmental demands. The way children are raised in any particular setting, will reflect some of the beliefs, norms, practices and other dimensions of that culture. It is as complex as a multifaceted diamond, where each angled surface has the ability to refract light. Similarly culture is multifaceted, which adds to its complexity and fascination.

Source: Molitor, A. & Hsu, H. (2011). Child development across cultures. Chapter 5 in: Keith, K.D. (Ed.) Cross-cultural psychology: Contemporary themes and perspectives. Chichester, U.K.: Wiley-Blackwell.

interactional styles based on various parenting approaches. During infancy, the focus emphasized safety and physical needs, whereas during early childhood and the school-age years, it expands to include increasingly social and psychological demands.

Landmarks of Middle Childhood

■ During this developmental stage, parents are charged with the responsibility of teaching their children skills such as regulation of emotions and coping mechanisms. The influence of peers becomes increasingly more important as children seek acceptance and create deeper bonds with other school-age children. Through continuous, open communication, parents can help children develop healthy mindsets and values on topics such as sexuality, friendship, and peer pressure.

■ Although infancy and its central focus on survival are in the past, parents should continue to put great effort into the health and well-being of their school-aged children. Both hunger and obesity are problems plaguing this age group, either as a result of poverty

or poor parental lifestyle choices. Overall health care, including vision, dental, and yearly check-ups continue to play an important role in a child's healthy development.

The Developmental Characteristics of School-age Children

■ Parents must adjust their parenting styles due to the changes occurring in their child's development during this period. As a child begins to rely more heavily on the opinions of their peer group, it is important for parents and teachers to counter the negative effects of bullying and harassment through awareness and possible intervention.

Cognitive Skills

■ The amount of information that a school-age child can absorb is seemingly limitless as they obtain greater critical thinking skills. By utilizing various thought processes, children begin to understand more concrete as well as abstract concepts.

The World of School

■ Social development in middle childhood relates to adjustment in school and other learning environments, establishing peer relations, and refining the self-concept. During this age (pre-adolescence) the normally developing brain has virtual superpowers to acquire new skills. Educational contexts should be used to promote the building and expansion of these skills. Parents and teachers collaborate in promoting children's academic performance and success.

Typical Behavioral Problems

■ Many behavioral problems in school-age children are linked to difficulties in achieving developmental tasks; other such problems relate more specifically to difficulties with interactions with parents and peers. Behavioral problems that are related to learning disorders are often displayed in the classroom. A variety of methods may be helpful in dealing with these problems.

Parenting Exceptional Children

■ Parents of children with special needs deal with issues in child rearing that are not usually confronted by other parents. Child rearing in these circumstances can be difficult but can also have unique rewards. Families experience challenges that influence the quality and the nature of parent–child relations. Federal legislative efforts continue to provide much needed support.

Parental Employment and Childcare Support

■ Dual employment brings rewards as well as challenges. Adults are affected by changes in their family roles and the use of their time. Mothers in non-egalitarian relationships may experience role strain and overload. Parents who are *mutually supportive* experience role enhancement in both their work and their family roles. Working outside the home has economic benefits, widens social networks, and provides intellectual stimulation. Children benefit in various ways from their parents' employment status, both economically and socially. Maternal employment can contribute to more gender-equal role perceptions by their children.

USEFUL WEBSITES

Websites are dynamic and change

Association for Middle Level Education
http://amle.org
Middle childhood education

Boy Scouts of America and Girls Scouts of America
www.scouting.org
www.girlscouts.org
Work ethic, discipline, soft skills

Federal Interagency Forum on Children and Family Statistics
www.childstats.gov
America's children in brief: Key national indicators of well-being

Learning Disabilities Association of America
www.ldaamerica.org
Learning disabilities, special education

National Alliance for Grieving Children
https://childrengrieve.org
Support for families and children dealing with grief

National Association of State Boards of Education
State School Healthy Policy Database
www.nasbe.org/healthy_schools/hs/
Special Education, Exceptional Children

National Association for Gifted Children
www.nagc.org
Talents, Gifted Children,

National Crime Prevention Council
www.ncpc.org
Bullying, Cyberbullying,

National Resource Center on ADHD
www.help4adhd.org
ADHD

National Safe Place
www.nationalsafeplace.org
Child Safety

Stop Bullying
www.stopbullying.gov
Bullying, School Safety

Stop Cyberbullying
www.stopcyberbullying.org/index2.html

Cyberbullying, Internet Safety

Cyberbullying Research Center
www.cyberbullying.us
Cyberbullying, Internet Safety

U.S. Department of Education
www.ed.gov
Gifted Children, Exceptional Children, Special
  Education

CHAPTER 10

Parenting Adolescents and Teens as Parents

Learning Outcomes

. . . .

After completing this chapter, you should be able to

1. Describe a parent's role in helping adolescents avoid risky behaviors.
2. Illustrate the cognitive attributes of adolescence.
3. Determine the appropriate balance of nurture and structure parents should provide for adolescents.
4. Assess the factors that contribute to unhealthy adolescent sexual behavior.
5. Propose positive communication strategies for emerging adults and their parents.
6. Analyze the current research surrounding teen pregnancy and parenthood.
7. Measure the benefits of various programs offering assistance to adolescent parents.

. . . .

THE PROMISE OF THE FUTURE

As parents of teenagers we are privileged to share and observe their journey, as they will bring fresh ideas into our world; they will "keep us in the loop." Adolescents are a wondrous mix of a little bit of child, a little bit of adult, and a whole lot of emerging personhood in between.

During adolescence we can catch a clear glimpse of the adult they will become. For parents, this is an exciting and also rewarding period of parenting as the investments of previous years are being integrated, the child is maturing, and autonomy is increasing. For parents, it also signals the phase of preparing the child for launch and independence, even though the parenting relationship will continue while changed in form and function.

Adolescence is the stage of the lifespan that represents a transitional period between childhood and adulthood. Chronologically, it begins at age 13 and extends through age 18. Development occurs gradually so that early and late adolescence can seem like two different stages. Early adolescence has some qualities of childhood, whereas late adolescence begins to model emerging adulthood (Arnett, 2000) The developmental event of puberty, which is usually in progress by early adolescence, signals the end of childhood. During this time, individuals become sexually mature and capable of reproduction. The term *puberty* refers to maturation in terms of physical sexual characteristics, whereas the term *adolescence* refers to the entire period between late childhood and early adulthood and includes social and emotional aspects as well as the physical dimension of puberty.

The stage of adolescence is technically divided into two periods:

1. *Early adolescence* typically encompasses puberty and involves a variety of physical changes associated with sexual maturation. The onset of puberty varies. The average age at which breast development in girls begins is age 10, but can be as early as age 8. The average age of menarche (the first menstrual period) is about 12, or earlier. The average age for male puberty is 12, but onset as young as age 9 is within the normal range. It typically ends at age 16.
2. *Late adolescence,* which begins at age 16 and continues until age 18, involves many psychosocial changes as individuals seek increasing independence. This stage then proceeds toward emerging adulthood.

Parents and adolescents are part of the same dynamic family system, and they influence each other (Sigel, McGillicuddy-DeLisi, & Goodnow, 2014; Seiffge-Krenke & Pakalniskiene, 2011). Traditionally, the period is described as stormy and stressful for teens, their parents, and the family system. Parents may fear for the safety of their increasingly independent children, whereas adolescents may feel invincible and want to declare their independence from overprotective parents (Brazelton, 2013; Koepke & Denissen, 2012).

A more contemporary view of adolescence describes this stage as one of expanding autonomy as children gain increasing degrees of personal responsibility at a time of significant transition (Kroger, Martinussen, & Marcia, 2010; McLean & Syed, 2014). Parents may view these gains apprehensively, being aware of the many hazards that can threaten the health and well-being of adolescent children. As with other stages of the lifespan, adolescence presents both children and their parents with unique challenges for growth and adaptation.

The Teenage Brain

Some of the limitations and idiosyncrasies of the adolescent's cognitive functioning are thought to be the product of the unique neurological makeup of the teenage brain, which has not yet reached full maturity. It is thought that some teenagers are more irresponsible in their cognitive processes, do not think through consequences, and may feel invincible (Blakemore, 2012a). There are many individual differences, and adolescents' cognitive abilities vary depending on their personal makeup and maturity. For that reason, it is best not to overgeneralize.

According to cognitive neuroscience, the adolescent brain continues its neurological development toward maturity, and changes in several cortical regions occur gradually (Blakemore, 2012b). A number of adolescents are responsible and mature beyond their years, defying the stereotypes.

Teenage decision making is thought to differ from that of adults. It can be impulsive, focused on the immediate, lacking consideration of long-term detrimental outcomes, and short of the anticipatory judgment required to think through consequences. Sadly, some decisions can have lifelong effects; for example, binge drinking, substance abuse, texting while driving, and reckless driving can all have dire consequences. Car insurance for young drivers, particularly young males, is expensive because they lack extensive driving experience and may not always exhibit the better judgment that is supposed to come with maturity (Bonnie & Scott, 2013).

Of special note is that substances such as alcohol and drugs can have far greater and also far more damaging effects on the developing mind of an adolescent. To illustrate this, if a teenager and a grown-up who each weighed the same and both ingested the same amount of alcohol, the teenage brain would react differently and be at greater risk than the adult brain. In other words, brain immaturity is also linked to brain vulnerability (Gilpin, 2014; Jensen & Nutt, 2015). Adolescents need to know that their margins are so much slimmer than for older adults and that they cannot afford to binge drink or get involved with the illicit use of prescription and other drugs, or even tobacco use. All these substances can be highly addictive when first taken during the teenage years, and they can easily derail a promising young life (Andersen, 2016; Spear, 2016).

Parents need to have ongoing conversations with their growing children, in which they explain how the human brain is a chemically driven machine, that is very sensitive to any input. Concussions, illicit substances, tobacco and alcohol can all do enormous damage to this finely tuned chemical masterpiece. Some of the damage may not be undone, and early drug addiction has been known to precipitate depression and related mental disorders (Temple, 2015).

As parents, we are often advised to give our children the "facts of life speech," by which is typically meant sex and relationship education. But the "facts of life speech" should also address our vulnerabilities toward drugs, alcohol, and tobacco; all of which can steer a young person onto an undesirable path where undoing or just controlling the harm may prove to be an ongoing battle. As parents, our responsibility is to model moderation in our behaviors, and we have a role to coregulate and care for the well-being of those youngsters entrusted to us. Our teenagers may appear like grownups as their bodies may seem fully grown; but they are still emerging on the path toward maturity, and our ongoing vigilance is essential.

The teenage brain has often been stereotyped as being impulsive and erratic (Van Leijenhorst et al., 2010). These emotional behaviors can occur, but can also be overshadowed by the cognitive strengths of a fast computing mind, an excellent memory, and the willingness to think outside the box. Young tech entrepreneurs have proved to the world that the mind of a late adolescent or an emerging adult can be a very powerful mind indeed.

Brain Development in Adolescence

- During the first years of life, the brain is in optimal learning mode; learning is easy and new tasks get mastered readily (Jensen & Nutt, 2015, p. 71). This lays the foundation for all that is to follow.

- For adolescents, similar learning conditions exist neurobiologically. The teenage brain is a learning machine that is highly efficient (Jensen & Nutt, 2015, p. 80).

- Although the adolescent brain is in great shape and very efficient, other aspects of functioning may be less optimal. For example, attention span, self-discipline, self-regulation, emotional balance, and task completion may be erratic at times, to the frustration of the parents (Jensen & Nutt, 2015, p. 80).

- The teenage brain has its strengths but also its vulnerabilities. For instance, it is more susceptible to addictions, and alcohol and drugs can do far greater harm to the developing mind (Volkow, Koob & McLellan, 2016).

- Alcohol and drugs can be deleterious and teenagers need to understand this so that they can protect themselves. Binge drinking can be extremely dangerous for adolescents, for the simple reason that alcohol can do greater damage to their developing brains (Jensen & Nutt, 2015 p. 135).

- Tobacco can be more addictive to the developing and immature brain, and it can be extremely difficult to break a smoking habit once it has been established (Jensen & Nutt, 2015, p. 115). Similarly, marijuana and hard drugs can flip the addiction switch in this age group, and pave the way to much greater problems (Volkow, et al, 2016).

- Cognitive strengths: The cognitive abilities, such as learning another language or mastering a musical instrument, are great. The teenage brain is very adept at learning new skills, sometimes more so than later in life. But these cognitive skills do not equate to emotional or social maturity (American Psychological Association, 2012).

- Social and emotional immaturity can put the teenager at risk, because poor choices, a sense of invulnerability, and impulsivity can put a young person in harm's way. For instance, the seemingly irresistible urge to text while driving can prove to be fatal (Gupta, Burns, & Boyd, 2016).

- Adolescents think they can do "all nighters" and study or work through the night. In reality, they need regular and enough sleep to function well and remain focused (Jensen & Nutt, 2015, p. 87).

■ Teenagers are susceptible to stress, they need to adopt healthy lifestyles and focus on wellness, for the same reasons adults may focus on these endeavors. Stress has different effects on teenagers than on adults, and self-medicating in adolescence is dangerous (Jensen & Nutt, 2015, p. 173; Romeo, 2013; Walsh & Walsh, 2014).

Primarily based on: Jensen, Frances with Nutt, A. (2015). *The Teenage Brain: A Neuroscientist's Survival Guide to Raising Adolescents and Young Adults*. New York, NY: Harper Collins.
    http://www.npr.org/sections/health-shots/2015/01/28/381622350/why-teens-are-impulsive-addiction-prone-and-should-protect-their-brains

Focus Point.   As children become young adults and lead more autonomous lifestyles, the role of parents shifts. Parents are advised to keep an open line of communication, enabling them to steer their adolescents toward desirable outcomes and away from harmful activities, including illegal and impulsive behavior that could be destructive. Being aware of the learning potential and plasticity of the adolescent's brain allows us to see the strengths and special capabilities of this developmental stage.

DEVELOPMENTAL LANDMARKS OF ADOLESCENCE

Three features distinguish development during adolescence:

■ *Rapid physical and psychological change.* Adolescence is a period of metamorphosis in an individual's life that involves dramatic changes in body proportions and physical size, sexual maturation, and personality shifts.
■ *Individual emancipation.* Western culture emphasizes the teenage years as the appropriate time for establishing independence as a mature person and assuming full responsibility.
■ *Experimentation, idealism, and uncertainty.* These changing and developing ideals often bring teens into conflict with adults, especially their parents.

Adolescence is a transitional period between childhood and adulthood that has few guidelines for how to behave, what to expect, and how to remain secure about what the future holds. Adolescents are known for unrealistic expectations and aspirations. These attitudes are expressed in relationships with peers and family members. High hopes for the future lead teenagers to create dreams and idealistic notions about their own abilities and skills in coping with the world.

Adolescents are known for self-exploration and self-expression, and the tendency to experiment is seen in their choice of clothing, musical tastes, friendships, and awakening sexuality. The specific developmental tasks and milestones that individuals encounter in adolescence focus on acquiring and refining more advanced skills, abilities, and attitudes that lead toward preparation for adulthood.

Focus Point.   As adolescents move from childhood to adulthood, their transitions are characterized by physical and psychological changes. They begin to solidify their thoughts and ideals concerning themselves and the surrounding world, and many use this time to explore aspects of their identity, philosophies concerning their existence, and life and career goals.

PARENTING ADOLESCENTS

When discussing parents' relationships with their teens, we need to look at both family status and family process. Family status is defined by aspects of family structure and positioning, such as marital union, single parenthood, socioeconomic resources, employment, and education. Family *process* concerns the relationships within the family. These relationships can occur *intergenerationally*, as when the grandparents are involved, and *intra-generationally*, as between siblings (Kail & Cavanaugh, 2015; Sigelman & Rider, 2014). Many parents anticipate conflict when a child reaches adolescence because this stage can be associated with rebellion, tension, and emotional turmoil. While some teenagers are rather extreme in their behaviors and attitudes, most adolescents do not act out, and the stereotypes do not normally apply.

Parenting styles and behaviors must adapt once again to meet the needs of a now maturing child. The adaptation is typically initiated by the adolescent, who may demand to be treated with more trust and respect,

Szefei/123RF.com

Skilled parents adapt child-rearing strategies, methods, and interaction styles to meet the particular needs of the adolescent. During adolescence, parents respond to expanding autonomy by becoming more authoritative, less authoritarian, and, eventually, more permissive.

which is perceived as independence. The developmental need for autonomy and individuation from the family system presents unique, yet rewarding, challenges, and adolescents put a high value on being respected by their parents (Schwartz, Luyckx, & Vignoles, 2011). Most parents understand that adolescents continue to need guidance, rules, and support during this process of growing toward maturity. The manner in which this guidance is offered needs to be respectful and acknowledge the emerging aspects of maturity, while being cognizant of the unique qualities that characterize adolescent thinking. The safety and shelter of parental guidance should allow appropriate self-exploration and autonomy (Inguglia, Ingoglia, Liga, Coco, & Cricchio, 2015).

Even though adolescents say that, and act as though, they want to be independent, they continue to thrive on parental and coparental attention and meaningful family relationships. Although the actual amount of time spent with parents as an adolescent, was less critical than the quality of that time; parental engagement had many *nuanced* influences related to better outcomes. Time spent with mothers was

studied and engaged maternal time was related to fewer delinquent behaviors (Milkie, Nomaguchi & Denny, 2015). In other words, parenting has not been completed by adolescence and early adulthood; constructive parental, coparental and family involvement remains a predictor of favorable child rearing and parenting outcomes (Mollborn & Jacobs, 2015).

Professionals who work with families stress that one of the more difficult challenges of parenting adolescents is the fine line that parents walk between being supportive of a teen's efforts to individuate and maintaining certain boundaries for appropriate behavior (Lebowitz & Omer, 2013). Adolescents need to learn how to make personal decisions, but sometimes their decisions can have drastic consequences. Family systems become unhealthy when there is a demand for complete conformity among all members, when everyone is expected to adhere to the same beliefs, values, and behaviors. Although parents and adolescents must agree on rules and other family patterns, this agreement ideally develops through negotiation and input from all concerned (O'Connell & Brannen, 2014).

**Focus On
10–1**

Developmental Characteristics of Adolescence

- Establishing a sense of personal identity.
- Establishing more mature relationships with peers of both genders.
- Accepting the physical changes that accompany puberty.
- Defining gender roles and accepting one's sexuality.
- Initiating the process of individuation.
- Initiating financial independence.
- Preparations for higher education and/or an occupation.
- Manifesting socially responsible behaviors.
- Continuing to acquire and develop the skills for healthy relationships.
- Continuing to solidify a set of values and an ethical system that will guide behavior.

Video Example 10.1

Watch this video of Mike Riera talking about parenting teens. When teens distance themselves from their parents, the parents have to find a context and a meaning for that behavior. Explain both the context and the meaning.

(https://www.youtube.com/watch?v=pVGY0Y Dq-Jk)

Revised Parenting Styles

Skilled parents adapt child-rearing strategies, methods, and interaction styles to meet the particular needs of the adolescent. Because of the expanding autonomy of adolescents, parents have to alter their parenting style as well. Parents become more authoritative, less authoritarian, and, eventually, more permissive.

Parents must discover ways to help teens learn to make decisions that minimize the potential harm to themselves and others. Communication between parents and teens requires patience and effort to achieve effective functioning in this microenvironment (Keijsers & Poulin, 2013). Parents must gradually relinquish control and place increasing amounts of personal responsibility onto teens so that they become self-regulating.

Some parenting styles are more common in subsets of society. Middle-class families tend to use methods based on persuasion and negotiation, including democratic,

egalitarian, and authoritative styles. Under economic strain, stressful influences can contribute to parenting styles that emphasize control, especially by forceful, power-assertive methods (Park & Walton-Moss, 2012). Financial independence may be valued if families are struggling, and they may expect that their adolescent children become financially independent at an earlier age. Parents with college educations tend to encourage their children to pursue further education, and the parents serve as role models (Rockwell, 2011).

Conflicts between parents and young adolescents occur more frequently than when children were younger (Marceau, Dorn, & Susman, 2012). These clashes can happen because of the intense focus of young adolescents on identity formation. Predictably, many parents initially react to such efforts by using styles that are strict and controlling.

Research consistently shows that parent–adolescent relations are best when decisions are perceived by both parties as being consistent, fair, and collaborative and the needs of all family members are respected (McKinney & Renk, 2011). As in previous stages of parenting children, the authoritative parenting style continues to be associated with positive adolescent outcomes.

Historic Research. The sociologist Glen Holl Elder (b. 1934) is best known for his historic work, *Children of the Great Depression* (1974, 1999). He studied human development against the backdrop of changing environments, and he showed how these changes in the environment could change lives. Elder examined how the chronosystem (time-related influences, according to Bronfenbrenner's family ecological theory) affected the outcomes of development over the life span. For instance, if all members of a cohort had to face a major life experience, such as the Great Depression, what influence would that have on their lives? He conducted a classic demographic study (1962) that described the styles commonly used by parenting adolescents. At a time when mainstream thinking undervalued the role of fathers as parents, and parent–child interaction was thought to be predominantly unidirectional, he studied the dimensions of parenting on a large scale. Elder's study included 7,400 adolescents from homes that had two parents, and it classified parenting styles on a continuum that differed in the degree of control exercised by the adults. According to the study, at least seven styles could be observed:

- *Autocratic.* Teens are allowed no freedom to express their opinions or to make any decision that affects how they conduct their lives.
- *Authoritarian.* Teens are allowed to express their opinions, but parents continue to make decisions that affect their lives.
- *Democratic.* Teens and parents share power, but parents have veto power over the decisions made by teens.
- *Permissive.* Teens take an increasing degree of responsibility for their decisions and actions, but with the understanding that parents continue to have input into the decision-making process.
- *Egalitarian.* Teens and parents have equal power and status, and they make decisions through joint effort.
- *Laissez-faire.* Teens take complete control and responsibility for making decisions about their lives and conduct. Parents understand that they can contribute information and opinions, which teens can freely disregard.
- *Ignoring.* Parents take no part or have no interest in an adolescent's behavior.

Most of the parents in this study used democratic or egalitarian styles. The stricter styles were more prevalent in larger family systems, among those with low incomes, and among those who had younger adolescents. Stricter parenting styles may be used more commonly in larger family systems because adults have greater time and resource management pressures. Contemporary family life is hectic when adolescents are present. Stricter methods among larger groups may facilitate family

functioning to a certain degree, but this may occur at the expense of an adolescent's achievement of high level individuation.

....

Focus Point.   Some of the challenges in parent–teen relationships relate to providing structure and nurture. A significant task involves the ability of parents and teens to communicate effectively. Adults who use democratic styles usually have more positive interactions. Authoritarian styles generate more conflict, which can be partly attributed to the adolescent's attempts at individuation. Parenting approaches need to adjust to developmental stage and acknowledge individual and contextual variations.

....

Meeting the Needs of Adolescents

Meeting Nutritional Needs.   The focus on *competent eating* is important, and the nutritional foundation laid down by parents during earlier phases will now pay dividends. Family meals, family food choices, and positive parental role models remain important influential factors in spite of peer group pressures. The appetites increase dramatically during adolescence. With appropriate discussion and modeling, modern adolescents are increasingly interested in healthy eating; although without this influence, they may be tempted by easy-to-access and generally less nutritious food. Because adolescents are very peer oriented, it may be challenging to encourage appropriate nutrition unless their peers care about healthy food choices. Most adolescents want to be like their friends, including their food choices. Because of greater body awareness, linked to self-concept, there is a greater risk of eating disorders, especially in adolescent females (Smink, van Hoeken, Oldehinkel, & Hoek, 2014). Obesity is increasing in both genders and can cause shame and erode the self-concept (Birbilis, Moschonis, Mougios, & Manios, 2013).

Health and Safety Concerns.   Health and safety issues influence present as well as future outcomes. Continued health monitoring is a good practice that facilitates early recognition and treatment of any irregularities, while also insuring that required immunizations are received. These visits can address confidential and personal issues and building a trusted relationship with a health care professional will facilitate the conversations. This in turn can play an important role in supporting teens' acquisition of a healthy lifestyle, including safer sexual practices and awareness of drug, prescription meds, and alcohol abuse.

Substance Abuse and Binge Drinking. Parents and other members of society are extremely concerned about adolescent drug, prescription meds, and binge drinking episodes. The extent of drug and prescription drug abuse and illegal underage drinking of alcohol among teenagers is considerable (see Figure 10-1). The misuse of prescription drugs and accidental fatal overdoses from these substances is on the rise and has become a new health endemic among teens and older age groups (Substance Abuse and Mental Health Services Administration, 2015). Additionally, the developing teenage brain is more vulnerable to the effects of these substances (Jensen & Nutt, 2015). An episode of binge drinking or drug use does more harm to the developing brain of an adolescent than it would do to an older person. Teenagers should be informed and know that they are not as invulnerable as they would like to think they are and they need to be proactive in protecting their brains.

Despite the influences of the media and peers, adolescents who have been raised by parents who rely on an authoritative style appear to have stronger internalized values that help to insulate them from peer pressure (Chan & Chan, 2013). Teens do care what parents think

about smoking and drinking and are less likely to drink alcohol, smoke cigarettes, or use drugs if the parental role models are appropriate.

Adolescents are also at increased risk for injury and death from accidents involving alcohol and/or drug use and automobiles (U.S. Census Bureau, n.d.). Such accidents are still the leading cause of death among teenagers in the United States, resulting in much grief when the lives of friends, siblings, and children are cut short. In addition to accidents and fatal injuries involving automobiles, teen text messaging while driving is taking its toll. Some states have enacted legislation to prohibit this practice.

Suicide. Suicide is the third leading cause of death, following fatal accidents and homicides among individuals between 11 and 24 years of age (Kochanek, Murphy, Xu, & Tejada-Vera, 2016), and the documented rate is thought to have tripled over the past 30 years. Males are more likely to succeed in their suicide attempts. The National Institute for Mental Health states that, for every 25 suicides attempted, one is fatal (www.nimh.nih.gov). A teen suicide attempt should always be recognized as an expression of extreme distress that necessitates professional intervention (www.teensuicide.us).

Suicide may be related to a variety of factors, including clinical depression, which distorts the ability to reason logically. Life frequently seems hopeless to persons who are clinically depressed, and suicide may seem to be

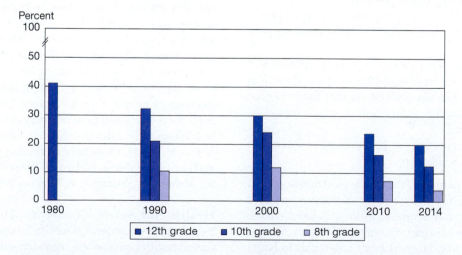

FIGURE 10–1. Percentage of 8th-, 10th-, and 12th-grade students who reported having five or more alcoholic beverages in a row in the past two weeks by grade, 1980–2014.

Source: National Institute on Drug Abuse, Monitoring the Future Survey.

the only possible escape. Some mental illnesses first present during late adolescence and can be contributory factors.

Suicide among adolescents is also related to substance abuse, which is frequently accompanied by depression and increased impulsivity (National Alliance on Mental Illness, 2017). Young people who identify themselves as LGBT (lesbian, gay, bisexual, or transgendered) or present with gender identity concerns, are more likely to attempt suicide than the average adolescent population. These youths experience anguish and inner turmoil and anticipate negative reactions from family and friends. A more informed and understanding society needs to reach out supportively and compassionately. Crisis hotlines are available to take emergency calls 24/7.

Suicide can be the outcome of *bullying*, where victims feel overwhelmed by the shaming and social abuse from peers. Social awareness, respect for human and civil rights, and a growing acceptance of diversity make it very clear that abusive behavior is unacceptable and cannot be tolerated. Heightened awareness and empathy among peers has been shown to exert a protective influence, and increasingly schools are adopting a zero-tolerance stance against bullying behavior.

Eating Disorders.   Some adolescents have a distorted body image (Grogan, 2016) and experience low self-esteem related to concerns about weight that may make them vulnerable to eating disorders. **Eating disorders** can be played out in the family system as a means of control. Eating disorders are increasingly recognized as a mental health disorder and should be treated seriously.

Anorexia nervosa and *bulimia* are serious eating disorders that affect the health, well-being, and lives of teenagers. Both conditions present predominantly in teenage girls, although young men especially those with gender role concerns have also been subject to these conditions (Crowther, Hobfoll, Stephens, & Tennenbaum, 2013). Eating disorders have serious consequences that can disturb normal adolescent behavior and development, and anorexia nervosa can result in death

Anorexic teenage girls appear to be obsessed with their body weight and have a distorted body image (Ferguson, Muñoz, Garza, & Galindo, 2014). The condition begins with dieting to achieve a particular weight, but continues to a point where it threatens their health and well-being. Controlling their weight and what they eat becomes the central life focus. Several factors interact:

- Strong cultural pressures emphasize slim figures.
- Within the family system, girls may react against strict, overprotective parents, the lack of adequate personal boundaries, or their inability to individuate and attain personal autonomy (Tetley, Moghaddam, Dawson, & Rennoldson, 2014).

Anorexia is a psychological disorder that can have fatal consequences if left untreated. Therapy can involve hospitalization to treat malnutrition and individual psychotherapy to help a teenage girl become more autonomous in less self-destructive ways. Family therapy and cognitive behavioral therapy can be helpful in resolving enmeshed familial relationships, improving communication, and helping the family system acquire healthy ways of resolving conflict (Lock & Grange, 2015). Psychiatrists may be involved to treat comorbid depression and anxiety disorders.

Bulimia involves consuming huge amounts of food that are then purged from the body by vomiting or using excessive amounts of laxatives (Hoste, Labuschagne, & Grange, 2012). Consumption occurs in periodic binges and during stressful situations as a means of coping. Unlike persons with anorexia, individuals with bulimia know that their behavior is not appropriate. They binge and purge in secret to avoid discovery and suffer from feelings of shame and guilt. The condition is similar to anorexia because it, too, revolves around the need to control one's eating and is motivated by a distorted body image.

Bulimia is a common method for weight control among adolescent girls. Many adolescents with bulimia are clinically depressed and have a tendency toward perfectionism. They are described as having an obsessive desire to control and manage themselves, as well as others in their lives. They are considered to be heavily dependent on the approval of others as the basis of their self-worth. This condition, like anorexia, responds to treatment through group, family, and individual psychotherapy and is also responsive to certain antidepressant medications (Couturier, Kimber, & Szatmari, 2013).

Cultural and family values influence the development of eating disorders, especially among female children (Crowther et al., 2013). These factors can combine in a family ecology to produce a behavioral problem in adolescence. A critical family environment, coercive parental controls, and a dominating discourse about body weight within the household can work together to increase the likelihood of an adolescent developing an eating disorder. Research also points to biological influences that may cause a genetic predisposition. As with many conditions, several factors interact to precipitate the behavior (Rohde, Stice, & Marti, 2015). With proper medical and psychotherapeutic treatment, both of these disorders can be brought under control and individuals can return to healthy, productive lives.

Focus Point. A variety of issues affect the health and safety of adolescents. A significant number of adolescents behave in ways that have short- and long-term adverse effects on their development. Substance abuse, depression and suicide, and eating disorders are tragically common during this developmental phase.

Family Climate

Family climate, rather than family structure, is related to the well-being of the members of the family, and is of greater importance in emotional satisfaction (Kreppner & Lerner, 2013). According to the U.S. Census Bureau (n.d.), about every fourth child under the age of 18 lives with only one parent. The cohesion of a family system is threatened when any change takes place that affects the system's functioning and equilibrium. Systems have a strong tendency to maintain the status quo because change in any aspect threatens the system's integrity. Family systems do face challenges that call for changes. When a child becomes an adolescent, the desire for individuation poses a serious threat to the family's functioning and the ability to maintain systemic cohesion.

Parents may seem particularly reluctant to release a teen from the controls, limits, and boundaries that were established in earlier developmental stages. Although many parents realize that this change must take place eventually, the equalization and transfer of power toward greater self-regulation occurs more slowly than most teens prefer. Parents who struggle with giving the child autonomy, may also present as helicopter parents, hovering over their children to keep them from any real or perceived harm (Van Ingen et al., 2015).

The benefits of authoritative parenting styles in mediating positive developmental outcomes for children continue while parents make alterations in response to the individuation process of their teenagers (Hiltz, 2015). For example, the behavioral problems of adolescents appear to diminish while academic competence can be enhanced when parents maintain *detached involvement* or supervision. This variation on the authoritative parenting method relates to the perception that adolescents have regarding their parents' involvement in their lives, while allowing them enough slack from parental supervision in order to feel autonomous. Parents are still providing structure for adolescents, but the structure is perceived as being fairly administered, yet firm and warm in its tone (see Figure 10-2).

Parenting Reflection 10–1

Is there such a thing as a *generation gap*, or is this a media fabrication? How would this influence interactions, communication, and mutual understanding among the generations?

Parenting Reflection 10–2

How can parents guide their teenage children toward making constructive decisions while also discouraging them from making unwise choices?

Peer Group Influences. The peer group plays a special role in the process of personal identity formation among adolescents. The interactions with peer groups in adolescence are similar to those during middle childhood, but the peer group takes on additional functions for teens (Albert, Chein, & Steinberg, 2013; Smith, Chein, & Steinberg, 2014). Teenagers use their peers as a device for making self-evaluations. In adolescence, this group becomes a new source for redefining the teen's personal identity. Teens view their peers as an extension of their own self-image. There is an enmeshment of personal identity of the self with others (Vaughans & Spielberg, 2014).

The push for autonomy reaches its peak in adolescence. This change gives a teenager freedom to test

Suicidal thoughts, attempts, and related injuries among high school students (grades 9–12), 2013 and 2015		
Percent of high school students who report they seriously considered attempting suicide (during the 12 months before the survey)	2013	2015
Total	17%	18%
Male	12%	12%
Female	22%	23%
Percent of high school students who report they attempted suicide one or more times (during the 12 months before the survey)	2013	2015
Total	8%	9%
Male	5%	6%
Female	11%	12%
Percent of high school students who report they attempted suicide resulting in an injury, poisoning, of overdose that had to be treated by a doctor or nurse (during the 12 months before the survey)	2013	2015
Total	3%	3%
Male	2%	2%
Female	4%	4%

FIGURE 10–2. Suicidal thoughts, attempts, and related injuries among high school students (grades 9-12), 2013 and 2015.

Source: Centers for Disease Control and Prevention. (2017c). 1991–2015 High School Youth Risk Behavior Survey data.

Cultural Snapshot 10–1

Cultural Competence: A Dance of Communication

Part of parenting emerging adults, is having to celebrate that our children are becoming independent, with thoughts and opinions of their own. Importantly, we have to give our children space and appropriate guidance as they explore their emerging identities and define their preferences. Learning to respectfully communicate with these emerging adults has many similarities with becoming *culturally competent*. We may not feel the same, we may cherish different worldviews; yet the respect to value the differentness of the other person's thinking and cultural identity is important in finding that bridge in communication that leads us to an area where we can share and connect.

Cultural communication is like dancing to the tune of a certain genre; switching midstep to another mode can be hard to do. While being in a comfort zone of competence while waltzing, it may be a challenge to change over to a tango. Not only our feet have to move to the sound of a different drum, our head and heart need to be supportive as well. We may still regard the waltz as our favorite, but we need to be open to respecting the person who favors a tango, and even try some steps or listen to the accompanying

music. The eminent anthropologist Edward Hall (1959/1973) summed it up: "*Communication is culture and culture is communication.*"

The researcher Chung (2011) uses a similar metaphor to describe this process:

...how can we be flexible, competent communicators when we interact with cultural strangers. This is no easy task, a bit like learning how to dance. During our cross-cultural encounters, we may step on people's toes, feel out of sync, or have mismatched ideas about our own ethnocentric viewpoint. With time and struggle, we learn to observe how to act appropriately, flow in our encounters, and adjust our perspective. Thankfully culture is not a static web. It is a dynamic, evolutionary process. Similarly, human beings are not static individuals—we change. In learning about another culture, or about dissimilar groups, we can expand our ways of thinking and find new insights to strengthen our own identity (Chung, 2011, p. 403).

Reference: Chung, L. C. (2011). Crossing boundaries: Cross-cultural communication. In: Keith, K. (Ed). *Cross-Cultural Psychology: Contemporary Themes and Perspectives*. Malden, MA: Wiley-Blackwell. Pp. 400–419.

> **PARENTS OF ADOLESCENTS**
>
> The parenting style should be adjusted to meet the developmental needs of the adolescent. Some behaviors that provide appropriate structure and nurture include:
>
> - Supporting the emerging identity of the adolescent.
> - Supporting positive self- and body-image formation.
> - Introducing adolescents to adult roles and modeling appropriate behavior.
> - Guiding adolescents toward educational and career goals.
> - Modeling respectful and gender-equal behavior.
> - Communicating age appropriately and respectfully.
> - Explaining the consequences of behavior and setting appropriate boundaries.
> - Providing a home environment that supports social and academic learning.
> - Teaching adolescents appropriate decision making.
> - Discussing the dangers of underage drinking and substance abuse.
> - Discussing values, sexual decision making, and safer sex practices.
> - Guiding adolescents toward sound financial decision making and modeling that behavior.
> - Encouraging adolescents to achieve appropriate autonomous behavior.
> - Supporting interests and peer group relationships/friendships.
> - Teaching adolescents pro-civic behaviors and values.
> - Facilitating engagement in prosocial groups in civic and/or religious contexts.

FIGURE 10–3. The Behaviors of Parents of Adolescents.

limits, discover areas of ability and weakness, and make mistakes while learning many skills and problem-solving strategies (Kisner, 2011). The boundaries between the self and the parents become more distinct, while the boundaries between the individual and the peer group begin to blur in early adolescence. Allegiance once felt toward the parents shifts to the peers. This change creates tension between an adolescent and the family system. Peer pressure to conform to established or imagined standards is high. Acceptance and validation from others bolster self-confidence,

while rejection elicits strong feelings of alienation (Silk et al., 2012).

By late adolescence, changes in cognitive abilities occur. Peer opinions augment an adolescent's beliefs, attitudes, and perceptions of the self. These result in crystallization of personal identity as boundaries are drawn between the self and the social group. Experiences within the family, school, and social systems bring adolescents into their own as individuals. "Who am I" and "where will I go with my life" are existential questions that seem to preoccupy teens. The sense of identity that emerges from adolescent experiences is a foundational attitude that young adults retain throughout their lifespan. Young adults continue to acquire, develop, and refine other roles, as well as develop an understanding about the self, which becomes integrated into their basic personal identity during the years of adulthood.

Promoting Individuation. The experiences of adolescence are a struggle toward the eventual emancipation of a teenager from the family of origin. The process leading to emancipation, or **individuation**, is part of the identity formation that is central to adolescent development. Although this process begins in adolescence, it may not be completed until later in adulthood. Some individuals never completely achieve the degree of emancipation or individuation they truly desire or that is expected of them by society. Becoming an individual who develops a personal belief system to guide decisions and behaviors, acquires financial independence, and assumes emotional self-care is a complex challenge.

Often a teen's advancement toward emancipation includes working at full- or part-time jobs. Making social decisions, such as choosing one's friends and dating, also helps teenagers take greater developmental steps toward maturity and personal autonomy.

Supporting Cognitive Changes. During adolescence, important changes take place in an individual's cognitive abilities. Thinking and comprehension during early and middle childhood are governed by perceptions. Children use their perceptions of the environment to develop hypotheses about their world and create a concrete understanding. In adolescence, an individual's understanding of people, events, and circumstances becomes more flexible, and abstract reasoning becomes possible.

Cognitive processes during this time become increasingly abstract, characterized by scientific reasoning. The emergence of true deductive reasoning gives

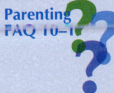

My teen has become secretive, seems to have a constant shortage of money, and is looking to his peer group as role models. I am most concerned about substance abuse. What now?

This is tough for any parent, and the threat of substance abuse is a serious situation that rings alarm bells; serious enough to immediately involve professional consultation. Secretiveness and excessive financial demands are warning signs because the child is clearly trying to hide something from the parent, or having unusual expenses. Encourage your teen to socialize with peers in situations and places where you can more closely observe, such as in your own home. His peers may seem to be the overriding influence socially, especially during adolescence. Encourage him to invite his friends home, and in turn create a home environment that is welcoming. There are many factors that influence your child's social development. Civic engagement can foster resilience. You and your family have a history with this child that is not discarded, despite his contact with his peers. Find ways to spend time with your teen and talk about your concerns; follow up on your hunches. If you suspect that your child is becoming involved in dangerous activities with his friends, you should access professional help immediately. Many a young life has been lost because drugs were involved.

the teen the ability to generate hypotheses and logically work toward an acceptable conclusion. Experimentation helps adolescents rehearse this type of thinking. Scientific reasoning gives rise to an increasing flexibility in thought. This requires divorcing oneself from reality and playfully considering various possibilities. For example, it is common for an adolescent to play the role of devil's advocate in discussions on moral issues. Teens who are developing advanced cognitive skills apply these to a variety of problems, including moral decisions, understanding the actions and words of others, and developing a basic belief or value system to guide their own behavior. An advanced, flexible thinking style can emerge.

Cognitive Egocentrism. As in middle childhood, cognitive egocentrism can distort or hinder mature thinking. In adolescence, egocentrism can manifest itself in these ways, although many adolescents are remarkably mature in their thinking and reasoning:

■ *Exaggeration and dramatization.* This tendency to interpret something in more complex ways than is necessary or intended is "making a mountain out of a molehill" thinking that can persist as a habitual way of reacting to problems and the behavior of others. This can precipitate disproportionate emotional reactions.
■ *Imaginary audience.* Adolescents typically believe that they are the center of everyone's attention and that every move they make is under the scrutiny of an imaginary audience. This contributes to self-consciousness about appearance, what they say, and with whom they

are seen (Galanaki, 2012). It contains strong elements of egocentrism.

■ *Incongruence.* Teenagers show a certain degree of apparent hypocrisy, meaning that there is incongruence between what they say they believe and how they act. Congruence refers to "realness" and "authenticity." This may be observed in arguments with adults, especially parents. Teens can be very critical of parental insensitivity, but may be oblivious of the other person's feelings, which could include parents. These types of behaviors contain elements of egocentrism as well.
■ *Personal invincibility.* Adolescents typically fall under the spell of a belief in their personal invincibility. They think that bad things happen only to other people and that they are protected or exempt from harm or injury when they take chances with risky behaviors. This cognitive flaw perhaps explains why some adolescents undertake risky experimentation with drugs, sexual activity, and reckless driving. Cognitive neuroscience indicates that the adolescent brain is not yet fully mature, which explains some of the irresponsible behavior and the sense of invincibility (Blakemore & Robbins, 2012).

Puberty is a central developmental milestone of adolescence. Puberty refers to the physical maturation process occurring during adolescence. In this developmental event, a child becomes a sexually mature individual with the possibility of being able to reproduce sexually. Although puberty is a physical process pertaining to the growth of the body, it is accompanied by psychological aspects. The psychological dimension influences the identity formation process. Because adolescents are not yet emotionally mature, the feelings that accompany the physical changes of puberty can be confusing and conflicting (Goddings, Burnett Heyes, Bird, Viner, & Blakemore, 2012). Many parents are unsure about how to help their adolescent child handle the various aspects of puberty. It is important for a parent to maintain open lines of communication so that issues can be discussed openly and honestly.

••

Focus Point. Parents must walk the fine line of promoting the increasing autonomy of their adolescent and providing helpful guidelines that foster health and safety. By modeling appropriate behaviors, warning against unhealthy habits, and teaching values and morals, parents prepare these young people to thrive in the world of adulthood. Civic engagement can also promote resilience.

••

RELATIONSHIPS AND SEXUALITY

Adolescent romance is important as it represents part of the ongoing developmental tasks, and can be influenced by factors in the family of origin (Underwood & Rosen, 2011). Dating is frequently the first interpersonal social experience that also addresses sexuality. Teens typically socialize in informal ways. Much of this socialization is in the context of a peer group rather than as individuals. The age at which adolescents begin to date is a significant predictor of the age at which sexual activity is initiated. Adolescent romances are foundational in adult union formation (Madsen & Collins, 2011). Dating practices vary culturally. Predictors of early sexual involvement include opportunity (being in a steady relationship), sexually permissive attitudes, lack of adult guidance and supervision, and alcohol use (Hipwell, Keenan, Loeber, & Battista, 2010).

Many teenagers are sexually active at younger ages than most adults imagine, and early sexual activity occurs more frequently amongst girls. As both groups mature, the figures for both genders level out. Instead of promiscuity, most adolescents become intensely involved with one person over a period of time and the relationship includes sexual intimacy. About one fourth of all teenage girls have had intercourse by age 15, and two thirds have had intercourse by age 19 (Martinez & Abma, 2015). These estimates contrast with the figures for teenage boys. By age 15, fewer boys than girls of that age have had intercourse. By age 19, both genders were more or less tied when it came to the numbers having participated in intercourse. Sexual activity becomes increasingly common with age during this period of life (Guttmacher Institute, 2016a).

Relationship and Sex Education for Teens

Because puberty has made them capable of reproduction, sexuality is no longer an abstract idea (Fortenberry, 2013). Exploration and experimentation during adolescence are behavioral components that support identity formation. Compounding the need for sex education is the fact that teens do not think logically about hypothetical concerns (Vivancos, Abubakar, Phillips-Howard, & Hunter, 2013). Sexual choices involve some of the same abstract decision-making skills. Teens may obtain information in sex education courses. Some adults fear that if teens are given information about sexual behavior or methods of birth control, they will become more curious, which may encourage sexual activity; but in reality, the research does not support this response (Stanger-Hall & Hall, 2011). Exposure to sexual information may delay the age at which adolescents become sexually active and support safer decisions (Campero, Walker, Atienzo, & Gutierrez, 2011).

Parents are an important link in providing teens with the skills to make healthy sexual decisions by creating trusting relationships and modeling responsible behavior. For some parents, this means helping their teen understand the reasons for sexual abstinence. For other parents, it means being sure that their adolescent understands the importance of safer sex practices. Each family system needs to determine how it will deal with this aspect of an adolescent child's identity development.

In a study on first exposure to explicit sexual images, the researchers found that young adults in a human sexuality class recalled that their first early exposure to these types of images typically happened unsupervised, and with visual material that was available in the parental home. More alarming was how young the children were. On average the events occurred when they were elementary school age (Allen & Lavender-Stott, 2015). This in itself is a lesson for parents. Be careful concerning unrestricted internet access, and preempt these occurrences by having age appropriate conversations about things in the big wide world that could be shocking or harmful to children. Make your own home a safe zone and have discussions about cyber safety. It hardly needs to be said that pornography has no place in a child friendly environment. In fact, creating an environment that allows for inadvertent exposure to inappropriate material amounts to neglectful and harmful parenting.

Relationship and Sex Education (RSE).   What's in a name? It is preferable to discuss sexuality within the context of relationships. Hence, current trends focus on: "Relationship and Sex Education" (RSE) to acknowledge the bigger picture (Arnab et al., 2013). This also allows for discussion of the implications and responsibilities of sexual partnering. Parents of contemporary adolescents need to be updated on the sexual information they should discuss with their teen children.

Equally important is the balancing of information that is strictly factual with that which addresses the emotional and values-related aspects of sexuality. Teens need support as they explore their first romantic encounters as these encounters deal with so much more than a mere expression of sexuality. They reflect values, societal and cultural norms. Additionally, the respect with which a romantic partner is treated while also considering the partner's wishes and concerns, are important aspects of preventing dating violence.

Adolescents from unstable home environments where parental role models might be absent or less than optimal may be influenced by their family of origin with regard to romantic relationships (Latack & Davila, 2016). Appropriate and formal relationship and sex education may support later outcomes of healthier partnering choices, including responsible sexual choices.

Sexually Transmitted Infections (STIs)

Sexually Transmitted Infections (STIs) are also known as Sexually Transmitted Diseases (STDs). The abbreviation STD is in common use and a matter of preference. The tendency toward using the STI term is because it may have less stigma, and because many of these conditions may appear to be silent and not always present with what is commonly associated with a disease. "The word *disease*

implies that a person has a set of distinctive, identifiable symptoms, and most of the time, sexually transmitted infections do not present any symptoms," (Deal, 2017, Sexually transmitted diseases branch of the National Institutes of Health's National Institute of Allergy and Infectious Diseases). Nevertheless, the abbreviation STD commonly appears in much of the literature, and on websites, including the 2017 version of the website of the Centers for Disease Control (CDC.gov).

The high frequency of unprotected sexual encounters and multiple sex partners result in equally alarming rates of STIs among adolescents. Adolescents represent about 25 percent of all sexually active individuals. Almost one-half of all new STIs reported are contracted among those between 15 and 24 years of age (Centers for Disease Control and Prevention, 2010). The high incidence results from *cognitive factors* such as lack of information, ignorance, denial, and a misplaced sense of personal invincibility, as in "that won't happen to me." *Social factors*, such as coercion and peer pressure, are a reality. Lack of planning and inappropriate shame associated with safer sexual practices play contributory roles.

A growing number of high schools have school-based health clinics that provide sex education, STI screening and treatment, and in some cases condoms. The increased use of condoms may reflect the influence of more effective sex education programs that provide factual information, especially regarding the transmission of HIV. A vaccine protecting against some types of the human papilloma virus (HTP) is an option for both male and female adolescents (Holman et al., 2014). Abstinence or responsible sexual practices, including condom use, contribute to safer outcomes. Importantly, an informed teen can make better informed choices concerning their own health and well-being, and that includes sexual choices.

Dating Coercion and Violence

Increasingly high school campuses and college environments have focused on the prevention of interpersonal *coercion* and *violence*, especially in dating contexts (DeGue et al., 2014; Vagi et al., 2013). Sexual expression should be mutually respectful, and, importantly, with mutual *consent*. If a partner says "No" that means "No," and the decision should be respected (New York State, 2017). Coercion and power inequalities in sexual relationships pave the way toward intimate partner violence and rape. Most schools and colleges have adopted a "no tolerance" policy, and young people need to be fully aware of what this means in practice and what their responsibilities are.

Young women especially need to know that they have the *right* to decline a sexual encounter and deserve support in their decisions. Young men need to understand that they need to respect the sexual decisions of their partner and that non-consensual sexual activity can amount to rape. Some high-profile court cases of youngsters involved in coercion and bullying of partners into sexual compliance, have signaled that there is no place for such harmful and humiliating behavior in our current society (Katz & Tirone, 2010). According to the Rape, Abuse and Incest National Network (RAINN) (n.d.), these activities are punishable by law.

Teenage Contraceptive Use

Teens who want to adopt mature roles that include sexuality, also need to have the maturity to be able to talk about values, the advantages of abstinence, sexual consent, and safer sexual practices with their partners. Embarrassment is misplaced and counterproductive. Contraception use is an admission of sexual activity and reflects the understanding of consequences, such as pregnancy and disease (Lawrence, Rasinski, Yoon, & Curlin, 2011). Seeking and obtaining contraception is a social, economic, and psychological responsibility that outweighs the risks and costs of an unplanned pregnancy. The personal attitudes of adolescents play an important role in influencing their use, or nonuse of contraceptives (Ott, Sucato, & Committee on Adolescence, 2014).

Teenagers may be influenced in their sexual activity and use of contraception by a variety of *cognitive* distortions and beliefs about their ability to become pregnant. These distortions relate to a flaw in cognitive processing at this life stage called the *personal fable*. They may not use contraception because of the erroneous, irrational belief that only other people become pregnant whereas they are invulnerable (Bay-Cheng, Livingston, & Fava, 2011). Perceiving oneself as being sexually active, and having the cognitive and psychological maturity to acknowledge this, influences the use of birth control. If teens are able to delay becoming sexually active until later adolescence, they are more likely to use contraception as they have developed the skills that promote effective sexual decision making.

Adolescents from low-income family systems may have feelings of fatalism, depression, and apathy.

These attitudes work against the effective use of contraception (Hall, Moreau, Trussell, & Barber, 2013). If teenagers from disadvantaged backgrounds can be assisted in continuing their education and schooling, their chances of using contraception also improve, as both behaviors display aspects of responsible behavior. Families can influence the use of contraception by providing or failing to provide information concerning sexual choices in their ongoing conversations with their children. Parents' openness to communicate and their support of safer sexual decision making tends to increase adolescents' use of contraception. When parents do not communicate with adolescents about sexual activity and pregnancy, peers provide information and are influential (Silk & Romero, 2014). When peers approve of the use of contraception, teenagers appear to be influenced by their peers as well. When teenagers who are sexually active have access to family-planning services and information regarding sexual choices, either in their schools or their communities, there is a greater likelihood of preventing pregnancy and STDs (Brakman & Gold, 2015; Koh, 2014). School sex education programs can promote safer and more informed choices concerning health and sexuality (Brakman & Gold, 2015).

Gender Roles and Sexual Orientation

During adolescence, gender roles become more clearly established. Sexual orientation serves as the foundation of **sexual identity**. **Sexual orientation** is influenced by interacting genetic, biological, and environmental factors beginning prenatally. As a society, we have become more understanding of the continuum on which sexual identity may be expressed, and our social values have adjusted accordingly. Adolescents who identify themselves as LGBT or who express **gender dysphoria**, require the same emotional acceptance and support offered to any adolescent in search of their identity (Drescher & Byne, 2012). Likewise, adolescents who identify as LGBT should be afforded equivalent types of social experiences available to heterosexual teens.

As is the case for most humans, young adolescents are similarly concerned about peer acceptance and tend to relate to a supportive peer group (Kingery, Erdley, & Marshall, 2011). Family rejection is regarded as one of the most harmful risk factors for LGBT young adults and young people expressing gender dysphoria (Snapp et al., 2015). Encouraging though, is that family, friend, and peer group support can be tremendously influential and can be identified as a predictor to positive outcomes and a protective factor.

Of all the forms of support, the *strongest* overall influence is exerted by *family acceptance* (Snapp et al., 2015). There is a very important lesson in this; the home and the family are the closest layers of love and support enveloping an emerging adult. As parents, we need to get it right and create an environment of unconditional acceptance of our children, including their sexual orientation. Ultimately, with individual and societal support, a fully integrated personal identity and related positive life outcomes should be the desired outcome for all adolescents, irrespective of their gender identity.

Video Example 10.2

Watch this video advice for parents on teens, relationships, and sex. Name some ways in which appropriate "Relationship and Sex Education" (RSE) can prepare teenagers for constructive relationship choices, specifically healthy sexual relationship choices.

(https://www.youtube.com/watch?v=_8c1_6KLUI0)

Parenting Reflection 10-3

The transmission of HIV and other STIs has affected the long-running debate on what public schools should teach in relationship and sex education (RSE) courses and what material is appropriate for which age group. Both parents and schools can play important roles in providing information pertaining to healthy lifestyle choices, including sexual matters. As a parent of a teenager, what relationship and sex education approach would you welcome?

Focus Point.   The current trend is to refer to this area as "Relationship and Sex Education" (RSE), acknowledging the context of sexuality. Developing a sexual identity is a key milestone in the path toward adulthood. The communication lines between teens and parents should remain open as these young adults navigate the world of dating, romance, and sexuality. Parents and schools can foster an environment in which healthy and mature choices are made based on correct information. Educating teens on relationships and sexual expression, including contraceptive use, STIs, and unintended pregnancy, is a responsibility to promote informed choices concerning sexual health.

Cathy Yeulet/123RF.com

Because the peer group plays a special role in the process of personal identity formation among adolescents, parents of adolescents may provide appropriate structure and nurture by supporting peer-group relationships and friendships with other adolescents with common interests.

PARENTING EMERGING ADULTS

We recognize a portion of early adulthood as **emerging adulthood.** This stage was first described by developmental psychologist Jeffrey Jensen Arnett (Arnett, 2000). Much of his research was carried out in collaboration with his partner Lene Arnett Jensen. In writing essentially about college-aged individuals, Arnett believed that a new developmental period in Western societies occurred between adolescence and adulthood, roughly the time between ages 18 and 25. During this advanced transition stage, individuals experience five defining characteristics: (a) exploring one's identity, (b) encountering feelings of instability, (c) focusing on one's self, (d) feeling emotionally in between adolescence and adulthood, and (e) experiencing a range of life's possibilities. Many of the traditional hallmarks that formerly defined one's entrance into adulthood have been altered. The age of first marriage has risen, often following the completion of one's education or military service. More young adults focus on exploring what life has to offer, for an extended period of time, sometimes called a "gap year" (O'Shea, 2011).

Arnett Jensen (2010) questions the generally negative view often held by older adults regarding the character of young people and attributes these negative views to four factors:

- Later entrance into adult roles is misinterpreted by older adults as selfishness.
- Exploration of identity during emerging adulthood is misinterpreted as self-indulgence.
- Young adults who seek identity-based work are seen by older adults as being less motivated.
- Elders interpret the high hopes of young adults regarding their lives as grandiosity.

While Arnett believes that many young adults do hold high hopes for themselves, most adjust these dreams to fit with reality by the time they reach their 30s. Emerging adulthood is an important transition phase that is characterized by the later age of finding a life partner and first marriage, widespread postsecondary education, and the search for satisfying work (Arnett, 2000).

Prolonged Parental Dependency

By the time a child has reached early adulthood (ages 18 to 45), the day-to-day involvement of a parent ceases, but parenthood does not come to a complete halt on the child's 18th birthday or when reaching legal age. The transformation of the relationship between parent and child has been taking place all along, in sync with the developmental changes occurring over time. The parenting relationship continues in an altered form. When children approach adulthood, the overall goal of guiding them toward autonomy should have been accomplished. Dependencies continue in modified form, and there is some degree of similarity in all intimate relationships among adults in the family; the relationship transforms from one originally based on power and responsibility toward one of shared balanced interactions defined by adult characteristics.

Most adult children experience the first years of adulthood as a transition period while they complete the final aspects of individuation from their family systems; hence the reason why the term *emerging adulthood* is so appropriate. Many are not yet married and have not been employed long enough to build a sound financial base or establish themselves in occupations that ensure an optimistic financial future. Parents continue to provide support and often financial assistance to young adult children. When young adult children temporarily return to live in the family home (boomerang children) the structure is shifted to a renested family system.

Parents are sometimes unsure about how to communicate with adult children who are partially dependent yet also independent adults. They continue to give advice to their adult children, who may or may not find this helpful. Adult children face similar conflicting emotions; they may want to confide in parents, but also feel hesitant if advice is intrusive or judgmental.

Essentially, most healthy parents want their child-rearing responsibilities to end at some point. Some parents continue to remain actively involved in a care-giving role. Parents ideally shift away from authoritarian styles to more democratic and egalitarian approaches. Egalitarian parenting styles support a child's individuation by shifting the source of social power to a more balanced position between the parent and the child.

Failure to Launch.

Unhealthy prolonged dependency can take place in some relationships. Parents can maintain this state of dependency by providing financial and emotional support that exceeds normal expectations. Sometimes situations beyond the control of the family system maintain these ties. For example, higher education is extremely costly, and young adults may seek assistance from their parents to meet financial obligations. Other situations can also prolong dependency, such as overparenting that promotes dependencies.

Some parents foster extended dependency of adult children by remaining overinvolved. They may have showered the child with material possessions yet the relationship lacked structure and boundaries. They may not have encouraged individuation (Scabini & Manzi, 2011) which should have led to a redefined, more adult relationship between parents and adult child. Prolonged dependency is not created and maintained only by the parents. A child can also play a part in maintaining a prolonged dependency role, for fear of assuming responsibility and making decisions. Additionally, depression, addictions, and related disorders can be influencing factors (Kloep & Hendry, 2010).

Parents may be partially responsible for creating the dependency of adult children. Boundaries can be adapted to reflect less involvement in the affairs of adult children and making a conscious and demonstrable change toward a more egalitarian stance (Kloep & Hendry, 2010). Another approach is to set a deadline for certain tasks to be accomplished, such as finding a job, moving into different quarters, and taking greater responsibility. When young adults struggle to achieve individuation from dysfunctional parents and family systems, they can find therapeutic assistance. In this case, the adult child, not the parent, struggles to let go of dependencies and inappropriate patterns. At times, adult children make aggressive attempts to individuate from unhealthy parents. When one person in an unhealthy family system attempts to make changes, the system often reacts to the loss of equilibrium by becoming even more chaotic. In some families, emotional factors stifle development, and children are never truly launched into adulthood.

The term "adult children" can also refer to adults who maintain certain aspects of the dependency of childhood, sometimes simply because circumstances dictate it. For instance, a child with Down syndrome, or a child with a serious disability, may require support throughout the lifespan.

Parenting FAQ 10–2

I boomeranged home and am job hunting. I'm having a hard time with my parents. They're trying to enforce rules as if I were a teen . . . which I'm not.

Persevere in being willing to work on this new relationship as everyone involved must learn to forge new roles, new rules, and new boundaries. Here are some additional thoughts to consider:

- Be willing to contribute to the work of the household in as many ways as possible, especially if you can't contribute financially. Show by your actions that you are trustworthy and mature.
- Talk rationally and keep a level head when you are discussing how you want to see this new relationship operate.
- Be willing to listen and contribute to the new relationship.
- Be willing to negotiate new rules and boundaries for your behavior that are acceptable to all involved.
- Suggest that new rules and boundaries be tested first, and then be willing to renegotiate any rule or boundary that doesn't seem to be working.

Parenting Reflection 10–4

What happens when a family system does not accept or support the efforts of young adults to individuate completely from the family of origin? What are the short- and long-term effects of such prolonged dependence among family members?

Parenting Reflection 10–5

Generations from different periods can be identified by what defines them as a group. For instance, "baby boomers" were all born after World War II. Members of generation "X" were born after the baby boomers (1960–1970). A stereotype is formed concerning the commonalities of people born in the same decade. Thinking of your own generation, what sociological and other influences characterized your relationship with your own parents in your family of origin, and what influences do you expect will influence the relationships with your own children?

Focus Point. Emerging adults require an extended period for education and career preparation. They may be somewhat financially independent, while also being reliant on parents. Emerging adult children who fail to transform and mature, may put the relationship with their parents in limbo. Restructuring this relationship, while acknowledging appropriate developmental outcomes, can be beneficial to all. Both parents and adult children contribute to the outcomes.

Guest Reflection 10–1

Things That Make Adolescents Thrive

I had seen Brian, 14, for a few visits about a routine matter, so I didn't know him well. Months later, his father, a man in his late 30s, called to tell me that he was dying of cancer and asked me if I would see his son again. The father died the morning after that call. I had hoped to have some visits with his son while the father was ill but instead found Brian in my office just two days after his father's death.

On arrival, Brian looked understandably tense and was barely holding back tears. I was not prepared when he sat in my office and unloaded his rage on me. Understand: He wasn't screaming about his father. He was screaming about me.

He yelled at me about how stupid it was that his mother made him come and how dumb I was and how pointless it all was. When he was done I told him I was wrong to agree to see him so quickly. I said I should have known better, because young people want to be with their friends after someone close to them dies and they hardly want to talk to an adult they barely know. I apologized. I told him I was shocked and sorry his father died. Brian's anger dissipated and the tears of rage turned into tears of loss.

Then, instead of reflecting back his feelings, or asking a probing question, or waiting him out silently—all of the things I was trained to do—I asked him if he wanted to just blow off the session and play cards. By the end of the session, he was laughing with me about strange turns of the cards. Some sessions later, we talked about his sorrow and grief.

There are things that help adolescents thrive and they aren't much different from what helps any of us thrive. Among those is respect. Teenagers do not get much respect. Our culture fears them. We embrace myths about them and talk about "teenagers today" as if they are all the same. We abuse the research on "the teenage brain," by telling teens they are incapable of making sound decisions until they reach the magic age of 25. We believe they are all mentally unbalanced and that their hormones, always "raging," will suddenly overtake them and cause family mayhem.

If you want to work with adolescents, I offer this. Bring your authentic self to each encounter. Treat teenagers with the respect due any fellow human being. Recognize that they make good decisions most of the time and that, when they make bad decisions, it is not so much because they are adolescents as because they are human beings. Presume they intend well and are more capable than our prejudices lead us to believe. From that frame, working with adolescents can be immensely rewarding.

Dale Wisely, Ph.D. has been a child and adolescent clinical psychologist for over three decades. Used with permission.

ADOLESCENTS AS PARENTS

Adolescence is a transitional period between childhood and adulthood that facilitates extended, tentative exploration of adult roles and culminates in emerging adulthood. If this exploration leads to adult responsibilities in the form of parenthood, the consequences may be overwhelming. An adolescent who is still searching for a niche in the world of employment, education, relationships, and other complex societal demands can be extremely challenged if the responsibility of an infant is added to this formula. Frequently, something gives way, and the loss may be in terms of further education and career preparation. A support network, including possible coparents and grandparents, is crucial to help adolescents become the best parents they can be.

Teen Pregnancy

Pregnancy among adolescents has been described as a problem with short- and long-term consequences for the adolescent parents, their child, and their families of origin. Teen pregnancies have declined, and this good outcome is attributable to better sex education and surprisingly reality television shows that depict teenage parents (Kearney & Levine, 2015). Adolescents learn from these peer models in the television shows, and the challenges of raising a baby while also being economically fragile are not romantic or worth emulating.

Most pregnancies among teenagers occur because of a failure to use contraception. The explanations are related to the meanings that adolescents attach to the use of contraception. Teen pregnancy continues to be a matter of concern for society, schools, adolescents, and their families and is accompanied by many short- and long-term consequences (Federal Interagency Forum on Child and Family Statistics, 2011).

Incidence, Causes, and Outcomes of Teenage Pregnancy.   There are consequences when teenagers assume a parental role (Assini-Meytin & Green, 2015). According to the Committee on Adolescence and the Committee on Early Childhood there are short- and long-term considerations regarding parenthood for teenagers (Pinzon & Jones, 2012).

The rate of adolescent pregnancy, as well as related teenage marriages, has declined and has reached a current low point (see Figure 10-4). As of 2014, the birth rate for women aged 15–19 years was about 24 per 1,000 women in this age group. The general lower teenage pregnancy rates may be attributed to several factors (Centers for Disease Control and Prevention, 2017b):

■ Increased participation in programs that emphasize responsible sexual decision making.
■ Postponement of sexual activity in teenage girls.
■ Wider use of contraceptives among sexually active teens.

Families are more supportive of pregnant teenagers by providing emotional, financial, and physical assistance, especially their own mothers and grandparents who care for the baby, fully integrating the child into the family. A variety of community programs assist both expectant teenagers and those who have become parents. Some programs offer teens the opportunity to continue their education with as few disruptions as possible.

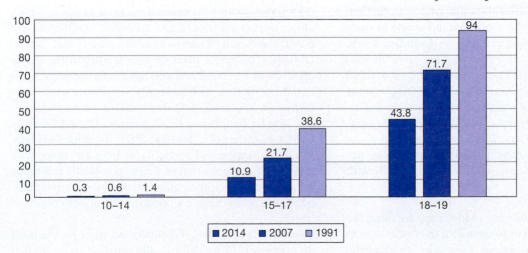

FIGURE 10–4.
Birth Rates for Women Aged 10-19, by Age of Mother, 1991, 2007, and 2014.
Source: National Vital Statistics Reports, Vol. 65, No. 3, June 2, 2016, CDC.

Halfpoint/Shutterstock

Families can support adolescent pregnancies by providing emotional, financial, and physical assistance. Once the child is born, fully integrating the child into the family through care from both parents and grandparents can help to ensure a smooth transition.

Marriage and Family Relations. Adolescent pregnancy hastens early marriage, but this option is not necessarily an optimal solution. Teenage marriages are likely to be high risk, unstable, and prone to end in divorce (Dahl, 2010; Molina Cartes & González Araya, 2012). When the teen father is involved in the pregnancy and is active in parenting following childbirth, then a stable relationship is more likely (Lewin, Mitchell, Burrell, Beers, & Duggan, 2011). Most frequently, the decision not to marry but to continue the pregnancy is influenced by a teenage girl's mother and the baby's father.

Regardless of whether teens marry or not, this group tends to encounter the poorest socioeconomic outcomes. Marriage does not significantly improve their situation; to the contrary it may be high risk and prone to early divorce (Dahl, 2010; Molina Cartes & González Araya, 2012). Teenagers who are unmarried are more likely to receive welfare benefits. The decision not to marry and to carry a pregnancy to term implies that teenagers must rely on their families of origin for assistance. In reality, unmarried teens receive less assistance from their families than those who marry. Public assistance can be an essential resource. It may be helpful to consult an agency or health care professional who deals specifically with these matters.

Educational Implications. More than anything the new parents need support to complete their education to ensure improved future options. Pregnancy appears to be

the most common reason why adolescent girls drop out of school (Kane, Philip Morgan, Harris, & Guilkey, 2013). The younger the mother, the less likely she is to return to school following the birth of her baby. Some school systems support continued education. Special programs, such as *Even Start* by the U.S. Department of Education, promote the continuation of schooling by providing child care during school hours and teaching parenting and family life skills, as well as assisting in vocational development. School attendance can be encouraged when teen mothers prioritize their educational goals and remain in school to complete their education (Hudgins, Erickson, & Walker, 2014; Kane et al., 2013). In addition, the teen parents are required to participate in parenting education and interactive literacy activities involving parent and child. (www2.ed.gov/programs/evenstartformula/index.html).

Work and Economic Consequences. When teenage parents drop out of school because of pregnancy, their future is jeopardized. Being able to provide adequate incomes for themselves and their children becomes virtually impossible. The income of adolescent mothers is about one half that of mothers who have their first child in early adulthood (U.S. Census Bureau, 2016). In the long run, teenage parents can expect to hold low-paying, low-level jobs in which little satisfaction or economic gain is evident.

Health Considerations. Early studies of adolescent pregnancy reported many adverse physical complications for the young mother which tend to be directly linked to lack of prenatal care, often because the mother is secretive about the pregnancy (Lee & Grubbs, 1995). Other factors contributing to increased health risks are poverty and lack of access to health care (Pilon, 2011). Obtaining adequate prenatal care is likely if the girl is open about her condition and has family support. Inadequate nutrition also presents significant problems (Whisner, Bruening, & O'Brien, 2016).

Mental health can be negatively affected by early childbearing (Siegel & Brandon, 2014). Teen mothers have less social support and personal resources for coping with stress. The accumulation of major, potentially traumatic events could precipitate other mental health conditions. Substance abuse further jeopardizes the unborn child.

Historic Research. The historical work by Vladimir de Lissovoy (1973a, 1973b) is illuminating, as he studied

Focus On 10–2   Contributing Causes of Teenage Pregnancy

Most adolescent girls become pregnant because no birth control was used. For some, the pregnancy is the result of rape. The basic reasons why teenagers become pregnant include:

- Increased frequency of sexual intercourse at earlier ages.
- Increased social acceptance of teen pregnancy.
- Lack of adequate knowledge of contraceptives and non-use by sexually active teenagers.
- Personal attitudes about sexuality, pregnancy, and parenthood.
- Serious emotional problems, lack of adequate social adjustment, isolation, loneliness, and low self-esteem.
- Embarrassment about sexual matters; reluctance to obtain information about contraception.
- Religious beliefs associated with guilt, enhancing a reluctance to be informed about sexual matters.
- Eagerness to participate in sexual activity, impulsivity, and peer pressure.
- Feelings of resentment and anger toward a parent, which can facilitate a desire to punish the parent.
- A desire to prove one's masculinity or femininity, and adult social status.
- An attempt to create a captive love or to "trap" a mate.
- Perceiving a baby as a substitute for parental, partner, or marital love.
- Behavioral problems, e.g. conduct disorders, delinquency, criminal activity, acting-out behavior, substance abuse.
- Certain social background markers, e.g. single-parent family of origin, level of parental education, early sexual activity by a parent or older siblings, low parental supervision, and low educational involvement.
- Adolescents' cognitive and emotional development usually lags behind physical development. For example, cognitive distortion may give them a sense of invulnerability.
- The family of origin is influential in shaping a teenager's attitudes about sexual activity, as it models behaviors that influence the adolescent's choices concerning sexual behavior.
- Peer influences may affect a teen's sexual involvement. Many feel a great deal of social pressure to become sexually active, especially girls, who may be particularly susceptible to coercion by males.
- Sociocultural factors, such as religious participation, ethnic background, or the family of origin's socio-economic status, may influence the probability of a teen's participation in sexual activity.

adolescent parents in depth during the seventies. His work is better understood in the context of the time during which he completed his research. Since then, social attitudes have shifted, and access to information concerning childcare has become easier. In de Lissovoy's research, both adolescent mothers and fathers were questioned shortly after the birth of their baby regarding their knowledge of the developmental norms and growth of infants. This research found that teenagers were grossly ignorant about when to expect certain developmental events during infancy, a fact that had broad implications regarding the ability of these young parents to provide quality, nurturing caregiving for infants and children. For example, teenage parents indicated that toilet training should begin at 24 weeks (6

months) of age and that teaching infants about obedience to parental direction should begin at either 26 weeks or 36 weeks. The need for correct information and child care training is important, including for the fathers. In contrast to the time when this research was done, current teen parents have greater access to information. Nevertheless, teen parents may require guidance to access appropriate parenting material.

Adolescents and Parenting.   Adolescent parents typically demonstrate a range of nurturing, caregiving behaviors toward children (East & Felice, 2014). Some immature and self-centered parenting styles may occur if the teen parent is emotionally immature. Other works suggest that, rather than being at immediate risk of abuse

Parenting FAQ 10–3

Our 16-year-old daughter recently revealed that she is pregnant. We worry that she will not continue her education and that she is too young for this responsibility. We like the boy who's the father. What do we need to know?

Most teenage parents choose to raise their children and tend not to choose adoption as an alternative family plan. In some cases, the fathers or grandparents request custody if that is in the best interests of the child. In open adoptions, the birth mother can remain in contact with the adoptive parents and can participate in some aspects of the child's life, even though her parental rights are limited. The rights of the biological father are determined by his legal status in the child's life, for instance whether his name appears on the birth certificate, or whether he is married to the mother of his child. Whatever avenue the family decide to follow, it is important that they support each other, and seek out professional guidance.   This family challenge is constructively handled if resources are pooled in the best interests of the new arrival and those who carry her well being at heart.

and neglect because of parental ignorance, children of teenage parents may experience some developmental delays because they have not been engaged in ongoing constructive and teaching/learning oriented interactions with the caretaking parent (A. L. Brown 2015; Mollborn, Lawrence, James-Hawkins, & Fomby, 2014). Social class may produce differences in children's development manifested via maternal knowledge, attitudes, and behaviors that determine the quality of the parenting experience. Parenting knowledge can be gained through participation in special education programs. When teen mothers have the support and involvement of grandmothers in providing care for their infants, their parenting competence appears to improve considerably (Reid, Schmied, & Beale, 2010). The less positive outlook can be reflected in adolescent mothers' perceptions of their infants as being more difficult, and this in turn can contribute to a negative self-concept in the child.

Adolescent Fathers

Adolescent fathers have not received the same degree of attention from researchers as young mothers (Bellamy & Banman, 2014; Kiselica & Kiselica, 2014). Studies examine personality characteristics, a father's involvement during a girl's pregnancy and after the child's birth, his role in pregnancy resolution decisions, his problems, and social outcomes associated with becoming an adolescent father (Bastos Silva et al., 2014; Santos Souza, Magalhães Silva, Rodrigues da Mata, & Oliveira Amaral, 2016).

Although most adolescent girls who become mothers choose to retain custody of their baby and do not marry, young fathers increasingly acknowledge their role in the pregnancy. The quality of a teen father's relationship with the mother of their child prior to their child's birth appears to positively influence the coparenting following the birth (Fagan, 2014). Once children are born, the majority of young fathers have contact with their child and the mother. In addition, the extent, nature, and context of the teen fathers' involvement with his child may be highly dependent on the mother's support and expectations.

Adolescent fathers who have been involved in an intimate relationship with their child's mother for a long time frequently continue this relationship after the child's birth. Although many young men state that they love the mother, the relationship is often characterized by a lack of commitment and little promise for continuation into the future (Lewin, Mitchell, Burrell, Beers, & Duggan, 2011; Mallette, Futris, Brown, & Oshri, 2015). The grandfather's support and his example as a role model may increase the likelihood of a young teen father's involvement with his child.

Some adolescent fathers may be uncaring, uninvolved, and immature, partly because they lack clarity concerning their role as the father, or are too immature to take on the responsibility. Some teen fathers make a remarkable transformation to becoming committed coparents to their child. In addition, they develop an ability to empathize with their coparenting partner.

A variety of social and educational programs have been developed to help teenage fathers address the changes in their lives when they become parents (Kiselica & Kiselica, 2014).

While not all teen males who experience these kinds of circumstances become fathers, the combined and interactive pressures put them at high risk. The following factors and social conditions can increase the likelihood for early fatherhood:

- Having parents who assumed the parenthood role early in life.
- Having parents with little formal education or educational disadvantage for the young man.
- Behaving in a delinquent or deviant manner (e.g., a history of arrest, gang involvement, having spent time in detention, living in a juvenile home, drug use, early sexual activity).
- Experiencing adverse childhood conditions (e.g., household members who were substance abusers, mentally ill, or have criminal records).

Implications for Children.   Although adolescent mothers may be competent in some aspects of parenting, the child born to an adolescent is at risk in numerous ways. These children are at greater biological, developmental, and psychological risk than those born to an older mother (Federal Interagency Forum on Child and Family Statistics, 2015). An infant is more likely to be born with health challenges if the mother is 15 years or younger and especially if the mother received no prenatal care. Several factors account for the high rate of health problems for infants born to teenage mothers: the developmental immaturity of the mothers, their lack of adequate knowledge about the importance of prenatal care, their tendency to seek prenatal care later in the pregnancy, and their poor nutrition during pregnancy. Other consequences can include circumstances that support low socioeconomic status and related challenges.

Researchers have also identified *protective factors* that can influence the adjustment of children born to teen parents, which include developing resiliency, having a father who is involved in their upbringing, having some type of religious affiliation, civic engagement, having mentors and close ties to individuals in their communities (Development Services Group, Inc., & Child Welfare Information Gateway, 2015; East & Felice, 2014).

Guest Reflection 10–2

Journey of Resilience: An Adolescent Father's Reflections

Love is everything in a child's life. I know that being a parent has been the most blessed, most challenging thing in my entire life. I live where every day is a new day, and my family is my life.

In the parenting class, I became more confident as a parent. I realized that there was a whole body of knowledge to help us face parenting challenges. Becoming more skilled as a parent improved my relationship with my daughter. I was going through a joint custody battle, and the stressors involved with custody agreements are like none other. In my local county family court, the process included very few court sessions, but long periods of waiting that seemed eternal. The presiding judge was not a supporter of 50/50 custody so we were at a stalemate. Two years later, another judge understood and supported our plans for joint custody. Although the custody battle was not caused by divorce, an agreement was necessary to protect my rights as an involved and responsible father. My name did not appear on my daughter's birth certificate, which meant that I had to actively prove my rights and intentions as an involved parent.

The stigmas of being a single father do not really work in my favor. The despondent research outcomes I had read about do not put teenage fathers in the best light. These negative preconceptions of adolescent parents have driven me far beyond what I thought I was capable of doing several years ago. Single fathers have assumed more responsibility, and it is a changing world. I like to think that we do not represent the stereotype of uninvolved and absent fathers, but it is up to us as fathers to bring about that change. Being a single father is one thing, and reading textbook statistics is another. Without strong will and motivation, a single father becomes the self-fulfilling prophecy the research describes. Single fathers should understand that a growth mindset and maturity ahead of our teenage years is required. I will always make it my mission to be the exception to the statistics. I want to be the best father I can be, and I am committed to that for life.

Perhaps the most important lesson I learned from parenting class would be to have a growth mindset throughout the experience. You remember the past but live in the present with plans that may succeed or fail. Whatever the outcome in each scenario, a pivotal moment allows us to choose the better option.

Life has taken off from the moment I knew I was going to be an adolescent parent to this day. Eight years later I am married to the most loving and caring wife, we have a newborn in addition to my daughter from my adolescence. Education was very important, and both my wife and I have advanced degrees that have provided us with the knowledge and mindset to make good decisions from which we have benefitted as a family. I would say the most important thing in adulthood that also directly impacts your family is having the best possible relationship with your spouse. The relationship of the parents affects the children. With a teammate, productive communication is essential. Looking back, I was extremely fortunate to have found the companion who understood and embraced the challenges of our blended family. So many children are the victims of poor decisions their parents made, and the children have no control. A healthy relationship with the biological parent in a split family situation must be maintained for that child to grow up in a positive environment.

From an adolescent parent to an established adult, I understood that hardships were going to be faced, but learning to face them head on with selfless intentions provided me with the maturity to become the person I am today. Adolescents facing similar experiences need to understand the value of an education and that it increases our rate of learning. Having a growth mindset throughout the challenges of parenthood, helps us deal with situations that do not resemble anything else in our lives. Learning from older generations is beneficial but can also be outdated, as some scenarios are influenced by the present environment. Hearing other parents openly discuss their experiences played a major role in understanding the parenting hardships and challenges; I was not alone, this was something we as parents shared. Parenthood is tough, no matter your situation, background, gender, or age. But in a lifetime, I believe that it counts amongst the most rewarding and exciting journeys a human can ever undertake.

The father who reflected on his experiences in this essay, P.W., had a child in late adolescence. Used with permission.

● ●

Focus Point. While teenage pregnancy rates in the United States continue to fall, many young adults find their lives upended by an unintended pregnancy. Teen mothers may have to sacrifice or postpone their education and related career goals. Children born to young mothers can be at a greater risk for biological, developmental, and psychological stressors. These risks can be minimized by consistent pre- and post-natal care, involved fathers, and positive social support, especially from coparents and grandparents.

SUPPORT FOR ADOLESCENT PARENTS

A teenager who becomes a parent receives more support from his or her community today than in the past. Until about 20 years ago, the only type of assistance available was a residential program where an adolescent could live while awaiting the birth of her baby. Today, this type of service may continue to be helpful to some pregnant adolescents, especially those who have left their family or have dropped out of school. Services also target teens with substance abuse problems, those who are abused by their family or boyfriend, and those who have run away from home. In many places, community services have been expanded to include a number of other social and human services programs that address the needs of pregnant teens and those who become parents. Some of these programs also assist in preventing repeat teen pregnancy and parenthood (Centers for Disease Control and Prevention, 2013b).

These programs may address educational needs, interpersonal skills, and/or parenting skill development. Regardless of the type of program, researchers identify those that are successful in achieving their goals as (a) providing individual attention to the participants, and (b) being multicomponent, multiagency, community-wide programs involving parents, schools, and religious groups to reach those teens most in need of services (Youthgov. org, n.d.). Programs that attempt to facilitate change in the lives of families with teenage mothers are also effective in minimizing the deleterious effects of adolescent pregnancy on the quality of life.

Programs that provide counseling, peer education, or services to increase contraceptive use seem to be more effective in preventing adolescent pregnancy than abstinence approaches. Programs that inform teenagers that there is a high risk of contracting sexually transmitted diseases and that pregnancy can ruin their lives appear to be effective (Guttmacher Institute, 2012b). In addition, abstinence-only sex education programs appear to influence sexually active teens to delay or neglect the use of contraceptives, which increases their risk of contracting an STD and becoming pregnant (Stanger-Hall & Hall, 2011). In essence, sex-education programs that address both abstinence and contraceptive use comprehensively have been found to help teens delay becoming sexually active, reduce their numbers of sexual partners, and increase their use of contraceptives when they do become sexually active (Guttmacher Institute, 2012a).

Some programs specifically target teenage fathers or boys who potentially could become teen fathers. Such programs are based on:

- Changing sexual habits of young men to include the use of condoms, not only to prevent the spread of STDs, but also to reduce pregnancy.
- Requiring males to assume financial responsibility for their children as motivation to avoid future unintended pregnancies.
- Increasing enforcement of statutory rape charges to reduce pregnancies and births.
- Strengthening the role of fathers in all families.
- Teaching teen fathers how to become more involved with their children.

Programs that promote the availability and use of resources such as housing, child care, and financial support appear to facilitate teen parents' educational experiences, especially for teen fathers.

Educational Programs

Many different types of programs have been developed to mainstream pregnant adolescents into public schools or to maintain the public school educational programs of those who are already parents (Jennings, Howard, & Perotte, 2014). Some programs support the continuation of a teenager's education while providing child development and parenting information that promotes competent caregiving skills (Youthgov.org, n.d.). The main function of these programs is to lower the high dropout rate observed among teenage girls who become pregnant. Disruption of schooling has long-range, largely negative effects on teen parents and their children. Other programs, such as Even Start, offer child care services to promote school attendance while also providing students with opportunities to observe infant and child behavior as part of child development and parenting courses (U.S. Department of Education, 2016).

Childcare services can provide practical experiences with infants and young children. One experimental program pairs adolescent mothers with older women who serve as mentors, role models, and friends (FamilyWise, 2017). This helps the young mothers learn parenting skills and acquire child development knowledge, motivates their participation in educational experiences, and results in fewer behavioral problems. When teenagers participate in such programs, they tend to return to, or stay in, school programs that lead to a high school diploma. Research reports that subsequent births among teen mothers are diminished when they remain in school, live at home with their parents, and are engaged in educational or work activities (East & Felice, 2014; Lewis, Faulkner, Scarborough, & Berkeley, 2012).

Promoting Parenting Skills

Participation in special programs can help teenagers who are pregnant or who already have children improve their parenting skills and prevent future unplanned pregnancies (Barlow et al., 2011). Support and mentoring by grandparents is also an important protective factor (East & Felice, 2014). When teenagers have information about sexuality, child development, contraception, and parenting, that knowledge may result in improved outcomes:

- An increase in the number of teens using birth control.
- A reduction in the number of repeat pregnancies.
- A reduction in the number of child-abuse cases.

These programs are as effective with teen fathers as they are with teen mothers. More programs are aimed at meeting the needs of adolescent mothers (Finigan-Carr et al., 2015). Many programs include information about child development and expectations regarding infant and child behavior. This information improves parenting skills and attempts to prevent abuse by teen parents (Ruedinger & Cox, 2012). Programs give teen parents and expectant teens opportunities to observe infants and young children. They offer lectures about child development and use special learning tools to promote appropriate parental attitudes and expectations.

The dilemma of adolescent parenthood can be most effectively addressed by implementing programs directed at the root of the issue: adequate sex education for teenagers that encourages them to postpone sexual relationships, and if sexually active to follow effective contraceptive practices. Youths who participate in sex-education programs have been found to delay sexual activity and are able to make more informed choices concerning sexual activity.

For many parents these are controversial issues. For that reason, parental conversations, imparting of values, civic engagement, involvement in your child's life, and an open ear for their concerns are important components in shaping and guiding not only the expression of their sexuality specifically, but of their overall behavior in general.

Cultural Snapshot 10–2

Dancing the Chisungu

Read these descriptions of adolescent rites of passage which vary in different cultures.

> Dancing the *Chisungu* is the ritual of female initiation—girls' puberty rites—among the matrilineal Bemba of northern Zambia and neighbouring peoples. The ceremony could take many weeks, involves the segregation of the novices, makes great use of clay figurines and consists of a mass of symbolic usages whereby girls just prior to marriage are formally taught both 'the things of womanhood' and 'the things of the garden'. There is no form of circumcision. Chisungu is understood as a necessary handing on, sanctioned and required by the ancestors, of the norms required for marriage and good living (Hinnells, 1995).

> Although the girl may continue to do the same kinds of tasks as she did as a child, she now has to do them as a responsible adult. The rites are thus the means by which the girl publicly accepts her new legal role. As with boys, girls' initiation rites also teach them what they will need to know as adults. Bemba women [in northern Zambia, Central Africa] explain their elaborate girls' initiation rite called *Chisungu* by saying that '*they make girls clever*.' The word they use means '*to be intelligent and socially competent and to have knowledge of etiquette*.' (Nanda & Warms, 2014, p. 202).

Initiation rites are also common amongst the Murik people in Papua, New Guinea. In this group, initiation rites are not only reserved for puberty, but mark various transitional stages of life. These lifelong rituals address both genders. For young women, for instance, the rites surrounding puberty will be followed by other important lifespan events; including the celebration of reproduction, marriage, and birth (Nanda & Warms, 2014, pp. 202).

Sources: Hinnells, John R. (1995). *A New Dictionary of Religions.* Oxford, U.K.: Blackwell. Retrieved online.

Nanda, S., & Warms, R. L. (2016). *Cultural Anthropology.* 11th ed. Belmont, CA: Wadsworth/Cengage.

Focus Point. Programs that address the needs of adolescent parents are available in many communities in the United States. These programs offer a number of social and human services that assist adolescent parents and help prevent future pregnancies. Public school systems provide programs that help teen parents pursue their educational goals and offer psychological support and training in parenting skills.

CHAPTER FOCUS POINTS

The Promise of the Future

■ As children become young adults and lead more autonomous lifestyles, the role of parents shifts. Parents are advised to keep an open line of communication, enabling them to steer their adolescents toward desirable outcomes and away from harmful activities, including illegal and impulsive behavior that could be destructive. Being aware of the learning potential and plasticity of the adolescent's brain allows us to see the strengths and special capabilities of this developmental stage.

Developmental Landmarks of Adolescence

■ As adolescents move from childhood to adulthood, their transitions are characterized by physical and psychological changes. They begin to solidify their thoughts and ideals concerning themselves and the surrounding world, and many use this time to explore aspects of their identity, philosophies concerning their existence, and life and career goals.

Parenting Adolescents

■ Some of the challenges in parent–teen relationships relate to providing structure and nurture. A significant task involves the ability of parents and teens to communicate effectively. Adults who use democratic styles usually have more positive interactions. Authoritarian styles generate more conflict, which can be partly attributed to the adolescent's attempts at individuation. Parenting approaches need to adjust to developmental stage and acknowledge individual and contextual variations.

■ A variety of issues affect the health and safety of adolescents. A significant number of adolescents behave in ways that have short- and long-term adverse effects on their development. Substance abuse, depression and suicide, and eating disorders are tragically common during this developmental phase.

■ Parents must walk the fine line of promoting the increasing autonomy of their adolescent and providing helpful guidelines that foster health and safety. By modeling appropriate behaviors, warning against unhealthy habits, and teaching values and morals, parents prepare these young people to thrive in the world of adulthood. Civic engagement can also promote resilience.

Relationships and Sexuality

■ The current trend is to refer to sex education as "Relationship and Sex Education" (RSE), acknowledging the context of sexuality. Developing a sexual identity is a key milestone in the path toward adulthood. The communication lines between teens and parents should remain open as these young adults navigate the world of dating, romance, and sexuality. Parents and schools can foster an environment in which healthy and mature choices are made based on correct information. Educating teens on relationships and sexual expression, including contraceptive use, STIs, and unintended pregnancy, is a responsibility. The results promote informed choices concerning sexual health.

Parenting Emerging Adults

■ Emerging adults require an extended period for education and career preparation. They may be somewhat financially independent, while also being reliant on parents. Emerging adult children who fail to transform and mature, may put the relationship with their parents in limbo. Restructuring this relationship, while acknowledging appropriate developmental outcomes, can be beneficial to all. Both parents and adult children contribute to the outcomes.

Adolescents as Parents

■ Although teenage pregnancy rates in the United States continue to fall, many young adults find their lives upended by an unintended pregnancy. Teen mothers may have to sacrifice or postpone their education and related career goals. Children born to young mothers can be at a greater risk for biological, developmental, and psychological stressors. These risks can be minimized by consistent pre- and post-natal care, involved fathers, and positive social support, especially from coparents and grandparents.

Support for Adolescent Parents

■ Programs that address the needs of adolescent parents are available in many communities in the United States. These programs offer a number of social and human services that assist adolescent parents and help prevent future pregnancies. Public school systems provide programs that help teen parents pursue their educational goals and offer psychological support and training in parenting skills.

USEFUL WEBSITES

Websites are dynamic and change

ABCD Parenting Young Adolescents
http://abcdparenting.org
Parenting young adolescents, provides programs in several languages

Adolescent Counseling Services
www.acs-teens.org
Counseling services for adolescents

Big Brothers Big Sisters of America
www.bbbs.org
Supporting a child, Becoming a big, Community-based support

Boys Town
www.boystown.org
Families in crises, Familial support

Educating Communities for Parenting
http://ecparenting.org
Parenting education and youth development programs, Empowering parents

Parent Involvement Matters
www.parentinvolvementmatters.org
Family and community engagement, Student achievement

Society for Adolescent Health and Medicine
www.adolescenthealth.org
Adolescent health and medicine

YMCA of the USA
www.ymca.net
Community support for family and children, Nutrition and exercise programs.

PART III

The Challenges of Parent–Child Relations

Families can be incredibly strong, yet simultaneously fragile. Qualities similar to what we find in porcelain and glass objects. A porcelain vase or a glass vessel can endure centuries on the ocean floor; but expose it to major blows, and it shatters. Families can be harmed, broken, hurt, challenged, and more. Effective parenting can be interrupted or impaired for a number of reasons, and every time the family has to find ways of regrouping, finding hidden strengths and resources, and trying to stabilize and survive against all odds. Many families experience problems that affect their ability to function in healthy ways.

Each family is unique. There is diversity in the family members, as well as in family form and function. Families are blended, sandwiched, children boomerang back into the home, same-sex parents raise families, and international children are welcomed into loving homes. Skipped generation parenting encourages grandparents to step in for their own children, and coparent their grandchildren for a variety of legitimate reasons. Solo parents, who want to enrich their lives with a child, make single-parenthood a conscious choice. The effects of globalization and a changing world reach into our personal lives as well.; for instance, astronaut parents orbit around their families from the distance of an international job.

Effective parenting may be difficult when the odds stack up to counteract the optimal goal. Some parents fail in their duties and responsibilities as parents and their parental rights may be suspended. In extreme and tragic situations, parents abuse their children physically, sexually, and/or emotionally. An adult parent's addictive disorders and mental health challenges can make them emotionally absent and unable to parent. These serious parental shortcomings harm all family members.

Ultimately, many facets of the future of humankind lie within the sacred bonds of kinship. Can we learn from best practices in other countries and societies? How do families display resilience in overcoming challenges? What have we done well in supporting the building blocks of society, namely, the family, and where do we need to venture in the future?

"There can be no keener revelation of a society's soul than the way in which it treats its children."

Nelson Mandela (1918–2013)

CHAPTER 11

Parenting: Family Composition and Dynamics

Learning Outcomes

After completing this chapter, you should be able to

1. Illustrate the implications surrounding the average number of children per household.
2. Compare the dynamics and challenges of single-mother and single-father households.
3. Discuss the implications of parental separation on custody arrangements.
4. Distinguish the role of a grandparent from that of a parent.
5. Describe the effects of role strain on parenting, with special reference to the sandwich generation.

THE DYNAMICS OF RATIO

Families, and therefore parenting, can vary significantly depending on how many parents, coparents, and other supporters are on the parenting team, versus how many children are being parented. Additionally, the personalities, interests, gender, and other attributes of the children can subtly influence the parenting styles and outcomes. It is a complicated formula, where the number of participants adds to the complexity of the parenting challenge at hand.

To illustrate the ratio concept, consider a single parent raising an only child. That picture will look a whole lot different to two parents raising six children, of which one is a child with special needs. It also means that we cannot jump to conclusions about single parents, only children, or any of the many categories that define family life. Single parenthood has often been seen as the black sheep of family constellations; after all the demographics lead us to believe that single parents face several social challenges. In reality it may not be the singleness as such that is the leading red flag, it may be all the concomitant factors determining the credit rating of that particular family system. The single, professional mother who has access to a well-educated childcare provider and has maintained a supportive relationship with the coparent father raises her two children in an entirely different scenario than the single mom trying to achieve this feat without educational or financial resources. In these two examples, one family is in credit while the other is in the red concerning available resources. In short, context is very important and codetermines outcomes.

The Resources Within a Family System

There is so much more to a family system than meets the eye. We have to look at available resources within a particular system, and the number of parents and coparents on the team can definitely represent valuable resources. A family can be economically well off, but if they are emotionally bankrupt, that can spell trouble too. It has to do with parental engagement, time invested in children, modeling of values, building the self-esteem of the child; all things that theoretically require more diversified resources. Hence, good or not-so-good parenting can cross the boundaries of the economic divide; there is indeed hope for the parent–child combination that displays engagement, responsiveness, and true concern for the child's well-being (Hagan, Roubinov, Adler, Boyce, & Bush, 2016).

Poverty is often perceived as the magnet attracting a whole host of other social problems. In reality, it is a chicken and egg situation and it is difficult to determine which comes first and which factors maintain the cycle of poverty. Despite these dire prospects, for children growing up in poverty, but with parents who are modeling good values and who take an active and constructive interest in their offspring, it is possible to rise out of poverty through education and parental and civic engagement (Dawson-McClure et al., 2015). There is a window of hope.

Sibling Ratios

Siblings can be a protective as well as a distractive factor in family functioning. When the number of siblings are such that all children can get the quantity and quality time and care they deserve, then the family is probably in a good position. Compare that to an overburdened family system, where the family resources cannot stretch to meet the family needs.

Increasingly, middle class families are getting smaller—two children per family on average, with many families opting for only one child. A number of affluent west European countries have negative growth rates, because not enough children are born to balance out the

The beauty of sibling relationships is that later in life, these are the people who remember and know the details of our youth; they share childhood memories from a similar period in time.

population numbers lost through death (Haase, Kabisch, & Haase, 2013). China, for instance, is worried that only children cannot carry the burden of looking after four aging grandparents, and the shrinking numbers will have a direct outcome on the general economy, with bleak prospects for any economic growth (Zhao & Gao, 2014).

Paradoxically, the largest families are frequently found in the poorest circumstances, such as in developing countries. Some northern African and Middle-Eastern countries have explosive birth rates, but also burgeoning poverty. Clearly, very large families are a problem when children have to commit to child labor and forfeit an education in order to contribute to the meager resources of a family struggling to survive against all odds.

In a nutshell then, family resources are an important consideration in family outcomes. Resources are varied and include interpersonal, social, economic, civic, educational, spiritual, health and more, and these resources interact on different systemic levels, such as those within the family as opposed to those within a society at large.

Birth Order.   Birth order can matter in terms of parental resources. It is often said, almost anecdotally, that the first born children are more responsible, have better language development and may be more precocious than their younger siblings. But consider the ratio in which these children were initially raised before the next sibling interrupted their world of being the only child getting all the attention. The larger the family, the more divided the resources; although the resources can also grow as a result of sibling participation. Siblings can provide for each other in ways that parents cannot, and they form a valuable subsystem with its own intrinsic resources (Hindle & Sherwin-White, 2014).

Single Child Families

Being an only child has advantages as well as disadvantages which are linked to the unique position within the nuclear as well as the extended family context. As a family form, the single-child family is gaining dominance. Gradual, yet persistently declining, family sizes have been observed in developed countries over the second half of the 20th century and leading into the 21st century, with the exception of the baby boom after WWII (Gerhardt, 2016e). During the Great Depression of the 1930s in the United States, parents opted

Guest Reflection 11.1

A Change of Plans

My husband and I went from no kids to four kids in only 19 months—and all our best laid plans went out the window. With a toddler and three infants, a nanny became a necessity. As parents we jointly tackled the evening hours, and my mother-in-law took the weekend shift. Eating, sleeping, bathing, dressing—everything times four—was physically and mentally exhausting. We never seemed to measure up to our previous parenting ideal. Our first son was lavished with attention to make his childhood the best possible foundation for a successful adult life. When the triplets arrived, our goal became simply to survive the day.

In those rare moments when all four children slept in tandem, our thoughts raced ahead—to four college tuitions, to a retirement postponed, to a well-planned future that had to be reinvented. Our marriage bond was stretched to its limits by exhaustion, by the constant presence of the support persons required to keep our family afloat, and by mourning the life we thought we'd lead. Our dream of a small family who traveled widely was replaced with a reality where even a short trip to the mall was a logistical stretch.

Preschool became a bright star on our horizon. Like dominos falling, new milestones clicked into place. Running, jumping, reading, writing. Regular date nights gave us a chance to reconnect as people rather than as parents; the strain in our marriage dissipated, leaving an even stronger bond. When we started our parenting journey, we were rigid in our expectations and our planning. Now, we've learned that flexibility is paramount. We've made adjustments for one son's autism, and we regularly take an emotional temperature reading of each child. Our boys have learned that using words effectively is the key to having needs met. Most importantly, they've learned that mom and dad are simply people trying their best, but who sometimes fail.

I recently knocked on my oldest child's door. "I'm sorry," I said to the still closed door. After a bit of shuffling, it opened a crack, and one tear-filled eye peeped through. Addressing the eye, I added, "If I could go back in time, I'd have handled that a lot differently and hopefully a lot better." The door opened and my first born baby, now almost as big as me, enveloped me in a bear hug. "That's okay mom," he said. "It can't be easy having this many kids to deal with at one time."

He's right. It's never easy. But gradually this life I never anticipated has become the only life I could ever want.

Jodi Burrus, parent of four sons, including triplets. Published with permission.

for much smaller and therefore more sustainable families. The United Nations, in an analysis of characteristics pertaining to children in the 35 richest countries in the world concluded that in the post millennial era, about 85% of these countries produced fewer offspring than was required for the replacement of the existing population. Changing demographic patterns contributing to one-child families include family formation at a later age because of educational and career demands, economic considerations, reliance on assisted reproductive technologies, and societal trends and pressures. Additionally, the incidence of one parent–one child families is increasing. China's Planned Birth policy, enacted into law in 1979, has drawn the attention of researchers to this family form, as research studies with very large samples are possible. Valuable conclusions have been drawn from the meta-analyses of numerous previous studies and literature reviews of research to date.

Siblings exert numerous influences on each other. Being part of a complex system of interrelated family members encourages the acquisition of diverse skills in the developing child (McAlister & Peterson, 2013). Additionally, siblings represent peer relationships within a highly select group who have experienced similar influences in their families of origin. In all likelihood, a sibling system will be a cohort for their entire lifespan. These and other premises contributed to the historical notion that only children are deprived of very valuable family connections which can exert a variety of far reaching influences.

Historical Underpinnings.   Alfred Adler (1870–1937), one of the early psychoanalysts and a contemporary of Sigmund Freud, stated in his research on birth order that being an only child could have detrimental effects on aspects of personality development, ultimately presenting in adulthood as a lack of life skills. A pioneer in American psychology and the first president of the American Psychological Association, G. Stanley Hall (1844–1924), made the controversial statement in 1898 that being an only child was a disease unto itself.

These eclipsed opinions are better understood against the backdrop of their historical time. At a time when infant mortality rates were very high, family planning was virtually nonexistent, and gender role inequality was persistent, one-child families were regarded with some suspicion and intolerance. It was also a time when large, especially rural agricultural, families were prevalent.

Changing Attitudes.   Currently, the attitudes towards single-child families are undergoing significant changes challenging former stereotypes and inconsistent findings often stemming from methodological variables in the research. The research of previous decades presented presumed differences between only children and children growing up with siblings in several areas including social, cognitive, and emotional dimensions. The popular stereotype was that only children were overindulged and their every whim catered to, presenting in permissive (or laissez faire) parenting. Chinese male children from one-child families were occasionally called "Little Emperors." Health concerns focused on the tendency towards obesity. Parents were likely to seek medical advice for their only children sooner and this could be read as overprotection. The reference to "4-2-1" denotes the ratio of participants in the intergenerational family; four grandparents and two parents focused on the only child. The one-child policy in China revealed previously unanticipated challenges (Feng, Gu, & Cai, 2016). The historic Chinese cultural preference for male offspring contributed to a large and growing gender imbalance, which in adulthood presented as a shortage of appropriate life partners (Yu & Winter, 2011).

The extensive work with large samples supported what, with hindsight, one could intuitively surmise; namely that there were no significant personality differences that could be attributed to the only child status apart from the expected variances of sample heterogeneity. Allowing for some cultural influences, only children in China and the United States displayed many more similarities than differences (Falbo, 2012). Academic achievement, responsibility, and diligence may be slightly more pronounced in only children, probably because of the parental attention and investment (Trent & Spitze, 2011). The negative outcome may be stress and coping difficulties if family and self-imposed demands are unrealistically high and unbalanced in terms of overall life management. Only children may benefit from constructive opportunities to learn to negotiate, share resources, and manage conflict. Having trusted friends and confidantes outside the nuclear family may add to resilience at times when the only child requires a support network but cannot rely on siblings.

Current research on one-child family systems seeks to correct bygone stereotypes and points towards several valuable implications surrounding parenting techniques and therapeutic outcomes. Ongoing overindulgence and inappropriate parenting are detrimental to any child, irrespective whether the child is a single child or part of a sibling system. The level of intensity could be too high when all attention from both grandparents and parents is focused on the one recipient of well-intended but also potentially damaging aspirations and affections (Clarke, Dawson, & Bredehoft, 2004/2014). The lesson to be learned is that what is appropriate in terms of good parenting outcomes is similar for all children, irrespective of their birth status within a family. Children grow up in the context of a family system, and that system is typically multigenerational and extended, exerting numerous influences (Lawson & Mace, 2010). Additionally, children are part of several systems ranging from micro level to macro level, as referenced by the ecological family systems theory. These systems include all the relevant persons, organizations, policies, and the like that may influence the child at various points of the lifespan.

Challenges for Only Children.   When seen against the backdrop of lifespan development, the only child may face different challenges. During childhood and adolescence, parents of single children should ensure adequate provision for catastrophic events, such as the child being orphaned. During middle adulthood the adult-only child may be sandwiched between the interests and demands of preceding as well as subsequent generations. Looking after aging parents is more challenging if the burden is not spread among siblings, and elderly parents should initiate appropriate measures for their own elder care, including long term health and financial provisions. Loss of elderly parents may feel like the loss of an entire generation, without the balancing effects of a peer sibling system who are part of the family of origin. Parents, in turn, are faced with devastating loss in the case of the death of their only offspring (Li, 2013). Major life transitions tend to pull families together. The effects of traumatic life passages can be exacerbated because only children tend to seek out fewer extended family contacts than their counterparts hailing from sibling systems (Yu & Winter, 2011). Friends and trusted confidantes will necessarily play a more pronounced role for the only child.

For only children, including adult-only children, their peer group, friends, extended family, educational and career environments, extramural activities, cultural norms, and social policies, to mention but a few subsystems, may all add subtle layers of influence which combine towards the final outcome (Feng, Gu, & Cai, 2016). Parents of only children can create wider networks for their children by encouraging opportunities for interaction on several platforms. Balancing these influences means that the only child hopes to experience a rewarding and varied lifespan; with the promise of an optimal developmental outcome.

Acknowledgment: This section on single child families was first published in Shehan, C. L. (2016). *The Wiley Blackwell Encyclopedia of Family Studies*. Chichester, UK: Wiley Blackwell. In this volume: Gerhardt, C. "Only Children." Volume III. Pp. 1533–1536. Used with permission of the publishers, John Wiley & Sons, Inc.

Focus Point.   Family resources are an important consideration in family outcomes. Resources are varied and include interpersonal, social, economic, civic, educational, spiritual, health and more, and these resources interact on different systemic levels, such as those within the family as opposed to those within a society at large. Compared to the large families of yesteryear, the average American family now consists of two children. Only children face unique challenges which parents can combat by creating networks of socialization and support. Advances in medical care, much lower infant mortality, and changes in social norms have played contributing roles. Challenges abound in all families, irrespective of size.

Families with only children, in contrast to families with multiples, display complex reciprocal interactions, which also influence parent–child relationships.

Elisabeth Schmitt/Moment/Getty Images

Cultural Snapshot 11–1

China's One-Child Policy

Consider how the dynamics of a family is changed by the number of children in that family, as well as the genders of those children. As a result of population pressure, China introduced a one-child policy in 1979, which has been changed to a two-child policy as of 2016 (Feng, Gu, & Cai, 2016). The approach is controversial, and it has allowed researchers to study families with only children in greater depth. One major and unanticipated problem that arose out of these policies is that the average Chinese family shows a strong gender preference towards boys, based on cultural customs and religious beliefs. Historically, daughters got married and moved to the homes of their in-laws. Sons on the other hand stayed close to home, possibly inheriting the land the father cultivated, and were seen as a living pension for elderly parents and grandparents. Sons had a duty to look after the older generations. Additionally, cultural and religious beliefs placed a strong emphasis on the male heir for continuation of the family line (Shiraev & Levy, 2016, pp. 216–217).

Gender preferences led to selective gender-based pregnancy terminations, because gender could be determined prenatally. In some countries, prenatal gender determination has been outlawed for that precise reason. Female children were increasingly abandoned, and international adoptions of Chinese girls increased. Fast forward three to four decades and the gender imbalance has caused alarming social problems. One estimate is that the surplus of men

of marriageable age is about 30 million and young men cannot find brides. Illegally kidnapped girls are a major human rights concern. Women from neighboring countries have also been targeted as marriage partners.

In terms of parenting, the single child policy has created a generation of indulged children; sometimes referred to as "little emperors." All parental and grandparental hopes and aspirations are lavished on them, creating the ideal opportunity for unbalanced and permissive parenting practices. In turn, many of the children tend to display characteristics of being spoiled and self-centered. Once the older generations require care, the entire burden of elder support is concentrated on the only child with a support ratio that cannot be sustained; another problematic scenario. Because of the ecological interrelatedness of systems, this is a good example of how personal choices on a micro level, translate to major challenges and imbalances on a macro systemic level (Nanda & Warms, 2014, p. 348).

Based on the following sources: Nanda, S., & Warms, R. (2014). *Cultural Anthropology.* 11th ed. Belmont, CA: Wadsworth/Cengage. Chapter 15: Culture, Change, and the Modern World.

Shiraev, E. B., & Levy, D. A. (2017). *Cross-cultural Psychology: Critical Thinking and Contemporary Applications.* 6th ed. New York , NY: Routledge. Chapter 7: Motivation and Behavior.

Multiples

Every year, since 1976, the world's largest reunion of twins and multiples is held in Twinville, Ohio, USA (http://www.twinsdays.org/). At this event, a number of research institutions take advantage of the unique opportunities for scientific research and multiples who are willing can participate. The Netherlands register of twins and multiples is also focused on facilitating research, and twins and multiples are often recruited as early as a few weeks after birth (http://www.tweelingenregister.org/). The composer Johann Sebastian Bach and his wife Maria

Magdalena had twins. Sadly, with the lack of medical care at that time (1713), one baby died at birth and the other about three weeks later.

The birth of multiples holds special challenges for parents; instead of parenting children consecutively, these parents do so simultaneously. With assisted reproductive techniques the incidence of multiples has increased, although elective single embryo transfer is generally thought to have more favorable outcomes for both mother and infant. Parents of twins, whether they were conceived naturally or through ART, can face greater parental distress and may require additional support (Kehoe, Dempster, McManus, & Lewis, 2016). Support groups for parents of twins and multiples can enhance parental attitudes and coping skills (http://www.multiplesofamerica.org/).

Parents with adequate support systems and resources in terms of emotional and financial backup, seem to have a better cushion to deal with the stressors of multiples. In a study done in China it appeared that parental involvement was decreased if economic status and educational level of the parents was lower (Wang, Deng, & Yang, 2016). Mothers and fathers who were aware of the parenting challenges, displayed equal engagement towards both twin children. It seems intuitive that parenting differs in twin versus singleton relationships, especially if the first born child was an only child. Parents who have had a child before they had twins as compared to parents who only experienced parenting multiples, seemed to fare slightly better during this new and possibly overwhelming challenge. Parents dealing with newborns for the first time, irrespective whether they are twins or singletons, learn from this experience and are then better able to cope with a subsequent birth (Anderson, Rueter, Connor, & Koh, 2016).

For the twins and multiples themselves, a unique sibling system is formed. Twins who are identical have a different experience than fraternal twins. Dizygotic or fraternal twins develop from two fertilized eggs, and have two distinctly different sets of genes. For that reason, twins of both genders, i.e., a boy and a girl as part of the same twin pair, are always dizygotic. Hence, these children show the same variations that other singletons within one family may display. Even monozygotic twins (formed from one fertilized egg that split into two) may not be totally identical, as the reflection "One of Two" describes. A meta-analysis of the heritability of traits, which was based on 50 years of twin studies, points towards the importance of the clusters of inherited traits, but also emphasizes the complexity of these situations as far as genetic variations are concerned, and to what extent individual differences can be ascribed to a variety of factors (Polderman, et al., 2015). Some parents may think that their twins are identical, until DNA testing reveals the contrary. The effects of *epigenetics* may also add subtle layers of difference; namely the expression of genes can vary depending on a variety of subsequent influences.

In the context of family dynamics, various combinations can be at play, namely the dynamics between the multiples, between the parents themselves, and between the parents and their twins or multiples. In a longitudinal study of over six thousand twin pairs, it was shown that children and their parents have different perceptions concerning the qualities of the parent–child relationships in which they participated (Hannigan, McAdams, Plomin, & Eley, 2016). Parenting is not an objective exercise, and psychotherapists know that each participating member of a family constellation may have a unique subjective reality concerning what is happening within that family and the associated emotions. Children see it one way, parents see it another, and then different children within one family system may also have various interpretations of what really happened on the home front. Subjective as well as objective realities display variations, as the quality of parenting may differ from one child to another. There is a reciprocal interaction too, in that some parent and child personalities may be more compatible and the nuances within the various relationships thus differ.

The beauty of sibling relationships is that later in life, these are the people who remember and know the details of our youth: they shared the same childhood during a similar time period or chronosystem. In the study, child- and parent-specific perceptions of parenting tended to be more similar for identical twins. Importantly, there was a stability in how parent–child interactions were interpreted by the identical twins themselves, and these perceptions persisted over time, emphasizing the influence of the shared genetic heritage. Families, and especially families with multiples, display complex reciprocal interactions, and these, just as in any other family, influence parent–child relationships. It appears that in families there is a shared as well as an individual reality, also concerning parenting. For twins, and especially identical twins, this shared reality is stronger than for singleton siblings (Hannigan, McAdams, Plomin, & Eley, 2016).

The parenting skills that parents display can be based on their own experiences of having been parented, be influenced by their own personality traits and emotional and interpersonal styles, and also be unique in response to a specific child and that child's personality and interactional patterns. Parents in this same study reported that they thought they treated multiples very similarly. Contrast this with the impression by the twins or multiples themselves, who perceived parenting styles to apply both individually and jointly. In other words, perceptions of parenting varied depending on which participant was asked to comment; parents may think they are doing one thing whereas children may perceive that same situation slightly differently, also influenced by their developmental stage. It would appear that:

For twins and multiples themselves, a unique sibling system is formed. Twins who are identical have a different experience than fraternal twins.

Lakomanrus/Shutterstock

"Evidently, child-driven effects are complex enough to drive both stability and change in the parenting relationship, and to be both jointly or individually perceived" (Hannigan, McAdams, & Plomin, 2016).

The Mixed-up Twins of Bogota.   The interaction between nature and nurture was dramatically illustrated when two sets of identical twins from Bogota, Colombia, were inadvertently separated at birth and raised by two sets of parents. Each parent pair raised a biological and a non-biological child, while under the impression that they were fraternal twins. Through a series of serendipitous events, each person was reunited with their identical twin, albeit having been raised in noticeably different environments with very different outcomes. The article and photos of the identical twins who were mixed up at birth can be accessed at: can be accessed at Video Example 11-1

Video Example 11.1

Watch this video of Twins of Bogota meeting for the first time. What does this example of twins separated at birth show us about nature and nature and how it places into the formation of a person?

(https://www.nytimes.com/2015/07/12/magazine/the-mixed-up-brothers-of-bogota.html)

Guest Reflection 11–2

One of Two

As a twin, my childhood and subsequent adulthood, has always been very different than that of my peers. I have always been one of two. I am an identical mirror twin, so my sister and I look physically alike. Some attributes are mirrored, for instance one of us is left- and the other right handed. If I have a beauty spot on my right cheek, Megan has a similar one but located on her left side.

Our personalities are very different, but complementary, and we have always been very in sync when it comes to thoughts, ideas, feelings, and emotions. My mom always expresses a mixture of confusion and amazement when Megan and I tell her about the same ideas or share like-minded thoughts within minutes of each other—no matter if we are in different rooms or different states. We've always done similar things without meaning to, and to this day, we unintentionally wear the same outfits and call each other with the same questions.

I love being a twin and would not change my experience for the world. I do not understand what it's like to have a "normal" sibling and do not easily relate to people who are not as close as Megan and I. We share a special bond that cannot be completely explained or understood by outsiders. We are womb-mates, and the biological closeness definitely carries over well after birth. We connect to each other in a way that non-multiple siblings cannot imitate. We can communicate without actually speaking and frequently know each other's thoughts and feelings. There is a biological bond from which we cannot escape.

We do have different skills and areas of expertise. We are both artistic—Megan in the visual arts, I am more literary. We are both smart, but in very different ways. I am academic and love excelling at school, Megan is sports minded, and can easily manage an athletic department. We are both organized, but in our own ways. Megan is extroverted and extremely outgoing; the life of a party. I tend to be introverted, love small gatherings and one-on-one conversations. We are so similar yet so different: we overlap in every way. There is such a unique connection physically, emotionally, and mentally that it can be hard to comprehend unless you have experienced a similar bond yourself.

My mom talks about our different personalities as children. We were each other's best friends and worst enemies. We could get mad at each other, but any time anyone tried to insult or hurt one of us, the other intervened. We ganged up on our parents and never let them get too harsh towards our twin. We could be angry one minute, and backing each other up the next. We played off each other and distracted our parents long enough that they forgot to punish us.

My childhood as a twin was the best and I cannot imagine it any other way. I loved having a built-in best friend and someone who literally cannot get rid of me. I have a person who I do not have to explain myself to and who knows what I am thinking and feeling without exchanging actual words. My childhood was filled with adventures and experiences that helped mold the woman I am. That wouldn't be possible without Megan—my womb-mate.

Nicole Smith, M.A. (Educational Counseling) and one of identical mirror twins. Published with permission.

• •

Video Example 11.2

Watch this video on the topic of twins. Why is it important for parents to support their twins' individuality?
(https://www.youtube.com/watch?v=UlrqbXO4Dhg)

SINGLE PARENT FAMILIES

A single-parent family system can be created in several ways:

- Conscious choice to form a single parent family
- Death of one of the parents; widowed
- Divorce, desertion, or separation of the adults

Single-by-Choice

Parents who are single by choice are a part of the "new normal." When they consciously decide to travel the parenthood journey solo, they do so with pride and with the support of their friends and family. About a century ago, this would have been unthinkable or regarded as a scandalous decision, and children were dropped off in foundling homes, although it broke the hearts of their mothers. Other children were welcomed into the family households, typically of the mother of the child (Frost, 2009).

The majority of single-parent families in which women have sole custody or are the physical custodian of children amount to about 80 percent, although there are significant increases in families where single men head the household. These families can include an unmarried adult partner of the parent, especially when adults live together in a household.

See Figure 11–1 for statistics on family types in the United States.

Single After the Death of a Partner

Children who become part of blended families as a result of the death of one parent and the subsequent remarriage of the surviving parent also face unique emotional challenges. About a quarter of children will react with associated mental health problems after the death of a parent or of a sibling (Stikkelbroek, Bodden, Reitz, et al., 2016), although that may be related to level of support and also if there were pre-existing mental health problems in pre-loss functioning.

Pre-loss factors are very important and include aspects such as if the marriage had been happy and whether the family was functioning well. Even under difficult circumstances, bereaved families tend to idealize the person who died. Adjustment following death of a parent includes a grieving process. Most therapists would advise not to start another blended family until most of the grieving work has been completed, and that includes both the surviving parent as well as the children. The developmental ages of the children are important, as teenagers tend to react differently than their younger siblings. When the death of a parent is anticipated (as in cancer) teenagers would prefer to be told when the loss is near, and expressed that they wanted to be given information not only by the remaining parent but also by professionals. This may have implications for family care pre- and post-bereavement (Bylund-Grenko et al., 2015).

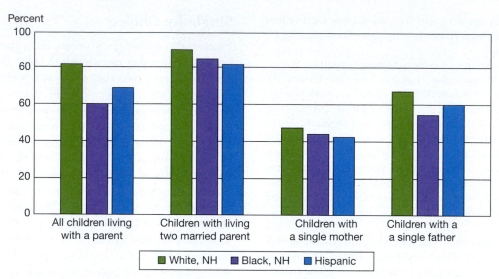

FIGURE 11–1. Percentage of children ages 0–17 living with at least one parent employed year round, full time by family structure and race and Hispanic origin, 2014.

Note: The abbreviation NH refers to non-Hispanic origin. Year-round, full-time employment is defined as usually working full time (35 hours or more per week) for 50 to 52 weeks. Children living with a single mother or single father includes some families in which both parents are present in the household but are unmarried partners.

Source: Bureau of Labor Statistics, Current Population Survey, Annual Social and Economic Supplement.

In short, the death of a parental figure involves the entire family, and will influence later blended family functioning. Strengthening family resilience is important and this can be facilitated through communication and emotional support (Walsh, 2016). Human vulnerability includes suffering, and the notion that people simply bounce back after loss is not accurate. Loss involves the whole person; in her relationships and in her emotional well-being (Galvin, Braithwaite, & Bylund, 2015; Walsh, 2016).

Single Post-divorce

The single parent category includes those families with single parents as a result of desertion and separation, as well as the leading factor, namely divorce. Separation and desertion frequently precede divorce.

The increasing rate of divorce has resulted in larger numbers of *binuclear* or single-parent families that are created when spouses go their separate ways (U.S. Census Bureau, n.d.). Traditional families that consist of two parents and their children with both parents in their first marriage constitute a distinct minority, accounting for only 21 percent of all families in the United States (U.S. Census Bureau, n.d.).

In this family form, children are members of two separate and distinct households or families, hence *binuclear* family—one headed by the father and the other headed by the mother. These are separate one-parent households. Increasingly, both parents hold joint custody of the children. The designated physical custodian could be the parent at whose house the children reside most of the time. These arrangements could change when the adults concerned remarry. Children may have divided responsibilities in two households.

Divorce is a stressful experience that can be uncomfortable for the family system because old familiar patterns are dismantled. Family systems theory describes divorce as an event that produces disruption in a family system. When a marriage is dissolved, a new family form evolves, namely the single-parent family, with new patterns, rules, and roles.

In 1970, approximately 3.8 million families were headed by a single parent. In 2014, 64 percent of all children in the United States lived with two married parents in comparison to the 24 percent who lived with either a single-parent mother or the 4 percent who lived with a single-parent father (Federal Interagency Forum on Child and Family Statistics, 2015).

A family system that loses one adult's presence has to adjust in distinct ways. Divorce, in particular, forces unique adaptation in the new single-parent family system. Divorce is one of the most difficult processes a family system can experience (Hetherington & Arasteh, 2014). It has short- and long-term effects for both the original first-marriage family system and any subsequent relationships. In keeping with family systems theory, it is predicted that divorce will affect everyone in a family system.

<hr>

Parenting Reflection 11–1

Are there any advantages to single parenthood in comparison with a marriage?

<hr>

Parental Adaptations Following Divorce

Divorce affects both adults and children. All members are affected when one key member experiences a major change. Divorce dissolves the effective functioning of the committed relationship between the adult partners. In turn, it disrupts the functioning of parent–child relationships. Emotional reactions such as depression, weight fluctuations, sleep disturbances, and an increase in the likelihood of addiction disorders may occur. Anger and hostility may color interactions between the divorcing adults and can take a long time to dissipate. Lifestyle-changes occur as a result of altered financial status of both adults. Single mothers may struggle financially and are often overrepresented among the impoverished.

Because divorce affects all family members, adults need to be aware of what is happening to their children and understand the changes taking place (Hetherington & Arasteh, 2014):

- **Facing reality.** Family members acknowledge that divorce is imminent and that the adults no longer share similar feelings of love and attachment. Feelings of insecurity, sadness, relief, even anger and hate may surface.
- **Physical separation.** Disruptive effects occur as the family dismantles. Removing one parent's presence from the nuclear family system can leave children with feelings of abandonment.
- **Family reorganization.** Divorced adults forge a new relationship with children. The recently formed single-parent family adapts by evolving new rules, roles, interaction patterns, and living conditions.
- **Family redefinition.** Both the custodial as well as the noncustodial parent reorganizes and explores the family system from a new angle. Children learn two sets of patterns and rules because they are now members of two single-parent family systems.

<hr>

Parenting Reflection 11–2

Explain the factors that precipitate a breakdown of a marriage. Describe the effects on the family.

<hr>

A major challenge for divorcing parents is to acknowledge that they continue to share parenting responsibilities and relationships with their children, even though their marriage has been dismantled (Martínez-Pampliega et al., 2015). The relationship is transformed in several ways:

- The visitation rights force some type of contact with the former spouse.
- Children may perpetuate the remnants of the relationship by sharing information about one parent with the other and discussing life and events in their new family system.
- With joint custody, spouses commit to sharing major decisions regarding the children.
- While parents attend to their own adjustment to the divorce, they need to be mindful of their children's reactions as well.
- Involving children in the details of the emotional divorce occurring between the two adult parents is inadvisable. Children should not be the go-betweens, or worse still the targets of misdirected anger.

<hr>

Focus Point.   Divorce elicits emotional and transitional adjustments as parents exchange their couple identity for single status, a transition with great implications on the parenting role. Divorced parents must communicate expectations clearly and learn to adjust to their new roles. Even though adults adjust differently, they continue to share a connection through their child. A couple can seldom be completely divorced when children are involved.

Parenting Implications.   During and following a divorce some parents increase the level of structure and control, as if they try to stabilize the family system with their control. They can become over-strict and/or over-protective of the children. Other parents, especially the non-custodial parents, may react by becoming indulgent towards the children, especially as they try to catch up on two weeks' worth of parenting in a single weekend when they have visitation rights with their children (Leonoff, 2015). An effect of role strain is the increased reliance on more authoritarian patterns of interacting with children. As the new family system evolves, new patterns establish a degree of stability, and single-parent mothers generally shift to more authoritative styles. This promotes healthier, well-adjusted children.

Some of the difficult patterns that were present before the separation, or which led to the separation may persist. When the marriage breaks up because of financial issues or addiction disorders such as alcoholism that affect one of the parents, those problems will have to be resolved before the parenting outcome will be significantly changed. For some families, the breakup serves as an opportunity to regroup and find healthier and more normal ways of going about life. The decision to divorce is never taken lightly, and the children in the household must have observed many episodes of disharmony. Typically, there are few secrets in families, and if children live in a household where the parental marriage has become a battleground, then they know about it (Katz & Gottman, 1993).

After divorce, single-parent mothers tend to change the boundaries, patterns, and rules that define the usual adult and child roles (Kavas & Gündüz-Hoşgör , 2013). A mother may redefine her role, particularly in relation to the oldest child, who may become a peer/partner and confidante. The mother increasingly relies on this child for emotional support and assigns her much of the missing adult partner's responsibilities. As a result, the child may be forced into interaction patterns that call for developmental maturity beyond his years.

When a mother transforms the child's role to one similar to the absent adult partner's, a conflict emerges that imitates the marital conflicts with the former spouse. The child discovers that it is a no-win situation. Some children may not feel comfortable expressing their feelings of frustration and confusion. They respond with psychosomatic symptoms and acting-out behaviors that reflect their concerns and fears (Deshpande & Pandey, 2014). Not surprisingly, when mothers disclose intimate details about personal problems, such as financial matters or negative feelings about ex-husbands, daughters report strong feelings of emotional distress (Lougheed, Koval, & Hollenstein, 2016). Parents may respond negatively to children who remind them of the former spouse, or they can develop over dependence on their children, children may appear to be a burden, as the parent focuses on survival rather than on parenting.

Children's Adaptations.   About one-fourth (24 percent) of American children lived only with their mothers, 4 percent lived only with their fathers, and 4 percent lived with neither of their parents (Federal Interagency Forum on Child and Family Statistics, 2015]). The number of single-parent families in the United States has increased considerably over the past half century. The marital status of the parents influences where children will live and with whom, as well as the quality of life they will experience. In line with the increase in single-parent families, there has been a concomitant decrease in the number of children living with two parents. In 2014, for example, 74 percent of Caucasian, non-Hispanic children, 58 percent of Hispanic children, and 34 percent of African American children lived with two married parents (Federal Interagency Forum on Child and Family Statistics, 2014).

Children's reactions to parental divorce include a gradual adjustment to change. This process is tempered by factors such as the child's age, gender, and past experiences. For many children, parental divorce involves significant loss, and children experience a variety of grief reactions. Children appear to undergo this process in three distinct stages:

■ The *initial stage* occurs after parents inform the child of their decision to separate. It is marked by high levels of stress, during which aggressive conflict and unhappiness increase markedly.
■ The *transition stage* commences about 1 year after the parents' separation and lasts for up to 3 years. Emotions normalize, and the restructuring process includes evolving new family patterns, changing the quality of life, and establishing visitation routines with the noncustodial parent.
■ The *restabilization stage* occurs about 5 years after the separation, when the new single-parent family system or blended family is more stable (Papernow, 2015).

Divorce may be one of the few major family crisis events in which adults become more focused on their own needs than on those of their children.

The functioning of the parent–child relationship is disrupted because of this changed focus. Children of divorcing parents can react uniquely in ways that express their own personalities (Tein, Sandler, Braver, & Wolchik, 2013). Several factors appear to influence the course of children's adjustment to this family crisis:

- Gender and age of the child when the parental divorce occurs.
- Adults' use of available social support networks to help the child adjust.
- Cultural attitudes toward divorce and single-parent families.

The effects of parental divorce on children may be short- or long-term, positive or detrimental. Short-term effects include behavioral difficulties at home and at school that present in association with the initial reaction to parental separation.

Long-term effects may not appear until adolescence or adulthood, when individuals experience difficulties in establishing intimate relationships (Whitten & Burt, 2015). The child's age at the time of the parental divorce seems to be one of the driving factors in how a child reacts and adjusts. Regressive behaviors, such as increased aggression; fretting; and negative attention-getting behaviors, such as whining or destroying toys, may be observed among preschoolers whose parents are divorcing. School-age children may fear abandonment or rejection by their absent parent and experience a drop in school performance, adverse interactions with peers, or boundary shifts with one of the parents. Adolescents may manifest similar feelings, and present with delinquency and negative acting-out behaviors, heightened conflicts with their parent, decline in school performance, and depression (Vélez, Wolchik, & Sandler, 2014). The first year after parental divorce may be the most difficult and stressful for both children and parents, especially if the parents continue to exhibit discord.

Divorce is more problematic for adolescents (Mashego & Taruvinga, 2014), and the context of the parent–child relationship is altered. Teenage girls may target the custodial parent with the anger they feel for the noncustodial parent. Adolescent girls may resent the change in their relationship with their mothers and experience boundary blurring. Some adolescents have divided allegiances to both parents. This division is aggravated if conflict and hostility is high, and the parents do not collaborate.

Many adolescents make adequate adjustments in the years following a divorce and become competent adults. A poorly managed, hostile divorce leaves children and adolescents emotionally sensitive to future dating relationships. On the other hand, the poor family climate that surrounds parents who are at war also has a high emotional price tag.

· ·

Parenting Reflection 11–3

Can growing up in a single-parent family be a healthy experience for children? What benefits might they gain from this experience?

· ·

The effects of divorce on children present as a negative and depressing scenario. Parents who are considering divorce should be aware that complications await them:

- Children experience the effects of parental divorce in ways that can be disruptive and stressful.
- Divorce is a process rather than an event, affecting the entire family system not just the divorcing couple.
- Divorce has immediate and long-term effects on children. The effects vary depending on the age and gender of the child at the time of the divorce, and how the parents manage the divorce.
- Children whose parents divorce during their developing years almost always see it as a milestone event that shaped developmental aspects of their adulthood.

It is safe to state that not all children whose parents divorce react negatively. It is equally safe to conclude that no child of divorced parents completely escapes the disruption that divorce has on a family system. The manner in which the divorcing adults maintain their roles as parents will determine part of the disruption, stress, and trauma that divorce can elicit. Parents who succeed in a collaborative divorce, will also reduce the potential damages that divorce can inflict on all concerned (Alba-Fisch, 2016).

· ·

Focus Point.   Parental divorce affects children in a number of ways. Age at the time of the divorce is an important factor. Parents fear that their children will experience harmful outcomes as a result of the divorce. Researchers generally find that divorce is disruptive, but that most children adapt and adjust in a resilient way. The manner in which the adults continue to fulfill their roles as parents and form a constructive working relationship as coparents, is an important factor in determining outcomes.

· ·

CUSTODY ARRANGEMENTS

Parents must confront a major decision when they divorce: Who will have custody of the children, and how will the noncustodial parent and the children have access to each other for visitation? The Family Law Section of the American Bar Association lists several standards that court officials may apply in determining the custody arrangements of children following the divorce of their parents (American Bar Association, n.d.). This includes the following:

■ Custody should be awarded to one parent or both parents according to the best interests of the child.

■ Custody may be awarded to persons other than the father or mother, whenever such award serves the best interests of the child. For instance, in some cases the grandparents get custody of the children.

■ If a child is old enough and able to reason and form an intelligent preference, her wishes concerning custody should be considered by the court.

■ Any custody award should be subject to modification or change whenever the best interests of the child require or justify such a change.

■ Reasonable visitation rights should be awarded to the noncustodial parent and to persons legitimately interested in the welfare of the child, at the discretion of the court.

Parenting Reflection 11–4

What can divorced parents do to prevent their child from feeling like a ball that is tossed from one parent to the other to meet the requirements of joint custody or noncustodial visitation?

Children Should Not Fight Parental Battles. Parental battles should shelter the children, not involve them. Even though mothers stand a good chance of being awarded legal custody, both parents can share custody which is a constructive arrangement if the parents can maintain an amicable divorce that affects children minimally. Divorcing couples must negotiate a decision, keeping the best interests of the child in mind.

The children should not have to continue taking sides or be poisoned by the conflict between the parents. The parents must reach visitation and support decisions, and consider other important details related to meeting the best interests of the child. Details regarding child support include how each parent will contribute to the child's medical, educational, and other expenses, and what percentage of the costs each party will contribute. It can be challenging for couples to reach these decisions in an objective and amicable manner. They may arrive

---

Cultural Snapshot 11–2

Child Custody a Century Ago

Before the 1920s, custody was automatically awarded to the father; the mother had virtually no legal rights. At that time, women could neither vote nor sign contracts. In subsequent years, women have gained legal status in the United States, and the child custody situation has changed tremendously and continues to transform as new family forms and functions evolve.

> Description of a domestic situation prior to 1920 in an impoverished part of London: "When households broke up, it was usually the bigger children who went into the workhouse, while their baby siblings were absorbed into the homes of neighbors or relatives" (Ross, 1993, p.134).

The acknowledgment that care for children gave adults rights over them generated many ambiguities about the definition of parenthood. Some of the paid nurses became very attached to their babies, and officials found many who had sacrificed dearly to support infants whose mothers had ceased making payments . . . Biological and nurse mothers regularly found themselves in battles for custody in the Old Bailey [Courthouse in London] or involved in assault cases that terminated in the magistrates' courts (Ross, 1993, p. 136).

Source: Ross, Eileen (1993). *Love and Toil: Motherhood in Outcast London, 1870–1918.* Oxford , England: Oxford University Press.

Pixelheadphoto digitalskillet/Shutterstock

Custody may be awarded to one or both parents, or a significant person who can take on the role of coparent and legal guardian. Custody decisions should serve the best interests of the child.

at this decision with the help of mediation professionals, therapists, or even the intervention of the legal profession and the court.

When divorcing parents consider custody issues, several factors frequently favor one parent over the other:

- The preferences of the child.
- Whether or not a parent wants or is able to have custody.
- The perceived need to place a child with the same-sex parent.
- A parent's ability to provide stable, continued support in the same residence or geographical area.

Joint Custody

One approach to custody decisions is **joint custody**, or awarding the responsibility for childcare and supervision to *both* parents. In many cases, joint custody, rather than single-parent custody, may be a viable solution that is in the best interests of the children (Fransson, Turunen, Hjern, Östberg, & Bergström, 2016). This alternative has advantages, as well as disadvantages, in its implementation and execution. The advantages outweigh the problems if the parents can work together in the best interests of their children. Advantages include:

- More contact between ex-spouses.
- Father's cooperation in meeting the financial-support agreement is more likely.

- Sharing of child-care responsibilities; children are exposed to the influences of both parents.
- Greater access to constructive interactions between children and both their parents.

Parenting Reflection 11–5

Should joint custody be the norm among divorced parents with children? Justify your answer.

Focus Point.   Children should be sheltered from custody battles between divorcing parents; encounters which often become hostile. Parents who share joint custody are more involved with parenting responsibilities, have more contact with their children, and use parenting resources extensively. Fathers in joint custody arrangements are more likely to be financially responsible towards the children, preventing a poverty-level existence.

Parenting Reflection 11–6

Is it right to force men to pay child support when they fall behind? Should a noncustodial mother pay child support to a custodial father even though she earns less than he does? Would noncustodial fathers be more willing to pay for child support if the federal government made this a line-item credit on annual tax returns?

Joint custody can involve the following challenges:

- It is expensive because each parent must supply housing and other essentials for children.
- It requires a connection with the ex-spouse that requires maturity and tolerance.
- Adults need to maintain civil discussions concerning child rearing.
- Constraints on relocation to another state can impair decision making.
- Children have commitments to two family systems instead of one.
- Children have to transition from one family system to another.
- Split living arrangements can contain their own challenges.

Post-divorce Coparenting. Coparenting is performed jointly. Resources are shared, and parents collaborate. It is a legitimate form of parenting and often occurs in binuclear families (two households). It typically has legal implications concerning parental rights and responsibilities, and the coparent can make decisions of influence.

At the heart of coparenting lies the ongoing commitment to a child's well-being. Coparents can be biological parents in binuclear families who take on the parenting roles based from two households because of divorce or separation. The adults could have a biological link to the children, but they need not have this connection. For instance, parents and stepparents in a postdivorce situation may coparent. Unmarried parents may coparent from two separate homes. Coparenting is undertaken by two or more adults who take on the care and upbringing of children for whom they share responsibility (McHale & Lindahl, 2011).

Managing Coparenting Arrangements. It is imperative that divorcing parents establish new rules and boundaries regarding their coparenting relationship. They must resist the temptation to involve children in the adult business of the divorce, making the children captive pawns. This is unhealthy for children as well as parents. Many children feel obliged to take sides with one parent, which is detrimental to all concerned. The problems of the parents should not cross the hierarchical parental boundaries to contaminate the children, even though the children will feel many of the aftershocks of a divorce.

Parenting Reflection 11–7

Are two parents really better for children than a single parent? Justify your answer.

When parents are separating in preparation for divorce, it is important that they maintain open lines of communication to resolve their differences. Children are inevitably a part of the matters discussed. To avoid the feelings of anger, frustration, and guilt that can accompany these discussions, divorcing parents might limit the topics to the health needs and educational concerns of the children, and sharing time with the children

(McHale & Lindahl, 2011). When these new rules and boundaries are followed, additional rules, patterns, and boundaries can be shaped to redefine the relationship between each individual parent and the children. This should allow for the development of new single-parent family systems.

Post-divorce Conflict

Many of the problems associated with sole custody reflect the noncustodial father's resentment, anger, and frustration in dealing with the perceived no-win situation. Some fathers feel that they are systematically disenfranchised and have minimal input into making important decisions concerning their children and are prevented from having access to quality interaction with their children.

As a result, post-divorce conflict with the ex-spouse continues or escalates, which affects the manner and context of children's interactions with their fathers. Noncustodial fathers typically disengage from the parenting relationship because their ability to function adequately in this role is greatly diminished when they withdraw from the former family system (Régnier-Loilier, 2015). The dismal record of defaulting on child-support payments by noncustodial fathers makes matters worse (Threlfall & Kohl, 2015). Many fathers feel they are cut out of their children's lives and should not have to maintain financial support. They often use this claim when they live out of state.

A single parent's sole custody of a child can create problems that appear to outweigh the advantages. Single-parent families, especially those headed by women, can experience problem-ridden, stressful, and challenging custody negotiations.

Sometimes divorcing parents are tempted to express their hurtful feelings about their divorce and the divorcing partner by playing "pain games" that can interfere with effective parenting. Basically, three types of games may serve as unhealthy ways to express the unpleasant feelings associated with divorce:

- **Discounting.** One parent discounts the other parent to a child, such as by making negative comments or using derogatory labels. When children hear such statements, they feel that these also apply to them as well because they are half of each parent.
- **Messenger or go-between.** One parent solicits a child to be a messenger or go-between with the

other parent. Children can sometimes distort innocent, simple messages that they might be asked to give to the other parent. It is not healthy for children to play the go-between role in the altered relationship between divorcing parents.

■ *I Spy.* Divorcing parents may be tempted to use a child as a source of information about the other parent. This is a ploy to find out what the other parent is doing, whether they are dating, what purchases they are making, and so forth. Asking children to spy on the other parent violates parental trust.

Single-parent Families Headed by Mothers

The majority of single-parent families in the United States are headed by women who have either never married or are divorced (Federal Interagency Forum on Child and Family Statistics, 2015). Among these families, quality of life is a major concern. Divorced and single-parent women appear to face more economic and related employment difficulties than men. Family income is lowest among single-parent families headed by women (Kramer, Myhra, Zuiker, & Bauer, 2016). Because of the low level of income among these mothers, these family systems experience poverty-level existences that seriously affect the standard of living of children (see Figure 11–2).

Financial Difficulties. Single-parent families headed by mothers can expect financial difficulties (West, 2015). A father's child support and maintenance payments are important sources of income and help provide an adequate standard of living. They do not adequately reflect the typical expenditures made by mothers who are physical custodians. Because of this dependence on inadequate support payments and other factors, such as less education or fewer years in the labor force, most single-parent families headed by women have lower annual incomes than those headed by men (Kramer et al., 2016). Child-support payments by the father can be absent or erratic (Kim, Cancian, & Meyer, 2015).

Child support is determined at the time a divorce is finalized by court decree (Boes, Collins-Camargo, & Thomas, 2015). The divorcing individuals arrange a settlement that is finalized in a legally, binding contract. Either party may agree to something that has adverse financial consequences due to the emotional coerciveness of negotiations. It may be wise to request the assistance of a divorce mediator to help the couple reach objective decisions regarding child support and secure arrangements that help ensure adequate financial support.

The most common reason for failure to pay regular child support is attributed to the financial problems of the noncustodial parent. Some parents fail to honor their child support agreement for other reasons, including

■ Withholding payment as a means of expressing anger toward the custodial ex-spouse.
■ Feelings of discrimination about the amount awarded by the court.
■ Unemployment or underemployment.

A divorce means that most women with children will seek employment to provide support for their families. Typically, they earn wages and salaries at lower levels

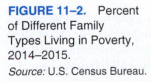

FIGURE 11–2. Percent of Different Family Types Living in Poverty, 2014–2015.

Source: U.S. Census Bureau.

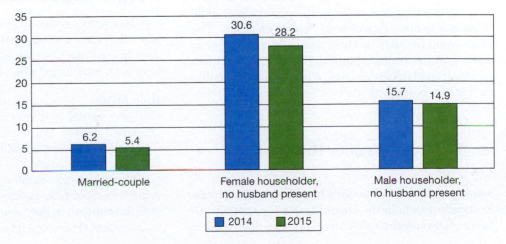

than men, often because of different levels of education, training, and work experience. Economic conditions are a primary source of stress among single-parent families headed by women (Schleider, Patel, Krumholz, Chorpita, & Weisz, 2015). Single-parent families headed by women are much more likely to live in poverty than two-parent families. This factor may contribute to a decrease in the quality of life and social functioning of the family, and it affects the parent–child relationship as well. Essentially, numerous ripple effects emanate from the dire financial conditions in single-parent families headed by mothers.

Role Strain. Single-parent mothers experience additional role strain within their new binuclear family system. Divorced women experience different degrees of role strain than divorced men. What was stressful in managing competing roles in a two-parent family system is even more stressful after divorce. The time demands in such systems are particularly exhausting (Federal Interagency Forum on Child and Family Statistics, 2015). There is less time for most activities, and employment responsibilities receive the highest priority. Child care and personal needs receive the least time; although the quality of the attention paid to children does not appear to decline. As with role strain in intact families with children, performance in all of the competing roles falls as role strain and stress increases (Nomaguchi & Johnson, 2016).

Focus Point. Lack of education, poorly paying jobs, lack of work experience, and inadequate alimony all contribute to the likelihood that more custodial mothers have family incomes at or below the poverty level. Role strain is also often experienced by these mothers. The relationship between mothers and children changes as the boundaries become blurred. Previously established adult and child roles transform. While many women find their status as single mothers stressful, most eventually manage to adjust.

Single-parent Families Headed by Fathers

Single-parent families headed by fathers is an increasing family system in the United States (Doucet, 2016). In comparison with single-parent mothers, single-parent

fathers earn considerably higher incomes, and this promotes a different standard of living, influencing the family's quality of life.

Although children in general tend to live with the mother, the children who are likely to live with a custodial father tend to be males (Nouman, Enosh, & Niselbaum-Atzur, 2016) Professionals within the legal system have become more flexible in awarding custody with the best interests of the child in mind. The quality of the parent–child relationship and the resources available to the custodial parent in providing a stable family life play a role in determining the best interests of the child.

Parenting Reflection 11–8

Divorced fathers are increasingly being granted sole custody of children. Why are women reluctant to relinquish full custody to the father?

Men assume the custodial parenting role for a variety of reasons. Unlike single-parent mothers, single-parent fathers gain custody of their children through two likely avenues:

- Men may assert their right to gain custody of children because they feel capable and motivated to parent their children effectively, although the mother may contest their ability.
- Men may assume custody when the mother shows no desire to continue parenting or is deemed unable to do so because of physical problems, mental illness, or addictive disorders.

Men adjust better to being custodial single fathers when they have a strong desire for this role. Many men wish to continue positive parenting activities that may have been established when the children were born.

Role Strain. Single-parent fathers and single-parent mothers experience role strain differently. Like the single-parent mother, the single-parent father must adjust to the additional responsibilities of child rearing while providing for the family.

Many single-parent fathers were not involved in managing household tasks before the divorce, but they have little difficulty when they assume responsibility for home management (Haire & McGeorge, 2012). Single-parent fathers tend to share household management tasks with children rather than secure help from outside resources. Single-parent mothers, in comparison, tend to perform these tasks themselves rather than expecting children to help, which promotes greater levels of role strain. Single-parent fathers expect daughters to help more than sons and to assist with household management tasks, possibly due to differences in the socialization of children. Trends in single-parent households run by a father appear to be:

■ Single-parent fathers may intentionally not involve their children in tasks in an effort to prove their own competence as household managers.

■ These fathers may attempt to ease the transition and tensions that children experience when they shift to new family patterns after the divorce.

■ Children have difficulty becoming familiar with the routines and patterns of two different households.

Arranging childcare may be a major problem, particularly for fathers with young children. Rather than hiring housekeepers or sitters, single fathers generally rely on the same childcare resources as other parents. These resources can include nonparental care, as well as support from their immediate and extended families. Frequently grandparents take on a significant caregiving role. Single fathers of older children typically rely on afterschool activities, such as dance instruction or athletics, to bridge the supervision gap.

Fathers and Gender-neutral Parenting.   Single-parent fathers can perform childcare responsibilities effectively (Gatrell, Burnett, Cooper, & Sparrow, 2015). Most men take on caregiving responsibilities in a competent manner that is healthy and beneficial to the children. Fathers are particularly competent when they have been actively involved in providing care since a child's infancy and when they willingly accept child custody after divorce. Because individuals in our society have moved increasingly toward gender-equal parenting roles, many men have learned how to provide for children's needs and to express nurture in caregiving.

Single-parent fathers promote different expectations for their children than single-parent mothers. For example, single-parent fathers demand more independence from children. As many gain experience in child-rearing activities, they shift away from authoritarian methods to an authoritative approach. They become less traditional, less discipline oriented, and more concerned

about the quality of the care they provide and the experiences children have with nonparental caregivers. They are more interested in children's educational experiences and more protective about dangerous situations to which children might be exposed (Hill, 2015).

The number of single-parent families headed by fathers has grown significantly. When making the transition to this type of family, fathers must consider whether they are able to take on caregiving responsibilities in a competent manner that is healthy and beneficial to children.

Many single-parent fathers also express concerns about raising a daughter in a family system that lacks the gender-role model provided by an adult woman. They wonder how they can provide socialization experiences for girls that will help them learn appropriate gender-role behaviors.

The Challenges of Nonresidential, Noncustodial Fathers

Fathers who do not share a home with their child face the risk of gradually fading from their child's life, other than for the obligatory child support. A troubling picture emerges. Being a nonresidential, noncustodial father seems to increase men's risk of injury, addiction, and premature death (Julion et al., 2016). These destructive lifestyles may be a reaction to the loss and grief experienced by nonresidential fathers, but it could also be a reflection of the type of irresponsible behavior that contributed to the divorce. Children's contact with their nonresidential father is important to both parties and has significant benefits (Westphal, Poortman, & van der Lippe, 2014). The nonresidential fathers' payment of child support and emotional involvement are positively associated with the well-being of the children.

Fathers may discover new dimensions in the relationship with their child. Nonresidential fathers transform the little time they have with their children into the most positive experiences possible. These fathers also tend to approach parenting from an adult-companion position. Positive outcomes are observed in the children's well-being when nonresidential fathers can maintain an age-appropriate parenting relationship.

The Challenges of Single-parent Families

The problems and challenges faced by single-parent families often overshadow the strengths (Lange, Dronkers, & Wolbers, 2014). The challenges provide opportunities for people to grow in ways they might not have done otherwise. Women state that their single-parenting experience helped build personal strengths and confidence.

There are several differences between children raised in various family structures, but they have to be qualified as there is no simple way to rank order the most advantageous family forms. In an exceptionally large study in the United States, data was collected from close to 200,000 children aged birth to 17, as part of the National Health Interview Survey (www.cdc.gov). Outcomes in nine family structures were examined. Specific attention was focused on the areas of health, schooling, and cognitive outcomes. These family forms included married couples, cohabiting couples, single moms, single dads, grandparental involvement, and skipped generation families where the middle generation was not present and the children were raised by grandparents. The results were at times counterintuitive. On average, if family functioning was good, the married couples seemed to have an advantage over single parents. Of the single parents though, the children who lived with their fathers, on average had better health outcomes. Surprisingly the presence of grandparents did not consistently provide the expected buffer against adversity that was expected, and socioeconomic factors could only explain some of the disparities. As far as the grandparents were concerned, much depended on their health, both physically and mentally; ailing grandparents were an added strain to family resources, and in such cases grandparents would be a last resort fill-in for parents, and the outcomes for those children were not ideal. Clearly the quality of parenting and grandparenting that occurs in the relationships with the children influences outcomes (Krueger, Jutte, Franzini, Elo, & Hayward, 2015).

The adverse effects or disadvantages that children are subjected to vary greatly in different family structures, as well as the reasons for living within a particular family structure. Death, chronic illness, addiction disorders, mental illness, and various other reasons may all contribute to family strain and the reason why a particular family form occurred. With so many interacting factors and variables, it would be shortsighted to doom one or the other family form while lauding others for best outcomes. There is no simple answer, especially as not all parents have the luxury of choosing the ideal family form for their offspring. In short, the level of disadvantage can vary and factors other than family form (importantly quality of parenting behavior) co-contribute to the

outcomes (Krueger et al., 2015). The conclusion in the research by these authors is sobering:

> U.S. children increasingly live in family structures that are associated with poor child well-being. The links between childhood circumstances and socioeconomic and health outcomes in later life mean that children's disadvantages may persist throughout their lives. Growing diversity in U.S. family structures suggests the need to better understand the associations between children's wellbeing and their family contexts (Krueger et al., 2015).

In well-functioning married-couple households, there seem to be support systems in place as a result of two parents both fulfilling parenting roles and contributing to the parenting resources for that particular family. This family form holds the promise of better outcomes. As far as single parent families are concerned, modeling gender-equal roles to children may offer benefits that promote well-being far beyond the years of childhood and adolescence. If the emotional climate within that single parent family was constructive and promoted child well-being, and additional mentors and family members offered consistent support and possibly coparenting, children are likely to acquire resilience from their experiences in growing up in single-parent families, a life skill that hopefully may serve them well in adulthood. There is no simple or easy answer to these complex challenges concerning family form and function.

....

Focus Point. Family systems headed by custodial fathers are increasing. Single-parent fathers are typically better educated than single-parent mothers and earn higher incomes. Men may gain custody of children after a divorce because they actively seek it or because the mother has defaulted on her parental rights by not being a responsible parent. Single-parent fathers can experience role strain as they add child rearing to their other responsibilities. The fostering of gender equality and resilience are among the positive outcomes that may be accomplished in single-parent families.

....

GRANDPARENTING

At some point, it is likely that many parents will become grandparents. It is possible for someone in their early 40s to be a grandparent. Rather than taking a sedentary approach to life, today's grandparents might be physically active, still employed, and at times providing full-time care for grandchildren (Mccarthy, 2013).

Considering the greater life expectancy, it is likely that children will have the opportunity to know and have a relationship with both sets of grandparents. The vast majority of Americans aged 65 years or older are grandparents. The most frequent activities that grandparents report sharing with grandchildren include having meals together, playing games and sports, and reading together. A majority of those studied see a grandchild at least once a week, but many live long distances away, which prevents regular visits. Because grandparents usually have an empty nest, they can allocate more time to their grandchildren.

The high divorce rate in contemporary society has changed the nature of grandparents' relationships with their grandchildren. The legal status of grandparents is a nebulous issue, and few states have enacted statutes that outline grandparental rights with regard to visitation with grandchildren (Beiner, Lowenstein, Worenklein, & Sauber, 2014).

Skipped generation parenting, implies that the grandparents step in for their own children, and take over parental roles for their grandchildren. Many grandparents take an active role in raising and providing care for grandchildren (Federal Interagency Forum on Child and Family Statistics, 2015). A substantial increase in the number of households headed by grandparents who provide primary care for their grandchildren has occurred, regardless of whether the children's parents are present or absent. Grandparents report that with regard to taking care of grandchildren, they are more relaxed, more involved, and wiser than when they parented their own children.

Although some grandparents are not especially involved with their grandchildren and their role is downplayed in family life, other grandparents make important contributions to family life and have a significant influence on the family system, such as:

- Accepting the behaviors and traits of grandchildren that the parents are not able to tolerate.
- Providing nurture for grandchildren that parents may not be able to provide.
- Providing instruction to grandchildren on values, ethics, and morals.
- Providing backup support for parents.
- Providing wisdom and advice if asked, and being the family historian.
- Acting as an equalizer to provide balance within a family system.

The Role of Grandparents

When the parents raise their own children, the role of the grandparent is part time and less demanding. Being a grandparent lacks clear definitions and boundaries in terms of the role, and depends on the nature of the relationship with each particular grandchild (Bates & Taylor, 2016). Grandparents, like parents, may have a unique relationship with each grandchild and appreciate the differences that each child brings to the relationship.

For many, the transition to grandparenthood begins when they learn that the adult child is becoming a parent for the first time. The older adults fantasize about what they will experience as grandparents. Because this is the first time, the first grandchild often has a special place in the lives of the grandparents. Some find the experience difficult, if becoming a grandparent is perceived as being developmentally off-time (Ben-Ari, Findler, & Shlomo, 2013).

Childhood experiences with grandparents influence the future involvement of men and women with their own grandchildren. Individual's pattern their grandparenting role and behavior on the models they observed as children (Soliz, 2015). Several prominent components can be found:

- Grandparents may act as the family caretaker, providing support to adult children and grandchildren when needed, and ameliorating the negative effects of problems experienced by the adult child, such as addiction disorders, divorce, or chronic mental or physical illness.
- Grandparents may provide nurture to all family members, which may not be available from other adults in the family.
- Grandparents serve as family historians, acting as a bridge between the past and the present that aids in developing a sense of family identity.
- Grandparents may provide companionship for grandchildren in shared social activities that promote close emotional attachment.

This evolution of grandparenting styles changes in tandem with grandchildren's development. Grandparenting styles may be mediated by a variety of factors.

Gender may temper how someone approaches the grandparenting role. Women may be more actively involved with grandchildren than men because of their socialization and past experiences in parenting children.

Grandfathers may emphasize interactions related to tasks outside the family, while grandmothers may emphasize issues related to interpersonal dynamics within the family. As gender-equality and shared-gender roles extend through the generations, these roles may blend over time.

Physical proximity is an important factor that mediates how the grandparent–grandchild relationship will unfold. The physical distance between the grandparents and the grandchildren will frequently determine how involved the older adults are and how interactions occur. Culture influences grandparenting style as well.

Grandparents have few legal rights to visit or be a part of their grandchildren's lives following the divorce of adult children. Because grandparents may play a very active role in the lives of their grandchildren, separation can be emotionally difficult for both parties. Unless a state has enacted legislation outlining such rights, grandparents may not be allowed to see their grandchildren if the custodial parent disapproves. If visitation rights are granted, the court allows such visitation because continuing to see the grandparents is perceived to be in the best interests of the child.

Step-grandparenting

Divorce among adult children and the grandparents themselves can temper how the grandparent–grandchild relationship will play out. When the grandparents themselves divorce after years of marriage, some may reduce their involvement with grandchildren because of the circumstances surrounding the divorce. When adult children divorce, many grandparents are uncertain about their visitation rights. The relationship of paternal grandparents and the grandchildren is often under greater duress than the relationship between the maternal grandparents and the grandchildren (Jappens & Van Bavel, 2016).

Divorce among the adult children can also strengthen the involvement of the grandparents and their relationship with the grandchildren. Grandparents may assume major caretaking responsibilities with regard to the grandchildren in the absence of one of the children's parents (Silverstein & Giarrusso, 2013). Grandparents may not be as capable of supporting grandchildren in school activities, and the age gap may present difficulties. These arrangements typically occur when some type of serious family problem affects the adult child. Quality of life often becomes a prominent concern because of financial constraints. Older adults may be on fixed incomes or dependent on public assistance, so their financial planning did not include providing for additional children.

Parenting Reflection 11–9

How is the family system affected when three generations reside in the family home and the grandparents provide ongoing care for their grandchildren?

Step-grandparenting has received relatively little attention from researchers. Because step-grandchildren are usually older when an adult-child remarries, there may be little opportunity for the step-grandparents to form a relationship with step-grandchildren. Because both parties have had experiences with this relationship prior to

---

Focus On 11–1 **The Role of Grandparents in the Extended Family**

Parental responsibilities	Coparenting, supporting their adult children in rearing the grandchildren
Positive experiences	Because they are grandparenting part time, they can focus on enjoyable moments, leaving disciplinary matters to the parents
Family historian	Knowing the family history and passing it on, ancestry
Disengaged or distant	Emotionally disengaged and/or living far away
Aging with health concerns, dependent	Health concerns can make grandparents dependent on their own children, needing help and support

parental divorce, it is likely that both wish to take advantage of opportunities for the new relationship to develop.

•••

Focus Point.   Many grandparents are overjoyed when grandchildren are introduced into their family system. Their roles within the family often include encouraging the grandchildren, supporting the parents, and acting as teachers in the passing down of family history and heritage. Grandparents have few legal rights over visitation, and therefore may not be allowed to visit grandchildren following a divorce or family conflict. Divorce settlements may spell out the details.

•••

CARING FOR AGING PARENTS

It is highly likely that, at some point, adult children will be called upon to provide care for an elderly parent. The American population is aging, and life expectancy is longer, with current averages in the mid-80s (Vespa, Lewis, & Kreider, 2013). Not all families can afford caregiving services for the elderly, and children have some responsibility to provide for aging parents (Pearson, 2013).

Relationships between adult-child caregivers and elderly parents are characterized by some of the following:

■ Because more people are living longer, family relationships are more numerous and complex. Younger members maintain ties with elderly parents, grandparents, great-grandparents, and older relatives.

■ Increased life expectancy means that people may experience more health problems and have an inadequate pension.

■ Ethnic minorities tend to provide more care in-home for their elderly parents.

■ Female adult children are more frequently the caregivers for the elderly.

■ Most adult-child caregivers are middle-aged, married, parents themselves, and working full time.

Providing emotional support, services, and financial assistance to the elderly is referred to as *eldercare* (Zacher & Schulz, 2015). Such care includes assisting the parent with personal hygiene, running errands, taking the parent to appointments, housekeeping, and paying bills. Adult-child caregivers can expect to perform informal caregiving for an estimated 18 hours a week or more, depending on the needs of the elderly parent. When this type of caregiving is not feasible, adult children hire caregivers to meet the needs of the parent, which adds financial stress. Many adult-child caregivers rely on siblings to help with these responsibilities. Some siblings are not reliable, making the burden of care especially heavy for the principal adult-child caregiver.

The relationship between the elderly parent and the adult-child caregiver follows a trajectory, beginning with concern about the welfare of an elderly parent and the expression of this concern to the siblings and others. This progresses to giving advice to the elderly parent on conducting their affairs. The adult-child caregiver assumes increasingly greater responsibilities and often consults with family members and professionals in making decisions. Conflicts between the elderly parent and the adult-child caregiver can emerge. The elderly parent may become resentful regarding her loss of power and control, and feel threatened by the loss of independence.

Many adults who are sandwiched between caring for both the younger generation (their children) and older generation (their parents), may experience role strain. This is more likely if they are also juggling career, parenting, and partnership responsibilities.

The elderly parent may also disagree with the adult-child caregiver's decisions, causing increasing stress and tension in the relationship. Dementia, Alzheimer's and related conditions add yet another level of strain and responsibility.

The Sandwich Generation

The middle generation is *sandwiched* between the needs and demands of the previous, as well as the following, generation (Kingsmill & Schlesinger, 2015). Many employed parents experience role overload and role strain as they continue to perform family roles in addition to work roles. Fueling the problems is the significant role reversal that takes place as the adult-child caregiver assumes greater responsibility, especially if chronic illness and disability is present. Burnout contributes to poor-quality caregiving. When the adult-child caregiver works full time, tries to maintain a marital relationship, seeks to conduct their own parent–child relationships, and receives little assistance from siblings or a spouse, they are overburdened. They are referred to as the **sandwich generation** because of the demands from both the older and the younger generations (Kingsmill & Schlesinger, 2015).

Video Example 11.3

Watch this video on the sandwich generation. What are the struggles that come with caring for aging parents while also caring for your own children?

(https://www.youtube.com/watch?v=bCBoeBrZ4KU)

Elder Abuse

Occasionally, excessive caregiver stress leads to emotional, physical, and/or verbal acting out, which can escalate to harmful **elder abuse** (Bennett & Kingston, 2013). Several options may alleviate such situations and minimize caregiver burnout. These might include

- Encouraging men to become as involved as women in providing eldercare.
- Involving broader community support, such as eldercare and respite programs.
- Providing more funding for programs that educate persons involved with eldercare.
- Making eldercare financially manageable through tax credits and other incentives.

Focus Point.   Many adults caring for both the younger generation (their children) and older generation (their parents), may experience role strain and eventual burnout. This is more likely if they are also juggling career obligations and partnerships or marriages. Elder abuse is a distressing reality. Involving more men and community members in the care of the elderly, as well as providing greater access to education and funding, may reduce the unacceptable actions related to elder abuse.

> **"We are caught in an inescapable network of mutuality, tied in a single garment of destiny. Whatever affects one directly, affects all indirectly."**
>
> *Martin Luther King Jr.*
> *Letter from Birmingham City Jail, April 16, 1963*

CHAPTER FOCUS POINTS

The Dynamics of Ratio

- Family resources are an important consideration in family outcomes. Resources are varied and include interpersonal, social, economic, civic, educational, spiritual, health, and more, and these resources interact on different systemic levels, such as those within the family as opposed to those within a society at large. Compared to the large families of yesteryear, the average American family now consists of two children. Only children face unique challenges which parents can combat by creating networks of socialization and support. Advances in medical care, much lower infant mortality, and changes in social norms have played contributing roles. Challenges abound in all families, irrespective of size.

Single Parent Families

- Divorce elicits emotional and transitional adjustments as parents exchange their couple identity for single status, a transition with great implications on the parenting role. Divorced parents must communicate expectations clearly and learn to adjust to their new roles. Even though adults adjust differently, they continue to share a connection through their child. A couple can seldom be completely divorced when children are involved.

- Parental divorce affects children in a number of ways. Age at the time of the divorce is an important factor. Parents fear that their children will experience harmful outcomes as a result of the divorce. Researchers generally find that divorce is disruptive, but that most children adapt and adjust in a resilient way. The manner in which the adults continue to fulfill their roles as parents and form a constructive working relationship as coparents, is an important factor in determining outcomes.

Custody Arrangements

- Children should be sheltered from custody battles between divorcing parents; encounters which often become hostile. Parents who share joint custody are more involved with parenting responsibilities, have more contact with their children, and use parenting resources extensively. Fathers in joint custody arrangements are more likely to be financially responsible towards the children, preventing a poverty-level existence.
- Lack of education, poorly paying jobs, lack of work experience, and inadequate alimony all contribute to the likelihood that more custodial mothers have family incomes at or below the poverty level. Role strain is often experienced by these mothers. The relationship between mothers and children changes as the boundaries become blurred. Previously established adult and child roles transform. While many women find their status as single mothers stressful, most eventually manage to adjust.
- Family systems headed by custodial fathers are increasing. Single-parent fathers are typically better educated than single-parent mothers and earn higher incomes. Men may gain custody of children after a divorce because they actively seek it or because the mother has defaulted on her parental rights by not being a responsible parent. Single-parent fathers can experience role strain as they add child rearing to their other responsibilities. The fostering of gender equality and resilience are among the positive outcomes that can be accomplished in single-parent families.

Grandparenting

- Many grandparents are overjoyed when grandchildren are introduced into their family system. Their roles within the family often include encouraging the grandchildren, supporting the parents, and acting as teachers in the passing down of family history and heritage. Grandparents have few legal rights over visitation, and therefore might not be allowed to visit grandchildren following a divorce or family conflict. Divorce settlements may spell out the details.

Caring for Aging Parents

- Many adults caring for both the younger generation (their children) and older generation (their parents), may experience role strain and eventual burnout. This is more likely if they are also juggling career obligations and partnerships or marriages. Elder abuse is a distressing reality. Involving more men and community members in the care of the elderly, as well as providing greater access to education and funding, may reduce the unacceptable actions related to elder abuse.

USEFUL WEBSITES

Websites are dynamic and change

Educating Communities for Parenting
http://ecparenting.org
Empowering parents and communities

Center on the Developing Child, Harvard University
http://developingchild.harvard.edu
Developing children, innovation in development

OnlyDads and OnlyMums (United Kingdom)
www.onlydads.org and www.onlymums.org
Support for separated/divorced parents

SingleFather.org
www.singlefather.org
Support for single fathers

Single Parents Alliance of America
www.spaoa.org
Support and resources for single parents

SingleParents.org
www.singleparents.org
Online single parent support

CHAPTER 12

Parenting Interrupted and Fragile Families

Learning Outcomes

After completing this chapter, you should be able to:

1. Discuss the implications on the family system when parenting is interrupted.

2. Explain what is considered a "fragile family" and how it affects child well-being.

3. Illustrate how adverse childhood experiences can influence healthy functioning throughout the lifespan.

4. Summarize the role of both internal and external developmental assets.

5. Describe phases for a family in crisis.

6. Describe the ways grief and loss affect families.

7. Evaluate the role of open communication in fighting drug abuse within families.

8. Examine the implications of parental addiction on children and families.

9. Categorize the various areas of child abuse and their ramifications.

PARENTING INTERRUPTED

Humans require a lot of "handholding" and protection until they can function independently. If we think of the average lifespan as being about 75 years, and children thinking they can do things independently at about age 15 (whether this is true or not), then we spend at least a fifth of our lives getting ready for adult-hood. We can do the same calculation again and be a little more generous on time periods involved. If we are lucky enough to reach 80, and we think we are adults by age 20, then we have still spent a quarter of our lives in delightful childhood and adolescent activities before the responsibilities of adulthood hit us full force.

Twenty years is a long time for parents to remain committed and on task. Things happen. As children, we thought that grownups knew everything. In a way, they were omnipotent and kind of perfect; after all, they had all the power. As young adults, and especially during our own training as family related professionals, we see the reality of parents struggling to parent; even if they started out with the best intentions.

Sometimes parents have to be in two places at the same time. They would like to be at home with the children, but their work occupies them elsewhere, or if they are military parents their deployment may call them away for days, months, or even years. Some par-ents are distant as in being incarcerated, and they too have been removed from the family table for years. Illness and especially mental health challenges take their toll. The depressed parent, the chronic pain suf-ferer, the parent using a wheelchair, the parent with a serious mental or physical disability; they are all forced to become "part time parents" of sorts, as there will be times when their condition forces them away from active, involved, and continuous family life (Fields, 2015).

When this happens, the family system has to redis-tribute its power and all the remaining family members pool their resources to keep the boat afloat. The family has to find a new homeostasis or equilibrium. What affects one family member in particular, will directly or indirectly affect the entire family system within which that individual is embedded. The temporary or perma-nent loss of one person in a strong, dedicated, and resourceful family system can be tragic, but it need not damage that entire system permanently.

More serious is when the entire family system is slowly poisoned by the demands or disabilities of one overruling family leader. The father who is aggressive and violent, or the mother who is emotionally absent and incapable of nurturing, while also dealing with addic-tions; these parents do not have the resources required to nurture and sustain their dependents. By being who they are at that moment in family life, they have the

destructive power to run their entire family into the ground, to harm the fragile and developing children and to destroy the hope for better outcomes.

Parents can be "hijacked" by their own addictions, where they become so dependent that they are con-trolled by their vices. Other parents have such problems with anger management that their toxicity spills out in abuse, including maltreatment of the most vulnerable members of that family system, namely the children. These scenarios are not pretty, and that is why they are often referred to as *toxic parenting*, or *poisonous pedagogy*.

If the support required to interrupt the cycle of destruction cannot be found within the family, society steps in, especially to protect the children. Our solutions are not ideal, but then we are dealing with the most destructive parenting practices, and there is no quick solution to those.

Historic Research

The Vaillant Study. This study is also known as the Harvard Grant Study. In one of the well-known longitu-dinal studies in the social and medical sciences, namely the Harvard Grant Study, 268 mentally- and physically healthy Harvard sophomores from the classes 1939–1944, were followed over a period of 75 years. The lead researcher was George Vaillant (b. 1934), a psychiatrist and professor in Harvard's medical school. Hence the study is often referred to as the Vaillant Study. Famously, one of the study's participants was future President John F. Kennedy, though the individual results of the study were anonymous and protected for privacy.

In the study, several domains were studied, including overall adult adjustment, career functioning/success, creativity, social relations, mental health, and of interest to this discussion, substance abuse, now known as substance-related and addictive disorders according to the *DSM-5* (Soldz & Vaillant, 1999). The study focused on nicotine (smoking) and alcohol specifically. The other aspect of relevance to this discussion were the relationships of the study participants with their own parents. Two important findings pertinent to this discussion were:

■ "Alcoholism is a disorder with great destructive power," negatively influencing almost all life and career outcomes of the participants in the Vaillant study (Stossel, 2013).

■ The quality of the parental relationship lasts into adulthood, with good relationships having positive and protective effects.

In other words, parenting, specifically nurturing and what was labelled as "warm" parental relationships, carried over into adulthood and seemed to affect social and other functioning. Those persons with good histories of having been parented appropriately and well ultimately reported happier lives. The qualities expected from mothers versus fathers seemed to have been somewhat influenced by gender norms of the time (Vaillant, 2012).

Vaillant (2012) continued to assess this group far beyond conventional retirement age and the findings are published in his book: *Triumphs of Experience: The Men of the Harvard Grant Study*. This book illuminates yet another dimension, in that several of the participants gave permission for their individual lives to be featured and discussed. Hence, there are individual case studies. Two important core findings are:

■ Recovery from negative childhood experiences is possible.
■ Memories of a happy childhood will sustain and inspire individuals throughout their lifetimes.

Hence, investing in the total well-being of families is always a noble pursuit, as the dividends are significant.

Video Example 12.1

Watch this video on Vaillant's longitudinal study on human development. What were the important findings of the Vaillant study? What was surprising according to Vaillant?

(https://www.youtube.com/watch?v=VyhBZCfIatk)

Focus Point. When parenting takes a back seat or is "interrupted" due to, for instance, career obligations, health issues, or substance abuse, the results could have lifetime implications for the children. The family system has to redistribute its power and all the remaining family members pool their resources to find a new homeostasis or equilibrium. The Vaillant study offers valuable insight into the connection between parent–child relationships and adult functioning, further displaying how childhood experiences greatly influence the entire life story.

FRAGILE FAMILIES

Families can be fragile. Even so, families are frequently represented as happy groups of people committed to nurturing, sustaining, and supporting each other. This is the romanticized version that we prefer to hear about. The darker side reveals unpleasant and also destructive realities. An effective parenting outcome presumes a parental system that is healthy, resilient, and able to meet the requirements demanded by the parenthood role. Many families experience problems and situations that affect their ability to function in healthy ways. Effective parenting in these families is difficult to achieve because several factors counteract this optimal goal, and often the parenting is interrupted.

Families can be considered as *fragile*, *high risk*, or *vulnerable* because of economic, health, psychological, or social factors. These, singly or in combination, challenge effective functioning. Many families find they can cope by seeking help from professionals, social networks, relatives, and other sources. They learn to use healthy means for dealing with difficult circumstances. Other families fail to respond to such challenges in constructive ways and their status becomes even more endangered. While every family can expect to experience crises, each family reacts in different ways to resolve critical situations.

These challenges are significant and have detrimental effects on parent–child relations. Poverty can have pervasive effects on the actual quality of life, as well as the aspirations of growing children. Financial constraints infiltrate into numerous areas of family life and significantly affect the children of those families (Wagmiller & Adelman, 2009). No family system is perfect, but many face problems that threaten the ability to function effectively and actually verge toward destruction and even illegal behavior.

Fragile Families

In *fragile families*, the family system cannot withstand the numerous assaults on its well-being and may become dysfunctional or disintegrate. In this context, fragile means "liable to break." In extreme cases, the family becomes a dangerous place for children. Typically, several risk factors interact to escalate the detrimental effects on the family. One risk factor leads to another. Some of the factors that increase the fragility of families are:

- Poverty and all of the factors linked to limited resources, economic or otherwise.
- Limited education, dropping out of school, and under-served schools.
- Unwed parenthood, lack of commitment to the family, and absent fathers.
- Lack of knowledge concerning childcare and parenting.
- Lack of vocational skills, low-income jobs, and difficulty finding and retaining employment.
- Poor conditions in the family of origin and no role models for a healthy family life.
- Chronic illness, disability, depression, and children with behavioral problems.
- Mental illness, frequently untreated or noncompliant patients who stop treatment.
- Use of illicit substances and addictive disorders, alcoholism, and prescription drug abuse.
- Social isolation, lack of support systems, and dependence on welfare.
- Lack of integration into a social or civic community, for example, a social, religious, or other group that supports family values.

Based on Mitchell, C., McLanahan, S., Notterman, D., Hobcraft, J., Brooks-Gunn, J., & Garfinkel, I. (2015). Family structure instability, genetic sensitivity, and child well-being. *American Journal of Sociology, 120*(4), 1195–1225.

The original study: The official *"Fragile Families and Child Wellbeing Study"* (FFCWS) was initiated by Princeton and Columbia Universities. It followed about 5,000 children born in the United States between 1998 and 2000 and is a longitudinal birth cohort study (www.fragilefamilies.princeton.edu).

Fragile Families and Child Wellbeing Research

The official *"Fragile Families and Child Wellbeing Study"* (FFCWS) was initiated by Princeton and Columbia Universities. It followed about 5,000 children born in the United States between 1998 and 2000 and is a longitudinal birth cohort study (www.fragilefamilies.princeton.edu). In this study the term *"fragile families"* was used to describe families who were at greater risk than more traditional families to face poverty, probably accompanied by marital and family breakup. The study included 5-year, 9-year and 15-year follow ups (completed in 2017), and also looked at parental relationships including marital status and, importantly, the outcomes for children in these families. The effects of policies and environmental conditions also came under the spotlight. About ten themes were studied but key themes from the research are also of relevance to parenting.

The Risks of Family Instability. When the relationships of the parents are *unstable*, the children are at risk. The numbers of children born outside a marriage relationship is increasing and at the time of the study almost 40% of children were born to unmarried parents, although many of these couples lived in marriage-like relationships, and were committed to each other (Waldfogel, Craigie, & Brooks-Gunn, 2010). The important implication for children is that these relationships tend to promise *less stability and continuity*, and for children the outcomes are less advantageous if compared to the outcomes for children growing up in stable homes with married parents. In the five-year follow up studies, less than 35% of the couples were still living with the same partner as when the child was born. Couples who stay together in committed constructive relationships are more likely to be able to produce shared wealth and reduce the chances of poverty becoming a factor in family instability.

These parental partnerships offered less continuity, and it followed that unmarried parents were more likely to have children with other partners, giving the child concerned half siblings. Importantly, the parents were more likely to have become parents during their teens, exponentially increasing the challenging factors. Linked factors were poverty, substance abuse, depression, and incarceration.

Particularly disconcerting is that the child's socioemotional and cognitive development can be adversely affected by parental instability, although in a related study using some of the same sample data, the researchers found that family instability mattered more than family structure for cognitive and health outcomes. When it concerned parenting by a single mother, irrespective of whether that family structure was stable or unstable at times, the instability could precipitate behavior problems in the children (Waldfogel, Craigie, & Brooks-Gunn, 2010).

The presence of a child with special needs within a family may also add to relationship stress and affect parental cohesion. The concept of "spill-over effect" implies that with stress originating from any area within the family, such as from the parental union, the problem and adaptive behaviors the family is facing can affect and tax the entire family system and reduce its systemic ability to cope constructively (Mitchell, Szczerepa, & Hauser-Cram, 2016). Paying attention to overall family climate through respite and self-renewal time and activities is especially important in families facing great challenges.

Union Instability and Disruptions.   Within-partner relationship instability and disruptions are significant contributors to family stress. This type of partner instability has occasionally been labeled as "churning" to denote the agitation occurring and the on-again, off-again nature of the relationship. Based on the Fragile Families and Child Wellbeing Study discussed earlier, 16% of the biological parents had experienced **union instability** by a child's 5th year. Union instability and disruptions appear to produce more stress than stable separation, as there is an unpredictability to the relationship that also influences the children's well-being. Parenting stress is precipitated by relationship instability, especially instability within one relationship that picks up and drops off again randomly (Halpern-Meekin & Turney, 2016).

Additionally, instability may influence child–parent attachment. Some of these patterns of inconsistent parental responsibility are found in the parents of children who are subjected to foster care; the unpredictability of the parents may cause repeated episodes of foster care, as the biological parents may be unreliable in terms of their true parenting commitment. Absent parenting, as precipitated through incarceration, in other words imprisonment, is another example of unreliable parenting that exerts stress on the family (Geller, Cooper, Garfinkel, Schwartz-Soicher, & Mincy, 2012). More fathers than mothers serve prison sentences, and it destabilizes children and their families. The FFCWS study confirmed what one would predict intuitively, namely that children tended to live with the parent who displayed fewer problems. If drugs, alcohol, or multiple partners were involved, then the child tended to be raised by the parent displaying the more stable parenting behavior (Goldscheider, Scott, Lilja, & Bronte-Tinkew, 2015).

Fathers who are nonresident, yet also maintain complex relationships with multiple mothers of their children, increase the complexity of their relationships as they clearly are not committed to a monogamous relationship. The financial and emotional burdens of multiple children, and parenting roles in different families can be overwhelming as the logistics of such relationships are clearly very complex. If a greater number of coparents are involved to take over some of the parenting responsibilities in the various families, higher parenting efficacy may occur (Fagan, Levine, Kaufman, & Hammar, 2016). These types of relationships are not always apparent in the research, as many studies tend to focus on the quality of one set of parents.

Children of the Great Recession

Historic Research.   The historic work of Elder (1998), documented outcomes of children of the *Great Depression* (1929 until late 1930s). Children had to support parents in maintaining economic viability of the family, with all the accompanying hardships of financial insecurity (which led to food and shelter insecurity). Unemployment occurred on a dramatic scale. Elder studied adults who had been children during this stressful time. He also examined how these stressors impacted family life and the effects on those who had experienced it.

Similarly, the *Great Recession* (during and after the financial crisis of about 2006–2008) represented the longest economic downturn in U.S. history since the Great Depression. The recession's impact on families was far-reaching. Apart from economic factors, related factors such as how it negatively affected parenting quality and child well-being were examined. As far as gender equality and dual income families was concerned, the research showed that, in families where the mother was college-educated, the families' income only dropped by 5%, whereas the losses for those families without college education were about three- to fourfold. *Economic insecurity* was an important factor linked to negative outcomes. Related instability also had negative outcomes for children's health. As unemployment rose and stressed family wellbeing, the likelihood of clinically meaningful child mental health problems would also increase substantially.

Children are part of a family system and what affects that system affects all its members as well (Burgard, 2012, Goldman-Mellor, Saxton, & Catalano, 2010).

Protective Factors.   It follows that college educated parents, especially families that included a college educated mother, fared better in economically challenging times. Stability of the parental dyad, and hence the family overall, was a major protective factor (Garfinkel, McLanahan, & Wimer, 2016).

In short, factors which influence family well-being are:

- **Parental resources.** Parents with college education, who have better employment opportunities, which in turn provide benefits such as health insurance. Civic and social support, extended family networks are valuable resources. These parents are more likely to be able to provide support in the form of books, clothing, and extracurricular activities, and may possibly live in areas with better-served schools.
- **Parental mental health.** Parental mental health influences all families, across family types. Depression does not support engaged parenting. Addiction disorders affect both quantity and quality of parenting engagement.
- **Parenting quality.** Parents who are warm and nurturing while also providing appropriate structure, and who provide stability for the children in the home, create the child friendly environments. The better the partnership quality of the parents, the more likely it is to carry over into a good environment in which to raise children.
- **Father involvement.** The father who is not residing with the mom, can still bring enormous benefits to the children if he remains actively involved. In other words, the quality of the involvement can override the family structure. Importantly, this includes the relationship with the mother. One of the biggest gifts we can give our children, is if we, as parents, get on well with the other parent of the child. Divorce is a reality, but spousal warfare is toxic for children. In the interest of the children, work it out, even if parents live apart.
- **Family stability.** Family structure at the time of the child's birth is highly indicative of stability and future father involvement. Family structure most likely to be associated with child well-being, is that of a stable married parental dyad. Exceptions can occur if the

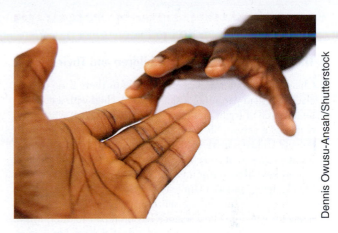

Dennis Owusu-Ansah/Shutterstock

Parents in fragile families may not be emotionally available to their children. If a consistent mentor invests in the child's well-being, this adult can provide the lifeline towards better outcomes. In turn, this fosters resilience and a sense of continuity for the child.

lead parent can succeed in creating stability, but typically that requires extensive social and other resources. See Guest Reflection 12–1. The greater the number of episodes of major family transitions, the more likely the occurrence of behavioral problems, which could also affect cognitive scores on tests. Hence, the potential problems when foster children have to transition repeatedly. See Guest Reflection 12–1.

"Family Stability is crucial for child well-being."
(Waldfogel, Craigie & Brooks-Gunn, 2010).

Focus Point.   The term *"fragile families"* is used to describe families who are at greater risk than more traditional families to face poverty, probably accompanied by marital and family breakup. Many elements can play a role in putting families at risk of becoming vulnerable, including socioeconomic challenges, physical health, and psychological well-being. Protective factors such as stability and availability of resources, civic engagement, and family support, act as mediating agents and promote family prosperity.

Guest Reflection 12–1

The Underrated Miracle of Children and Their Parents

Challenges abound in parenting. Perhaps there is no greater challenge than parenting a sick child. A child with a cold can be a source of fright and worry to any parent, but what if the child has a severe, life-threatening illness, or a terrible birth defect? Unlike a mere cold, these things don't get better in a few days, so parent and child may be faced with a life-long (and sometimes, life-shortening) disease. Such disease is always life-changing, and also family-changing.

As a physician who specializes in congenital heart defects, many for which medical science has no repair to offer, I have often thought, how do parents, and indeed their children, muster the incredible fortitude to deal with the daily struggles of a chronic illness, and the occasional terror of a serious setback, or the need for a death-defying surgery or procedure to treat that life-threatening disease? The answer isn't obvious.

Even though most parents not only manage but become self-taught experts at parenting a child with a chronic illness, some do not. That parent, usually but not always a single parent, stops coming to medical visits, and often drops out of the child's life completely. Someone else, a family member or a foster parent, steps in to tackle the job. The fact that this is rare is amazing. Most parents faced with this challenge rise to the occasion and never seem to look back. It's a daunting task. They, after all, must learn how to parent, perhaps having never been parents before; they must learn about medical issues and how to render home care while at the same time taking care of all the normal needs of the child and siblings.

Parents of a newly diagnosed child are perceptive and smart and always seem to ask the same questions, even if the parents are from a different culture and speak a different language. I find myself anticipating the next question—perhaps from the look on the parent's face and the body language, or maybe from having heard the litany of concerns many times before, "Is this problem life threatening?" (usually asked more than once), "Will my child lead a normal life?," "What do I need to watch for?," and so on.

My answers to these questions allow me opportunity to give a new parent hope, because I have had the enormous privilege of seeing patients grow and follow the journey with their parents, who themselves grow as parents, until one day that young adult patient returns for a medical visit without his or her parents. I know that patient has not only grown to be responsible for their own health care, but also that their parents have done what parents live to do, to see their children, in spite of challenges such as disease, become independent and capable, and I'm thankful yet again to have witnessed the underrated miracle of children and parents passing this fabulous milestone.

Walter H. Johnson, MD, Pediatric Cardiologist, Children's of Alabama. Published with permission.

Cultural Snapshot 12–1

Parental Gifts and Sources of Strength

In our families of origin, we learn the unique cultural customs of our ancestors, resources for strength and resilience. When we reach transitional points in our lives, we can rely on the customs that we experienced in our childhood home to be a guiding force. When families migrate, and children are raised in host cultural environments, they have to renegotiate many of these customs as they are blending the old and the new, the familiar with the less familiar. What customs and rituals withstand the test of time, which ones are so important that we want to pass them on to our children? Sona Pai wrote a short story with the title "Under the Mandap" and discussed precisely these questions regarding the parental gifts that her Indian parents gave her, and which also provide her with strength and resilience. Traditional Hindu weddings are held under a *mandap*, which is a canopy or open tent-like festive structure.

> "Growing up, I had always thought of my life between two cultures as a role without a script. Now, at twenty-seven, it becomes clear to me that this was not really the case. As my hyphenated identity took shape over the years, clues were everywhere. Pop culture and peer pressure taught me what was cool and American; parental expectations and family traditions taught me what was proper and Indian. At school with my friends and at home with my family, I always did what I thought I was supposed to do, and I had plenty of guides to provide direction" (2005, pp. 126–127).

These cultural choices become more ambiguous and difficult when we reach transitional points in the lifespan. Celebrating a marriage, the birth of a child, mourning a loss or facing family difficulties and grief; what does the cultural script dictate for those times? Will the new hybrid culture and identity provide the same comfort and resources from our childhood?

> "After growing up wondering if I could ever be American enough to fit in with my friends, now I wonder if I can ever be Indian enough to give my children the culture of their ancestors. I can cook a full Indian meal, but I need all day to do it. I can speak a little Gujarati and even less Hindi, but barely enough to complete a full sentence. I can wear a sari, but only if someone else puts it on for me. I wonder if I am ready for this leap from daughter and sister to wife and mother" (2005, p. 127).

Culture is not static, and the emotional language between parents and their children will be transmitted across the divides created by bicultural contexts. Each next generation will drift a little further from that original cultural well of their culture of origin. But in exchange they will drift closer to the culture of their adopted homeland; and that too provides great and unexpected wealth in its own right.

Source: Pai, Sona. (2005). Under the Mandap. In Fountas, A. J. (Ed.). *Waking up American: Coming of Age Biculturally*. Emeryville, CA: Avalano/Seal Press.

ADVERSE CHILDHOOD EXPERIENCES

The Centers for Disease Control (CDC) and Kaiser-Permanente, a group involved with health care, launched a large-scale study into Adverse Childhood Experiences, also referred to as the ACE study. It comprised responses from over 17 thousand participants. The essence of the findings indicate the interactive roles of adverse childhood experiences with various consecutive life events and health choices. Everything that follows the initial adverse childhood experience can add increasing layers of risk, and the likelihood of a number of risk-related events increases. The sequence from conception and birth, throughout life to eventual death can be layered in the following manner and is visually presented in the ACE study in the form of a pyramid, showing how health and well-being is influenced throughout the lifespan (www.cdc.gov/violenceprevention/acestudy/about.html). See Figure 12–1.

Adverse childhood experiences from conception onwards can lead to disrupted neurodevelopment, which can pave the way for social, emotional, and cognitive impairment. These risk factors can facilitate the adoption of high risk behaviors. This in turn can facilitate disease, disability and social problems. Ultimately, all the described factors can contribute to a shorter life span, or early death.

FIGURE 12–1. The ACE Pyramid.

Source: Centers for Disease Control and Prevention, National Center for Injury Prevention and Control, Division of Violence Prevention. https://www.cdc.gov/violenceprevention/acestudy/about.html

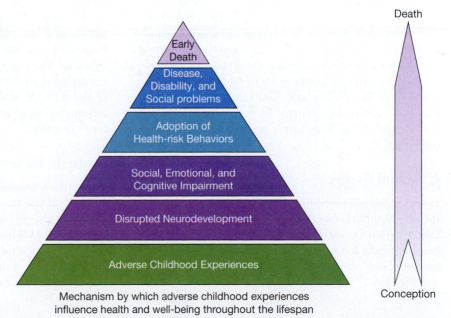

Mechanism by which adverse childhood experiences influence health and well-being throughout the lifespan

Many behaviors related to violent or abusive behavior throughout the lifespan can be particularly toxic and lead to poor outcomes. These include child maltreatment, intimate partner violence (IPV), sexual violence, elder abuse, and also global violence.

In parenting terms this is an important outcome: "Positive relationship factors may help break the cycle of child maltreatment" (Merrick, Leeb, & Lee; 2013). Safe, stable, and nurturing relationships are the foundation for positive childhood experiences and can also break the cycle of intergenerational abuse (Jaffee, Caspi, Moffitt, Polo-Tomás & Taylor, 2007). (www.cdc.gov/violenceprevention/acestudy)

• •

Focus Point. As a snowball builds when rolling down a hill, adverse childhood experiences contribute to more negative outcomes that ultimately contribute to early death. However, mediating factors such as positive familial relationships could aid in breaking the cycle of negative experiences, thus halting the "snowball" of risk.

• •

ASSETS CONTRIBUTING TO HEALTHY DEVELOPMENT

The Search Institute has identified the factors that contribute to healthy development. They refer to them as building blocks, or *developmental assets* (www.search-institute.org). They have built up detailed lists of developmental assets for various age groups including forty assets for adolescents. The assets are grouped into two main areas, namely external and internal assets. The external assets refer to factors in the environment of the children and their families that can support good outcomes. Internal factors refer to qualities and attitudes that may foster resilience and positive scenarios.

External Assets

External assets, according to the Search Institute (n.d.), include Support, Boundaries and Expectations, and Constructive Use of Time. Clearly, each of these subheadings calls for resources in a number of areas that involve family, civic engagement, educational systems, and the like.

Internal Assets

Internal assets according to the Search Institute (n.d.) include Commitment to Learning, Positive Values, Social Competencies, and Positive Identity. Each of these relate to intra- as well as interpersonal dimensions and influence outcomes (www.search-institute.org).

• •

Focus Point. Both internal and external development assets contribute to positive outcomes and foster environments dedicated to health and success.

• •

PHASES IN FAMILY FUNCTIONING

Families confront many stressor events and changes throughout the lifespan; such as an adult's job loss, moving, the chronic illness of one member, divorce, and other happenings which can act as *disruptors* or as *catalysts*. Catalysts are events that set a secondary series of events in motion. Positive events such as marriages and births, can be stressful as well, as they elicit *eustress* (a term coined by Hans Selye) (Selye, 1983). Eustress typically involves a level of arousal that is not overwhelming and can be motivating and even invigorating.

A model of family crisis management demonstrates the common ways of reacting when families are challenged by a significant stressor event. This proposed model depicts the paths towards various outcomes that can occur following a stressor event. The family system's reaction to the stressor event is a response or process based on these complex interactions. This model is a streamlined, updated, and slightly more intuitive version of the ABC-X model. It represents a family system's interpretation of how stressor events influence the system's reactions.

Historic Research

The ABC-X model was first described by Reuben Hill in 1947, at the time a professor at Minnesota University. It is also referred to as the family stress adaptation theory. Hill had studied family outcomes following the major societal disruptions of the Great Depression. He came to the conclusion that families varied in the *buffers* that they could access, and, importantly, their perceptions of themselves as families (Boss, 2014). Those who felt hopeless, disempowered, and depressed had poorer prospects. Because of this model's emphasis on how families deal with adversity, such as crisis situations, Hill is also referenced as "the father of family stress and coping theory" (Rosino, 2016, p. 3).

One cannot help but notice some similarity of this line of thinking with the work of Viktor Frankl (1905–1997), the psychiatrist and holocaust survivor, who stated that if all was lost, the individual still had a choice concerning the meaning and dignity with which they infused the unfortunate circumstances. Frankl's book *Man's Search for Meaning* (1959) elaborated on these principles.

This model and the expanded versions are still relevant in family-related research. The model has been further refined and expanded through the inclusion of the family's social context (Rosino, 2016). In the original ABC-X model of crisis the letters had the following meaning:

- A = the stressor event
- B = the resources available to the family
- C = the family's perceptions of the stressor
- X = the likelihood of a crisis

Most of the visual depictions of the original ABC-X model are complex, but intend to show that three factors will interact, namely the Stressor event (A), Resources (B), and the Perception of the stressor (C). Together, these three will determine how the crisis (X) is handled (Rosino, 2016).

Phases in Family Functioning

A model of phases in family functioning during a crisis (see Figure 12–2) depicts the sequencing of events. Note that it is *not* intended to be a duplicate of the ABC-X model, instead this is a sequential interpretation.

The family functioning model predicts that families will go through a phase of disorganization during and after a stressful event or impactful period of their lives. The family will then be in a temporary state of disorganization, until it can regroup and adapt. The adaptation can be an improved version of former functioning, in which case the outcome is hopeful. Some families settle back into that with which they were familiar, and lastly in the worst scenario, families sink to a lower detrimental level of functioning. Importantly, the role of the family's intrinsic coping skills and other resources to overcome the crisis, will also mediate the outcome. Clearly, the family rich in buffers and resources has a better chance than the one bankrupted by lack of buffers and resources, emotional and otherwise.

Family coping strategies differ in reaction to stressor events. These strategies include withdrawing from persons outside the system, discussing the situation only among the adults (which can lead to family secrets), denying that there is a problem, and using anger and other negative emotions. In keeping with the predictions made by the original ABC-X model, the degree to which a family system interprets a stressor as disruptive becomes a self-fulfilling prophecy. In these instances, the outcomes are likely to be negative.

Constructively, alternatives consist of seeking assistance from peers and professionals outside the system,

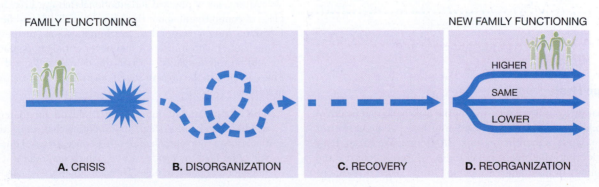

FIGURE 12–2. Phases in Family Functioning.

extending support systems such as civic engagement, and finding meaning and fulfillment in a spiritual life or religious involvement. These coping strategies may be protective factors if they are constructive.

In summary, the family's phases in functioning can follow this path:

■ **Crisis**. The family faces a stressor event, depicted by an exploding star.
■ **Disorganization.** A phase of disorganization occurs.
■ **Recovery**. This is followed by a phase of recovery.
■ **Reorganization**. The family's new functioning which is modified by factors such as resources and resilience.

One can also access aspects of Olson's *Family Circumplex Model* in this context (Olson, 2000). His premise is that during times of crisis healthy families tend to rally around each other, they become even closer and more supportive in a temporarily *enmeshed* manner that serves to deal with the crisis. The families that become insular and *disengaged* would face poorer outcomes because they lacked family and societal support. For example, when a family death occurs, supportive families are close and nurturing as they weather the crisis and deal with their loss.

∙∙

Focus Point. Stressors that impact a family system can either be positive, such as a birth of a child, or negative, such as illness and the death of a loved one. According to the ABC-X model, factors such as the type of stressor, availability of family resources, and perception of the stressor or crisis event all affect how the family functions following the stressor. Ideally, the family will utilize its available resources and reorganize to continue functioning on a healthy level.

∙∙

∙∙

Guest Reflection 12–2

Hope Heals

As parents, our first concern is for the well-being and health of our children. The weighty burden of how we might protect them lands squarely on our shoulders. We're so busy considering what might befall them, we rarely consider the possibility of the trauma happening to us. When it does, our

response may well be one of the most important things we could ever give our children. In our own experiences, we've seen that when parents and thus entire family systems experience trauma, it can be one of the most positively transformational experiences for a child.

When parents model resilience and flourish, despite suffering in the midst of it, a child gets a firsthand opportunity to see that the worst-case, nightmare scenario does not have to be the end to the story. Rather, it can signal a new kind of beginning, one that can have unexpected beauty, virtues, and compassion that could not have been experienced otherwise. Children start to see that their own fears of the unknown are less influential than what they have seen in their parents' model of post-traumatic growth and they can live lives informed by hope rather than lives fueled by fear and later, regrets.

My son James was 6 months and 5 days old when I nearly died. Out of the blue, I suffered a massive brainstem stroke brought on from a rare, congenital defect in my brain called an AVM. I had no symptoms or history. I was a perfectly healthy and active 26-year-old woman. In an instant, the dreams my husband and I had for our futures were left hanging by a thread.

Miraculously, I survived 16-hours of micro brain surgery, but parts of my brain had to be removed to save my life and the deficits that would remain were great. I was in hospitals and brain rehab settings for nearly 2 years after the stroke, relearning how to walk, swallow, speak, and live in a body that could not do what it had previously done. Throughout, a village of family and friends helped take our place as parents, giving James so many things we desperately wanted to give him but could not at that time.

As painful as the physical aspects were, losing my motherhood hurt most profoundly. I spent my first Mother's Day in the ICU and struggled for months early on to figure out how I could breastfeed my baby in his short, daily visits. My brain didn't comprehend that I no longer fed him and that for months he had been cared for by friends. For years, I was not his primary caregiver, and I felt a profound sense of loss, even shame, that I could not be the mom I had always thought I would be.

After years of physical and emotional therapy, I reached a place of contentment about this "new normal" life and family. I was no longer trapped in my longings for the past or disenchanted with a future I had never anticipated. Rather, I could be fully engaged with all the unique skills and love I have to offer in the present state I am in. I wrote these words in February of 2012:

> The other day, Jay, James, and I walked up to our neighborhood coffee shop, a mini-outing that seems to make its way into our schedule at least once a week. James will often hold my hand as I walk, which I wonder if it's more for his benefit or mine. He has a mommy who needs

him in ways that he can't fully give right now. So he takes my hand and though I'm too slow for him, he walks beside me, saying" Be Careful Mommy!" Precious and humbling. Nonetheless, as I take my son by the hand, cross the street, and buy him a cakepop (all under Jay's watchful supervision, don't worry), I get lost for a moment in the feeling of being a normal mommy again, and it is so blissfully sweet. The coffee and cakepop are gone too fast, as is that feeling of being a totally healthy, able-bodied mother out for a quick coffee stop. I'm not that mommy, but I do get to be James' mommy, and we do get to have our own special coffee date in our own normal way.

Despite having a myriad of health issues and struggles, we felt compelled to grow our family. Under the guidance of many doctors, I got pregnant and had a miracle baby, John, in the summer of 2015. In some ways, it feels like redemption for our family, though the reality is that nothing can fully restore the losses James experienced as a young child; the scars which he—and we all—will carry forever. And yet we have found redemption in the reality that scars do not have to make us victims, rather they can remind us that we have overcome. They can be the catalyst of bitterness and fear, or the birthplace of gratitude and compassion.

But how do we learn compassion? How do we teach it? Compassion is learned through presence, particularly in the midst of great hardship. Compassion sinks into our fibers and souls as we receive it, and learn to give it away ourselves. It cannot be forced or memorized or beat into someone. It comes through osmosis, through touch, like a parent to a child, like a child to a parent. And thankfully, there is compassion for us who fumble in acting compassionately ourselves. To suffer with each other—"com-passion"—might be the greatest gift we teach our children, but it also might be the most profound thing we learn from them.

Katherine and Jay Wolf. Authors of Hope Heals (2016), Zondervan Publishers. Their platform "Hope Heals" is multifaceted and includes summer camps for children and families facing challenges (www.hopeheals.com). Used with permission.

● ●

FAMILY STRESSORS: GRIEF AND LOSS

Parenting can be interrupted when a parent or significant caretaker is lost through illness, disability, or death. This interrupts parenting and disrupts the family system, which then has to reorganize and find a new balance. Frequently, it changes economic conditions within the family and may also necessitate moving. The loss of a sibling can also be devastating to a family and siblings as well as parents may carry the pain of this loss with them for years to come.

Grief in Children

Children's grief looks different at various developmental levels. For children, they are not only dealing with intense emotions that they may have never felt before, but they are also learning what death is and what it means to be dead. That is why it is important to choose the words used to describe death very carefully when talking with children and allow them to ask questions and be honest with them.

Children should be encouraged to participate in funeral rituals. Children that were invited to have some part in the planning can be helpful in the aftermath of a significant death. It is important to explain to children what they will see and experience at the visitation, wake, funeral, or memorial ceremony. If the child is resistant to attend, it is recommended not to force them to go. For young children, a trusted friend or family member should be available to remove the child from the service or visitation if needed (Walter & McCoyd, 2015).

Development can play a powerful role in how a child experiences and expresses his or her grief. Whereas adults may experience intense grief over a sustained period of time that may takes months, a child experiences grief in intense bursts throughout his or her developmental experience. Grief may be revisited at developmental milestones and significant events, such as graduation, wedding days, etc.

The death of a significant caregiver, such as a mother or father, can bring with it secondary losses that may have an effect on a child. Loss of income and changing homes and/or schools are just a few changes that a child might experience. These other losses will cause the child to emotionally adjust to his or her new environment. (Davey, Kissil, & Lynch, 2016)

It is important for all children to feel a sense of control in how they are able to grieve. Caregivers should involve children in memorial activities and give them choices of how they would like to remember the deceased person. Here are some things to keep in mind when interacting with children of different ages and developmental stages.

Very Young Children. Use the words dead and death, and explain to them what it means to be dead (Walter & McCoyd, 2015). Explain how it is different than sleep and help them understand the finality of death. Using euphemisms (e.g., "he's at rest," "we lost her," or "God took him") can slow a child's understanding of death and can be confusing to them. This may result in a more intense grief response due to the misunderstanding of death.

A significant death often results in a loss of security for a young child, which may result in regressive behaviors such as thumb-sucking, bedwetting, or increased clinginess to caregivers (Porter, 2016). Maintaining a routine as much as possible can be helpful in reducing a child's anxiety.

Young children are learning about the world around them and may ask the same question multiple times. The concept of death is no different. Be patient with repetition and answer their questions honestly each time. Death is seen as temporary for this age range (Davey, Kissil, & Lynch, 2016). Repetitive questions are not a sign of denial but rather a child revisiting a concept and trying to understand it.

Elementary School. Around the time a child enters school, he or she tends to understand the concept that death is irreversible. However, euphemisms can still be confusing and should be avoided.

A child may be observed expressing emotions for a short period of time that may seem random to a caregiver. Usually, a child will express emotions related to grief in short "bursts" and then return to normal activities such as play. Allow children the ability to express their emotions in healthy ways and comfort them as needed. Follow their lead in how long they spend with thoughts and feelings related to grief.

Although a child is developing a larger vocabulary, play is still an important vehicle for a child to express thoughts and emotions. Children are often observed utilizing play to revisit a traumatic event to help them understand it. Allowing a child to openly play out a scary or traumatic event, such as the death of a loved one, can help them move through grief and understand the event they experienced.

A child might glamorize the relationship he had with a deceased relative, even if the actual relationship was strained or not that close. Honor a child's need to connect with the deceased by sharing real memories or facts about the person who died. Confronting a child's inaccuracies in a harsh manner may cause the child to minimize his or her emotional expression around you.

Because children are egocentric, they may believe that they caused the death or could have stopped the death in some way (Porter, 2016). If a child had been "bad" or argued with someone before the death, he may blame himself.

Middle School. During the grieving process, pre-teen and early teens focus more heavily on social relationships outside of the family. They often begin to confide in friends in addition to close family. It is important for caregivers to get to know their children's friends to monitor from whom the child might be seeking emotional support.

During this period, most children understand the finality of death. This will minimize questions about revisiting the deceased, or of them returning. However, because of a more mature understanding of death, there may be questions regarding details about the death and/or the body of the deceased. It is important to answer the questions honestly on a level that is appropriate for the child's age.

Because this is the time puberty often begins, there are many changes going on inside the child's body as well. Oftentimes, these changes can have an emotional impact on the individual, which can cause grief reactions to be more intense. Understand that there is not a clear line between the effects of puberty and grief. Rules and expectations should remain stable even through emotional times so that the child feels safe and secure. Although discipline should be maintained to create stability, a child at this age needs permission to express powerful emotions in healthy ways.

High School. Adolescents experience grief at a more mature level; and their ability to understand their own mortality is just beginning to solidify. A significant death can challenge their worldview, spurring anxiety, fear, loss of identity, and questions of purpose and meaning. It is important to allow teenagers to explore these emotions and thoughts in a safe way.

Adolescents strongly gravitate to peer groups for emotional support. It is uncommon for individuals at this age to confide in close family members or parents. It is important for caregivers to know their teenager's friends to monitor from whom he or she is seeking emotional support.

A well-developed self-esteem can have a positive effect on the way an adolescent copes with the death of a significant person. Providing opportunities and activities to build self-esteem can build important coping mechanisms that can aid in a healthy grief experience (Davey, Kissil, & Lynch, 2016).

Unhealthy behaviors may become apparent during an adolescent's grief. Adolescents are more prone to risk-taking behaviors such as drug use or increased sexual activity. It is important for teenagers to be given choices in how to express their emotions such as journaling, art, music, talk, or physical activity.

"The horrors of war, pale beside the loss of a [parent]."

Anna Freud, Psychoanalyst (1895–1982)

Focus Point.   Children's and adolescents' grief looks different at various developmental levels. For children, they are not only dealing with intense emotions that they may have never felt before, but they are also learning what death is and what it means to be dead. Adolescents experience grief at a more mature level; and their ability to understand their own mortality is beginning to solidify. A significant death can challenge their worldview, spurring anxiety, fear, loss of identity, and questions of purpose and meaning.

Matthew Bunt, M.Ed., LPC-S, *authored the section on "Grief and Loss." He serves at the Amelia Center, a comprehensive grief counseling center for children and their families, affiliated with Children's of Alabama. (www.ameliacenter.org). Published with permission.*

SUBSTANCE-RELATED AND ADDICTIVE DISORDERS

Various addiction disorders have become a major concern of contemporary American society. Typically, alcohol, drugs, nicotine, and prescription medications come to mind when thinking of substance-related disorders. People can also struggle with excessive dependence on things, events, and experiences, as well as substances.

It is not possible to determine the exact number of adults in the United States who present with a substance-related or addictive disorder.

The good news is that, as a nation, the United States has had promising results reducing smoking habits of especially the younger generation, and generally there is greater awareness of the addictive qualities of nicotine and the long-term harmful effects of smoking, especially on our lungs. The bad news is that another addictive disorder is taking its place, in the form of opioid use disorder, or the more general dependency on prescription drugs and pain medications. Heroin related deaths are climbing as well (National Institute on Drug Abuse at: www.drugabuse.gov).

During 2016, the Centers for Disease Control made it known that these addictions were taking on endemic proportions and needed to be addressed on several fronts. Some of the disconcerting facts:

■ Overdose from opioid related substances were highest in the early to middle adult groups (25–54 years).
■ In 2014 alone, almost 2 million Americans were dependent or abused prescription opioids.
■ Every day in the United States about a thousand people are medically treated for misusing prescription opioids.
■ Currently half of all overdose related deaths are linked to prescription opioid (www.cdc.gov/drugoverdose/data).

Preventing Drug Abuse Through Positive Parenting

A program was developed by the Child and Family Center at the University of Oregon called *Family Checkup*, with the subtitle: "Positive parenting prevents drug abuse" (http://cfc.uoregon.edu/services.html). The premise is that positive parenting can be our first line of defense against substance and related abuse. Some of the questions parents are encouraged to ask themselves include:

■ Can I communicate calmly and clearly with my teenager concerning relationship problems?
■ Do I encourage positive behaviors in an ongoing manner?
■ Can I work towards a solution with my teenager, by negotiating emotional conflicts?
■ Can I calmly set limits, especially when defiant and disrespectful behavior occurs?

- Can I calmly set limits for more serious threats, like problem behavior or drug use?
- Do I monitor my child and ensure that there is not too much unsupervised time with peers, especially peers I do not personally know? (Dishion, Nelson, & Kavanagh, 2003).

(Based on: The National Institute on Drug Abuse who also has a site especially for teens called: NIDA for Teens accessible at: https://teens.drugabuse.gov/. Also at http://easyread.drugabuse.gov)

In essence, the importance is ongoing relationship building that contains structure and boundaries to minimize undesirable behaviors but also allows an open and accepting environment for ongoing conversations. The talks about the dangers of drug abuse need to recur at various developmental stages so that the teenagers themselves are aware of the risks and can make informed decisions that facilitate health and well-being.

With many of the destructive behaviors that can occur in families, it may be a chicken and egg situation; which comes first and at which point can we try to intervene with best outcomes in mind. If parents can provide constructive, ongoing, and supportive parenting, then we have a good chance for improved outcomes. Problems arise when the parents themselves are at risk—if they model undesirable behavior and they are only parenting intermittently, their own addictive disorders will hijack them and take them away from their parenting responsibilities. In this way their parenting will be interrupted and incomplete.

The price of substance use and addictive disorders is high, especially to the family. The affected individual experiences health problems. When a serious addiction has developed, the economic costs can be enormous and adversely affect the family's quality of life, sometimes to the point of bankruptcy. The U.S. government has developed a series of video clips that parents can access that show how positive versus negative examples of a skill can lead to different outcomes. This source also has material available to support and enhance positive parenting skills (https://teens.drugabuse.gov/videos).

Video Example 12.2

Watch this video on the brain and the systems it uses to process rewards. How does the feeling of pleasure motivate us? How does the brain process rewards?

(https://www.youtube.com/watch?v=DMcmr P-BWGk)

The emotional costs are incalculable, long lasting, and reach into adulthood. Chemical dependencies and other addictions may have behavioral, as well as genetic/biological, components and a genetic sensitivity may be at play. When a parent experiences such problems, the children are at risk for developing similar addictions because they are presented with the role models of their parents and other adult family members.

It is estimated that almost 7 percent of the U.S. population is, to some degree, dealing with alcohol use disorder, as reflected by 12-month prevalence estimates using the criteria from the *Diagnostic and Statistical Manual of Mental Disorders* (American Psychiatric Association, 2013). According to the National Institute on Alcohol Abuse and Alcoholism (2015), 7.2% of adults 18 years or older have an alcohol use disorder. The highest alcohol consumption is found among ages 18–29. Underage drinking and alcohol-related motor vehicle accidents are problems that affect adolescents (National Institute on Alcohol Abuse and Alcoholism, 2015).

The abuse of substances and the development of an addiction lead to a crisis and problems that chronically affect all family members and put the children at risk. Among the most serious is the violence and/or antisocial behavior that almost always accompanies many of these problems.

Children are especially vulnerable to emotional damage growing up in a family that is affected by parental addiction, and they may model the behavior. Although adolescents are vulnerable to developing dependencies and addictions, we will focus on families in which one or both parents have developed this problem and will examine some of the effects on the family. Additionally, the parent dealing with an addiction disorder is not fully and emotionally available as a parent, he or she may be partially sedated or experiencing a number of side effects related to the intake of these substances.

Focus Point.   Due to high levels of drug abuse across the country, programs such as Family Check Up have begun to formulate ways for families to maintain healthy practices. By encouraging open and honest communication concerning the risks of drug abuse, these programs help give parents the knowledge and skills to minimize the danger of substance abuse that threatens their families.

FAMILY STRESSORS AND ADDICTIVE DISORDERS

Substance-related and Addictive Disorders

When an adult family member develops a *substance-related and addictive disorder*, as defined by the *DSM-5* (American Psychiatric Association, 2013), it implicates the entire family. Organizations such as Alcoholics Anonymous provide support groups not only for the identified person seeking to adopt a sober lifestyle, but they also offer support to spouses and families, as such conditions affect the entire system within which they occur.

Definition.   A **substance use disorder** is defined as "a complex condition, a brain disease that is manifested by compulsive substance use despite harmful consequences" (American Psychiatric Association, 2013). It affects the functioning of the user in their work, school, and home roles, and in the context of the family it can lead to neglect of the children and the household. Social and interpersonal roles can be impaired as a result of the effects of the substance; for instance, anger can be aggravated, leading to physical fights and abuse or neglect of the children or a spouse. Persons can become secretive and dishonest to hide their behavior, and engage in risky behavior to maintain their addiction disorder. A great deal of time and money is spent on obtaining the substance, leading to the depletion of financial resources and neglect of the family and the household. *Tolerance* of the substance may develop, meaning that there is a need for an increase in the amount ingested because the same dose fails to have the desired effect. *Withdrawal* may have severe physical and emotional side effects (American Psychiatric Association, n.d.).

Persons can develop dependencies and addictions to a variety of things and activities other than illicit drugs. Prescription medication has become a big headache for U.S. users, especially now that tobacco use has become less popular. The compulsive use of events, people, experiences, and nonchemical substances such as food can, in certain circumstances, qualify as dependencies which are hard to control and which activate a reward center in the brain. In some individuals, the excessive use of electronic media, and constant web presence, can take on addictive proportions. The resultant feelings can become irresistible, and seem to hold their own reward. Persons become addicted to the thrill of illicit relationships, the experience of falling in love, gambling, work, shopping, and a variety of other things. As long as the substance or the experience is capable of alleviating some kind of emotional need or even pain, and seems to reinforce itself by activating the reward center in the brain, it serves as the basis for the problematic relationship that the person develops with the substance or the experience.

According to neuroscientific research, some mechanism in the pleasure centers of the brain seems to be triggered in addictive behaviors, even if these behaviors do not involve chemical substances such as drugs or medications (Volkow, Koob, & McLellan, 2016). It is also thought that various chemical substances made by the body can be released and can enhance a pleasurable effect and reduce pain. These substances are thought to bind to opiate receptors in the brain. When we talk about an "endorphin rush" in popular language, we are referring to the release of endorphins by the body that makes the person feel exhilarated. This may explain why the same agent causes some people no problem but becomes the focal point of addictions for others. Although there is a genetic basis for some portion of an addiction, it is the interaction with the environmental experiences that can ensure that the addiction is maintained.

Implications for Children

Children may not be aware that one or both of their parents have a substance-related and addictive disorder, because their parents deny it. These children are affected by living in a home where this problem exists, but the parents pretend that it does not exist. Because they observed destructive patterns modeled by their parents, it is unlikely that they know what constitutes healthy family life. They become more vulnerable and are susceptible to getting involved with relationships where a future partner behaviorally resembles one or both parents in the family of origin.

The atmosphere in homes where one or both parents have an addictive disorder can be chaotic and abusive for children. Alcohol dependence disorder is associated with an increased likelihood of physical and sexual maltreatment of children. Emotional damage is also inflicted on the children living in these families. Dependent and addicted family systems have very rigid rules that enable the system to function in unhealthy ways. The problem becomes a *family secret*, one that eats away at the integrity of the system as a whole and the individuals who are a part of it (Imber-Black, 1993). It also implies that children are not likely to seek help from school counselors or relatives because they are not allowed to breathe a word about what really happens at home. The patterns can be similar to spousal abuse. Three basic rules are strictly enforced in such families:

■ Do not talk about the parent's problem because it is a family secret.
■ Do not trust anyone outside the family to understand the problem.
■ Do not feel anything because this will destroy the integrity of the family.

Children typically become assigned to a special role in these dysfunctional families that helps to maintain the system's unhealthy homeostasis and protect the family secret from becoming public. While these roles can be observed in almost every kind of unhealthy family system, they are especially significant in dependent and addiction disordered families because they help children cope with the chaotic climate of the family home.

These children often personalize the problems their families experience by feeling that they should be perfect children. When parents are intoxicated or high, children frequently presume that they are the cause of such behavior, and that somehow they ought to be able to correct the parents' problem and make their family healthy and whole again. Children who grow up in such situations may exhibit their own set of problematic behaviors and thinking, including indecision, difficulty in thinking clearly, and hypervigilance and may do poorly at school by underachieving.

Among the most successful support programs, which have a long history of effectiveness in helping people overcome dependencies, are Alcoholics

An effective parenting outcome presumes a parental system that is emotionally healthy, resilient, and able to meet the requirements of the parenthood roles. The Wolf family transformed trauma into strength. Their platform "Hope Heals" includes camps for children and their families facing challenges. See Guest Reflection 12–2.

Anonymous (www.aa.org) and other related 12-step programs. Rational Recovery is another approach to dealing with addictions. These programs exist in communities throughout the United States. In addition, auxiliary programs are available for partners and children of addicted family members.

Focus Point.   When an adult develops an addictive disorder, all members of the family unit are affected. The parent concerned will be more focused on fulfilling his or her own needs that feed the addiction, than providing for the children. Children growing up in this environment develop patterns that help them cope with their dysfunctional family. Typically, a child's emotional development is seriously affected, and the opportunity of a normal childhood is often forfeited. Because these children have experienced chaotic, unpredictable parenting by adults who have possibly abandoned them emotionally, they are left without the usual parental supports that can also promote resilience.

To report abuse or to get help in the United States, contact Childhelp: National Child Abuse Hotline at 1–800–4–A–CHILD (1–800–422–4453).

THE BATTLEGROUND OF ABUSE

For some, the family is a battleground where atrocities occur with all-too-frequent regularity. Others feel free to harm each other in physical, sexual, emotional, or other inappropriate ways only within the intimacy and secret shelter of the family system (Aadnanes & Gulbrandsen, 2017). The impact of child abuse and maltreatment is far reaching. Not only is the child harmed in the immediate context, but their hopes and dreams for the future are pulled into the battle as well. Violence within families has effects on partnerships, future marriage formation, cohabitation, and parenting. The cycle of abuse may be perpetuated.

Early explanations of family functioning recognized conflict as an inevitable human condition. When personal interests and needs override the welfare of the group, tension ensues. Research on family violence aims to learn more about this unsavory aspect of family life so that the cycle of harm can be interrupted and possibly stopped (Finkenauer et al., 2015).

Historic Research

In 1860, Ambroise Tardieu, a forensic physician and radiologist, published his findings concerning 32 cases who displayed suspicious injuries and conditions. Tardieu ascribed these radiologic and forensic findings to neglect and abuse, and he tried to raise awareness amongst his colleagues. He is quoted as stating:

> But it remains that these cases are multiplying, that they provoke indignation, that they must not catch off guard the physician, often the only one capable of denouncing the crime to the legal authorities, and that they must not remain unknown to the forensic expert enjoined by the courts to explain its true character and to unveil all the circumstances of the deed (Roche, Fortin, Labbé, Brown, & Chadwick, 2005; quoted by Paul & Adamo, 2014).

An early article published in 1962 by physician C. Henry Kempe, described findings in children that could not be ascribed to accidents. All the caregivers and parents adamantly denied inflicting harm to the children, highlighting that this form of abuse is typically executed in secret. The nature and location of the injuries pointed towards the nonaccidental nature of the trauma. Dr. Kempe and his colleagues' historic article was published with the title: "The Battered Child Syndrome" (Kempe, Silverman, Steele, Droegemueller, & Silver, 1962).

But in 1946, even earlier than the article by Kempe et al., a pediatric radiologist, Dr. John Caffey had published his findings of unexplained and suspicious trauma in six infants. He warned his colleagues that guardians and parents confabulated false histories to lead the physician astray and to deflect blame. In 1974, Caffey coined the term "whiplash shaken infant syndrome" (Paul & Adamo, 2014).

These early articles contributed to greater awareness, leading the path towards establishment of laws to protect children in the United States. It is also associated with the obligation to call in authorities or the "*duty to inform.*" This mandates reporting actual or suspected maltreatment or abuse. Professionals in childcare related professions, school teachers, social workers, and members of the medical team, may interact with children who appear to have been maltreated in some way or another. As part of their professional ethics, they have a duty to inform authorities. Parental rights may be suspended if these suspicions are validated. Maltreatment and abuse, often linked to parental substance related and addictive disorders, are leading causes why children are placed in foster care.

Family Violence

Several cultural and social factors have promoted an interest in studying violence in families, including the women's movement and increased gender equality. Public attention was drawn towards the issues of violence toward women and children, especially intimate partner violence, marital rape, and incest.

Child maltreatment or abuse is defined as "behavior that causes significant harm to a child. It also includes when someone knowingly fails to prevent serious harm to a child" (Children's Bureau, 2016). The World Health Organization (2016) states that child maltreatment or abuse constitutes "all forms of physical and/or emotional ill-treatment, sexual abuse, neglect, or negligent treatment or commercial or other exploitation, resulting in actual or potential harm to the child's health, survival, development or dignity in the context of a relationship of responsibility, trust or power." The World Health Organization considers *maltreatment* to be synonymous with *abuse.*

Non-accidental trauma (NAT) is a medical term used to describe trauma that is willfully inflicted. Typically the victims are young defenseless children.

Maltreatment and abuse delineates four areas of cruelty to children:

- ***Physical abuse:*** hurting, injuring, inflicting pain, smothering, drowning, poisoning.
- ***Sexual abuse:*** direct or indirect sexual exploitation, coercion, or corruption by involving children in inappropriate sexual activities.
- ***Emotional abuse:*** repeatedly rejecting, humiliating, and denying their worth and rights as human beings.
- ***Neglect:*** the persistent lack of appropriate care of children, including love, stimulations, safety, nourishment, warmth, education, and medical attention (Barlow, Turow & Gerhart, 2017).

Note too that a child can be abused in more than one area simultaneously. Discrimination, harassment, and *bullying* are also abusive and can harm a child, both physically and emotionally (Kim, Mennen, & Trickett, 2016).

Neglect refers to acts of parental negligence, such as failing to supervise children or properly provide for their nutritional needs. While this is a basic premise of abuse, *maltreatment* of children and adolescents is the term increasingly used, which includes those acts that define abuse and neglect, as well as radical parental acts, such as excessive punishment, child abandonment, infanticide, murder of children, and abandonment of a child's corpse.

Violence is a rather broad concept that includes acts of force against family members, which often fall under the guise of discipline and parental control of children. The term also relates to illegitimate acts of violence occurring as part of a family conflict. Some dysfunctional families regard hitting as acceptable behavior and they consider spanking a child a necessary parental practice. Of particular concern is that the incidence of abuse is higher among children with disabilities (Corr & Santos, 2017). The vulnerability of these children seems to bring out qualities of parental outrage, despair, and burnout.

A Canadian review of 37 studies on child abuse and neglect found that a child was likely to be removed from the home and placed into foster care if there was evidence of harm to the child, if the living quarters were unsafe, if there were older children involved, and if the parents were found to be negligent or incapable of parenting appropriately (Tonmyr, Quimet, & Ugnat, 2012).

Shockingly the greater majority of perpetrators are parents—about 80 percent (See Figure 12–3), and about two thirds of cases involved children under the age of ten (See Figure 12–4).

Family or domestic violence represents any abusive, violent, coercive, forceful, or threatening act or word inflicted by one member of a family or household on another (U.S. Department of Justice, n.d.). Some definitions include *dating violence* as well. Examples of such acts include spanking, shoving, hitting, slapping, pinching, shooting, cutting, or pulling, as well as acts that cause psychological harm.

Violence in families can be directed at both children and adults, and perpetrators are typically parents or adolescent children. Child abuse and neglect have received a great deal of attention from both researchers and the media. Even though there is a wide range of abusive acts, a general categorization of physical and psychological abuse has emerged. This especially pertains to those acts that constitute child abuse and maltreatment.

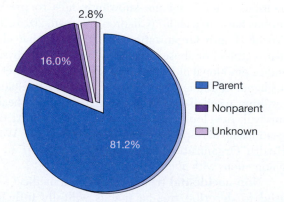

FIGURE 12–3. Perpetrators of Violence by Relationship to Victims, 2010.
Source: National KIDS COUNT.

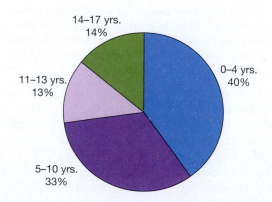

FIGURE 12–4. Ages of Children Confirmed by Child Protective Services as Victims of Maltreatment, 2014.

Models of Family Violence

Several theoretical models focus on reasons why parents and families display interpersonal violence (Lawson, 2012):

1. The **psychiatric model** assumes that abusive individuals in a family system are mentally and emotionally ill. This model isolates the personality characteristics of the offender as the primary cause of the abusive behavior. It attempts to link personality patterns or traits with the tendency to perform abusive acts and with other behavior patterns, such as borderline personality disorder, alcoholism, substance abuse, and mental illness.

2. The **ecological model** explores the child's development within the family system and the family within its community. From this viewpoint, abuse is a family problem that affects everyone, and the entire family must receive treatment in order to promote healthier outcomes.

3. The **sociological model** states that cultural and social norms may prevail, for instance violence may be seen as a way of settling disputes and conflicts with others. Adults' violent behavior toward children could be a reaction to stress and frustration. Family structure and organization can influence violent behavior. Crowded living conditions, high levels of unemployment, strained financial resources, and social isolation from other families place additional stress on the parent–child microenvironment, which can trigger abusive behavior. Additionally, stressful life situations such as being an adolescent parent, or living in a stepfamily situation may increase incidence of violence.

4. The **social psychological model** states that interaction patterns, the transmission of violent behavior from one generation to the next, and environmental stress serve as prime motivators of violent behavior. Violence is learned through modeling and serves as a coping mechanism in response to stress. Child abuse is considered a product of inconsistent and excessive punishment. Violence may be learned within the family of origin as a problem-solving approach.

5. The **patriarchy model** emphasizes that violence occurs in families as a result of the traditional social dominance of adult males, which places women in a subordinate position and condones the use of violence to support male dominance.

6. The **exchange/social control model** suggests that violence occurs in families when the behavior is condoned. For example, the rewards of violent behavior might be assuming superiority, revenge, and expressing anger and frustration. The costs might include being arrested and jailed or a divorce. These costs act as social controls to prevent and limit the violent behavior. Factors that tend to support the violence include (a) gender inequality; (b) the privacy of the family; and (c) subscription to cultural beliefs that are expressed in aggressive, hostile, and violent ways.

7. The **information-processing approach** proposes that neglectful parents fail to process information about children's need for care, which leads to physical neglect, a form of maltreatment. Reasons include ignoring the behavioral cues provided by children and choosing an inappropriate response.

Factors Associated With Family Violence

A **cycle of violence** can be manifested in two basic ways:

1. Individuals who experienced violent and abusive childhoods in their family of origin tend to perpetuate the pattern in their own families.

2. A three-phase sequence in the expression of violent behavior begins with increasing tension, a loss of control accompanied by violent behavior, and a reconciliation period of regret and forgiveness.

Researchers describe several psychosocial variables that are related to the incidence and variety of violent behaviors expressed in families (Ferreira & Buttell, 2016):

■ The *socioeconomic status* of a family system is associated with expressions of violence, particularly in families from lower socioeconomic groups where the quality of life, environmental stressors, and cultural conditioning or standards may be felt more keenly than they are in other social groups.

■ *Stress* is closely related to domestic violence. Acts of violence or abuse form part of a person's coping mechanism for stress. Sources of stress may include poverty, unemployment or part-time employment, financial problems, pregnancy and childbirth, single parenthood, or a child with a disability.

■ *Social isolation* from other families increases the risk of abusive behavior directed toward children or a spouse. This may be a contributing factor to the likelihood of abuse occurring in single-parent families. The interactions provided by social networks and contact with other families tend to act as a control mechanism to reduce the risk of such behavior.

Substance abuse. There is also an association between substance abuse and addictive disorders in parents and the physical abuse and neglect of children. Substance abuse or chemical dependency may play a role in 50 percent to 90 percent of cases of physical abuse of children by parents. Intoxication and chemical dependency impair judgment, increase irritability, and enhance depressive reactions, increasing the likelihood that children will be mistreated (Herrenkohl, Hong, Klika, Herrenkohl, & Russo, 2013).

Family form. Another factor associated with child abuse and neglect is family form. The majority of reported cases of child abuse occur in single-parent families. Rather than being a function primarily of single-parent household status, abuse of children may occur in these homes because of the effects of poverty on single-parent families. Stepfathers are more likely to abuse children than biological fathers.

Intergenerational. There is strong evidence of intergenerational transmission of abusive behavior (Widom, Czaja, & DuMont, 2015). From this perspective, a child learns such behavior by being abused by his or her parents, and the maltreatment in the family of origin serves as a model for later aggressive behavior. This abusive behavior is replicated when the abused child becomes a parent. In this way, abuse is passed from one generation to the next.

● ●

Parenting Reflection 12–1

You are grocery shopping and have just witnessed a parent viciously slapping and shaking her preschool-aged boy. The child is screaming and crying, and the parent is continuing to yell at the child, calling him names and shaming him. What should you do?

● ●

Abusive Parents

The antecedents that lead up to the violent or abusive outbursts are an important link in the pattern of abuse. Researchers observe several characteristics in adults who abuse their children. The child-rearing patterns typically reflect a rigid, harsh, authoritarian approach. For example, abusive mothers characteristically express inconsistency and hostility, together with surprising protectiveness toward their children. They

seek to gain control over their children's behavior by eliciting anxiety and guilt in the child or through physical punishment (Beckerman, van Berkel, Mesman, & Alink, 2017).

Neglect of Children. Physical and emotional neglect of children constitutes the most frequently reported type of maltreatment. This accounts for more than 75 percent of all reported child abuse in the United States (Children's Bureau, 2015). Parents who neglect their children fail to physically provide for their basic needs, such as sufficient food, supervision, or medical care. Such inadequate care and physical abuse results in fatalities. A child who is physically neglected is almost always also emotionally neglected because the inattentiveness and disinvested attitude of the parents. Good parenting requires ongoing *responsiveness* to the child, and this dimension is absent.

Parents living in poverty experience high levels of stress that are accompanied by depression and anxiety. Aggravating circumstances include unemployment, inadequate nutrition, substance abuse, and low incomes. These are multi-problem families with chaotic home environments and low personal functioning. The families are socially isolated and maintain closed boundaries and do not access community support. (See Figure 12–3).

Physical Abuse of Children. Parents who physically abuse children are not aware that what they are doing is wrong and harmful. They see it as their parental responsibility to be in control of their children. They use physical punishment. These parents generally have a low tolerance for children's misbehavior. They are impatient, quick to anger, have poor empathy and are insensitive to children's needs. **Physical abuse** of children usually occurs when these parents are responsible for young children and they find themselves in situations that are highly stressful, without sufficient support, and without adequate coping skills (Meinck, Cluver, Boyes, & Ndhlovu, 2015). Several factors interact in abusive actions (Hesselink & Booyens, 2016). See Focus On 12–1.

Emotional Abuse of Children. Parents who emotionally abuse children experience low levels of self-esteem (Manczak, DeLongis, & Chen, 2016). They have poor coping skills and lack child management techniques. These deficiencies lead to situations in which parents express their anger and impatience with

Focus On 12–1 — Facts about Child Abuse and Neglect

- More than 4 million reports of child maltreatment are received by state and local agencies in the United States each year. That is nearly six reports every minute, although not all are substantiated.
- An estimated 740,000 victims of child abuse or neglect are treated in hospital emergency rooms in the United States each year. Of course, not all victims receive medical care as needed.
- In 2015, 683,000 children were found to be victims of maltreatment by child protective services.
- Seventy-eight percent of child victims experienced neglect. Almost 17% were physically abused; fewer than 10% were sexually abused.
- Children from birth to age 1 had the highest rates of victimization at 20 per 1,000 children. Girls were slightly more likely to be victims than boys.
- About 1 in 50 infants in the United States are neglected or abused; nearly one third of these are newborns.
- Caucasian (44.8%), African American (21.9%), and Hispanic (21.4%) children had the highest rates of victimization.
- Child fatalities are the most tragic consequence of maltreatment. In 2014, an estimated 1,580 children died from abuse or neglect.
- Three quarters (79.4%) of children who were killed as a result of abuse were younger than 4 years old.
- Infant boys (birth to age 1) had the highest rate of fatalities.
- Of child fatalities, 32.6% were exclusively attributed to neglect. Physical abuse and sexual abuse were major contributors to fatalities.
- More than 40% of child fatalities were caused by multiple types of maltreatment.
- Of the perpetrators, 80% were the biological parents. Female perpetrators, mostly mothers, outnumbered men.
- Of all parents who were perpetrators, fewer than 8% inflicted sexual abuse.
- More than one half of all reports of child abuse and neglect were made by professionals such as medical personnel, teachers, police, attorneys, and social services staff. The remainder was reported by neighbors, friends, or relatives.

Based on Centers for Disease Control and Prevention. (2014a). Child abuse and neglect prevention (https://www.cdc.gov/violenceprevention/childmaltreatment/); Childhelp Foundation. (2014). Retrieved from https://www.childhelp.org/child-abuse-statistics/; Children's Rights Foundation. (2015). Retrieved from http://www.childrensrights.org/newsroom/fact-sheets/child-abuse-and-neglect/; American Society for the Positive Care of Children. (2014). Retrieved March 14, 2017, from http://americanspcc.org/child-abuse-statistics/

children in ways that damage children's self-esteem. The attainment of adulthood does not automatically confer emotional maturity. Some parents experienced abuse in their family of origin that impaired them developmentally.

When parents become emotionally abusive, they express their impatience, frustration, rage, personal hurt, and disappointment toward their children in ways that damage the children's trust and well-being. Discounting a child's feelings and actions through name-calling, or sarcasm is considered **emotional and verbal abuse**. Telling children they will never amount to anything is abusive. Other examples include shaming children when they make mistakes; handing down punishments that are humiliating; not allowing children to express their feelings; ostracizing children by not speaking to them or ignoring their presence; and destroying their favorite toys. When children are abused in these ways, it increases the likelihood of depression (Sperry & Widom, 2013). Because depression is associated with suicidal ideation, these children are also at greater risk of suicide.

Sexual Abuse of Children.   For most people, it is abhorrent to even think that adults could abuse children in a sexual context and perform incestuous acts. There is a strong taboo against incest in almost all societies. **Incest** is sexual activity between members of the same family (bloodline) and is considered to be an aspect of **sexual abuse** involving children. Children cannot give consent to such activity. In families where children are taught to obey their parents and other elders, children are incapable of declining and may not understand the intentions of the adult perpetrator. Sexual abuse by a parent is most frequent, occurring in more than 80% of reported abuse cases (Childhelp, 2014). The majority of adults who sexually molest children are relatives and familiar nonrelatives.

Until half a century ago, researchers thought that sexual abuse or incestuous activity rarely occurred in American families. When child-abuse legislation was instituted at this time that required such cases to be reported, researchers discovered that sexual abuse of children was more widespread than they had anticipated. Victims have become more open in disclosing sexual abuse in childhood. Several high-profile court cases, some accusing persons from religious groups as well as eminent celebrities, have shared the stories, and thrown light on these "silent" atrocities. The shocking aspect is that some persons not only abused children, but also used their positions of trust to perpetrate their crimes. Sexual abuse involves inappropriate sexual touching and insinuations between parents and children. There are many risks involved with such

activities, especially for the child. In cases where children have been diagnosed with STDs, health-care professionals have a duty to report the parents to the authorities, and the legal system will intervene (Renvoize, 2017). See Figure 12–5.

Treatment and Intervention

Services include medical care, counseling, psychotherapy, marriage and family therapy, mediation, support groups, a crisis hotline, childcare, parenting education, and temporary foster care for the children. Some programs emphasize skill development that enhances prosocial parental attitudes and relationships. Other programs address family support for early intervention and prevention. Where there is legal involvement, the courts may order participation in therapeutic programs.

Some critics observe that most treatment programs are not particularly successful. Programs that emphasize parent education and early intervention may be more effective than others, especially in producing short-term effects. Many communities have safe houses that provide temporary shelter and initial assistance to women and their children who have been in abusive

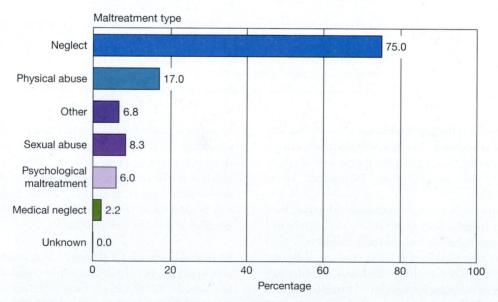

FIGURE 12–5. Reported Child Maltreatment by Type, 2010.

When one family member faces extreme challenges, all members of that family unit are affected. The family may have to find a new balance, or a new "normal." Marital support, civic engagement, and a network of social support provide constructive buffers for all involved.

Otnaydur/123RF.com

Someday, maybe, there will exist a well-informed, well considered and yet fervent public conviction that the most deadly of all possible sins is the mutilation of a child's spirit; for such mutilation undercuts the life principle of trust, without which every human act, may it feel ever so good and seem ever so right is prone to perversion by destructive forms of conscientiousness.

Erik Erikson, Psychologist (1902–1994)

Focus Point.   Child abuse and neglect justly receive a great deal of attention. Several psychosocial factors are associated with violent behaviors directed towards children and spouses. Parents who abuse and neglect children display characteristics, such as hostility and a need for control. The types of abuse range from physical neglect and maltreatment to emotional and sexual abuse of children. Unfortunately, many children who experience abuse grow up to repeat the same harmful behaviors and continue the cycle of abuse. While intervention and treatment programs have been developed, the limited success reflects the resistance and complexity of these types of destructive behavior patterns.

family situations (Hackett, McWhirter, & Lesher, 2016). When families are treated by a competent therapist, all of the elements of the abuse become part of the intervention strategy: the perpetrator, the victim, and the relationship.

Focus On 12–2

Classifications of Child Abuse and Neglect

- *Physical abuse:* Inflicting harm through burns, cuts, bites, etc.
- *Sexual abuse:* Forcing, tricking, or coercing sexual behavior between a young person and an older person, with an age difference of at least 5 years between the perpetrator and the victim, includes fondling, penetration, and behaviors such as voyeurism or pornography
- *Physical neglect:* Failure to provide a child with an adequate and nurturing home environment, including the basic necessities of food, clothing, shelter, and supervision
- *Medical neglect:* Failure to provide a child with medical treatment and withholding care, either of which action could be life threatening to the child
- *Emotional abuse:* Speech, actions, and interactions that affect emotional well-being and a sense of self-worth, and hamper healthy personal and social development
- *Emotional neglect:* Failure to show concern for a child and his or her activities
- *Abandonment:* Failure to make provisions for the continual supervision of a child
- *Multiple maltreatments:* A combination of several types of abuse or neglectful acts

Based on Featherstone, B. (2016). Telling different stories about poverty, inequality, child abuse and neglect. *Families, Relationships and Societies,* 5(1), 147–153; Radford, L. (2017). Child Abuse and Neglect: Prevalence and Incidence; and Sabyrkulova, S., Talbert, J., Dahle, S., Williams, A., & Flamand, K. (2016). Determining Child Abuse Potential with the Child Guidance Interview Subscales.

Focus On 12–3

Characteristics of an Abusive Parent

- Unhappy childhood, being mistreated or abused in the family of origin.
- Parents failed to model good parenting; used violence instead.
- Socially isolated: Few friends, little support from family, friends, neighbors.
- Low self-esteem; feels inadequate, unlovable, incompetent, or worthless.
- Emotionally immature with a dependent personality.
- Sees little joy or pleasure in life; may be clinically depressed.
- Holds distorted perceptions and unrealistic expectations of children.
- Supports physical punishment as discipline. Authoritarian parenting.
- Minimal nurturing behaviors; frequent outbursts of temper.
- Limited empathy, general insensitivity towards others and own children.

Based on American Psychological Association, Understanding and preventing child abuse and neglect. http://www.apa.org/pi/families/resources/understanding-child-abuse.aspx, Retrieved 12/13/2017.

Cultural Snapshot 12–2

Broken Courage, Soul Loss and Other Afflictions

Major illnesses such as schizophrenia, bipolar disorder, anxiety disorders, and depression, affect mental well-being and implicate the entire family system. The World Health Organization has documented that many of these conditions and symptom-clusters occur universally and in various cultures. The names and meanings attached to these conditions can vary as specific cultural interpretations are added. In some cultures, variations of mental illness are described in culturally unique ways, and are attempts to give meaning and gain understanding of feelings and behavior that express or display distress.

Amok is a sudden intense display of aggression, even homicidal aggression and has been described in countries such in Asia (Malaysia, Philippines and Thailand). *Baksbat* is seen in Cambodia and is a condition that is described by the local culture as "broken courage." Symptoms can include fear, submissiveness, and being distrustful. *Susto* is the result of an event that was intensely traumatic and results in "soul loss." All these descriptions have a poetic quality, and there is a universality and validity in the descriptors that allows us to empathize and try to understand the distress they describe.

"Broken courage" and "soul loss" are also descriptions of qualities that can make their appearance within depression or even post-traumatic stress. When these qualities are voiced by members of a specific cultural group, they describe the emotional pain experienced in the metaphors of that culture. They are culture specific or *emic* expressions. The distress of mental illness on the other hand is *etic* or culture universal.

Based on Matsumoto, D., & Juang, L. (2017). *Culture and Psychology*. 6th ed. Boston, MA: Cengage. Chapter 12: Culture and psychological disorders, p. 298. See also Kirmayer, J., & Ryder, A. G. (2016). Culture and psychopathology. *Current Opinion in Psychology*, 8, 143–148.

CHAPTER FOCUS POINTS

Parenting Interrupted

- When parenting takes a back seat or is "interrupted" due to, for instance, career obligations, health issues, or

substance abuse, the results could have lifetime implications for the children. The family system has to redistribute its power and all the remaining family members pool their resources to find a new homeostasis or equilibrium. The Vaillant study offers valuable insight into the connection between parent–child relationships and adult functioning, further displaying how childhood experiences greatly influence the entire life story.

Fragile Families

■ The term *"fragile families"* is used to describe families who are at greater risk than more traditional families to face poverty, probably accompanied by marital and family breakup. Many elements can play a role in putting families at risk of becoming vulnerable; including socioeconomic challenges, physical health, and psychological well-being. Protective factors such as stability and availability of resources, civic engagement and family support, act as mediating agents and promote overall family prosperity.

Adverse Childhood Experiences

■ As a snowball gathers mass when rolling down a hill, adverse childhood experiences contribute to more negative outcomes that ultimately contribute to early death. However, mediating factors such as positive familial relationships could aid in breaking the cycle of negative experiences, thus halting the "snowball" of risk.

Assets Contributing to Healthy Development

■ Both internal and external development assets contribute to positive outcomes and foster environments dedicated to health and success.

Phases in Family Functioning

■ Stressors that impact a family system can either be positive, such as a birth of a child, or negative, such as the death of a loved one. According to the ABC-X model, factors such as the type of stressor, availability of family resources, and perception of the stressor all affect how the family functions following the stressor or crisis event. Ideally, the family will utilize its available resources and reorganize to continue functioning on a healthy level.

Family Stressors: Grief and Loss

■ Children's and adolescents' grief looks different at various developmental levels. Children are not only dealing with intense emotions that they may have never felt before, but they are also learning what death is and what it means to be dead. Adolescents experience grief at a more mature level; and their ability to understand their own mortality is beginning to solidify. A significant death can challenge their worldview, spurring anxiety, fear, loss of identity, and questions of purpose and meaning.

Substance-Related and Addictive Disorders

■ Due to high levels of drug abuse across the country, programs such as Family Checkup have begun to formulate ways for families to maintain healthy practices. By encouraging open and honest communication concerning the risks of drug abuse, these programs help give parents the knowledge and skills to minimize the danger of substance abuse that threatens their families.

Family Stressors and Addictive Disorders

■ When an adult develops an addictive disorder, all members of the family unit are affected. The parent concerned will be more focused on fulfilling his or her own needs that feed the addiction, than providing for the children. Children growing up in this environment develop patterns that help them cope with their dysfunctional family. Typically, a child's emotional development is seriously affected, and the opportunity of a normal childhood is often forfeited. Because these children have experienced chaotic, unpredictable parenting by adults who have possibly abandoned them emotionally, they are left without the usual parental supports that can also promote resilience.

The Battleground of Abuse

■ Child abuse and neglect justly receive a great deal of attention. Several psychosocial factors are associated with violent behaviors directed towards children and spouses. Parents who abuse and neglect children display characteristics such as hostility and a need for control. The types of abuse range from physical neglect and maltreatment to emotional and sexual abuse of children. Unfortunately, many children who experience abuse grow up to repeat the same harmful behaviors and continue the cycle of abuse. While intervention and treatment programs have been developed, the limited success reflects the resistance and complexity of these types of destructive behavior patterns.

USEFUL WEBSITES

Websites are dynamic and change

Centers for Disease Control and Prevention, Injury and Violence Prevention and Control
www.cdc.gov/injury
Injury prevention and control

Child Welfare Information Gateway
www.childwelfare.gov
Supporting and preserving families

Childhelp: National Child Abuse Hotline, 1–800–4–A–CHILD (1–800–422–4453)
www.childhelp.org
Protecting a child, Child Abuse Hotline

Children's Bureau, Administration for Children and Families
www.acf.hhs.gov/
Prevention and treatment of child abuse

FRIENDS: National Resource Center for Community-based Child Abuse Prevention
www.friendsnrc.org
Community-based child abuse prevention, Resources and education

National Council on Alcoholism and Drug Dependence
www.ncadd.org
Alcoholism and Drug dependency support/resources

National Institute on Alcohol Abuse and Alcoholism
www.niaaa.nih.gov
Alcohol abuse resources, Support and treatments

Search Institute
www.search-institute.org
Research and resources for what kids need to succeed

CHAPTER 13

Blended and Intergenerational Family Systems

Learning Outcomes

After completing this chapter, you should be able to:

1. Report the incidence of divorce and remarriage in the United States.
2. Illustrate the various avenues by which blended families are formed.
3. Summarize the role of conflict as experienced in blended families.
4. Assess the cultural, social, and economic factors influencing intergenerational families.

Families grow in various ways and different groups of people can establish alliances to form *blended families*. There are several variations on the theme, where we depart from the formula of two biological parents with biological offspring.

A new family system can be formed when a person repartners, or when a single parent remarries. A family can expand by fostering or adopting children. A *reconstituted* or **blended family** system typically brings together children who may have had different families of origin, and/or adults who have been partnered or married previously, or have children from previous relationships. They blend their resources to form a new family. Instead of focusing on how the children joined the blended family (repartnering, remarriage, adoption, fostering), this chapter concentrates on the dynamics and challenges involved in blended family formation.

This blended formation can also include intergenerational additions to the family, as when a grandparent joins the household, or in skipped generation parenting, when grandparents raise the grandchildren.

Typically, each one of the parents in a blended family can be the biological parent of some of the children while *stepparenting* the new spouse's children. Alternatively, neither parent has a biological link to the child, as in the case of adoption and fostering. Not all of the roles within the blended family are step relationships.

The repartnering and remarriage of adults restores the adult family role that was vacant in a single-parent family. Because the vast majority of single-parent families in the United States are headed by women, the person usually filling the vacant adult role is a man who probably has been previously partnered or who may or may not have been previously married. Occasionally, two single parents and their families are merged by repartnering or the remarriage of the adults. Other variations of blended families are families who adopt and who foster children.

The problems and challenges facing blended families are different from those of other family systems. The adults face the usual tasks of establishing an intimate relationship as a newly partnered or married couple. This process is complicated by children who are not gradually introduced into the family structure, but who join the new family system with many memories of a former family system. The ability of the new blended family system to survive and cope with these challenges occupies much of the time, attention, and resources of the system, especially in the early years following the new blended family formation.

THE CHARACTERISTICS OF BLENDED FAMILY SYSTEMS

Repartnering and Remarriage

Where there are partnerships, repartnering can occur. Where there are marriages, there are also remarriages. Importantly, blended families are also formed through variations where persons regroup to form new alliances that function like families. With the many major changes in family form and function, blended families are not only the result of a divorce. As partnerships form, new groups of people may form kinship-like bonds, usually referred to as **families-by-choice**. Blended families can represent many variations of family groupings, not only

biological and stepparent family formations. In LGBT partnerships, just as in other family groups, family membership can regroup and can be formed by choice, as opposed to being formed through kinship.

More information is available about blended families after divorces, as marital dissolutions are formally recorded in the legal system. Partnered living arrangements do not typically have extensive legal implications that are as trackable.

Remarriage. In the past, many married adults became widowed and remarried after the death of a spouse. In recent decades, divorce has become the leading cause for single status after a first marriage (Lehrer & Son, 2017). Remarriage is more likely to occur if an adult has been divorced rather than if they were widowed. Women who were under age 25 at the time of the divorce are more likely to remarry than women older than age 25. Remarriage is more likely if divorced women live in communities with lower rates of male unemployment, poverty, and welfare dependence. Interestingly, women living in non-urban areas are more likely to remarry than those living in cities; possibly because in rural communities the sense of community may be stronger. These patterns may be explained in part by the age of the individuals when they become single. People who are widowed are usually in late adulthood and especially the women are less likely to remarry because of their advanced age. Divorced individuals tend to be a younger demographic. Remarriages are considered to be high-risk relationships as they have an even greater chance of ending in divorce (Hiyoshi, Fall, Netuveli, & Montgomery, 2015). Our knowledge of the factors that lead to second and even third divorces are limited (Jensen, Shafer, Guo, & Larson, 2017).

The couples who have stable, functional remarriages report having higher satisfaction and greater pride in their new relationship than first-marriage couples. Their developmental lifespan stage may also contribute to this subsequent success. Being more mature, and having learned from a previous marriage, they may be more motivated to improve communication and conflict resolution, supporting enhanced marital outcomes.

Almost two thirds of the persons who divorce each year in the United States eventually remarry. In the typical divorcing couple, the man is in his late thirties, whereas the woman is in her early thirties, and they have at least one child (Federal Interagency Forum on Child and Family Statistics, 2010). This suggests that many men and women remarry when they are about 10 years older than when they were first married. Generally, remarriage is more likely to occur among younger, rather than older, individuals (Brown & Lin, 2013). The median interval between divorce and remarriage is about 3 years for women, with about half remarrying within 5 years of their divorce.

Cohabitation and Remarriage.   **Cohabitation** occurs more commonly post-divorce, and at greater rates than before first marriages (Langlais, Anderson, & Greene, 2016). This may reflect the desire to test a relationship before making a marital commitment. Cohabitation prior to remarriage appears to have little effect on a couple's relationship (Shafer, Jensen, & Larson, 2014). Another distinction of courtship prior to remarriage is the influence of the children's presence. Not only do single parents, especially those who hold custody of children, have a more challenging time in locating prospective partners, they have other considerations as well. Single parents must be considerate of the developmental stages of their own children and the values they model when becoming involved in a serious relationship.

Alternatively, how does one explain to children that the relationship has dissolved, especially if the children have developed an attachment to the potential partner? Children can also contribute to the stress experienced within a marriage or a cohabiting partnership, and partnership satisfaction may be lowered during the stressful years of raising a family. Once children leave the home, parents seem to regain higher levels of satisfaction than during the active child rearing years. The post-child-rearing years can also mean greater financial stability for a couple as children become fiscally independent. Couples who remain together, as opposed to having had to deal with a divorce, are more likely to be able to create financially stable outcomes. Financially supporting members of a previous marriage choice, in addition to current obligations, can be a great responsibility (Zissimopoulos, Karney, & Rauer, 2015).

Remarriages are characterized by the difference in developmental levels of the adults at the time of remarriage in comparison with those during their first marriage. Because of what they have experienced during their first marriage and because of developmental changes, divorced persons tend to have different expectations of remarriage and of themselves (Garneau, Higginbotham, & Adler-Baeder, 2015). Women who have children, and who remarry, may have stronger and more definite career goals than during their first marriage. Many know that they can

survive a divorce and are more committed to making another marriage work successfully. Their ideas of what a marriage requires are clearer in comparison to during their first marriage (Theunis, Pasteels, & Van Bavel, 2015).

The number of children involved in these diverse family arrangements is very high. These children have dual roles in that they can be a stepchild to one parent and a biological child to the other parent. Additionally, about 1.5 million adopted children have joined families in the United States (Kreider & Lofquist, 2014). As greater numbers of families cohabit and are involved in relationships that may cycle fairly rapidly, the children can be exposed to structural instability, as precipitated by union disruptions. These youngsters are becoming accustomed to multiple living arrangements, and exposed to different parenting styles and expectations. Family stability may not be the most outstanding characteristic in these situations, and the children have to adjust accordingly with varying outcomes (Brown, Manning, & Stykes, 2015).

Solidifying Stepfamily Bonds.   Usually the blended family consists of children from previous partnerships. Some newly partnered couples have a child together, and that child is said to cement or *solidify* their relationship. The child born into this blended family unites the parties as the child is genetically linked to both the mother and the father (Ganong & Coleman, 2017a). The children in these blended families have various roles and influence the family in subtle as well as overt ways.

The "percolator" effect refers to the brewing at the base of the family system, which then bubbles to the top, resulting in either negative or positive impacts. In the context of stepfamilies, the parenting may be influenced strongly by the children, in other words, come from the bottom up, as children influence and express their needs to their parents. This is in contrast to the original two parent families where some of the parenting initiatives flow from the parent toward the child, or from the top down to the bottom. In this manner, the children can gain a fairly dominant power base within the stepfamily. The percolator effect can also be maintained by the relationships between stepsiblings. In other words, in these step families, the children can play a decisive role in contributing to the climate within the stepfamily. This has been described by Ganong and Coleman (2017a), who are leading researchers in the field of stepfamilies and the intricacies of their relationships.

Additionally, the factors that affect siblings in the first marriages, can potentially be perpetuated in a subsequent marriage. Events from the first marriage can infiltrate and have an effect on the second or subsequent marriages (Ganong & Coleman, 2017a). For instance, problems in custodial arrangements, financial responsibilities and alimony to spouses from previous marriages, can influence the tone of the subsequent marriage. In blended families the nonbiological or stepparent may find it particularly challenging to provide guidance to children who may not see this stepparent as having any authority. New relationships need to be forged before parental responsibilities and privileges of the stepparent gain the same legitimacy as interventions initiated by the biological parent.

When blended families are formed, the children in that family have several trajectories of how their relationships with the new stepparent might play out. These relationships can vary from being warm and welcoming, to being hostile and rejecting. Researchers have identified six patterns in stepfamily development: accepting of the stepparent, virtual immediate affinity or liking, ambivalent acceptance, changing feelings concerning the stepparent, and as the most hostile in this lineup openly rejecting and coexisting under the same roof under duress (Ganong, Coleman, & Jamison, 2011). Children who are living in complex family arrangements with stepsiblings, and possibly half siblings, have to deal with family dynamics on numerous levels which can contribute to adjustment challenges within the blended family (Nixon & Hadfield, 2016). These dynamics between stepsiblings and possibly half siblings are further influenced by the temperaments

HDeser/Shutterstock

This sand ceremony at a wedding, symbolizes the merging of families. With the many major changes in family form and function, blended families may be a result of variations where persons regroup to form new alliances that function like families. Blended families can represent many different types of family groupings, not only biological and stepparent family formations.

Ganong, Lawrence, & Coleman, Marilyn. (2017a). *Stepfamily Relationships: Development, Dynamics and Interventions.* 2nd ed. New York, NY: Springer.

Papernow, Patricia. (2015). *Becoming a Stepfamily: Patterns of Development in Remarried Families.* New York, NY: Routledge.

FIGURE 13–1. Resources for Blended Families.

of the children and the general quality of the parenting that occurs within the blended family system.

Parenting Reflection 13–1

Distinguish between a blended family and a first-marriage, biological family.

Because remarriage most frequently involves individuals who have been previously divorced, it is likely that the children of one adult or both will be included as part of the new family system. Several characteristics of blended families distinguish them from first-marriage families (Papernow, 2015):

1. *A new family system is created instantaneously.* The typical timeline for family formation is seldom the norm, as new family members are there from the word "Go." In the developmental lifespan of first marriages, adults can gradually develop new patterns (rules, boundaries, and roles) for their family system that affect functioning. Blended families are challenged by the immediacy of developing patterns without gradually adding children to the system. In many cases, the patterns formed for one adult's single-parent family system after divorce is a template for those initially used in the new stepfamily system.

2. *There is a new configuration of individual lifespan tasks and goals.* There may be a conflict between what is required for healthy, individual adult development and what is required to establish a new marital relationship in the newly formed blended system.

3. *Ex-spouses and ex-grandparents continue to be part of the extended family.* Unlike the family systems based on first marriages, family functioning is complicated by the influence of past relationships and former family systems. For example, the adults may continue to be influenced by their former

partners because they still share the biological parenthood of children who are part of the new blended family system.

4. ***Both children and adults may have mixed feelings of allegiance.***   Children in blended families can have divided loyalties because they are members of two separate and distinct family systems. Children may feel torn in several directions, which tests the strength of their personal boundaries. It is not uncommon for remarried men to feel torn between the need to provide for their biological children from their previous marriage and to meet the needs of the new family system to which they now belong. Whereas some men are relieved that their former relationship has ended, others continue to resent the continuing degree of involvement with that severed relationship through children and financial responsibilities.

5. ***Children may not be willing participants in the new blended family system.***   Although adults may consult children about a potential partner, they often do not seek a child's approval before deciding to remarry. Typically, children may feel ambivalent about accepting the new marriage. Many children of divorced parents fantasize that their biological parents will somehow be reunited and that their family life will return to its former state.

6. ***Role confusion can be challenging.***   A major task of the system is to establish new patterns and this task is common to all blended family systems. The role of a stepmother or stepfather is not clear; new rules must be established that promote healthy family functioning. Boundaries are a special challenge to effective stepfamily functioning. They may relate to personal property, psychological intimacy, and family routines or traditions. Clear communication, a commitment to the new family system, and a willingness to discuss issues and reach agreeable solutions are necessary to establish new patterns.

••

Focus Point.   Nearly two thirds of divorced individuals remarry, and a large majority of these unions include children from previous relationships. Babies born in remarriages typically create a stronger bond between the couple and solidify their commitment. Challenges such as tested allegiance and role conflict are common themes in newly formed blended families.

••

Cultural Snapshot 13–1

Love and Marriage

About 90% of persons in societies across the world get married or follow an equivalent custom reflecting long-term commitment (Matsumoto & Juang, 2017, p. 342). In many societies, especially in developing countries, fertility is an important factor to strengthen the bonds, and infertility may be reason to dissolve the commitment. Romantic love and the tumultuous feelings that may accompany the event of "falling in love" have also been described virtually universally, as attested by poetry and music. Even so, in India for example, arranged marriages still occur, and these couples are expected to learn to love their betrothed, as opposed to the Western notion of marrying the person with whom you fall in love.

The Inuit from the northwestern parts of the continent of North America regard all marriage relationships as permanent and favor extended family organization. After marriage, men typically join the extended families of their wives. The concept of "divorce," as known in mainstream American contexts and accompanied by legal implications, does not exist in traditional Inuit societies. Instead couples can be "separated." The practical implications are that marriages are *reactivated* when the couple reunites. Marriage appears to be a flexible arrangement that also requires considerable goodwill between partners. When partners remarry, but not to each other as in the first marriage, then the subsequent relationships define the partners as "co-husbands" and "co-wives." Importantly separations attempt to maintain family connections, which is beneficial to the offspring (Guemple, 1995, pp. 21 and 24).

Based on the following sources:

Matsumoto, D., & Juang, L. (2017). *Culture and psychology.* 6th ed. Boston, MA: Cengage.

Guemple, L. (1995). Gender in Inuit Society. In Klein, L. F., & Ackerman, L. A. (Eds.) *Women and Power in Native North America.* Norman, OK: University of Oklahoma Press.

BLENDED FAMILY FORMATION

The problems that challenge blended family systems are unique, and these systems may experience a greater level of stress than usually encountered by first-marriage family systems. Problems are linked to the following (Ganong & Coleman, 2017c):

■ Merging different family cultures and identities as the new system establishes roles and patterns.
■ Developing new ways of distributing time, energy, material goods, finances, and affection.
■ Establishing new bonds of loyalty while managing loyalty bonds to former family systems.

Blended family system formation involves different structures than in first-marriage systems. First-marriage families have had time to allow the adults to develop an intimate relationship and areas of shared interests and values, and habitual patterns that guide interactions and conflict resolution. The gradual addition of children to a biological family allows the adults to develop and adapt to parenting roles, learn to resolve differences, and create a shared value system (Stewart, 2007).

When a first-marriage couple divorces, they create two single-parent family systems that most prominently affect the children, who become members of two distinct *binuclear* systems. A major consequence is the dismantling of the usual generational boundaries between adults and children. Adults often look toward children for the support and nurture formerly provided by the spouse. Potentially negative consequences are children being triangulated between parents in two households; it is difficult to form allegiances to both with equal loyalty.

At the beginning of a blended family's life, the stepparent at first seems to be an outsider to the existing alliance between the biological parent and his or her children. This alliance is based on the patterns established in the former single-parent family system and has its own history, rules, boundaries, patterns, and operational styles firmly in place. The greatest challenge to the survival and effective, healthy functioning of a blended family system may be overcoming the obstacles and resistance encountered in adapting previously established patterns and styles.

Video Example 13.1

Watch this video on blended families. What benefits do children in blended families experience when all family members become an integral part of their lives?

(https://www.youtube.com/watch?v=gPIPStOAyjk)

Families may at times be separated by the professional demands of the breadwinners, or by deployment. One parent may be "parenting-at-a-distance," while a grandparent may take on additional parenting responsibilities.

Tropical studio/Shutterstock

Focus Point.   The structure of blended families has its own unique qualities. Single-parent families are created when adults separate, divorce or are widowed. When parents repartner, another variation of a family unit is created, with concomitant shifts in the relationship between the biological parents and their children. When a biological parent's marriage to a new partner forms a blended family, additional changes in the parent–child subsystem emerge.

COPARENTING AND BLENDED FAMILY ROLES

Coparents agree to take on the parenting tasks together. Coparents are also characterized by two key factors, namely that ideally they have a deep and ongoing interest in the child's well-being, and that they may be instrumental in effecting change or making decisions that affect the child.

In blended family systems, there may be two coparenting dyads at play. The first refers to the biological parents, who have to find ways to coparent successfully from binuclear households. The second dyad refers to the two persons fulfilling parental roles within the blended family, of whom one will be a biological parent and the other a stepparent. Coparenting has the best success rate if the best interests of the children are considered, and if parental systems can maintain the parental hierarchical boundaries. This means that the personal problems and challenges within the parental dyad should not spill over into the relationships with the children. Children should not be pulled into the intimacy problems of parents or be turned into go-betweens for warring parents. As responsible adults, the coparents have to set their personal agendas aside when it comes to parent–child relations and focus on the needs of the children, keeping their best interests in mind (Kuehnle, Kirkpatrick, & Drozd, 2014).

A stepparent's role has a high degree of role ambiguity (Schrodt, 2016). Our culture promotes many stereotypical images of stepparents that are largely negative. These images can be found in stories and fairy tales told to children. Stepparents, particularly stepmothers, are depicted as evil, uncaring, self-centered individuals who mistreat stepchildren. To a certain degree, popular television shows and movies can reflect the lack of clarity in the stepparent role. The stepmother role is made more difficult by these myths. Successful stepmothers go through a process of establishing an identity and gaining trust in the newly blended family. One of the potential obstacles in blended families, is that the incoming stepparent may be tempted to overparent. Children may feel resentful of this new influence within the family system, and the well intentioned overparenting initiatives may be met with resentment (Segrin, Givertz, Swaitkowski, & Montgomery, 2015).

Parenting FAQ 13–1

I'm seriously considering marriage to a woman with school-age children. I've never been married before and have no clue about parenting, much less what is involved in being a stepfather. What can I expect?

Your unique position may be to your advantage. Because you have never parented your own child, you may rely on influences from your family of origin, your own experiences of having been parented, and your observations concerning this role. This is an instant family situation. You are the newcomer in an already established and long-term relationship between the children and their mother. As authority figures in parental roles, your new bride and you should spend time talking about these things and discuss your wishes for your newly formed family. Show the amount of affection that is comfortable for all involved. When it comes to discipline, consider that the children may have divided loyalties, so make it a joint decision with your spouse. Gain clarity with your spouse concerning financial obligations and responsibilities. Roles will transition toward greater informality and trust as you communicate and get to know each other better. A blended family is a work in progress. Family meetings where all members can convey their opinions can be helpful, if a collaborative and optimistic atmosphere is maintained.

Belief in these negative stereotypes vary according to a person's current family situation. Perceptions about stepparents, and particularly those about stepmothers, are generally negative when compared with perceptions about biological parents. Negative perceptions about stepparents seem to decrease as people become more sensitive, familiar, and vested in blended families and find their own reality (Ganong & Coleman, 2017c).

Stepparents are expected to share equally in the parental status of the new family system. Some stepparents are less involved than the biological parent (Jensen, Shafer, & Holmes, 2015). Special parenting problems may arise for a person who occupies the vacant role in a former single-parent family system. Both men and women who become stepparents may approach their new role hesitantly as they seek and find trust. For example, a single-parent mother who marries or remarries has to relinquish her role as sole authority, and share decision-making responsibilities with her new partner. Although many women welcome this change, others take longer to realign their role to be in synch with the new partner. Family systems tend to resist any change in the current homeostasis or functioning, even if they are healthy and welcome changes.

• •

Parenting Reflection 13–2

Why are clearly defined roles, functions, and behaviors for stepparents so challenging? Could these preconceived ideas of what the roles entail become self-fulfilling prophecies?

• •

Families in which the mother role is filled by a stepmother have more problems than those with a stepfather. This may relate to the differences in the ways in which stepfamilies are formed. Fathers who gain custody of children after remarriage often do so because the mother has difficulties such as addiction disorders, which prove to be detrimental in the relationships with her biological children. Another challenging situation among families with stepmothers involves a woman who has never had children of her own but who quickly assumes a parenting role after her first marriage or remarriage (Sanner, 2016).

Relationships with stepchildren may vary depending on the gender of the children. Stepmothers and stepdaughters are found to have the least favorable relationship. Some of the girls in these relationships do not feel loved and report more feelings of hostility and lower self-esteem. Importantly, blended families have to find solutions that work for their unique challenges.

The age of stepchildren is a factor that influences the relationship with the stepmother, especially among those who have live-in stepmothers. Preschool-age children have the least problems interacting with stepmothers, while school-age and adolescent children have poorer relationships with their stepmothers. The stepmothers of these older children have more disagreements with their spouses, more conflicts over ways of disciplining children, and less satisfaction with their marriages than stepmothers of younger children.

There are successful stepmothers who adapt well to their new role and make significant contributions to their new family (Whiting, Smith, Barnett, & Grafsky, 2007). The methods most often used by these mothers include supports from outside, as well as inside, their family system; positive attitudes; the use of positive communication styles; and working toward the quality of the marital relationship.

Stepfathers

Stepfathers encounter similar problems in developing and performing their family role (King, Amato, & Lindstrom, 2015). The stepfather–stepchild relationship may be at risk for as long as 2 years following the remarriage. Unlike the stepmother, the stepfather may not be as shackled by myths and stereotypes regarding his new role and may be seen in a more positive manner, for instance as the provider (Gold & Adeyemi, 2013). The fact that this role is less structured has both advantages and disadvantages. On the positive side, he can forge a new identity and impression when establishing a relationship with his spouse's children. Stepfathers are less likely to be authoritative in parenting style than biological fathers. Establishing disciplinary patterns and using controls related to stepchildren's behavior are often prime problem areas for stepfathers. Disagreements with the spouse may occur over how the stepfather disciplines the stepchildren.

Stepfathers also experience problems with financial affairs. Many make child support payments for their biological children from a former marriage. This money may be very much needed by the new blended family and can produce feelings of resentment about the former marriage. Guilt derives from the sense that the biological children have been abandoned after the new blended family system was formed. Some men feel that when another man becomes involved as a stepfather to their biological children, this man should help bear the financial costs of caring for these children. Research suggests that biological fathers reduce their social and economic investments in children if they no longer live with them and when they become involved in a blended family. Biological fathers in new blended families are likely to adjust child support payments to nonresidential children to accommodate the financial needs of supporting the new biological children produced in the subsequent marriage (Ellman & Braver, 2015).

Stepgrandparents

If we acknowledge that the family role of grandparents in contemporary times is ambiguous, consider the unique role of stepgrandparents. The legal status of stepgrandparents is not clear. Stepgrandparents are more likely to view young stepgrandchildren as a welcome addition to the family when an adult child remarries. When stepgrandchildren live with the adult child, the likelihood of a relationship between stepgrandparents and stepgrandchildren increases (Pashos, Schwarz, & Bjorklund, 2016).

Research suggests that stepgrandparents can improve their relationship with their stepgrandchildren by increasing their active participation, including establishing a closer relationship with their adult child and increasing their visits with the stepgrandchild at family gatherings and during the holidays (Chapman et al., 2016). The quality of the stepgrandparent–stepgrandchild relationship appears to be influenced to a greater extent by the adult child than by any factors that are exclusive to the stepgrandparent–stepgrandchild relationship. Stepgrandchildren perceived the quality of the relationship with their biological grandparents to be stronger than their relationship with their stepgrandparents. Stepgrandparents may have limited legal rights, depending on the context of their precise family situation.

Stepchildren and Stepsiblings

Usually, the quality of life for children is thought to be enhanced when their biological mother remarries. Single-parent families headed by a woman typically experience either a poverty-level existence or a borderline standard of living. When children live in these conditions, they fare less well than children living in more affluent families in terms of quality of life, medical care, nutrition, education, and economic security (Federal Interagency Forum on Child and Family Statistics, 2016).

Researchers report that children from stepfamilies fare neither better nor worse than children from single-parent families in terms of well-being (Brown, Manning, & Stykes, 2015). When compared with children from intact, first-marriage families, children from both blended families and single-parent families are rated as less well adjusted. It should be stressed that most children in these family forms do not have serious problems.

Children are expected to make a series of adjustments when biological parents divorce and later remarry. These adjustments typically focus on making a transition in family structure and functioning. These adjustments are stressful and affect school performance, behavior, and other socioemotional factors (Anthony, DiPerna, & Amato, 2014). Children living in intact, first-marriage families do not experience anything comparable that can affect their development.

Children, especially girls who grow up in blended families, tend to reject their stepfather and leave the blended family at an earlier age than those growing up in single-parent or two-parent households. They leave to establish their own homes and lifestyles or to get married. These early departures may be the result of the tensions between them and their parents and stepparents. Exiting the blended family is seen as a more viable way to resolve these tensions. The friction that exists in blended families involving female children is attributed to the disruption of the mother–daughter relationship by the mother's male sexual partner who has an ambiguous relationship with the daughter. The quality of the mother's relationship with her adolescent children while entering into a new blended family set-up, is also influenced by what the relationships were like *before* she repartnered. A parent who repartners, will probably continue to have a good relationship with the children if the quality of that relationship was constructive and nurturing prior to the events that led to repartnering. This is turn influences the relationships with the incoming stepparent (King, Amato, & Lindstrom, 2015).

The relationship among stepsiblings is complex when blended families are formed. Forging stepsibling relationships presents other challenges for blended families.

The problems observed in biological sibling relationships, such as rivalry and jealousy, can become even more intense when stepsiblings are involved. It is not unusual for coalitions to form, creating a "my children are being mistreated by your children" scenario. Sexual tensions can exist when stepsiblings are pubertal or adolescent. On a more positive note, stepsiblings can also develop strong relationships where mutual support can be found and friendships flourish (Ganong & Coleman, 2017b).

Video Example 13.2

Watch this video on stepparent/child relationships. What are the key components of a healthy stepparent/stepchild relationship? How does one build such a constructive relationship?

(https://www.youtube.com/watch?v=pDJ1vSZOn0A)

Ex-spouses and Ex-in-laws

For persons in blended families, the relationships with ex-spouses and ex-in-laws are altered rather than severed. It is typical to feel displaced and alienated when divorce transforms the relationship. Although the rights and boundaries that define the altered relationship between ex-spouses begin with the divorce agreement, few legal rights or clear distinctions inform ex-in-laws about their altered relationship.

It is not uncommon for ex-spouses to experience feelings of jealousy, anger, and competition with their former partners (Berger, 2000). Likewise, ex-in-laws may harbor similar feelings of resentment. In other situations, ex-spouses and ex-in-laws collaborate to make the situation tolerable and even amicable.

Focus Point. Coparenting in a remarriage often involves a complete restructuring of expectations and roles. Although homes with stepmothers tend to experience more problems than those with stepfathers, both types of blended families experience unique challenges and obstacles to intimacy. Ex-spouses and ex-in-laws, as well as stepgrandparents, also have to redefine their roles and relationships in the new family structure.

Challenges and Adjustments

The ability of blended families to adjust to their new status, roles, and patterns depends on three central themes:

- Giving up unrealistic expectations for the new family system.
- Clarifying the feelings and needs of each family member.
- Committing to new rules, roles, boundaries, and routines.

Members of blended families experience challenges as new relationships are defined and developed. Additional loyalties have to be forged, while also maintaining ties with members of the original family unit.

Monkey Business Images/Shutterstock

Blended family systems must accomplish several tasks to successfully transition from early disillusionment to total commitment to the new family system (Zeleznikow & Zeleznikow, 2015).

Sources of Support.   For blended families who actively seek support beyond their own extended family and friends, there are several choices. Support for blended families can come from support groups, self-help publications, educational experiences, and therapeutic interventions. Educational strategies assist individuals in developing more realistic expectations of stepfamily life that facilitate the creation of long-term goals. Marriage and family enrichment programs are offered by churches and other organizations, and assist development. Family therapy can be helpful in restoring family balance and in guiding family members toward optimal functioning with one another.

Stepchildren are typically included in therapeutic programs. Children can call on teachers for help. Teachers can play an important role in helping children understand that the problems of blended family life can be resolved. Teachers may work with parents as well.

Because stepchildren complain about problems in their new family, it may appear as if the blended family home is a negative environment. Adjustment problems are more prevalent among children in blended families, and stressors can affect school performance. The children are not necessarily harmed by having a blended family experience. Blended families can find online and community support through organizations that provide information concerning the following topics: judicial information, the importance of parenting time, legislation pertaining to blended families, and information on child support and custody.

Additionally, each family develops its own communication patterns. In some ways, entering and joining a new blended family can be as disorienting as moving cultures; as participants joining a blended family are also changing family culture. The rules and patterns that worked in one family are different in another. Participants may become less fluent in the rules of their former families, while adopting the rules and patterns of their new blended family. This has similarities with changing cultures and, therefore, languages. In the transition, some family members become cultural translators in a bicultural context, similar to what is described in the Cultural Snapshot 13–2, in this chapter.

Focus Point.   The success of a blended family may depend on its ability to overcome obstacles that challenge the development of the new family system. The blended family may use several strategies, such as therapeutic and support groups, to promote healthy family functioning.

Parenting Reflection 13–3

What are some indicators that a blended family needs professional assistance to support them in their new family structure?

Cultural Snapshot 13–2

Dynamic Cultural Heritage: Gaining and Losing Languages

Freud is credited with stating that language is "the royal road to the subconscious." Language is a cognitive modality; it is the communication tool with which we make our thoughts, goals, and wishes known. It is the bridge between our inner self and the outer world. With language come so many other cultural gifts, like getting a better grasp of the host country's ways, making friends, and truly connecting. Ultimately, this new rootedness will bring with it varying degrees of cultural assimilation and integration. It may stretch over a few generations, as each generation becomes more deeply immersed in the host culture until by the third and fourth generations the grand- and great grandchildren of the original immigrants see only their own home culture, where their grandparents had thought of it as a new and possibly alien culture. The "old country," as it is sometimes lovingly called is no longer their home, they were not born there, and they no longer have a direct cultural connection.

(Continued)

Language is how we connect with our fellow humans. When families migrate, there is a major emphasis on learning the language of the new adopted country. For neurolinguistic reasons, the children and teens of that family can do so with greater ease than the parents and possibly the grandparents. For them, the window of opportunity for language acquisition is semi-frozen at a much smaller aperture. We put much emphasis on English as a Second Language (ESL) for immigrants. But what happens to the mother tongue, the first and beloved language in which they have the freedom and familiarity like no other language can offer? There is a fairly predictable pattern: first generation immigrants hold onto their mother tongue and may struggle with the language of the host country. Second generation are cultural translators and have access to both languages, that of the host and of the country of origin. The third generation drifts further and further away from the original language source. With only their parents as teachers, and probably losing their grandparents who were native speakers; the language input is progressively diluted. Hence, by the third generation, the language of the original country is typically falling into disuse as assimilation into the host culture is nearing completion (Koppelman, 2017, p. 80).

Note how this learner of the Chinese language grapples with the nuances of language in the following description:

> In Chinese, my vocabulary was still so limited that I had to learn to live without all of these nuances of language. I missed my ability to hint at paradox—like the sense that my life was determined both by factors beyond my control and by my own free will. I also missed a certain candidness and friendliness that I began to associate with Americans … Only in China did I realize how American I was (Kellor, 2005, p. 145).

As much as multilingualism and cultural diversity are valued, each new generation becomes part of a changing cultural dynamic, where some traditional skills and values fall into disuse as new dimensions are incorporated.

References:
Kellor, A. L. (2005). Rising and falling. In Fountas, A. J. (Ed.). *Waking Up American: Coming of Age Biculturally*. Berkeley, CA: Seal Press.

Based on Koppelman, K. (2017). *Understanding Human Differences: Multicultural Education for a Diverse America*. 5th ed. Pearson.

INTERGENERATIONAL FAMILIES

The intergenerational or multigenerational family form is rapidly increasing in the United States, due to longer life expectancy as well as economic, emotional, and social demands. Historically, extended families were the norm and functioned as economic units, especially in rural and agricultural contexts. Changing demographic patterns include dual-career, single-parent, adolescent parent, and deployed military family structures. These serve as incentives to access temporary or permanent *intergenerational support systems*, even to form intergenerational households.

Three generations can form a cohesive unit providing benefits from pooled resources. This family form can deal with childcare needs, which can solidify intergenerational relations. Stressors increase when the middle generation in this triad feels sandwiched between caring for the older and younger generations. Family dynamics change over the life span, especially in grandparents' interactions with adult grandchildren. Research in the early twenty-first century emphasizes the influence of multigenerational family dynamics on participating parties, the sociological/psychological implications, and optimal intergenerational parenting outcomes.

Lifespan and Multigenerational Parenting

An intergenerational or **multigenerational family** is typically a family unit composed of several generations. They can function as a unit with distinct and dynamic intergenerational patterns. They may live under one roof or separately. What makes an intergenerational family system distinctive is that several generations are involved. The dynamics of intergenerational or multigenerational family systems are best understood from a family systems perspective. Relationships within intergenerational family systems are bidirectional in nature; each participating party or generation exerts and receives influences from all the contributing generations. (Barnett, Scaramella, Neppl, Ontai, & Conger, 2010).

The interactions progress over the lifespan of the participating members and the parenting and grandparenting are developmental; they adjust to the life-span stage of each participating party. Several variations of relationships take place including relationship partners on the same generational level, such as siblings or the marital dyad. Additionally, relationships can skip a generation, reflected in grandparent–grandchild bonds. Interactions also take place with both the generation above and the generation below, which is the case for the middle generation, which is sandwiched between the oldest and the youngest generations. Within any intergenerational system, several subsystems can be identified, such as the nuclear family, the spousal dyad, and the sibling system, to mention a few.

Complexity.   Intergenerational family systems are complex, and they require ongoing adaptation and change to function optimally. In a systemic model, the presumption is that a family cannot be reduced to one or two generations, as there are numerous influences from the families of origin, extending through to the family of procreation. Each generation in such an intergenerational family model has its own anticipated life span, and the generations are staggered typically between 20 and 30 years apart. When the fourth or youngest generation is born, the oldest generation (the great grandparents of the newborn) may be dealing with end-of-life challenges. Seen against the backdrop of individual life spans, the members of each generation are facing their own challenges that reflect their position in their personal development and lifespan.

It is possible to look at a family that is intergenerational and see a representative moment in developmental time. These intergenerational moments are particularly poignant during family rituals such as marriages and funerals, when distinctive life events are ritualized and all the generations participate. For the younger generations in this intergenerational family constellation, these moments may become part of their family history and a way of connecting to preceding generations. For the older generations, it instills a sense of hope to see the continuance of the family line and to pass on values that enhance the sense of family belonging.

Intergenerational families renew themselves. As a younger generation is added to the family line, the oldest generation eventually passes on. Much like a cohort of students is replenished by entering freshmen and downsized by graduating seniors, the intergenerational family evolves over time. This sequence is not always fixed, and premature death in any generation may prove to be particularly challenging as such deaths defy the anticipated course of a typical life span. For

example, an adult can reasonably expect to eventually bury his/her elderly parents but in the intergenerational family it is unexpected and tragic if a parent has to bury a child. Intergenerational families can also be likened to a layered structure (Laszloffy, 2002); new layers are added on top as younger generations join the family, whereas the older, foundational generations gradually melt away from the bottom, with life-span completion marked by death causing this attrition.

Nuclear and Extended Family Contexts

Being in an intergenerational family system elicits challenges that are linked to the unique position of a member within the nuclear as well as the extended family contexts. As a family form, the multigenerational family is regaining dominance, especially in some cultural subgroups within the United States. Intergenerational families are on the rise because of changing family demographics. Longer life expectancy, later marriages or later partnership formation, later adoption of parenthood roles, teen pregnancy, and dual-career families may make it more likely that the middle generation will be "sandwiched," looking up the generational line toward their own parents for help and support in childrearing, as well as economic support.

Cultural Variations.   Cultural and ethnic values influence whether intergenerational families will be accepted as the norm. Sharing resources may ease the threat of poverty and enhance survival of all the participating members. Latino families, for example, are more likely to have three generations living under one roof; the practice makes economic sense and is in line with the cultural values of this group. African American families may have strong intergenerational cohesion. Across ethnicities, higher levels of education in the older generation may support the expression and appreciation of the value of intergenerational relationships. Even so, the results from various ethnic groups need to be controlled for socioeconomic status, specifically poverty (Edin and Kissane, 2010), in order to place these relationships within their larger context. Clearly, a number of factors interact in the expression of closeness between generations.

Intergenerational parenting is unique in migrant families, who at times leave their young children with the grandparents in the country of origin while trying to establish their own futures in an adopted homeland to which they immigrate. These parents may have to requalify professionally if they have higher education to establish credentials in the country they are migrating to. Alternatively, they may wish to establish themselves financially and set up a home with an infrastructure that can support a family. In other cases, immigrants ask their parents to follow them once they have established themselves and their offspring. The possibilities are strongly dependent on immigration legislation.

In immigrant families, the intergenerational family system can become part of the support that enables parents to seek gainful employment, with the grandparents taking over the childrearing roles. The youngest generation is typically acculturated most rapidly, or is born in the newly adopted homeland. The youngest generation may absorb local customs and cultural content more rapidly than the older generations, and most likely will be fluent in the language of the new country. In this manner, children frequently become the literal as well as the metaphorical translators of the family system. They can explain the nuances of the new culture to the rest of the family, and because of their bilingualism they feel at home in both cultural contexts. In this instance, it is the youngest generation in the intergenerational triad that may have the greatest chance of becoming competent in the new environment, and in turn they may be looked on to give back and offer support to the generations above them.

When it comes to interpersonal relationships within the intergenerational system, it can safely be said that this system exerts power over its members and the members in turn influence the family system in a bidirectional manner. For that same reason, any change in a multigenerational family system has the ability to influence the nuclear family system that is locked within this greater intergenerational constellation. This system not only functions in terms of family roles, it is an emotional system as well.

Functions: Parenting the Fragile

An intergenerational family system fulfills a number of important functions for its members, irrespective of the generation to which individual members belong. As a system, it offers exchanges that can represent emotional, social, and financial support. It also offers caregiving exchanges, where any member that is in need of care can be sheltered by the umbrella of family cohesion. The youngest generation may be the most in need of caretaker support while its members have not yet emerged as adults, but then the oldest generation

will require care as well, as its members move into positions of frailty, whether physical, emotional, or cognitive, for instance in cases of dementia and Alzheimer's disease.

In a decade review of articles pertaining to aging and family life, Silverstein and Giarrusso (2010) identified several overarching themes. Their review findings can be summarized as follows:

- Emotional relationships of varying complexity.
- Diversity between and within intergenerational systems.
- Interdependence between the roles fulfilled by various members of this system.
- Outcomes and patterns pertaining to care giving and nurturing relationships (pp. 1039–40).

In short, there is no simple blueprint for intergenerational family structure, as these families are also defined and characterized by their *diversity*. The diversity in turn is influenced by cultural factors and processes that morph and change from generation to generation.

Caregiving Relationships

When the nurturing or care-giving relationships are further examined, it is noteworthy that an attribution bias occurs in reporting these relationships. Adult children focus more strongly on the amount of support they give, and tend to overreport these acts. On the other hand, they underreport, and may underestimate, the help they receive. These perceptions can subtly influence the power dynamics within the generations. Each of the adult generations (parent or grandparent) may see themselves as providing the most support while receiving the least support. Similarly, the perception of the emotional closeness and cohesion of the relationships between the generations will shift and change. The middle generation feels less vested, whereas the members of the oldest generation feel that they contribute greatly. In this manner, there is a discrepancy in how the members of each generation view their contributions within the intergenerational system (Giarusso, Feng, & Bengston 2005). In research studies, the oldest generation typically overreports the help and support they give toward the generations below them, while also underreporting the help and support they receive. Thus, an attribution or self-serving bias is at play, where the perceptions are colored to benefit the image of the person doing the reporting.

Sandwich Generation.   Investments in intergenerational relationships change as time progresses. Typically, the oldest generation continues to invest emotionally whereas the middle generation is sandwiched between demands from the generations above and below (Fingerman, Pillemer, Silverstein, & Suitor, 2012). As far as models for conceptualizing these relationships are concerned, one of the important models is a comprehensive scheme for describing a variety of feelings, attitudes, behaviors, values, and structural arrangements in intergenerational relationships. It is based on the work of Bengtson, Biblarz, and Roberts (2002) and provides a formal way of conceptualizing the many complex layers of these types of relationships.

Another area of research has been the ambivalence that occurs in intergenerational relationships. Seemingly conflicting emotions may occur depending on the context and the parties involved. This theme was conceptualized in an intergenerational solidarity paradigm (Connidis & McMullin, 2002). Several research studies have followed and have provided tools for intergenerational researchers in terms of a variety of dimensions.

Eldercare and Role Strain.   Silverstein and Giarrusso (2010), in their important decade review of family life involving an aging generation, state that the notion that intergenerational families are predominantly characterized by harmonious relationships has been challenged. Postmillennial research has pointed toward ambivalence and ambiguity, role strain, divided loyalties, emotional discordance, and stressful outcomes for members of intergenerational family systems who juggle roles and demands and at times do so involuntarily and driven by necessity. For instance, grandparents raising grandchildren where the middle generation is absent through incarceration, problems related to addictive disorders, deployment, mental health issues, or physical challenges may do so with ambiguous feelings if not outright resentment. Additionally, the generations may experience so-called *structural ambivalence,* which refers to the competing demands on resources such as finances, time, and space management.

Another parameter of ambivalence is "collective ambivalence," which goes beyond interpersonal relationships and extends into larger and more complex social systems in which these relationships are nested (Silverstein & Giarrusso, 2010). This refers to those systems that are larger than the innermost microsystem, according to a socioecological model of interrelated systems. In other words, all relationships, including dyadic relationships, are contained within larger societal systems, and the bidirectional influence can be felt in intergenerational relationships as well.

A number of factors influence grandparent–grandchild relationships including geographical proximity, frequency of contact, cohabitation among the elderly, and financial considerations.

XiXinXing/Shutterstock

Focus Point.   Intergenerational families cover a broad range of family types, varying in size, structure, and function. Many adults find themselves "sandwiched" between caring for their own children and caring for their aging parents, a situation which often leads to role strain.

Grandparent-headed Families

A grandparent who is obliged to raise a grandchild may feel that his/her entire life in all its dimensions has been affected (Buchanon & Rotkirch, 2016). According to demographics and census findings, a grandparent raising a grandchild in the absence of the middle or parental generation is a family form that is on the increase. The 2010 U.S. Census revealed that most of the children in the United States permanently living with grandparents were under the age of six. The stressors for an aging generation of having to take responsibility for a very young generation are apparent, and these "skipped-generation" households certainly carry their share of burdens.

Of the parties participating in these intergenerational relationships, siblings at any level of the generations may vie for attention and position. Siblings who are adults may remember favoritism in their nuclear family and carry these competitive feelings into their adult relationships. Siblings on one generational level may also feel that they compete with nieces and nephews in terms of dominance and esteem within a given generation. Clearly, family-of-origin issues can influence later intergenerational relationships.

Societal pressures and trends are reflected in the changing demographics surrounding the family—specifically, significantly declining family size. Research consistently points toward changes on the macrosystemic level that trickle down to families. Large-scale, cross-national studies have revealed sociocultural factors that are contributing to variations in the levels of contact and support between the cohorts in intergenerational family systems. Studies on intergenerational families from various sociocultural and economic backgrounds reflect the entire spectrum of support through public welfare provisions; such support ranges from strong public support networks with sociodemocratic values through to provisions that support greater individual choice and responsibility with accompanying decreased public safety nets. Clearly, these larger sociopolitical systems have a direct impact on the smaller units of their society, namely the building blocks comprising individual and intergenerational families. Generally, countries with weaker social welfare supports place greater emphasis on the family network to provide intergenerational care giving for members (of any generation) requiring support, whether for disability, illness, or aging-related factors.

Financial Considerations.   When it comes to financial considerations, it is most likely that in the United States the older generations typically support the younger ones and that the financial support metaphorically flows downstream. The support can range from small gifts and financial support to large sums, such as paying for tuition or helping offspring buy their first home. In the case of temporary or permanent absence of the middle generation, grandparents may have to bridge the void with their own resources and provide a much-needed safety net, which in turn can have an impact on their own economic viability in terms of retirement provision. They may also find themselves being the stabilizers of a system in flux. Past and current relationship quality may determine the willingness of the participating generations to invest, be it emotionally or economically.

Little formal research has been done into whether and how members of the youngest generation may compete for possible inheritance benefits and implied financial gain from grandparents. Additionally, grandparents can provide grandchildren with a priceless legacy in terms of family history and personal identity. As the oldest living generation, they are the repository of ancestral history. When grandchildren learn certain activities, family rituals, and possibly religious rites from grandparents, it contributes to intergenerational learning and enhances feelings of belonging and connectedness within the family. On the other hand, the youngest generation may keep the grandparents in the proverbial loop, familiarizing them with technological advances and current expressions, such as verbal slang, fashion, and other trends that mark and display changes in a society. Both generations learn from each other and mutual socialization occurs, much to the benefit of participating generations.

Grandparental Support.   Increasingly, families are becoming smaller, many choosing one-child family structures or no children as the preferred family form.

In these families, the intergenerational relationships are also affected. Only children may experience a greater burden, being sandwiched between a younger and an older generation. On the other hand, for dual-career families, the backup systems that one or two sets of grandparents can provide can prove to be invaluable. Additionally, divorce rates have climbed since the mid-twentieth century, and increasingly couples marry later or cohabit. After a divorce, the formation of a blended family is a possibility, and again members of the oldest generation may have to adjust to the choices their children make. Once a blended family is formed after a divorce, loyalties may be divided.

Grandparents may feel loyalties toward all their grandchildren but the time they have available to interact with this youngest generation may be limited and they may have to negotiate the new relationships and family additions brought about by subsequent marriages. Variables that may have an impact on the effects of divorce on grandchildren and grandparents include proximity, family structure, and the pressures derived from need (Buchanon & Rotkirch, 2016).

Geographic Proximity and Frequency of Contact.
Geographic proximity is an additional factor influencing frequency of contact. The variety of electronic communication possibilities may make it easier to bridge the long-distance communication gap, if the oldest generation is able and willing to become or remain technologically engaged. The research indicates that frequency of contact is more important than proximity in determining the emotional closeness between the oldest and the youngest generations. A wise adage concerning parenting also applies to grandparenting: "If there isn't enough quantity, there can't be enough quality." Sustaining a meaningful and rewarding intergenerational relationship requires an investment of (especially) time, reflected in frequency of contact.

Admittedly, geographical closeness may facilitate frequency of contact and support mutual assistance. Even so, the frequency with which the grandparental generation interacts with other generations will be mediated by other factors such as cultural and ethnic value systems, gender, and social class, and it is possible that the dimension of expression of closeness between the generations is overemphasized.

Generally, the research indicates that grandmothers tend to initiate and maintain greater frequency of contact than grandfathers. Of all the dyads, grandmothers and granddaughters report the closest bonds and this has been referred to as the "*matrifocal tilt*" (Sheehan & Petrovic, 2008, p. 108). There may be a gender-based role definition in this older generation that shapes this generation's perception of the demands of the grandparental role.

Cohabitation among the Elderly.
Cohabitation is also occurring in the oldest generation. Some of the members of this group have been widowed and may not want to enter another marriage later in life as it may affect their financial assets, unless clear legal provisions are put in place. Members of the oldest generation in the intergenerational system may be more concerned with societal opinion and judgment if they cohabit, but generalizations are difficult to make as cultural and socio-economic factors play a strong role in these choices.

In data comparing attitudes toward cohabitation in the elderly over a two-decade period, researchers found that support for cohabitation accelerated (Brown & Wright, 2016). Two decades previously in the mid-nineties, only 20 percent of the elderly questioned expressed support or acceptance of cohabitation. That figure steadily increased to approximately the 50 percent mark two decades later. Later opinions are influenced by the kind of cultural and societal values experienced when this group was younger. For instance, each generation such as the baby boomers (born between 1946 and 1960) versus Generation X (born between 1960 and 1980), are exposed to different societal climates, which in turn influence their values. This acceptance of cohabitation is accompanied by greater numbers of elderly cohabiting in later life. Current estimates are that one in three baby boomers are single. The reasons for this vary and include divorce, but increasingly also widowhood as members of this generation lose their life partners to death.

Living apart together (LAT) is another variation on the theme favored by older adults (Brown & Wright, 2016). In these instances, the elderly may share companionship in a variety of social situations, but prefer to remain in their own living arrangements, while keeping their financial affairs separate as well. This may have to do with pension and other insurance related constrictions. Some of the elderly, especially women, who have nursed a spouse over a long period of time, and are now widowed, do not want to revisit this pattern with a next partner, and definitely do not want to co-reside. Elderly men on the other hand, welcome co-residential arrangements, possibly because they become accustomed to having a wife take care of domestic responsibilities (Brown & Wright, 2016).

It seems then that the lifecycle needs between the genders are not fully in synch and gender equality is less pronounced amongst this age group. In the early marriage days, many women express a need for intimacy and closeness, while the men value their independence. Later in life, amongst the elderly, this pattern is often reversed with women valuing their autonomy and being hesitant to commit to co-residence.

Boomerang Children

Boomerang kids, those children who return to their parental home after having been launched, are another variation contributing to intergenerational family life. These emerging adults may be forced by financial reasons such as unemployment, a job market without prospects, and increasingly high study debt burdens to rejoining their family of origin in order to survive economically. This move has far-reaching effects on dating patterns and the ability of the emerging adults to be launched into family formation as well as gainful employment. The generation they return to, typically the middle generation, may have some resentments as their parental responsibilities seem to have become never-ending. Frequently, parents resume overprotective and controlling roles when dealing with their returning children, which can be an added stressor and requires skillful negotiation and balance across generations.

Multiple Family Roles

The complexities of relationships that bridge several generations are intricate and there may be a number of implicit and explicit rules that have to be respected by all participants. Participants in intergenerational relationships typically wear several hats. They fulfill several roles, some within their own generation and others across generations. One person may simultaneously face all the responsibilities and privileges of being a spouse, a sibling, a parent, and an adult child of aging parents. Being part of, and contributing to, an intergenerational system brings both rewards and challenges.

Clearly, the social institution of the family has undergone numerous changes and there is heterogeneity of family forms. This demands new ways of conceptualizing roles, challenges, resilience, and positive outcomes within the complexity of the intergenerational family system.

Focus Point. The older generations are increasingly becoming more involved in assisting the younger generation in a variety of capacities. The number of grandparents caring for their grandchildren is on the rise, and more adult children are moving back home with their parents due to either need or desire. The complexity of these growing family types calls for continual examination of current theories and policies relating to individuals and families.

Acknowledgment: Sections of this chapter were first published in a slightly different format in: Shehan, C. L. (2016). *The Wiley Blackwell Encyclopedia of Family Studies.* Chichester, UK: Wiley Blackwell. In this volume: Gerhardt, C. Intergenerational relationships. Volume III. Pp. 1159–1166. Used with permission of the publishers, John Wiley & Sons, Inc.

CHAPTER FOCUS POINTS

Characteristics of Blended Family Systems

■ Nearly two thirds of divorced individuals remarry, and a large majority of these unions include children from previous relationships. Babies born in remarriages typically create a stronger bond between the couple and solidify their commitment. Challenges such as tested allegiance and role conflict are common themes in newly formed blended families.

Blended Family Formation

■ The structure of blended families has its own unique qualities. Single-parent families are created when adults separate, divorce or are widowed. When parents repartner, another variation of a family unit is created, with concomitant shifts in the relationship between the biological parents and their children. When a biological parent's marriage to a new partner forms a blended family, additional changes in the parent–child subsystem emerge.

Coparenting and Blended Family Roles

■ Coparenting in a remarriage often involves a complete restructuring of expectations and roles. Although homes with stepmothers tend to experience more problems than those with stepfathers, both types of blended families experience unique challenges and obstacles to intimacy. Ex-spouses and ex-in-laws, as well as stepgrandparents, also have to redefine their roles and relationships in the new family structure.

■ The success of a blended family may depend on its ability to overcome obstacles that challenge the development of the new family system. The blended family may use several strategies, such as therapeutic and support groups, to promote healthy family functioning.

Intergenerational Families

■ Intergenerational families cover a broad range of family types, varying in size, structure, and function. Many adults find themselves "sandwiched" between caring for their own children and caring for their aging parents, a situation which often leads to role strain.

■ The older generations are increasingly becoming more involved in assisting the younger generation in a variety of capacities. The number of grandparents caring for their grandchildren is on the rise, and more adult children are moving back home with their parents due to either need or desire. The complexity of these growing family types calls for continual examination of current theories and policies relating to individuals and families.

USEFUL WEBSITES

Websites are dynamic and change

Center for the Improvement of Child Caring
www.ciccparenting.org
Parenting education, training, and support

Harvard Family Research Project
www.hfrp.org
Family involvement, Community-based support

HelpGuide: Harvard Health Publications and Harvard Medical School
www.helpguide.org
Stress management, Helping troubled teens, Self-help suggestions

Parent Further
www.parentfurther.com
Strengthen relationships, Preparing for your child's future

Search Institute: Discovering What Kids Need to Succeed
www.search-institute.org
Developmental assets, Developmental relationships, Developmental communities

CHAPTER 14

Family Formation and Parenting in LGBT Contexts

Learning Outcomes

After completing this chapter, you should be able to:

1. Summarize the changing legal landscape, and concomitant legal implications, as they pertain to LGBT.
2. Summarize the various research findings concerning factors contributing to sexual orientation.
3. Describe the continuum of gender identity.
4. Describe the impact that coming out could have on a family system.
5. Evaluate the similarities and differences between same-sex and heterosexual parenting outcomes.

A family is traditionally considered to be the one place where people are nurtured emotionally, being accepted and loved unconditionally. It typically is the shelter within which we can develop our strengths, reveal our weaknesses, and trust those closest to us without wearing masks and pretending to be someone else. Family formation appears to be intertwined with our human condition; as humans, we seek the togetherness of a group of people who are closest and dearest to us. These persons of significance accept and nurture us for who we are, and love us as we are. They accept and respect the total person, which includes one's sexual orientation.

The emotional climate of the family appears to be more important than the structure of the family in determining the well-being of family members, including the children (Patterson & Farr, 2015). Importantly, a summary of more than two decades of research did not reveal significant differences in the adjustment or development of children or adolescents reared by same-sex couples when these groups were compared to the offspring of heterosexual parents (Patterson & Farr, 2015). In essence, the outcomes of parent–child relationships are determined by the *quality* of the parenting and the family relationships, which have a stronger influence than the sexual orientation of the parents, and no difference was found in terms of parenting practices between heterosexual and same-sex adopting couples (Gates, 2015a). In other words, the quality of the parenting behavior is the significant variable, not the sexual orientation of the parents. What one would intuitively expect is supported by research, namely that the children of parents who had good and close relationships with their children reported child social adjustment in more positive terms. In short, positive outcomes in parent–child relations are strongly influenced by the quality of the parenting.

Parenting in LGBT (lesbian, gay, bisexual, and transgender) contexts also pertains to raising a child who identifies as LGBT. The parents who form a family and identify as LGBT or a child within a family who comes out as LGBT, provide two perspectives; both addressed in research. Supporting a child toward optimal functioning, autonomy, and self-efficacy in a loving and accepting environment, is one of the primary tasks of a family; and this applies to any family and any child, irrespective of the gender identification of the child or of the parents.

LEGAL MATTERS

Some important trends are emerging in a changing legal landscape, and pertain especially to relationship recognition, adoption, and parental rights. In 2015, the U.S Supreme Court ruled same-sex marriage to be legalized nationwide. Additionally, state bans on same-sex marriages were declared unconstitutional. The decision rests partly on the interpretation of the 14th Amendment, which states that limiting marriage only to heterosexual couples violates the amendment's guarantee of equal protection under the law (Pew Research Center, 2015a).

Internationally to date, about two dozen countries have legalized same-sex marriages, and the movement is gaining momentum (Pew Research Center, 2015c). In 2004, Massachusetts became the first state to officially sanction marriage equality legislation and eleven years later the entire United States followed suit. Marriage equality as a matter of civil rights has both supporters and opponents. It follows that legal and social policy contexts can vary vastly with the jurisdiction within which they occur (Pew Research Center, 2015a). If a union is legally sanctioned as a marriage, it has a ripple effect that also involves aspects pertaining to family formation (Tasker & Figueroa, 2016).

By 2016, close to 60% of the population supported same-sex marriage with the strongest support coming from the younger generation, namely the millennials, whereas the older generations and conservative religious groups were more cautious in their opinions (Kelly, 2015; Perry & Whitehead, 2016). According to Flores (2014) public support for the LGBT community has doubled over the past three decades, and, importantly, the support is greater than for any other surveyed group. Contrast that to the turn of the millennium, when the majority of people polled were opposed to same-sex marriage (Pew Research Center, 2015b). The "Don't Ask, Don't Tell Act," which affected armed services personnel, was officially ended in September 2011, making the armed services inclusive (Goldbach & Castro, 2016). Many religious groups have inclusive policies and welcome all persons into their places of worship. Increasingly, persons identifying as LGBT request the same constitutional rights and privileges that others have as members of a diverse society.

Increasingly persons identifying as LGBT are adopting children, or are finding a path toward parenthood through a number of other avenues (Patterson & Farr, 2015), including reproductive technologies, ovum and sperm donation, and/or surrogate mothers. In most states, biological parents in a same-sex relationship usually have parental rights. The legal premise of "in the best interests of the child" is applicable as well. Nevertheless, a great number of states do not grant same-sex couples the opportunity to adopt jointly (Movement Advancement Project, n.d.).

Cultural Snapshot 14–1

Marriage Equality Worldwide

In 2017, same-sex marriage was legal in over two dozen countries internationally, mostly in Europe and the Americas. The number of countries granting legal recognition to gay marriage is growing, and are as far afield as Greenland (2015), Malta (2017), New Zealand (2013), and South Africa (2006) (Pew Research Center, 2017). In 2017, Germany became the 15th nation in Europe to support same-sex marriage. In some countries gay marriage is only legal in some jurisdictions. The number of countries enacting legislation in support of gay marriage is anticipated to grow, reflecting societal acceptance and gradually changing cultural norms.

Source: Pew Research Center. (2017). *Gay marriage around the world.* Retrieved from http://www.pewforum.org/2017/08/08/gay-marriage-around-the-world-2013/

With same-sex couples, the challenges of family formation (for instance, adoption and coparenting situations) may necessitate some ingenuity. Parenthood in same-sex unions is changing traditionally held beliefs concerning family formation and the millennial or younger generation appears to have more tolerant attitudes toward same-sex parenting (Schoephoerster & Aamlid, 2016). In a study of 28 European countries, social acceptance of the adoption of children by same-sex couples paralleled the official adoption policies of that country, ranging from acceptance to rejection of said practices (Takács, Szalma, & Bartus, 2016).

History

Historically, it is important to note that in 1973 the American Psychiatric Association declassified homosexuality as a mental disorder. By implication, no label based on a disease model or a normative value in terms of normality/abnormality could or should be attached to homosexuality.

Looking back over the centuries, it is apparent that homosexuality has always been recognized as an aspect of human nature and sexuality (Pickett, 2015). Using anthropological reports, the presence or absence of male homosexual preference was researched in 107 societies. The findings indicated (among other things) that a positive relationship was found between the level of social stratification in a particular society, and the presence of male homosexual preference (Barthes, Crochet, & Raymond, 2015). In cultures with a strong Judeo-Christian heritage, homosexuality was labeled most negatively. The occurrence of homosexual behavior has been described in the cultures of the ancient Greeks and Romans. Detailed research papers describe the occurrence of homosexual behavior in various cultures and contexts (Pickett, 2015; Kapila & Kumar, 2015).

Ignorance, intolerance, and fearfulness can underlie negative feelings and behaviors (Francis, 2017). With increasing respect for diversity in its many expressions, including sexual orientation, our society is increasingly displaying cultural competence and understanding.

Photograph part of the "Living in Limbo" exhibition displayed at the Birmingham Civil Rights Institute in Alabama (2012). Used with permission of the photographer, Carolyn Sherer (2017).

Focus Point.   Major legal strides have been made in terms of relationship recognition, marriage, adoption, and parental rights. As far as parenting is concerned, the outcomes of parent–child relationships are determined by the *quality* of the parenting and the family relationships, which have a stronger influence than the sexual orientation of the parents.

THE DETERMINANTS OF SEXUAL ORIENTATION

The majority of current research on sexual orientation seems to focus on several specific areas, including genetic influences; variations in brain structure; the role of prenatal hormones on the developing fetus during critical prenatal developmental stages; epigenetics; and maternal and individual variables, including life experiences. Despite ongoing investigations, there remains no simple answer to the etiology of sexual orientation. Several complex interacting genetic, epigenetic, hormonal, and other biological factors seem to underlie sexual orientation, and later environmental and social factors can add subtle layers to this complexity.

Biological Perspectives

Brain Structure and Genes.   With the use of modern brain-imaging techniques, as well as through postmortem studies, the brains of persons who are homosexual have been examined to determine whether there are any significant identifiers in terms of structure. Carter (2010) addresses research findings concerning brain structure. She refers to the early and classic studies by Simon LeVay (1991) that compare the structure of the nucleus in the hypothalamus of the brain. LeVay found that there are structural differences in the nucleus of men who are gay versus men who are heterosexual. Other researchers have found similar differences in the structure of the human brain in individuals who identify themselves as gay versus heterosexual. Using neuroimaging techniques, current research on structural brain phenotypes is continuing and shows subtle differences in a number of areas. A meta-analysis combining the results of several studies also confirmed structural differences (Guillamon, Junque, & Gómez-Gil, 2016).

Male homosexual preference has been regarded as being partially heritable (Barthes, Crochet, & Raymond, 2015). Chromosomal linkage studies suggested that a particular gene on the X chromosome (Xq28) may be responsible for the inheritance of homosexuality. An X-linked inheritance model has been proposed in the work of Chaladze (2016).

Epigenetics.   Epigenetics, or the effects of the environment on gene expression, probably contribute to the expression of the genetics of homosexuality. Epigenetic effects, so called "chemical modifications of the human genome that alter gene activity without changing the DNA sequence, may sometimes influence sexual orientation" (Balter, 2015). This was shown in a study of 37 pairs of identical male twins where one was gay and the other straight. This variance was ascribed to the effects of epigenetic principles (Balter, 2015).

Another example concerns the exposure to estrogen in fetal and early postnatal life in certain critical windows, which turns on and turns off various genes that are important in sexual differentiation and the development of adult sexual behaviors in both males and females (Rice, Friberg, & Gavrilets, 2016). The sensitivity of the estrogen receptor to estrogen plays a dominant role because all fetuses are exposed to maternal estrogens.

Although the understanding of the role of genetics in determining sexual orientation is incomplete, some contribution, at least in some individuals, is highly likely.

Hormonal Influences and Genes.   When people can attribute causation to genetic factors it can favorably influence the immutability and stereotypical judgments about groups, including judgments about gays and lesbians (Joslyn & Haider-Markel, 2016). The neurohormonal theory of brain sexual differentiation is a key area of research in understanding the brain in relation to gender (Guillamon, Junque, & Gómez-Gil, 2016). Additionally, hormones such as oxytocin have been implicated in bonding behavior which supports attachment and parenting, including caregiving behaviors (Feldman, Monakhov, Pratt, & Ebstein, 2016).

Research has thus far failed to conclusively prove the link between sexual orientation in either sex and exposure to sex hormones (testosterone and estrogen). The presence of these hormones *in adulthood* may be linked to the intensity of sexual desire, but they have not been found to be connected to sexual orientation

(Rathus, 2016). Exposure to varying concentrations of sex hormones *prenatally*, particularly during certain critical windows, may contribute to gender identity and/or sexual orientation (Rice, Friberg, & Gavrilets, 2016).

Human sexual development begins in the first trimester of pregnancy. The genetic sex (usually XX or XY) determines whether the bipotential gonads will become testes (in the presence of the SRY gene found on the Y chromosome) or ovaries (in the absence of the SRY gene). The differentiated gonads begin to produce hormones in utero at about 7 weeks of gestation (Kelly, 2010). Until differentiation of the external genitalia occurs, the genitalia of all fetuses are identical and are referred to as *bipotential*, meaning that the same tissues have the ability to differentiate into either male or female genitalia (Moore, Persaud, & Torchia, 2015). Current research is focused on understanding whether the human brain may have an analogous window of differentiation into male and female, leading to gender identity and ultimately perhaps to sexual orientation.

Female fetuses with 21 hydroxylase deficiency CAH (Congenital Adrenal Hyperplasia) are exposed to testosterone in utero, an exposure that would typically only occur for male fetuses. This causes not only virilization of their external genitalia (some appear as typical males and would be identified as boys at birth), but also creates early prenatal exposure for the developing female brain to testosterone. Postnatal exposure to testosterone continues until the condition is detected and treated. In almost all states, most individuals with CAH are identified and treated as infants, because CAH is screened for by newborn screening programs (Held et al., 2015; Pearce et al., 2016).

Endocrine Disruptors. An intriguing new area of research is in the area of the so-called *endocrine disruptors*, which are chemicals in the environment (such as the compound Bisphenol A found in hard plastic food and beverage containers) that may alter the usual course of pre- and postnatal hormone exposure. "BPA is widely acknowledged to be an endocrine disrupting chemical, broadly defined as compounds that interfere with one or more hormone actions" (Vandenberg & Prins, 2016). According to these same authors, hundreds of scientific studies have confirmed the disturbing fact that low doses of BPA can alter a range of hormone sensitive endpoints in a significant manner. The National Institute of Environmental Health Sciences, under the auspices of the National Institutes of Health, has created a study section that is dedicated to this research (www.niehs.nih.gov/health/topics/agents/endocrine/index.cfm).

Multifactorial Influences. Many groups have tried to understand the delicate balance of the influence of genetics, sex hormones, and socialization on gender identity and sexual orientation. Without a complete understanding, the classic nature versus nurture debate continues, although both biology and the environment appear to play a role (Garretson & Suhay, 2016).

The etiology of gender identity and sexual orientation is complex, with multifactorial influences that include some contribution from genetics, epigenetics, exposure to prenatal and postnatal sex hormones, other environmental factors, and individual variables, including life experiences. Additionally, we may have subjective biases based on societal conditions, political events, and how the groups with which we identify behave. All these factors can add to the attributions that are formed concerning this complex topic (Joslyn & Haider-Markel, 2016).

This is a cutting-edge research area; although we expect further findings to clarify aspects of sexual orientation, at this point, we have many leads but the picture is neither clear nor conclusive.

Parenting Reflection 14–1

The following hypothetical question illustrates the complexity of a particular situation: If an XX genetically female individual with male external genitalia, who was raised as a male (but is only reproductively capable as a female), chooses a female sexual partner, is this person heterosexual or homosexual? Even for an expert, this is such a complex topic that there is no clear-cut answer.

Psychological Perspectives

Historically, and from a more *psychological* angle, the *psychoanalytic* view, based on the work of Sigmund Freud, suggests that family influences, in particular, play a significant role. This approach proposed that male homosexual orientation occurred because an individual had an extremely dominant mother and a relatively submissive, emotionally distant, or absent father (Domenici & Lesser, 2016).

Other approaches proposed that sexual orientation is *learned behavior* among males and females, which suggests that individuals can willfully choose, as well as change, their sexual orientation. Considerable, yet erroneous, popular support persists for the latter view that environmental factors are the sole cause of a homosexual orientation. There is no conclusive scientific support for such an opinion. Although learning is an important facet of adolescent and adult sexual behavior, learning theorists have not been able to conclusively point to a link between learned experiences and adult sexual orientation (Pilkey, 2014; Rathus, Nevid, & Fichner-Rathus, 2014). Evidence continues to grow that numerous factors interact to present the very complex scenario of sexual and gender identification.

Queer Theory.   The word *queer* has been used in previous decades in colloquial language to refer to homosexuals. It was especially used in British English, while its use in American speech is often viewed as derogatory, simple, or overly artsy. The word has regained attention because a very popular television show, which focused on home and personal makeovers, used this word in its title (Rathus et al., 2014), and the team doing the makeovers were proudly gay. The word has slipped back into mainstream use through reference to *Queer Theory*, and by referring to lesbian, gay, bisexual, transgender, and queer (LGBTQ), as well as to lesbian, gay, bisexual, and queer (LGBQ).

Queer theory, which started circulating in the early 1990s, tries to normalize the connotation of the concept of homosexuality by stating that it is not an opposite or another variant of heterosexuality. Queer theory is a critique, among other things, of *heteronormativity*. In other words, heterosexuality should not be the central point of reference (Pilkey, 2014; Miller, Taylor, & Rupp, 2016). This would be similar to ethnocentrism, where one's own culture (often the dominant culture) is used as the norm as well as the reference point. An ethnocentric view implies that one sees the world through a limited and very personal perspective; everything can be colored by this worldview. Putting this same type of thinking into the context of queer theory would mean that the world is generally viewed through heterosexual lenses, as it were, and heterosexuality then becomes the mainstream point of reference. Similarly, the historic marginalization of persons with disabilities resembles the marginalization of homosexuality. It is proposed that the dichotomies of hetero- and homosexuality are deconstructed to allow more flexible and universal constructs that bypass restricting connotations (Pilkey, 2014; Miller, Taylor, & Rupp, 2016).

Queer theory states that the approach whereby a categorization is made between hetero- and homosexuality should be challenged because they are social constructs. Queer theory acknowledges a continuum in sexual identification and expression, implying that sexuality is more varied than denoted by one label, and one can claim a *Q identity* (Miller, Taylor, & Rupp, 2016). The concept of *gender fluidity* denotes this flexible approach.

Focus Point.   Available research concerning sexual orientation indicates that multifactorial aspects may play varying roles in influencing an individual's sexual orientation and gender expression. Interacting factors including genetics and epigenetics, hormonal influences during critical developmental periods, and social and psychological factors can be some of the contributory factors.

THE CONTINUUM OF GENDER IDENTITY

A large number of family systems in the United States today include a child who identifies as LGBT. From historical sex research by Alfred Kinsey more than half a century ago, it was estimated that individuals with exclusively homosexual orientation made up 7 to 12 percent of the male population and 5 to 7 percent of the female population (Kinsey, Pomeroy, & Martin, 1948; Kinsey, Pomeroy, Martin, & Gebhard, 1953).

Data from the 2011–2013 National Survey of Family Growth which reported information from over ten thousand participants (aged 18–44 years) in the United States, reported lower figures for persons identifying as exclusively gay or lesbian, than those reported historically. The added category for bisexual orientation indicated that 5.5% of women and 2.0% of men said that they were bisexual (Copen, Chandra, & Febo-Vazquez, 2016). Earlier reports did not consistently differentiate the groups in this manner, and if the LGBT categories are clustered together, the incidence is more aligned with what was historically reported.

Assuming that these individuals come from average-size families of about four persons, the potential number of persons with a relative or close friend identifying themselves as LGBT is nearly a quarter to a third of the population of the United States. In addition, about 25 percent of the LGBT population of the United States claim biological parenthood for children from heterosexual relationships. There may be upwards of 6 million children in the United States who have a gay or lesbian parent (Gates, 2013).

There is no clear estimate of the number of families who know they have a member who identifies as LGBT because not all have disclosed their orientation to family members. Nonetheless, those who make their orientation known cause change in the identity of their families of origin as family members adapt and emotionally readjust to the greater sexual diversity within their own family. Those individuals who are fully integrated and have strong support groups may be able to disclose their sexual orientation more easily and without fear of discrimination. This carries over into the relationships with their children where disclosure and openness may be adjusted to the level of acceptance and support within their communities (Telingator & Patterson, 2008; Kelly, 2010).

Toward Gender Authenticity

In contrast to "sex," "*gender*" is a concept that includes "cultural ideas of masculinity and femininity that are used to organize identities, behaviors and social roles" (Diamond, Pardo, & Butterworth, 2011). Hence, gender expression is how gender identity is exhibited or enacted, and this can change over a lifespan (McGuire, Kuvalanka, Catalpa, & Toomey, 2016). Importantly, the meaning a family assigns to gender identity will facilitate *family acceptance*, which is crucial to ensure healthy emotional development.

Gender ideology, or how we think about gender, is changing. Because it is in flux, there is dissent among opinions. The following statements are quoted from an article by McGuire and colleagues, and represent but one approach among several, concerning gender identity:

■ "Gender is not inherently binary."
■ "The development of gender expression and identity may not be purely social."
■ "Gender variance can emerge throughout the lifespan."
■ "Family acceptance of a trans*person depends on family meaning" (McGuire, et al., 2016).

Note: Trans*, i.e. Trans with an asterisk, is used by some authors to denote a variety of identities. In this instance "Trans*" is a "broader umbrella term" (Ryan, 2014). It is a linguistic variation that is inspired by computer language, and how the asterisk can be used in online searches.

It is important to note in this context, that how we approach and possibly permanently intervene in situations concerning gender ideology, can have permanent and long-lasting outcomes, not all of them desirable or even foreseeable. For instance, early and drastic physical interventions in pre- and pubertal children by means of surgery and hormone treatments can foreclose their later decisions regarding their own potential to procreate. In the wrong hands, an inappropriate approach to the complexity of gender ideology has the potential to harm children. Parents are recommended to seek out opinions from teams of highly qualified experts; typically only found in leading research and academic hospitals across the United States.

The American College of Pediatricians has published a statement, which was updated in January 2017, concerning gender ideology as it pertains to chemical and surgical interventions that can never be reversed. It includes the following statement and justification supporting this point of view: "The American College of Pediatricians urges healthcare professionals, educators and legislators to reject all policies that condition children to accept as normal a life of chemical and surgical impersonation of the opposite sex." (American College of Pediatricians, 2017). The document deserves careful study as it is complex. It can be accessed at the website of the American College of Pediatricians, seeking out the position statement on gender ideology (www.acpeds.org). The above position statement refers to surgical and chemical interventions of a *permanent* nature, of which long term emotional outcomes are not entirely foreseeable.

Importantly, and according to the American College of Pediatricians, some of the gender ideology concerns in children resolve spontaneously after puberty. Clearly children and adolescents struggling with gender identity concerns deserve emotional and social support. Emotionally accepting and supportive parents, educators, and other societal contexts, are crucial in reducing the potential for suicide (a very real threat), bullying, and general unhappiness related to gender identity concerns. Educational resources are being created for parents of transgender and gender nonconforming youth. The Gender Creative Parenting Curriculum can be accessed through the researchers in a study on educational support (Murphy Pantoja, 2016).

In short, parental acceptance is a *protective* factor that supports best outcomes for youth dealing with the multifaceted emotional concerns of gender identity.

Heteronormativity and **Cisnormativity** refer to the traditional approach of allocation of one of two labels to an individual; they are either male or female. According to this approach, the norm or what is perceived as "normal," is what occurs most frequently. The fact that something occurs in greater numbers does not necessarily mean that it is the only way to be; there may be valid variations on the theme of gendered attributions.

The existing and prevalent notions concerning the development of gender in families were traditionally based on the gendered norms of being either male or female. Recent approaches to gender identification and sexuality, do not necessarily view these as an either/or choice, like a binary system, hence the concept Non-Binary. Instead, sexuality can be expressed on a *continuum* and perceptions of gender need to be broadened to include a wider range of possibilities and variations (Savin-Williams, 2016). The term Non-Binary is also in use. For families who have a member identifying as LGBT, whether it is a parent or a child, a spouse or a sibling, *gender authenticity* and gender socialization in families need to be inclusive, supportive, and accepting (McGuire et al., 2016).

The traditional approach implies that within family units each family member is perceived in terms of gendered familial and societal attributions of what is expected of girls/women versus boys/men (McGuire et al., 2016).

Cisgender implies that "each individual's identified gender is aligned with the sex assigned at birth, e.g. an individual assigned as a female identifies as a girl/woman" (McGuire et al., 2016).

Transgender or trans* are the terms used to describe "the spectrum of individuals whose assigned sex at birth does not align with their own sense of gender identity and those who do not conform to societal gender norms" (Bockting, 2014; McGuire et al., 2016).

Gender dysphoria refers to a "discomfort with one's gender assigned at birth. Individuals who have persistent gender dysphoria typically have an experienced gender identity that differs significantly from the sex they were assigned at birth, and may consider changing their gender role and feminize or masculinize their body to achieve greater comfort with self and identity" (Bockting, 2014). The *DSM-5* lists gender dysphoria as a formal diagnosis. This diagnostic category was controversial, but has been retained in the *DSM-5* (American Psychiatric Association, 2013).

FAMILY SYSTEMS WITH CHILDREN IDENTIFYING AS LGBT

It is common for parents to develop and acquire a variety of expectations about themselves and their children. These expectations shape parenting behavior and may serve as self-fulfilling prophesies for those involved in a family subsystem. Generally, these expectations are positive and reflect wishes, hopes, and dreams for parents, as well as for children. Most parents do not include an expectation that any of their children will reveal an LGBT identity or orientation upon reaching puberty. When it is revealed by a child that she identifies as LGBT, the entire family system has a duty to support and accept this family member, as *family acceptance* ranks high amongst protective factors (Snapp, Watson, Russell, Diaz, & Ryan, 2015).

Disclosing this information and sexual identity to others, especially to family members, is known as *coming out* and once it has been disclosed as *being out*. For the person concerned, the act of coming out can be a key developmental milestone (Kosciw, Palmer, & Kull, 2015). For persons who identify as LGBT, the significance of the disclosure lies in presenting themselves to others as a whole, integrated person with a positive self-concept. They share this act of intimacy in the hope that the disclosure will result in honest acceptance and unconditional love (Snapp et al., 2015). Clearly it would help to promote good self-esteem and other interpersonal strengths if acceptance can be found within the close and trusted family circle, as well as in the wider societal network (Kelly, 2015).

Coming out can hold the risk of greater victimization, especially for rural youth, or in unsupportive environments. Despite this negative possibility, being out appears to promote well-being, as the person can live a congruent life. Being out can develop individual resilience, but contextual community influences and ecological circumstances, which may be more or less supportive, play important roles (Kosciw, Palmer, & Kull, 2015). Schools with anti-bullying policies, and professional development and awareness campaigns, have lower incidence of reported victimization (Kosciw & Pizmony-Levy, 2016). Acceptance and support are cornerstone components in preventing suicide amongst this group. Parents and family play an important role in helping a child attain selfhood in a congruent manner (Solomon, 2012).

An important resource for families is the "Family Acceptance Project," under the auspices of the San Francisco State University (https://familyproject.sfsu.edu/). This project provides education, access to research and resources, and features video clips from families who have constructively dealt with the coming out of their child. This group has the following goals, as presented on their website, which cites "building healthy futures for youth" as their core mission:

- "Research on family acceptance and rejection;
- Education and training to decrease the risk and promote well-being by increasing family acceptance;
- Family oriented services to help diverse families support their LGBT children;
- Informed public policy, to promote well-being—not just protect from harm."

The group's work has been honored by the American Foundation for Suicide Prevention, and was placed on the Registry of Best Practices, specifically for suicide prevention (https://familyproject.sfsu.edu/). On this site, familyacceptanceproject.org, watch a video called "Always My Son," about a family's acceptance of their child, who identifies as LGBT. What did the parents of this child have to overcome?

• •

Parenting Reflection 14–2

How can we best support a friend or close family member who has disclosed that one of their siblings identifies as LGBT?

• •

Family Systems Theory predicts that when one family member experiences change in some manner, all other members of the system are also affected to a greater or lesser degree. A child's disclosure of sexual orientation is unlikely to be part of the vision that most parents hold for their child or for themselves as parents (Kosciw, Palmer, & Kull, 2015). These beliefs and stereotypes may govern initial reactions of family members, but in a

society more accustomed to, and accepting of, diversity, the positive overrides. Family members and friends like to maintain the positive image they already have about the child as an individual and as a family member. Several factors predict the nature and strength of a family's determination to constructively deal with a child's disclosure:

- There may be feelings of *ambiguous loss* as the family has to reinterpret gender (McGuire, Catalpa, Lacey, & Kuvalanka, 2016).
- The more a family system and wider societal circles subscribe to traditional, conservative teachings about gender identification, the more negative the reactions to, and interpretations of, an individual's disclosure (Gibbs & Goldbach, 2015; McGuire et al., 2016).
- The situation can escalate in communities where bias, discrimination, and violence may persist, and is aptly described in research which includes the phrase: "When love meets hate … " (Levy & Levy, 2017).
- The rules that govern the functioning of a family system can influence the likelihood of negative reactions to disclosure. For example, some family rules relate to maintaining an image or reputation in the community, or which roles are followed by each family member (Kuo et al., 2016).
- The age and gender of family members can influence reactions in positive or negative ways. Generally, the younger children and much older adults in a family system may be more accepting and react more favorably to the disclosure than others. Members of the same sex as the child identifying as LGBT can occasionally react more negatively than members of the opposite sex.

In some instances, a child who identifies as LGBT may feel forced to withdraw his participation in the family system due to the negative, unaccepting reactions of members. In more extreme situations, a family system's unhealthy resolution may contribute to the likelihood of serious depression in the child. This depression can escalate toward suicide, which may account for the high suicide rate among adolescents who have difficulty accepting their LGBT orientation (Gibbs & Goldbach, 2015). Ten per cent of men attempting suicide cited depression as a factor, but generally gay men are at higher risk for suicide as compared to the general population. The top three reasons cited are social and interpersonal reasons, love and relationship problems, and difficulty in accepting one's sexual orientation (Wang, Plöderl, Häusermann, & Weiss, 2015). Because many jurisdictions have acknowledged legal marriages for LGBT couples, the adolescent suicide rate for LGBT youths has dropped (American Foundation for Suicide Prevention). One hypothesis is that the normalcy that these civil rights convey, support young people in finding and acknowledging their true sexual and gender identity.

Childhood abuse and victimization, especially concerning LGBT identity, can also be a contributing factor for attempted suicide (Flynn, Johnson, Bolton, & Mojtabai, 2016). This distressing trend is counteracted by high-profile individuals publicly acknowledging their homosexual orientation and actively contributing to the understanding and acceptance of sexual diversity. The power and positive effects of supportive family and friend relationships can be emphasized yet again.

Those systems which resolve the crisis in healthy ways may reach levels in recovery that are similar to, or greater than, what existed before the crisis. These families turn the crisis into learning experiences that can result in personal growth and appreciation for all family members.

Ambiguous Loss and Subsequent Healing.   Parents, in their role as caregivers, must find constructive ways to express their need to provide unconditional love, nurture, and visible support to a child who identifies as LGBT (Russell & Fish, 2016). Parents most likely need to express their grief about any losses that they may be experiencing, for example, the possibility of not becoming grandparents, no longer having a child who is conventionally similar to other children in the family, and no longer being like other parents of children who are heterosexual. Parents must allow this ***ambiguous loss*** to proceed to grieving and mourning processes in order to ultimately heal and find resolution. By doing so, they facilitate the healing of their family system and the reconstruction of a role definition for their child as an accepted, loved, and respected family member (McConnell, Birkett, & Mustanski, 2015).

....

Focus Point.   Families supporting the coming out of a family member identifying as LGBT, do well to foster an environment in which gender authenticity is encouraged and emotional support is demonstrated. Being informed concerning heteronormativity is an important step in becoming more inclusive and promoting equalities in our society. All family members should be supported and accepted for who they are, including their sexual identity.

....

FAMILY FORMATION IN SAME-SEX COUPLES

Parenting forms the core of family life for most American adults. Regardless of sexual orientation, it can be a very rewarding aspect of adulthood (Patterson & Farr, 2011). Persons identifying as LGBT participate in family forms that are very similar to those typically found in our society (Fedewa, Black, & Ahn, 2015). As applied to family life, same-sex couples have reinvented the notion of what it means to be a family, how this family functions, and who participates in the family (Gates, 2015b). These families are referred to as *families of choice* and represent a form of kinship formation (B. P. Allen, 2015; Orel & Coon, 2016).

Membership, roles, and rules governing this type of family structure are custom designed according to mutually agreed-upon conditions. As such, families of choice are formed by a conscious decision about who constitutes the family, how it is defined, and what it means to each participant. Many persons who identify as LGBT do not feel the need to conform to family structure based on consanguinity or legally sanctioned marriage. They focus instead on providing a social support network based on compatibility, love, intimacy, emotional warmth, interest, and a sense of community. According to societal norms, these elements compose the *essence of family life*. When children are involved, it is difficult to distinguish families with same-sex parents from stepfamilies where the parents are heterosexual, except concerning the same-sex composition of the adults who act as parents (Reczek, Spiker, Liu, & Crosnoe, 2016). Indeed, the parenting challenges and skills of same-sex couples are similar to those of heterosexual couples (Domenici & Lesse, 1995). In brief, " … regardless of gender, sexual orientation, and route to parenthood, new parents experience similar, positive changes in perceived [parenting] skills … " (Goldberg, 2010, p. 861).

The beginning of LGBT *kinship formation* takes place when an individual initiates what is known as the coming-out process. Persons who identify as LGBT develop a personal identity based on their sexual orientation, similar to that experienced by individuals who are heterosexual. Part of this identity is the desire to become emotionally close to another person (Khajehei, 2016). Same-sex couples participate in loving, committed relationships that often endure for long periods of time and resemble those found among heterosexuals. Some distinct differences are found in same-sex committed relationships. Primarily, their committed relationships strongly emphasize *egalitarian* functions because they are not forced to adopt and maintain the traditional gender-role models typically found among heterosexuals that emphasize differences in social power in the relationship (Miller, Kors, & Macfie, 2016).

Like other families, those formed by persons who identify as LGBT bring strengths, as well as challenges, to family members (Mitchell, 2016). By expanding the very idea of a family that transcends traditional limitations, same-sex couples demonstrate how to deal with societal challenges in healthy ways.

Mixed-Orientation Marriage

Diversity in Family Forms.   Mixed-orientation marriage, sometimes referred to as a *hetero-gay* relationship, is one in which one of the spouses or partners identifies him- or herself as heterosexual, while the other spouse or partner may be lesbian or gay (Vencill & Wiljamaa, 2016). They conceive and raise children together and their sexualities may be expressed in ways

Photograph part of the "Living in Limbo" exhibition displayed at the Birmingham Civil Rights Institute in Alabama (2012). Used with permission of the photographer, Carolyn Sherer (2017).

that suit the individual needs of each partner. They may or may not share a common physical residence. If the couple is not legally married, this family type represents a variation of a *nonmarital family*. Part of the complexity of the situation revolves around how each partner wishes to express him- or herself within the marriage and the qualities they seek from a marital union (Tornello & Patterson, 2012). Partners may seek a biological parent for their children who will also help them coparent. Because these families appear to be like heterosexual families to outsiders, they capture the characteristics of both traditional and nontraditional families. Researchers indicate that the children of these families appear to benefit from their family structure; they have a stable and predictable family environment with a father who is involved in their upbringing and shares in their financial support, and have generally positive psychosocial and developmental functioning (Parker, 2016).

Parent–Child Relations in Same-Sex Couples

Not all parents are heterosexual; some are gay or lesbian. Their families are not significantly different from other family systems, although unique challenges are particular to their situations (Patterson, 2016). The experiences of fathers who are gay are similar to those of mothers who are lesbian. Each type of family system faces unique challenges. Homosexuality per se does not prevent or hinder someone from being an effective parent. Research strongly confirms that it is the *quality* of the parent–child relationship that determines success (Parker, 2016). Additionally, the *resilience* of the children is promoted with constructive parenting techniques, and the stability of the family provides a protective factor (Ungar, 2016). Regardless of sexual orientation, the difficulties in parent–child relations usually find their origins within the realms of psychological and/or psychiatric difficulties (Bos, Knox, van Rijn-van Gelderen, & Gartrell, 2016), the many societal and economic constraints that put families at *high risk*, and the various stressors that influence *fragile* families.

Because we are transitioning into greater acceptance and understanding of homosexuality, many people are reconciling their ideas concerning parenthood for adults who are gay or lesbian (Costa, Pereira, & Leal, 2015). The following discussion examines the issues related to parenthood in same-sex couples and how their sexual orientation affects their children.

Fatherhood and Men Who Are Gay.   The father who is gay is a relatively new emergent figure in homosexual culture. Males who are gay and are fathers have a unique and complex psychosocial environment. Their challenges of adjustment relate to identity issues, acceptance of self, acceptance by other men who are gay, and matters related specifically to parenting and child custody concerns (Miller, Kors, & Macfie, 2016). Other challenges focus on the development of a long-term, committed relationship with another man who is gay, who accepts and copes with the children as being a central component of the relationship.

Some of the more historic research on the topic maintained that the process of *identity development* for a father who is gay required a reconciliation of perceptions. Because each identity, homosexual and heterosexual, is perceived with caution by the other group, the task of integrating both identities into a cognitive concept of the *father who is gay* can be challenging. This process is referred to as *integrative sanctioning* (Tornello & Patterson, 2015). It involves the man's disclosure of his gay orientation and identity to non-gays and his identity as a father to gays, thus forming close liaisons with persons who tolerate or accept both identities simultaneously. It also involves distancing himself from those who are intolerant.

An estimated 20 percent of men who are gay marry women at some point, and approximately 2 million families are affected by the upheavals resulting from *mixed-orientation marriages*, other marriages involve *bisexual* spouses. These marriages face greater challenges than heterosexual marriages, and ultimately about half end up in divorce court. The reasons for these marriages are varied (Adler & Ben-Ari, 2016). He may be denying his true sexual orientation, while also pursuing a genuine desire to be a parent. A number of fathers who are gay, have children from a former heterosexual marriage (Kissil & Itzhaky, 2015). After a failed mixed orientation marriage, some try open relationships and others stay together platonically for the sake of family commitments.

The adjustment of men who divorce and pursue a homosexual lifestyle is difficult as the man acquires a new identity as a father who is gay (Daly, MacNeela, & Sarma, 2015). These men enter the gay subculture at some disadvantage because they come out at later ages. They usually seek to replicate the kind of relationships they experienced or desired in their heterosexual marriages. They may experience discrimination and rejection from other gays who are not fathers. Many fathers who are gay are successful in forging a partnership with another man who is gay, based on long-term commitment, emotional and sexual exclusivity, and economic cooperation.

Little is known about the nature of these relationships or about the gay blended family system that may emerge from its formation (Few-Demo & Demo, 2015). It appears that the satisfaction of all persons involved in a gay blended family is improved when efforts are made to include the stepfather who is gay (Ganong & Coleman, 2016). This is similar to what is found in heterosexual blended families.

Motherhood and Women Who Are Lesbian.   The parenting experiences of mothers who are lesbian are generally similar to those of fathers who are gay; but researchers observe some differences in family dynamics (Tasker & Delvoye, 2015; Delvoye & Tasker, 2016) Women who are lesbian differ from men who are gay in the ways in which they become involved as parents. For example, although many women acknowledge their homosexual orientation after being married to a man and having children, other lesbians use artificial insemination as a means of achieving parenthood (Somers et al., 2016). Adoption may also be a preferred option.

Couples who are lesbian face legal and social challenges when they use artificial insemination to conceive children within a committed relationship (Johnson, O'Connor, & Tornello, 2016). The laws of most states commonly recognize the biological mother's legal custody of the child, which leaves the non-biological or social mother with no legal parental rights unless she legally adopts the child conceived by her partner (Schwartz, 2016). Many states do not permit the names of two women to appear on a child's birth certificate or allow adoption by a nonbiological mother. The custody rights of fathers are relatively unclear in these situations as well, even if the identity of the father who was the sperm donor is known. Legal testing of these rights continues in various court cases that will set precedents for the future. Generally speaking, if the father is known to the lesbian-led family, it is possible to create legal documents that spell out the legal rights and responsibilities of the father, for example, regarding custody and visitation.

For many couples who are lesbian, parenthood via insemination is a well-planned, deliberate, and complex life decision. They address topics such as who the biological mother will be and how to choose a donor (known or anonymous). Children are greatly valued and desired; motivation to attain parenthood may be a positive prerequisite for successful parenting outcomes.

Children of Same-Sex Parents

Children of same-sex parents do not differ significantly from children of heterosexual parents on key psychosocial developmental outcomes (Scott & Saginak, 2016). Fathers who are gay are as effective as fathers who are heterosexual in their ability to parent children and provide care. They are believed to be nurturing with children and less traditional in perceiving the provider role as a prime aspect of their parenting role. They have positive relationships with children and are motivated to create stable home lives for them (Tornello, Sonnenberg, & Patterson, 2015). Some contributing reasons could be that parents who are gay may feel additional pressure to be proficient in their parenting roles because they face numerous obstacles to create their own families, and the children they raise are typically desired and welcomed children. Additionally, they may feel guilty about the difficulties that disclosure and a possible related divorce may have created for their children. The scrutiny by ex-spouses and others, as well as the genuine desire for a family, can be motivators to display optimal parenting skills and create a harmonious and supportive family environment.

Children of parents identifying as LGBT, live in family systems with matching diverse parenting experiences (Umberson, 2016). No differences in general adjustment, gender-role identity, or cognitive or behavioral functioning are consistently reported in studies comparing children of lesbian and nonlesbian mothers (Bos, Gelderen, & Gartrell, 2015). Children who display some behavioral issues add to the stress of their parents; this occurs regardless of the sexual orientation of the parents (Patterson & Farr, 2015).

Four principal issues are relevant to children of mothers who are lesbians (Bos et al., 2015): (1) dealing with the parent's disclosure of her sexual orientation, (2) dealing with the uniqueness of having lesbian parents

and the effect on the parent–child relationship, (3) coping with custody concerns, and (4) dealing with the reactions of others.

Like the children of fathers who are gay, those growing up in same-sex family systems headed by women face the challenges of coping with parental divorce and the fact that their parents may be perceived as different from other parents. Sons are more accepting than daughters when their mother establishes a lesbian partnership. Researchers generally find that the more accepting and relaxed the mother is about her sexuality, the more accepting the child will be (Powell, Hamilton, Manago, & Cheng, 2016).

When children are conceived by artificial insemination by donor, the information children are given about their father needs to be consistent. It is a unique situation, but most children react positively if this disclosure is appropriately managed. Child custody is a central concern of mothers who come out. Many children of mothers who are lesbian wish to remain in their care and establish stable family relationships. This relates directly to custody and parental rights, which are matters that can threaten the continuation of a meaningful parent–child relationship in a family system that is headed by same-sex parents.

Because same-sex parental systems exist in a social environment that can vary in the amount of support it provides, these parents may turn to their children for implicit approval of their sexual orientation. At the same time, mothers do not want their children to feel different from other children (Gilmore, Esmail, & Eargle, 2016). For adolescents this can be a more difficult situation to handle as they are dealing with identity as well as peer group opinions (Farr, Oakley, & Ollen, 2016). The child should not necessarily be expected to accept the parent's sexual orientation completely. It is important that the child respects the parents' lifestyle and the ways in which it is expressed. Some children need assistance in working through the ambivalent feelings they have for their mother, precipitated by her sexual orientation, and the guilt that accompanies these feelings (Fedewa, Black, & Ahn, 2015).

A common concern expressed in court proceedings, which determines the custody of children with a father who is gay, is that the children will also develop a homosexual orientation. The consensus of research is that although the causes of sexual orientation are complex, sexual orientation does not seem to be transmitted from parents with a particular orientation to the children they raise (Degner & Dalege, 2013). The parents of most homosexuals are heterosexual. The same patterns found in the general population concerning the incidence of homosexual orientation, appears to be replicated among sons of gay fathers (Regnerus, 2012). More than 90 percent of adult sons of fathers who are gay reportedly have a heterosexual orientation. This data strongly suggests that the sons of fathers who are gay do not adopt the homosexual orientation by modeling their fathers, nor does living with a father who is gay appear to contribute in a substantial way to the sexual orientation developed by sons.

Gender-equal Behavior

One of the advantages that fathers who are gay offer to children of both sexes, is the modeling of gender-equal behavior (Ghaziani, Taylor, & Stone, 2016) and their acceptance of gender nonconformity (Richards, Jonathan, & Kim, 2015). Fathers who are gay may also be more gender equal in their approach to parenting. Their child-rearing styles may incorporate a greater degree of expressiveness and nurture (Richards, Rothblum, Beauchaine, & Balsam, 2016). On the other hand, these couples may not function in a manner that is as genderless as is often believed (Puolimatka, 2016).

Fathers who are gay can combine both *emotional expressiveness* and *goal instrumental behaviors* in their behavioral repertoire; children can learn to adopt these gender-equal behaviors as well and adopt gender-equal language. Research does indicate that clear and appropriate gender roles are expressed, while still incorporating gender equality as a value (Grossman, 2016). The data indicates that the sexual orientation of children, and that of sons in particular, is not transmitted by being parented by a father who is gay.

Historically, the work of Bem (1975) identified *androgyny* as an ideal gender role. **Androgynous** individuals manifest characteristics associated with both genders regardless of their biological sex. Researchers have identified advantages to having such gender role flexibility. Gender-equal attitudes are perceived more positively (Qian, 2016). Adult males who are gender equal are described as showing greater flexibility in considering options to solving problems, and having a deeper respect for individual differences. They are also described as having an accepting attitude about sexual behavior, sexual relationships, and interpersonal relationships with others in general.

The benefits offered by fathers who are gay relate to their ability to expand their interpretations of what it means to be a father beyond the limited traditional meanings of this family role (Goodfellow, 2015). The benefits to children are likely to become even more apparent upon reaching adulthood, when their relationships with others can be expected to be based on equality rather than on who holds the most social and physical power (Patterson & Farr, 2015). Researchers have found that couples in which one or both persons are gender equal have higher levels of relationship satisfaction, divide decision making equally, de-emphasize the use of power by either partner in the relationship, and have greater long-term life satisfaction (Westwood, 2016). In terms of parenting, same sex parents can generally be expected to incorporate greater degrees of gender-equal behavior and identification than their heterosexual parenting peers (Barker, 2015).

This does not mean that children of mothers and fathers who are homosexual do not have adjustment issues that relate to their parents' sexual orientation.

Photograph part of the "Living in Limbo" exhibition displayed at the Birmingham Civil Rights Institute in Alabama (2012). Used with permission of the photographer, Carolyn Sherer (2017).

Cultural Snapshot 14–2

Cultural Context Concerning Sexuality

"Different cultures may promote specific attitudes toward particular types of sexual orientations" (Shiraev & Levy, 2016, p. 216). Concerns that are treated differently in varying sex cultures include: expression of sexuality, premarital and extramarital sex, homosexuality, and chastity. Depending on the cultural context, beliefs about sex and sexual orientation may vary greatly. Similarly, the willingness to talk about these topics or to express one's sexual identity may be culturally nuanced. Cultures vary between being open and accepting of a variety of sexual expressions to being guarded and restrictive. Non-traditional sex cultures veer toward permissive expressions of sexuality (countries such as Holland, Sweden, Russia, Australia, Scandinavia, and others are regarded as non-traditional) whereas areas in the Middle East and Africa are regarded as traditional sex cultures. Sex culture and general attitudes toward sex and sexual identity include whether these expressions are heavily regulated, even prohibited, or not. Despite this, the terms traditional and non-traditional can be misleading and individual variances within mainstream cultures abound. Research on sexuality and gender related topics may be influenced by these cultural variations, in that topics that can or cannot be discussed will vary, and the honesty and frankness with which subjects respond in research involving this type of subject matter will vary greatly.

"Every culture has its own set of requirements, beliefs, symbols, and norms regarding sexuality and its expression. This set of characteristics is called the culture. Sex cultures vary greatly across the world and are influenced by the religious, ideological, political, and moral values developed by society" (Shiraev and Levy, 2016, p. 214).

Based on Shiraev, E. B., & Levy, D. A. (2017). *Cross-cultural Psychology: Critical Thinking and Contemporary Applications.* 6th. ed. New York, NY: Routledge. Chapter 7: Motivation and Behavior.

Like children coming from other minority group families, these children face unique challenges. Adjustments are often facilitated if both parents are committed to providing high-quality care and supervision (Farr, Tasker, & Goldberg, 2016). With greater tolerance of diversity and greater awareness of the dangers of discrimination and bullying, this problem should decrease noticeably as adult role models encourage desirable attitudes and competencies.

Family Dynamics in Same-Sex Couples

Families formed by same-sex couples share common qualities with heterosexual blended families (Umberson & Kroeger, 2016). This is especially so for mothers who are lesbian, who more frequently have custody of children from a former heterosexual relationship (Mosovsky, Nolan, Markovic, & Stall, 2016). Other similarities may involve relationship concerns in the new blended family. The partner of the lesbian biological mother (the children's stepparent, coparent, or social parent) is rejected by the stepchildren, the stepchildren and stepparent compete for the attention and affection of the biological mother, and conflicts erupt over territoriality in the home.

Distinct characteristics within same-sex family systems headed by lesbians distinguish them from other family forms:

■ They may experience a lack of legitimacy because their community might not recognize them as a family unit. This presents unique problems, such as in dealings with school systems.

■ Fathers who are gay and who do not have full-time child custody do not usually experience these same challenges. Parents often instruct children to keep the adults' sexual orientation a secret from outsiders. Same-sex parents who are lesbian may isolate themselves and their children and may not invite their children's friends home to play because they fear exposure. The pressure of maintaining family secrets is unhealthy and counteracts the effective functioning of the family. These mothers may fear losing custody of their children, which represents a continual threat (Chamberlain, Miller, & Rivera, 2015).

- These families can experience strained relationships with ex-spouses and other relatives. The negative feelings of ex-spouses may be compounded during post-divorce interactions. Despite all these problems, the children of mothers who are lesbian are well adjusted, and families typically find creative and healthy ways for responding to the crises they experience.
- The division of labor and parental roles take on unique assignments and situations. For example, each family must decide what each mother will be called and determine which parent will function as the primary caregiver.

Same-sex couples base the structure of their committed relationship on the gender-equal principle of *equality of partners* (Sells & Ganong, 2016). This differs considerably from the structure typically found among heterosexual couples that use gender to determine who does what in the relationship. Families that are headed by lesbians report sharing household responsibilities, but the biological mother can be expected to be more involved in child care, while the nonbiological mother reports working longer hours outside the home. Children are found to be better adjusted when both mothers divide the childcare responsibilities equally (Ball, 2016).

Video Example 14.1

Watch this video on differing roles in same sex couples. What are some of the roles that are required of all parents in same sex relationships?

(https://www.youtube.com/watch?v=th0vpHDmE z8&t=3s)

Challenges for Parents Identifying as LGBT

- The age of the children at the time of disclosure may affect their reaction. Those who have not experienced puberty may be more accepting and tolerant.
- Children may have some difficulty relating to peers once it has been disclosed that their parents identify as LGBT. Generally, the children cope successfully, if supported by their families and friends. It may be

important for parents to have age appropriate conversations with their children to pre-empt these situations.

Parenting Skills and Effectiveness

- No empirical or descriptive evidence proves that being raised by, or living with, a parent identifying as LGBT, is detrimental to the development of children. The quality of the parenting relationship is the crucial factor (Domenici & Lesse, 1995; Goldberg, 2010).
- Most parents identifying as LGBT, have positive relationships with their children; they make serious attempts to create stable home lives.
- Parents identifying as LGBT, tend to be nontraditional and more responsive to children's needs and provide more explanations for rules.
- Sexual orientation is not a factor in determining the quality of parenting behavior and relationships (Domenici & Lesse, 1995; Goldberg, 2010).

In a Nutshell.   Research shows that the *quality* of the relationship between parents and children is a top indicator of success, regardless of the parents' sexual orientation. While these families may experience unique challenges, such as legal obstacles, children raised in same-sex households display the same levels of adjustment and behavior as children with heterosexual parents.

Video Example 14.2

Watch this video of children of parents identifying as LGBT. What is the main message these children are trying to send to the world about being raised by parents identifying as LGBT? How did their parent's sexual orientation shape their childhood?

(https://www.youtube.com/watch?v=MJnkp6D3j7c)

Parenting Reflection 14–3

Suppose you are an attorney who is representing a parent who is gay or lesbian in a custody hearing. What evidence would you present to demonstrate the ability of this parent to raise a child in a developmentally appropriate manner?

Focus Point. In general, parenting among same-sex couples is similar to heterosexual parenting in terms of function and nature. Research shows that the quality of the relationship between parents and children is a top indicator of success, regardless of the parents' sexual orientation. While these families experience unique challenges, such as possible legal obstacles, children raised in same-sex households display the same levels of adjustment and behavior that children with heterosexual parents exhibit.

CHAPTER FOCUS POINTS

Legal Matters

■ Major legal strides have been made in terms of relationship recognition, marriage, adoption, and parental rights. As far as parenting is concerned, the outcomes of parent–child relationships are determined by the *quality* of the parenting and the family relationships, which have a stronger influence than the sexual orientation of the parents.

The Determinants of Sexual Orientation

■ Available research concerning sexual orientation indicates that multifactorial aspects may play varying roles in influencing an individual's sexual orientation and gender expression. Interacting factors including genetics and epigenetics, hormonal influences during critical developmental periods, and social and psychological factors can be some of the contributory factors.

Family Systems with Children identifying as LGBT

■ Families supporting the coming out of a family member identifying as LGBT do well to foster an environment in which gender authenticity is encouraged and emotional support is demonstrated. Being informed concerning heteronormativity is an important step in becoming more inclusive and promoting equalities in our society. All family members should be supported and accepted for who they are, including their sexual identity.

Family Formation in Same-Sex Couples

■ In general, parenting among same-sex couples is similar to heterosexual parenting both in function and nature. Research shows that the quality of the relationship between parents and children is a top indicator of success, regardless of the parents' sexual orientation. While these families experience unique challenges, such as possible legal obstacles, children raised in same-sex households display the same levels of adjustment and behavior that children with heterosexual parents exhibit.

USEFUL WEBSITES

Carolyn Sherer
http://www.carolynsherer.com/
Website of photographer who provided photos for this chapter
"Art and Activism," art and diversity

Family Acceptance Project
https://familyproject.sfsu.edu/
Suicide prevention and support for families, Information on risks and challenges facing LGBT youth

Family Equality Council
www.familyequality.org
Advocacy for family equality, Regional LGBT parent groups

Human Rights Campaign: Working for Lesbian, Gay, Bisexual, and Transgender Equal Rights
www.hrc.org
Equality in the workplace

National Center for Lesbian Rights
www.nclrights.org
Lesbian rights, Legal help, Youth resources

National Gay and Lesbian Taskforce
www.thetaskforce.org
Advocacy, action, and events for LGBTQ

Parents, Families and Friends of Lesbians and Gays (PFLAG)
https://www.pflag.org/
LGBTQ support, Community and individual education, Community advocacy

CHAPTER 15

Toward Better Outcomes

Learning Outcomes

After completing this chapter, you should be able to

1. Name the characteristics of a responsive "serve-and-return" approach to parent–child relations.
2. Describe the risk and resilience model in terms of good parenting outcomes.
3. Explain the interrelated factors that contribute to individual resilience.
4. Evaluate the major protective factors supporting effective parenting and family resilience.

CREATING OPTIMAL ENVIRONMENTS

Children thrive in environments where they are acknowledged, supported, and valued. Many geographical, cultural, ethnic, and other variables contribute to childhoods that are unique, yet the predictability of lifespan development adds a universal quality. Children's brains are wired to be appropriately stimulated, and they need to be able to initiate as well as respond in an ongoing feedback loop; give and take, "*serve* and *return*" (Center on the Developing Child at Harvard University, 2016b). They need to interact backwards and forwards, as players in the complexities of the game of life. Variations of neglect, ranging from occasional to extreme, are grouped as child maltreatment, and neglect causes harm that will destabilize the child in immediate and later contexts. On the positive side, neighborhood social influences can act as buffers (Maguire-Jack & Negash, 2016) as well as extended relationships with meaningful mentors. Early inputs, prenatally and even before the third year of life, can affect future outcomes, including physical and mental health, as well as learning. These early influences also affect gene expression, or *epigenetics*.

If all other factors were equal, the child who is raised in a fairly stress free, responsive and supportive environment, can anticipate better outcomes than the child subjected to ongoing stress and uncertainty. So important is the stress element, that in order for healthy brain development to occur, the child needs to be subjected to an environment that is not only stimulating, but is also as stress free as possible ("Center on the Developing Child at Harvard University 2016b, p. 2). Clearly, ongoing stressful situations like being displaced or trapped in a cycle of poverty, or the uncertainty of whether food and shelter will be available, can have far-reaching repercussions. Children of homeless and refugee parents would be an example of the latter (Johnson, Beard, & Evans, 2016). But even in these instances, the children did better if at least one of the parents displayed effective coping mechanisms while navigating turbulent times (Masten, 2015, p. 107).

What does it take to increase resilience in a child? Surprisingly, the demands are relatively modest. Although resilience is often visualized as a stand-alone trait; it may be more helpful to regard it as a process which involves a number of attributes. Masten (2015) identifies resilience as the "ordinary magic," also the title of her book summarizing decades of research on resilience and related topics. Resilience can be compared to a journey of coping by displaying qualities such as self-regulation, focus, social problem-solving skills, competence, a sense of humor, motivation to adapt, the ability to delay gratification, and more (Masten, 2015, p. 71). These factors contribute to the "ordinary magic" that will support the process of resilience, although in some contexts these seemingly every day, yet valuable assets may require extraordinary determination to take effect. This broader conception of resilience imparts greater hope for future outcomes:

> Human resilience usually arises from the operation of ordinary and common adaptive systems, both inside and outside people, and not from rare or extraordinary actions, resources, or processes. Thus, there are reasons for optimism about the possibilities of shifting the odds in favor of success for young people at risk due to adversities in the past, present, or yet to come. (Masten, 2015, p. 305).

Importantly, appropriate *responsiveness* by parents ranks high among the parenting traits that are likely to elicit resilient behavior in children. An appropriate response is a reply to a cue that the child emits. It is an acknowledgment of the child and her needs. It continues into behaviors that seek to fulfil the requirements of the child appropriately and in a timely manner. Children who experience this cycle feel that they are in a trusted environment, that is also predictable and safe, and, here is that word again, *stress-free*. The parents are doing what good parents are supposed to be doing; namely creating the optimal environment to unfold the potential of a developing person. Secure parent–child attachments can act as buffers and mitigate potentially harmful intrusions (Hostinar & Gunnar, 2015). Parents who have welcomed children with difficult pasts into their home, through adoption and fostering, have witnessed improvements as the children responded to loving environments (Thompson, 2015a).

The implication for parenting is that good parent–child relations are *active* and *responsive*. Parents learn to understand the cues their infants, toddlers, and growing children emit. As their parenting skills improve, they also learn to respond in the most constructive ways. Working toward better outcomes for our children means that we begin with our own immediate relationships with the children in our lives; whether those are in personal family contexts or professional work environments. We start in our own backyard, small and humble, one child at a time. Give this youngster our time and our attention. By doing this we can encourage, develop and strengthen core life skills, another important link in the chain of resilience (Center on the Developing Child at Harvard University 2016b),

So often we hear the refrain: "It's about quality time, not quantity time." Indeed, quality is of utmost importance, as we have learnt by comparing the outcomes of high-quality versus marginal childcare settings (Forry et al., 2013). Even so, if there is not enough quantity time with a child, then the quality eventually also suffers. Quality requires a certain amount of quantity in terms of investment. Children are time consuming, they deserve some of our focus when it is our privilege to be interacting with them.

Supporting the parents and caregivers who look after the children by being a trusted mentor, or supporting them toward some time for self-renewal, is an important link in making a difference. Cumulatively, these investments enhance the quality of our relationships with children, and can lead to better outcomes (Center on the

Developing Child at Harvard University, 2016b, p. 2). According to the Center on the Developing Child at Harvard University, three interacting factors play an integral role in fostering optimal outcomes:

- Responsive caregiving and relationships
- Striving toward stress- free environments
- Strengthening core life skills.

For parents that means providing a responsive and stable environment for children, which includes economic stability. This in turn will provide children with the opportunity for healthy development which fosters educational achievement (Center on the Developing Child at Harvard University, 2016b), Each process feeds off the other, forming a system that supports optimal outcomes for the families involved.

Additionally, parents should create environments in which core life skills can be acquired.

Focus Point.   Children are surprisingly resilient in the face of various adversities, particularly if a caregiver exhibits healthy coping strategies. Relative lack of stress in their environment also contributes to the forming of resilience. Positive parent–child relationships are fostered when parents invest both quality and quantity time with their children.

Video Example 15.1

Watch this video on how resilience is built. What factors (people and things) influence resilience in children? (https://www.youtube.com/watch?v=xSf7pRpOgu8)

THE RISK AND RESILIENCE MODEL

"Early childhood is a time of great promise and rapid change, when the architecture of the developing brain is most open to the influence of relationships and experiences" (Center on the Developing Child at Harvard University, 2016b, p. 4). Just as positive experiences during childhood can set the stage for healthy later development, adverse experiences can be destructive in their own right. The bar for functioning well in a complex society is constantly raised. Millennials have a greater chance of a middle class lifestyle if they have a college

education. This in turn promises better outcomes for their children, with education and stable households being contributing protective factors (Lavner, Bradbury, & Karney, 2015).

Societies are made up of the building blocks of families. Families, in turn, rely on societies to anchor them, allowing for a hopeful future. Responsible and informed parenthood is supported and rests within all the systems of a larger society. There is a constant mutual influence. Raising and maintaining a healthy family truly requires the entire village, it is not a task lightly undertaken. As a society, and as individual members within that society, we need to give all of the support we can to obtain the best outcomes. The "serve and respond" rule that we mentioned for parent–child relations can also apply on a macro-systemic level. Societies ideally need to respond to the needs of families through family friendly public policies that serve to support family outcomes that seek to enhance well-being for all the members.

Optimal parenting cannot be the exclusive responsibility of an isolated family because it is bidirectionally locked within the society where it occurs. We can try to refer to a "universal child" or a "universal family," but only if we add a string of qualifiers. The outcome of each parenting experience will have traits that are family and culture specific. The cultural, geographic, economic, and other situational differences can be large enough to coat families with unique layers of socialization and enculturation; this, in turn, will influence parenting outcomes for the next generation. There is no way of oversimplifying family life complexity when it comes to individual outcomes.

We examine some of the factors that promote both risk and resilience, with an emphasis on resilience.

Ecological Perspective.   Parenting is embedded within the family, which, in turn, is cushioned by societal institutions like educational facilities, places of civic engagement, centers for religious life, and many more. This collection is nested within the larger society, which exerts societal values and pressures, which with its social policies can be family friendly and supportive. It can create policies, allocate resources from national budgets, and turn a listening ear to the risk factors, which, in some ways, concern all of us, and which have to be addressed to allow resilience to rise like the mythological Phoenix.

Both risks and protective factors exert an influence during childhood. Individual, interpersonal, and social factors, as well as environmental factors, interact (Jenson & Fraser, 2015). It is a similar approach to that of Urie

Bronfenbrenner's ecological model in which influential factors can operate in micro, meso, exo, and macro systems. These two approaches have been combined in Figure 15–1.

As researchers in the field of parenting and family-related topics, we can study the ways in which individuals, families, and communities intersect and interface (Karney, 2013; Lavner, Karney, & Bradbury, 2015). Some relevant topics are intergenerational relationships, family stress, adaptation, and community resilience. Additionally, Karney addresses the ways in which stressors outside the relationship affect the relationship itself. There is a spillover effect, and factors such as chronic financial strain, or limited skills in communicating constructively, influence marital systems (Karney, 2013).

Bidirectional and Dynamic Interaction.   In an ecological and systemic model, the different levels interact in a *bidirectional* and a *dynamic* manner. It is an ongoing, interactive process of give and take between all parties involved. Our society influences us as individuals and as members of that society. But we, as individuals, shape the larger society as well. It is a constant and often almost imperceptible back and forth movement. Like the changing tides in the ocean, we see little if we watch the ocean from minute to minute; yet long term, the changes have remarkable effects. In the parent–child relationship both participating parties are shaped by each other.

Changes also occur because they are instigated by the need for adaptation to different circumstances, and

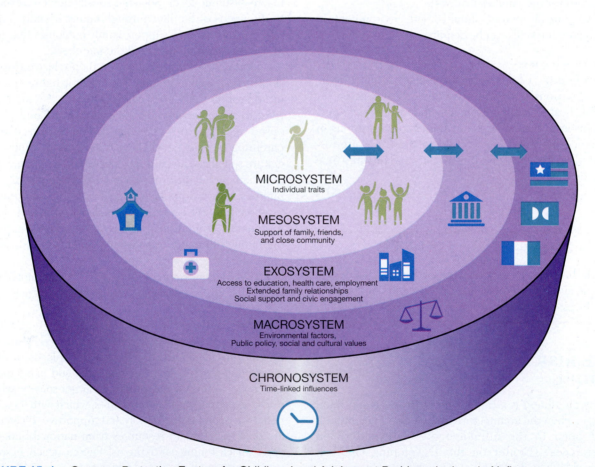

FIGURE 15–1.   Common Protective Factors for Childhood and Adolescent Problems by Level of Influence.

Diagram adapted by C. Gerhardt and based on Jenson, J. M., & Fraser, M. W. (2015). A Risk and Resilience Framework for Child, Youth, and Family Policy. Chapter 1 in Jenson, J. M., & Fraser, M. W. (eds.). (2015). *Social Policy for Children and Families: A Risk and Resilience Perspective*. 3rd ed. Los Angeles, CA: SAGE.

Berk, L. (2014). Chapter 1: History, Theory and Research Strategies, Figure 1–5, page 19. Structure of the environment in ecological systems theory. In *Exploring Lifespan Development*. 3rd ed. Upper Saddle River, NJ: Pearson.

the adaptation enhances outcomes. Adaptation means a reorganization based on dynamic feedback. Charles Darwin (1809–1882) was attributed as describing the evolutionary process in the simplest of terms: "*Adapt or die.*" The broader context of this quote was Darwin's statement: "It is not the strongest of the species that survives, nor the most intelligent that survives. It is the one that is the most adaptable to change."

Protective Factors

A glass of water is either half full or half empty, depending on how we look at it. Some youth seem to find it within them to use the half glass of water constructively and toward good outcomes, whereas others complain of thirst because they see the glass as half empty. The factors that contribute toward good outcomes despite adversity are **protective factors**. As members of the helping professions and groups that engage in matters of social concern, and as policy makers and members of this society, we will do well if we can strengthen those protective factors. Masten (2014, p. 148) summarizes various research studies and lists factors that contribute to resiliency and those systems that aid adaptation.

According to Masten (2014) resilience factors are displayed in good parenting, which displays effective caretaking and is of high quality in terms of engagement. Relationships with significant caretakers, mentors, and other adults, as well as a circle of friends and, in adolescence and emerging adulthood, relationships with romantic partners all show the importance of social connections and community. Other factors that will support the individual are problem-solving skills, paired with intelligence, emotional regulation, and self-control, and combined with self-efficacy. On a larger societal scale, effective schools, neighborhoods, and opportunities for civic involvement support youth in exploring good outcomes which also improve their self-image and motivates them toward higher aspirations leading to better outcomes (Emery, Trung, & Wu, 2015).

The ability to work toward better outcomes can also be compared to playing a good game with what may be a poor deck of cards. In major bridge competitions, each table gets the same set of cards, in that they are presorted so that the sequencing of cards is identical for each table. The outcomes of the games that are played depend on the skill and teamwork of the players. Life similarly may not provide us with an easy starting point, but by seeking constructive social contexts, some strength may be found in the mere act of mutual support. Viktor Frankl

(1905–1997) described some of these mental processes in his reflections on his experiences as a Holocaust survivor in his celebrated book: *The Will to Meaning* (1969/2014). When he had lost virtually everything (including his pregnant wife, closest family, freedom, and intellectual property) he maintained that he still had the choice of the dignity with which he would face adversity. In his own words:

> Everything can be taken from a man but one thing: the last of the human freedoms—to choose one's attitude in any given set of circumstances, to choose one's own way … every day, every hour, offered the opportunity to make a decision, a decision which determined whether you would or would not submit to those powers which threatened to rob you of your very self, your inner freedom. *Viktor Frankl*

The above examples display adaptive systems in both micro and macro contexts; where social connections, family and peer support, and expanded networking circles such as schools, churches, and civic contexts, strengthen engagement behavior that promises improved opportunities and can thus also change future outcomes (Masten, 2014, p. 171).

Risk and Resilience. Research from the 1980s indicated that despite adversity, the presence of risk seemed to be lessened by the presence of the almost magical catalyst identified as resilience. Initially, it was thought that risk and resilience were opposite ends of the continuum. According to Jenson and Fraser (2015), social researchers asked whether these protective factors could be identified and measured. They also asked if risk and resilience go hand in hand or whether we could separate the constructs in our research and our policies. Rather than describing **resilience** as a personal asset such as a personality trait or characteristic, Masten (2014) felt that it was best described as a *process*. It is a process that engages personality traits, personal resources, and other aspects from the larger ecological system. "Risk factors are individual, school, peer, family and community influences that increase the likelihood that a child will experience a social or health problem" (Jenson & Fraser, 2015, Chapter 1, p. 6). They supply a second definition adapted from Frazer and Terzian's (2015,) earlier work, and which is still relevant:

> Broadly defined, the term *risk factor* relates to any event, condition, or experience that increases the probability that a problem will be formed, maintained or exacerbated (emphasis added) (Jenson & Fraser, 2015, p. 6).

Importantly though, research emphasizes the social connectedness that imparts resilience (Center on the Developing Child at Harvard University, 2016b). The ability to resurface is not attributed solely to inner and stoic strength, but can be found in the meaningful and core relationships that nurture, encourage, and provide self-esteem. The child who feels safe and protected in an environment is more likely to be able to rely on his inner resources that may have been strengthened in social contexts with caring adults. *Self-regulation* and *executive functioning* are cornerstone qualities, but they seem to find expression through ongoing responsive relationships such as constructive parenting behavior.

A key insight is that protective factors act as *buffers*; they stand between the youth or the family and adversity. They absorb the shock, like the crumple zone of a good car fender. In other words, protective factors are resources that the individual and the environment can access, which will then minimize or reduce the risk of impact. We can identify and name many of the buffering agents, and the intervention lies in implementing these protective buffers in high-risk situations. As with all complicated challenges, this may be easier said than done, but it is a beginning nonetheless, and a hopeful point of departure. Fraser and Terzian (2005) identify three steps, namely *Reduce*, *Interrupt*, and *Prevent*. We added illustrative metaphors for learning purposes:

■ **Reduce** whatever will cause the impact. If we are going to be hit by a truck, try to get the truck to slow down, or maybe it could be a smaller truck. Or reduce the amount of traffic and set speed limits. Reduction of the harmful agent will allow for a better outcome. In the parenting context it may be something obvious like reducing the unhealthy food kept in the home, or limiting visits to fast food outlets to enhance better nutritional outcomes. If television exposure is becoming the unofficial child-minder, then put structure into this activity and reduce it to levels where it remains fun, constructive, and a learning experience. Some selected television input can be educational so it would be difficult to cut out this activity entirely. It can also be compared to the effects of immunization, we cannot prevent the child from being exposed to certain illnesses, but having been vaccinated the child will have built up an immunity and can overcome the health threat which in itself has been reduced because of the intervention.

■ **Interrupt** the chain of risk. If we are going to get in harm's way, make sure there is a stop sign or a traffic light for the truck and the pedestrian. These will interrupt the chain of connected risks. In the parenting context, the child who is having a meltdown may be encouraged to "Take-a-minute" so that they can stop, reflect, and regroup. Hopefully, this interrupts the sequence of emotional outbursts that would escalate if unchecked.

■ **Prevent** or block the factors that will cause the harm. No large vehicles are allowed in a pedestrian area; no unaccompanied children are allowed in traffic areas. Legislation makes this possible, and the system enforces it (Terzian et al., 2015, quoted in Jenson & Fraser, 2015, p. 9). In educational contexts for example, we can initiate a zero tolerance policy for bullying behavior. Empathy training and prosocial behavior by peer group leaders and role models will hopefully prevent bullying behavior before it can even gain a foothold. To prevent drug use in schools, the entire area around a school is a drug free zone. Another example, to prevent accidents when children embark or disembark from a school bus, traffic in both lanes has to obey mandatory traffic rules and stop. Introducing this measure has reduced accidents related to children getting on and off school buses dramatically.

> *"One who gains strength by overcoming obstacles possesses the only strength which can overcome adversity."*
>
> Albert Schweitzer (1875–1965),
> Physician, Organist, Nobel Laureate,
> Founder of the Schweitzer Hospital "Lambarene" in Gabon, Africa

Focus Point.   Parenting is largely impacted by (and, in turn, impacts) a range of outside influences, from children's school teachers to the state of the economy. When an outside source introduces negativity or adversity, protective factors such as safety and nurture act as buffers to foster resilience in both individuals and family units.

Cultural Snapshot 15-1

Resilience and a Multicultural Identity

The world of the 21st century is becoming increasingly multifaceted and technologically advanced. Adolescents have to navigate their way through these complexities while also transitioning toward their own cultural identity. This highly mobile world, where people move to other countries for a job, for better opportunities, or out of the necessity of survival, exposes a maturing generation of children to all the influences of multiple agents of socialization. These influences can be contradictory as in trying to merge cultures of origin with host cultures. These emerging adults grapple with forming a multicultural identity that is coherent. At the same time, this generation of multinational adolescents and young adults become cultural translators with the skills to navigate multicultural worlds. They can rise to the challenge in ever changing contexts and contribute meaningfully while simultaneously molding their particular society (Miller, 2011, p. 520).

> Over the course of our lives, we inhabit several worlds, including the world that revolves around our family, the world of education, the job world and the world created by our culture. Our experiences in each of these several worlds influences our understanding of who we are and form the basis of

our identity. As a result of globalization, assimilation, cross-cultural marriages, and immigration, we live in an increasingly interconnected world. Growing up in an independent, coherent, and stable culture has become less typical than it once was. The process of globalization alone, which includes the expansion of mass tourism, creation of multinational corporations, the emergence of multilateral governmental and non-governmental agencies, as well as the unprecedented availability of multicultural, media-based influences, has changed the processes by which individuals form a sense of identity (Miller, 2011, p. 509).

Precisely because they have a multicultural identity, they may display the self-efficacy and resilience perfected during immigration and translocation processes. The repeated transitions can be double edged as they can demand a price especially in terms of rootedness, while also contributing to coping and adaptation skills.

Source: Miller, R. L. (2011). Multicultural Identity Development. In Keith, K. D. (Ed.), *Cross-cultural Psychology: Contemporary Themes and Perspectives*. West Sussex, England: Wiley-Blackwell.

ENHANCING INDIVIDUAL RESILIENCE

"Education is a powerful driver of development and is one of the strongest instruments for reducing poverty and improving health, gender equality, peace, and stability." (The World Bank, n.d.). It is undisputed that learning is the key to improving socioeconomic outcomes. It is a powerful buffering agent. But in order to benefit fully from formal education, the opportunities for learning should also exist. These opportunities vary tremendously between developed and developing nations. Individuals can be held hostage by illiteracy because there are no facilities or opportunities to break the debilitating cycle. This educational disadvantage can be passed on from generation to generation unless the

larger society implements those elements that will foster better educational outcomes.

The different ecological layers influence the outcomes as well. On the micro and individual levels, family and personal factors interact to keep children in (or out of) school. For parents who missed out on their own education, helping their children reach their educational goals can be a major parental gift.

Parents need to be involved with the school and be attentive to their child's progress. The parent who prevents tardiness and absenteeism and supports the child in simple things like catching the school bus on time and making sure the child has had adequate rest, meals, and clean clothes, is encouraging behavior patterns that send the message that the needs of the child and the role of schooling are important. Providing an environment that is conducive to learning, a time for age-appropriate play, and the support of pro-social values are important parental responsibilities. Children are quick to pick up these messages. It becomes difficult if the child has unsupported special needs or is exposed to parental examples where negative patterns may be reenacted.

Timing of education is very important. Ideally early child development programs should provide the foundation for later learning, as the window of opportunity for learning (including brain development) is wide open during these tender years of infancy and early childhood.

The legislative building blocks for school attendance in the United States are in place, as mandatory and predominantly free schooling is available to all children until the minimum age of 16 or 17, depending on the state. The minimum age for employment is 15 (or 14 in some states). There typically is a 1-year gap. It is the state's intention that children are encouraged to attend schools at least until the minimum full-time employment age so that there is a seamless transition and no added temptation to leave school early for the lure of a paycheck. Worldwide, countries differ in enforcing mandatory school attendance. In many developing countries, the minimum age for employment is fairly low, encouraging children to enter the workforce to contribute to the family income. This, in itself, can perpetuate poverty through limited literacy.

For children and youngsters who reveal talent and motivation, many scholarships and educational support systems can be called upon. Legislation like the No Child Left Behind Act of 2001 in the United States, which sets goals and standards for best practices, seeks to improve outcomes for disadvantaged students and, in essence, supports literacy. The full title of this legislation is An Act to Close the Achievement Gap with Accountability, Flexibility, and Choice, So that No Child Is Left Behind (Planty et al., 2008).

In addition to the inner family circle, support from teachers and schools can make the difference between success and failure. Underserved schools in poor neighborhoods present greater challenges in focusing on factors contributing to resilience because of fewer resources and often uninvolved parents. If a child is consistently mentored by someone who is truly interested in their well-being, even in the absence of a parent, this may be the catalyst for the child to obtain a better educational outcome (Coller & Kuo, 2014). Organizations such as Big Brothers Big Sisters of America (www.bbbs.org) provide mentoring that encourages positive self-image formation

and better outcomes through role models and interpersonal encouragement. YMCA of the USA (www.ymca.net) operates after school programs and many other programs to contribute to "development, healthy living, and social responsibility," as reflected by their mission statement. Some of these programs provide a much needed and welcome support system to working parents. The "Communities in Schools" initiative (www.communitiesinschools .org), works hard to keep children and youths in school, encouraging them to graduate and in so doing access greater opportunities and better futures.

> *"The function of education is to teach one to think intensively and to think critically. Intelligence plus character—that is the goal of education."*
>
> *Martin Luther King Jr. (1929–1968)*

Civic Organizations

Head Start (www.nhsa.org) and similar organizations step in to ensure that the foundation for early childhood education is solid. Head Start estimates that more than 33 million children in the United States have taken part in their programs since its inception in 1965, and that many of these children have progressed to positions of leadership and/or national eminence (Early Childhood Learning and Knowledge Center, 2016). Another organization that has positively affected the lives of thousands is Teach for America (www.teachforamerica.org). Students who have graduated in a variety of fields spend 2 transitional years teaching in low-income communities, contributing their skills and enthusiasm toward providing an education for children from underserved schools. This organization estimates that only 8 percent of children growing up in low-income communities in America will graduate from college by age 24, and that about 16 million American children "face the extra challenges of poverty" (Teach for America, n.d.).

The influence of socioeconomic class, parental education, and related opportunities for children, creates large educational disparities. The differences in terms of access to education and the likelihood to access education between the bottom and the top quartile are profound (Pell Institute for the Study of Opportunity in Education). Again, the bidirectional effect can be seen in operation. Virtually all of the participants who took on the teacher role as part of the Teach for America initiatives, state that they, too, were enriched by the experience, that it broadened their understanding and their compassion, and they felt rewarded by contributing to the greater good. It is very encouraging that a society such as illustrated here, can find it within in its own resource systems to make a palpable difference.

The W. K. Kellogg Foundation (www.wkkf.org) supports family stability through financial education, early learning, and child-care options. Through their investment and support, they encourage education and learning, and they use national organizations and their networks to achieve this goal. Part of their mission statement is "Whole child development, family literacy, and educational advocacy." Similarly, the Annie E. Casey Foundation (www.aecf.org) supports many social initiatives. They have produced a body of research that outlines some of the challenges and successes. They focus on children, but also on the communities that can bring about changes in children's lives. They have examined factors that pertain to juvenile justice, economic security, and education. They foster leadership and have set up networking sites where the poorest families can make connections and regain a sense of civic involvement. This is a key factor in feeling connected and wanting to make a difference at each level, even in the direst of circumstances. This organization estimates that 15 million children lived in poverty in the United States in 2015, representing 21 percent of all children (Annie E. Casey Foundation, 2016). On the cautiously encouraging side, these figures decreased by 2% between 2011 and 2015. In short, this foundation exemplifies that change has to occur on many levels to be truly effective because there is a reciprocal influence. Another estimate is that 45% of people who spend at least half of their childhood in poverty, will still live in poverty at age 35 (Child Defense Fund, 2016; National Center for Children in Poverty, n.d.).

The United Nations have developed a list of sustainable development goals described in "The Millennium Development Goals Report" of 2009 (Griggs et al., 2013). The Millennium Declaration initially set its target date as 2015, and this has been extended to 2030. The targets are interrelated and each one in turn affects other domains, like a challenging global and ecological puzzle. Among the initial global targets were the following:

- **Education:** A goal of education for all children, and disparities in this area are still great. Improvements have been witnessed since the inception of the development goals. In the developing world primary education is becoming more available, although high school education still needs to be developed further.
- **Employment:** Increased employment opportunities especially for young people and women and in developing countries. Productive work environments create a domino effect of change.
- **Food Production:** Hunger and food insecurity, which especially impacts the poor.
- **Life Expectancy:** Reduction of maternal mortality, especially in Sub Saharan Africa and Southern Asia. Infant and child mortality has been reduced through major health initiatives such as vaccination programs.
- **Living Conditions:** Improved sanitation and living conditions for the poor. On the positive side, extreme poverty has declined somewhat since the early nineties, although about a quarter of the world's population live in extreme poverty.
- **Resources:** Preserving the natural resource base as water scarcity has been increasing and resources are finite.

These are a few select examples from countless organizations, initiatives, and foundations that are seeking to improve outcomes for people and the planet. It is apparent that the key to change lies predominantly with education, as this capstone piece of the interrelated global challenges has the power to influence virtually all other areas of concern.

Worldwide, children face very diverse educational challenges. In developing countries, many children have no prospects of receiving an education; there simply are no schools or teachers to accommodate them. Others are forced into child labor or to enlist as soldiers in armed conflict. Based on 2013 data, an estimated 124 million children worldwide are *not* attending school (UNESCO, 2015). These youngsters are referred to as "out-of-school children." Forty million of these children live in areas of civil conflict or war. Education is often compromised or unavailable. Children who are crippled by the effects of poverty, famine, and disease will not be able to reach their educational potential (UNESCO, 2015). In those societies where maternal educational levels were increased, infant mortality was lowered and children had

Societies are made up of the building blocks of families. Education should be a priority as it strengthens individuals, families, as well as societies.

Image Source/Alamy Stock Photo

better nutrition and improved health outcomes. The Bill and Melinda Gates Foundation (www.gatesfoundation.orgw) applies substantial resources to improving outcomes for children on a global platform with numerous initiatives, including major vaccination programs. According to UNESCO,

> Education is a universal human right. However, enjoyment of that right is heavily conditioned by the lottery of birth and inherited circumstance. Opportunities for education are heavily influenced by where one is born and by other factors over which children have no control, including parental income, gender, and ethnicity (UNESCO, 2015, p. 26).

"Education is the most powerful weapon which you can use to change the world."

Nelson Mandela (1918–2013)

Gender Equality in Educational Outcomes

The public consensus concerning the movement toward the changing role of women in society has been supportive, and nearly three-quarters of American adults state that the trend of women entering the workforce is a welcome development. About 62 percent of adults in the United States believe that dual-income families have a more satisfying life and that both spouses should contribute to household and family-related chores (The Pew Charitable Trusts, 2013).

The outcomes of gender equality in the workplace in the United States are cautiously optimistic. It is encouraging that women, in greater numbers than ever before in history, are seeking out tertiary or higher education and are graduating and entering the workforce in positions that match their expertise. They can be found in careers that had been male-dominated in the past, such as in engineering, research, business, academia, and some of the medical specialties. Almost a quarter of small businesses list women as owners or co-owners (U.S. Census Bureau, n.d.).

Less encouraging is that in key influential contexts, such as in boardrooms, in legislature, and in upper management, women's voices are in the minority. There are many contributing factors apart from education and work equality. The family life cycle tends to put much responsibility for family emotional wellness on the shoulders of women. Throughout the childbearing years, women's careers may be repeatedly interrupted, while social supports such as quality child care are limited and expensive. If women do have a career outside the home, they are frequently left managing their career and their family, and role overload ensues. With the fragility of families, single parenthood adds numerous difficulties to the challenges of fulfilling the parental role successfully, and single mothers and their children are more likely to live in poverty. There are always those who defy the norm, and children raised by single mothers have managed to reach their potential because they saw the parental sacrifices from close quarters and knew that the best way to thank their parent was to use the challenges of poverty or limited opportunity to strengthen them in their resolve to carve out different lives for their own families.

Around the world, the picture is bleak, especially for women in developing countries. Worldwide, women account for the majority of illiterate persons because of persistent gender disparities in accessing education. When these disadvantaged women become parents, their children perpetuate that same cycle of deprivation: infant mortality is higher, illnesses take their toll, and ultimately the chances of these children going to school are diminished (UNESCO, 2009, p. 28). Parents may hold universal dreams for their children, but some are shackled by the constraints of poverty.

Additionally and importantly, the more veiled benefit of education, namely development of the self, self-reflection, self-actualization and a greater awareness of how education can contribute to a meaningful life, in turn provides the motivation to pursue further learning. These facets are succinctly captured by Iris Murdoch, Irish-born author and winner of the Booker Prize for Literature:

> Education doesn't make you happy, and nor does freedom. We don't become happy just because we're free, if we are, or because we've been educated, if we have, but because education may be the means by which we realize we are happy. It opens our eyes, our ears … tells us where delights are lurking … convinces us that there is only one freedom of any importance whatsoever … that of the mind … and gives us the assurance, the confidence, to walk the path our mind … our educated mind … offers.
> *Dame Iris Murdoch, DBE (1919–1999)*

Generational Differences

Research indicates that a cohort, or a generation of people, has a personality, in a similar manner to how individuals have personalities. There is a collective identity that defines these groups, and the group, in turn, is shaped by the many interactive layers of the community. Each group or cohort may reveal specific values, subtle cultural differences, attitudes, and visions of their own and of the larger world. One of the latest identified generations in the United States is the **Millennial Generation**, born between 1981 and 2000, the beginning of the new millennium, right at the cusp of the Internet paradigm shift (The Pew Research Center, 2014b). Characteristic of this group that grew up in the shadow of the World Wide Web is that they are hyperconnected, and this digital connectedness influences real face-to-face relationships.

The questions asked by the researchers of The Pew Charitable Trusts are about the current early adult generation: who they are, how they differ from their parents, how they are similar to their parents, how they are influencing the shaping of our society, how they are they being shaped in a bidirectional manner, and what their influence will be in the decades ahead (The Pew Research Center, 2014b). The characteristics that differentiate this generation are as follows:

■ A third of Millennials over the age of 26 have a four-year college degree. Computer skills represent the new literacy, and they have been dubbed "digital natives."

■ As a cohort, they are the best educated group in the history of the United States; they also have record amounts of student debt.

■ Millennials face some employment challenges; hence, the boomerang effect of returning to the parental home.

■ Jobs are blocked by an aging, non-retiring workforce. Advanced technical skills become highly sought after.

■ Millennials are technologically more connected, but also think people disclose too much about themselves on social media.

■ This generation wants both a career and a family: 74% indicate they want children.

■ In reality, only 26% were married, lower percentages than in previous decades.

■ Almost half describe themselves as political independents, and show strong support for social issues of their concern (e.g., legalization of same-sex marriage, marijuana legalization).

■ Almost 3 in 10 (29%) say that they are not affiliated with any religion.

■ Millennials are the most racially diverse group in America.

Source: The Pew Charitable Trusts: Pew Research Center (2014). *"Millennials in Adulthood."*

Focus Point. A good education can bolster resilience and fight poverty. Unfortunately, the quality of available education is often linked to one's socioeconomic status. Parenting also plays a substantial role in education, as encouraging words or acts exhibited by parents can help instill an appreciation for, and love of, learning in their children.

ENHANCING FAMILY RESILIENCE

For men and women of all age groups, being a good parent and having a successful marriage continue to rank high on their list of priorities, often more important than being successful or having a high-paying job or career. Women are placing more emphasis on their careers, sometimes at the expense of marriage and the family. In 2012, almost one in five married women was better educated than her husband and earned more (Pew Research, 2014a). The factor that best predicts marital success is level of education. College-educated spouses seem to have more resources at their disposal with which to create successful and rewarding marriages, while their education also protects them from poverty and related debilitating challenges (Lavner, Bradbury, & Karney, 2015).

Many men have stepped up to the challenge of family-related responsibilities by becoming involved with the nurturing and interactional aspects of child rearing. Frequently, these men are better educated and have been exposed to the role models of their own mothers who had been educated and have had careers outside the home. These men have expressed the pleasure that they experience in being involved in all facets of fatherhood.

Fathers are more visibly involved in their families, from the birthing room to the schoolroom. This means that they are present and involved during pregnancy, birth, and beyond. Men are better educated concerning child rearing, with programs such as "Boot Camp for New Dads" (www.bootcampfornewdads.org) contributing to the empowerment of fathers. When fathers are in the boardroom, they make it known that their families are important to them and their lives cannot be dictated by work demands. Public figures in high-visibility roles have been good role models for fathers. Increasingly, fathers are seeking a balance between work and their families. Some fathers have taken on the primary nurturing and caretaking role for their families by raising young children in the home while their partners become breadwinners, working outside the home. There is greater flexibility in matching personal preferences, economic opportunities, and the needs of the family.

Looking at the global picture, there is great variety in the educational and economic realms. In some countries, women are part of the top leadership, while, simultaneously, great economic and educational disparity between classes and genders persist. Some developed countries have made exceptional progress in these areas, and there are valuable lessons to be learned from their more successful approaches to providing family support and family-friendly work environments. In some countries, the effects of unrest place great burdens on families and children. Family life, parenting, and schooling are interrupted by war. Military families face separation and have to deal with distance coparenting and the risks of war to their survival and health (Trail, Meadows, Miles, & Karney, 2015).

Family Structure

Family structure has changed dramatically over the last half century. Some key factors related to family stability are race, ethnicity, immigration status, men's and women's earnings, and family structure. Some of the characteristics of current families are:

- Households are smaller and more fluid.
- Household composition and size change more frequently.
- Greater variation in the assignment of the parenting or primary caretaker role.
- Greater variation in family structure.
- Adults and children are more disconnected.
- Less family time, more television and media time.
- High rates of disruption in the parental union, including divorce.
- More children from non-marital unions and many single mothers.
- Fathers' roles vary from being involved and responsible to being disengaged.
- Social connections and social support have atrophied.
- Little extended-family support.
- Families often live geographically far apart.
- Economic stressors, crises with the mortgage, and unemployment.

To maintain stability in the family unit, access to family support is an important strategy. That, in turn, is linked to health-promoting behaviors and general well-being. Higher high school dropout rates, less education, and poorer job prospects facilitate economic disparities (Neff & Karney, 2017; Lavner, Karney, Williamson, & Bradbury, 2016) College-educated parents promote better educational and occupational aspirations in their offspring and, generally, marital quality as well as long term economic well-being is better among the educated and those couples who do not face marital disruption (Zissimopoulos, Karney, & Rauer, 2015).

Increasingly, institutional marriages that are supposed to last a lifetime are being replaced by non-marital relationships. In practice, this means that blended and reconstituted families are more likely. The numbers of couples who choose to marry are declining, with more marriages occurring at a later age among the college educated. Americans still tend to marry for love, and when that love fades, divorce rates increase (Sprecher & Hatfield, 2017).

Marriage and Family.   As marriage rates decline and couples are tying the knot later in life, family formation and the living arrangements of the children are affected. In 2015, about half of adults age 18 and older were married, which was much lower than the almost three in four, recorded in 1960 (Livingston & Caumont, 2017). There is a widening of the "marriage gap," with college-educated adults marrying later. They also tend to marry other college-educated adults, often leading to dual-career and dual-income couples. Many single mothers have less education and are in the lower income groups (The Pew Charitable Trusts, 2013).

Karney (2013) interprets some of the findings of the U.S. Census Bureau (n.d.) and research by The Pew Charitable Trusts. He states that lower socioeconomic status and concomitant poverty add to the probability of divorce and to lack of satisfaction within the marriage. Based on the Building Strong Families study, it was found that marriage education curricula offered in order to decrease divorce rates had less of an effect than was hoped for because many couples could not attend because of lack of childcare, holding down multiple poorly paying jobs, transportation problems, and a generally lower motivation to attend (Karney, 2013). The unique problems of low-income relationships were identified as follows:

- Problems related to money and the effects of poverty.
- Addiction disorders (alcohol and drugs).
- Little investment in a monogamous, trusting relationship; infidelity and concomitant marital problems.
- Fewer friends, social isolation.
- Lack of connectedness with civic organizations that provide social cohesion and support.

All relationships, regardless of the educational level or socioeconomic status, had difficulties or faced challenges in the following areas: spending time together, intimate marital relations, problems with parents or in-laws, problems with children and parenting children, communication, and the fair division of household chores (Karney, 2013). It appears that if there are problems in paying for food for the next meal, the luxury of relationship skills falls by the wayside. Low-income families face so many problems linked to survival that these problems take precedence, while independent relationship skills and attitudes are placed on the back burner (Karney, 2013). As stress and poverty add to the survival demands of families, husbands and wives, or committed partners, increasingly communicate in negative ways. It confirms what intuition would lead us to believe, namely, that stress aggravates problems that might otherwise have been surmountable. Individuals from low-income communities report that negative life events and mental health incidents perpetuate the cycle of stress. We presume from the literature that couples in stressful environments communicate less and they do so less constructively, problem resolution is on a downward spiral, and stress then inhibits the adaptive process (Neff & Karney, 2017). So at a time when it is most important to cope, the stress makes some couples less capable of coping. These are some of the factors that so clearly contribute to **caretaker despair**, where parents and caretakers feel overwhelmed by a tsunami of difficulties.

Marriage-friendly environments are created by taking care of the wolf howling at the door. Health care, quality child care, and a living wage for working people are the cornerstones that hold up the marital structure (Lavner, Karney, & Bradbury, 2015). We cannot pin all the blame on the socioeconomic aggregate of the neighborhood. What seems to be important is the level of engagement or attachment by members of the community. Are they investing in their community, or have they taken the approach of blaming the community, which

Strong levels of community investment and civic engagement provide social cohesion and support.

Monkey Business Images/Shutterstock

ends up immobilizing the entire system? Other dimensions of the community experience seem to matter, especially civic engagement and emotional investment.

The separation of family status and family process can seem artificial. It follows along the same lines as the parenting argument concerning quality time. Researchers have found that if there is not enough quantity, which is not enough time spent in parent–child relations, then it impacts the quality. Parents who have to hold down daytime and nighttime jobs cannot spend time with children, and there is an effect in terms of parenting outcomes in this scenario, unless consistent and trusted caretakers step in. Sometimes this role is allocated to the grandparents.

We can maintain that the family climate overrides the family structure, but in some family structures, the cards are stacked against them, making it more difficult to maintain a good climate. For instance, for single parents the role overload and the effects of poverty can be so overwhelming that this family form can face greater challenges than a family where two parents share parenting tasks, resources, and skills. Even if the parents part ways, it is always in the best interests of the child that the parents work out responsible ways of fulfilling the dual-household parenting roles. This means that the battles of the adults should never be fought with the children as go-betweens or pawns.

Video Example 15.2

Watch this video on family resilience. What does family resilience look like? What does resilience in the family provide for children?

(https://www.youtube.com/watch?v=cM8fY4C5mVo)

The Power of Family Support

Raising children successfully is a task that requires a thousand characteristics and more; among them responsibility, dedication, patience, foresight, and a sense of humor. If families are systems, and the members of each system are influenced by each other, then it follows that the support of the family can lighten the load and enable us to be more effective in our parent–child relations. Raising children successfully is a relay race. Even though the parents are the primary coaches, there is so much value in intergenerational parenting. Children can connect to the wisdom and grace of their own ancestors, while the grandparents are reminded that they have an important role to fulfill that extends to the third generation. They can be the link to ancestry and relay the family oral history, reminding us of our roots, which uniquely belong to each individual. As the

Cultural Snapshot 15–2

A Vision for Better Outcomes

Urie Bronfenbrenner was a Russian-born developmental psychologist who immigrated to America. Because of his bicultural background he was very aware of cultural influences in the context of child development. He allocated special significance to culture in especially the macrosystemic influences as described in his ecological systems theory. Cultural values and beliefs influence parenting outcomes. The following quotations by Bronfenbrenner reflect some of his views.

■ "If the children and youth of a nation are afforded opportunity to develop their capacities to the fullest, if they are given the knowledge to understand the world and the wisdom to change it, then the prospects for the future are bright. In contrast, a society which neglects its children, however well it may function in other respects, risks eventual disorganization and demise."

■ "Development, it turns out, occurs through this process of progressively more complex exchange between a child and somebody else—especially somebody who's crazy about that child."

■ "If we can stand on our own two feet, it is because others have raised us up. If, as adults, we can lay claim to competence and compassion, it only means that other human beings have been willing and enabled to commit their competence and compassion to us—through infancy, childhood, and adolescence, right up to this very moment."

Quotes by Urie Bronfenbrenner (1917–2005): Russian-born, American Developmental Psychologist

---

American population is graying, it is more likely that grandparents can play a more active role in family relationships and also in sharing some of the childcare roles (Gerhardt, 2016d).

Siblings, too, can be a stabilizing factor for children. Children learn from brothers and sisters. There is a model for language, and they can interact in play. Later in life, the siblings become the reference group that uniquely understands how it was growing up in the family of origin. Siblings are cohorts who travel through time in a synchronized manner. They are the support when parents fall away. Even though much has been written about family position and children, each child may have different perspectives on the parents; the positives are that they represent the family of origin, and there normally is cohesiveness. Older siblings learn to share and empathize with the needs of younger siblings.

During normal, stable times, families oscillate in a range of connectedness, drawing closer or farther apart as the occasion demands. Typically, during key ritual and transitional moments in the family life span, the family will draw closely together, being almost enmeshed, as they go through the transition as a group. Transitional events can be happy ones, such as births, graduations, and marriages. There are also sad events, such as illness, loss, and death, when the family draws on each other for support, hope, and courage. These are times when the extended family is typically also involved. They know the family secrets, they know the code and the ritual; they subscribe to the same family culture. See (Figure 15–3).

Ideally, the nuclear and the extended families should fulfill some of the following roles:

■ They provide nurture and structure.
■ For growing children in these systems, there is the bond with primary caregivers.
■ They should encourage and support a child's education.
■ The family is the most intimate place, providing stability, shelter, and a sense of belonging.
■ The family provides specific protective factors, such as celebrating and mourning together.
■ Families communicate through the secret and overt codes of the family culture.
■ Families are based on a business model, including financial obligations.
■ Families provide a sense of control and provide the scaffolding upon which to acquire skills.
■ Families provide support that is anchored in a network of traditions.

Emily 9 years old

Emily 13 years old

Emily's drawings depict her nuclear family, which provides nurture, structure, stability, shelter, and a sense of belonging that is essential to healthy socialization. The illustrations were created four years apart and also reflect the developmental changes taking place in Emily's artistic skills.

• •

Guest Reflections 15–1

Of Time and Children

As one rabbi recently said, "Happy weddings are a dime a dozen. Happy marriages barely exist."

With this in mind, I gave my oldest daughter away this year. I approached the wedding day with joy but also a little trepidation. How could my wife and I entrust our precious first born to another adult for a lifetime? What could we do to make her marriage and her full launch into adulthood as successful as ours had been? The answer I found was to focus on the long "process of marriage" rather than the event of the wedding. Remember: happy weddings are a dime a dozen.

Our daughter's journey toward marriage started more than 20 years ago. When our children were very young, it occurred to me that there is no such thing as "quality time." So many people talk about spending "quality time" with their children. It's as if we can balance out with "quality time" all the time we spend doing other things—like chasing jobs, buying cars, and paying mortgages. How do you place a value on "quality time"? At what level of richness does time become "quality"?

Newsflash: children don't understand the concept of "quality time." To them, there is only quantity time. As a result of this approach, I was able to take a long view of my daughter's transition to life as an adult. I realized that her transition to independence and adulthood was a continuation of my transition to adulthood and everything that came with it. Pushing her in a stroller through the neighborhood, driving her to school every morning, attending numerous choir concerts, helping her study for exams, moving her into the dorm at college were all part of the process of her marriage to another. Simply put, we were preparing her to move on.

When the wedding ceremony took place, nothing was "over." The event simply took its place on the continuum of life's transitions—the "process of marriage." Now that she is blooming with emotional and intellectual independence, our quantity time is of course less—as it should be. It is time for her to pass on the gift of quantity time with someone else.

David S. Shipley, Ph.D.
Assoc. Professor, Journalism and Mass Communication.
Samford University
Used with permission.

• •

The Power of Social and Civic Connectedness

Families and the children within families are more resilient if they can access and belong to organizations that emphasize social connectedness and promote civic engagement. These organizations can model appropriate behavior, provide a sense of belonging, and allow the children and the family to address developmental challenges while having a peer group for support as role models and as a reality check.

Schools are not only places of learning. They are social laboratories in which to learn how to connect interpersonally with peers and adults. Parents who become actively involved in their children's schools may find good connections with fellow parents that provide support and extend the child's social network. Any organization that promotes appropriate social engagement can act as a support system to the family and strengthen parent–child relations. A sense of belonging is an important component of the social nature of the family. Families will choose those settings that best meet their needs and where they, too, can contribute to the fabric of society. Such settings include youth groups, social support groups, cultural organizations, volunteer opportunities, after school centers, and places of worship and communities with religious values.

School based prevention programs can be very successful, as they provide social and educational contexts, and peer feedback can be harnessed for a good cause. Anti-bullying programs had remarkably positive outcomes if social opinion leaders were involved. Similarly, programs designed to reduce aggressive behavior and focus on appropriate self-regulation and social information processing promised improved outcomes for participants (Terzian, Li, Fraser, Day, & Rose, 2015). Any time a social environment is used optimally it can mitigate and envelop the participating child with buffers.

Research in the field of psychology indicates that the sense of knowing there is concern and empathy from peers is an important part of getting support. A load shared is a load halved. Families who do not have extended family support nearby may form alliances with several other families who are facing similar challenges. They become each others' family and the children know that there are persons other than their parents who will look out for them.

In unfortunate situations where children and youth do not feel safe within their own homes, National Safe Place (based in the United States) has made it their mission to provide places of safety and shelter to support adolescents and to "create a safety net for youth" (www.nationalsafeplace.org). Typically, these shelters can be found at fire stations, police stations, schools, libraries, grocery stores, public transit, YMCAs, and other youth-friendly businesses. They are clearly identified by a yellow-and-black, diamond-shaped Safe Place sign. These sites are supported by qualified agencies that provide social services and trained volunteers.

Severe and frequent stress, experienced both in the formative years and in adulthood, can have ripple effects affecting many other areas of functioning. Despite these adverse influences, the sunnier side of the picture reveals that there is no expiration date when it comes to extending core capabilities in adults, as these investments translate into their parenting skills and influence the younger generation (Center on the the Developing Child at Harvard University, 2016b). Two among several desirable qualities that will serve adults well in their parenting tasks, are self-regulation and executive function. Self-regulation in adults is similar to how it presents in children and it refers to a cluster of processes including the ability to postpone immediate rash and impulsive behavior to focus on the better outcome. It also implies that we can postpone immediate need gratification to work toward the better long term outcome. In terms of parenting, it translates as not being over-impulsive in discipline. Lashing out in anger can easily escalate to abusive behavior. Additionally, if we can model calm control for our children it tends to defuse a potentially inflammable situation.

Expanding executive skills is important in all walks of life, be it for civic engagement, work situations, or dealings with peers and colleagues. It encompasses several higher order thinking capabilities such as mental flexibility and inhibitory control, a type of self-regulatory behavior which counteracts impulsive spur-of-the-moment decisions which might not represent the best choices in the long term (Harvard, 2016, p. 5). The World Bank (n.d.) in their report on suggestions that may have long ranging influence and effects, also mentions decision making skills which are more thought-through and less impulsive. These, in turn, can influence life decisions and parenting behavior, as well as the aspirations parents have for their children.

The Harvard Report on "Building core capabilities for life" states:

We know from science that it is never too late to help adults build up their core capabilities, and that we can have a lifelong intergenerational impact if adults support the development of these skills in children." (2016a, p. 4).

Search Institute: Developmental Assets

The Search Institute, with its half century history of research, has identified the many and varied "Developmental Assets" children and adolescents require to succeed. They have identified over forty markers and refined these to match different developmental age groups.

The asset areas in Figure 15–2 pertain to adolescents and are grouped into key areas. Similar asset lists are available for other developmental age groups.

EXTERNAL ASSETS
Support: Family support, positive family communication, other adult relationships, caring neighborhood, caring school climate, parent involvement in schooling.
Empowerment: Community values youth, youth as resources, service to others, safety.
Boundaries and Expectations: Family, school and neighborhood boundaries, adult role models, positive peer influence, high expectations.
Constructive Use of Time: Creative activities, youth programs, religious community, time at home.

INTERNAL ASSETS
Commitment to Learning: Achievement motivation, school engagement, homework, bonding to school, reading for pleasure.
Positive Values: Caring, equality and social justice, integrity, honesty, responsibility, restraint.
Social Competencies: Planning and decision making, interpersonal competence, cultural competence, resistance skills, peaceful conflict resolution.
Positive Identity: Personal power, self-esteem, sense of purpose, positive view of personal future.

The complete and detailed lists can be found at: www. search-institute.org. This list is an educational tool. It is not intended to be nor is it appropriate as a scientific measure of the developmental assets of individuals.

FIGURE 15–2.　Search Institute: Developmental Assets for adolescents.

Based on the following source: The Developmental Relationships Framework. Copyright © 2016 Search Institute®, 615 First Avenue NE, Suite 125, Minneapolis, MN 55413; 800-888-7828; www.search-institute.org. All rights reserved.

Research Trends in the Family Sciences

Research on families highlight two important areas, namely *family structure* and *family process*. How our families are changing and evolving affects the children within those family structures. How those families function determines the quality of the relationships that occur within that context. These two areas overlap and influence each other. Five trends in family-related research are (Crosnoe & Cavanagh, 2010):

1. *Research into the meaning of parental behavior.* Two parents may do similar things as part of their parenting behavior, but their motives may differ, and possibly the outcomes may differ. Self-disclosure is a product of positive parenting. Involvement and trust are foundations that develop and contribute to intimacy, which creates a sense of safety that allows disclosure and enhances emotional investment within the family.

2. *Relational components of the parent–child relationship.* Shared family time is important. Shared time is positive for young people if it is actively and purposefully chosen and does not occur merely by default. Less family time signals problems if it is a symptom of disengagement. Even adolescents and young adults want some family time, although their developmental needs may determine different types of shared activities. Family time is also reflected in the sharing of family meals and the celebration of rituals, events, and personally significant moments together. Parents do indeed learn from relationships and seem to parent better with subsequent children as reflected by chosen time spent together.

3. *Importance of the father's role.* Fathers are becoming increasingly visible, partaking in various roles, such as stepparenting, cohabiting, and adopting multiple father roles for different children in different contexts. The link between the father's involvement and parenting outcomes is of great importance. By the same token, absent fathers escalate problems in single-parent families.

4. *Unique strengths and qualities.* The research is no longer simply dividing ethnicities or races by contrasting or comparing one group with another. Instead, there is an acknowledgment of specific strengths and unique qualities within the groups. Cultural expectations and strengths, as well as challenges stemming from the assimilation and blending of cultural heritage, address challenges that immigrant populations may face. With almost 20 percent of children having one foreign-born parent, this affects a much larger group than previously anticipated.

5. *Exploring diversity within general patterns of parent–child relationships.* Increasingly, we respect the many ways that diverse groups parent. There may be differences in terms of timing, what is done when, and qualitative differences. Acknowledgment of the validity of different parental practices with differing outcomes add to the complexity of the unique parent–child relationship.

Select Global Initiatives for Young People

With regard to research that pertains to global development and the empowerment of the next generation, some meaningful suggestions have been made (The World Bank, n.d., http://www.worldbank.org/):

■ *Civic engagement: Be a part of the solution, not a part of the problem.* Expand opportunities for developing and engaging human capital. This is done by focusing on education and health care, and facilitating employment planning. The fresh element added to this mix is to involve youth in this planning, making their voices heard, because they need to be emotionally vested in these civic actions to ensure greater success rates. Young people need to feel that they are a *part of the solution*, and they need opportunities to participate in contexts where their input is valued. They need to feel that they are part of the initiative and the change. If we fail to do this, the younger generation will misread well-intended interventions as yet another form of authority, and the youth may rebel.

■ *Empowerment through constructive decision-making skills.* Develop leadership skills in the younger generation, and guide them to choose well among the given choices. Their decision-making skills require strengthening so that when they do come to a fork in the road, they will choose the constructive option. They need to understand what is involved in decision making and the *consequences and outcomes*. They need to be well informed, have sufficient resources, and a sense of civic engagement. Hopefully, these principles come into play when young people face health- and lifestyle-related choices, such as the decision not to smoke or binge drink, and to adopt safe and responsible sexual practices. By empowering young people through the development of their decision-making skills, they will feel that they have control over their lives by making better decisions (World Bank, 2016).

■ *Second chances and a purposeful life.* Develop a system of *second chances* that works hand in hand with rehabilitation. If young people have made mistakes, there needs to be a way back into the system through programs that target young people who have made poor choices or have had bad luck. Given another opportunity, they may regain a sense of hope and purpose.

Policies and Programs

Several initiatives focus on improving outcomes for young people. The Harvard University: Center for the Developing Child (2016b) has published core principles which serve to inform policymakers and facilitate program development. Greater details can be found in their report: "From best practices to breakthrough impacts" (2016). Here is a summary of the cornerstone areas, quoting the five subheadings verbatim (printed in bold and in quotes), as provided in the report (2016b, pp. 20–29):

■ *"Build caregiver skills":* Provide the appropriate support to those who care for children, be they parents, educators, or other childcare related professionals. Design programs that support these roles and persons and provide linked professional development opportunities. Centers that offer child focused services, like child care and educational settings, could also provide opportunities for parent engagement and the opportunity to build skills and find support. Pay attention to those groups facing difficult situations in childcare, such as challenging behavior.

■ *"Match interventions to sources of significant stress":* Some families face stressful situations that exceed the resources of the individual family. Examples are families dealing with poverty, a special needs child, and parents or caregivers who themselves have to deal with mental problems, such as chronic depression or social isolation. Other specific challenges can comprise parents with addiction disorders and substance abuse, child maltreatment, and intimate partner violence.

■ *"Support the health and nutrition of children and mothers before, during, and after pregnancy":* pre-, peri-, and postnatal care deserves intensified efforts as these are crucial periods of development, also in terms of epigenetics, and can influence future outcomes. Incorporation of the latest scientific and medical findings should guide interventions and support.

■ *"Improve the quality of the broader caregiving environment":* The settings and the people providing childcare are very varied in terms of context and persons providing the care. This group has the potential of initiating positive life outcomes, and better outcomes are associated with stable and responsive childcare. The characteristics of the care are more important than where that care is provided; hence, high quality stable childcare environments can support parents who work full time and rely on childcare outside the home.

■ *"Establish clear goals and appropriately targeted curricula":* All children benefit from curricula built on insights from best educational practices. These learning situations allow for optimal brain development during critical periods and form the foundation for later learning and life. Children vary in the care and attention they receive in their home environments. Quality childcare can endeavor to bridge some of the shortcomings experienced by families facing a variety of stressful challenges.

Focus Point. As the culture shifts, so does the structure of the family. More women are now part of the workforce, and fathers are taking on greater responsibilities in parenting and homemaking. While all relationships have conflict, families of low socioeconomic status often feel the effects of dissension to a greater extent than those with more resources. The level to which families are invested in their communities also has a large impact on the resilience of each member.

Core Concepts

Serve-and-return

■ Children thrive in environments where they are acknowledged, supported, and valued. Children's brains are wired to be appropriately stimulated, and they need to be able to initiate as well as respond in an ongoing feedback loop; give and take, "serve-and-return." Variations of neglect cause harm that will destabilize the child in immediate and later contexts. On the positive side, neighborhood social influences and extended relationships with meaningful mentors can act as buffers and contribute to resilience.

Risk and resilience

■ Resilience can be regarded as a process which involves a number of attributes including qualities such as self-regulation, focus, social problem-solving skills, competence, a sense of humor, motivation to adapt, the ability to delay gratification, and more. These factors support the process of resilience, although in some contexts these seemingly everyday, yet valuable, assets may require extraordinary determination to take effect. Appropriate responsiveness by parents ranks high among the parenting traits that are likely to elicit resilient behavior in children. An appropriate response is a reply to a cue that the child emits and continues into behaviors that seek to fulfil the requirements of the child appropriately and in a timely manner.

Promoting good parenting

■ Parenting is embedded within the family, which, in turn, is cushioned by societal institutions like educational facilities, places of civic engagement, centers for religious life, and many more. This collection is nested within the larger society, which exerts societal values and pressures. Both risks and protective factors exert an influence during childhood. Individual, interpersonal, and social factors, as well as environmental factors, interact. It is a similar approach to that of Urie Bronfenbrenner's ecological model in which influential factors can operate in micro, meso, exo, and macro systems.

Supporting good parent–child relations

■ To maintain stability in the family unit, access to family support is an important strategy. That, in turn, is linked to health-promoting behaviors and general well-being. If families are systems, and the members of each system are influenced by each other, then it follows that the support of the family enables us to be more effective in our parent–child relations.

Grandparents and siblings

■ Even though the parents are the primary coaches, there is so much value in intergenerational parenting and many grandparents can play an active role in family relationships while also sharing some of the childcare roles. Siblings, too, can be a stabilizing factor for children. Later in life, the siblings become the reference group that uniquely understands how it was growing up in the family of origin. They are the support when parents fall away.

FINAL THOUGHTS

When best parenting practices are examined with a special focus on risk and resilience perspectives, it is apparent that in the United States, a number of major initiatives address the diverse challenges faced by parents and their children. Numerous public, educational, and social policies place the family into contexts that attempt to anchor and engage family life in civic networks that endeavor to cushion and sustain.

We have an outstanding network of information available in the public domain through websites maintained by major professional organizations and charitable foundations. Much of the research and the multitude of reports published on these websites and elsewhere point us in the right direction. Numerous gifted researchers have given these challenging questions their attention and have come up with tentative suggestions. We have learned from our past, both in terms of best practices and from outcome-based interventions.

Many systems interact to form a basis for good parenting. Parental love and structure may be a starting point, but it may not be strong enough to overcome the challenges of economic survival. Smaller families make it possible to give children the quality care and nurture they deserve for a better future, using the available resources. Families are culturally anchored and in some ways they differ widely. But in other ways they face the same challenges of providing support and nurture to offspring. These goals are universal for all parents, regardless of their resources.

Ultimately, many facets of the future of humankind lie within the sacred bonds of kinship and civic responsibility. Can we learn from best practices in other contexts, are there ways in which we can empower and support the building blocks of society, namely the family? As we are educating the next generation of parent

Many geographical, cultural, ethnic, and other variables contribute to childhoods that are unique, while also displaying a universal quality. We do well striving toward best outcomes, as families represent our hope for the future.

Dashu Xinganling/Shutterstock

educators, we hope that they, too, will venture toward securing improved outcomes for children and their parents.

After all, public wisdom tells us that there is no better investment than allocating appropriate resources to our children, who, in turn, hold the promise of becoming the next generation of parents.

CHAPTER FOCUS POINTS

Creating Optimal Environments

■ Childhood resilience can be cultivated in the face of adversity, especially if a caregiver exhibits healthy coping strategies. An environment lacking stress also contributes to the forming of resilience. Good parent–child relationships are fostered when both quality *and* quantity of time are invested by the parents.

The Risk and Resilience Model

■ Parenting is largely impacted by (and, in turn, impacts) a range of outside influences, from children's school teachers to the state of the economy.

When an outside source introduces negativity or adversity, protective factors such as safety and nurture act as buffers to foster resilience in both individuals and family units.

Enhancing Individual Resilience

■ A good education can bolster resilience and fight poverty. Unfortunately, the quality of available education is often linked to one's socioeconomic status. Parenting also plays a substantial role in education, as encouraging words or acts exhibited by parents can help instill an appreciation for, and love of, learning in their children.

Enhancing Family Resilience

■ As the culture shifts, so does the structure of the family. More women are now part of the workforce, and fathers are taking on greater responsibilities in parenting and homemaking. While all relationships have conflict, families of low socioeconomic status often feel the effects of dissension to a greater extent than those with more resources. The level to which families are invested in their communities also has a large impact on the resilience of each member.

USEFUL WEBSITES

Websites are dynamic and change

The Annie E. Casey Foundation
www.aecf.org
Economic opportunities

Big Brothers Big Sisters of America
www.bbbs.org
Mentorship, enhancing self-esteem

The Bill and Melinda Gates Foundation
www.gatesfoundation.org
Global support, major health and other initiatives

Center on the Developing Child at Harvard University
www.developingchild.harvard.edu
Child development initiatives, best practices, and break-through impacts

Child Welfare Information Gateway, Administration for Children and Families, U.S. Department of Health and Human Services
www.childwelfare.gov
Child Welfare, family and caretaker support

Communities in Schools
www.communitiesinschools.org
Encouraging youths to complete their education and graduate

Healthy Marriage Initiative, Administration for Children and Families, U.S. Department of Health and Human Services
www.acf.hhs.gov/healthymarriage
Family assistance

Jumpstart
www.jstart.org
Building language and literacy skills. Provides books to underserved communities.

National Fatherhood Initiative
www.fatherhood.org
Fatherhood support

National Head Start Association
www.nhsa.org
Family empowerment initiative, family learning

National Responsible Fatherhood Clearinghouse
www.fatherhood.gov
Fatherhood support

National Safe Place
www.nationalsafeplace.org
Response for youth in crises

Search Institute
www.search-institute.org
Discovering what kids need to succeed

Teach for America
www.teachforamerica.org
Impacting under-resourced youth, teaching in under-served schools

W.K. Kellogg Foundation
www.wkkf.org
Resources for early childhood

YMCA of the USA
www.ymca.net
Youth development, healthy living, social responsibility

Glossary

CHAPTER 1

Bidirectional The flow of influence goes both ways, or in both directions; adults and children influence each other; parents and their offspring have mutual influence.

Binuclear families allow children to have access to two families, typically each family living in their own household. Usually as a result of parental divorce.

Coparents take on permanent and semi-permanent roles with a serious commitment to a child's upbringing. Coparents are characterized by two factors: executive function and an emotional attachment/commitment to the child they coparent.

Coparenting A very legitimate caretaking system born out of the need to ensure constructive outcomes for parenting challenges while also keeping the best interests of the child in mind. For the child it ensures ongoing access to a figure who is committed to taking on parental responsibilities.

Developmental the changes that parents and children undergo with time- and lifespan progressions.

Ecological approach The interrelatedness of individuals, families, and other social groups as seen within changing environmental systems with bidirectional influence. Members of a family can be perceived as forming a system.

Family systems theory The family can be perceived as a unit or system. The relationship between parents and children is a subsystem of the larger social system that we call a family. Family systems theory describes family functioning in ways that resemble other systems found in nature.

Lifespan the anticipated journey from conception to death; it stretches over the time period of an individual's life.

Nuclear family The smallest unit of a family living together. Typically this excludes the extended family members, who do not share the same household.

Parental dyad Usually the two persons at the head of the household, who act as parents to a child in that family.

Parents Two people, as part of a family system, who take on the responsibility of raising children. Parenthood can occur in diverse contexts. Traditionally it referred to a man and a woman who produced offspring together, but the definition now includes a much wider range of possibilities.

Parenthood The responsibility of parents for nurturing, teaching, and acting as guardians for their children until they reach the age of legal maturity. Parenthood is a developmental role that changes over time, usually in response to the evolving developmental needs of both the children as well as the parents.

polygamy involves a marriage that may include several adults, as opposed to two persons as typically represented in a legal marriage agreement.

Subsystem A subsystem is a microcosm of the larger family system that mirrors the functioning of this group.

Unidirectional model of socialization typically represents an adult assuming responsibility. The flow of information is predominantly from parent to child and provides the adult with significant power over the child. In contrast, the subordinated child lacks social power. This can be a characteristic of an authoritarian parenting style.

CHAPTER 2

Abusive parents harm children emotionally, physically, and even sexually. These parents were often abused by their own parents and are prone to repeating such actions. Professionals working with families and children have a mandatory duty to report suspected or actual abuse.

Authoritarian parenting This parenting style uses control and social power over children's behavior and is anchored in traditional methods and ideologies of child-rearing. It is characterized by high structure, and low nurture.

Authoritative parenting The most favored parenting style. It represents a balance of structure and nurture. This parenting style tends to promote children who are self-reliant, self-controlled, content, and curious about learning and exploring their environment.

Cognitive Behavioral Approaches connect elements of cognition (thinking) and behavior (expressive actions), to help both parents and their children reframe their thinking and restructure their actions.

Constructive Criticism providing positive comment or correction with good outcomes in mind.

Corporal punishment Physical punishment such as spanking, slapping, or hitting, applied as a form of discipline. In most contexts it is unlawful and is not socially sanctioned. Also refers to physical punishment in an educational setting by teachers or administration; this is typically not tolerated in the United States.

Critical parents interact with children by finding fault, being judgmental and belittling. This tactic is used as a means to gain control over children. It is likely destructive and contains elements of bullying.

Demanding parents typically conduct authoritarian child rearing. They require children to live their lives according to the adult's standards and conform to parental ideas of what is acceptable and appropriate.

Discipline Actions used to guide and shape children. Discipline is most effective when provided to children in a caring, responsive and nurturing environment. Discipline should be developmentally appropriate and constructive.

Disengaged parents are emotionally uninvolved or even absent. These individuals appear to be too busy or self-absorbed to function adequately as parents.

Ineffective parents are incapable of constructively meeting the needs of children and do not accept the range of responsibilities required by responsible parenting.

Multimodal Approaches combine elements of various approaches and theoretical models, to reach best outcomes in an eclectic manner.

Negative reinforcement A term first described by B. F. Skinner. Negative reinforcement occurs when an unpleasant stimulus is removed or stopped. This, in turn, increases the likelihood of the desired behavior reoccurring or being maintained.

Negotiable Rules flexibility in enforcement of rules; commands can change depending on context.

Nonnegotiable Rules inflexibility in enforcement of rules; commands remain constant even in changing contexts.

Nurture relates to all the ways in which we demonstrate love, not only for others, but also for ourselves. Nurturing behavior represents actions that are emotionally replenishing, and represent caring in healthy and appropriate ways.

Overfunctioning parents can be overprotective. This behavior sends consistent messages to children concerning their ineptitude and can hinder the normal progression towards appropriate autonomy.

Parenting styles Approaches to parenting, used in shaping children's developmental behaviors. These styles can range from low to high in structure, as well as low to high in nurture.

Permissiveness lenient and very flexible parenting where the child is given free reign, while the adult provides minimal structure or guidance.

Permissive parenting An indulgent style that displays nurture without the benefit of accompanying structure. This approach avoids excessive control, does not enforce obedience to externally defined standards, and basically allows children to regulate their own activities. In so doing, it can encourage self-indulgent and poorly regulated behavior.

Positive parental discipline is a parental approach that focuses on and predominantly uses positive and constructive methods in providing guidance and hence discipline.

Positive reinforcement A reward that immediately follows a positive behavior, strengthens or reinforces that desired behavior and increases the likelihood that a particular behavior will occur again. Example: praising a child for using good table manners.

Reinforcement Literally means "to strengthen." It is a way to strengthen or maintain a desired behavior. A reward following a specific behavior increases the likelihood that that behavior will reoccur. There are two types of reinforcements. Positive reinforcement and negative reinforcement.

Relationship-based approaches apply principles used in counseling and are characterized by active listening and respectful dialogue.

Relationship-based parenting approaches focus on listening and communication skills. Many basic principles in counseling are applied to parent-child communications.

Responsive care A parent can provide care for a child's needs because of the feedback loop between parent and child. This involves noticing and listening to the child and understanding the cues and requests that the child offers; or appropriately *responding* to the child.

Social Learning Approaches use positive alternatives to traditionally punitive inputs. Can include modeling, and strengthening appropriate and desired behavior.

Social learning based approaches are based on principles that include use of positive reinforcement, negotiation, and finding alternatives to punishment. It can also include modeling behavior by example, and creating an environment with positive social cues and feedback. It uses the social interaction between the parent/caretaker and the child to facilitate constructive learning outcomes.

Social learning theory This theory is based on the work of Albert Bandura. It explores socialization and how appropriate behaviors are learned through modeling. The individual responds to a number of unique and complex stimuli in forming associations between appropriate and inappropriate behaviors. Conscious thoughts, rather than an automatic response to a stimulus, assist in shaping behaviors and actions.

Structure is provided through the internalized boundaries and controls that people acquire through socialization experiences which guide their behavior. Appropriate structure in combination with appropriate nurture, are the cornerstones of good parent-child relations.

Uninvolved parenting An emotionally absent or disengaged parenting style. These parents do not provide much input; neither positive nor negative. In an extreme form this can be a variation of neglect.

CHAPTER 3

Collectivism A cultural trait that emphasizes interdependence of a larger community. Collectivism is frequently associated with cultural groups in Asia.

Culture An expression of what individuals and families value. It provides guidelines and contexts to social behavior, through customs, beliefs, rituals and more. Culture is a virtual shorthand between persons sharing the same cultural context. It is not static; it can change and there is a bidirectional influence between a culture and those subscribing to that cultural content.

Ethnic identity This concept is closely related to cultural, racial and group identity and contains elements of these concepts. It can refer to how one sees oneself and subgroup identification. In the context of the family, it is an ecological factor that influences how most family systems are organized and function.

Globalization The increasing interconnectedness worldwide. Globalization is a flexible and evolving process that defies a tight and permanent definition. Currently, it appears to be a progressive process, as nations become more connected and communicate more easily across borders and cultures.

Individualism A cultural trait that values the person and what can be accomplished on one's own. Individual identity, autonomy, self-expression, and self-actualization are valued. Individualism is frequently associated with the mainstream North American cultural context.

Parent-child relationship A relationship that mirrors the larger family process and in turn aspects of cultural norms. This relationship provides an opportunity for psychosocial development for both the participating child and the parent. It is a developmental process and tends to represent a lifelong commitment.

Socialization The set of interpersonal processes through which cultural meaning and social values are evolved and passed on. It allows participants to blend, understand and function well within a given interpersonal or social context.

CHAPTER 4

Attachment theory Initially based on the work of John Bowlby, Mary Ainsworth and others. It presumes that children brought up with consistent, loving parents or significant, reliable caregivers can develop a foundation of trust and attachment and can grow up to be well-adjusted adults, capable of forming trusting and loving relationships. If for any reason the stability is interrupted, problems can manifest. The first two years of life are particularly important for the formation of attachment.

Behavior modification *See* operant conditioning.

Bidirectional Influence and interchange occurs and flows in both directions; it is a back and forth or reciprocal influence. It can occur between individuals, subsystems, and systems.

Chronosystem Refers to the time dimension within the ecological systems model and encompasses the entire network of other systems. This time context involves the organization of events and changes over the lifespan of an individual at a particular historical time. A cohort who for example lived during a major war, are linked through their experiences of living in that particular time period. Some cohorts move through time as a group; for instance, the Baby Boomers or the Millennials.

Cognitive theory A theoretical approach that explains how people acquire thought processes and problem-solving abilities, in addition to organizing and using information. In short, it refers to the thinking dimension, as related to an aspect of the brain's functioning.

Contact comfort An infant's need for soft, comforting, nurturing sensations provided by a caregiver. For newborns parents are encouraged to provide skin-to-skin contact, as it soothes the infant and promotes attachment and bonding.

Developmental interaction (developmental parenting) Interactions or social relationships that change as the child along with the parent progresses through lifespan stages. Thus, the relationship is never static or the same. These represent developmental lifespan differences. Developmental parenting implies parenting that acknowledges the lifespan stage of the child and is appropriate for that particular age group.

Dynamic Refers to movement or change. In constructive contexts, these changes will contribute to better outcomes, and hence appropriate family adaptation or stability.

Ecological systems theory Proposed by Urie Bronfenbrenner. Different environments affect individual and family functioning, including parent-child relations. Bronfenbrenner's theory represents interrelated nested systems, with bidirectional influence. Starting with the individual and her family, then circle outward to extended social influences and ultimately the social culture within which a nation is embedded.

Exosystem This layer in Bronfenbrenner's model acts as the buffer zone between the inner circles known to the individual and society at large (macrosystem).

Explicit rules Known, stated, and outlined clearly; rules that all people in the family know and understand. Can also be referred to as overt rules.

Harlow Monkey Experiments A study done by Harry Harlow that explored the dependency of monkeys on their mothers. The monkeys preferred the more tactile softer surrogate monkey frames for comfort, and only went to the wire mesh surrogates for food. The presumption underlines the social and tactile needs of infant primates. These experiments are thought to have contributed to the implementation of rules guiding the ethical treatment of laboratory animals.

Implicit rules   Unspoken and often inferred from nonverbal behavior. Not usually discussed openly, yet everyone is expected to know and obey these rules. Can also be referred to as covert rules.

Little Albert   A case study in the 1920's by psychologist John B. Watson, showing the effects of generalization of conditioned responses on the subject "Little Albert." Important long-term outcomes of this experiment were the subsequent implementation of stringent ethical guidelines concerning experimentation with children.

Macrosystem   The largest context of the nested layers that affect an individual. The influence is often indirect. This environment involves the larger culture in which the individual lives and encompasses all the other systems. It can for instance include values and policies on a national scale.

Mesosystem   This is the middle layer sandwiched between the smallest (micro) and the outer (exo) layers. It functions to connect the structures in the child's world. For instance, the teachers and the parents could be connected to each other through the mesosystem, yet both have an influence on the child.

Microsystem   The innermost and smallest setting in which a child is embedded. This is comprised of the very personal influences and environments provided by immediate family and to an extent peers, a school, or a neighborhood.

Negotiable rules   Flexible enforcement of rules by parents which can be contested by children. The context will typically determine whether negotiation is feasible and appropriate.

Nonnegotiable rules   Rigid enforcement that cannot be contested. These rules might require children to always inform parents of their whereabouts when away from home. Rules that concern the safety of children are non-negotiable in that they cannot be broken or changed without consequences.

Operant conditioning   is a powerful tool that parents can use to shape children's behavior. It can occur by using rewards (positive) or punishment (negative). Both these inputs can strengthen the desired behavioral outcome because an association is formed between the behavior and the consequence.

psychosocial crisis   Erikson suggests a developmental theme or challenge requiring resolution within each of the eight life stages described in his theory. If resolved constructively it enhances a person's ability to confront the challenges of the next stage. If not resolved it hinders progression.

Readiness   biological, social, and psychological readiness facilitates further progression on the developmental path, and is significantly influenced by social environment.

Scaffolding   Any parental behavior that supports a child's effort towards more advanced skill acquisition and competency.

Significant others   persons who are singularly important to an individual and assist or inhibit the developmental progress at each life stage.

Social learning theory   This theory explains how learning and socialization may occur when there is no visible reinforcer or reward. Typically, modeling and imitation play an important role, and learning appropriate behaviors based on family beliefs and values are attributed to this process.

Sociocultural theory   Based on the work of Lev Vygotsky. This approach emphasizes the social and cultural aspects of cognitive development. The values and beliefs within a group are important in co-determining what happens between people.

Systemic family development theory   A model that describes how families change over time. This systemic model proposes that families are both similar and diverse in their intergenerational composition and functioning. Just as an individual changes in responses to lifespan development, a family unit or system can change over the lifespan of that family and its members.

Zone of proximal development (ZPD)   This concept supports the child's learning potential. It emphasizes the interpersonal context in which learning occurs by implying that learning is a shared experience. A supportive interaction creates a 'zone' or area in which one can safely learn. Proximal refers to closeness. Combined the words refer to a close area or space, in which the child can learn optimally because she is supported and feels safe.

CHAPTER 5

Age of majority   In the eyes of the law, the age at which a child is treated as an adult, and assumes adult responsibilities. The age of majority in the United States is typically 18, but some states extend it to the age of 21.

Beneficence   The principle of best interests regarding the child, the child's wellbeing, and the wellbeing of the larger context of family and society. It can imply the concept "Best Interests of the Child." Literally, it contains the same root ("Bene") as the word "beneficial," meaning "good" in a specific context.

Collaborative divorce   is a more recent approach to resolving conflicts in family law. It allows divorcing couples to negotiate and work together in finding solutions and best outcomes. It is the opposite of an adversarial or acrimonial split, where couples fight and are vindictive. Clearly a collaborative divorce is preferable if children are involved.

Convention on the Rights of the Child   A document drafted by the United Nations Children's Fund (UNICEF, 1959) and formally adopted in 1990. This document reflects a concern with the global well-being of children and is an intentional approach to create and maintain a comprehensive national agenda for children. The rights address the best interests of the children, the protection of rights, nondiscrimination, parental guidance, and survival and development of these minors.

Legal custody   Typically, custody decisions are awarded by a court of law. It refers to decision making and responsibilities concerning the major aspects of a child's life such as medical, educational, religious, and extracurricular activities. Legal custody can be granted to one parent or shared by both parents as in dual-custody arrangements and are determined by what would serve the best interests of the child.

Maleficence   Harm or evil done to a child, the child's wellbeing, or the wellbeing of the larger context of family and society.

Mediation   is a process in which couples negotiate and work together to create a parenting plan, divide the family assets, and settle other post-divorce issues with the facilitation of a trained neutral third person, the mediator.

Nonmaleficence   Inflicting or doing no harm; typically used in ethical contexts.

Parallel parenting   Co-parenting with limited contact between each parent. Communication is usually by email or through a third party. In a very high conflict situation, this approach to parenting may be the safest and preferred way for a child to have access to both parents.

Physical custody   refers to where and with which parent a child will live.

Putative father   An alleged father of a child, but without legal determination of paternity.

Responsibilities (of parenting)   Upheld by laws that hold parents accountable for meeting the basic needs of their children. These laws are mostly at the state level, but federal legislation has provisions for state adherence in areas of child abuse, foster care, child support, education, and interstate custodial issues.

Right (to parent)   Parental rights including health care, education, religious affiliation, extra-curricular activities, and the like. It embodies much more than just the right to decide with whom a child may visit.

Visitation rights   Legally mandated access and right of parents to spend specific times with their child, if they do not have physical custody of that child.

CHAPTER 6

Disinhibited Social Engagement Disorder   An attachment disorder that is characterized by indiscriminate, random or impulsive attachment. The disinhibited social behavior can be characterized by repeated violations of conventional interpersonal boundaries. This disorder can form in children who have experienced traumatic or neglected early childhoods.

Family of creation   Also known as 'family of procreation' and 'family of making'. This denotes the union of individuals with the intent of creating a family, typically sharing a household.

Foster parents   Individuals who raise or offer a temporary home to children. Prospective foster parents may be single or married, come from all social backgrounds, undergo foster care and parenting training, have no criminal record or history of child maltreatment, and have an income. The latter reduces the risk of fostering for the wrong reasons. Fostering is temporary, in contrast to adoption which is a permanent and legally binding commitment.

Inter-national adoption (also known as *inter-country adoption*) Adoption that occurs outside the United States. These adoptions are noted for their high risk and difficulty, because transnational welfare practices are not universal. Also referred to as international adoptions.

Miscarriage Also known as spontaneous abortion. These are terms used for a pregnancy that spontaneously ends within the first 20 weeks of gestation, although most miscarried pregnancies end within the first trimester.

Postpartum depression A type of clinical depression can arise post-childbirth and can include feelings of not wanting to provide care for the infant, severe mood swings, continual fatigue, lack of joy in life, and/or withdrawal from relationships. This is a serious condition that requires medical intervention. If postpartum depression goes unacknowledged and untreated, there can be very serious repercussions for both the mother and the infant.

Postpartum psychosis A serious psychiatric condition that can cause mothers who suffer from this disease to lose contact with reality. Delusions and hallucinations can occur. Some mothers with this disease have harmed their children and themselves during psychotic episodes.

Rainbow baby A healthy baby following a previous infant loss or miscarriage.

Reactive Attachment Disorder An attachment disorder that is characterized by withdrawn behavior and restricted positive affect. This disorder can occur in children who have been subjected to traumatic or neglected early childhoods. This has been known to occur in inter-country or international adoptions where early childhood experiences of emotional trauma and neglect were present.

Role strain occurs when adults attempt to succeed at a multitude of social roles. It can lead to overload as they are trying to juggle various roles.

Transracial Adoption (also referred to as *Interracial adoption*) The placement of a child from one racial or ethnic group, with parents of another racial or ethnic group.

CHAPTER 7

Attachment An attraction to someone based on psychological bonding. It is also described as a strong affectionate tie between infants and their primary caregivers. Attachment is important in establishing an infant's sense of basic trust in people and the environment, and feeling secure in exploring the environment. There are several types of attachment: secure attachment, insecure/avoidant attachment, insecure/resistant attachment, and disorganized attachment.

Cognitive development As it pertains to intellectual capabilities. Jean Piaget is known for his theory of cognitive development. The current thinking about cognitive development includes emphasis on neuropsychology. Parents and caregivers play a big role in facilitating cognitive development by providing "serve and return" loops. The process is bidirectional in that all participating parties initiate actions which require appropriate responses.

Infancy is the period of the lifespan that extends between birth and the first year following birth.

Nonaccidental trauma (nonaccidental injury) The most common cause of mortality and morbidity associated with child abuse or maltreatment. This type of trauma or injury is willfully inflicted.

Self efficacy refers to the ability of the child to manage certain tasks independently and age appropriately.

Self regulation refers to the ability to appropriately manage emotions, also in an age-appropriate manner.

Sucking reflex One of the earliest reflexes to appear during prenatal development. This reflex is easily elicited by almost any stimulation to the lips, cheeks, or mouth area, and ensures the infant can obtain nourishment for example by nursing.

Toileting The act of going to the bathroom and using the toilet versus being in a diaper. Toileting usually begins between 19 and 30 months of age and is typically completed by 36 months.

CHAPTER 8

Aggression A hostile action that can elicit fear. Aggression can be verbal and/or physical.

Gender identity The knowledge or assigned role associated with a specific gender. Traditionally this was thought of as either male or female. Gender identity tends to be used in psychological, cultural and sociological contexts, as opposed to sexual identity, which tends to focus on the genetic and anatomical identifiers.

Gender roles A set of stereotypes or roles specific to gender that represent what it means to be male or female. These roles/stereotypes can vary from one culture or sociological context to another. Contributing factors to a child's gender are multifactorial.

Montessori approach (to schooling) Based on the work of Italian educator Maria Montessori. This approach emphasizes the independence and autonomy of the child within a developmentally appropriate context. Complex tasks are broken down into simple, easy-to-follow educational steps. Children can pace themselves.

Reggio Emilia approach (to schooling) Named after an Italian village where the first preschool was located, that was based on the methods and philosophy of Italian educator Loris Malaguzzi. This approach emphasizes that children should be actively engaged and have control over their learning, which is facilitated using their five senses. Relationships with other children are encouraged to support opportunities for self-expression.

Sexuality refers to the broad aspects of sexual interest, attitudes, and activities that are an expression of a person's total being. Sexuality plays a significant psychological role throughout an individual's lifespan, not just following puberty.

Socialization refers to the process of acquiring personal values, attitudes and behaviors that reflect the demands of the cultural environment. Parents and teachers take an active role in facilitating socialization in preschoolers.

Temper tantrums A reaction to over stimulation or exhaustion. There are two aspects of a tantrum. 1) Intense frustration that can be linked to kicking, yelling, screaming, throwing objects, or pulling things over. 2) Seeking comfort through whimpering and sadness. These aspects are not necessarily sequential but they can occur together. As self-regulation improves, temper tantrums may lessen.

Toxic parenting Adult caregivers who exhibit negligence or destructive interactional patterns, potentially scarring and traumatizing those in their care.

Waldorf approach (to schooling) Based on the teachings of the founder of anthroposophy, Rudolf Steiner, and popular in the early 1900's. Children are encouraged to develop critical thinking skills and empathic understanding. This approach presumes that the child has multiple intelligences which need to be addressed and stimulated.

CHAPTER 9

Antisocial behaviors promote ill will, interfere with effective communication and interaction, constitute negative ways of getting attention, and serve as a means of expressing anger and hostility. They can also be an attempt to cope with frustration and anxiety.

Bullying Teasing/harassment that occurs predominantly during the school-aged years. Individuals are victimized, especially if they seem vulnerable and defenseless. The predators often act in groups. Schools should have zero tolerance for bullying.

Childhood obesity A condition that is becoming more prevalent in middle-childhood, often combined with lack of exercise. Ethnic heritage can play a role in obesity, especially related to cultural food practices. Socioeconomic class, knowledge about and access to healthy nutrition, and parental role modeling represent powerful contributory influences.

Co-regulation is exerted by parents of children, specifically middle-aged children. The parents guide the children towards regulation or age-appropriate control of emotions in socially appropriate ways. Parents can anticipate difficulties and mediate outcomes making co-regulation successful.

Cyberbullying The relentless harassment, intimidation, humiliation, and tormenting of an individual over the Internet via social media or by use of other digital technologies.

Emotional intelligence is expressed through social interactions and social insight. Parents play an important role in supporting and modeling these skills.

Exceptional This inclusive term can describe potential that ranges over a wide spectrum beyond what is regarded as typical. Children displaying special needs, sensory impairments, as well as students displaying high potential or special talents, are groups that can be described as exceptional.

Exceptional children Children with emotional, developmental, and intellectual disabilities, or learning disorders, which may require a tailored educational approach. Alternatively, children displaying high potential.

Exceptionalities can involve difficulties in visual, auditory, speech, and motor abilities, or in providing self-care that can create unusual demands on educational and family systems, including on parents and educators.

Food insecurity Not knowing where the next meal is coming from. This is more prevalent in the USA than one would intuitively think, despite alarming obesity rates among the general population.

Inclusion Including school-age children with exceptionalities in existing public school programs to the greatest possible extent. Formerly known as mainstreaming.

Lead-parent The parent who is most readily available to meet the day-to-day needs and demands of the child, and for that reason could potentially spend more time with the child.

Neurodevelopmental disorders Disorders with neurobiological and genetic bases. Attention deficit disorder (ADD) and attention deficit/hyperactivity disorder (ADHD) are both neurodevelopmental disorders.

Noncompliance Children who fail to comply with parental requests and who disobey the rules established by the family system.

Peer groups subcultures that form in the middle years of childhood. They can be formed spontaneously, as with neighborhood children who play together, or formally, as when children are grouped by age in elementary school. In the early part of middle childhood, these groups are less structured and adherence is looser. Peer groups help children learn social lessons and can exert a mutual influence on members.

Puberty A period of time that includes developmental events and changes that begin the journey toward sexual maturation, increased maturity and responsibilities. Onset tends to occur at age 10 onward, but for some children it is earlier. Girls tend to be slightly ahead of boys when it comes to the onset of puberty. Puberty refers to the physical changes that accompany the unfolding of sexual maturity.

Respite care A community service for families and individuals with disabilities. It provides temporary relief and emergency care, allowing for self-renewal of caretakers.

Self-regulation the developmental ability to manage and control emotions and urges in socially appropriate ways.

Soft skills Skills that are connected with social interaction and express the emotional intelligence of the child. These interactions include for example good manners, punctuality, a good work ethic, respect and appropriate concern for others.

Special Education is a highly specialized field, helping children with disabilities require professional assessment and interventions.

Talents Special gifts possessed by exceptional children.

Work-family balance allows for and prioritizing family time. While work is important, family should occupy an equally important role.

CHAPTER 10

Anorexia An eating disorder accompanied by body image distortions. It is characterized by starvation resulting in low body mass, and is frequently accompanied by excessive exercising. This serious condition can be life threatening and may require hospitalization.

Adolescence is the stage of the lifespan that represents a transitional period between childhood and adulthood. Chronologically, it begins at age 13 and extends through age 18. The entire period between late childhood and early adulthood could be included and it involves social and emotional aspects, as well as the physical dimension of puberty.

Bulimia An eating disorder in which very large amounts of food are consumed and subsequently purged by vomiting or excessive laxative use. Consumption occurs in periodic binges and during stressful situations as a means of coping. Individuals with bulimia, unlike anorexia, know that their behavior is not healthy; hence they tend to be secretive about it.

Eating disorders A group of mental health disorders that involve distorted body image, accompanied by low self-esteem and weight concerns. Two types of eating disorders are anorexia nervosa and bulimia.

Emerging adulthood Described by psychologist Jeffrey Jensen Arnett, as an additional developmental period that occurs between adolescence and adulthood, ages 18–25. This stage has several defining characteristics including exploring one's identity, focusing on one's self, and feeling emotionally positioned between adolescence and adulthood.

Family climate Describes the well-being of the members of the family on an emotional level. It assesses emotional satisfaction among family members.

Gender dysphoria Occurs when a person's emotional, social, and psychological identity as male/female may not be in agreement with that individual's genetic or anatomical sexual identity.

Individuation An adolescent's transitional journey toward emancipation. For teens this normally includes working, making social decisions, and developmental steps toward maturity and personal autonomy.

Sexually Transmitted Infections (STI's) Also known as Sexually Transmitted Diseases (STDs). These infections/diseases conditions may appear to be silent. These diseases are typically contracted through sexual activities between two or more individuals.

Sexual identity The knowledge or assigned role associated with a specific sex; typically male or female. Sexual identity tends to focus on genetic and anatomical identifiers. Gender identity in contrast, tends to be used in psychological, cultural and sociological contexts.

Sexual orientation is multifactorial and thought to be influenced by interacting genetic, biological, prenatal and environmental factors. Research on this complex topic is ongoing.

CHAPTER 11

Elder abuse The emotional, physical, and/or verbal abuse, or violation of rights, of adults typically during middle and especially late adulthood.

Joint custody Awarding the legal responsibility for child care and supervision to both parents when they divorce.

Sandwich generation The middle generation who care for their own children, as well as for their aging parents. These individuals are responsible for the demands of both the older and the younger generations.

Skipped generation parenting Grandparents who step in for their own children, taking over parental roles for their grandchildren. This can occur because parents are incapacitated, deceased, deployed or otherwise incapable of taking on the full responsibility of raising their own children.

CHAPTER 12

Child abuse Behavior that causes significant psychological and/or physical harm to a child. It includes neglect and situations when someone knowingly fails to prevent serious harm to a child.

Child maltreatment See Child abuse.

Cycle of violence A cycle that can be manifested by individuals who experienced violent and abusive childhoods in their family of origin and who perpetuate this in their own families of creation. A typical three-phase sequence in the expression of violent behavior can occur, beginning with increasing tension, a loss of control accompanied by violent behavior, and finally a reconciliation period of regret and forgiveness, after which the cycle can repeat.

Ecological model A model that explores the child's development within the family system and the family within its larger community. It acknowledges the greater context within which individuals and their families are embedded.

Emotional and verbal abuse Repeatedly rejecting, humiliating, and denying children's worth and rights as human beings. This can occur through critical and hateful verbal engagement, emotional neglect and creating or maintaining an unsafe and threatening environment.

Exchange/social control model A model that suggests that violence occurs in families when this type of behavior is condoned. An example is the reward of violent behavior which might present by assuming superiority, revenge, and/or expressing anger and frustration.

Family or domestic violence Any abusive, coercive, violent, threatening, or forceful act or word inflicted by one member of a family/household on another. Sometimes, dating violence is included in this definition.

Fragile families Families who are more vulnerable or at a higher risk because of economic, health, psychological, or social factors.

Incest is unlawful sexual activity between members of the same family (bloodline). When children are the victims, it is considered to be an aspect of sexual abuse and there is a mandatory obligation to report this suspected behavior to authorities.

Information-processing approach in the context of child maltreatment proposes that neglectful parents fail to process information about their children's need for care. This in turn leads to physical neglect, a form of maltreatment.

Non-accidental trauma (NAT) is a medical term used to describe trauma that is willfully inflicted. Victims are typically young defenseless children.

Neglect refers to acts of parental negligence, such as failing to supervise children or adequately provide for their needs for food, shelter, safety, education and the like. If a parent or guardian fails to protect the child from harmful situations, this also amounts to neglect.

Union instability Partner relationships that are unstable, conflict laden or rocky. They cause family stress because of the on-again, off-again nature of the relationship.

Patriarchy model In the context of abusive behavior, this model implies that violence occurs in families as a result of the traditional social dominance of adult males, which places women in a subordinate position and condones the use of violence towards them.

Physical abuse The act of hurting, injuring and inflicting pain through behaviors such as smothering, starvation, physical confinement, near-drowning, and the like. It is inappropriately used as a way of controlling the victims, who are often children or other defenseless persons.

Psychiatric model In the context of family abuse this model assumes that abusive individuals in a family system are mentally or emotionally ill. This model isolates the personality characteristics of the offender as the primary cause for the abusive behavior.

Sexual abuse In the context of children this refers to direct or indirect sexual exploitation, coercion, or corruption by involving children in inappropriate sexual activities.

Sociological model In the context of family violence, this model states that cultural and social norms may prevail, for instance violence may be seen as a way of settling disputes and conflicts with others. Family structure and organization can influence violent behavior.

Social psychological model In the context of family violence, this model states that interaction patterns, the transmission of violent behavior from one generation to the next, and environmental stress serve as prime motivators of violent behavior. Violence is learned through modeling and serves as a coping mechanism in response to stress.

Substance use disorder The maladaptive pattern of substance use leading to clinically significant impairment or distress (American Psychiatric Association, 2013, DSM-5).

Union instability partnerships lacking in commitment and characterized by unpredictable involvement and turmoil; on-again/off-again relationships.

Violence In the context of the family, violence refers to a broad concept that includes acts of force against family members, which often fall under the guise of discipline and parental control of children. This also relates to the illegitimate acts of violence, occurring as part of family conflict.

CHAPTER 13

Blended family Also known as a reconstituted family. This type of family brings together children who may have had different families of origin, and/or adults who have been previously partnered or married, or have children from previous relationships.

Boomerang kids Children who return to their parental home after having been launched. Children may return to the home after graduating, while planning the next phase of their lives, or because of financial constraints.

Cohabitation Living with a significant other before marriage, or without getting married.

Families-by-choice Kinship-like bonds among people who are not necessarily biologically related or family.

Multigenerational family Also called an Intergenerational family. A family unit composed of several generations.

CHAPTER 14

Ambiguous loss When a child identifies as LGBT, parents may initially experience a sense of loss because their anticipated developmental outcomes for their child may not follow a predictable path. The relationship may require redefinition towards mutual acceptance, love, respect and support.

Androgynous Individuals who have psychological characteristics associated with both genders regardless of their biological sex.

Cisgender Implies that "each individual's identified gender is aligned with the sex assigned at birth, e.g. an individual assigned as a female identifies as a girl/woman" (McGuire et al., 2016).

Cisnormativity See Heteronormativity.

Queer theory states that homosexuality is not an opposite or another variant of heterosexuality. It is a critique of heteronormativity. This theory or approach started circulating in the early 1990s.

Heteronormativity (or Cisnormativity) The traditional approach of allocation of one of two labels to an individual; that of being either male or female.

Transgender (trans) Used to describe "the spectrum of individuals whose assigned sex at birth does not align with their own sense of gender identity and those who do not conform to societal gender norms." (McGuire et al., 2016).

CHAPTER 15

Caretaker despair Stress that comes with the responsibility of caring for another person in such an ongoing manner that temporary overload or burnout occurs. Caregiver despair can occur because caretakers get overtired and exhausted. A judgmental attitude toward caregiver despair is unhelpful and not supportive, and it is important to have good support systems in place to interrupt or preferably prevent the despair before it occurs.

Millennial Generation The generation born from 1981-2000; around the beginning of the new millennium. This group is characteristically hyper-connected; coming of age in the shadow of the Word Wide Web. This in turn influences communication patterns and real face-to-face relationships.

Protective factors Factors that contribute toward good outcomes despite adversity.

Resilience A process that engages personality traits, personal resources, and other aspects from the larger ecological system to ensure good outcomes despite adversities.

Risk and Resilience Model A theoretical model highlighting the dynamic interplay between negative and positive factors. Qualities and processes associated with emotional strength allow an individual to overcome challenging and potentially debilitating situations.

Risk factors Factors that relate to any event, condition, or experience that could increase the probability that a problem or issue will be precipitated, maintained, or exacerbated.

References

Aadnanes, M., & Gulbrandsen, L. M. (2017). Young people and young adults' experiences with child abuse and maltreatment: Meaning making, conceptualizations, and dealing with violence. *Qualitative Social Work*, 1473325016683245. https://doi.org/10.1177/1473325016683245

Abraham, E., Hendler, T., Shapira-Lichter, I., Kanat-Maymon, Y., Zagoory-Sharon, O., & Feldman, R. (2014). Father's brain is sensitive to childcare experiences. *PNAS Proceedings of the National Academy of Sciences of the United States of America*, 111(27), 9792–9797. https://doi.org/http://dx.doi.org/10.1073/pnas.1402569111

Adler, A. (1930a/2006). *Education for prevention: Individual psychology in the schools. The education of children*. Bellingham, WA: The Classical Adlerian Translation Project.

Adler, A. (1930b/2015). *The education of children*. New York, NY: Routledge.

Adler, A., & Ben-Ari, A. (2016). The Myth of Openness and Secrecy in Intimate Relationships: The Case of Spouses of Mixed-Orientation Marriage [Abstract]. *Journal of Homosexuality, 64*(6), 804–824. doi:10.1080/00918369.2016.1236585

AdoptUSKids. (n.d.). Who can adopt and foster? Retrieved from http://www.adoptuskids.org/adoption-and-foster-care/overview/who-can-adopt-foster

Ager, P., & Brückner, M. (2013). Cultural diversity and economic growth: Evidence from the US during the age of mass migration. *European Economic Review, 64*, 76–97. https://doi.org/10.1016/j.euroecorev.2013.07.011

Ainsworth, M. D. S. (1973). The development of infant–mother attachment. In B. Caldwell & H. Riciuti (Eds.), *Review of child development research* (Vol. 3). Chicago, IL: University of Chicago Press.

Ainsworth, M. D. S. (1977). Attachment theory and its utility in cross-cultural research. In P. Leiderman, S. Tulkin, & A. Rosenfield (Eds.), *Culture and infancy: Variations in the human experience*. New York, NY: Academic Press.

Ainsworth, M. D. S. (1983). Patterns of infant–mother attachment as related to maternal care: Their early history and their contribution to continuity. In D. Magnusson & V. L. Allen (Eds.), *Human development: An interactional perspective* (pp. 35–55). New York, NY: Academic Press.

Ainsworth, M. D. S. (1993). Attachment as related to mother–infant interaction. *Advances in Infancy Research, 81*.

Ainsworth, M. D. S., Blehar, M. C., Waters, E., & Wall, S. (1978/2015). *Patterns of attachment: A psychological study of the strange situation*. Oxford, England: Lawrence Erlbaum.

Akkermans, M. D., van der Horst-Graat, J. M., Eussen, S. R., van Goudoever, J. B., & Brus, F. (2016). Iron and vitamin D deficiency in healthy young children in Western Europe despite current nutritional recommendations. *Journal of Pediatric Gastroenterology and Nutrition*, 62(4), 635–642.

Alabama Hall of Fame for Social Work (2002). *Inductees*. Retrieved from http://socialwork.ua.edu/6962-2/1527-2/2002-inductees/

Alba, R., & Holdaway, J. (2013). *The children of immigrants at school: A comparative look a integration in the United States and Western Europe*. New York, NY: New York University Press.

Alba-Fisch, M. (2016). Collaborative divorce: An effort to reduce the damage of divorce. *Journal of Psychology, 72*(5), 444–457.

Albert, D., Chein, J., & Steinberg, L. (2013). The teenage brain: Peer influences on adolescent decision making. *Current Directions in Psychological Science, 22*(2), 114–120. https://doi.org/10.1177/0963721412471347

Alldred, P., Fox, N., & Kulpa, R. (2016). Engaging parents with sex and relationship education: A UK primary school case study. *Health Education Journal, 75*(7), 855–868. https://doi.org/10.1177/0017896916634114

Allemand, M., Hill, P. L., & Lehmann, R. (2015). Divorce and personality development across middle adulthood. *Personal Relationships, 22*(1), 122–137. https://doi.org/10.1111/pere.12067

Allen, B. P. (2015). *Personality theories: Development, growth, and diversity* (5th ed.). New York, NY: Routledge.

Allen, K. R. (2015). Fictive kin. *The Encyclopedia of Adulthood and Aging*. 1–4. Hoboken, NJ: John Wiley & Sons

Allen, K. R., & Lavender-Stott, E. S. (2015). Family contexts of informal sex education: Young men's perceptions of first sexual images. *Family Relations, 64*(3), 393–406. https://doi.org/10.1111/fare.12128

Allen, T. D., & Eby, L. T. (2016). *The Oxford Handbook of Work and Family*. Oxford, England: Oxford University Press.

Allen, T. D., Lapierre, L. M., Spector, P. E., Poelmans, S. A. Y., O'Driscoll, M., Sanchez, J. I., Woo, J.-M. (2014). The link between national paid leave policy and work–family conflict among married working parents. *Applied Psychology, 63*(1), 5–28.

Allgaier, K., Zettler, I., Wagner, W., Püttmann, S., & Trautwein, U. (2015). Honesty–humility in school: Exploring main and interaction effects on secondary school students' antisocial and prosocial behavior. *Learning and Individual Differences, 43*, 211–217. https://doi.org/10.1016/j.lindif.2015.08.005

Amato, P. R. (2014). The demography of contemporary fatherhood. *Men as Fathers*, 23. Retrieved from https://jacobsfoundation.org/app/uploads/2017/06/Jacobs-Foundation_Conference_2014.pdf

Amato, P. R., & Patterson, S. E. (2016). The intergenerational transmission of union instability in early adulthood. *Journal of Marriage and Family*. http://dx.doi.org/10.1111/jomf.12384

Ambert, A. M. (2001). *The effect of children on parents* (2nd ed.). New York, NY: Routledge.

American Academy of Pediatrics (2012a). *Healthy child care America: Fostering language development of 3- to 5-year-olds*, Standard 2.1.3.6.

American Academy of Pediatrics (2012b). Breastfeeding and the use of human milk: Section on breastfeeding. *Pediatrics, 129*(3), 827–841.

American Academy of Pediatrics, American Public Health Association, National Resource Center for Health and Safety in Child Care and Early Education (2014). *Caring for our children: National health and safety performance standards; Guidelines for early care and education programs* (3rd ed.). Elk Grove Village, IL: American Academy of Pediatrics; Washington, DC: American Public Health Association. Also available at http://nrckids.org.

American Academy of Pediatrics (2017a). AAP expands guideline for infant sleep safety and SIDS risk education. Retrieved from https://www.aap.org/en-us/about-the-aap/aap-press-room/Pages/AAP-Expands-Guidelines-for-Infant-Sleep-Safety-and-SIDS-Risk-Reduction.aspx

American Academy of Pediatrics (2017b). AAP policy on breastfeeding. Retrieved from https://www2.aap.org/breastfeeding/PolicyOnBreastfeeding.html

American Academy of Pediatrics (2017c). American Academy of Pediatrics supports childhood sleep guidelines. Retrieved from https://www.aap.org/en-us/about-the-aap/aap-press-room/pages/American-Academy-of-Pediatrics-Supports-Childhood-Sleep-Guidelines.aspx

American Academy of Pediatrics (2017d). Safety and prevention. Retrieved from http://www.healthychildren.org/English/Pages/default.aspx

American Association of Neurological Surgeons. (2017). Shaken baby syndrome. Available from https://www.aans.org/Patients/Neurosurgical-Conditions-and-Treatments/Shaken-Baby-Syndrome

American Bar Association (n.d.). Child custody and support. Retrieved from https://www.americanbar.org/groups/public_education/resources/law_issues_for_consumers/child.html

American College of Pediatricians (2017). Gender ideology harms children. Retrieved from http://www.acpeds.org/the-college-speaks/position-statements/gender-ideology-harms-children.

American Humane Association. (2016). History and milestones. Available from http://www.americanhumane.org/about-us/history/

American Pregnancy Association. (2017). Pre-conception health for women. Available from http://americanpregnancy.org/getting-pregnant/women-preconception-health/ml

American Pregnancy Association: Promoting Pregnancy Wellness (2017). Available from http://americanpregnancy.org/

American Psychiatric Association (n.d.). What is addiction? Retrieved from https://www.psychiatry.org/patients-families/addiction/what-is-addiction

American Psychiatric Association (Eds.). (2013). *Diagnostic and statistical manual of mental disorders: DSM-5* (5th ed.). Washington, DC: American Psychiatric Association.

American Psychological Association (n.d.). Understanding and preventing child abuse and neglect. Available from http://www.apa.org/pi/families/resources/understanding-child-abuse.aspx

American Psychological Association (2012). Judging adolescents' actions: Teens mature intellectually before they mature emotionally. *Journal of Family Psychology*, *30*(4), 453–469. https://doi.org/10.1037/fam0000191

American SPCC (2017). Statistics & facts about child abuse in the U.S. [Data file]. Retrieved from http://americanspcc.org/child-abuse-statistics/

Andersen, S. L. (2016). Commentary on the special issue on the adolescent brain: Adolescence, trajectories, and the importance of prevention. *Neuroscience & Biobehavioral Reviews*, *70*, 329–333. https://doi.org/10.1016/j.neubiorev.2016.07.012

Anderson, C., Turner, A. C., Heath, R. D., & Payne, C. M. (2016). On the meaning of grit and hope and fate control and alienation and locus of control and self-efficacy and effort optimism. *The Urban Review*, *48*(2), 198–219. https://doi.org/10.1007/s11256-016-0351-3

Anderson, K. N., Rueter, M. A., Connor, J. J., & Koh, B. D. (2016). Observed mother– and father–child interaction differences in families with medically assisted reproduction-conceived twins and singletons. *Family Process*. https://doi.org/10.1111/famp.12254

Anderst, J., & Moffatt, M. (2014). Adequate supervision for children and adolescents. *Pediatric Annals*, *43*(11), e260–e265. https://doi.org/10.3928/00904481-20141022-09

Annie. E. Casey Foundation (2016). 2016 KIDS COUNT data book. Retrieved from http://www.aecf.org/m/resourcedoc/aecf-the2016-kidscountdatabook-2016.pdf

Anthony, C. J., DiPerna, J. C., & Amato, P. R. (2014). Divorce, approaches to learning, and children's academic achievement: A longitudinal analysis of mediated and moderated effects. *Journal of School Psychology*, *52*(3), 249–261. https://doi.org/10.1016/j.jsp.2014.03.003

Anthony, S. (2013). *The child's discovery of death: A study in child psychology*. New York, NY: Routledge.

Aries, M. B. C., Aarts, M. P. J., & Van Hoof, J. (2015). Daylight and health: A review of the evidence and consequences for the built environment. *Lighting Research and Technology*, *47*(1), 6–27.

Aries, P. (1962). *Centuries of childhood: A social history of family life*. New York, NY: Random House, Inc.

Arnab, S., Brown, K., Clarke, S., Dunwell, I., Lim, T., Suttie, N., … de Freitas, S. (2013). The development approach of a pedagogically-driven serious game to support Relationship and Sex Education (RSE) within a classroom setting. *Computers & Education*, *69*, 15–30. http://dx.doi.org/10.1016/j.compedu.2013.06.013

Arnett, J. J. (2000). Emerging adulthood: A theory of development from the late teens through the twenties. *American Psychologist*, *55*(5), 469–480. https://doi.org/10.1037/0003-066X.55.5.469

Arnon, I., Casillas, M., Kurumada, C., & Estigarribia, B. (Eds.). (2014). *Language in interaction: Studies in honor of Eve V. Clark*. Amsterdam: John Benjamins.

Assini-Meytin, L. C., & Green, K. M. (2015). Long-term consequences of adolescent parenthood among African American urban youth: A propensity matching approach. *The Journal of Adolescent Health: Official Publication of the Society for Adolescent Medicine*, *56*(5), 529–535. https://doi.org/10.1016/j.jadohealth.2015.01.005

Astington, J. W. (1993). *The child's discovery of the mind*. Cambridge, MA: Harvard University Press.

Attané, I. (2016). Second child decisions in China. *Population and Development Review*, *42*(3). 519–536. https://doi.org/10.1111/j.1728-4457.2016.00151.x

Aughinbaugh, A., Robles, O., & Sun, H. (2013). Marriage and divorce: Patterns by gender, race, and educational attainment. *Bureau of Labor Statistics*, *136*, 1–19.

Autor, D. H. (2014). Skills, education, and the rise of earnings inequality among the "other 99 percent." *Autor via Kate McNeill*. Retrieved from http://dspace.mit.edu/handle/1721.1/96768

Bales, R. F., & Parsons, T. (2014). *Family: Socialization and interaction process*. New York, NY: Routledge.

Ball, C. A. (Ed.). (2016). *After marriage equality: The future of LGBT rights*. New York, NY: New York University Press.

Ballard, M. B., Fazio-Griffith, L., & Marino, R. (2016). Transgenerational family therapy: A case study of a couple in crisis. *The Family Journal*, *24*(2), 109–113. http://dx.doi.org/10.1177/1066480716628564

Balter, M. (2015). Homosexuality may be caused by chemical modifications to DNA. *Science*. https://doi.org/10.1126/science.aad4686

Bandura, A. (1977). *Social learning theory*. Englewood Cliffs, NJ: Prentice Hall.

Banschick, M. R., & Tabatsky, D. (2010). *The intelligent divorce: Taking care of your children*. Stamford, CT: Intelligent Book Press.

Barak-Levy, Y., & Atzaba-Poria, N. (2015). The effects of familial risk and parental resolution on parenting a child with mild intellectual disability. *Research in Developmental Disabilities*, *47*, 106–116. https://doi.org/10.1016/j.ridd.2015.09.006

Barbel, I., & Piaget, J. (2013). *The growth of logical thinking from childhood to adolescence: An essay on the construction of formal operational structures*. New York, NY: Routledge.

Barbera, F., Bernhard, F., Nacht, J., & McCann, G. (2015). The relevance of a whole-person learning approach to family business education: Concepts, evidence, and implications. *Academy of Management Learning & Education*, *14*(3), 322–346. https://doi.org/10.5465/amle.2014.0233

Barker, D. P. (2004). The developmental origins of chronic adult disease. *Acta Paediatrica. Supplement*, *93*(s446), 26–33.

Barker, D., Eriksson, J., Forsén, T., & Osmond, C. (2002). Fetal origins of adult disease: Strength of effects and biological basis. *International Journal of Epidemiology*, *31*(6), 1235–1239.

Barker, G. (2015). Globalized fatherhood. *Gender & Development*, *23*(2), 397–399. https://doi.org/10.1080/13552074.2015.1053271

Barlow, J., Smailagic, N., Bennett, C., Huband, N., Jones, H., & Coren, E. (2011). Individual and group based parenting programmes for improving psychosocial outcomes for teenage parents and their children. In *Cochrane Database of Systematic Reviews*. John Wiley & Sons, Ltd. Retrieved from http://onlinelibrary.wiley.com/doi/10.1002/14651858.CD002964.pub2/abstract

Barlow, M. R., Turow, R. G., & Gerhart, J. (2017). Trauma appraisals, emotion regulation difficulties, and self-compassion predict posttraumatic stress symptoms following childhood abuse. *Child Abuse & Neglect*, *65*, 37–47.

Barn, R., & Tan, J.-P. (2015). Foster youth and drug use: Exploring risk and protective factors. *Children and Youth Services Review*, *56*, 107–115. https://doi.org/10.1016/j.childyouth.2015.07.007

Barnes, G. (2016). Narratives of attachment and processes of alienation in post-divorce parenting disputes. In A. Vetere & E. Dowling (Eds.), *Narrative Therapies with Children and Their Families: A Practitioner's Guide to Concepts and Approaches*. New York, NY: Routledge.

Barnett, M. A., Scaramella, L. V., Neppl, T. K., Ontai, L., & Conger, R. D. (2010). Intergenerational relationship quality, gender, and grandparent involvement. *Family Relations*, *59*(1), 28–44. https://doi.org/10.1111/j.1741-3729.2009.00584.x

Barr, R. G., Rajabali, F., Aragon, M., Colbourne, M., & Brant, R. (2015). Education about crying in normal infants is associated with a reduction in pediatric emergency room visits for crying complaints. *Journal of Developmental & Behavioral Pediatrics*, *36*(4), 252–257. https://doi.org/10.1097/DBP.0000000000000156

Barthes, J., Crochet, P., & Raymond, M. (2015). Male homosexual preference: Where, when, why? *PLOS ONE*, *10*(8). doi:10.1371/journal.pone.0134817

Bastos Silva, T., Nagib Boery, E., Narriman Silva de Oliveira Boery, R., Cruz Santos, V., Ferraz dos Anjos, K., & Benemérita Alves Vilela, A. (2014). Social, economic and affective impact of pregnancy in the father teenager. *Journal of Nursing UFPE*, 8(9), 2957–2963. https://doi.org/10.5205/reuol.5960-55386-1-ED.0809201401

Bates, J. S., & Taylor, A. C. (2016). Grandparent–grandchild relationships. In *Encyclopedia of Family Studies*. John Wiley & Sons, Inc. https://doi.org/10.1002/9781119085621.wbefs448

Baumrind, D. (1966). Effects of authoritative parental control on child behavior. *Child Development*, 37, 887–907.

Baumrind, D. (1996). The discipline controversy revisited. *Family Relations*, 45, 405–414.

Baumrind, D., & Thompson, A. R. (2002). The ethics of parenting. In M. Bornstein (Ed.). *Handbook of Parenting: Volume 5. Practical Issues in Parenting* (2nd ed.). (pp. 3–487). Mahwah, NJ: Lawrence Erlbaum Associates.

Bavis, R. W., & MacFarlane, P. M. (2016). Developmental plasticity in the neural control of breathing. *Experimental Neurology*. https://doi.org/10.1016/j.expneurol.2016.05.032

Bay-Cheng, L. Y., Livingston, J. A., & Fava, N. M. (2011). Adolescent girls' assessment and management of sexual risks: Insights from focus group research. *Youth & Society*, 43(3), 1167–1193. https://doi.org/10.1177/0044118X10384475

Bean, H., Softas-Nall, L., Eberle, K. M., & Paul, J. A. (2016). Can we talk about stay-at-home moms? Empirical findings and implications for counseling. *The Family Journal*, 24(1), 23–30.

Beckerman, M., van Berkel, S. R., Mesman, J., & Alink, L. R. A. (2017). The role of negative parental attributions in the associations between daily stressors, maltreatment history, and harsh and abusive discipline. *Child Abuse & Neglect*, 64, 109–116. https://doi.org/10.1016/j.chiabu.2016.12.015

Becvar, D. S., & Becvar, R. J. (2012). *Family therapy: A systemic integration*. (8th ed.). Boston, MA: Pearson.

Beginning - Elementary and Secondary Education Act (ESEA). (2008). [Laws]. Retrieved from https://www2.ed.gov/policy/elsec/leg/esea02/beginning.html

Beiner, S. F., Lowenstein, L., Worenklein, A., & Sauber, S. R. (2014). Grandparents' rights. Psychological and legal perspectives. *The American Journal of Family Therapy*, 42(2), 114–126. https://doi.org/10.1080/01926187.2013.857907

Bellamy, J. L., & Banman, A. (2014). Advancing research on services for adolescent fathers: A commentary on Kiselica and Kiselica. *Psychology of Men & Masculinity*, 15(3), 281–283. https://doi.org/10.1037/a0037334

Belsky, J. (1984). The determinants of parenting: A process model. *Child Development*, 55(1), 83–96. https://doi.org/http://dx.doi.org/10.2307/1129836

Belsky, J., & Barends, N. (2002). Personality and parenting. In M. H. Bornstein (Ed.). (2012). *Handbook of parenting: Volume 3: Being and becoming a parent* (2nd ed.). (pp. 415–438). Mahwah, NJ: Lawrence Erlbaum Associates.

Belsky, J., & de Haan, M. (2011). Annual research review: Parenting and children's brain development: The end of the beginning. *Journal of Child Psychology & Psychiatry*, 52(4), 409–428.

Belsky, J., & Rovine, M. (1990). Patterns of marital change across the transition to parenthood: Pregnancy to three years postpartum. *Journal of Marriage and Family*, 52(1), 5–19. https://doi.org/10.2307/352833

Bem, S. L., & Lewis, S. A. (1975). Sex role adaptability: One consequence of psychological androgyny. *Journal of Personality and Social Psychology*, 31(4), 634–643. http://dx.doi.org/10.1037/h0077098

Ben-Ari, O. T., Findler, L., & Shlomo, S. B. (2013). When couples become grandparents: Factors associated with the growth of each spouse. *Social Work Research*, 37(1), 26–36. https://doi.org/10.1093/swr/svt005

Benefits.gov. (2017). Healthcare. Retrieved from https://www.benefits.gov/benefits/browse-by-category/category/18

Bengtson, V. L. (2002). Beyond the nuclear family: The increasing importance of multigenerational bonds. *Journal of Marriage and Family*, 63(1), 1–16. https://doi.org/10.1111/j.1741-3737.2001.00001.x

Bengtson, V. L., Biblarz, T. J., & Roberts, R. L. (2002). *How families still matter: A longitudinal study of youth in two generations*. New York, NY: Cambridge University Press.

Bennett, G., & Kingston, P. W. (1993/2013). *Elder abuse: Concepts, theories and interventions*. New York, NY: Springer.

Berger, R. (2000). Remarried families of 2000: Definitions, description, and interventions. In W. C. Nichols, M. A. Pace-Nichols, D. S. Becvar, & A. Y. Napier (Eds.), *Handbook of family development* (pp. 371–390). New York, NY: Wiley.

Berk, L. (2014). *Exploring lifespan development*. (3rd ed.). Upper Saddle River, NJ: Pearson.

Bernard, K., Lind, T., & Dozier, M. (2014). Neurobiological consequences of neglect and abuse. In J. E. Korbin & R. D. Krugman (Eds.). *Handbook of Child Maltreatment* (pp. 205–223). Springer Netherlands. https://doi.org/10.1007/978-94-007-7208-3_11

Bhutta, Z. A., Das, J. K., Rizvi, A., Gaffey, M. F., Walker, N., Horton, S., Black, R. E. (2013). Evidence-based interventions for improvement of maternal and child nutrition: What can be done and at what cost? *The Lancet*, 382(9890), 452–477. https://doi.org/10.1016/S0140-6736(13)60996-4

Biebel, K., & Alikhan, S. (2016). Paternal postpartum depression. *Journal of Parent and Family Mental Health*. Retrieved from https://works.bepress.com/kathleen_biebel/56/

Biehle, S. N., & Mickelson, K. D. (2012). First-time parents' expectations about the division of childcare and play. *Journal of Family Psychology*, 26(1), 36–45. https://doi.org/10.1037/a0026608

Bigner, J. J., & Gerhardt, C. (2014). *Parent-child relations: An introduction to parenting* (9th ed.). Boston, MA: Pearson.

Bigner, J. & Wetchler, J. L. (Eds.) (2012). *Handbook of LGBT-affirmative couple and family therapy*. New York, NY: Routledge.

Bingham, T., & Conner, M. (2015). *The new social learning: Connect. Collaborate. Work*. (2nd ed.). Alexandria, VA: Association for Talent Development.

Birbilis, M., Moschonis, G., Mougios, V., & Manios, Y. (2013). Obesity in adolescence is associated with perinatal risk factors, parental BMI and sociodemographic characteristics. *European Journal of Clinical Nutrition*, 67(1), 115–121. https://doi.org/10.1038/ejcn.2012.176

Birchler, G. (2015). Handling resistance to change. In I. R. H. Falloon, *Handbook of behavioural family therapy* (pp. 128–155). Chapter 6. New York, NY: Routledge.

Black, C., & Zeanah, C. H. (2015). Reactive attachment disorder and disinhibited social engagement disorder. *The encyclopedia of clinical psychology*. Hoboken, NJ: John Wiley & Sons.

Blakemore, S.-J. (2012a). Development of the social brain in adolescence. *Journal of the Royal Society of Medicine*, 105(3), 111–116. https://doi.org/10.1258/jrsm.2011.110221

Blakemore, S.-J. (2012b). Imaging brain development: The adolescent brain. *NeuroImage*, 61(2), 397–406. https://doi.org/10.1016/j.neuroimage.2011.11.080

Blakemore, S.-J., & Robbins, T. W. (2012). Decision-making in the adolescent brain. *Nature Neuroscience*, 15(9), 1184–1191. https://doi.org/10.1038/nn.3177

Blatchford, P., Pellegrini, A. D., & Baines, E. (2015). *The child at school: Interactions with peers and teachers* (2nd ed.). New York, NY: Routledge.

Blyaert, L., Van Parys, H., De Mol, J., & Buysse, A. (2016). Like a parent and a friend, but not the father: A qualitative study of stepfathers' experiences in the stepfamily. *Australian and New Zealand Journal of Family Therapy*, 37(1), 119–132. https://doi.org/10.1002/anzf.1138

Bockting, W. O. (2014). Transgender identity development. In D. L. Tolman, L. M. Diamond, J. A. Bauermeister, W. H. George, J. G. Pfaus, & L. M. Ward (Eds.), *APA handbook of sexuality and psychology, Vol. 1: Person-based approaches* (pp. 739–758). Washington, DC: American Psychological Association.

Boes, C., Collins-Camargo, C., & Thomas, T. A. (2015). Evaluation of implementation of the Kentucky court rules of procedure and practice: An approach to assessing the impact of court reform efforts. *Juvenile and Family Court Journal*, 66(4), 1–16. https://doi.org/10.1111/jfcj.12048

Bogan, V. L. (2015). Household asset allocation, offspring education, and the sandwich generation. *The American Economic Review*, 105(5), 611–615. https://doi.org/10.1257/aer.p20151115

Bohn, A., & Berntsen, D. (2013). The future is bright and predictable: The development of prospective life stories across childhood and adolescence. *Developmental Psychology*, 49(7), 1232–1241. https://doi.org/10.1037/a0030212

Bohr, Y., & Tse, C. (2009). Satellite babies in transnational families: A study of parents' decision to separate from their infants. *Infant Mental Health Journal*, 30(3), 265–286. https://doi.org/10.1002/imhj.20214

Bonnie, R. J., & Scott, E. S. (2013). The teenage brain: Adolescent brain research and the law. *Current Directions in Psychological Science*, 22(2), 158–161.

Boonstra, H. D. (2015). Advancing sexuality education in developing countries: Evidence and implications. In *Evidence-based approaches to sexuality education: A global perspective*. Chapter 21. New York, NY: Routledge.

Bornstein, M. H. (Ed.). (2012). *Handbook of parenting: Volume I: Children and parenting* (2nd edition). New York, NY: Routledge.

Bornstein, M. H. (2014). Human infancy … and the rest of the lifespan. *Annual Review of Psychology*, 65(1), 121–158. https://doi.org/10.1146/annurev-psych-120710-100359

Bos, H., Gelderen, L. van, & Gartrell, N. (2015). Lesbian and heterosexual two-parent families: Adolescent–parent relationship quality and adolescent well-being. *Journal of Child and Family Studies*, 24(4), 1031–1046. https://doi.org/10.1007/s10826-014-9913-8

Bos, H. M. W., Knox, J. R., van Rijn-van Gelderen, L., & Gartrell, N. K. (2016). Same-sex and different-sex parent households and child health outcomes: Findings from the National Survey of Children's Health. *Journal of Developmental and Behavioral Pediatrics*, 37(3), 179–187. http://dx.doi.org/10.1097/DBP.0000000000000288

Boss, P. (2014). Family stress. In A. C. Michalos (Ed.), *Encyclopedia of quality of life and well-being research* (pp. 2202–2208). Springer Netherlands. https://doi.org/10.1007/978-94-007-0753-5_1008

Bottoms, B. L., Goodman, G. S., Tolou-Shams, M., Diviak, K. R., & Shaver, P. R. (2015). Religion-related child maltreatment: A profile of cases encountered by legal and social service agencies. *Behavioral Sciences & the Law*, 33(4), 561–579. https://doi.org/http://dx.doi.org/10.1002/bsl.2192

Bouchard, G. (2016). Transition to parenthood and relationship satisfaction. In *Encyclopedia of family studies*. John Wiley & Sons, Inc. https://doi.org/10.1002/9781119085621.wbefs007

Bouchard, M.-C., Gallagher, F., Soubhi, H., Bujold, L., & St-Cyr, D. (2015). Collaborative practice in secondary schools in the promotion of healthy eating and physical activity. *Journal of Research in Interprofessional Practice and Education*, 5(1). Retrieved from http://jripe.org/jripe/index.php/journal/article/view/184

Bowen, M. (2013). *The origins of family psychotherapy: The NIMH Family Study Project*. J. Butler (Ed.). Lanham, MD: Jason Aronson, Inc.

Bowen, M. (2015). Psychotherapy—Past, present, and future. In *Evolution of psychotherapy: The 1st conference* (p. 32). New York, NY: Routledge.

Bowlby, J. (1952). *Maternal care and mental health: A report prepared on behalf of the World Health Organization as a contribution to the United Nations programme for the welfare of homeless children*. Geneva, Switzerland: World Health Organization.

Bowlby, J. (1982). *Attachment and loss*. New York, NY: Basic Books.

Brakman, A., & Gold, M. (2015). Access to contraception and school-based health: One strategy for preventing teen pregnancy. *Contraceptive Technology Update*, 36(6), 8–9.

Bramlett, M. D., & Radel, L. F. (2014). *Adverse family experiences among children in nonparental care, 2011–2012* (National Health Statistics Reports No. 74). U.S. Department of Health and Human Services Centers for Disease Control and Prevention National Center for Health Statistics. Retrieved from http://www.cdc.gov/nchs/data/nhsr/nhsr074.pd

Brazelton, T. B. (2013). *Toddlers and parents: A declaration of independence*. New York, NY: Random House Publishing Group.

Breggin, P. R. (2015). The biological evolution of guilt, shame and anxiety: A new theory of negative legacy emotions. *Medical Hypotheses*, 85(1), 17–24. https://doi.org/10.1016/j.mehy.2015.03.015

Breyer, R. J., & MacPhee, D. (2015). Community characteristics, conservative ideology, and child abuse rates. *Child Abuse & Neglect*, 41, 126–135. https://doi.org/10.1016/j.chiabu.2014.11.019

Briere, J. N., & Scott, C. (2014). *Principles of trauma therapy: A guide to symptoms, evaluation, and treatment (DSM-5 Update)*. SAGE Publications.

Britto, P. R., Lye, S. J., Proulx, K., Yousafzai, A. K., Matthews, S. G., Vaivada, T., … Bhutta, Z. A. (2016). Advancing early childhood development: From science to scale 2: Nurturing care: Promoting early childhood development. *The Lancet*, 389(10064), 91–102. http://dx.doi.org/10.1016/S0140-6736(16)31390-3

Bronfenbrenner, U. (1979). *The ecology of human development*. Cambridge, MA: Harvard University Press.

Bronfenbrenner, U. (1985). The parent–child relationship and our changing society. In L. E. Arnold (Ed.), *Parents, children, and change*. Lexington, MA: Lexington Books.

Bronfenbrenner, U. (1986). Ecology of the family as a context for human development: Research perspectives. *Developmental Psychology*, 22(6), 723–742. http://dx.doi.org/10.1037/0012-1649.22.6.723

Bronfenbrenner, U. (1993). Ecological systems theory. In R. H. Wozniak (Ed.), *Development in context* (pp. 44–78). Hillsdale, NJ: Lawrence Erlbaum.

Bronfenbrenner, U. & Evans, G. W. (2000). Developmental science in the 21st century: Emerging questions, theoretical models, research designs and empirical findings. *Social Development*, 9(1), 115–125. https://doi.org/10.1111/1467-9507.00114

Brown, A. (2014, June 26). U.S. Hispanic and Asian populations growing, but for different reasons. Retrieved from http://www.pewresearch.org/fact-tank/2014/06/26/u-s-hispanic-and-asian-populations-growing-but-for-different-reasons/

Brown, A. L. (2015). The impact of early intervention on the school readiness of children born to teenage mothers. *Journal of Early Childhood Research*, 13(2), 181–195.

Brown, J. E. (2016). *Nutrition through the life cycle* (5th ed.). Stamford, CT: Cengage Learning.

Brown, R. (2015). Building children and young people's resilience: Lessons from psychology. *International Journal of Disaster Risk Reduction*, 14, Part 2, 115–124. https://doi.org/10.1016/j.ijdrr.2015.06.007

Brown, S. L., & Lin, I.-F. (2013). Age variation in the remarriage rate, 1990–2011. *National Center for Family & Marriage Research*, FP-13-17. Retrieved from http://www.firelands.bgsu.edu/content/dam/BGSU/college-of-arts-and-sciences/NCFMR/documents/FP/FP-13-17.pdf

Brown, S. L., Manning, W. D., & Stykes, J. B. (2015). Family structure and child well-being: Integrating family complexity. *Journal of Marriage and Family*, 77(1), 177–190. https://doi.org/10.1111/jomf.12145

Brown, S. L., & Wright, M. R. (2016). Older adults' attitudes toward cohabitation: Two decades of change. *The Journals of Gerontology. Series B, Psychological Sciences and Social Sciences*, 71(4), 755–764. https://doi.org/10.1093/geronb/gbv053

Browne, C. H. (2016). The strengthening families approach and protective factors framework: A pathway to healthy development and well-being. In C. J. Shapiro & C. H. Browne (Eds.), *Innovative Approaches to Supporting Families of Young Children* (pp. 1–24). Springer International Publishing. https://doi.org/10.1007/978-3-319-39059-8_1

Brownell, C. A., & The Early Social Development Research Lab. (2016). Prosocial behavior in infancy: The role of socialization. *Child Development Perspectives*, 10(4), 222–227. https://doi.org/10.1111/cdep.12189

Bruner, J. S. (1966). *Studies in cognitive growth: A collaboration at the Center for Cognitive Studies*. Oxford, England: John Wiley & Sons.

Brunton, P. J. (2013). Effects of maternal exposure to social stress during pregnancy: Consequences for mother and offspring. *Reproduction*, 146(5), R175–R189. https://doi.org/10.1530/REP-13-0258

Buchanon, A., & Rotkirch, A. (Eds.). (2016). *Grandfathers: Global perspectives*. New York, NY: Springer.

Bunting, L. (2010). Parenting programmes: The best available evidence. *Child Care in Practice*, 10(4), 327–343. https://doi.org/10.1080/1357527042000285510

Burgard, S. (2012). *Health, mental health and the great recession*. Stanford, CA: Stanford Center on Poverty and Inequality.

Burgess, E. W. (1926). The family as a unity of interacting personalities. *The Family, 2,* 3-9.

Burgoon, J. K., Guerrero, L. K., & Floyd, K. (2016). *Nonverbal communication.* New York, NY: Routledge.

Burke, H., Leonardi-Bee, J., Hashim, A., Pine-Abata, H., Chen, Y., Cook, D. G., & McKeever, T. M. (2012). Prenatal and passive smoke exposure and incidence of asthma and wheeze: Systematic review and meta-analysis. *Pediatrics, 129*(4), 735–744. https://doi.org/10.1542/peds.2011-2196

Burke, R. J., & Major, D. A. (2014). *Gender in organizations: Are men allies or adversaries to women's career advancement?* Northhampton, MA: Edward Elgar Publishing.

Burkle, C., & Pope, T. (2015). Brain death: Legal obligations and the courts. *Seminars in Neurology, 35*(2), 174–179. https://doi.org/10.1055/s-0035-1547537

Burnett Heyes, S., Lau, J. Y. F., & Holmes, E. A. (2013). Mental imagery, emotion and psychopathology across child and adolescent development. *Developmental Cognitive Neuroscience, 5,* 119–133. https://doi.org/10.1016/j.dcn.2013.02.004

Bylund-Grenklo, T., Kreicbergs, U., Uggla, C., Valdimarsdóttir, U. A., Nyberg, T., Steineck, G., & Fürst, C. J. (2015). Teenagers want to be told when a parent's death is near: A nationwide study of cancer-bereaved youths' opinions and experiences. *Acta Oncologica (Stockholm, Sweden), 54*(6), 944–950. https://doi.org/10.3109/0284186X.2014.978891

Cabrera, N. J., & Tamis-LeMonda, C. S. (Eds.). (2013). *Handbook of father involvement: Multidisciplinary perspectives* (2nd ed.). New York, NY: Routledge.

Calisto, J. L., & Gaines, B. (2015). The new science of concussion and mild brain injury in children. *Current Surgery Reports, 3*(10), 33. https://doi.org/10.1007/s40137-015-0111-4

Callaway, E. (2012). Fathers bequeath more mutations as they age. *Nature, 488*(7412), 439.

Campbell, A. F. (2015). More Women Are Earning More Than Their Husbands. *The Atlantic.* Retrieved from https://www.theatlantic.com/politics/archive/2015/11/more-women-are-earning-more-than-their-husbands/433491/

Campbell, C. S. (2017). Limiting the right to die: Moral logic, professional integrity, societal ethos. In M. J. Cholbi (Ed.). *Euthanasia and assisted suicide: Global views on choosing to end life.* (Chapter 9). Denver, CO: Praeger.

Campero, L., Walker, D., Atienzo, E. E., & Gutierrez, J. P. (2011). A quasi-experimental evaluation of parents as sexual health educators resulting in delayed sexual initiation and increased access to condoms. *Journal of Adolescence, 34*(2), 215–223. https://doi.org/10.1016/j.adolescence.2010.05.010

Capuzzi, D., Stauffer, M. D., & Cass Dykeman. (2016). Chapter 13: Family theory. In *Counseling and Psychotherapy: Theories and Interventions* (pp. 339–366). Hoboken, NJ: John Wiley & Sons.

Carl, J. D. (2012). *A short introduction to the U.S. Census.* Upper Saddle River, NJ: Pearson Education.

Carlo, G., White, R., Streit, C., Knight, G. P., & Zeiders, K. H., (2017). Longitudinal relations among parenting styles, prosocial behaviors, and academic outcomes in US Mexican adolescents. *Child Development.* Hoboken, NJ: Wiley Online.

Carlson, D. L., Miller, A. J., Sassler, S., & Hanson, S. (2016). The gendered division of housework and couples' sexual relationships: A reexamination. *Journal of Marriage and Family, 78*(4), 975–995. https://doi.org/10.1111/jomf.12313

Carneiro, P., & Ginja, R. (2014). Long-term impacts of compensatory preschool on health and behavior: Evidence from head start. *American Economic Journal: Economic Policy, 6*(4), 135–173. https://doi.org/10.1257/pol.6.4.135

Carr, D. (2015). Marital transitions: Widowhood, divorce, and remarriage. In *The Encyclopedia of Adulthood and Aging.* Hoboken, NJ: John Wiley & Sons. Retrieved from http://onlinelibrary.wiley.com/doi/10.1002/9781118521373.wbeaa289/abstract

Carter, R. (1998/2010). *Mapping the mind.* Los Angeles, CA: The University of California Press.

Cartwright, C., & Gibson, K. (2013). The effects of co-parenting relationships with ex-spouses on couples in step-families. *Family Matters,* (92), 18. Retrieved from http://search.informit.com.au/documentSummary;dn=442088432086929;res=IELAPA

Center for Injury Research and Prevention (2017). Retrieved from https://injury.research.chop.edu/

Center on the Developing Child at Harvard University (2016a). *Building core capabilities for life: The science behind the skills adults need to succeed in parenting and in the workplace.* Retrieved from https://developingchild.harvard.edu/resources/building-core-capabilities-for-life/

Center on the Developing Child at Harvard University (2016b). From best practices to breakthrough impacts: A science-based approach to building a more promising future for young children and families. Retrieved from http://developingchild.harvard.edu/resources/from-best-practices-to-breakthrough-impacts/

Center on the Developing Child at Harvard University. (2017). *Serve and return interaction shapes brain circuitry.* Retrieved from http://developingchild.harvard.edu/resources/serve-return-interaction-shapes-brain-circuitry/

Centers for Disease Control and Prevention. (2008). National marriage and divorce rate trends. Retrieved from https://www.cdc.gov/nchs/nvss/marriage_divorce_tables.htm

Centers for Disease Control and Prevention. (2010). STDs in adolescents and young adults. Retrieved from https://www.cdc.gov/std/stats10/adol.htm

Centers for Disease Control and Prevention. (2012). CDC childhood injury report. Retrieved from www.cdc.gov/safechild/Child_Injury_Data.html

Centers for Disease Control and Prevention. (2013a). Preventing repeat teen births. Retrieved from https://www.cdc.gov/vitalsigns/teenpregnancy/index.html

Centers for Disease Control and Prevention. (2013b). Vaccination coverage among children in kindergarten - United States, 2012-13 school year. *MMWR. Morbidity and Mortality Weekly Report, 62*(30), 607–612.

Centers for Disease Control and Prevention. (2014a). Child maltreatment: Facts at a glance. Retrieved from https://www.cdc.gov/violenceprevention/pdf/childmaltreatment-facts-at-a-glance.pdf

Centers for Disease Control and Prevention (2014b). Health effects & risks: Zika virus. Retrieved from http://www.cdc.gov/zika/healtheffects/index.html

Centers for Disease Control and Prevention. (2015a). CDC childhood injury report. Retrieved from https://www.cdc.gov/safechild/child_injury_data.html

Centers for Disease Control and Prevention. (2015b). Unintended pregnancy prevention. Retrieved from https://www.cdc.gov/reproductivehealth/unintendedpregnancy/

Centers for Disease Control and Prevention. (2016). Pregnancy and infant loss. Retrieved from https://www.cdc.gov/features/pregnancy-infant-loss-day/index.html

Centers for Disease Control and Prevention. (2017a). Breastfeeding. Retrieved from https://www.cdc.gov/breastfeeding/

Centers for Disease Control and Prevention. (2017b). Reproductive health: Teen pregnancy. Retrieved from https://www.cdc.gov/teenpregnancy/about/

Centers for Disease Control and Prevention. (2017c). Suicide prevention. Retrieved from https://www.cdc.gov/violenceprevention/suicide/

Chadwick, E. (2011). *Lady of the english.* Naperville, IL: Sourcebooks Landmark.

Chaladze, G. (2016). Heterosexual male carriers could explain persistence of homosexuality in men: Individual-based simulations of an x-linked inheritance model. *Archives of Sexual Behavior, 45*(7), 1705–1711. https://doi.org/10.1007/s10508-016-0742-2

Chamberlain, J., Miller, M. K., & Rivera, C. (2015). Same-sex parents' sentiment about parenthood and the law: Implications for therapeutic outcomes. In M. K. Miller, J. A. Blumenthal, & J. Chamberlain (Eds.), *Handbook of community sentiment* (pp. 183–197). New York, NY: Springer. https://doi.org/10.1007/978-1-4939-1899-7_13

Chan, S. M., & Chan, K. W. (2013). Adolescents' susceptibility to peer pressure: Relations to parent–adolescent relationship and adolescents' emotional autonomy from parents. *Youth & Society, 45*(2), 286–302. https://doi.org/10.1177/0044118X11417733

Chapman, A., Sanner, C., Ganong, L., Coleman, M., Russell, L., Kang, Y., & Mitchell, S. (2016). Exploring the complexity of stepgrandparent-stepgrandchild relationships. In *Divorce, separation, and remarriage: The transformation of family*

(Vol. 10, pp. 101–130). Bingley, United Kingdom: Emerald Group Publishing Limited. https://doi.org/10.1108/S1530-353520160000010005

Chapman, G. D., & Campbell, R. (2016). *The 5 love languages of children: The secret to loving children effectively.* Chicago, IL: Moody Publishers.

Chen, F. J. (2016). Maternal voices in personal narratives of adoption. *Women's Studies, 45*(2), 162–187. https://doi.org/10.1080/00497878.2015.1122504

Chen, W. W. (2015). The relations between perceived parenting styles and academic achievement in Hong Kong: The mediating role of students' goal orientations. *Learning and Individual Differences, 37*, 48–54. https://doi.org/10.1016/j.lindif.2014.11.021

Cheng, S., & Powell, B. (2015). Measurement, methods, and divergent patterns: Reassessing the effects of same-sex parents. *Social Science Research, 52*, 615–626. https://doi.org/10.1016/j.ssresearch.2015.04.005

Cherlin, A. J. (2012). Goode's world revolution and family patterns: A reconsideration at fifty years. *Population and Development Review, 38*(4), 577–607. https://doi.org/http://dx.doi.org/10.1111/j.1728-4457.2012.00528.x

Cheung, H., Siu, T. S. C., & Chen, L. (2015). The roles of liar intention, lie content, and theory of mind in children's evaluation of lies. *Journal of Experimental Child Psychology, 132*, 1–13. https://doi.org/10.1016/j.jecp.2014.12.002

Child Defense Fund (2016). Child poverty in America: National analysis. Retrieved from http://www.childrensdefense.org/library/data/child-poverty-in-america-2015.pdf

Child Welfare Information Gateway. (2012). *Obtaining background information on your perspective adopted child.* Washington, DC: US Department of Health and Human Services, Children's Bureau

Child Welfare Information Gateway. (2013). *Impact of adoption on birth parents.* Washington, DC: US Department of Health and Human Services, Children's Bureau. Retrieved from https://childwelfare.gov/pubs/f-impact/

Child Welfare Information Gateway. (2014a). *Parental substance use and the child welfare system.* Washington, DC: U.S. Department of Health and Human Services, Children's Bureau. Retrieved from https://www.childwelfare.gov/pubs/factsheets/parentalsubabuse/

Child Welfare Information Gateway. (2014b). *The rights of unmarried fathers: State statutes.* Washington, DC: US Department of Health and Human Services, Children's Bureau. Retrieved from https://www.childwelfare.gov/topics/systemwide/laws-policies/statutes/putative/

Child Welfare Information Gateway. (2016). *Mandatory reporters of child abuse and neglect.* Washington, DC: US Department of Health and Human Services, Children's Bureau. Retrieved from https://www.childwelfare.gov/topics/systemwide/laws-policies/statutes/manda/

Childhelp (2014a). Child abuse statistics and facts [Data file]. Retrieved from https://www.childhelp.org/child-abuse-statistics/

Children's Bureau. (n.d.). Retrieved from https://www.acf.hhs.gov/cb

Children's Bureau. (2015). The AFCARS report #22. Retrieved from https://www.acf.hhs.gov/cb/resource/afcars-report-22

Children's Bureau (2017). Child Maltreatment 2015. Retrieved from https://www.acf.hhs.gov/sites/default/files/cb/cm2015.pdf

Children's Defense Fund. (n.d.). Retrieved from http://www.childrensdefense.org/

Children's Rights (2015). Child abuse and neglect. Retrieved from http://www.childrensrights.org/newsroom/fact-sheets/child-abuse-and-neglect/

Childstats.gov (n.d.). Family structure and children's living arrangements. *America's Children: Key National Indicators of Well-Being 2015.* Retrieved from https://www.childstats.gov/americaschildren15/family1.asp

Chilton, M., Knowles, M., Rabinowich, J., & Arnold, K. T. (2015). The relationship between childhood adversity and food insecurity: "It's like a bird nesting in your head." *Public Health Nutrition, 18*(14), 2643–2653. https://doi.org/10.1017/S1368980014003036

Choe, D. E., Olson, S. L., & Sameroff, A. J. (2013). The interplay of externalizing problems and physical and inductive discipline during childhood. *Developmental Psychology, 49*(11), 2029–2039. https://doi.org/10.1037/a0032054

Choi, M., Sprang, G., & Eslinger, J. G. (2016). Grandparents raising grandchildren: A synthetic review and theoretical model for interventions. *Family & Community Health, 39*(2), 120–128. https://doi.org/10.1097/FCH.0000000000000097

Chomsky, N. (1975). *Reflections on language.* New York, NY: Pantheon Books.

Chung, L. C. (2011). Crossing boundaries: Cross-cultural communication. In K. Keith (Ed.). *Cross-Cultural Psychology: Contemporary Themes and Perspectives* (pp. 400–419). Chichester, England: Wiley-Blackwell.

Claridge, G., & Canter, S. (1973/2013). *Personality differences and biological variations: A study of twins.* W. I. Hume (Ed.). Elmsford, NY: Pergamon Press.

Claridge, G., Canter, S., Hume, W. (1973/2013). *Personality differences and biological variations: A study of twins.* W. I. Hume (Ed.). Elmsford, NY: Pergamon Press.

Clarke, J. I., & Dawson, C. (1998). *Growing up again: Parenting ourselves, parenting our children* (2nd ed.). Center City, MN: Hazelden Information and Educational Services.

Clarke, J., Dawson, C., & Bredehoft, D. (2004/2014). *How much is too much? [previously published as How much is enough?]: Raising likeable, responsible, respectful children—from toddlers to teens—in an age of overindulgence.* Boston, MA: Da Capo Press.

Clifford, S., Lemery-Chalfant, K., & Goldsmith, H. H. (2015). The unique and shared genetic and environmental contributions to fear, anger, and sadness in childhood. *Child Development, 86*(5), 1538–1556. https://doi.org/10.1111/cdev.12394

Cohen, D. (2013). *Family secrets: Shame and privacy in modern Britain.* Oxford, England: Oxford University Press.

Cole, S. Z., & Lanham, J. S. (2011). Failure to thrive: An update. *American Family Physician, 83*(7). Retrieved from http://www.aafp.org/afp/2011/0401/p829.html

Colker, L. (2014). The world gap: The early years make the difference. *Teaching Young Children, 7*(3). Retrieved from https://www.naeyc.org/tyc/article/the-word-gap

Coller, R. J., & Kuo, A. A. (2014). Youth development through mentorship: A Los Angeles school-based mentorship program among Latino children. *Journal of Community Health, 39*(2), 316–321. https://doi.org/10.1007/s10900-013-9762-1

Coller, R. J., Stewart-Brown, S. L., & Blair, M. (2015). *Child health: A population perspective.* Oxford, England: Oxford University Press, Inc.

Collier-Harris, C. A., & Goldman, J. D. G. (2016). Puberty and sexuality education using a learning and teaching theoretical framework. *Educational Review*, 1–18. https://doi.org/10.1080/00131911.2016.1225672

Connidis, I. A., & McMullin, J. A. (2002). Sociological ambivalence and family ties: A critical perspective. *Journal of Marriage and Family, 64*(3), 558–567. https://doi.org/10.1111/j.1741-3737.2002.00558.x

Cook, R., Bird, G., Catmur, C., Press, C., & Heyes, C. (2014). Mirror neurons: From origin to function. *The Behavioral and Brain Sciences, 37*(2), 177–192. https://doi.org/10.1017/S0140525X13000903

Cooke, J. E., Stuart-Parrigon, K. L., Movahed-Abtahi, M., Koehn, A. J., & Kerns, K. A. (2016). Children's emotion understanding and mother–child attachment: A meta-analysis. *Emotion, 16*(8), 1102–1106. https://doi.org/10.1037/emo0000221

Cooper, C., Phillips, D., Osmond, C., Fall, C., & Eriksson, J. (2014). David James Purslove Barker: Clinician, scientist and father of the "fetal origins hypothesis." *Journal of Developmental Origins of Health and Disease, 5*(3), 161–163.

Copen, C. E., Chandra, A., & Febo-Vazquez, I. (2016). Sexual behavior, sexual attraction, and sexual orientation among adults aged 18–44 in the United States: Data from the 2011–2013 National Survey of Family Growth. *National Health Statistics Reports,* (88), 1–14.

Corr, C., & Santos, R. M. (2017). Abuse and young children with disabilities: A review of the literature. *Journal of Early Intervention, 39*(1), 3–17. https://doi.org/10.1177/1053815116677823

Cosmi, E., Fanelli, T., Visentin, S., Trevisanuto, D., & Zanardo, V. (2011). Review article: Consequences in infants that were intrauterine growth restricted. *Journal of Pregnancy, 2011.* Retrieved from http://www.hindawi.com/journals/jp/2011/364381/ref/

Costa, P. A., Pereira, H., & Leal, I. (2015). "The contact hypothesis" and attitudes toward same-sex parenting. *Sexuality Research and Social Policy*, *12*(2), 125–136. https://doi.org/10.1007/s13178-014-0171-8

Courage, M. L., Bakhtiar, A., Fitzpatrick, C., Kenny, S., & Brandeau, K. (2015). Growing up multitasking: The costs and benefits for cognitive development. *Developmental Review*, *35*, 5–41. https://doi.org/10.1016/j.dr.2014.12.002

Courtney, M., Dworsky, A., Brown, A., Cary, C., Love, K., & Vorhies, V. (2011). *Midwest evaluation of the adult functioning of former foster youth: Outcomes at age 26*. Chicago, IL: Chapin Hall at the University of Chicago. Retrieved from http://www.chapinhall.org/sites/default/files/Midwest%20Evaluation_Report_4_10_12.pdf

Couturier, J., Kimber, M., & Szatmari, P. (2013). Efficacy of family-based treatment for adolescents with eating disorders: A systematic review and meta-analysis. *International Journal of Eating Disorders*, *46*(1), 3–11. https://doi.org/10.1002/eat.22042

Coyne, C. A., & D'Onofrio, B. M. (2012). Some (but not much) progress toward understanding teenage childbearing: A review of research from the past decade. *Advances in Child Development and Behavior*, *42*, 113–152.

Cozolino, L. (2014). *The Neuroscience of human relationships: Attachment and the developing social brain* (2nd ed.). New York: NY: W.W. Norton & Company.

Crosnoe, R., & Cavanagh, S. E. (2010). Families with children and adolescents: A review, critique, and future agenda. *Journal of Marriage and Family*, *72*(3), 594–611.

Crowther, J. H., Hobfoll, S. E., Stephens, M. A., & Tennenbaum, D. L. (Eds.). (1992/2013). *The etiology of bulimia nervosa: The individual and familial context: Material arising from the second annual Kent Psychology Forum, Kent, October 1990*. Washington, DC: Taylor & Francis.

Cunningham, H. (2005). *Children and childhood in western society since 1500*. New York, NY: Pearson Longman.

Czeizel, A. E. (1995). Folic acid in the prevention of neural tube defects. *Journal of Pediatric Gastroenterology and Nutrition*, *20*(1), 4–16.

Dagdeviren, H., Donoghue, M., & Promberger, M. (2016). Resilience, hardship and social conditions. *Journal of Social Policy*, *45*, 1–20. http://dx.doi.org/10.1017/S004727941500032X

Dahl, G. B. (2010). Early teen marriage and future poverty. *Demography*, *47*(3), 689–718.

Daly, S. C., MacNeela, P., & Sarma, K. M. (2015). When parents separate and one parent "comes out" as lesbian, gay or bisexual: Sons and daughters engage with the tension that occurs when their family unit changes. *PLOS ONE*, *10*(12). Retrieved from http://search.proquest.com.fetch.mhsl.uab.edu/docview/1764149893/D00EE4F41761479BPQ/1

Daniels, S. R. (2016). The editors' perspectives: The barker hypothesis revisited. *The Journal of Pediatrics*, 173, 1–3. https://doi.org/10.1016/j.jpeds.2016.04.031

Davey, M., Kissil, K., & Lynch, L. (2016). *Helping children and families cope with parental illness: A clinician's guide*. New York, NY: Routledge.

Davidson, J., & Wood, C. (2003). Helping families cope: A fresh look at parent effectiveness training. *Family Matters*, (65), 28–33.

Davis, G. A., Rimm, S. B., & Siegle, D. B. (2010). *Education of the gifted and talented* (6th ed.). Upper Saddle River, NJ: Pearson.

Davis, T. J., Morris, M., & Drake, M. M. (2016). The moderation effect of mindfulness on the relationship between adult attachment and wellbeing. *Personality and Individual Differences*, *96*, 115–121. https://doi.org/10.1016/j.paid.2016.02.080

Dawson, A., Sharma, P., Irving, P. G., Marcus, J., & Chirico, F. (2015). Predictors of later-generation family members' commitment to family enterprises. *Entrepreneurship Theory and Practice*, *39*(3), 545–569. https://doi.org/10.1111/etap.12052

Dawson, P. (2016). The first eight years ~ Giving kids a foundation for a lifetime success resource review. *Journal of Youth Development*, *8*(3), 134–136. https://doi.org/10.5195/jyd.2013.90

Dawson-McClure, S., Calzada, E., Huang, K.-Y., Kamboukos, D., Rhule, D., Kolawole, B., … Brotman, L. M. (2015). A population-level approach to promoting healthy child development and school success in low-income, urban neighborhoods: Impact on parenting and child conduct problems. *Prevention Science*, *16*(2), 279–290. https://doi.org/10.1007/s11121-014-0473-3

De Bellaigue, C. (2015). Charlotte Mason, home education and the Parents' National Educational Union in the late nineteenth century. *Oxford Review of Education*, *41*(4), 501–517. https://doi.org/10.1080/03054985.2015.1048117

De Bolle, M., De Fruyt, F., McCrae, R. R., Löckenhoff, C. E., Costa Jr., P. T., Aguilar-Vafaie, M. E., Terracciano, A. (2015). The emergence of sex differences in personality traits in early adolescence: A cross-sectional, cross-cultural study. *Journal of Personality and Social Psychology*, *108*(1), 171–185. https://doi.org/10.1037/a0038497

De Lissovoy, V. (1973a). Child care by adolescent parents. *Children Today*, *2*(4), 22–25.

De Lissovoy, V. (1973b). High school marriages: A longitudinal study. *Journal of Marriage and Family*, *35*(2), 245–255. https://doi.org/10.2307/350653

Degner, J., & Dalege, J. (2013). The apple does not fall far from the tree, or does it? A meta-analysis of parent–child similarity in intergroup attitudes. *Psychological Bulletin*, *139*(6), 1270. https://doi.org/10.1037/a0031436

DeGue, S., Valle, L. A., Holt, M. K., Massetti, G. M., Matjasko, J. L., & Tharp, A. T. (2014). A systematic review of primary prevention strategies for sexual violence perpetration. *Aggression and Violent Behavior*, *19*(4), 346–362. https://doi.org/10.1016/j.avb.2014.05.004

DeHaan, L. G., Hawley, D. R., & Deal, J. E. (2013). Operationalizing family resilience as process: Proposed methodological strategies. In D. S. Becvar (Ed.), *Handbook of family resilience* (pp. 17–29). New York, NY: Springer. https://doi.org/10.1007/978-1-4614-3917-2_2

Deliens, G., Gilson, M., & Peigneux, P. (2014). Sleep and the processing of emotions. *Experimental Brain Research*, *232*(5), 1403–1414. https://doi.org/10.1007/s00221-014-3832-1

DeLoache, J. S., & Gottlieb, A. (2000). Gift from the gods: A Balinese guide to early child rearing. In *a World of Babies: Imagined Childcare Guides for Seven Societies*. Cambridge, England: Cambridge University Press.

Delvoye, M., & Tasker, F. (2016). Narrating self-identity in bisexual motherhood. *Journal of GLBT Family Studies*, *12*(1), 5–23. https://doi.org/10.1080/1550428X.2015.1038675

Demick, J., Bursik, K., & DiBiase, R. (Eds.). (2014). *Parental development*. New York, NY: Psychology Press.

Dere, J., Ryder, A. G., & Kirmayer, L. J. (2010). Bidimensional measurement of acculturation in a multiethnic community sample of first-generation immigrants. *Canadian Journal of Behavioural Science/Revue Canadienne Des Sciences Du Comportement*, *42*(2), 134–138.

Dermott, E. (2014). *Intimate fatherhood: A sociological analysis*. 2nd ed. New York, NY: Routledge.

Deshpande, A., & Pandey, N. (2014). Psychological impact of parental divorce on children: A qualitative study. *Indian Journal of Health and Wellbeing*, *5*(10), 1201–1205. Retrieved from http://search.proquest.com/openview/d8edc721640d-434925946cd4979d9e82/1?pq-origsite=gscholar

Devaney, E. (2015). *Ready for work? How after-school programs can support employability through social and emotional learning. Beyond the bell: Research to practice in the afterschool and expanded learning field*. American Institutes for Research. Retrieved from http://eric.ed.gov/?id=ED563829

Development Services Group, Inc., & Child Welfare Information Gateway. (2015). *Promoting protective factors for pregnant and parenting teens: A guide for practitioners*. Washington, DC: Department of Health and Human Services, Administration on Children, Youth and Families, Children's Bureau. Retrieved from https://www.childwelfare.gov/pubs/factsheets/guide-teen/

DeVoe, E. R., & Ross, A. (2012). The parenting cycle of deployment. *Military Medicine*, *177*(2), 184–190.

Diamond, J. (2010). The benefits of multilingualism. *Science*, *330*(6002), 332–333.

Diamond, L. M., Pardo, S. T., & Butterworth, M. R. (2011). Transgender experience and identity. In S. J. Schwartz, K. Luyckx, & V. L. Vignoles (Eds.), *Handbook of identity theory and research* (pp. 629–647). New York, NY: Springer. https://doi.org/10.1007/978-1-4419-7988-9_26

Dishion, T. J., Nelson, S. E., & Kavanagh, K. (2003). The family check-up with high-risk young adolescents: Preventing early-onset substance use by parent monitoring [Special Issue]. *Behavior Therapy, 34*, 553–571.

Doepke, M., & Zilibotti, F. (2014). *"Parenting with style: Altruism and paternalism in intergenerational preference transmission." Working paper*. National Bureau of Economic Research. doi:10.3386/w20214.

Doh, H. S., & Falbo, T. (1999). Social competence, maternal attentiveness, and overprotectiveness: Only children in Korea. *International Journal of Behavioral Development, 23*(1), 149–162. https://doi.org/10.1080/016502599384044

Domenici, T. & Lesser, R. C. (Eds.). (1995). *Disorienting sexuality: Psychoanalytic reappraisals of sexual identities*. New York, NY: Routledge.

Dominus, S. (2015). The mixed-up brothers of Bogotá. *The New York Times*. Retrieved from http://www.nytimes.com/2015/07/12/magazine/the-mixed-up-brothers-of-bogota.html

Döring, A. K., Schwartz, S. H., Cieciuch, J., Groenen, P. J. F., Glatzel, V., Harasimczuk, J., … Bilsky, W. (2015). Cross-cultural evidence of value structures and priorities in childhood. *British Journal of Psychology, 106*(4), 675–699. https://doi.org/10.1111/bjop.12116

Döring, A. K., Uzefovsky, F., & Knafo-Noam, A. (2015). Values in middle childhood: Social and genetic contributions. *Social Development, 25*(3), 482–502. Retrieved from https://dx.doi.org/10.1111/sode.12155

Doss, B. D., & Rhoades, G. K. (2017). The transition to parenthood: Impact on couples' romantic relationships. *Current Opinion in Psychology, 13*, 25–28. https://doi.org/10.1016/j.copsyc.2016.04.003

Doucerain, M., Dere, J., & Ryder, A. G. (2013). Travels in hyper-diversity: Multiculturalism and the contextual assessment of acculturation. *International Journal of Intercultural Relations, 37*(6), 686–699.

Doucet, A. (2016). Single Fathers. In *Encyclopedia of family studies*. John Wiley & Sons, Inc. https://doi.org/10.1002/9781119085621.wbefs396

Downey, D. B., & Condron, D. J. (2004). Playing well with others in kindergarten: The benefit of siblings at home. *Journal of Marriage and Family, 66*(2), 333–350. https://doi.org/10.1111/j.1741-3737.2004.00024.x

Downs, J. O. (2015). Positive behavioral interventions and supports vs. corporal punishment: A literature review. *International Journal for Cross-Disciplinary Subjects in Education (IJCDSE), 6*(1). Retrieved from http://infonomics-society.ie/wp-content/uploads/ijcdse/published-papers/volume-6-2015/Positive-Behavioral-Interventions.pdf

Dreikurs, R. (1946). *Manual of child guidance*. Ann Arbor, MI: Edward Bros.

Dreikurs, R. (1948). *The challenge of parenthood*. New York, NY: Duell, Sloan, & Pearce.

Drescher, J., & Byne, W. (2012). Gender dysphoric/gender variant children and adolescents: Summarizing what we know and what we have yet to learn. *Journal of Homosexuality, 59*(3), 501–510. https://doi.org/10.1080/00918369.2012.653317

Drozd, L., Olesen, N., & Saini, M. (Eds.). (2016). *Parenting plan evaluations: Applied research for the family court* (2nd ed.). New York, NY: Oxford University Press.

Duckworth, A. (2016). *Grit: The power of passion and perseverance*. New York, NY: Scribner.

Duncan, M. L. (2016a). Adoption, GLBT. In *Encyclopedia of family studies*. John Wiley & Sons, Inc.

Duncan, M. L. (2016b). Reproductive rights. *In Encyclopedia of Family Studies*. John Wiley & Sons, Inc. Retrieved from http://onlinelibrary.wiley.com/doi/10.1002/9781119085621.wbefs440/abstract

Duncan, S., & Fiske, D. W. (2015). *Face-to-face interaction: Research, methods, and theory*. New York, NY: Routledge.

Dunsworth, H. M. (2016). Thank your intelligent mother for your big brain. *Proceedings of the National Academy of Sciences, 113*(25), 6816–6818. https://doi.org/10.1073/pnas.1606596113

Dwyer, L., Oh, A., Patrick, H., & Hennessy, E. (2015). Promoting family meals: A review of existing interventions and opportunities for future research. *Adolescent Health, Medicine and Therapeutics, 6*, 115–131. https://doi.org/10.2147/AHMT.S37316

Early Childhood Learning and Knowledge Center. (2016). Head start program facts fiscal year 2015. Retrieved from https://eclkc.ohs.acf.hhs.gov/hslc/data/factsheets/2015-hs-program-factsheet.html

East, P. L. & Felice, M. E. (2014). *Adolescent pregnancy and parenting: Findings from a racially diverse sample*. New York, NY: Psychology Press.

Edin, K., & Kissane, R. J. (2010). Poverty and the American family: A decade in review. *Journal of Marriage and Family, 72*(3), 460–479. https://doi.org/10.1111/j.1741-3737.2010.00713.x

Elder, G. H. (1998). *Children of the Great Depression, 25th anniversary edition*. Boulder, CO: Westview Press.

Elkind, D. (2011). *The child's reality: Three developmental themes*. New York, NY: Psychology Press.

Ellis, A., Chebsey, C., Storey, C., Bradley, S., Jackson, S., Flenady, V., Siassakos, D. (2016). Systematic review to understand and improve care after stillbirth: A review of parents' and healthcare professionals' experiences. *BMC Pregnancy and Childbirth, 16*. https://doi.org/10.1186/s12884-016-0806-2

Ellis, B. J., Boyce, W. T., Belsky, J., Bakermans-Kranenburg, M. J., & Van Ijzendoorn, M. H. (2011). Differential susceptibility to the environment: An evolutionary–neurodevelopmental theory. *Development and Psychopathology, 23*(1), 7–28. https://doi.org/10.1017/S0954579410000611

Ellis, B. J., Volk, A. A., Gonzalez, J. M., & Embry, D. D. (2015). The meaningful roles intervention: An evolutionary approach to reducing bullying and increasing prosocial behavior. *Journal of Research on Adolescence, 26*(4), 622–637. doi:http://dx.doi.org/10.1111/jora.12243.

Ellman, I. M., & Braver, S. L. (2015). Child support and the custodial mother's move or remarriage: What citizens believe the law should be. *Psychology, Public Policy, and Law, 21*(2), 145–60. doi:http://dx.doi.org/10.1037/law0000045

Emery, A. E. H. (2013). Hippocrates and the oath. *Journal of Medical Biography, 21*(4).

Emery, C. R., Trung, H. N., & Wu, S. (2015). Neighborhood informal social control and child maltreatment: A comparison of protective and punitive approaches. *Child Abuse & Neglect, 41*, 158.

Erford, B. (2014). *Orientation to the counseling profession: Advocacy, ethics, and essential professional foundations* (2nd ed.). New York, NY: Pearson.

Erikson, E. (1950/1993). *Childhood and society*. New York, NY: W. W. Norton & Company, Inc.

Erikson, E. (1959) Identity and the life cycle: Selected papers. *Psychological Issues, 1*(1), 1–171.

Erikson, E. (1964). *Insight and responsibility*. New York, NY: W. W. Norton & Company, Inc.

Erikson, E. (1982). *The life cycle completed*. New York, NY: W. W. Norton & Company, Inc.

Erikson, E., Erikson, J., & Kivnick, H. (1986). *Vital involvement in old age*. New York, NY: W. W. Norton & Company, Inc.

Ermisch, J. F. (2003/2016). *An economic analysis of the family*. Princeton, NJ: Princeton University Press.

Fabiano, G. A., Waxmonsky, J. G., Greiner, A. R., Gnagy, E. M., Pelham, W. E., Coxe, S., … Murphy, S. A. (2016). Treatment sequencing for childhood ADHD: A multiple-randomization study of adaptive medication and behavioral interventions. *Journal of Clinical Child & Adolescent Psychology, 45*(4), 396–415. https://doi.org/10.1080/15374416.2015.1105138

Fagan, J. (2014). Adolescent parents' partner conflict and parenting alliance, fathers' prenatal involvement, and fathers' engagement with infants. *Journal of Family Issues, 35*(11), 1415–1439. https://doi.org/10.1177/0192513X13491411

Fagan, J., Levine, E. C., Kaufman, R., & Hammar, C. (2016). Low-income, nonresident fathers' coparenting with multiple mothers and relatives: Effects on fathering. *Journal of Family Psychology, 30*(6), 665–675. https://doi.org/10.1037/fam0000231

Falbo, T. (2012). Only children: An updated review. *The Journal of Individual Psychology, 68*(1), 38–49.

Family Equality Council. (2013). *The outspoken generation*. Retrieved from https://www.youtube.com/watch?v=MJnkp6D3j7c

FamilyWise. (n.d.). *Youth services: Bright beginnings young parent mentoring program*. Retrieved from http://familywiseservices.org/programs-services/youth-services/

Farr, R. H., Oakley, M. K., & Ollen, E. W. (2016). School experiences of young children and their lesbian and gay adoptive parents. *Psychology of Sexual Orientation and Gender Diversity 3*(4), 442–47. doi:http://dx.doi.org/10.1037/sgd0000187.

Farr, R. H., Tasker, F., & Goldberg, A. E. (2016). Theory in highly cited studies of sexual minority parent families: Variations and implications. *Journal of Homosexuality*, 1–37. https://doi.org/10.1080/00918369.2016.1242336

Featherstone, B. (2016). Telling different stories about poverty, inequality, child abuse and neglect. *Families, Relationships and Societies*, 5(1), 147–153. https://doi.org/10.1332/204674316X14540714620085

Federal Interagency Forum on Child and Family Statistics. (2010). *America's children: Key national indicators of well-being, 2010*. Washington, DC: US Government Printing Office.

Federal Interagency Forum on Child and Family Statistics. (2011). *America's children: Key national indicators of well-being, 2011*. Washington, DC: US Government Printing Office.

Federal Interagency Forum on Child and Family Statistics (2012). *America's children at a glance, 2012*. Washington, DC: US Government Printing Office.

Federal Interagency Forum on Child and Family Statistics. (2015). *America's children: Key national indicators of well-being, 2015*. Washington, DC: US Government Printing Office.

Federal Interagency Forum on Child and Family Statistics. (2016). *America's children: Key national indicators of well-being, 2016*. Washington, DC: US Government Printing Office.

Fedewa, A. L., Black, W. W., & Ahn, S. (2015). Children and adolescents with same-gender parents: A meta-analytic approach in assessing outcomes. *Journal of GLBT Family Studies*, 11(1), 1–34. https://doi.org/10.1080/1550428X.2013.869486

Feldman, R. (2015). The adaptive human parental brain: Implications for children's social development. *Trends in Neurosciences*, 38(6), 387–399. https://doi.org/10.1016/j.tins.2015.04.004

Feldman, R. (2017). The neurobiology of human attachments. *Trends in Cognitive Sciences*, 21(2), 21,80–99. doi.org/10.1016/j.tics.2016.11.007

Feldman, R., Monakhov, M., Pratt, M., & Ebstein, R. P. (2016). Oxytocin pathway genes: Evolutionarily ancient system impacting on human affiliation, sociality, and psychopathology. *Biological Psychiatry*, 79(3), 174–184. https://doi.org/10.1016/j.biopsych.2015.08.008

Feldman, R., Rosenthal, Z., & Eidelman, A. I. (2014). Maternal-preterm skin-to-skin contact enhances child physiologic organization and cognitive control across the first 10 years of life. *Biological Psychiatry*, 75(1), 56–64. http://dx.doi.org/10.1016/j.biopsych.2013.08.012

Felfe, C., Nollenberger, N., & Rodríguez-Planas, N. (2015). Can't buy mommy's love? Universal childcare and children's long-term cognitive development. *Journal of Population Economics*, 28(2), 393–422. https://doi.org/10.1007/s00148-014-0532-x

Feng, W., Gu, B., & Cai, Y. (2016). The end of China's one-child policy. *Studies in Family Planning*, 47(1), 83–86. https://doi.org/10.1111/j.1728-4465.2016.00052.x

Ferguson, C. J., Muñoz, M. E., Garza, A., & Galindo, M. (2014). Concurrent and prospective analyses of peer, television and social media influences on body dissatisfaction, eating disorder symptoms and life satisfaction in adolescent girls. *Journal of Youth and Adolescence*, 43(1), 1–14. https://doi.org/10.1007/s10964-012-9898-9

Fernald, A., Marchman, V. A., & Weisleder, A. (2013). SES differences in language processing skill and vocabulary are evident at 18 months. *Developmental Science*, 16(2), 234–248. https://doi.org/10.1111/desc.12019

Ferrari, P. F., & Coudé, G. (2011). Mirror neurons and imitation from a developmental and evolutionary perspective. In A. Vilain, J.-L. Schwartz, C. Abry, J. Vauclair, A. Vilain, J.-L. Schwartz, … , J. Vauclair (Eds.), *Primate communication and human language: Vocalisation, gestures, imitation and deixis in humans and non-humans.* (Vol. 1, pp. 121–138). Amsterdam, The Netherlands: John Benjamins Publishing Company.

Ferraro, G., & Andreatta, S. (2014). *Cultural anthropology: An applied perspective*, (10th ed.). Stamford, CT: Cengage Learning.

Ferreira, R. J., & Buttell, F. P. (2016). Can a "psychosocial model" help explain violence perpetrated by female batterers? *Research on Social Work Practice*, 26(4), 362–371. https://doi.org/10.1177/1049731514543665

Ferrera, M. (2005). *Peoples of the world*. Vercelli, Italy: White Star.

Few-Demo, A. L., & Demo, D. H. (2015). Family diversity. In *The Wiley Blackwell encyclopedia of race, ethnicity, and nationalism*. John Wiley & Sons, Ltd. Retrieved from http://onlinelibrary.wiley.com/doi/10.1002/9781118663202.wberen464/abstract

Fields, J. (2015). *Families living with mental and physical challenges*. Broomall, PA: Mason Crest Publisher, Inc.

Figley, C. R., & McCubbin, H. I. (2016). *Stress and the family: Coping with catastrophe*. New York, NY: Routledge.

Fillo, J., Simpson, J. A., Rholes, W. S., & Kohn, J. L. (2015). Dads doing diapers: Individual and relational outcomes associated with the division of childcare across the transition to parenthood. *Journal of Personality and Social Psychology*, 108(2), 298–316. https://doi.org/10.1037/a0038572

Fine, M. J. (1989/2014). *The second handbook on parent education: Contemporary perspectives*. San Diego, CA: Academic Press.

Fingerhut, H. (2016). Support steady for same-sex marriage and acceptance of homosexuality. *Pew Research Center*. Retrieved from http://www.pewresearch.org/fact-tank/2016/05/12/support-steady-for-same-sex-marriage-and-acceptance-of-homosexuality/

Fingerman, K. L., Kim, K., Tennant, P. S., Birditt, K. S., & Zarit, S. H. (2016). Intergenerational support in a daily context. *The Gerontologist*, 56(5), 896–908. https://doi.org/10.1093/geront/gnv035

Fingerman, K. L., Pillemer, K. A., Silverstein, M., & Suitor, J. J. (2012). The baby boomers' intergenerational relationships. *The Gerontologist*, 52(2), 199–209. https://doi.org/10.1093/geront/gnr139

Finigan-Carr, N. M., Murray, K. W., O'Connor, J. M., Rushovich, B. R., Dixon, D. A., & Barth, R. P. (2015). Preventing rapid repeat pregnancy and promoting positive parenting among young mothers in foster care. *Social Work in Public Health*, 30(1), 1–17. https://doi.org/10.1080/19371918.2014.938388

Finkenauer, C., Buyukcan-Tetik, A., Baumeister, R. F., Schoemaker, K., Bartels, M., & Vohs, K. D. (2015). Out of control: Identifying the role of self-control strength in family violence. *Current Directions in Psychological Science*, 24(4), 261–266. https://doi.org/10.1177/0963721415570730

Fisch, H., Hyun, G., Golden, R., Hensle, T. W., Olsson, C. A., & Liberson, G. L. (2003). The influence of paternal age on Down syndrome. *The Journal of Urology*, 169(6), 2275–2278. https://doi.org/10.1097/01.ju.0000067958.36077.d8

Fitz, B. M., Lyon, L., & Driskell, R. (2016). Why people like where they live: Individual- and community-level contributors to community satisfaction. *Social Indicators Research*, 126(3), 1209–1224. https://doi.org/10.1007/s11205-015-0922-9

Flores, A. (2014). National trends in public opinion on LGBT rights in the United States. *The Williams Institute*. Retrieved from https://williamsinstitute.law.ucla.edu/research/census-lgbt-demographics-studies/natl-trends-nov-2014/

Flournoy, J. C., Pfeifer, J. H., Moore, W. E., Tackman, A. M., Masten, C. L., Mazziotta, J. C., … Dapretto, M. (2016). Neural reactivity to emotional faces may mediate the relationship between childhood empathy and adolescent prosocial behavior. *Child Development*, 87(6), 1691–1702. https://doi.org/10.1111/cdev.12630

Flynn, A. B., Johnson, R. M., Bolton, S., & Mojtabai, R. (2016). Victimization of lesbian, gay, and bisexual people in childhood: Associations with attempted suicide. *Suicide and Life-Threatening Behavior*, 46(4), 457–470. https://doi.org/10.1111/sltb.12228

Fogleman, S., Santana, C., Bishop, C., Miller, A., & Capco, D. G. (2016). CRISPR/Cas9 and mitochondrial gene replacement therapy: Promising techniques and ethical considerations. *American Journal of Stem Cells*, 5(2), 39–52.

Forry, N., Iruka, I., Tout, K., Torquati, J., Susman-Stillman, A., Bryant, D., & Daneri, M. P. (2013). Predictors of quality and child outcomes in family child care settings. *Early Childhood Research Quarterly*, 28(4), 893–904. https://doi.org/10.1016/j.ecresq.2013.05.006

Fortenberry, J. D. (2013). Puberty and adolescent sexuality. *Hormones and Behavior*, 64(2), 280–287. https://doi.org/10.1016/j.yhbeh.2013.03.007

Foster Care to Adopt. (2017). Retrieved from https://www.togetherwerise.org

Fragile Families and Child Wellbeing Study (n.d.). Fact sheet. Retrieved from http://fragilefamilies.princeton.edu/sites/fragilefamilies/files/ff_fact_sheet.pdf

Francis, D. A. (2017). Shifting positions of inclusion. In *Troubling the teaching and learning of gender and sexuality diversity in South African education*, 71–87. Queer Studies and Education. New York, NY: Palgrave Macmillan US. doi:10.1057/978-1-137-53027-1_5.

Frankl, V. (1959). *Man's search for meaning*. Boston, MA: Beacon Press.

Frankl, V. E. (1969/2014). *The will to meaning: Foundations and applications of logotherapy*. New York, NY: Penguin Group.

Fransson, E., Turunen, J., Hjern, A., Östberg, V., & Bergström, M. (2016). Psychological complaints among children in joint physical custody and other family types: Considering parental factors. *Scandinavian Journal of Social Medicine*, 44(2), 177–183. https://doi.org/10.1177/1403494815614463

Fréchette, S., Zoratti, M., & Romano, E. (2015). What is the link between corporal punishment and child physical abuse? *Journal of Family Violence*, 30(2), 135–148. https://doi.org/10.1007/s10896-014-9663-9

Freese, J. S., Smith, A. M., & Grzywacz, J. G. (2016). Maternal employment and child health: Conceptual and empirical foundations for work and family "Weaving Strategies." In C. Spitzmueller & R. A. Matthews (Eds.), *Research perspectives on work and the transition to motherhood* (pp. 171–197). Switzerland: Springer International Publishing. https://doi.org/10.1007/978-3-319-41121-7_9

Frost, G. S. (2009). *Victorian childhoods*. Westport, CT: Praeger.

Fukuyama, F. (1995). *Trust: The social virtues and the creation of prosperity*. New York, NY: Free Press.

Gabor, A. M., Fritz, J. N., Roath, C. T., Rothe, B. R., & Gourley, D. A. (2016). Caregiver preference for reinforcement-based interventions for problem behavior maintained by positive reinforcement. *Journal of Applied Behavior Analysis*, 49(2), 215–227. https://doi.org/10.1002/jaba.286

Gadzikowski, A. (2013). Preschool: Differentiation strategies for exceptionally bright children. *YC Young Children*, 68(2), 8–14.

Gaillard, A., Le Strat, Y., Mandelbrot, L., Keïta, H., & Dubertret, C. (2014). Predictors of postpartum depression: Prospective study of 264 women followed during pregnancy and postpartum. *Psychiatry Research*, 215(2), 341–346. https://doi.org/10.1016/j.psychres.2013.10.003

Galanaki, E. P. (2012). The imaginary audience and the personal fable: A test of Elkind's theory of adolescent egocentrism. *Psychology*, 3(6), 457. https://doi.org/10.4236/psych.2012.36065

Galinsky, E. (1987). The six stages of parenthood. In R. L. Newman (Ed.), *Building relationships with parents and families in school age programs* (pp. 56–69). Reading, MA: Perseus Books.

Galinsky, E. (2010). *Mind in the making: The seven essential life skills every child needs*. New York, NY: HarperStudio.

Galinsky, E. (2016). Research to action: Review of research conducted by the families and work institute. In T. Allen & L. Eby (Eds.), *The Oxford Handbook of Work and Family*. Chapter 15. Oxford, United Kingdom: Oxford University Press. Retrieved from http://www.oxfordhandbooks.com/view/10.1093/oxfordhb/9780199337538.001.0001/oxfordhb-9780199337538-e-24

Galvin, K. M., Braithwaite, D. O., & Bylund, C. L. (2015). *Family communication: Cohesion and change*. New York, NY: Routledge.

Ganong, L., & Coleman, M. (2016). Gay and lesbian couples in stepfamilies. In *Stepfamily relationships*, 111–124. New York, NY: Springer. doi:10.1007/978-1-4899-7702-1_6.

Ganong, L. & Coleman, M. (2017a). *Stepfamily relationships: Development, dynamics and interventions* (2nd ed.). New York, NY: Springer.

Ganong, L., & Coleman, M. (2017b). Siblings, half-siblings, and stepsiblings. In *Stepfamily relationships* (pp. 191–204). New York, NY: Springer. https://doi.org/10.1007/978-1-4899-7702-1_10

Ganong, L., & Coleman, M. (2017c). The dynamics of stepparenting. In *Stepfamily relationships* (pp. 143–173). New York, NY: Springer. https://doi.org/10.1007/978-1-4899-7702-1_8

Ganong, L. H., Coleman, M., & Jamison, T. (2011). Patterns of stepchild–stepparent relationship development. *Journal of Marriage and Family* 73(2), 396–413. doi.org/10.1111/j.1741-3737.2010.00814.x.

García, J. L., Heckman, J. J., Leaf, D. E., & Prados, M. J. (2016). *The life-cycle benefits of an influential early childhood program*. Rochester, NY: Social Science Research Network. Retrieved from https://papers.ssrn.com/abstract=2884880

Gardner, R. (Ed.). (2016). *Tackling child neglect: Research, policy and evidence-based practice*. Philadelphia, PA: Jessica Kingsley Publishers.

Garfinkel, I., McLanahan, S. S., & Wimer, C. (Eds.). (2016). *Children of the great recession*. New York, NY: Russell Sage Foundation.

Garneau, C. (2016). Remarriage. In *Encyclopedia of Family Studies*. John Wiley & Sons, Inc. doi:10.1002/9781119085621.wbefs256.

Garneau, C. L., Higginbotham, B., & Adler-Baeder, F. (2015). Remarriage beliefs as predictors of marital quality and positive interaction in stepcouples: An actor–partner interdependence model. *Family Process*, 54(4), 730–745. https://doi.org/10.1111/famp.12153

Garretson, J. (1701/1983). *The school of manners, or rules for childrens behaviour: At church, at home, at table, in company, in discourse, at school, abroad, and among boys, with some other short and mixt precepts* (4th ed.). London, England: Oregon Press for the Victoria and Albert Museum.

Garretson, J., & Suhay, E. (2016). Scientific communication about biological influences on homosexuality and the politics of gay rights. *Political Research Quarterly*, 69(1), 17–29.

Gartstein, M. A., Bell, M. A., & Calkins, S. D. (2014). EEG asymmetry at 10 months of age: Are temperament trait predictors different for boys and girls? *Developmental Psychobiology*, 56(6), 1327–1340. doi:10.1002/dev.21212.

Gaspari, A. (2016). Inheriting your mother's eyes, hair, and drug addiction: Protecting the drug-exposed newborn by criminalizing pregnant drug use. *Family Court Review*, 54, 96.

Gates, G. (2013). LGBT parenting in the United States. *The William Institute*. Retrieved from http://williamsinstitute.law.ucla.edu/research/census-lgbt-demographics-studies/lgbt-parenting-in-the-united-states/

Gates, G. (2015a). Lesbian, gay, bisexual, and transgender family formation and demographics. In W. Swan (Ed.), *Gay, Lesbian, Bisexual, and Transgender Civil Rights: A Public Policy Agenda for Uniting a Divided America* (pp. 21–34). Boca Raton, FL: CRC Press.

Gates, G. J. (2015b). Marriage and family: LGBT individuals and same-sex couples. *The Future of Children*, 25(2), 67–87.

Gatrell, C. J., Burnett, S. B., Cooper, C. L., & Sparrow, P. (2015). The price of love: The prioritisation of childcare and income earning among UK fathers. *Families, Relationships and Societies*, 4(2), 225–238. https://doi.org/10.1332/204674315X14321355649771

Geel, M. van, Toprak, F., Goemans, A., Zwaanswijk, W., & Vedder, P. (2016). Are youth psychopathic traits related to bullying? Meta-analyses on callous-unemotional traits, narcissism, and impulsivity. *Child Psychiatry & Human Development*, 1–10. https://doi.org/10.1007/s10578-016-0701-0

Geller, A., Cooper, C. E., Garfinkel, I., Schwartz-Soicher, O., & Mincy, R. B. (2012). Beyond absenteeism: Father incarceration and child development. *Demography*, 49(1), 49–76. https://doi.org/10.1007/s13524-011-0081-9

Geller, A., Garfinkel, I., & Western, B. (2011). Paternal incarceration and support for children in fragile families. *Demography*, 48(1), 25–47. https://doi.org/10.1007/s13524-010-0009-9

Gerhardt, C. (2016a).Circumplex model of marital and family systems. In C. L. Shehan (Ed.). *Encyclopedia of family studies*, 1, 356–358. Hoboken, NJ: John Wiley & Sons, Inc.

Gerhardt, C. (2016b). Family of procreation. In C. L. Shehan (Ed.). *Encyclopedia of family studies*, 2, 755–757. Hoboken, NJ: John Wiley & Sons, Inc. Retrieved from http://onlinelibrary.wiley.com/doi/10.1002/9781119085621.wbefs223/abstract

Gerhardt, C. (2016c). Globalization and families. In C. L. Shehan (Ed.). *Encyclopedia of family studies*, 2, 979–986. Hoboken, NJ: John Wiley & Sons, Inc. Retrieved from http://onlinelibrary.wiley.com/doi/10.1002/9781119085621.wbefs236/abstract

Gerhardt, C. (2016d). Intergenerational relationships. In C. L. Shehan (Ed.). *Encyclopedia of family studies*, 3, 1159–1166. Hoboken, NJ: John Wiley & Sons, Inc.

Gerhardt, C. (2016e). Only children. In C. L. Shehan (Ed.). *Encyclopedia of family studies, 3,* 1533–1536. Hoboken, NJ: John Wiley & Sons, Inc.

Gerhardt, C. & Gerhardt, C.M. (2009). *Creativity and group dynamics in problem-based learning context.* In O.Tan (Ed.), Problem-based learning and creativity (pp. 109-126). Singapore: Cengage Learning.

Gershoff, E. T. (2013). Spanking and child development: We know enough now to stop hitting our children. *Child Development Perspectives, 7*(3), 133–137. https://doi.org/10.1111/cdep.12038

Gershoff, E. T., & Grogan-Kaylor, A. (2016). Spanking and child outcomes: Old controversies and new meta-analyses. *Journal of Family Psychology, 30*(4), 453–469. doi:http://dx.doi.org/10.1037/fam0000191

Gerson, S. A., & Woodward, A. L. (2014). Learning from their own actions: The unique effect of producing actions on infants' action understanding. *Child Development, 85*(1), 264–277. https://doi.org/10.1111/cdev.12115

Ghaziani, A., Taylor, V., & Stone, A. (2016). Cycles of sameness and difference in LGBT social movements. *Annual Review of Sociology, 42*(1), 165–183. https://doi.org/10.1146/annurev-soc-073014-112352

Giarrusso, R., Feng, D., & Bengtson, V. L. (2005). The intergenerational-stake phenomenon over 20 years. In M. Silverstein & S. K. Warner (Ed.). *Annual review of gerontology and geriatrics, 2004: Focus on intergenerational relations across time and place,* 55–76. New York, NY: Springer. Retrieved from http://search.proquest.com.fetch.mhsl.uab.edu/docview/1760852003/8D02290774484DE4PQ/1.

Gibbs, J. J., & Goldbach, J. (2015). Religious conflict, sexual identity, and suicidal behaviors among LGBT young adults. *Archives of Suicide Research: Official Journal of the International Academy for Suicide Research, 19*(4), 472–488. https://doi.org/10.1080/13811118.2015.1004476

Giesbrecht, G. F., Miller, M. R., & Müller, U. (2010). The anger–distress model of temper tantrums: Associations with emotional reactivity and emotional competence. *Infant and Child Development, 19*(5), 478–497. https://doi.org/10.1002/icd.677

Gilmore, D. L., Esmail, A., & Eargle, L. A. (2016). Lesbian parents. In *Encyclopedia of family studies.* John Wiley & Sons, Inc. doi:10.1002/9781119085621.wbefs180

Gilpin, N. W. (2014). Brain reward and stress systems in addiction. *Frontiers in Psychiatry, 5*(79). doi:10.3389/fpsyt.2014.00079

Ginott, H. G. (1965). *Between parent and child: New solutions to old problems.* New York, NY: Three Rivers Press.

Glick, J. E. (2010). Connecting complex processes: A decade of research on immigrant families. *Journal of Marriage & Family, 72*(3), 498–515.

Glover, V. (2014). Maternal depression, anxiety and stress during pregnancy and child outcome; what needs to be done. *Best Practice & Research Clinical Obstetrics & Gynaecology, 28*(1), 25–35. https://doi.org/10.1016/j.bpobgyn.2013.08.017

Goddings, A. L., Heyes, S. B., Bird, G., Viner, R. M., & Blakemore, S. J. (2012). The relationship between puberty and social emotion processing. *Developmental Science, 15*(6), 801–811. https://doi.org/10.1111/j.1467-7687.2012.01174.x

Gold, J. M. (2015). Intergenerational attachments in stepfamilies facilitating the role of the step-grandparents. *The Family Journal, 23*(2), 194–200.

Gold, J. M., & Adeyemi, O. (2013). Stepfathers and noncustodial fathers: Two men, one role. *The Family Journal, 21*(1), 99–103. https://doi.org/10.1177/1066480712456829

Goldbach, J. T., & Castro, C. A. (2016). Lesbian, gay, bisexual, and transgender (LGBT) service members: Life after don't ask, don't tell. *Current Psychiatry Reports, 18*(6), 56. https://doi.org/10.1007/s11920-016-0695-0

Goldberg, A. E. (2010). *Lesbian and gay parents and their children: Research on the family life cycle.* Washington, DC: American Psychological Association.

Goldberg, J. S. (2015). Coparenting and nonresident fathers' monetary contributions to their children. *Journal of Marriage and Family, 77*(3), 612–627. https://doi.org/10.1111/jomf.12191

Goldfarb, W. (1945). Psychological privation in infancy and subsequent adjustment. *American Journal of Orthopsychiatry, 15,* 247–255.

Goldman-Mellor, S. J., Saxton, K. B., & Catalano, R. C. (2010). Economic contraction and mental health: A review of the evidence, 1990–2009. *International Journal of Mental Health, 39*(2), 6–31. doi:http://dx.doi.org/10.2753/IMH0020-7411390201.

Goldscheider, F., Scott, M. E., Lilja, E., & Bronte-Tinkew, J. (2015). Becoming a single parent: The role of father and mother characteristics. *Journal of Family Issues, 36*(12), 1624–1650. https://doi.org/10.1177/0192513X13508405

Gollin, E. (1981/2012). *Developmental plasticity: Behavioral and biological aspects of variations in development.* Cambridge, MA: Academic Press.

Goodfellow, A. (2015). *Gay fathers, their children, and the making of kinship.* New York, NY: Fordham University Press.

Gordon, T. (1975/2000). *Parent effectiveness training: The tested way to raise responsible children.* New York, NY: Wyden.

Goswami, U. (2014). *Cognition in children.* East Sussex, UK: Psychology Press.

Gottman, J. M. (1993). *What predicts divorce?: The relationship between marital processes and marital outcomes.* New York, NY: Psychology Press.

Green, J., Whitney, P., & Potegal, M. (2011). Screaming, yelling, whining, and crying: Categorical and intensity differences in vocal expressions of anger and sadness in children's tantrums. *Emotion, 11*(5), 1124–1133.

Greene, J. P. (2016). Teaching character: Grit is critical to how and why people succeed. *Education Next, 16*(4), 77. Retrieved from https://www.questia.com/library/journal/1G1-464163365/teaching-character-grit-is-critical-to-how-and-why

Griggs, D., Stafford-Smith, M., Gaffney, O., Rockström, J., Öhman, M. C., Shyamsundar, P., … Noble, I. (2013). Policy: Sustainable development goals for people and planet. *Nature, 495*(7441), 305–307. https://doi.org/10.1038/495305a

Grogan, S. (2016). *Body image: Understanding body dissatisfaction in men, women and children.* New York, NY: Routledge.

Gross, M. U. M. (2015). Characteristics of able gifted, highly gifted, exceptionally gifted, and profoundly gifted learners. In H. E. Vidergor & C. R. Harris (Eds.), *Applied practice for educators of gifted and able learners* (pp. 3–23). Sense Publishers. https://doi.org/10.1007/978-94-6300-004-8_1

Grossman, J. L. (2016). Parentage without gender. *Cardozo Journal of Conflict Resolution, 17*(3). Rochester, NY: Social Science Research Network. Retrieved from https://papers.ssrn.com/abstract=2807197

Groza, V., & Muntean, A. (2016). A description of attachment in adoptive parents and adoptees in Romania during early adolescence. *Child and Adolescent Social Work Journal, 33*(2), 163–174. https://doi.org/10.1007/s10560-015-0408-2

Grunwald, L., & Adler, S. J. (Eds.). (1999/2008). *Letters of the century: America 1900-1999.* New York, NY: The Dial Press.

Guemple, L. (1995). Gender in Inuit society. In L.F. Klein & L.A. Ackerman (Eds.). *Women and Power in Native North American* (pp. 17–27). Norman, OK: University of Oklahoma Press.

Guillamon, A., Junque, C., & Gómez-Gil, E. (2016). A review of the status of brain structure research in transsexualism. *Archives of Sexual Behavior, 45*(7), 1615–1648. https://doi.org/10.1007/s10508-016-0768-5

Gunderson, E. A., Gripshover, S. J., Romero, C., Dweck, C. S., Goldin-Meadow, S., & Levine, S. C. (2013). Parent praise to 1-to-3-year-olds predicts children's motivational frameworks 5 years later. *Child Development, 84*(5), 1526–1541. https://doi.org/10.1111/cdev.12064

Gupta, P. B., Burns, D. J., & Boyd, H. (2016). Texting while driving: An empirical investigation of students' attitudes and behaviors. *Information Systems Management, 33*(1), 88–101. https://doi.org/10.1080/10580530.2016.1117884

Gurman, A. S., & Kniskern, D. P. (2014). *Handbook of family therapy.* New York, NY: Routledge.

Guttmacher Institute. (2012a). March 2012 issue of perspectives on sexual and reproductive health. Retrieved from https://www.guttmacher.org/news-release/2012/march-2012-issue-perspectives-sexual-and-reproductive-health

Guttmacher Institute. (2012b). Perspectives on sexual and reproductive health. Retrieved from https://www.guttmacher.org/news-release/2012/december-2012-issue-perspectives-sexual-and-reproductive-health

Guttmacher Institute. (2016a). American teens' sexual and reproductive health. Retrieved from https://www.guttmacher.org/fact-sheet/american-teens-sexual-and-reproductive-health

Guttmacher Institute. (2016b). Unintended pregnancy in the United States. Retrieved from https://www.guttmacher.org/fact-sheet/unintended-pregnancy-united-states

Haase, D., Kabisch, N., & Haase, A. (2013). Endless urban growth? On the mismatch of population, household and urban land area growth and its effects on the urban debate. *PLOS ONE*, 8(6). https://doi.org/10.1371/journal.pone.0066531

Hackett, S., McWhirter, P. T., & Lesher, S. (2016). The therapeutic efficacy of domestic violence victim interventions. *Trauma, Violence, & Abuse*, 17(2), 123–132. https://doi.org/10.1177/1524838014566720

Hagan, M. J., Roubinov, D. S., Adler, N. E., Boyce, W. T., and Bush, N. R. (2016). Socioeconomic adversity, negativity in the parent child-relationship, and physiological reactivity: An examination of pathways and interactive processes affecting young children's physical health. *Psychosomatic Medicine*, 78(9), 998–1007. doi:http://dx.doi.org/10.1097/PSY.0000000000000379.

Haggbloom, S. J., Warnick, R., Warnick, J. E., Jones, V. K., Yarbrough, G. L., Russell, T. M., ... Monte, E. (2002). The 100 most eminent psychologists of the 20th century. *Review of General Psychology*, 6(2), 139–152. https://doi.org/10.1037/1089-2680.6.2.139

Haire, A. R., & McGeorge, C. R. (2012). Negative perceptions of never-married custodial single mothers and fathers: Applications of a gender analysis for family therapists. *Journal of Feminist Family Therapy*, 24(1), 24–51. https://doi.org/10.1080/08952833.2012.629130

Hall, E. T. (1959/1973). *The silent language*. New York, NY: Anchor Books.

Hall, K. S., Moreau, C., Trussell, J., & Barber, J. (2013). Role of young women's depression and stress symptoms in their weekly use and nonuse of contraceptive methods. *Journal of Adolescent Health*, 53(2), 241–248. https://doi.org/10.1016/j.jadohealth.2013.02.009

Halpern, H. P., & Perry-Jenkins, M. (2016). Parents' gender ideology and gendered behavior as predictors of children's gender-role attitudes: A longitudinal exploration. *Sex Roles*, 74(11–12), 527–542. https://doi.org/10.1007/s11199-015-0539-0

Halpern-Meekin, S., & Turney, K. (2016). Relationship churning and parenting stress among mothers and fathers. *Journal of Marriage and Family*, 78(3), 715–729. https://doi.org/10.1111/jomf.12297

Hamid, D. A. E. (2015). Emotional and behavioral problems of children with learning disabilities. *Journal of Educational Policy and Entrepreneurial Research*, 2(10), 66–74.

Hamzelou, J. (2016). '3-Parent baby' success. *New Scientist*, 232(3093), 8–9. https://doi.org/10.1016/S0262-4079(16)31769-9

Hannan, C. (2013). Gender equality in the welfare state? G. Pascall (Ed). Bristol, UK: PB - The Policy Press. *International Journal of Social Welfare*, 22(3), 329–30. doi:10.1111/ijsw.12026.

Hannigan, L. J., McAdams, T. A., Plomin, R., & Eley, T. C. (2016). Etiological influences on perceptions of parenting: A longitudinal, multi-informant twin study. *Journal of Youth and Adolescence*, 45(12), 2387–2405. https://doi.org/10.1007/s10964-016-0419-0

Hanson, M. A., & Gluckman, P. D. (2014). Early developmental conditioning of later health and disease. Physiology or pathophysiology? *Physiological Reviews*, 94(4), 1027–1076. https://doi.org/10.1152/physrev.00029.2013

Hanson, M. A., & Gluckman, P. D. (2015). Developmental origins of health and disease – Global public health implications. *Best Practice & Research Clinical Obstetrics & Gynaecology*, 29(1), 24–31. https://doi.org/10.1016/j.bpobgyn.2014.06.007

Hanus, M. D., & Fox, J. (2015). Assessing the effects of gamification in the classroom: A longitudinal study on intrinsic motivation, social comparison, satisfaction, effort, and academic performance. *Computers & Education*, 80, 152–161. https://doi.org/10.1016/j.compedu.2014.08.019

Hardy, K. V., & Laszloffy, T. A. (2002). Couple therapy using a multicultural perspective. *Clinical Handbook of Couple Therapy*, 3, 569–593.

Harkness, S., & Super, C. M. (2002). Culture and parenting. In M. H. Bornstein (Ed.). *Handbook of parenting: Biology and ecology of parenting, Vol. 2*, 2nd ed. (pp. 253–280). Mahwah, NJ: Lawrence Erlbaum Associates Publishers.

Harlow, H. F. (1958). The nature of love. *American Psychologist*, 13(12), 673–685.

Harlow, H. F., Harlow, M. K., & Hansen, E. W. (1963). *The maternal affectional system of rhesus monkeys*. New York, NY: Wiley.

Harlow, M., & Laurence, R. (Eds.). (2010). *A cultural history of childhood and the family in antiquity*. New York, NY: Bloomsbury Academics.

Harrington, B., Van Deusen, F., & Humberd, B. (2011). *The new dad: Caring, committed, and conflicted*. Boston, MA: Boston College Center for Work & Family.

Harris, C. E. (2016). LGBT parenting. In K. Eckstrand & J. M. Ehrenfeld (Eds.). *Lesbian, gay, bisexual, and transgender healthcare*, 115–24. Springer International Publishing. doi:10.1007/978-3-319-19752-4_9.

Harris, K. I. (2015). Focus on family: Peer play dates: Making friends and facilitating prosocial skills. *Childhood Education*, 91(3), 223–226. https://doi.org/10.1080/00094056.2015.1047317

Hart, B., & Risley, T. R. (1995). *Meaningful differences in the everyday experience of young American children*. Baltimore, MD: Paul H. Brookes Publishing.

Hart, R., & Norman, R. J. (2013). The longer-term health outcomes for children born as a result of IVF treatment. Part II: Mental health and development outcomes. *Human Reproduction Update*. https://doi.org/10.1093/humupd/dmt002

Hawes, K., McGowan, E., O'Donnell, M., Tucker, R., & Vohr, B. (2016). Social emotional factors increase risk of postpartum depression in mothers of preterm infants. *The Journal of Pediatrics*. https://doi.org/10.1016/j.jpeds.2016.07.008

Hawkins, A. O., Rabenhorst-Bell, M. M., & Hetzel-Riggin, M. D. (2015). Exploring racially diverse college students' perspectives on child discipline. *Journal of Child and Adolescent Trauma*, 8(1), 73–82. https://doi.org/10.1007/s40653-014-0034-8

Hayford, S. R., & Guzzo, K. B. (2016). Fifty years of unintended births: Education gradients in unintended fertility in the US, 1960–2010. *Population and Development Review*, 42(2), 313–341. https://doi.org/10.1111/j.1728-4457.2016.00126.x

Heaman, M. I., Sword, W., Elliott, L., Moffatt, M., Helewa, M. E., Morris, H., Cook, C. (2015). Barriers and facilitators related to use of prenatal care by inner-city women: Perceptions of health care providers. *BMC Pregnancy and Childbirth*, 15, 2. https://doi.org/10.1186/s12884-015-0431-5

Heath, P. (2012). *Parent-child relations: Context, research, and application* (3rd ed.). Boston, MA: Pearson.

Heckman, J. J. (2013). *Giving kids a fair chance*. Cambridge, MA: The MIT Press.

Heinicke, C. M. (1984). Impact of prebirth parent personality and marital functioning on family development: A framework and suggestions for further study. *Developmental Psychology*, 20(6), 1044–1053. doi:10.1037/0012-1649.20.6.1044.

Heinicke, C. M. (2002). The transition to parenting. In M. H. Bornstein (Ed.). *Handbook of parenting: Volume 3: Being and becoming a parent* (2nd ed.). New York, NY: Routledge.

Held, P. K., Shapira, S. K., Hinton, C. F., Jones, E., Hannon, W. H., & Ojodu, J. (2015). Congenital adrenal hyperplasia cases identified by newborn screening in one-and two-screen states. *Molecular Genetics and Metabolism*, 116(3), 133–138. https://doi.org/10.1016/j.ymgme.2015.08.004

Hergenhahn, B. R., & Henley, T. (2013). *An introduction to the history of psychology* (7th ed.). Belmont, CA: Wadsworth.

Herrenkohl, T. I., Hong, S., Klika, J. B., Herrenkohl, R. C., & Russo, M. J. (2013). Developmental impacts of child abuse and neglect related to adult mental health, substance use, and physical health. *Journal of Family Violence*, 28(2), 191–199. https://doi.org/10.1007/s10896-012-9474-9

Herrenkohl, T. I., Leeb, R. T. & Higgins, D. (2016). The public health model of child maltreatment prevention. *Trauma, Violence & Abuse*, 17(4), 363–365. doi:http://dx.doi.org/10.1177/1524838016661034.

Hesselink, A., & Booyens, K. (2016). When parents interchange love with abuse: An analysis of parental-child abuse for correctional intervention. *Child Abuse Research in South Africa*, 17(2), 103–114. Retrieved from https://journals.co.za/content/carsa/17/2/EJC198059

Hetherington, E. M., & Arasteh, J. D. (2014). *Impact of divorce, single parenting and stepparenting on children: A case study of visual agnosia*. New York, NY: Psychology Press.

Heywood, C. (2013). *A history of childhood: Children and childhood in the west from medieval to modern times*. New York, NY: John Wiley & Sons.

Hill, Deirdre R. (2015). *Hispanic single fathers experiences of parental involvement in the academic achievement of their children*. [Unpublished dissertation]. Capella University. http://search.proquest.com.fetch.mhsl.uab.edu/docview/1716316193/abstract/23D2C25D87C9426APQ/1.

Hiltz, J. (2015). Helicopter parents can be a good thing. *Phi Delta Kappan*, 96(7), 26–29.

Hindle, D., & Sherwin-White, S. (2014). *Sibling matters: A psychoanalytic, developmental, and systemic approach*. London, England: Karnac Books.

Hinnells, J. R. (Ed.). (1995). *A new dictionary of religions*. New York, NY: Wiley-Blackwell.

Hipwell, A. E., Keenan, K., Loeber, R., & Battista, D. (2010). Early predictors of sexually intimate behaviors in an urban sample of young girls. *Developmental Psychology*, 46(2), 366–378. https://doi.org/10.1037/a0018409

Hiyoshi, A., Fall, K., Netuveli, G., & Montgomery, S. (2015). Remarriage after divorce and depression risk. *Social Science & Medicine*, 141, 109–114. https://doi.org/10.1016/j.socscimed.2015.07.029

Hoffman, D. M. (2013). Power struggles: The paradoxes of emotion and control among child-centered mothers in the privileged United States. *Ethos*, 41(1), 75–97. https://doi.org/10.1111/etho.12003

Hoischen, A., Krumm, N., & Eichler, E. E. (2014). Prioritization of neurodevelopmental disease genes by discovery of new mutations. *Nature Neuroscience*, 17(6), 764–772. https://doi.org/10.1038/nn.3703

Holcomb, P., Edin, K., Max, J., Young A., D'Angelo, A. V., Friend, D., Clary, E., Johnson, W. E. (2015). *In their own voices: The hopes and struggles of responsible fatherhood program participants in the parents and children together evaluation*. Washington, DC: U.S. Department of Health and Human Services.

Holden, G. W., & Williamson, P. A. (2014). Chapter 39: Religion and child well-being. In A. Ben-Arieh, F. Casas, I. Frønes, & J. E. Korbin (Eds.), *Handbook of child well-being* (pp. 1137–1169). The Netherlands: Springer Netherlands. https://doi.org/10.1007/978-90-481-9063-8_158

Holland, D., Chang, L., Ernst, T. M., Curran, M., Buchthal, S. D., Alicata, D., … Dale, A. M. (2014). Structural growth trajectories and rates of change in the first 3 months of infant brain development. *JAMA Neurology*, 71(10), 1266–1274. https://doi.org/10.1001/jamaneurol.2014.1638

Holman, D. M., Benard, V., Roland, K. B., Watson, M., Liddon, N., & Stokley, S. (2014). Barriers to human papillomavirus vaccination among US adolescents: A systematic review of the literature. *JAMA Pediatrics*, 168(1), 76–82. https://doi.org/10.1001/jamapediatrics.2013.2752

Hoste, R. R., Labuschagne, Z., & Grange, D. L. (2012). Adolescent bulimia nervosa. *Current Psychiatry Reports*, 14(4), 391–397. https://doi.org/10.1007/s11920-012-0280-0

Hostinar, C. E., & Gunnar, M. R. (2015). Social support can buffer against stress and shape brain activity. *AJOB Neuroscience*, 6(3), 34–42. https://doi.org/10.1080/21507740.2015.1047054

Hott, B., Thomas, S., Abbassi, A., Hendricks, L., & Aslina, D. (2015). It takes a village: Counselor participation with students, families, and other school personnel in serving students with special needs. In *National Forum of Special Education Journal*, 26(1).

Howard, J. (2014). The importance of play. In P. Mukherji & L. Dryden, *Foundations of Early Childhood: Principles and Practice* (Chapter 7, pp. 122–142). Thousand Oaks, CA: Sage.

Hudgins, R., Erickson, S., & Walker, D. (2014). Everyone deserves a second chance: A decade of supports for teenage mothers. *Health & Social Work*, 39(2), 101–108.

Huffman, C. S., Schwartz, T. A., & Swanson, K. M. (2015). Couples and miscarriage: The influence of gender and reproductive factors on the impact of miscarriage. *Women's Health Issues*, 25(5), 570–578. https://doi.org/10.1016/j.whi.2015.04.005

Humes, K. R., Jones, N. A., & Ramirez, R. R. (2011) Overview of race and Hispanic origin: 2010 census briefs. *United States Census Bureau*, 1–24. Retrieved from https://www.census.gov/prod/cen2010/briefs/c2010br-02.pdf

Illingworth, R. (1960/2012). *The development of the infant and the young child: Normal and abnormal*. (10th ed.). M. K. C Nair & P. Russell (Eds.). Elsevier.

Imber-Black, E. (1993). *Secrets in families and family therapy*. New York, NY: W. W. Norton & Company, Inc.

Individuals with Disabilities Education Act of 2004, Pub. L. 108-446, 104 Stat. 1142.

Inglehart, R. (2015). *The silent revolution: Changing values and political styles among Western publics*. Princeton, NJ: Princeton University Press.

Inguglia, C., Ingoglia, S., Liga, F., Coco, A. L., & Cricchio, M. G. L. (2015). Autonomy and relatedness in adolescence and emerging adulthood: Relationships with parental support and psychological distress. *Journal of Adult Development*, 22(1), 1–13. https://doi.org/10.1007/s10804-014-9196-8

Iossifov, I., O'Roak, B. J., Sanders, S. J., Ronemus, M., Krumm, N., Levy, D.,Wigler, M. (2014). The contribution of de novo coding mutations to autism spectrum disorder. *Nature*, 515(7526), 216–221. https://doi.org/10.1038/nature13908

Jackson, C. (2015). Modernity and matrifocality: The feminization of kinship? *Development and Change*, 46(1), 1–24. https://doi.org/10.1111/dech.12141

Jackson, G. L., Trail, T. E., Kennedy, D. P., Williamson, H. C., Bradbury, T. N., & Karney, B. R. (2016). The salience and severity of relationship problems among low-income couples. *Journal of Family Psychology*, 30(1), 2–11. https://doi.org/10.1037/fam0000158

Jaffee, S. R., Caspi, A., Moffitt, T. E., Polo-Tomás, M., & Taylor, A. (2007). Individual, family, and neighborhood factors distinguish resilient from non-resilient maltreated children: A cumulative stressors model. *Child Abuse & Neglect*, 31(3), 231–253. https://doi.org/10.1016/j.chiabu.2006.03.011

Janov, A. (1970). *The primal scream*. New York, NY: Dell Publishing Company.

Janov, A. (1973). *The feeling child*. New York, NY: Simon and Schuster.

Jappens, M., & Van Bavel, J. (2016). Parental divorce, residence arrangements, and contact between grandchildren and grandparents. *Journal of Marriage and Family*, 78(2), 451–467. https://doi.org/10.1111/jomf.12275

Jennings, J. M., Howard, S., & Perotte, C. L. (2014). Effects of a school-based sexuality education program on peer educators: The teen PEP model. *Health Education Research*, 29(2), 319–329. https://doi.org/10.1093/her/cyt153

Jensen, A. L. (2010). *Bridging cultural and developmental approaches to psychology: New syntheses in theory, research, and policy*. New York, NY: Oxford University Press.

Jensen, F. E., & Nutt, A. E. (2015). *The teenage brain: A neuroscientist's survival guide to raising adolescents and young adults*. New York, NY: HarperCollins.

Jensen, L. A., & Arnett, J. J. (2012). Going global: New pathways for adolescents and emerging adults in a changing world. *Journal of Social Issues*, 68(3), 473–492. https://doi.org/10.1111/j.1540-4560.2012.01759.x

Jensen, T. M., Shafer, K., & Holmes, E. K. (2015). Transitioning to stepfamily life: The influence of closeness with biological parents and stepparents on children's stress. *Child & Family Social Work*. https://doi.org/10.1111/cfs.12237

Jensen, T. M., Shafer, K., Guo, S., & Larson, J. H. (2017). Differences in relationship stability between individuals in first and second marriages: A propensity score analysis. *Journal of Family Issues*, 38(3), 406–432. https://doi.org/10.1177/0192513X15604344

Jenson, J. M., & Fraser, M. W. (2015). *Social policy for children and families: A risk and resilience perspective*. Thousand Oaks, CA: SAGE Publications.

Jia, R., Kotila, L. E., Schoppe-Sullivan, S. J., & Kamp Dush, C. M. (2016). New parents' psychological adjustment and trajectories of early parental involvement. *Journal of Marriage and Family*, 78(1), 197–211. https://doi.org/10.1111/jomf.12263

Jin, H. J., Lee, J. H., & Kim, M. K. (2013). The prevalence of vitamin D deficiency in iron-deficient and normal children under the age of 24 months. *Blood Research*, 48(1), 40–45. https://doi.org/10.5045/br.2013.48.1.40

Johns, R. (2014). *Using the law in social work* (6th ed.). Thousand Oaks, CA: SAGE Publications.

Johnson, J. L., Beard, J., & Evans, D. (2016). Caring for refugee youth in the school setting. *NASN School Nurse*, 32(2), 122–128. https://doi.org/10.1177/1942602X16672310

Johnson, M. D. (2016). *Great myths of intimate relationships: Dating, sex, and marriage*. West Sussex, England: Wiley-Blackwell.

Johnson, S., O'Connor, E., & Tornello, S. (2016). Gay and lesbian parents and their children: Research relevant to custody cases. In L. Drozd, N. Olesen, & M. Saini, *Parenting Plan Evaluations: Applied Research for the Family Court* (pp. 514–532). New York, NY: Oxford University Press.

Jojic, M., Raj, A., Wilkins, K., Treadwell, R., Caussade-Rodriguez, E., & Blum, J. (2012). Demographics and treatment of the American family. *International Review of Psychiatry*, 24(2), 128–132. https://doi.org/10.3109/09540261.2012.659239

Jolly, S., Griffith, K. A., DeCastro, R., Stewart, A., Ubel, P., & Jagsi, R. (2014). Gender differences in time spent on parenting and domestic responsibilities by high-achieving young physician-researchers. *Annals of Internal Medicine*, 160(5), 344–353. https://doi.org/10.7326/M13-0974

Joslyn, M. R., & Haider-Markel, D. P. (2016). Genetic attributions, immutability, and stereotypical judgments: An analysis of homosexuality. *Social Science Quarterly*, 97(2), 376–390. https://doi.org/10.1111/ssqu.12263

Judd, S., Newton, J., Newton, F., & Ewing, M. (2016). Influence of parents on child eating practices in low ses communities: Identifying insights for health promotion campaigns. In C. Campbell & J. J. Ma (Eds.), *Looking Forward, Looking Back: Drawing on the Past to Shape the Future of Marketing* (pp. 352–355). Springer International Publishing. https://doi.org/10.1007/978-3-319-24184-5_92

Julion, W. A., Sumo, J., Bounds, D. T., Breitenstein, S. M., Schoeny, M., Gross, D., & Fogg, L. (2016). Study protocol for a randomized clinical trial of a fatherhood intervention for African American non-resident fathers: Can we improve father and child outcomes? *Contemporary Clinical Trials*, 49, 29–39. https://doi.org/10.1016/j.cct.2016.05.005

Jung, A. K., & Heppner, M. J. (2015). Work of full-time mothers: Putting voice to the relational theory of working. *The Career Development Quarterly*, 63(3), 253–267. https://doi.org/10.1002/cdq.12017

Kaerts, N., Vermandel, A., Van Hal, G., & Wyndaele, J.-J. (2014). Toilet training in healthy children: Results of a questionnaire study involving parents who make use of day-care at least once a week. *Neurourology and Urodynamics*, 33(3), 316–323. https://doi.org/10.1002/nau.22392

Kagan, J. (1976). The psychological requirements for human development. In N. Talbott (Ed.), *Raising Children in Modern America: Problems and Prospective Solutions*. Boston, MA: Little, Brown.

Kagitcibasi, C. (2013). *Family, self, and human development across cultures: Theory and applications.* (2nd ed.). New York, NY: Routledge.

Kail, R. V., & Cavanaugh, J. C. (2015). *Human development: A life-span view.* (7th ed.). Boston, MA: Cengage Learning.

Källén, B. (2016). The 'alert clinician.' In *Drugs During Pregnancy* (pp. 3–8). Switzerland: Springer International Publishing. https://doi.org/10.1007/978-3-319-40697-8_2

Kalmijn, M. (2015). Family disruption and intergenerational reproduction: Comparing the influences of married parents, divorced parents, and stepparents. *Demography*, 52(3), 811–833. https://doi.org/10.1007/s13524-015-0388-z

Kaminski, J. W., Valle, L. A., Filene, J. H., & Boyle, C. L. (2008). A meta-analytic review of components associated with parent training program effectiveness. *Journal of Abnormal Child Psychology*, 36(4), 567–589. https://doi.org/10.1007/s10802-007-9201-9

Kane, J. B., Philip Morgan, S., Harris, K. M., & Guilkey, D. K. (2013). The educational consequences of teen childbearing. *Demography*, 50(6), 2129–2150. https://doi.org/10.1007/s13524-013-0238-9

Kapila, G., & Kumar, D. A. (2015). Homosexuality: Road to visibility. *The International Journal of Indian Psychology*, 3(1), 69–97. https://doi.org/C03133V3I12015

Kaplan, M., & Haider, J. (2015). Creating intergenerational spaces that promote health and well-being. In R. Vanderbeck & N. Worth, *Intergenerational Space*. Chapter 3. New York, NY: Routledge.

Karney, B. R. (2013). Couples and stress: How demands outside a relationship affect intimacy within a relationship. In: Simpson, J. & Campbell, L. (Eds.), *The Oxford Handbook of Close Relations*. New York, NY: Oxford University Press.

Karney, B. R., & Crown, J. S. (2011). Does deployment keep military marriages together or break them apart? Evidence from Afghanistan and Iraq. In S. M. Wadsworth & D. Riggs (Eds.), *Risk and Resilience in U.S. Military Families* (pp. 23–45). New York, NY: Springer. https://doi.org/10.1007/978-1-4419-7064-0_2

Katz, J., & Tirone, V. (2010). Going along with it: Sexually coercive partner behavior predicts dating women's compliance with unwanted sex. *Violence Against Women*, 16(7), 730–742. https://doi.org/10.1177/1077801210374867

Katz, L. F., & Gottman, J. M. (1993). Patterns of marital conflict predict children's internalizing and externalizing behaviors. *Developmental Psychology*, 29(6), 940–950. https://doi.org/10.1037/0012-1649.29.6.940

Kavas, S., & Gündüz-Hoşgör, A. (2013). The parenting practice of single mothers in Turkey: Challenges and strategies. *Women's Studies International Forum*, 40, 56–67. https://doi.org/10.1016/j.wsif.2013.05.004

Kearney, M. S., & Levine, P. B. (2015). Media influences on social outcomes: The impact of MTV's 16 and Pregnant on teen childbearing. *The American Economic Review*, 105(12), 3597–3632. https://doi.org/10.1257/aer.20140012

Kehoe, A., Dempster, M., McManus, J., & Lewis, S. (2016). Stress and coping in parents of newly born twins. *Journal of Psychosomatic Obstetrics & Gynecology*, 37(3), 110–118. https://doi.org/10.1080/0167482X.2016.1175427

Keijsers, L., & Poulin, F. (2013). Developmental changes in parent–child communication throughout adolescence. *Developmental Psychology*, 49(12), 2301–2308. https://doi.org/10.1037/a0032217

Kellor, A. L. (2005). Rising and falling: In A. J. Fountas (Ed.). *Waking up American: Coming of age biculturally*. Berkeley, CA: Seal Press.

Kelly, G. (2015). *Sexuality Today* (11th ed.). New York, NY: McGraw-Hill Education.

Kelly, K. M., Chopra, I., & Dolly, B. (2015). Breastfeeding: An unknown factor to reduce heart disease risk among breastfeeding women. *Breastfeeding Medicine*, 10(9), 442–447. https://doi.org/10.1089/bfm.2015.0082

Kempe, C. H., Silverman, F. N., Steele, B. F., Droegemueller, W., & Silver, H. K. (1962). The battered-child syndrome. *JAMA*, 181(1), 17–24. https://doi.org/10.1001/jama.1962.03050270019004

Kennedy, S., & Ruggles, S. (2014). Breaking up is hard to count: The rise of divorce in the United States, 1980–2010. *Demography*, 51(2), 587–598. https://doi.org/10.1007/s13524-013-0270-9

Kerr, M., Stattin, H., & Özdemir, M. (2012). Perceived parenting style and adolescent adjustment: Revisiting directions of effects and the role of parental knowledge. *Developmental Psychology*, 48(6), 1540–1553. https://doi.org/10.1037/a0027720

Khajehei, M. (2016). Parenting challenges and parents' intimate relationships. *Journal of Human Behavior in the Social Environment*, 26(5), 447–451. https://doi.org/10.1080/10911359.2015.1083509

Khanlou, N., Haque, N., Sheehan, S., & Jones, G. (2015). "It is an issue of not knowing where to go": Service providers' perspectives on challenges in accessing social support and services by immigrant mothers of children with disabilities. *Journal of Immigrant and Minority Health*, 17(6), 1840–1847. https://doi.org/10.1007/s10903-014-0122-8

Kids Count Data Center. (2016). Children in poverty (100 percent poverty). Retrieved from http://datacenter.kidscount.org/data/Tables/43-children-in-poverty-100-percent-poverty

Kids In The House. (n.d.). *How Parental Roles Differ in Same Sex Relationship*. Retrieved from https://www.youtube.com/watch?v=th0vpHDmEz8&t=3s

KidsHealth (n.d.). Medical care and your newborn. Retrieved from http://kidshealth.org/en/parents/mednewborn.html?WT.ac=ctg#

Kim, K., Mennen, F. E., & Trickett, P. K. (2016). Patterns and correlates of co-occurrence among multiple types of child maltreatment. *Child & Family Social Work*, 22(1), 492–502. https://doi.org/10.1111/cfs.12268

Kim, P., Rigo, P., Mayes, L. C., Feldman, R., Leckman, J. F. & Swain, J. E. (2014). Neural plasticity in fathers of human infants. *Social Neuroscience*, 9(5), 522-535. doi:10.1080/17470919.2014.933713.

Kim, Y., Cancian, M., & Meyer, D. R. (2015). Patterns of child support debt accumulation. *Children and Youth Services Review*, 51, 87–94. https://doi.org/10.1016/j.childyouth.2015.01.017

Kindleberger, H. L. (2016). History of child development. In W.D. Woody, R.L. Miller, & W.J. Wozniak (Eds.), *Psychological Specialties in Historical Context: Enriching the Classroom Experience for Teachers and Students*. Retrieved from http://teachpsych.org/ebooks/psychspec

King, V., Amato, P. R., & Lindstrom, R. (2015). Stepfather–adolescent relationship quality during the first year of transitioning to a stepfamily. *Journal of Marriage and Family*, 77(5), 1179–1189. https://doi.org/10.1111/jomf.12214

Kingery, J. N., Erdley, C. A., & Marshall, K. C. (2011). Peer acceptance and friendship as predictors of early adolescents' adjustment across the middle school transition. *Merrill-Palmer Quarterly*, 57(3), 215–243. https://doi.org/10.1353/mpq.2011.0012

Kingsmill, S., & Schlesinger, B. (2015). *The family squeeze: Surviving the sandwich generation*. Toronto, Canada: University of Toronto Press.

Kinsey, A. C., Pomeroy, W. B., & Martin, C. E. (1948). *Sexual behavior in the human male*. Philadelphia, PA: Saunders.

Kinsey, A. C., Pomeroy, W. B., Martin, C. E., & Gebhard, P. H. (1953). *Sexual behavior in the human female*. Philadelphia, PA: Saunders.

Kirby, J. N., & Sanders, M. R. (2013). The acceptability of parenting strategies for grandparents providing care to their grandchildren. *Prevention Science*, 15(5), 777–787. https://doi.org/10.1007/s11121-013-0428-0

Kirmayer, L. J., & Ryder, A. G. (2016). Culture and psychopathology. *Current Opinion in Psychology*, 8, 143–148. https://doi.org/10.1016/j.copsyc.2015.10.020

Kiselica, A. M., & Kiselica, M. S. (2014). Improving attitudes, services, and policies regarding adolescent fathers: An affirming rejoinder. *Psychology of Men & Masculinity*, 15(3), 284–287. https://doi.org/10.1037/a0037359

Kisiel, C. L., Fehrenbach, T., Torgersen, E., Stolbach, B., McClelland, G., Griffin, G., & Burkman, K. (2013). Constellations of interpersonal trauma and symptoms in child welfare: Implications for a developmental trauma framework. *Journal of Family Violence*, 29(1),1–14. https://doi.org/10.1007/s10896-013-9559-0

Kisner, M. J. (2011). *Spinoza on human freedom: Reason, autonomy and the good life*. Cambridge, UK: Cambridge University Press.

Kissil, K., & Itzhaky, H. (2015). Experiences of the Marital Relationship among Orthodox Jewish Gay Men in Mixed-Orientation Marriages. *Journal of GLBT Family Studies*, 11(2), 151–172. https://doi.org/10.1080/1550428X.2014.900659

Klobas, J. E., & Ajzen, I. (2015). Making the decision to have a child. In D. Philipov, A. C. Liefbroer, & J. E. Klobas (Eds.), Reproductive decision-making in a macro-micro perspective (pp. 41–78). Switzerland: Springer Netherlands. Retrieved from http://link.springer.com/chapter/10.1007/978-94-017-9401-5_3

Kloep, M., & Hendry, L. B. (2010). Letting go or holding on? Parents' perceptions of their relationships with their children during emerging adulthood. *British Journal of Developmental Psychology*, 28(4), 817–834. https://doi.org/10.1348/026151009X480581

Kluckhohn, C. (2009). Queer Customs. In G. P. Ferraro, *Classic readings in cultural anthropology* (2nd ed., pp. 6–12). Boston, MA: Cengage Learning.

Kochanek, K. D., Murphy, S. L., Xu, J., & Tejada-Vera, B. (2016). Deaths: Final data for 2014. *National Vital Statistics Reports*, 65(4). Hyattsville, MD: National Center for Health Statistics. Retrieved from https://www.cdc.gov/nchs/data/nvsr/nvsr65/nvsr65_04.pdf

Kochanska, G., Kim, S., & Boldt, L. J. (2015). (Positive) power to the child: The role of children's willing stance toward parents in developmental cascades from toddler age to early preadolescence. *Development and Psychopathology*, 27(4), 987–1005. https://doi.org/10.1017/S0954579415000644

Koepke, S., & Denissen, J. J. A. (2012). Dynamics of identity development and separation–individuation in parent–child relationships during adolescence and emerging adulthood – A conceptual integration. *Developmental Review*, 32(1), 67–88. https://doi.org/10.1016/j.dr.2012.01.001

Koerner, A. F., & Schrodt, P. (2014). An Introduction to the Special Issue on Family Communication Patterns Theory. *Journal of Family Communication*, 14(1), 1–15. https://doi.org/10.1080/15267431.2013.857328

Koh, H. (2014). The teen pregnancy prevention program: An evidence-based public health program model. *Journal of Adolescent Health*, 54(3), S1–S2. https://doi.org/10.1016/j.jadohealth.2013.12.031

Koppelman, K. (2017). *Understanding human differences: Multicultural education for a diverse America* (5th ed.). Upper Saddle River, NY: Pearson.

Körner, A. (2016). Heirs and their wives: Setting the scene for Umbertian Italy. In Mehrkens, H., & Lorenz, F. (Eds.) *Sons and Heirs: Succession and Culture in Nineteenth Century Europe* (pp. 38-52). London, England: Palgrave Macmillan.

Kosciw, J. G., & Pizmony-Levy, O. (2016). International perspectives on homophobic and transphobic bullying in schools. *Journal of LGBT Youth*, 13(1–2), 1–5. https://doi.org/10.1080/19361653.2015.1101730

Kosciw, J. G., Palmer, N. A., & Kull, R. M. (2015). Reflecting resiliency: Openness about sexual orientation and/or gender identity and its relationship to well-being and educational outcomes for LGBT students. *American Journal of Community Psychology*, 55(1–2), 167–178. https://doi.org/10.1007/s10464-014-9642-6

Kotila, L. E., Schoppe-Sullivan, S. J., & Kamp Dush, C. M. (2013). Time in parenting activities in dual-earner families at the transition to parenthood. *Family Relations*, 62(5), 795–807. https://doi.org/10.1111/fare.12037

Kramer, K. Z., Myhra, L. L., Zuiker, V. S., & Bauer, J. W. (2016). Comparison of poverty and income disparity of single mothers and fathers across three decades: 1990–2010. *Gender Issues*, 33(1), 22–41. https://doi.org/10.1007/s12147-015-9144-3

Kray, L. J., Galinsky, A. D., & Thompson, L. (2002). Reversing the gender gap in negotiations: An exploration of stereotype regeneration. *Organizational Behavior and Human Decision Processes*, 87(2), 386–409. https://doi.org/10.1006/obhd.2001.2979

Kreider, R. M., & Lofquist, D. A. (2014). Adopted children and stepchildren: 2010. Retrieved from https://www.census.gov/prod/2014pubs/p20-572.pdf

Kreppner, K., & Lerner, R. M. (2013). *Family systems and life-span development*. New York, NY: Psychology Press.

Krizman, J., Skoe, E., & Kraus, N. (2016). Bilingual enhancements have no socioeconomic boundaries. *Developmental Science*, 19(6), 881–891. https://doi.org/10.1111/desc.12347

Kroger, J., Martinussen, M., & Marcia, J. E. (2010). Identity status change during adolescence and young adulthood: A meta-analysis. *Journal of Adolescence*, 33(5), 683–698. https://doi.org/10.1016/j.adolescence.2009.11.002

Krueger, P. M., Jutte, D. P., Franzini, L., Elo, I., & Hayward, M. D. (2015). Family structure and multiple domains of child well-being in the United States: a cross-sectional study. *Population Health Metrics*, 13, 6. https://doi.org/10.1186/s12963-015-0038-0

Krugman, S. D., & Lane, W. G. (2014). Fatal child abuse. In J. E. Korbin & R. D. Krugman (Eds.), *Handbook of Child Maltreatment* (pp. 99–112). Switzerland: Springer Netherlands. https://doi.org/10.1007/978-94-007-7208-3_5

Kuczynski, L., & Mol, J. D. (2015). Dialectical models of socialization. In R. M. Lerner (Ed.), *Handbook of Child Psychology and Developmental Science* (pp. 1–46). Hoboken, NJ: John Wiley & Sons, Inc. Retrieved from http://doi.wiley.com/10.1002/9781118963418.childpsy109

Kuehnle, K., Kirkpatrick, H. D., & Drozd, L. (2014). Child custody. In *The Encyclopedia of Clinical Psychology*. Hoboken, NJ: John Wiley & Sons, Inc. Retrieved from http://onlinelibrary.wiley.com/doi/10.1002/9781118625392.wbecp450/abstract

Kugelman, A., & Colin, A. A. (2013). Late preterm infants: Near term but still in a critical developmental time period. *Pediatrics*, 132(4), 741–751. https://doi.org/10.1542/peds.2013-1131

Kunzman, R., & Gaither, M. (2013). Homeschooling: A comprehensive survey of the research. *Other Education*, 2(1), 4–59.

Kuo, C., Atujuna, M., Mathews, C., Stein, D.J., Hoare, J., Beardslee, W., Brown, K.L. (2016). Developing Family Interventions for Adolescent HIV Prevention in South Africa. *AIDS Care*, 28(1), 106–110. https://doi.org/10.1080/09540121.2016.1146396.

LaFreniere, P., & MacDoald, K. (2013). A postgenomic view of behavioral development and adaptation to the environment. *Developmental Review*, 33(2), 89–109. https://doi.org/10.1016/j.dr.2013.01.002

Lahiri, J. (2003). *The namesake*. New York, NY: Houghton Mifflin.

Lamanna, M. A., Riedmann, A., & Stewart, S. D. (2014). *Marriages, families, and relationships: making choices in a diverse society*. Boston, MA: Cengage Learning.

Lamb, M. E., & Freund, A. M. (2010). *The handbook of life-span development* (Vol. 2). Hoboken, NJ: Wiley.

Lamb, M. E., Thompson, R. A., Gardner, W., & Charnov, E. L. (2013). *Infant-mother attachment: The origins and developmental significance of individual differences in strange situation behavior*. New York, NY: Routledge.

Lange, M. de, Dronkers, J., & Wolbers, M. H. J. (2014). Single-parent family forms and children's educational performance in a comparative perspective: Effects of school's share of single-parent families. *School Effectiveness and School Improvement*, 25(3), 329–350. https://doi.org/10.1080/09243453.2013.809773

Langlais, M. R., Anderson, E. R., & Greene, S. M. (2016). Consequences of dating for post-divorce maternal well-being. *Journal of Marriage and Family*, 78(4), 1032–1046. https://doi.org/10.1111/jomf.12319

Lanius, R. A., Vermetten, E., & Pain, C. (2010). *The impact of early life trauma on health and disease: The hidden epidemic*. Cambridge, UK: Cambridge University Press.

Larzelere, R. E., Gunnoe, M. L., Roberts, M. W., & Ferguson, C. J. (2017). Children and parents deserve better parental discipline research: Critiquing the evidence for exclusively "positive" parenting. *Marriage & Family Review; New York*, 53(1), 24–35. https://doi.org/http://dx.doi.org/10.1080/01494929.2016.1145613

Larzelere, R. E., & Kuhn, B. R. (2016). Parental discipline. In *Encyclopedia of Family Studies*. John Wiley & Sons, Inc. https://doi.org/10.1002/9781119085621.wbefs512

Lasagna, L. (1964). *Hippocratic oath: Modern version*. WGBH Education Foundation for PBS and NOVA Online. Retrieved from http://www.pbs.org/wgbh/nova/body/hippocratic-oath-today.html

Laszloffy, T. A. (2002). Rethinking family development theory: Teaching with the systemic family development (SFD) model. *Family Relations*, 51, 206–214.

Latack, J. A., & Davila, J. (2016). Predicting relational security among early adolescent girls: Parental relationships and romantic experiences. *Journal of Social and Personal Relationships*, 33(6), 792–813. https://doi.org/10.1177/0265407515597563

Lavner, J. A., Karney, B. R., & Bradbury, T. N. (2015). New directions for policies aimed at strengthening low-income couples. *Behavioral Science & Policy*, 1(2), 13–24. https://doi.org/10.1353/bsp.2015.0017

Lavner, J. A., Karney, B. R., Williamson, H. C., & Bradbury, T. N. (2016). Bidirectional associations between newlyweds' marital satisfaction and marital problems over time. *Family Process*. https://doi.org/10.1111/famp.12264

Lawrence Ganong, & Coleman, M. (2017). Siblings, half-siblings, and stepsiblings. In *Stepfamily Relationships* (pp. 191–204). New York, NY: Springer. https://doi.org/10.1007/978-1-4899-7702-1_10

Lawrence, R. E., Rasinski, K. A., Yoon, J. D., & Curlin, F. A. (2011). Adolescents, contraception and confidentiality: A national survey of obstetrician–gynecologists. *Contraception*, 84(3), 259–265. https://doi.org/10.1016/j.contraception.2010.12.002

Lawson, D. W., & Mace, R. (2010). Siblings and childhood mental health: Evidence for a later-born advantage. *Social Science & Medicine*, 70(12), 2061–2069. https://doi.org/10.1016/j.socscimed.2010.03.009

Lawson, J. (2012). Sociological theories of intimate partner violence. *Journal of Human Behavior in the Social Environment*, 22(5), 572–590. https://doi.org/10.1080/10911359.2011.598748

Le, Y., McDaniel, B. T., Leavitt, C. E., & Feinberg, M. E. (2016). Longitudinal associations between relationship quality and co-parenting across the transition to parenthood: A dyadic perspective. *Journal of Family Psychology*. https://doi.org/10.1037/fam0000217

Leach, P. (2015). *When parents part: How mothers and fathers can help their children deal with separation and divorce*. New York, NY: Knopf Doubleday Publishing Group.

Leaper, C. (2015). Gender and social-cognitive development. In R. M. Lerner, L. S. Liben, & U. Miller (Eds.), *Handbook of Child Psychology and Developmental Science* (Vol. 2). John Wiley & Sons, Inc. Retrieved from http://onlinelibrary.wiley.com/doi/10.1002/9781118963418.childpsy219/abstract

Lebel, C., & Beaulieu, C. (2011). Longitudinal development of human brain wiring continues from childhood into adulthood. *Journal of Neuroscience*, 31(30), 10937–10947. https://doi.org/10.1523/JNEUROSCI.5302-10.2011

LeBlanc, A. J., Frost, D. M., & Wight, R. G. (2015). Minority stress and stress proliferation among same-sex and other marginalized couples. *Journal of Marriage and Family*, 77(1), 40–59. https://doi.org/10.1111/jomf.12160

Lebowitz, E. R., & Omer, H. (2013). Childhood anxiety and family boundaries. In E. R. Lebowitz & H. Omer, *Treating Childhood and Adolescent Anxiety: A Guide for Caregivers* (pp. 139–149). John Wiley & Sons, Inc. Retrieved from http://onlinelibrary.wiley.com/doi/10.1002/9781118589366.ch9/summary

Lee, J. K., Wendelken, C., Bunge, S. A., & Ghetti, S. (2016). A time and place for everything: Developmental differences in the building blocks of episodic memory. *Child Development*, 87(1), 194–210. https://doi.org/10.1111/cdev.12447

Lee, S. H., & Grubbs, L. M. (1995). Pregnant teenagers' reasons for seeking or delaying prenatal care. *Clinical Nursing Research*, 4(1), 38–49. https://doi.org/10.1177/105477389500400105

Leeson, P. T., & Pierson, J. (2015). Economic origins of the no-fault divorce revolution. *European Journal of Law and Economics*, 1–21. https://doi.org/10.1007/s10657-015-9501-4

Lehrer, E. L., & Son, Y. (2017). *Marital instability in the United States: Trends, driving forces, and implications for children*. Rochester, NY: Social Science Research Network. Retrieved from https://papers.ssrn.com/abstract=2903125

Lenzi, M., Vieno, A., Pastore, M., & Santinello, M. (2013). Neighborhood social connectedness and adolescent civic engagement: An integrative model. *Journal of Environmental Psychology*, 34, 45–54. https://doi.org/10.1016/j.jenvp.2012.12.003

Leonoff, A. (2015). *The good divorce: A psychoanalyst's exploration of separation, divorce, and childcare*. London, England: Karnac Books.

Lercara, B. (2016). The adoption and safe families act: proposing a "best efforts" standard to eliminate

the ultimate obstacle for family reunification. *Family Court Review*, 54(4), 657–670. https://doi.org/10.1111/fcre.12208

Lereya, S. T., Copeland, W. E., Costello, E. J., & Wolke, D. (2015). Adult mental health consequences of peer bullying and maltreatment in childhood: Two cohorts in two countries. *The Lancet Psychiatry*, 2(6), 524–531. https://doi.org/10.1016/S2215-0366(15)00165-0

LeVay, S. (1991). A difference in hypothalamic structure between heterosexual and homosexual men. *Science*, 253(5023), 1034–1037.

Levinson, D. J. (1978). *The seasons of a man's life*. New York, NY: Ballantine Books.

Levy, B. L., & Levy, D. L. (2017). When love meets hate: The relationship between state policies on gay and lesbian rights and hate crime incidence. *Social Science Research*, 61, 142–159. https://doi.org/10.1016/j.ssresearch.2016.06.008

Lewin, A., Mitchell, S. J., Burrell, L., Beers, L. S. A., & Duggan, A. K. (2011). Patterns and predictors of involvement among fathers of children born to adolescent mothers. *Journal of Family Social Work*, 14(4), 335–353.

Lewis, C. M., Faulkner, M., Scarborough, M., & Berkeley, B. (2012). Preventing subsequent births for low-income adolescent mothers: An exploratory investigation of mediating factors in intensive case management. *American Journal of Public Health*, 102(10), 1862–1865. https://doi.org/10.2105/AJPH.2012.300914

Li, Y. (2013). A perspective on health care for the elderly who lose their only child in China. *ResearchGate*, 41(6). https://doi.org/10.1177/1403494813490252

Liben, L. S. (2016). We've Come a Long Way, Baby (But We're Not There Yet): Gender Past, Present, and Future. *Child Development*, 87(1), 5–28. https://doi.org/10.1111/cdev.12490

Linde, L. E., & Erford, B. T. (2018). Ethical and legal issues in counseling. In B. T. Erford, *Orientation to the Counseling Profession* (3rd. ed.). (pp. 70–112). Upper Saddle River, NJ: Pearson.

Lindert, P. H. (1978/2015). *Fertility and scarcity in America*. Princeton, NJ: Princeton University Press.

Lindsey, L. L. (2015). *Gender roles: A sociological perspective*. New York, NY: Routledge.

Lino, M. (2014). Expenditures on children by families, 2013. *U.S. Department of Agriculture, Center for Nutrition Policy and Promotion*. Retrieved from https://www.cnpp.usda.gov/sites/default/files/expenditures_on_children_by_families/crc2013.pdf

Liu, Q. (2015). Individual Education Plan (IEP) Use by general classroom teachers. *TSpace*. Retrieved from https://tspace.library.utoronto.ca/handle/1807/68679

Livingston, G., & Caumont, A. (2017). 5 facts on love and marriage in America [Fact Tank]. Retrieved from http://www.pewresearch.org/fact-tank/2017/02/13/5-facts-about-love-and-marriage/

Lock, J., & Grange, D. L. (2015). *Treatment manual for anorexia nervosa, second edition: A family-based approach*. New York, NY: Guilford Publications.

Locke, J. (1693). *Some thoughts concerning education* (2nd ed.). London, England: A. and J. Churchill, Oxford University.

Lofquist, D., Lugaila, T., O'Connell, M., & Feliz, S. (2012). Household and families: 2010. *United States Census Bureau*. Retrieved from https://www.census.gov/library/publications/2012/dec/c2010br-14.html

Lomanowska, A. M., Boivin, M., Hertzman, C., & Fleming, A. S. (2017). Parenting begets parenting: A neurobiological perspective on early adversity and the transmission of parenting styles across generations. *Neuroscience, 342*, 120–139. https://doi.org/10.1016/j.neuroscience.2015.09.029

Lonner, W.J. & Malpass, R.S. (Eds.) (1994). *Psychology and culture*. Boston, MA: Allyn & Bacon.

Lougheed, J. P., Koval, P., & Hollenstein, T. (2016). Sharing the burden: The interpersonal regulation of emotional arousal in mother–daughter dyads. *Emotion, 16*(1), 83–93. https://doi.org/10.1037/emo0000105

Lucier-Greer, M., Arnold, A. L., Mancini, J. A., Ford, J. L., & Bryant, C. M. (2015). Influences of cumulative risk and protective factors on the adjustment of adolescents in military families. *Family Relations, 64*(3), 363–377. https://doi.org/10.1111/fare.12123

Luijkx, J., Putten, A. A. J. van der, & Vlaskamp, C. (2016). "I love my sister, but sometimes I don't": A qualitative study into the experiences of siblings of a child with profound intellectual and multiple disabilities. *Journal of Intellectual & Developmental Disability, 41*(4), 279–288. https://doi.org/10.3109/13668250.2016.1224333

Lundberg, S., Pollak, R. A., & Stearns, J. (2016). Family inequality: Diverging patterns in marriage, cohabitation, and childbearing. *The Journal of Economic Perspectives, 30*(2), 79–101. https://doi.org/10.1257/jep.30.2.79

Lusby, C. M., Goodman, S. H., Yeung, E. W., Bell, M. A., & Stowe, Z. N. (2016). Infant EEG and temperament negative affectivity: Coherence of vulnerabilities to mothers' perinatal depression. *Development and Psychopathology; Cambridge, 28*(4pt1), 895–911. https://doi.org/http://dx.doi.org/10.1017/S0954579416000614

Luyten, P., Mayes, L. C., Fonagy, P., Target, M., & Blatt, S. J. (2015). Attachment disorders. In P. Luyten, L. C. Mayes, P. Fonagy, M. Target, & S. J. Blatt (Eds.). *Handbook of Psychodynamic Approaches to Psychopathology* (pp. 425–444). New York, NY: Guilford Publications.

Lynne, E. G., Gifford, E. J., Evans, K. E., & Rosch, J. B. (2015). Barriers to reporting child maltreatment: Do emergency medical services professionals fully understand their role as mandatory reporters? *North Carolina Medical Journal, 76*(1), 13–18. https://doi.org/10.18043/ncm.76.1.13

Maccoby, E., & Martin, J. A. (1983). Socialization in the context of the family: Parent–child interaction. In P. H. Mussen (Ed.), *Handbook of child psychology, Vol. 4: Socialization, personality, and social development* (4th ed., pp. 1–101). New York, NY: Wiley.

Macdowall, W., Jones, K. G., Tanton, C., Clifton, S., Copas, A. J., Mercer, C. H., … Wellings, K. (2015). Associations between source of information about sex and sexual health outcomes in Britain: Findings from the third National Survey of Sexual Attitudes and Lifestyles (Natsal-3). *BMJ Open, 5*(3). https://doi.org/10.1136/bmjopen-2015-007837

MacKenzie, M. J., Nicklas, E., Brooks-Gunn, J., & Waldfogel, J. (2015). Spanking and children's externalizing behavior across the first decade of life: Evidence for transactional processes. *Journal of Youth and Adolescence, 44*(3), 658–669. https://doi.org/10.1007/s10964-014-0114-y

Maclean, M. J., Drake, D., & Mckillop, D. (2016). Perceptions of stepfathers' obligations to financially support stepchildren. *Journal of Family and Economic Issues, 37*(2), 285–296. https://doi.org/10.1007/s10834-015-9451-6

Madsen, S. D., & Collins, W. A. (2011). The salience of adolescent romantic experiences for romantic relationship qualities in young adulthood. *Journal of Research on Adolescence, 21*(4), 789–801. https://doi.org/10.1111/j.1532-7795.2011.00737.x

Maguire-Jack, K., & Negash, T. (2016). Parenting stress and child maltreatment: The buffering effect of neighborhood social service availability and accessibility. *Children and Youth Services Review, 60*, 27–33. https://doi.org/10.1016/j.childyouth.2015.11.016

Maine Children's Growth Council. (2011). *Infant brain development-The critical intervention point*. Retrieved from https://www.youtube.com/watch?v=_0EYXx9iI64

Mallette, J. K., Futris, T. G., Brown, G. L., & Oshri, A. (2015). The influence of father involvement and interparental relationship quality on adolescent mothers' maternal identity. *Family Relations: An Interdisciplinary Journal of Applied Family Studies, 64*(4), 476–489. https://doi.org/10.1111/fare.12132

Mancillas, A. (2006). Challenging the stereotypes about only children: A review of the literature and implications for practice. *Journal of Counseling & Development, 84*(3), 268–275. https://doi.org/http://dx.doi.org/10.1002/j.1556-6678.2006.tb00405.x

Manczak, E. M., DeLongis, A., & Chen, E. (2016). Does empathy have a cost? Diverging psychological and physiological effects within families. *Health Psychology, 35*(3), 211–218. https://doi.org/10.1037/hea0000281

Mandela, N. (1995). *Long walk to freedom: The autobiography of Nelson Mandela* (Reprinted). Randburg, South Africa: Macdonald Purnell.

Mann, M. T., & Peabody, E. P. (1863/2015). *Moral culture of infancy, and kindergarten guide*. Andesite Press.

Manning, W. (2015). Cohabitation and child well-being. *The Future of Children, 25*(2), 51–66. Retrieved from http://www.jstor.org/stable/pdf/43581972.pdf

Marceau, K., Dorn, L. D., & Susman, E. J. (2012). Stress and puberty-related hormone reactivity, negative emotionality, and parent–adolescent relationships. *Psychoneuroendocrinology, 37*(8), 1286–1298. https://doi.org/10.1016/j.psyneuen.2012.01.001

Margolis, R. (2016). The changing demography of grandparenthood. *Journal of Marriage and Family, 78*(3), 610–622. https://doi.org/10.1111/jomf.12286

Marian, V., & Shook, A. (2012). The cognitive benefits of being bilingual. *Cerebrum: The Dana Forum on Brain Science, 2012*. Retrieved from http://www.ncbi.nlm.nih.gov/pmc/articles/PMC3583091/

Marland, S. P. (1971). Education of the Gifted and Talented - Volume 1: Report to the Congress of the United States by the U. S. Commissioner of Education. Retrieved from https://eric.ed.gov/?id=ED056243

Marshall, J. (2011). Infant neurosensory development: Considerations for infant child care. *Early Childhood Education Journal, 39*, 175–181.

Marta Maria Antonieta de, S. S., Denise, C. de B., Jamile, L. N., Miriam, R. B., & C., S. (2013). Impact of an intervention nutrition program during prenatal on the weight of newborns from teenage mothers. *Nutrición Hospitalaria*, (6), 1943. https://doi.org/10.3305/nh.2013.28.6.6860

Martinez, G. M., & Abma, J. C. (2015). *Sexual activity, contraceptive use, and childbearing of teenagers aged 15–19 in the United States*. (NCHS data brief No. 209). Hyattsville, MD: National Center for Health Statistics. Retrieved from https://www.cdc.gov/nchs/data/databriefs/db209.pdf

Martinez, P., & Wizer-Vecchi, J. (2016). Fostering family engagement through shared leadership in the district, schools, and community. *Bringing Transformative Family Engagement to Scale: Implementation Lessons from Federal i3 Grants, 6*.

Martínez-Pampliega, A., Aguado, V., Corral, S., Cormenzana, S., Merino, L., & Iriarte, L. (2015). Protecting children after a divorce: Efficacy of Egokitzen—An intervention program for parents on children's adjustment. *Journal of Child and Family Studies, 24*(12), 3782–3792. https://doi.org/10.1007/s10826-015-0186-7

Mashego, T. A. B., & Taruvinga, P. (2014). Family resilience factors influencing teenagers adaptation following parental divorce in Limpopo Province South Africa. *Journal of Psychology, 5*(1), 19–34.

Mason, J. & Tripper, B. (2014). Children as family members. In G. B. Melton, A. Ben-Arieh., J. Cashmore, G. S. Goodman, & N. K. Worley, N.K. *The SAGE Handbook of Child Research* (pp. 153–168). Thousand Oaks, CA: SAGE Publications.

Masten, A. S. (2014). Invited commentary: resilience and positive youth development frameworks in developmental science. *Journal of Youth and Adolescence*, 43(6), 1018–1024. https://doi.org/10.1007/s10964-014-0118-7

Masten, A. S. (2015). *Ordinary magic: Resilience in development* (Reprint ed.). New York, NY: Guilford Publications.

Matheson, B. E., Camacho, C., Peterson, C. B., Rhee, K. E., Rydell, S. A., Zucker, N. L., & Boutelle, K. N. (2015). The relationship between parent feeding styles and general parenting with loss of control eating in treatment-seeking overweight and obese children. *International Journal of Eating Disorders*, 48(7), 1047–1055. https://doi.org/10.1002/eat.22440

Matsumoto, D. R., & Juang, L. P. (2013). *Culture and psychology* (5th ed.). Belmont, CA: Wadsworth Cengage Learning.

Matsumoto, D., & Juang, L. (2017). *Culture and psychology* (6th Ed.). Belmont, CA: Wadsworth Publishing.

Mayo Clinic. (2011). *Mayo Clinic: Guide to a healthy pregnancy*. Intercourse, PA: Good Books.

Mayo Clinic. (2017a). Healthy pregnancy. Retrieved from http://www.mayoclinic.org/healthy-lifestyle/pregnancy-week-by-week/basics/healthy-pregnancy/hlv-20049471

Mayo Clinic. (2017b). Labor and delivery, postpartum care. Retrieved from http://www.mayoclinic.org/healthy-lifestyle/labor-and-delivery/expert-answers/doula/faq-20057910

McAlister, A. R., & Peterson, C. C. (2013). Siblings, theory of mind, and executive functioning in children aged 3–6 years: New longitudinal evidence. *Child Development*, 84(4), 1442–1458. https://doi.org/10.1111/cdev.12043

Mccarthy, A. (2013). Supporting roles of grandparents in holding the family together. In A. Singh & M. Devine (Eds.), *Rural Transformation and Newfoundland and Labrador Diaspora* (pp. 309–317). Sense Publishers. https://doi.org/10.1007/978-94-6209-302-7_27

McConnell, E. A., Birkett, M. A., & Mustanski, B. (2015). Typologies of social support and associations with mental health outcomes among LGBT youth. *LGBT Health*, 2(1), 55–61. https://doi.org/10.1089/lgbt.2014.0051

McDonald, L., Miller, H., & Sandler, J. (2015). A social ecological, relationship-based strategy for parent involvement: Families and Schools Together (FAST). *Journal of Children's Services*, 10(3), 218–230. https://doi.org/10.1108/JCS-07-2015-0025

McGinn, K. L., Ruiz Castro, M., & Lingo, E. L. (2015). Mums the word! Cross-national effects of maternal employment on gender inequalities at work and at home. Retrieved from https://dash.harvard.edu/handle/1/16727933

McGoldrick, M., & Gerson, R. (1985). *Genograms in family assessment*. New York, NY: W. W. Norton & Company, Inc.

McGuire, J. K., Catalpa, J. M., Lacey, V., & Kuvalanka, K. A. (2016). Ambiguous loss as a framework for interpreting gender transitions in families. *Journal of Family Theory and Review*, 8(3), 373–385. https://doi.org/10.1111/jftr.12150

McGuire, J. K., Kuvalanka, K. A., Catalpa, J. M., & Toomey, R. B. (2016). Transfamily theory: How the presence of trans* family members informs gender development in families. *Journal of Family Theory and Review*, 8, 60-73. doi:10.1111/jftr.12125

McHale, J. P. (1995). Coparenting and triadic interactions during infancy: The roles of marital distress and child gender. *Developmental Psychology*, 31(6), 985–996. https://doi.org/10.1037/0012-1649.31.6.985

McHale, J. P., Khazan, I., Erera, P., Rotman, T., DeCourcey, W., & McConnell, M. (2012). Coparenting in diverse family systems. In M. H. Bornstein (Ed.), *Handbook of Parenting, Volume 3: Being and Becoming a Parent* (2nd ed., pp. 75–107). New York, NY: Routledge.

McHale, J. P., & Lindahl, K. M. (Eds.). (2011). *Coparenting: A conceptual and clinical examination of family systems*. Washington, DC: American Psychological Association. https://doi.org/10.1037/12328-000

McIvor, O., & Parker, A. (2016). Back to the future: Recreating natural indigenous language learning environments through language nest early childhood immersion programs. *The International Journal of Holistic Early Learning and Development*, 3, 21–35. Retrieved from https://ijheld.lakeheadu.ca/article/view/1444

McKinney, C., & Renk, K. (2011). A multivariate model of parent–adolescent relationship variables in early adolescence. *Child Psychiatry & Human Development*, 42(4), 442–462. https://doi.org/10.1007/s10578-011-0228-3

McLean, K. C., & Syed, M. (2014). *The Oxford handbook of identity development*. New York, NY: Oxford University Press.

Mehrkens, H. & Muller, F. L. (Eds.). (2015). *Sons and heirs: Succession and culture in nineteenth century Europe*. United Kingdom: Palgrave Macmillan

Meinck, F., Cluver, L. D., Boyes, M. E., & Ndhlovu, L. D. (2015). Risk and protective factors for physical and emotional abuse victimisation amongst vulnerable children in South Africa. *Child Abuse Review*, 24(3), 182–197. https://doi.org/10.1002/car.2283

Merrell, K. W., & Gimpel, G. (1998/2014). *Social skills of children and adolescents: Conceptualization, assessment, treatment*. New York, NY: Psychology Press.

Merrick, M. T., Leeb, R. T., & Lee, R. D. (2013). Examining the role of safe, stable, and nurturing relationships in the intergenerational continuity of child maltreatment—Introduction to the special issue. *The Journal of Adolescent Health: Official Publication of the Society for Adolescent Medicine*, 53(4 Suppl), S1–3. https://doi.org/10.1016/j.jadohealth.2013.06.017

Meyer v. Nebraska. 262 U.S. 390. (1923). https://supreme.justia.com/cases/federal/us/262/390/

Meyer, M. H., & Abdul-Malak, Y. (2016). *Grandparenting in the United States*. New York, NY: Routledge.

Midgett, A., Doumas, D., Sears, D., Lundquist, A., & Hausheer, R. (2015). A bystander bullying psychoeducation program with middle school students: A preliminary report. *Professional Counselor*, 5(4), 486–500.

Mikkonen, H. M., Salonen, M. K., Häkkinen, A., Olkkola, M., Pesonen, A.-K., Räikkönen, K., … Kajantie, E. (2016). The lifelong socioeconomic disadvantage of single-mother background-the Helsinki Birth Cohort study 1934-1944. *BMC Public Health*, 16(1), 817. https://doi.org/10.1186/s12889-016-3485-z

Milevsky, A. (2016). Sibling issues in diverse families. In *Sibling Issues in Therapy* (pp. 78–93). London, England: Palgrave Macmillan. https://doi.org/10.1057/9781137528476_5

Milkie, M. A., Nomaguchi, K. M., & Denny, K. E. (2015). Does the amount of time mothers spend with children or adolescents matter? *Journal of Marriage and Family*, 77(2), 355–372. https://doi.org/10.1111/jomf.12170

Miller, A. (1990). *For your own good: Hidden cruelty in childrearing and the roots of violence*. New York, NY: Noonday Press.

Miller, A. (2015). *Stepmothers' perceptions and experiences of stepmothers stereotypes* (Thesis). ResearchSpace@Auckland. Retrieved from https://researchspace.auckland.ac.nz/handle/2292/26705

Miller, B. G., Kors, S., & Macfie, J. (2016). No differences? Meta-analytic comparisons of psychological adjustment in children of gay fathers and heterosexual parents. *Psychology of Sexual Orientation and Gender Diversity*, 4(1), 14-22. https://doi.org/10.1037/sgd0000203

Miller, P. M., & Commons, M. L. (2010). The benefits of attachment parenting for infants and children: A behavioral developmental view. *Behavioral Development Bulletin*, 16(1), 1–14. https://doi.org/10.1037/h0100514

Miller, R. L. (2011). Multicultural identity development. In K. D. Keith (Ed.). *Cross-cultural Psychology: Contemporary Themes and Perspectives*. West Sussex, England: Wiley-Blackwell.

Miller, S., Taylor, V., & Rupp, L. (2016). Social movements and the construction of queer identity. In J. Stets & R. Serpe (Eds.), *New Directions in Identity Theory and Research* (Chapter 16). New York, NY: Oxford University Press. Retrieved from https://global.oup.com/academic/product/new-directions-in-identity-theory-and-research-9780190457532

Mindell, J. A., Li, A. M., Sadeh, A., Kwon, R., & Goh, D. Y. T. (2015). Bedtime routines for young children: A dose-dependent association with sleep outcomes. *Sleep: Journal of Sleep and Sleep Disorders Research*, 38(5), 717–722. https://doi.org/http://dx.doi.org/10.5665/sleep.4662

Minuchin, S. (1974). *Families and family therapy*. Cambridge, MA: Harvard University Press.

Miodrag, N., Burke, M., Tanner-Smith, E., & Hodapp, R. M. (2015). Adverse health in parents of children with disabilities and chronic health conditions: a meta-analysis using the Parenting Stress Index's Health Sub-domain. *Journal of Intellectual Disability Research*, 59(3), 257–271. https://doi.org/10.1111/jir.12135

Mitchell, C., McLanahan, S., Hobcraft, J., Brooks-Gunn, J., Garfinkel, I., & Notterman, D. (2015). Family structure instability, genetic sensitivity, and child well-being. *American Journal of Sociology*, 120(4), 1195–1225. https://doi.org/10.1086/680681

Mitchell, D. B., Szczerepa, A., & Hauser-Cram, P. (2016). Spilling over: Partner parenting stress as a predictor of family cohesion in parents of adolescents with developmental disabilities. *Research in Developmental Disabilities*, 49–50, 258–267. https://doi.org/10.1016/j.ridd.2015.12.007

Mitchell, V. (2016). Couple therapy with same-sex and gender-variant (LGBT) couples: Sociocultural problems and intrapsychic and relational consequences. In K. T. Sullivan & E. Lawrence (Ed.) *The Oxford Handbook of Relationship Science and Couple Interventions* (Chapter 17, pp. 241–256). New York, NY: Oxford University Press.

Moffitt, R. A. (2015). The deserving poor, the family, and the U.S. welfare system. *Demography*, 52(3), 729–749. https://doi.org/10.1007/s13524-015-0395-0

Molina Cartes, R., & González Araya, E. (2012). Teenage pregnancy. *Endocrine Development*, 22, 302–331. https://doi.org/10.1159/000326706

Molina, J. A. (2015). Caring within the family: Reconciling work and family life. *Journal of Family and Economic issues*, 36(1), 1.

Mollborn, S., & Jacobs, J. (2015). "I'll be there for you": Teen parents' coparenting relationships. *Journal of Marriage and Family*, 77(2), 373–387. https://doi.org/10.1111/jomf.12175

Mollborn, S., Lawrence, E., James-Hawkins, L., & Fomby, P. (2014). How resource dynamics explain accumulating developmental and health disparities for teen parents' children. *Demography*, 51(4), 1199–1224. https://doi.org/10.1007/s13524-014-0301-1

Montessori, M. (1964/2013). *The Montessori method*. New Brunswick, NJ: Transaction Publishers.

Montessori, M. (2015). *To educate the human potential* (Chapter 2). Santa Barbara, CA: ABC-CLIO.

Montgomery, H. (2009). *An introduction to childhood: Anthropological perspectives on children's lives* (p. 1). Hoboken, NJ: John Wiley & Sons.

Moon, R. Y. (2016). How to keep your sleeping baby safe: AAP policy explained. Retrieved from http://www.healthychildren.org/English/ages-stages/baby/sleep/Pages/A-Parents-Guide-to-Safe-Sleep.aspx

Moore, K., Torchia, M., & Persaud, T. V. N. (2015). *The developing human: Clinically oriented embryology* (10th ed.). Philadelphia, PA: Saunders.

Moore, K. L., Persaud, T. V. N., & Torchia, M. G. (2015). *The developing human: Clinically oriented embryology* (10th ed.). Philadelphia, PA: Saunders.

Moore, Q., Bocchini, C., & Raphael, J. (2016). Development of an evidence-based early childhood development strategy. Retrieved from https://scholarship.rice.edu/handle/1911/92697

Moravcsik, A. (2015, October). Why I put my wife's career first. *The Atlantic*. Retrieved from http://www.theatlantic.com/magazine/archive/2015/10/why-i-put-my-wifes-career-first/403240/

Mosovsky, S., Nolan, B. A. D., Markovic, N., & Stall, R. (2016). RADICLE Moms study: Minority stress and implications for lesbian mothers. *Women & Health*, 56(8), 859–870. https://doi.org/10.1080/03630242.2016.1141827

Moutsiana, C., Johnstone, T., Murray, L., Fearon, P., Cooper, P. J., Pliatsikas, C., . . . Halligan, S. L. (2015). Insecure attachment during infancy predicts greater amygdala volumes in early adulthood. *Journal of Child Psychology & Psychiatry*, 56(5), 540–548. https://doi.org/10.1111/jcpp.12317

Movement Advancement Project. (n.d.). *Same-sex couples raising children*. Retrieved from http://www.lgbtmap.org/equality-maps/same_sex_couples_raising_children

Mowder, B. A., Rubinson, F. & Yasik, A. E. (2009). *Evidence-based practice in infant and early childhood psychology*. Hoboken, NJ: Wiley.

Mundasad, S. (2013, April 10). Babies' brains to be mapped in the womb and after birth. *BBC News*. Retrieved from http://www.bbc.com/news/health-21880017

Murphy, A. (2014, May). Parental Influence on the Emotional Development of Children | Developmental Psychology at Vanderbilt. Retrieved from https://my.vanderbilt.edu/developmentalpsychologyblog/2014/05/parental-influence-on-the-emotional-development-of-children/

Murphy Pantoja, K. (2016). Gender Creative Parenting: An Educational Curriculum for Parents of Transgender and Gender Nonconforming Youth. *MSW Capstones*. Retrieved from http://digitalcommons.tacoma.uw.edu/msw_capstones/20

Murray, J., Theakston, A., & Wells, A. (2016). Can the attention training technique turn one marshmallow into two? Improving children's ability to delay gratification. *Behaviour Research and Therapy*, 77, 34–39. https://doi.org/10.1016/j.brat.2015.11.009

Myers-Walls, J. A. and Myers-Bowman, K. S. (2015). War and Families. *The Wiley Blackwell Encyclopedia of Family Studies*. 1–4. https://doi.org/10.1002/9781119085621.wbefs529.

Myrskylä, M., & Margolis, R. (2014). Happiness: before and after the kids. *Demography*, 51(5), 1843–1866. https://doi.org/10.1007/s13524-014-0321-x

Nadan, Y., Spilsbury, J. C., & Korbin, J. E. (2015). Culture and context in understanding child maltreatment: Contributions of intersectionality and neighborhood-based research. *Child Abuse & Neglect*, 41, 40–48. https://doi.org/10.1016/j.chiabu.2014.10.021

Nagel, M. C. (2012). *In the beginning: The brain, early development and learning*. Australian Council for Educational Research.

Nanda, S., & Warms, R. L. (2014). *Cultural Anthropology* (11th ed.). Belmont, CA: Cengage Learning - Wadsworth.

Nasrallah, H.A. (2011). The Antipsychiatry Movement: Who and Why. Editorial Comment. *Current Psychiatry*, 10(12), 1–2.

National Alliance on Mental Illness. (2017). Risk of suicide. Retrieved from https://www.nami.org/Learn-More/Mental-Health-Conditions/Related-Conditions/Suicide

National Association of Children's Hospitals. (2015, March 11). Injury prevention facts and trends. Retrieved from https://www.childrenshospitals.org/issues-and-advocacy/population-health/injury-prevention/fact-sheets/injury-prevention-facts-and-trends

National Campaign to Prevent Teen and Unplanned Pregnancy. (2016). National & state data. Retrieved from https://thenationalcampaign.org/data/landing

National Center for Children in Poverty (n.d.). Child Poverty. Retrieved from http://www.nccp.org/topics/childpoverty.html

National Center for Education Statistics (n.d.). Programme of International Student Assessment (PISA) 2015 results. Retrieved from https://nces.ed.gov/surveys/pisa/pisa2015/index.asp

National Center for Health Statistics. (2016, June 13). Retrieved September 20, 2016, from http://www.cdc.gov/nchs/nvss/births.htm

National Center on Shaken Baby Syndrome. (2017). National Center on Shaken Baby Syndrome. Retrieved from https://www.dontshake.org/learn-more

National Conference of State Legislatures. (2014). Child support 101.2: Establishing paternity. Retrieved from http://www.ncsl.org/research/human-services/enforcement-establishing-paternity.aspx

National Conference of State Legislatures: Termination of Support- Age of Majority. (2015). Retrieved from http://www.ncsl.org/research/human-services/termination-of-child-support-age-of-majority.aspx

National Conference of State Legislatures. (2016). Mental health and foster care. Retrieved from http://www.ncsl.org/research/human-services/mental-health-and-foster-care.aspx

National Foster Parent Association, 2016. Retrieved from www.nfpaonline.org

National Institute of Child Health and Human Development (n.d.). Retrieved from https://www.nichd.nih.gov/Pages/index.aspx

National Institute on Alcohol Abuse and Alcoholism (NIAAA). (2015a). Alcohol Use Disorder |. Retrieved from https://www.niaaa.nih.gov/alcohol-health/overview-alcohol-consumption/alcohol-use-disorders

National Institute on Alcohol Abuse and Alcoholism (NIAAA). (2015b). Alcohol facts and stats. Retrieved from https://pubs.niaaa.nih.gov/publications/AlcoholFacts&Stats/AlcoholFacts&Stats.htm

National Medical Association. (2017). Breastfeeding. Retrieved from http://www.nmanet.org/?page=Breastfeeding

National Middle School Association. (2009). The power of looping and long-term relationships. *Middle Ground, 12*(3). Retrieved November 7, 2012, from www.nmsa.org/Research/ResearchSummaries/Looping/tabid/2090/Default.aspx

National Resource Center for Health and Safety in Child Care and Early Education. (2017). Safe sleep practices and SIDS risk reduction: Applicable standards from: Caring for our children: National health and safety performance standards; Guidelines for early care and education programs. 3rd Edition. Retrieved from http://cfoc.nrckids.org/StandardView/SpcCol/Safe_sleep

Nauck, B. (2016). Stages and transitions in the family life cycle in an international comparative perspective. Presented at the Third ISA Forum of Sociology (July 10-14, 2016), Isaconf. Retrieved from https://isaconf.confex.com/isaconf/forum2016/webprogram/Session6401.html

Neff, L. A., & Karney, B. R. (2017). Acknowledging the elephant in the room: how stressful environmental contexts shape relationship dynamics. *Current Opinion in Psychology, 13*, 107–110. https://doi.org/10.1016/j.copsyc.2016.05.013

Negy, C., Velezmoro, R., Reig-Ferrer, A., Smith-Castro, V., & Livia, J. (2016). Parental Influence on Their Adult Children's Sexual Values: A Multi-National Comparison Between the United States, Spain, Costa Rica, and Peru. *Archives of Sexual Behavior, 45*(2), 477–489. https://doi.org/10.1007/s10508-015-0570-9

Neumann, M. M. (2015). Young children and screen time: Creating a mindful approach to digital technology. *Australian Educational Computing, 30*(2). Retrieved from http://journal.acce.edu.au/index.php/AEC/article/view/67

New York State. (2017). What does a healthy relationship look like? Available from https://www.ny.gov/teen-dating-violence-awareness-and-prevention/what-does-healthy-relationship-look

Newman, L. K., Harris, M., & Allen, J. (2011). Neurobiological basis of parenting disturbance. *The Australian And New Zealand Journal Of Psychiatry, 45*(2), 109–122. https://doi.org/10.3109/00048674.2010.527821

Nixon, E. and Hadfield, K. 2016. Blended Families. *The Wiley Blackwell Encyclopedia of Family Studies*. 1–5 https://doi.org/10.1002/9781119085621.wbefs207.

Noddings, N. (2013). *Caring: A Relational Approach to Ethics and Moral Education*. Berkeley, CA: University of California Press.

Noddings, N. (2015). *The challenge to care in schools, 2nd Edition*. New York, NY: Teachers College Press.

Nomaguchi, K., & Johnson, W. (2016). Parenting Stress Among Low-Income and Working-Class

Fathers: The Role of Employment. *Journal of Family Issues, 37*(11), 1535–1557. https://doi.org/10.1177/0192513X14560340

Nouman, H., Enosh, G., & Niselbaum-Atzur, P. (2016). The role of parental communication, child's wishes and child's gender in social workers' custody recommendations. *Children and Youth Services Review, 70*, 302–308. https://doi.org/10.1016/j.childyouth.2016.09.034

Numis, A. L., and Sankar, R. (2016) Neurodevelopmental disorders. In R. P. Lisak, D. D. Truong, W. M. Carroll, and R. Bhidayasiri (Eds.), *International Neurology*. Chichester, England: John Wiley & Sons, Ltd. doi: 10.1002/9781118777329.ch162

O'Connell, O., Meaney, S., & O'Donoghue, K. (2016). Caring for parents at the time of stillbirth: How can we do better? *Women and Birth, 29*(4), 345–349. https://doi.org/10.1016/j.wombi.2016.01.003

O'Connell, R., & Brannen, J. (2014). Children's food, power and control: Negotiations in families with younger children in England." *Childhood, 21*(1), 87–102. doi:10.1177/0907568213476900.

O'Hara, M. W., & McCabe, J. E. (2013). Postpartum depression: Current status and future directions. *Annual Review of Clinical Psychology, 9*(1), 379–407. https://doi.org/10.1146/annurev-clinpsy-050212-185612

O'Neal, C. W., Lucier-Greer, M., Mancini, J. A., Ferraro, A. J., & Ross, D. B. (2016). Family relational health, psychological resources, and health behaviors: A dyadic study of military couples. *Military Medicine, 181*(2), 152–160. https://doi.org/10.7205/MILMED-D-14-00740

O'Reilly, J. R., & Reynolds, R. M. (2013). The risk of maternal obesity to the long-term health of the offspring. *Clinical Endocrinology, 78*(1), 9–16. https://doi.org/10.1111/cen.12055

O'Shea, J. (2011). Delaying the academy: A gap year education. *Teaching in Higher Education, 16*(5), 565–577. https://doi.org/10.1080/13562517.2011.570438

Obadina, S. (2013). Understanding attachment in abuse and neglect: implications for child development. *British Journal of School Nursing, 8*(6), 290–295.

Office on Women's Health in the Department of Health and Human Services. (2014). Why breastfeeding is important. Retrieved from https://www.womenshealth.gov/breastfeeding/breastfeeding-benefits.html

Ogden, C. L., Carroll, M. D., Lawman, H. G., Fryar, C. D., Kruszon-Moran, D., Kit, B. K., & Flegal, K. M. (2016). Trends in obesity prevalence among children and adolescents in the United States, 1988–1994 through 2013–2014. *JAMA, 315*(21), 2292–2299. https://doi.org/10.1001/jama.2016.6361

Ojha, S., Fainberg, H. P., Sebert, S., Budge, H., & Symonds, M. E. (2015). Maternal health and eating habits: Metabolic consequences and impact on child health. *Trends in Molecular Medicine, 21*(2), 126–133. https://doi.org/10.1016/j.molmed.2014.12.005

Okhovati, M., Zare, M., Zare, F., Bazrafshan, M. S., & Bazrafshan, A. (2015). Trends in global assisted reproductive technologies research: A scientometrics study. *Electronic Physician, 7*(8), 1597–1601. https://doi.org/10.19082/1597

Olson, D. H. (2000). Circumplex model of marital and family systems. *Journal of Family Therapy, 22*(2), 144.

Olson, D. H. (2011). FACES IV and the circumplex model: Validation study. *Journal of Marital and Family Therapy, 37*(1), 64–80. https://doi.org/10.1111/j.1752-0606.2009.00175.x

Olson, D. H., & Gorall, D. M. (2003). Circumplex model of marital and family systems. In F. Walsh (Ed.), *Normal family processes* (3rd ed., pp. 51–547). New York, NY: Guilford.

Olson-Sigg, A., & Olson, D. H. (2011). PREPARE/ENRICH Program for premarital and married couples. In D. K. Carson, M. Casado-Kehoe, D. K. Carson, & M. Casado-Kehoe (Eds.), *Case studies in couples therapy: Theory-based approaches*. (pp. 1–12). New York, NY: Routledge/Taylor & Francis Group.

Orel, N. A., & Coon, D. W. (2016). The challenges of change: How can we meet the care needs of the ever-evolving LGBT family? *Generations, 40*(2), 41–45.

Ortman, J. M., Velkoff, V. A., & Hogan, H. (2014). An aging nation: The older population in the United States. *United States Census Bureau*, 1–28. Retrieved from https://www.census.gov/prod/2014pubs/p25-1140.pdf

Oshri, A., Lucier-Greer, M., O'Neal, C. W., Arnold, A. L., Mancini, J. A., & Ford, J. L. (2015). Adverse childhood experiences, family functioning, and resilience in military families: A pattern-based approach. *Family Relations, 64*(1), 44–63. https://doi.org/10.1111/fare.12108

Ott, M. A., Sucato, G. S., & Committee on Adolescence. (2014). Contraception for adolescents. *Pediatrics, 134*(4), e1257–e1281. https://doi.org/10.1542/peds.2014-2300

Overall, C. (2012). *Why have children?: The ethical debate* Cambridge, MA: MIT Press.

Pai, S. (2005). Under the mandap. In A. J. Fountas (Ed.). *Waking up American: Coming of age biculturally: First-generation women reflect on identity* (pp. 126–127). Emeryville, CA: Seal Press.

Painter, G., & Corsini, R. J. (2015). *Effective discipline in the home and school*. New York, NY: Routledge.

Papernow, P. L. (2015). *Becoming A stepfamily: Patterns of development in remarried families*. New York, NY: Routledge.

Park, H., & Walton-Moss, B. (2012). Parenting style, parenting stress, and children's health-related behaviors. *Journal of Developmental & Behavioral Pediatrics, 33*(6), 495–503.

Park, H., Coello, J. A., & Lau, A. S. (2014). Child socialization goals in East Asian versus Western Nations from 1989 to 2010: Evidence for social change in parenting. *Parenting 14*(2), 69–91. https://doi.org/10.1080/15295192.2014.914345

Parker, J. (2016). The effects of same-sex parenting on child development. *IU South Bend Undergraduate Research Journal*, 16, 161–166. Retrieved from https://scholarworks.iu.edu/journals/index .php/iusburj/article/view/22204

Parker, K., & Wang, W. (2013). Modern parenthood. Retrieved from http://www.pewsocialtrends.org/2013/03/14/modern-parenthood-roles-of-moms-and-dads-converge-as-they-balance-work-and-family/

Parlee, S. D., & MacDougald, O. A. (2014). Maternal nutrition and risk of obesity in offspring: The Trojan horse of developmental plasticity. *Biochimica et Biophysica Acta (BBA) - Molecular Basis of Disease*, 1842(3), 495–506. https://doi .org/10.1016/j.bbadis.2013.07.007

Pasalich, D. S., Fleming, C. B., Oxford, M. L., Zheng, Y., & Spieker, S. J. (2016). Can parenting intervention prevent cascading effects from placement instability to insecure attachment to externalizing problems in maltreated toddlers? *Child Maltreatment*, 21(3), 175–185. https://doi .org/10.1177/1077559516656398

Pashos, A., Schwarz, S., & Bjorklund, D. F. (2016). Kin investment by step-grandparents—more than expected. *Evolutionary Psychology*, 14(1), 1474704916631213.

Patterson, C. J. (2016). Parents' sexual orientation and children's development. *Child Development Perspectives*. https://doi.org/10.1111/cdep.12207

Patterson, C., & Farr, R. (2015). Children of lesbian and gay parents: Reflections on the research-policy interface. In K. Durkin & H. R. Schaffer, *The Wiley Handbook of Developmental Psychology in Practice: Implementation and Impact* (pp. 121–142). Hoboken, NJ: John Wiley & Sons.

Paul, A. R., & Adamo, M. A. (2014). Non-accidental trauma in pediatric patients: a review of epidemiology, pathophysiology, diagnosis and treatment. *Translational Pediatrics*, 3(3), 195–207.

Pearce, M., DeMartino, L., McMahon, R., Hamel, R., Maloney, B., Stansfield, D.-M., . . . Tavakoli, N. P. (2016). Newborn screening for congenital adrenal hyperplasia in New York State. *Molecular Genetics and Metabolism Reports*, 7, 1–7. https:// doi.org/10.1016/j.ymgmr.2016.02.005

Pearson, K. C. (2013). *Filial support laws in the modern era: Domestic and international comparison of enforcement practices for laws requiring adult children to support indigent parents* Rochester, NY: Social Science Research Network. Retrieved from https://papers.ssrn.com/abstract=2079753

Perry, S. L., & Whitehead, A. L. (2016a). Religion and non-traditional families in the United States. *Sociology Compass*, 10(5), 391–403. https://doi .org/10.1111/soc4.12370

Perry, S. L., & Whitehead, A. L. (2016b). Religion and public opinion toward same-sex relations, marriage, and adoption: Does the type of practice matter? *Journal for the Scientific Study of Religion*, 55(3), 637–51. doi:10.1111/jssr.12215.

Peterson, G. W., Steinmetz, S. K., & Wilson, S. M. (2005). Cultural and cross-cultural perspectives on parent–youth relations. In G. W. Peterson, S. K. Steinmetz, & S. M. Wilson (Eds.), *Parent–youth relations: Cultural and cross-cultural perspectives*. Binghamton, NY: Haworth Press.

Pew Research Center (2014). Millennials in adulthood. Retrieved from http://www.pewsocialtrends.org/2014/03/07/millennials-in-adulthood/

Pew Research Center. (2015a). Half of unmarried LGBT Americans say they would like to wed. Retrieved from http://www.pewresearch.org/fact-tank/2015/06/26/half-of-unmarried-lgbt-americans-say-they-would-like-to-wed/

Pew Research Center. (2015b). Same-sex marriage, state by state. Retrieved from http://www .pewforum.org/2015/06/26/same-sex-marriage -state-by-state/

Pew Research Center. (2015c). The American family today. Retrieved from http://www.pewsocialtrends.org/2015/12/17/1-the-american-family-today/

Pew Research Center. (2017). Gay marriage around the world. Retrieved from http://www.pewforum.org/2017/08/08/gay-marriage-around-the -world-2013/

Pfefferbaum, B., Jacobs, A. K., Houston, J. B., & Griffin, N. (2015). Children's disaster reactions: The influence of family and social factors. *Current Psychiatry Reports*, 17(7), 57. https://doi .org/10.1007/s11920-015-0597-6

Philadelphia Research Initiative. (2014). Millennials in Philadelphia. Retrieved from http://www.pewtrusts.org/en/research-and-analysis/reports/2014/01/21/millennials-in-philadelphia-a-promising-but-fragile-boom

Piaget, J. (1967). *Six psychological studies*. New York, NY: Random House.

Piaget, J., & Inhelder, B. (1969). *The psychology of the child*. New York, NY: Basic Books.

Pickett, B. (2015). Homosexuality. In E. N. Zalta (Ed.), *The Stanford Encyclopedia of Philosophy*. Metaphysics Research Lab, Stanford University. Retrieved from https://plato.stanford.edu/archives/fall2015/entries/homosexuality/

Pieterse, J. N. (2015). *Globalization and culture: Global mélange*. Lanham, MD: Rowman & Littlefield.

Pilkey, B. (2014). Queering heteronormativity at home: Older gay Londoners and the negotiation of domestic materiality. *Gender, Place & Culture*, 21(9), 1142–1157. https://doi.org/10.1080/0966369X.2013.832659

Pilon, B. (2011). Removing the barriers to prenatal care and education for teens -- Rock-a-bye teens: An early SSTART program. *International Journal of Childbirth Education*, 26(4), 23–27.

Pinquart, M. (2016). Associations of parenting styles and dimensions with academic achievement in children and adolescents: A meta-analysis. *Educational Psychology Review*, 28(3), 475–493. https://doi.org/10.1007/s10648-015-9338-y

Pinzon, J. L., Jones, V. F., Committee on Adolescence, & Committee on Early Childhood. (2012). Care of adolescent parents and their children. *Pediatrics*, 130(6), e1743–e1756. https://doi .org/10.1542/peds.2012-2879

Planty, M., Hussar, W., Snyder, T., Provasnik, S., Kena, G., Dinkes, R., KewalRamani, A., and Kemp, J. (2008). The Condition of Education 2008 (NCES 2008-031). National Center for Education Statistics, Institute of Education Sciences, U.S. Department of Education. Washington, DC.

Polakoff, E. G. (2007). Globalization and child labor review of the issues. *Journal of Developing Societies*, 23(1–2), 259–283. https://doi.org/10.1177/0 169796X0602300215

Polderman, T. J. C., Benyamin, B., de Leeuw, C. A., Sullivan, P. F., van Bochoven, A., Visscher, P. M., & Posthuma, D. (2015). Meta-analysis of the heritability of human traits based on fifty years of twin studies. *Nature Genetics*, 47(7), 702–709. https://doi.org/10.1038/ng.3285

Pollak, S. D., Nelson, C. A., Schlaak, M. F., Roeber, B. J., Wewerka, S. S., Wiik, K. L., . . . Gunnar, M. R. (2010). Neurodevelopmental effects of early deprivation in post-institutionalized children. *Child Development*, 81(1), 224–236. https://doi .org/10.1111/j.1467-8624.2009.01391.x

Ponzetti, J. J. (2016). *Evidence-based parenting education : A global perspective*. New York, NY: Routledge.

Porter, J. (2016). Bereavement in the primary school: A critical consideration of the nature, incidence, impact and possible responses. *The STeP Journal*, 3(1), 11–17.

Posada, G., Longoria, N., Cocker, C., & Lu, T. (2011). Child–caregiver attachment ties in military families: Mothers' view on interactions with their preschooler, stress, and social competence. In S. MacDermid- Wadsworth (Ed.), *Stress in U.S. military families* (pp. 131–147). New York, NY: Springer.

Postpartum Support International (n.d.). Pregnancy & postpartum mental health. Retrieved from http://www.postpartum.net/learn-more/pregnancy-postpartum-mental-health/

Potegal, M., & Knutson, J. F. (2013). *The Dynamics of aggression: Biological and social processes in dyads and groups*. New York, NY: Psychology Press.

Pound, P., Langford, R., & Campbell, R. (2016). What do young people think about their school-based sex and relationship education? A qualitative synthesis of young people's views and experiences. *BMJ Open*, 6(9). https://doi.org/10.1136/bmjopen-2016-011329

Powell, B., Hamilton, L., Manago, B., & Cheng, S. (2016). Implications of changing family forms for children. *Annual Review of Sociology*, 42(1), 301–322.

Pratt, M., Apter-Levi, L., Vakart, A., Feldman, M., Fishman, R., Feldman, T., Zagoory-Sharon, O., & Feldman, R. (2015). Maternal depression and child oxytocin response; Moderation by maternal oxytocin and relational behavior. *Depression and Anxiety*, 32(9), 635–646. doi:http://dx.doi .org/10.1002/da.22392.

Preckel, F., Baudson, T. G., Krolak-Schwerdt, S., & Glock, S. (2015). Gifted and maladjusted? Implicit attitudes and automatic associations related to gifted children. *American Educational Research Journal*, *52*(6), 1160–1184. doi:10.3102/0002831215590413.

Prioste, A., Narciso, I., Gonçalves, M. M., & Pereira, C. R. (2015). Family relationships and parenting practices: A pathway to adolescents' collectivist and individualist values? *Journal of Child and Family Studies*, *24*(11), 3258–3267. https://doi.org/10.1007/s10826-015-0129-3

Puolimatka, T. (2016). The gender diverse and the genderless conceptions of marriage and children's right to develop their sexual identity. *New Educational Review*, *45*. https://doi.org/10.15804/tner.2016.45.3.02

Qian, G. (2016). The effect of gender equality on happiness: Statistical modeling and analysis. *Health Care for Women International*, 1–16. https://doi.org/10.1080/07399332.2016.1198353

Radford, L. (2017). Child abuse and neglect: Prevalence and incidence. In L. Dixon, L. A. Craig, D. F. Perkins, & C. Hamilton-Giachritsis (Eds.), *What Works in Child Protection: An Evidence-Based Approach to Assessment and Intervention in Care Proceedings*. John Wiley & Sons. Retrieved from http://eu.wiley.com/WileyCDA/WileyTitle/productCd-1118976177.html

RAINN (n.d.). Retrieved from https://www.rainn.org/

Raley, S. B., Mattingly, M. J., & Bianchi, S. M. (2006). How dual are dual-income couples? Documenting change from 1970 to 2001. *Journal of Marriage and Family*, *68*(1), 11–28. https://doi.org/10.1111/j.1741-3737.2006.00230.x

Ralston, D. A., Egri, C. P., Furrer, O., Kuo, M.-H., Li, Y., Wangenheim, F., . . . Weber, M. (2013). Societal-level versus individual-level predictions of ethical behavior: A 48-society study of collectivism and individualism. *Journal of Business Ethics*, *122*(2), 283–306. https://doi.org/10.1007/s10551-013-1744-9

Ramamurthy, D., Lin Chua, S. Y., & Saw, S.-M. (2015). A review of environmental risk factors for myopia during early life, childhood and adolescence. *Clinical and Experimental Optometry*, *98*(6), 497–506. https://doi.org/10.1111/cxo.12346

Rathbun, A., & Zhang, A. (2016). *Primary early care and education arrangements and achievement at kindergarten entry*. Washington, DC: National Center for Education Statistics.

Rathus, S. A. (2016). *Childhood and adolescence: Voyages in development*. Boston, MA: Cengage Learning.

Rathus, S. A., Nevid, J. S. & Fichner-Rathus, L. (2014). *Human sexuality in a world of diversity* (9th ed.). Upper Saddle River, NJ: Pearson.

Raudino, A., Fergusson, D. M., & Horwood, L. J. (2013). The quality of parent/child relationships in adolescence is associated with poor adult psychosocial adjustment. *Journal of Adolescence*, *36*, 331–340. https://doi.org/10.1016/j.adolescence.2012.12.002

Reckmeyer, M. (2016). *Strengths based parenting: Developing your children's innate talents*. New York, NY: Simon and Schuster.

Reczek, C., Spiker, R., Liu, H., & Crosnoe, R. (2016). Family structure and child health: Does the sex composition of parents matter? *Demography*, *53*(5), 1605–1630. https://doi.org/10.1007/s13524-016-0501-y

Redelmeier, D. A., & Raza, S. (2016). Concussions and repercussions. *PLoS Medicine*, *13*(8). https://doi.org/10.1371/journal.pmed.1002104

Regnerus, M. (2012). How different are the adult children of parents who have same-sex relationships? Findings from the New Family Structures Study. *Social Science Research*, *41*(4), 752–770. https://doi.org/10.1016/j.ssresearch.2012.03.009

Régnier-Loilier, A. (2015). When fathers lose touch with their children after separation. In A. Régnier-Loilier (Ed.), *The Contemporary Family in France* (pp. 139–157). Switzerland, Springer International Publishing. https://doi.org/10.1007/978-3-319-09528-8_7

Rehel, Erin M. (2014). When dad stays home too: Paternity leave, gender, and parenting. *Gender & Society*, *28*(1), 110–132. doi:10.1177/0891243213503900.

Reid, J., Schmied, V., & Beale, B. (2010). "I only give advice if I am asked": Examining the grandmother's potential to influence infant feeding decisions and parenting practices of new mothers. *Women and Birth*, *23*(2), 74–80. https://doi.org/10.1016/j.wombi.2009.12.001

Renvoize, J. (2017). *Innocence destroyed: A study of child sexual abuse*. New York, NY: Routledge.

Renzulli, J. S., & Reis, S. M. (2014). *The schoolwide enrichment model: A how-to guide for talent development*. Waco, TX: Prufrock Press, Inc.

Ribble, M. A. (1943). *The rights of infants, early psychological needs and their satisfaction*. New York, NY: Columbia University Press.

Ricci, M. C., & Lee, M. (2016). *Mindsets for parents: Strategies to encourage growth mindsets in kids*. Waco, TX: Prufrock Press, Inc.

Rice, W. R., Friberg, U., & Gavrilets, S. (2016). Sexually antagonistic epigenetic marks that canalize sexually dimorphic development. *Molecular Ecology*, *25*(8), 1812–1822. https://doi.org/10.1111/mec.13490

Richards, J. C., Jonathan, N., & Kim, L. (2015). Building a circle of care in same-sex couple relationships: A socio-emotional relational approach. In C. Knudson-Martin, M. A. Wells, & S. K. Samman (Eds.), *Socio-Emotional Relationship Therapy* (pp. 93–105). Switzerland, Springer International Publishing. https://doi.org/10.1007/978-3-319-13398-0_8

Richards, M. A., Rothblum, E. D., Beauchaine, T. P., & Balsam, K. F. (2016). Adult children of same-sex and heterosexual couples: Demographic "thriving." *Journal of GLBT Family Studies*, 1–15. https://doi.org/10.1080/1550428X.2016.1164648

Richter, L. (2004). *The importance of caregiver-child interactions for the survival and healthy development of young children: A review*. Geneva, Switzerland: World Health Organization.

Riem, M. M. E., Alink, L. R. A., Out, D., Ijzendoorn, M. H.V., & Bakermans-Kranenburg, M.

J. (2015). Beating the brain about abuse: Empirical and meta-analytic studies of the association between maltreatment and hippocampal volume across childhood and adolescence. *Development and Psychopathology*, *27*(2), 507–520. https://doi.org/10.1017/S0954579415000127

Rilling, J. K., & Young, L. J. (2014). The biology of mammalian parenting and its effect on offspring social development. *Science*, *345*(6198), 771–776. https://doi.org/10.1126/science.1252723

Rimm, S. (2007). When overempowerment yields underachievement-strategies to adjust. *Parenting for High Potential*, 6.

Riness, L. S., & Sailor, J. L. (2015). An exploration of the lived experience of step-motherhood. *Journal of Divorce & Remarriage*, *56*(3), 171–179. https://doi.org/10.1080/10502556.2015.1012702

Ripoll-Núñez, K., & Carrillo, S. (2016). Mother and father figures in biological and stepfamilies: Youths' perceptions of parent-child relationship quality and parental involvement. *Journal of Latino/Latin American Studies*, *8*(2), 30–46. https://doi.org/10.18085/1549-9502-8.2.30

Ritchhart, R. (2015). *Creating cultures of thinking: The 8 Forces we must master to truly transform our schools*. San Francisco, CA: Jossey-Bass.

Robinson, E. B., Lichtenstein, P., Anckarsäter, H., Happé, F., & Ronald, A. (2013). Examining and interpreting the female protective effect against autistic behavior. *Proceedings of the National Academy of Sciences*, *110*(13), 5258–5262. https://doi.org/10.1073/pnas.1211070110

Robinson, M. (1980). Systems theory for the beginning therapist. *Australian Journal of Family Therapy*, *1*(4), 183–194. https://doi.org/10.1002/j.1467-8438.1980.tb00024.x

Roche, A. J., Fortin, G., Labbé, J., Brown, J., & Chadwick, D. (2005). The work of Ambroise Tardieu: The first definitive description of child abuse. *Child Abuse & Neglect*, *29*(4), 325–34. doi:10.1016/j.chiabu.2004.04.007.

Rockwell, C. (2011). Factors affecting parental involvement with children's education: A qualitative study of parent's socioeconomic status, level of education, and parent-school relationship. *Perspectives (University of New Hampshire)*, 94.

Rodriguez, C. M. (2016). Predicting parent–child aggression risk: Cognitive factors and their interaction with anger. *Journal of Interpersonal Violence*. https://doi.org/10.1177/0886260516629386

Rodriguez, Y., & Helms, H. M. (2016). Co-parenting. In *Encyclopedia of Family Studies*. Hoboken, NJ: John Wiley & Sons. 2016. doi:10.1002/9781119085621.wbefs322.

Rogers, Carl (1961). *On becoming a person: A therapist's view of psychotherapy*. London, England: Constable.

Rogoff, B. (1990). *Apprenticeship in thinking: Cognitive development in social context*. New York, NY: Oxford University Press.

Rohde, P., Stice, E., & Marti, C. N. (2015). Development and predictive effects of eating disorder risk factors during adolescence: Implications for prevention efforts. *International Journal of Eating Disorders*, 48(2), 187–198. https://doi.org/10.1002/eat.22270

Romeo, R. D. (2013). The teenage brain: The stress response and the adolescent brain. *Current Directions in Psychological Science*, 22(2), 140-145. https://doi.org/10.1177/0963721413475445

Roopnarine, J., & Johnson, J. E. (2013). *Approaches to early childhood education*. Retrieved from https://works.bepress.com/jaipaul_roopnarine/2/

Rose-Greenland, F., & Smock, P. J. (2013). Living together unmarried: What do we know about cohabiting families? In G. W. Peterson & K. R. Bush (Eds.), *Handbook of Marriage and the Family* (pp. 255–273). New York, NY: Springer. https://doi.org/10.1007/978-1-4614-3987-5_12

Rosino, M. (2016). ABC-X model of family stress and coping. In *Encyclopedia of Family Studies*. Hoboken, NJ: John Wiley & Sons. https://doi.org/10.1002/9781119085621.wbefs313

Ross, E. (1993). *Love and toil: Motherhood in outcast London, 1870-1918*. New York, NY: Oxford University Press.

Ross, S. M. (2016). United states, military families in. In *Encyclopedia of Family Studies*. Hoboken, NJ: John Wiley & Sons. Retrieved from http://onlinelibrary.wiley.com/doi/10.1002/9781119085621.wbefs015/abstract

Ross-Cowdery, M., Lewis, C. A., Papic, M., Corbelli, J., & Schwarz, E. B. (2016). Counseling about the maternal health benefits of breastfeeding and mothers' intentions to breastfeed. *Maternal and Child Health Journal*, 1–8. https://doi.org/10.1007/s10995-016-2130-x

Rotz, D. (2016). Why have divorce rates fallen?. *Journal of Human Resources*, 51(4), 961-1002. https://doi.org/10.3368/jhr.51.4.0214-6224R.

Ruedinger, E., & Cox, J. E. (2012). Adolescent childbearing: Consequences and interventions. *Current Opinion in Pediatrics*, 24(4), 446–452. https://doi.org/10.1097/MOP.0b013e3283557b8

Ruf, D. L. (1999). If you're so smart, why do you need counseling? *Advanced Development*, 8, 63–75.

Ruf, D. L. (2009). *5 levels of gifted: School issues and educational options*. Tucson, AZ: Great Potential Press.

Ruprecht, K., Elicker, J., & Choi, J. Y. (2016). Continuity of care, caregiver–child interactions, and toddler social competence and problem behaviors. *Early Education and Development*, 27(2), 221–239. https://doi.org/10.1080/10409289.2016.1102034

Russell, S. T., & Fish, J. N. (2016). Mental health in lesbian, gay, bisexual, and transgender (LGBT) youth. *Annual Review of Clinical Psychology*, 12, 465–487. https://doi.org/10.1146/annurev-clinpsy-021815-093153

Ryan, A., Baner, J., Demko, Z., Hill, M., Sigurjonsson, S., Baird, M. L., & Rabinowitz, M. (2013). Informatics-based, highly accurate, noninvasive prenatal paternity testing. *Genetics in Medicine*, 15(6), 473–477. https://doi.org/10.1038/gim.2012.155

Ryan, H. (2014). What does Trans* mean, and where did it come from? Retrieved from http://www.slate.com/blogs/outward/2014/01/10/trans_what_does_it_mean_and_where_did_it_come_from.html

Ryder, A. G., & Dere, J. (2010). Canadian diversity and clinical psychology: Defining and transcending cultural competence. *The CAP Monitor*, 32(1), 6–13. Retrieved from www.cap.ab.ca/pdfs/capmonitor35.pdf

Ryder, A. G., Alden, L. E., Paulhus, D. L., & Dere, J. (2013). Does acculturation predict interpersonal adjustment? It depends on who you talk to. *International Journal of Intercultural Relations*, 37(4), 502–506. https://doi.org/10.1016/j.ijintrel.2013.02.002

Sabyrkulova, S., Talbert, J., Dahle, S., Williams, A., & Flamand, K. (2016). Determining child abuse potential with the child guidance interview subscales. *University of Montana Conference on Undergraduate Research*. Retrieved from http://scholarworks.umt.edu/umcur/2016/amposters/5

Saltzman, W. R., Lester, P., Milburn, N., Woodward, K., & Stein, J. (2016). Pathways of risk and resilience: Impact of a family resilience program on active-duty military parents. *Family Process*, 55(4), 633-646. https://doi.org/10.1111/famp.12238

SAMHSA. (n.d.). NREPP. Retrieved from http://nrepp.samhsa.gov/landing.aspx

Samuel, L. R. (2013). *The American middle class: A cultural history*. New York, NY: Routledge.

Sanagavarapu, P. (2010). What does cultural globalization mean for parenting in immigrant families in the 21st Century? *Australasian Journal of Early Childhood*, 35(2), 36–42.

Sandberg, J. G., Feldhousen, E. B., & Busby, D. M. (2012). The impact of childhood abuse on women's and men's perceived parenting: Implications for practitioners. *The American Journal of Family Therapy*, 40(1), 74–91.

Sanders, M. R. (2012). Development, evaluation, and multinational dissemination of the triple P-Positive Parenting Program. *Annual Review of Clinical Psychology*, 8, 345–379. https://doi.org/10.1146/annurev-clinpsy-032511-143104

Sanner, C. (2016). *(Re)constructing family images: Stepmotherhood before motherhood* (Thesis). University of Missouri--Columbia. Retrieved from https://mospace.umsystem.edu/xmlui/handle/10355/56186

Santos Souza, M., Magalhães Silva, H. D., Rodrigues da Mata, J., & Oliveira Amaral, M. (2016). Paternity in adolescence: Expectations and feelings face to this reality. *Journal of Nursing UFPE/Revista de Enfermagem UFPE*, 309–315. https://doi.org/10.5205/reuol.7901-80479-1-SP.1001sup201616

Satir, V., Gilmore, D., & Golden Triad Films, I. (2004). *Of rocks and flowers: dealing with the abuse of children*. Kansas City, MO: Golden Triad Films.

Savin-Williams, R. C. (2016). Sexual orientation: Categories or continuum? Commentary on Bailey et al. (2016). *Psychological Science in the Public Interest: A Journal of the American Psychological Society*, 17(2), 37–44. https://doi.org/10.1177/1529100616637618

Scabini, E., & Manzi, C. (2011). Family processes and identity. In S. J. Schwartz, K. Luyckx, & V. L. Vignoles (Eds.), *Handbook of Identity Theory and Research* (pp. 565–584). New York, NY: Springer. https://doi.org/10.1007/978-1-4419-7988-9_23

Scheidegger, A. R. (2014). Corporal punishment. In *The Encyclopedia of Criminology and Criminal Justice*. Hoboken, NJ: John Wiley & Sons, Inc. https://doi.org/10.1002/9781118517383.wbeccj323

Schleider, J. L., Patel, A., Krumholz, L., Chorpita, B. F., & Weisz, J. R. (2015). Relation between parent symptomatology and youth problems: Multiple mediation through family income and parent–youth stress. *Child Psychiatry & Human Development*, 46(1), 1–9. https://doi.org/10.1007/s10578-014-0446-6

Schmidt, B., Holroyd, C. B., Debener, S., & Hewig, J. (2016). I can't wait! Neural reward signals in impulsive individuals exaggerate the difference between immediate and future rewards. *Psychophysiology*. https://doi.org/10.1111/psyp.12796

Schoephoerster, E., & Aamlid, C. (2016). College students' attitudes toward same-sex parenting. *College Student Journal*, 50(1), 102–106.

Schonert-Reichl, K. A., Smith, V., Zaidman-Zait, A., & Hertzman, C. (2012). Promoting children's prosocial behaviors in school: Impact of the "Roots of Empathy" Program on the social and emotional competence of school-aged children. *School Mental Health*, 4(1), 1–21. https://doi.org/10.1007/s12310-011-9064-7

Schover, L. R. (2014). Cross-border surrogacy: The case of Baby Gammy highlights the need for global agreement on protections for all parties. *Fertility and Sterility*, 102(5), 1258–1259. https://doi.org/10.1016/j.fertnstert.2014.08.017

Schrodt, P. (2016). Coparental communication with nonresidential parents as a predictor of children's feelings of being caught in stepfamilies. *Communication Reports*, 29(2), 63–74. https://doi.org/10.1080/08934215.2015.1020562

Schwartz, C. R., & Gonalons-Pons, P. (2016). Trends in relative earnings and marital dissolution: Are wives who outearn their husbands still more likely to divorce? *The Russell Sage Foundation Journal of the Social Sciences*, 2(4), 218–236. Retrieved from http://www.ncbi.nlm.nih.gov/pmc/articles/PMC5021537/

Schwartz, E. (2016). LGBT Issues in surrogacy: Present and future challenges. In E. S. Sills, *Handbook of Gestational Surrogacy: International Clinical Practice and Policy Issues* (Chapter, 8, pp. 55–61). Cambridge, United Kingdom: Cambridge University Press.

Schwartz, S. J., Luyckx, K., & Vignoles, V. L. (Eds.). (2011). *Handbook of identity theory and research*. New York, NY: Springer.

Scott, S., & Saginak, K. (2016). Adolescence: Emotional and social development. In D. Capuzzi & M. D. Stauffer, *Human Growth and Development*

Across the Lifespan: Applications for Counselors (Chapter 12). Hoboken, NJ: John Wiley & Sons.

Search Institute. (n.d.). Retrieved from http://www.search-institute.org/

Seeskin, K. (2006). Maimonides. In E Zalta (Ed.) *The Stanford Encyclopedia of Philosophy* (Spring 2017 Ed.). Retrieved from https://plato.stanford.edu/archives/spr2017/entries/maimonides/

Segrin, C., Givertz, M., Swaitkowski, P., & Montgomery, N. (2015). Overparenting is associated with child problems and a critical family environment. *Journal of Child and Family Studies, 24*(2), 470–479. https://doi.org/10.1007/s10826-013-9858-3

Seiffge-Krenke, I., & Pakalniskiene, V. (2011). Who shapes whom in the family: Reciprocal links between autonomy support in the family and parents' and adolescents' coping behaviors. *Journal of Youth and Adolescence, 40*(8), 983–995. https://doi.org/10.1007/s10964-010-9603-9

Sells, T. G. C., & Ganong, L. (2016). Emerging adults' expectations and preferences for gender role arrangements in long-term heterosexual relationships. *Sex Roles*, 1–13. https://doi.org/10.1007/s11199-016-0658-2

Selye, H. (1983) The stress concept: Past, present and future. In C. L. Cooper (Ed.). *Stress research issues for the eighties* (pp. 1–20). New York, NY: John Wiley & Sons.

Sev'er, A. (2012). In the name of fathers: Honour killings and some examples from South-Eastern Turkey. *Atlantis: Critical Studies in Gender, Culture & Social Justice, 30*(1), 129–145.

Severson, R. L., & Lemm, K. M. (2016). Kids see human too: Adapting an individual differences measure of anthropomorphism for a child sample. *Journal of Cognition and Development, 17*(1), 122–141. https://doi.org/10.1080/15248372.2014.989445

Sevón, E. M. (2015). Who's got the power? Young children's power and agency in the child-parent relationship. *International Journal of Child, Youth and Family Studies, 6*(4–1), 622–645. https://doi.org/10.18357/ijcyfs.641201515049

Shafer, K., Jensen, T. M., & Larson, J. H. (2014). Relationship effort, satisfaction, and stability: Differences across union type. *Journal of Marital and Family Therapy, 40*(2), 212–232. https://doi.org/10.1111/jmft.12007

Shapiro, A. F., Gottman, J. M., & Fink, B. C. (2015). Short-term change in couples' conflict following a transition to parenthood intervention. *Couple and Family Psychology: Research and Practice, 4*(4), 239–251. https://doi.org/10.1037/cfp0000051

Sharaievska, I., & Stodolska, M. (2015). Redefining boundaries in families through social networking leisure. *Leisure Sciences, 37*(5), 431–446. https://doi.org/10.1080/01490400.2015.1021882

Sharma, R., Biedenharn, K. R., Fedor, J. M., & Agarwal, A. (2013). Lifestyle factors and reproductive health: Taking control of your fertility. *Reproductive Biology and Endocrinology, 11*, 66. https://doi.org/10.1186/1477-7827-11-66

Sheehan, N. W., & Petrovic, K. (2008). Grandparents and their adult grandchildren: Recurring themes from the literature. *Marriage & Family Review, 44*(1), 99–124. https://doi.org/10.1080/01494920802019590

Shehan, C. L. (Ed.). (2016). *The Wiley-Blackwell encyclopedia of family studies*. Hoboken, NJ: Wiley-Blackwell.

Sherif-Trask, B. (2010). *Globalization and families: Accelerated systemic social change*. New York, NY: Springer.

Shin, Wonsun. (2015). Parental socialization of children's internet use: A qualitative approach. *New Media & Society, 17*(5), 649–665.

Shiraev, E. B., & Levy, D. A. (2016). *Cross-cultural psychology: Critical thinking and contemporary applications* (6th ed.). New York, NY: Routledge.

Siegel, D. J. (2012). *The developing mind: How relationships and the brain interact to shape who we are*. New York, NY: Guilford Publications.

Siegel, D. J., & Bryson, T. P. (2014). *No-drama discipline: The whole-brain way to calm the chaos and nurture your child's developing mind*. New York, NY: Random House Publishing Group.

Siegel, R. S., & Brandon, A. R. (2014). Adolescents, pregnancy, and mental health. *Journal of Pediatric and Adolescent Gynecology, 3*, 138. https://doi.org/10.1016/j.jpag.2013.09.008

Sigel, I. E., McGillicuddy-DeLisi, A. V., & Goodnow, J. J. (2014). *Parental belief systems: The psychological consequences for children*. New York, NY: Psychology Press.

Sigelman, C. K., & Rider, E. A. (2014). *Life-span human development*. Boston, MA: Cengage Learning.

Silk, J., & Romero, D. (2014). The role of parents and families in teen pregnancy prevention: An analysis of programs and policies. *Journal of Family Issues, 35*(10), 1339–1362. https://doi.org/10.1177/0192513X13481330

Silk, J. S., Stroud, L. R., Siegle, G. J., Dahl, R. E., Lee, K. H., & Nelson, E. E. (2012). Peer acceptance and rejection through the eyes of youth: Pupillary, eyetracking and ecological data from the Chatroom Interact task. *Social Cognitive and Affective Neuroscience, 7*(1), 93–105. https://doi.org/10.1093/scan/nsr044

Silverstein, M., & Giarrusso, R. (2010). Aging and family life: A decade review. *Journal of Marriage and the Family, 72*(5), 1039–1058. https://doi.org/10.1111/j.1741-3737.2010.00749.x

Silverstein, M., & Giarrusso, R. (2013). *Kinship and cohort in an aging society: From generation to generation*. Baltimore, MA: John Hopkins University Press.

Simons, L. G., Burt, C. H., & Simons, R. L. (2008). A test of explanations for the effect of harsh parenting on the perpetration of dating violence and sexual coercion among college males. *Violence and Victims, 1*, 66.

Simons, R. (2015). *Blended families*. New York, NY: Simon and Schuster.

Simovska, V., & Kane, R. (2015). Sexuality education in different contexts: Limitations and possibilities. *Health Education, 115*(1), 2–6. https://doi.org/10.1108/HE-10-2014-0093

Skinner, B. F. (1938). *The behavior of organisms*. New York, NY: Appleton-Century-Crofts.

Smalley, B. K., & Schooler J. E. (2015). *Telling the truth to your adopted or foster child: Making sense of the past* (2nd ed.). Santa Barbara, CA: Praeger.

Smink, F. R. E., van Hoeken, D., Oldehinkel, A. J., & Hoek, H. W. (2014). Prevalence and severity of DSM-5 eating disorders in a community cohort of adolescents. *International Journal of Eating Disorders, 47*(6), 610–619. https://doi.org/10.1002/eat.22316

Smith, A. R., Chein, J., & Steinberg, L. (2014). Peers increase adolescent risk taking even when the probabilities of negative outcomes are known. *Developmental Psychology, 50*(5), 1564–1568. https://doi.org/10.1037/a0035696

Smutney, J. F., Walker, S. Y., & Honeck, I. E. (2015). *Teaching gifted children in today's preschool and primary classrooms: Identifying, nurturing, and challenging children ages 4-9*. Golden Valley, MN: Free Spirit Publishing.

Snapp, S. D., Watson, R. J., Russell, S. T., Diaz, R. M., & Ryan, C. (2015). Social support networks for LGBT young adults: Low cost strategies for positive adjustment. *Family Relations, 64*(3), 420–430. https://doi.org/10.1111/fare.12124

Snyder, T.D., & Dillow, S.A. (2015). Digest of education statistics 2013. *National Center for Education Statistics*. Retrieved from https://nces.ed.gov/pubsearch/pubsinfo.asp?pubid=2015011

Soldz, S., & Vaillant, G. E. (1999). The big five personality traits and the life course: A 45-year longitudinal study. *Journal of Research in Personality, 33*(2), 208–232. https://doi.org/10.1006/jrpe.1999.2243

Soliz, J. (2015). Communication and the grandparent–grandchild relationship. In *The International Encyclopedia of Interpersonal Communication*. Hoboken, NJ: John Wiley & Sons. Retrieved from http://onlinelibrary.wiley.com/doi/10.1002/9781118540190.wbeic221/abstract

Solomon, A. (2012). *Far from the tree: parents, children, and the search for identity*. New York, NY: Scribner.

Somers, S., Van Parys, H., Provoost, V., Buysse, A., Pennings, G., & De Sutter, P. (2016). How to create a family? Decision making in lesbian couples using donor sperm. *Sexual & Reproductive Healthcare, 11*, 13–18. https://doi.org/10.1016/j.srhc.2016.08.005

South, S. J., & Lei, L. (2015). Failures-to-launch and boomerang kids: Contemporary determinants of leaving and returning to the parental home. *Social Forces, 94*(2), 863–890. https://doi.org/10.1093/sf/sov064

Spear, L. P. (2016). Consequences of adolescent use of alcohol and other drugs: Studies using rodent models. *Neuroscience & Biobehavioral Reviews, 70*, 228–243. https://doi.org/10.1016/j.neubiorev.2016.07.026

Sperry, D. M., & Widom, C. S. (2013). Child abuse and neglect, social support, and psychopathology in adulthood: A prospective investigation. *Child*

Abuse & Neglect, 37(6), 415–425. https://doi
.org/10.1016/j.chiabu.2013.02.006

Spitz, R. (1945). *Hospitalism: An inquiry into the genesis of psychiatric conditions in early childhood.* New Haven, CT: Yale University Press.

Spitzer, M. (2016). Bilingual benefits in education and health. *Trends in Neuroscience and Education,* 5(2), 67–76.

Spock, B. (1946). *The common sense book of baby and child care.* New York, NY: Duell, Sloan, and Pearce.

Sprecher, S., & Hatfield, E. (2017). The importance of love as a basis of marriage: Revisiting Kephart (1967). *Journal of Family Issues,* 38(3), 312–335. https://doi.org/10.1177/0192513X15576197

Stabile, M., & Allin, S. (2012). The economic costs of childhood disability. *The Future of Children,* 22(1), 65–96.

Stacey, J. & Biblarz, T.J. (2001). (How) does the sexual orientation of parents matter? *American Sociological Review,* 66(2), 159–183. https://doi.org/10.2307/2657413.

Stahl, A. E., & Feigenson, L. (2015). Observing the unexpected enhances infants' learning and exploration. *Science,* 348(6230), 91–94. https://doi.org/10.1126/science.aaa3799

Stahl, M. J. (Ed.). (2003). *Encyclopedia of health care management.* Thousand Oaks, CA: SAGE Publications.

Stanford Children's Health. (2017). Newborn-sleep patterns. Retrieved from http://www.stanfordchildrens.org/en/topic/newborn-sleep-patterns

Stanger-Hall, K. F., & Hall, D. W. (2011). Abstinence-only education and teen pregnancy rates: Why we need comprehensive sex education in the U.S. *PLOS ONE,* 6(10). https://doi.org/10.1371/journal.pone.0024658

Stavrinides, P., Nikiforou, M., & Georgiou, S. (2015). Do mothers know? Longitudinal associations between parental knowledge, bullying, and victimization. *Journal of Social and Personal Relationships,* 32(2), 180–196.

Steiner, R. (2004). *Human values in education.* Great Barrington, MA: Antroposophic Press.

Sterling, E. W., & Best-Boss, A. (2013). *Your child's teeth: A complete guide for parents.* Baltimore, MD: Johns Hopkins University Press.

Sterrett, E. M., Kincaid, C., Ness, E., Gonzalez, M., McKee, L. G., & Jones, D. J. (2013). Youth functioning in the coparenting context: A mixed methods study of African American single mother families. *Journal of Child and Family Studies,* 24(2), 455–469. https://doi.org/10.1007/s10826-013-9857-4

Stevenson, R. G., & Cox, G. R. (Eds.). (2017). *Children, adolescents, and death: Questions and answers.* New York, NY: Routledge.

Steward, J. (2016). *Personal communication: Parenting.* Birmingham, AL: Samford University.

Stewart, L., & Thompson, J. (2015). *Early years nutrition and healthy weight.* Hoboken, NJ: John Wiley & Sons.

Stewart, N. (2011). *How children learn: The characteristics of effective early learning.* London, England: The British Association for Early Childhood Education.

Stewart, S. (2016). The secret trail to Machu Picchu. *Condé Nast Traveller.* Retrieved from http://www.cntraveller.com/recommended/amazing-journeys/machu-picchu-peru-tours-andes

Stewart, S. D. (2007). *Brave new stepfamilies: Diverse paths to stepfamily living.* Thousand Oaks, CA: SAGE Publishers.

Stikkelbroek, Y., Bodden, D. H., Reitz, E., Vollebergh, W. A., & van Baar, A. L. (2016). Mental health of adolescents before and after the death of a parent or sibling. *European Child & Adolescent Psychiatry,* 25(1), 49–59. https://doi.org/10.1007/s00787-015-0695-3.

Stoltenborgh, M., Bakermans-Kranenburg, M. J., van Ijzendoorn, M. H., & Alink, L. R. A. (2013). Cultural-geographical differences in the occurrence of child physical abuse? A meta-analysis of global prevalence. *International Journal of Psychology: Journal International De Psychologie,* 48(2), 81–94. https://doi.org/10.1080/00207594.2012.697165

Stossel, S. (2013). A 75-year harvard study finds what it takes to live a happy life. *The Atlantic.* Retrieved from http://www.businessinsider.com/grant-study-reveals-what-makes-us-happy-2013-4

Suarez-Orozco, M. M., Suarez-Orozco, C., & Qin-Hillard, D. (2014). *The new immigrant in American society: Interdisciplinary perspectives on the new immigration.* New York, NY: Routledge.

Substance Abuse and Mental Health Services Administration. (2015). Specific populations and prescription drug misuse and abuse. Retrieved from https://www.samhsa.gov/prescription-drug-misuse-abuse/specific-populations

Sun, J. X., Helgason, A., Masson, G., Ebenesersdóttir, S. S., Li, H., Mallick, S., . . . Stefansson, K. (2012). A direct characterization of human mutation based on microsatellites. *Nature Genetics,* 44(10), 1161–1165. https://doi.org/10.1038/ng.2398

Sun, J., Knowles, M., Patel, F., Frank, D. A., Heeren, T. C., & Chilton, M. (2016). Childhood adversity and adult reports of food insecurity among households with children. *American Journal of Preventive Medicine,* 50(5), 561–572. doi:10.1016/j.amepre.2015.09.024

Sun, M. H., bin Sallahuddin, M. A., & Kaur, M. (2016). To what extent do the benefits of multilingualism outweigh its disadvantages? *Universiti Sains Malaysia,* 1–13. Retrieved from https://www.researchgate.net/publication/311308759_To_what_extent_do_the_benefits_of_multilingualism_outweigh_its_disadvantages

Sung, V., Hiscock, H., Tang, M. L. K., Mensah, F. K., Nation, M. L., Satzke, C., . . . Wake, M. (2014). Treating infant colic with the probiotic Lactobacillus reuteri: Double blind, placebo controlled randomised trial. *BMJ,* 348. https://doi.org/10.1136/bmj.g2107

Suskind, D. (2015). *Thirty million words: Building a child's brain.* New York, NY: Penguin Publishing Group.

Suzumori, N., & Sugiura-Ogasawara, M. (2010). Genetic factors as a cause of miscarriage. *Current Medicinal Chemistry,* 17(29), 3431–3437.

Takács, J., Szalma, I., & Bartus, T. (2016). Social attitudes toward adoption by same-sex couples in Europe. *Archives of Sexual Behavior,* 45(7), 1787–1798. https://doi.org/10.1007/s10508-016-0691-9

Talaulikar, V. S., & Arulkumaran, S. (2013). Maternal, perinatal and long-term outcomes after assisted reproductive techniques (ART): implications for clinical practice. *European Journal of Obstetrics & Gynecology and Reproductive Biology,* 170(1), 13–19. https://doi.org/10.1016/j.ejogrb.2013.04.014

Tanner, J. L., & Arnett, J. J. (2016). Emerging adult clinical psychology. In J. C. Norcross, G. R. VandenBos, D. K. Freedheim, & M. M. Domenech (Eds.), *APA handbook of clinical psychology: Roots and branches* (Vol. 1, pp. 127–138). Washington, DC: American Psychological Association.

Tantibanchachai, C. (2014). Teratogens. *Embryo Project Encyclopedia.* Retrieved from http://embryo.asu.edu/handle/10776/7510.

Tasker, F., & Delvoye, M. (2015). Moving out of the Shadows: Accomplishing Bisexual Motherhood. *Sex Roles,* 73(3–4), 125–140. https://doi.org/10.1007/s11199-015-0503-z

Tasker, F., & Figueroa, V. (2016). [Review of the book *Modern families: Parents and children in new family forms*]. *Journal of GLBT Family Studies,* 12(1), 111–113. https://doi.org/10.1080/1550428X.2015.1103140

Taylor, C. A., Al-Hiyari, R., Lee, S. J., Priebe, A., Guerrero, L. W., & Bales, A. (2016). Beliefs and ideologies linked with approval of corporal punishment: A content analysis of online comments. *Health Education Research,* 31(4), 563–575. https://doi.org/10.1093/her/cyw029

Taylor, M., Harper, S., Jurecko, L., Melowsky, J., & Towler, C. (2015). The resource center for separating and divorcing families: Interdisciplinary perspectives on a collaborative and child-focused approach to alternative dispute resolution. *Family Court Review,* 53(1), 7–22. https://doi.org/10.1111/fcre.1212

Teach for America (n.d.). Retrieved from https://www.teachforamerica.org/

Tein, J. Y., Sandler, I. N., Braver, S. L., & Wolchik, S. A. (2013). Development of a brief parent-report risk index for children following parental divorce. *Journal of Family Psychology: JFP: Journal of the Division of Family Psychology of the American Psychological Association (Division 43),* 27(6), 925–936. https://doi.org/10.1037/a0034571

Telingator, C. J., & Patterson, C. (2008). Children and adolescents of lesbian and gay parents. *Journal of the American Academy of Child and Adolescent Psychiatry,* 47(12), 1364–1368. https://doi.org/10.1097/CHI.0b013e31818960bc

Telzer, E. H., Flannery, J., Humphreys, K. L., Goff, B., Gabard-Durman, L., Gee, D. G., & Tottenham, N. (2015). "The Cooties Effect": Amygdala reactivity to opposite- versus same-sex faces declines from childhood to adolescence. *Journal of Cognitive Neuroscience,* 27(9), 1685–1696. https://doi.org/10.1162/jocn_a_00813

Temple, E. C. (2015). Clearing the smokescreen: The current evidence on cannabis use. *Frontiers in Psychiatry, 6*. https://doi.org/10.3389/fpsyt.2015.00040

Terzian, M. A., Li, J., Fraser, M. W., Day, S. H., & Rose, R. A. (2015). Social information-processing skills and aggression: A quasi-experimental trial of the making choices and making choices plus programs. *Research on Social Work Practice, 25*(3), 358–369. https://doi.org/10.1177/1049731514534898

Tetley, A., Moghaddam, N. G., Dawson, D. L., & Rennoldson, M. (2014). Parental bonding and eating disorders: A systematic review. *Eating Behaviors, 15*(1), 49–59. https://doi.org/10.1016/j.eatbeh.2013.10.008

Tew, M. (2013). *Safer childbirth? A critical history of maternity care*. New York, NY: Springer.

The American Congress of Obstetricians and Gynecologists. (2017). Adolescent pregnancy, contraception, and sexual activity. *Committee Opinion, 699*, 1–8. Retrieved from http://www.acog.org/Resources-And-Publications

The American Speech-Language-Hearing Association. (n.d.). Preschool language disorders. Retrieved from http://www.asha.org/public/speech/disorders/Preschool-Language-Disorders/

The Children's Hospital of Philadelphia. (n.d.). Center for injury research and prevention research institute. Retrieved from https://injury.research.chop.edu/

The Pell Institute. (n.d.). Retrieved from http://www.pellinstitute.org/

The Pew Charitable Trusts. (2013). Faces of economic mobility. Retrieved from http://bit.ly/1wW5Oy3

The Stuart Foundation. (2013). At greater risk, California foster youth and the path from high school to college. Retrieved from http://stuartfoundation.org/greater-risk-california-foster-youth-path-high-school-college/

The Urban Child Institute. (2016). Baby's brain begins now: Conception to age 3. Retrieved from http://www.urbanchildinstitute.org/why-0-3/baby-and-brain

The World Bank (n.d.). *Overview*. Retrieved January 19, 2017, from http://www.worldbank.org/en/topic/education/overview#1

Theunis, L., Pasteels, I., & Van Bavel, J. (2015). Educational assortative mating after divorce: Persistence or divergence from first marriages? *Zeitschrift Für Familienforschung, 27*(Special Issue: Family Dynamics after Separation), 183–202.

Thompson, R. A. (2015a). *Counseling techniques: Improving relationships with others, ourselves, our families, and our environment*. New York, NY: Routledge.

Thompson, R. A. (2015b). Social support and child protection: Lessons learned and learning. *Child Abuse & Neglect, 41*, 19–29. https://doi.org/10.1016/j.chiabu.2014.06.011

Thompson, R. A. (2015c). Stress and child development. *The Future of Children, 24*(1), 41–59. https://doi.org/10.1353/foc.2014.0004

Threlfall, J. M., & Kohl, P. L. (2015). Addressing child support in fatherhood programs: Perspectives of fathers and service providers. *Family Relations, 64*(2), 291–304. https://doi.org/10.1111/fare.12119

Till, C. R., Everette, D., & Haas, D. M. (2015). Incentives for increasing prenatal care use by women in order to improve maternal and neonatal outcomes. In *Cochrane Database of Systematic Reviews*. Hoboken, NJ: John Wiley & Sons. https://doi.org/10.1002/14651858.CD009916.pub2

Titelman, P. (Ed.). (1998). *Clinical applications of Bowen Family Systems Theory*. New York, NY: Routledge.

Tobia, V., Riva, P., & Caprin, C. (2016). Who are the children most vulnerable to social exclusion? The moderating role of self-esteem, popularity, and nonverbal intelligence on cognitive performance following social exclusion. *Journal of Abnormal Child Psychology*, 1–13. https://doi.org/10.1007/s10802-016-0191-3

Tonmyr, L., Ouimet, C., & Ugnat, A. M. (2012). A review of findings from the Canadian Incidence Study of Reported Child Abuse and Neglect (CIS). *Canadian Journal of Public Health, 103*(2), 103–112.

Tornello, S. L., & Patterson, C. J. (2012). Gay fathers in mixed-orientation relationships: experiences of those who stay in their marriages and of those who leave. *Journal of GLBT Family Studies, 8*(1), 85–98. https://doi.org/ http://dx.doi.org/10.1080/1550428X.2012.641373

Tornello, S. L., & Patterson, C. J. (2015). Timing of parenthood and experiences of gay fathers: A life course perspective. *Journal of GLBT Family Studies, 11*(1), 35–56. https://doi.org/10.1080/1550428X.2013.878681

Tornello, S. L., Sonnenberg, B. N., & Patterson, C. J. (2015). Division of labor among gay fathers: Associations with parent, couple, and child adjustment. *Psychology of Sexual Orientation and Gender Diversity, 2*(4), 365–375. https://doi.org/10.1037/sgd0000109

Trail, T. E., Meadows, S. O., Miles, J. N., & Karney, B. R. (2015). Patterns of vulnerabilities and resources in U.S. military families. *Journal of Family Issues*. https://doi.org/10.1177/0192513X15592660

Trask, B. S. (2008/2010). *Globalization and families: Accelerated systemic social change*. New York, NY: Springer.

Treas, J., & Sanabria, T. (2016). Marital status and living arrangements over the life course. In M. H. Meyer & E. A. Daniele (Eds.), *Gerontology: Changes, Challenges, and Solutions [2 volumes]: Changes, Challenges, and Solutions* (Chapter 10, pp. 247–269). Santa Barbara, CA: ABC-CLIO.

Treffinger, D., Inman, T., Jolly, J., & Smutny, J. F. (2011). *Parenting gifted children: The authoritative guide*. Waco, TX: Prufrock Press.

Trent, K., & Spitze, G. D. (2011). Growing up without siblings and adult sociability behaviors. *ResearchGate, 32*(9), 1178–1204. https://doi.org/10.1177/0192513X11398945

Troxel v. Granville: Opinion of the U.S. Supreme Court on the rights of parents and grandparents to rear their children, Justices S. D. O'Connor, D. H. Souter, C. Thomas, J. P. Stevens, A. Scalia, A. M. Kennedy. (2001). *Historic Documents of 2000*.

Tudge, J. H., Mokrova, I., Hatfield, B. E., & Karnik, R. B. (2009). Uses and misuses of Bronfenbrenner's bioecological theory of human development. *Journal of Family Theory and Review, 1*(4), 198.

U.S. Bureau of Labor Statistics. (2015). Women in labor force: A databook. *BLS Reports*. Retrieved from https://www.bls.gov/opub/reports/womens-databook/archive/women-in-the-labor-force-a-databook-2015.pdf

U.S. Bureau of Labor Statistics. (2017). Employment characteristics of families: 2016. Retrieved from http://www.bls.gov/news.release/famee.nr0.htm

U.S. Census Bureau. (n.d.). *One-parent unmarried family groups with own children under 18, by marital status of the reference person: 2011*. Retrieved from http://www.census.gov/population/www/socdemo/hh-fam/cps2011.html

U.S. Census Bureau. (2011). *Section 23: Transportation*. Retrieved from www.census.gov/prod/2011pubs/11statab/trans.pdf

U.S. Census Bureau. (2014). 10 percent of grandparents live with a grandchild, census bureau reports. Retrieved from https://www.census.gov/newsroom/press-releases/2014/cb14-194.html

U.S. Census Bureau (2015). America's families and living arrangements: 2015: Children (C table series). Retrieved from https://www.census.gov/data/tables/2015/demo/families/cps-2015.html

U.S. Census Bureau. (2016). America's families and living arrangements: 2016: Family groups (FG table series). Retrieved from https://www.census.gov/data/tables/2016/demo/families/cps-2016.html

U. S. Const. amend. XIV, § 1. Retrieved from https://www.law.cornell.edu/constitution/amendmentxiv

U.S. Consumer Product Safety Commission (n.d.). Retrieved from https://www.cpsc.gov/

U.S Consumer Product Safety Commission. (n.d.). Safety education: Kids and babies. Retrieved from http://www.cpsc.gov/en/safety-education/safety-guides/kids-and-babies/

U.S. Declaration of Independence (1776). Retrieved from http://www.ushistory.org/declaration/document/

U.S. Department of Education. (n.d.). Even start. Retrieved from https://www2.ed.gov/programs/evenstartformula/index.html

U. S. Department of Justice. Retrieved from https://www.justice.gov/

U.S. Department of State, Bureau of Consular Affairs (n.d). Intercountry adoption statistics. Retrieved from https://travel.state.gov/content/adoptionsabroad/en/about-us/statistics.html

Umberson, D. (2016). *Stress and the provision of social support in gay, lesbian, and heterosexual marriages*. Presented at the Third ISA Forum of Sociology (July 10-14, 2016), Isaconf. Retrieved from https://isaconf.confex.com/isaconf/forum2016/webprogram/Paper76568.html

Umberson, D. D., & Kroeger, R. A. (2016). Gender, marriage, and health for same-sex and different-sex couples: The future keeps arriving. In S. M. McHale, V. King, J. V. Hook, & A. Booth (Eds.), *Gender and Couple Relationships* (pp. 189–213). Switzerland, Springer International Publishing. https://doi.org/10.1007/978-3-319-21635-5_12

Underwood, M. K., & Rosen, L. H. (Eds.). (2011). *Social development: Relationships in infancy, childhood, and adolescence.* New York, NY: Guilford Publications.

UNESCO Institute for Statistics. (2015). A growing number of children and adolescents are out of school as aid fails to meet the mark. *United Nations Educational Scientific and Cultural Organization, 22*(31), 1–13. Retrieved from http://www.uis.unesco.org/Education/Documents/fs-31-out-of-school-children-en.pdf

Ungar, M. (2015). Practitioner review: Diagnosing childhood resilience – A systemic approach to the diagnosis of adaptation in adverse social and physical ecologies. *Journal of Child Psychology and Psychiatry, 56*(1), 4–17. https://doi.org/10.1111/jcpp.12306

Ungar, M. (2016). Which counts more: Differential impact of the environment or differential susceptibility of the individual? *British Journal of Social Work.* https://doi.org/10.1093/bjsw/bcw109

UNICEF. (n.d). Convention on the rights of the child. Retrieved from http://unicef.org/crc

UNICEFeastcaribbean. (2011). *UNICEF: Developmental milestones in children.* Retrieved from https://www.youtube.com/watch?v=SBFnO2FCdeE

Vagi, K. J., Rothman, E. F., Latzman, N. E., Tharp, A. T., Hall, D. M., & Breiding, M. J. (2013). Beyond correlates: A review of risk and protective factors for adolescent dating violence perpetration. *Journal of Youth and Adolescence, 42*(4), 633–649. https://doi.org/10.1007/s10964-013-9907-7

Vaillant, G. E. (2012). *Triumphs of Experience: The men of the Harvard Grant Study.* Cambridge, MA: Harvard University Press.

Van Ingen, D. J., Freiheit, S. R., Steinfeldt, J. A., Moore, L. L., Wimer, D. J., Knutt, A. D., . . . Roberts, A. (2015). Helicopter parenting: The effect of an overbearing caregiving style on peer attachment and self-efficacy. *Journal of College Counseling, 18*(1), 7–20. https://doi.org/10.1002/j.2161-1882.2015.00065.x

Van Leijenhorst, L., Moor, B. G., Op de Macks, Z. A., Rombouts, S. A. R. B., Westenberg, P. M., & Crone, E. A. (2010). Adolescent risky decision-making: Neurocognitive development of reward and control regions. *NeuroImage, 51*(1), 345–355. https://doi.org/10.1016/j.neuroimage.2010.02.038

Vanassche, S., Corijn, M., Matthijs, K., & Swicegood, G. (2015). Repartnering and childbearing after divorce: Differences according to parental status and custodial arrangements. *Population Research and Policy Review, 34*(5), 761–784. https://doi.org/10.1007/s11113-015-9366-9

Vandenberg, L. N., & Prins, G. S. (2016). Clarity in the face of confusion: New studies tip the scales on Bisphenol A (BPA). *Andrology, 4*(4), 561–564. https://doi.org/10.1111/andr.12219

Vanderwert, R. E., Marshall, P. J., Nelson, III, C. A., Zeanah, C. H., & Fox, N. A. (2010). Timing of intervention affects brain electrical activity in children exposed to severe psychosocial neglect. *PLOS ONE, 5*(7), 1–5.

Vandivere, S., Yrausquin, A., Allen, T., Malm, K., & McKlindon, A. (2015). Children in nonparental care: A Review of the literature and analysis of data gaps. Retrieved from https://aspe.hhs.gov/basic-report/children-nonparental-care-review-literature-and-analysis-data-gaps

Vaughans, K., & Spielberg, W. (2014). *The psychology of black boys and adolescents.* Santa Barbara, CA: Praeger.

Vélez, C. E., Wolchik, S. A., & Sandler, I. N. (2014). Divorce effects on adolescents. In T. P. Gullotta & M. Bloom (Eds.), *Encyclopedia of Primary Prevention and Health Promotion* (pp. 1076–1085). New York, NY: Springer. https://doi.org/10.1007/978-1-4614-5999-6_230

Vencill, J. A., & Wiljamaa, S. J. (2016). From MOM to MORE: Emerging Research on Mixed Orientation Relationships. *Current Sexual Health Reports, 8*(3), 206–212. https://doi.org/10.1007/s11930-016-0081-2

Vernon, P. E., Adamson, G., Vernon, D. F. (1977/2015). *The psychology and education of gifted children.* New York, NY: Routledge.

Vespa, J., Lewis, V. M., Kreider, R. M. (2013). America's families and living arrangements: 2012. *United States Census Bureau,* 1-34. Retrieved from https://www.census.gov/prod/2013pubs/p20-570.pdf

Vitali, A., & Arpino, B. (2016). Who brings home the bacon? The influence of context on partners' contributions to the household income. *Demographic Research, 35*(41), 1213–1244.

Vivancos, R., Abubakar, I., Phillips-Howard, P., & Hunter, P. R. (2013). School-based sex education is associated with reduced risky sexual behaviour and sexually transmitted infections in young adults. *Public Health, 127*(1), 53–57. https://doi.org/10.1016/j.puhe.2012.09.016

Volk, A. (2011). The evolution of childhood. *Journal of the History of Childhood & Youth, 4*(3), 470–494.

Volk, A. A., Farrell, A. H., Franklin, P., Mularczyk, K. P., & Provenzano, D. A. (2016). Adolescent bullying in schools: An evolutionary perspective. In D. C. Geary & D. B. Berch (Eds.), *Evolutionary Perspectives on Child Development and Education* (pp. 167–191). Switzerland, Springer International Publishing. https://doi.org/10.1007/978-3-319-29986-0_7

Volkow, N. D., Koob, G. F., & McLellan, A. T. (2016). Neurobiologic advances from the brain disease model of addiction. *The New England Journal of Medicine, 374*(4), 363–371. https://doi.org/10.1056/NEJMra1511480

Volkow, N. D., Swanson, J. M., Evins, A. E., Delisi, L. E., Meier, M. H., Gonzalez, R., … Baler, R. (2016). Effects of cannabis use on human behavior, including cognition, motivation, and psychosis: A review. *JAMA Psychiatry, 73*(3), 292. doi:10.1001/jamapsychiatry.2015.3278

Von Bertalanffy, L. (1974). *General systems theory.* New York, NY: Braziller.

Vygotsky, L. S. (1962). *Thought and language.* Cambridge, MA: MIT Press.

Vygotsky, L. S. (1987). Thinking and speech. In R. W. Reiber & A. S. Carton (Eds.), *The collected works of L. S.Vygotsky: Problems of general psychology* (Vol. 1, pp. 37–285). New York, NY: Plenum.

Wadsworth, S. M., & Riggs, D. (Eds.). (2011). *Risk and resilience in U.S. Military families.* New York, NY: Springer. Retrieved from http://link.springer.com/10.1007/978-1-4419-7064-0

Wadsworth, S. M., Cardin, J.-F., Christ, S., Willerton, E., O'Grady, A. F., Topp, D., … Mustillo, S. (2016). Accumulation of risk and promotive factors among young children in US military families. *American Journal of Community Psychology, 57*(1–2), 190–202. https://doi.org/10.1002/ajcp.12025

Wagmiller, R. L., & Adelman, R. M. (2009). *Childhood and intergenerational poverty: The long-term consequences of growing up poor.* Retrieved from http://www.nccp.org/publications/pub_909.html

Wagmiller, R. L., Lennon, M. C., Kuang, L., Alberti, P. M., & Aber, J. L. (2006). The dynamics of economic disadvantage and children's life chances. *American Sociological Review, 71*(5), 847–866. https://doi.org/10.1177/000312240607100507

Wagner, M., Schmid, L., & Weiß, B. (2015). Exploring increasing divorce rates in West Germany: Can we explain the iron law of increasing marriage instability? *European Sociological Review, 31*(2), 211–229. https://doi.org/10.1093/esr/jcv014

Waldfogel, J., Craigie, T.-A., & Brooks-Gunn, J. (2010). Fragile families and child wellbeing. *The Future of Children, 20*(2), 87–112.

Waldinger, R. J., & Schulz, M. S. (2016). The long reach of nurturing family environments links with midlife emotion-regulatory styles and late-life security in intimate relationships. *Psychological Science, 27*(11), 1443–1450. https://doi.org/10.1177/0956797616661556

Walsh, D., & Walsh, E. (2014). *Why do they act that way? A survival guide to the adolescent brain for you and your teen* (2nd rev. upd. ed.). New York, NY: Atria Books.

Walsh, F. (2016). *Strengthening family resilience* (3rd ed.). New York, NY: Guilford Press

Walter, C. A., & McCoyd, J. L. M. (2015). *Grief and loss across the lifespan: A biopsychosocial perspective* (2nd ed.). New York, NY: Springer.

Wang, J., Plöderl, M., Häusermann, M., & Weiss, M. G. (2015). Understanding suicide attempts among gay men from their self-perceived causes. *The Journal of Nervous and Mental Disease, 203*(7), 499–506. https://doi.org/10.1097/NMD.0000000000000319

Wang, W., & Taylor, P. (2011). For millennials, parenthood trumps marriage. Retrieved from http://www.pewsocialtrends.org/2011/03/09/for-millennials-parenthood-trumps-marriage/

Wang, W., Parker, K., & Taylor, P. (2013). Breadwinner moms. Retrieved from http://www.pewsocialtrends.org/2013/05/29/breadwinner-moms/

Wang, Y., Deng, C., & Yang, X. (2016). Family economic status and parental involvement: Influences of parental expectation and perceived barriers. *School Psychology International, 37*(5), 536–553. https://doi.org/10.1177/0143034316667646

Washington, P. (1997). *Bach*. New York, NY: Knopf Publishers.

Watkins, C. S., & Howard, M. O. (2015). Educational success among elementary school children from low socioeconomic status families: A systematic review of research assessing parenting factors. *Journal of Children and Poverty, 21*(1), 17–46. https://doi.org/10.1080/10796126.2015.1031728

Watkinson, A. M., & Rock, L. (2016). Child physical punishment and international human rights: Implications for social work education. *International Social Work, 1*, 86.

Webster-Stratton, C. H., & Reid, M. J. (2011). The incredible years program for children from infancy to pre-adolescence: Prevention and treatment of behavior problems. In R. C. Murrihy, A. D. Kidman, & T. H. Ollendick (Eds.), *Clinical Handbook of Assessing and Treating Conduct Problems in Youth* (pp. 117–138). New York, NY: Springer. https://doi.org/10.1007/978-1-4419-6297-3_5

Weerdenburg, K., Schneeweiss, S. Koo, E. & Boutis, K. (2016). Concussion and its management: What do parents know? *Paediatrics & Child Health, 21*(3), E22.

Weimer, A. A., Parault Dowds, S. J., Fabricius, W. V., Schwanenflugel, P. J., & Suh, G. W. (2017). Development of constructivist theory of mind from middle childhood to early adulthood and its relation to social cognition and behavior. *Journal of Experimental Child Psychology, 154*, 28–45. https://doi.org/10.1016/j.jecp.2016.10.002

Weisleder, A., & Fernald, A. (2014). Social environments shape children's language experiences, strengthening language processing and building vocabulary. In *Language in Interaction: Studies in honor of Eve V. Clark* (pp. 29–41). John Benjamins Publishing Company.

Weissbluth, M. (2015). *Healthy sleep habits, happy child: A step-by-step program for a good night's sleep* (4th ed.). New York, NY: Random House Publishing Group.

Wentzel, K. R., & Ramani, G. B. (2016). *Handbook of social influences in school contexts: Social-emotional, motivation, and cognitive outcomes*. New York, NY: Routledge.

West, S. (2015). Financial fragility and emergency savings in households headed By single mothers. Presented at the 2015 Fall Conference: The Golden Age of Evidence-Based Policy, Appam. Retrieved from https://appam.confex.com/appam/2015/webprogram/Paper14000.html

Westphal, S. K., Poortman, A.-R., & van der Lippe, T. (2014). Non-resident father–child contact across divorce cohorts: The role of father involvement during marriage. *European Sociological Review, 30*(4), 444–456. https://doi.org/10.1093/esr/jcu050

Westwood, S. (2016). *Ageing, gender and sexuality: Equality in later life*. New York, NY: Routledge.

Whisner, C. M., Bruening, M., & O'Brien, K. O. (2016). A brief survey of dietary beliefs and behaviors of pregnant adolescents. *Journal of Pediatric & Adolescent Gynecology, 29*(5), 476–481. https://doi.org/10.1016/j.jpag.2016.03.002

Whiting, J. B., Smith, D. R., Barnett, T., & Grafsky, E. L. (2007). Overcoming the Cinderella myth: A mixed methods study of successful stepmothers. *Journal of Divorce & Remarriage, 47*(1/2), 95–109.

Whitten, K. M., & Burt, I. (2015). Utilizing creative expressive techniques and group counseling to improve adolescents of divorce social-relational capabilities. *Journal of Creativity in Mental Health, 10*(3), 363–375. https://doi.org/10.1080/15401383.2014.986594

Whittle, S., Simmons, J. G., Dennison, M., Vijayakumar, N., Schwartz, O., Yap, M. B. H., … Allen, N. B. (2014). Positive parenting predicts the development of adolescent brain structure: A longitudinal study. *Developmental Cognitive Neuroscience, 8*, 7–17. https://doi.org/10.1016/j.dcn.2013.10.006

Widom, C. S., Czaja, S. J., & DuMont, K. A. (2015). Intergenerational transmission of child abuse and neglect: Real or detection bias? *Science, 347*(6229), 1480–1485. https://doi.org/10.1126/science.1259917

Wiese, B. S., Burk, C. L., & Jaeckel, D. (2016). Transition to grandparenthood and job-related attitudes: Do grandparental sex and lineage matter? *Journal of Marriage and Family, 78*(3), 830–847. https://doi.org/10.1111/jomf.12307

Wilcoxon, S. A., Remley, T. P., & Gladding S. T. (2013). *Ethical, legal and professional issues in the practice of marriage and family therapy* (5th ed.). Upper Saddle River, NJ: Pearson.

Willerton, E., Wadsworth, S.M. & Riggs, D. (2011). Introduction: Military families under stress: What we know and what we need to know. In S. Wadsworth & D. Riggs (Eds.), *Risk and resilience in U.S. military families* (pp. 1–20). New York, NY: Springer.

Winnicott, D. W. (1953). Psychoses and child care. *British Journal of Medical Psychology, 26*(1), 68–74. doi:10.1111/j.2044-8341.1953.tb00810.x.

Winnicott, D. W. (1960). The theory of the parent-infant relationship. *The International Journal of Psycho-Analysis, 41*, 585–95.

Winnicott, D.W. (1971). *Playing and reality*. New Fetter Lane, London, England: Tavistock/Routledge.

Wittmer, D. S., Petersen, S. H., & Puckett, M. B. (2013). *The young child: Development from prebirth through age eight* (6th ed.). Boston, MA: Pearson.

Wolf, K. & Wolf, J. (2016). *Hope heals: A true story of overwhelming loss and an overcoming love*. Grand Rapids, MI: Zondervan.

Wong, S., & Logan, H. (2016). Play in early childhood education: An historical perspective. In T. Brabazon (Ed.), *Play: A Theory of Learning and Change* (pp. 7–26). New York, NY: Springer International Publishing. https://doi.org/10.1007/978-3-319-25549-1_2

World Health Organization. (2016). Child maltreatment. Retrieved from http://www.who.int/mediacentre/factsheets/fs150/en/

Yablonsky, A. M., Barbero, E. D., & Richardson, J. W. (2016). Hard is normal: Military families' transitions within the process of deployment. *Research in Nursing & Health, 39*(1), 42–56. https://doi.org/10.1002/nur.21701

Yavorsky, J. E., Kamp Dush, C. M., & Schoppe-Sullivan, S. J. (2015). The production of inequality: The gender division of labor across the transition to parenthood. *Journal of Marriage and Family, 77*(3), 662–679. https://doi.org/10.1111/jomf.12189

Younes, M. N., & Klein, S. A. (2014). The international adoption experience: Do they live happily ever after? *Adoption Quarterly, 17*(1), 65–83. https://doi.org/10.1080/10926755.2014.875090

Youthgov.org. (n.d.). *Promising strategies and existing gaps in supporting pregnant and parenting teens*. Retrieved from http://youth.gov/feature-article/promising-strategies-and-existing-gaps-supporting-pregnant-and-parenting-teens

Yu, L., & Winter, S. (2011). Gender atypical behavior in chinese school-aged children: Its prevalence and relation to sex, age, and only child status. *The Journal of Sex Research, 48*(4), 334–348. https://doi.org/10.1080/00224491003774867

Yuhas, D. (2015). Parental controls. *Scientific American, 312*(1), 18–18. https://doi.org/10.1038/scientificamerican0115-18

Zacher, H., & Schulz, H. (2015). Employees' eldercare demands, strain, and perceived support. *Journal of Managerial Psychology, 30*(2), 183–198. https://doi.org/10.1108/JMP-06-2013-0157

Zeanah, C. H., & Gleason, M. M. (2015). Annual research review: Attachment disorders in early childhood—clinical presentation, causes, correlates, and treatment. *Journal of Child Psychology and Psychiatry, and Allied Disciplines, 56*(3), 207–222. https://doi.org/10.1111/jcpp.12347

Zeleznikow, L., & Zeleznikow, J. (2015). Supporting blended families to remain intact: A case study. *Journal of Divorce & Remarriage, 56*(4), 317–335. https://doi.org/10.1080/10502556.2015.1025845

Zhao, S., & Gao, Y. (2014). Can adjustments of China's family planning policy truly relieve pressures arising from population aging? *International Journal of China Studies, 5*(3), 657–680. Retrieved from http://search.proquest.com/openview/30c33e105afbc0bdcb3270a37c667d66/1?pq-origsite=gscholar

Ziol-Guest, K. M. (2014). A commentary on "maternal work and children's diet, activity, and obesity." *Social Science & Medicine (1982), 107*, 205–208. https://doi.org/10.1016/j.socscimed.2014.02.038

Zissimopoulos, J. M., Karney, B. R., & Rauer, A. J. (2015). Marriage and economic well being at older ages. *Review of Economics of the Household, 13*(1), 1–35. https://doi.org/10.1007/s11150-013-9205-x

Zolfaghari, B., Möllering, G., Clark, T., & Dietz, G. (2016). How do we adopt multiple cultural identities? A multidimensional operationalization of the sources of culture. *European Management Journal, 34*(2), 102–113. https://doi.org/10.1016/j.emj.2016.01.003

Zottis, G. A. H., Salum, G. A., Isolan, L. R., Manfro, G. G., & Heldt, E. (2014). Associations between child disciplinary practices and bullying behavior in adolescents. *Jornal De Pediatria, 90*(4), 408–414. https://doi.org/10.1016/j.jped.2013.12.009

Name Index

Subject Index